Crime Prevention
in America

❖

DEAN JOHN CHAMPION

Texas A & M International University

PEARSON

Prentice
Hall

Upper Saddle River, New Jersey 07458

Library of Congress Cataloging-in-Publication Data

Champion, Dean J.
Crime prevention in America/Dean J. Champion.
    p. cm
    Includes bibliographical references.
    ISBN 0-13-225377-1
    1. Crime prevention—United States. I. Title.

HV7431 .C726 2007
364.40973—dc22   2006049404

Editor-in-Chief: Vernon R. Anthony
Executive Editor: Frank Mortimer, Jr.
Marketing Manager: Adam Kloza
Associate Editor: Sarah Holle
Editorial Assistant: Jillian Allison
Production Editor: Emily Bush, Carlisle Editorial Services
Production Liaison: Barbara Marttine Cappuccio
Director of Manufacturing and Production: Bruce Johnson
Managing Editor: Mary Carnis
Manufacturing Manager: Ilene Sanford
Manufacturing Buyer: Cathleen Petersen
Senior Design Coordinator: Mary Siener
Cover Designer: Eva Ruutopold
Cover Image: F. Schussler/Getty Images
Formatting: Carlisle Publishing Services
Printer/Binder: R. R. Donnelley & Sons Company

Pearson Education Ltd.
Pearson Education Singapore, Pte. Ltd.
Pearson Education Canada, Ltd.
Pearson Education—Japan

Pearson Education Australia PTY, Limited
Pearson Education North Asia Ltd.
Pearson Educación de Mexico, S.A. de C.V.
Pearson Education Malaysia, Pte. Ltd.

10 9 8 7 6 5 4 3 2 1
ISBN: 0-13-225377-1

Contents

❖

PREFACE   ix

PART I
CRIME PREVENTION: HISTORY AND THE MEDIA   1

    Chapter 1   "The History of Crime Prevention in the United
                  States."
                  Dean John Champion, 2006.   3

    Chapter 2   "The News Media's Coverage of Crime and
                  Victimization."
                  Washington, DC: U.S. Department of Justice, Office
                  of Justice Programs, National Victim Assistance
                  Academy. Anne Seymour, 2002.   29

    Chapter 3   "Media Consumption and Public Attitudes Toward
                  Crime and Justice: The Relationship Between Fear
                  of Crime, Punitive Attitudes, and Perceived Police
                  Effectiveness."
                  Journal of Criminal Justice and Popular Culture
                  10: 109–126. Kenneth Dowler, 2003.   39

PART II
LAW ENFORCEMENT AND CRIME PREVENTION   51

    Chapter 4   "Examining the Role of the Police in Reentry
                  Partnership Initiatives."
                  Federal Probation 68: 62–69.
                  James M. Byrne and Don Hummer, 2004.   53

    Chapter 5   "Defending Against Cybercrime and Terrorism: A
                  New Role for Universities."
                  FBI Law Enforcement Bulletin 74: 14–20.
                  Tony Aeilts, 2005.   66

Chapter 6   "Coordinated Terrorist Attacks: Implications for
                 Local Responders."
                 *FBI Law Enforcement Bulletin 74: 11–17. Brian K.
                 Houghton and Jonathan M. Schachter, 2005.*   72

Chapter 7   "Compstat Process."
                 *FBI Law Enforcement Bulletin 74: 12–21.
                 Jon M. Shane, 2004.*   78

Chapter 8   Crime Mapping and Analysis by Community
                 Organizations in Hartford, Connecticut.
                 *Washington, DC: U.S. Department of Justice,
                 Office of Justice Programs. Thomas Rich, 2001.*   86

Chapter 9   Homeland Security and Emergency Preparedness.
                 *Washington, DC: Department of Homeland Security,
                 2006. Homeland Security Office, 2006.*   97

Chapter 10   "Managing Joint Terrorism Task Force Resources."
                 *FBI Law Enforcement Bulletin 73: 5–10. James
                 Casey, 2004.*   101

Chapter 11   "The Future of Public/Private Partnerships."
                 *FBI Law Enforcement Bulletin 73: 7–10.
                 Al Youngs, 2004.*   107

**PART III
THE COURTS AND CRIME PREVENTION**   **113**

Chapter 12   "State Sentencing Schemes, Part I and II."
                 *American Jails 15: 23–28. J. W. Barbrey and Keith E.
                 Clement, 2001.*   114

Chapter 13   "The Imposition of Economic Sanctions in
                 Philadelphia: Costs, Fines, and Restitution."
                 Federal Probation 68: 21–26. R. Barry Ruback, 2004.   132

Chapter 14   "Listening to Victims: A Critique of Restorative
                 Justice Policy and Practice in the United States."
                 *Federal Probation 68: 32–38. Harry Mika, Mary
                 Achilles, Ellen Halbert, Lorraine Stutzman Amstutz,
                 and Howard Zehr, 2004.*   140

Chapter 15   "Are the Politics of Criminal Justice Changing?"
                 *Corrections Today 64: 74–76. Nicholas R. Turner and
                 Daniel F. Wilhelm, 2002.*   153

PART IV
CORRECTIONS AND CRIME PREVENTION   **159**

Chapter 16   "The University of Washington Vipassana Meditation
              Research Project at the North Rehabilitation Facility."
              American Jails 17: 13–17. George A. Parks, G. Alan
              Marlatt, Sarah W. Bowen, Tiara M. Dillworth, Katie
              Witkiewitz, Mary Larimer, Arthur Blume, Tracy
              L. Simpson, Heather Lonczak, Laura Marie
              MacPherson, David Murphy, and Lucia Meijer, 2003.   161

Chapter 17   "Prison-Based Therapeutic Community Substance
              Abuse Programs: Implementation and Operational
              Issues."
              Federal Probation 66: 1–8. William M. Burdon,
              David Farabee, Michael L. Prendergast, Nena P.
              Messina, and Jerome Cartier, 2002.   166

Chapter 18   "Adult Basic/Secondary Education Program for the
              Incarcerated in Sheboygan County, Wisconsin."
              American Jails 14: 57–61. Sharon Abel, 2001.   175

Chapter 19   "Understanding and Responding to the Needs of
              Parole Violators."
              Corrections Today 66: 84–87, 105. Kristofer Bret
              Bucklen, Gary Zajac, and Kathleen Gnall, 2004.   180

Chapter 20   "Offender Reentry: A Returning or Reformed
              Criminal?"
              FBI Law Enforcement Bulletin 73: 1–10. David M.
              Allender, 2004.   187

Chapter 21   "Offender Reentry Requires Attention to Victim
              Safety."
              APPA Perspectives 27: 24–29. Melissa Hook and
              Anne Seymour, 2003.   196

Chapter 22   "Managing Offender Resistance to Counseling:
              The '3R's.' "
              Federal Probation 66: 43–49. William N. Elliott, 2002. 207

PART V
JUVENILE DELINQUENCY AND ITS PREVENTION   **219**

Chapter 23   "Restorative Justice, Communities, and Delinquency:
              Whom Do We Reintegrate?"
              Criminology and Public Policy 1: 103–130. Nancy
              Rodriguez, 2005.   221

Chapter 24   "The Peer Court Experience."
              APPA Perspectives 27: 30–33. James P. Gray, 2003.   235

Chapter 25   Treatment, Services, and Intervention Programs
              for Child Delinquents.
              Washington, DC: U.S. Department of Justice.
              Barbara J. Burns, James C. Howell, Janet K. Wiig,
              Leena K. Augimeri, Brendan C. Welsh, Rolf Loeber,
              and David Petechuk, 2003.   241

Chapter 26   "Truancy Mediation: A Collaborative Approach
              to Truancy Intervention."
              APPA Perspectives 25: 34–36. Kathy Elton and Kerrie
              Naylor, 2001.   255

Chapter 27   "What Works in Juvenile Justice Outcome
              Measurement? A Comparison of Predicted Success
              to Observed Performance."
              Federal Probation 66: 50–55. Kristin Parsons
              Winokur, Ted Tollett, and Sherry Jackson, 2002.   260

PART VI
CRIME PREVENTION PROGRAMS FOR SELECTED OFFENSES:
PROGRAM EVALUATION AND POLICY IMPLICATIONS   **269**

Chapter 28   "Did *Ceasefire, Compstat,* and *Exile* Reduce
              Homicide?"
              Criminology and Public Policy 4: 419–450. Richard
              Rosenfeld, Robert Fornango, and Eric Baumer, 2005.   273

Chapter 29   "How Do We Know If It Works?: Evaluation Strategies
              for Making Evidence-Based Decisions."
              American Jails 18: 17–24. Jeanne B. Stinchcomb, 2004.   287

Chapter 30   "Mental Health Jail Diversion."
              American Jails 17: 35–41. Edward W. Szostak and
              Marisa L. Beeble, 2003.   296

Chapter 31   "Electronic Monitoring: Positive Intervention
              Strategies."
              Federal Probation 66: 21–25. Ralph Kirkland Gable
              and Robert S. Gable, 2005.   303

Chapter 32   "PROGRESS: An Enhanced Supervision Program
              for High-Risk Criminal Offenders."
              FBI Law Enforcement Bulletin 72: 20–24. Greg
              Hagenbucher, 2004.   311

Chapter 33 "Problem-Solving Probation: Overview of Four
Community-Based Experiments."
*APPA Perspectives 26: 26–34. Robin Campbell and
Robert Victor Wolf, 2002.* 315

Chapter 34 "Willingness-to-Pay for Crime Control Programs."
*Criminology 42: 89–109. Mark A. Cohen, Roland
T. Rust, Sara Steen, and Simon T. Tidd, 2004.* 331

Chapter 35 "Minor Crime in a Quaint Setting: Practices,
Outcomes, and Limits of Vermont Reparative Boards."
*Criminology and Public Policy 4: 655–686. David
R. Karp and Kevin M. Drakulich, 2004.* 340

Chapter 36 Restitution: Making It Work.
*Washington, DC: U.S. Department of Justice,
John W. Gillis, 2002.* 357

Chapter 37 "High Anxiety Offenders in Correctional Settings: It's
Time for Another Look."
*Federal Probation 68: 43–50. Shelley Johnson
Listwan, Kimberly Gentry Sperber, Lisa Murphy
Spruance, and Patricia Van Voorhis, 2004.* 363

Chapter 38 "Managing Offenders with Special Health Needs:
Highest and Best Use Strategies."
*Corrections Today 67: 58–61. Elizabeth Anderson
and Theresa Hilliard, 2005.* 371

Chapter 39 "Co-Occurring Substance Abuse and Mental
Disorders in Offenders: Approaches, Findings and
Recommendations."
*Federal Probation 67: 32–39. Stanley Sacks and
Frank Pearson, 2003.* 377

Chapter 40 "Debating the Effectiveness of Parole."
*APPA Perspectives 30: 54–61. Anne Morrison Piehl,
2006.* 389

Chapter 41 "Targeting for Reentry: Inclusion/Exclusion Criteria
Across Eight Model Programs."
*Federal Probation 68: 53–61. James M. Byrne and
Faye S. Taxman, 2004.* 399

Chapter 42 "Environmental Corrections: A New Paradigm for
Effective Probation and Parole Supervision."
*Federal Probation 66: 28–37. Francis T. Cullen,
John E. Eck, and Christopher T. Lowenkamp, 2002.* 412

Chapter 43   "Evaluation Report of the Juvenile Mediation
              Program."
              Corrections Compendium 27: 1–3, 19, 21. Robert R.
              Smith and Victor S. Lombardo, 2002.   426

Chapter 44   "Costs and Outcomes of a Work Ethic Camp: How
              Do They Compare to a Traditional Prison Facility?"
              Corrections Compendium 30: 1–5, 28–30. Kurt D.
              Siedschlaw and Beth A. Wiersma, 2005.   432

Chapter 45   Crimes Against Persons Age 65 or Older, 1993–2002.
              Washington, DC: Patsy Klaus, 2005.   441

Chapter 46   Financial Crimes Against the Elderly.
              Washington, DC: Kelly Dedel Johnson, 2003.   449

Chapter 47   What Is Telemarketing Fraud?
              U.S. Department of Justice, Criminal Division.
              Washington, DC. U.S. Department of Justice, 1998.   458

Chapter 48   What Kinds of Telemarketing Schemes Are Out There?
              U.S. Department of Justice, Criminal Division.
              Washington, DC. U.S. Department of Justice,
              Criminal Division, 1998.   461

Chapter 49   "Are Sex Offenders Dangerous?"
              Criminology and Public Policy 3: 59–82. Lisa L.
              Sample and Timothy M. Bray, 2003.   468

Chapter 50   Assault Prevention.
              Tempe, AZ: City of Tempe. City of Tempe, 2005.   484

Chapter 51   Model Peer-Led Sexual Assault Prevention Programs:
              Lessons for Engaging and Empowering Youth.
              Boston, MA: Massachusetts Department of Public
              Health. Michelle Harris and Mark Bergeron-Naper,
              1999.   494

BIBLIOGRAPHY   **505**

Preface

Crime Prevention in America is a collection of readings examining a contemporary view of the efforts of law enforcement, the courts, and corrections to prevent or minimize the occurrence of crime in the United States. Crimes are committed by adults and juveniles alike, and therefore some attention will be given to preventing delinquency, which is crime committed by juveniles.

There are many types of crime. Traditional crime categorizations distinguish between felonies and misdemeanors. However, there are many types of felonies. Some felonies are more serious than others. Rape, murder, robbery, and aggravated assault are qualitatively more serious compared with property crimes, such as vehicular theft, burglary, or larceny. Seriousness of crime is often equated with harm caused to one or more victims. Bodily injuries or death are frequent consequences of these serious felonies, although even less serious felonies may have serious consequences for victims, including substantial financial loss. Also, some felonies, such as terrorism, have both national and international consequences. Furthermore, it has been demonstrated repeatedly that in over two-thirds of all crimes, drug and alcohol dependencies have figured prominently in their commission. Closely associated with crime, especially violent crime, is the pervasiveness of gangs in the United States. Gangs include both youth and adult members, and their tentacles have spread not only throughout communities but also into prisons and among those under correctional supervision on probation and parole.

Our technological advances have created different breeds of criminals. Cybercrime and cyberterrorism are relatively new arrivals within the spectrum of criminal activities investigated by the police and other law enforcement agencies. Various strategies are or have been implemented to attack both crime and its causes. The major components of criminal justice—law enforcement, the courts, and corrections—have been continuously engaged in crime prevention and control strategies, using a variety of experimental methods to minimize crime. Some of these strategies have proved to be more successful than others for combating certain types of criminal activity.

Crime prevention is therefore multidimensional. Attacking crime is logically believed by many citizens to be a law enforcement function. And it is. Police officers fight crime and are known often as "crime fighters." But in recent decades, greater community involvement has been solicited by police organizations through the establishment of neighborhood watch programs and other community interventions. Police organizations have established community policing, whereby the visibility of police officers on city streets has been heightened and meaningful partnerships with community residents and leaders have been established. But the police and community residents cannot prevent crime on their own.

The courts have been involved in crime prevention as well. State legislatures and the U.S. Congress have enacted harsh laws and stiff penalties for committing certain types of crime, such as terrorism, child sexual abuse, murder, and crimes of violence in general. Sentencing schemes have been revised and incorporate new punishments for all types of offenders. Indeterminate sentencing schemes, where parole boards exert primary control over an inmate's early release from prison, have gradually been replaced with determinate sentencing, where the objectives sought have been to objectify early-release decision making and induce inmates to be more compliant and law-abiding while incarcerated. In a fourth of all states, parole boards have been abolished. Whenever certain inmates are released because of parole board discretion, and where these released offenders commit heinous crimes, parole boards are blamed for exercising poor decision making. A logical response from the public and some politicians is to replace parole boards and remove their discretionary authority to make early-release decisions. In their place, sentencing guidelines have been established to promote greater fairness and proportionality in sentencing offenders. Judges themselves, who have exhibited substantial disparity in the punishments they impose on convicted offenders, are frequent targets of sentencing guidelines schemes designed to generate greater fairness and equality in the sentencing process. But these measures, designed to control or prevent parole board and judicial discretionary abuses, may be tantamount to throwing the baby out with the bath water. Personal judgments rather than guidelines may be preferable to keeping certain prisoners incarcerated for longer periods. Under determinate or presumptive guidelines–based sentencing schemes, these more dangerous offenders will be freed regardless of the dangers they pose to communities. Judges may be restricted from imposing harsher sentences on certain convicted offenders who should receive more severe sentencing because of the heinousness of their criminal acts. But statutory or guidelines-based provisions are in place to ensure less severe penalties even though such penalties may be deserved and should be imposed.

Also, almost every state today has habitual offender or chronic offender laws, such as the "Three Strikes and You're Out" scheme adopted by California, Washington, and other state jurisdictions. Career criminals and persistent offenders are the targets of such mandatory-penalty laws, which include mandatory sentences of up to 5 years or more for using a firearm during a crime's commission. Virginia Exile is an exemplary program that makes such a provision. The intent of Virginia Exile and other "use a firearm and receive an additional 5 years" punishment schemes is to deter the use of dangerous weapons when offenders decide to commit crimes. If dangerous weapons are not used, it is reasoned, then the likelihood of personal injuries and death to victims is reduced. Thus, these mandatory sentencing laws contribute in their own ways to crime prevention, or at least help to minimize various potentially serious outcomes to victims.

Furthermore, both federal and state governments have enacted truth-in-sentencing provisions in their criminal codes to ensure that offenders serve greater proportions of their sentences. During the 1990s and earlier, many state and federal inmates were being released from prison after serving about a third of their maximum sentences imposed. Today, many states emulate the federal sentencing guidelines that call for sentenced prisoners to serve at least 85 percent of their sentences before being considered for early release. These tougher laws and penalties have been designed as deterrents to crime, although their value in this regard is a continuously debated and unresolved issue.

The correctional community, including prisons, jails, and probation/parole organizations, has attempted to do its part in preventing crime. Because this segment of the criminal justice system manages convicted offenders, their concerted efforts have been directed toward the noble aims of offender rehabilitation and reintegration. Useful vocational and educational programs have been established in most prisons and some larger jails. Prison industries have been established to assist some offenders in acquiring useful skills to make them more employable when they are eventually released. Individual and group counseling, anger management, and other forms of psychological and social assistance programs have been implemented in correctional institutions. Drug and alcohol dependencies among inmates have been addressed by therapeutic treatment programs, since decreasing one's dependence on drugs/alcohol is believed to be a significant factor in reducing recidivism. And in fact, such efforts by corrections agencies and organizations have often been rewarded positively by increased law-abiding behavior among clients participating in such interventions.

At the same time, probation and parole agencies have engaged in aggressive efforts to professionalize their officers who supervise offenders and to offer the means whereby offenders under probation/parole (PO) supervision can receive needed treatments. Successful community reintegration is regarded by paroling authorities as critical in the process of offender reentry. But the public is less forgiving and resists accepting offenders back into their neighborhoods. The NIMBY syndrome, "Not in My Back Yard," is a consistent theme echoed by citizens in most communities throughout the United States. The public doesn't want criminals living among them.

Employers are reluctant to hire persons with criminal records. Frustrated because of pervasive rejection by the public, many parolees turn to committing new crimes to obtain resources to survive on the streets. Thus a vicious cycle of crime occurs, which makes corrections a revolving door. Former criminals commit new crimes, often related to societal rejection, and they are convicted and reincarcerated. Released later, they continue their pattern of recidivism and the revolving-door phenomenon recurs. Increasingly aware of these frustrations among parolees and other criminal clients, probation and parole agencies have engaged in greater networking with community and business leaders aimed at making one's transition from institutional living to community living occur more smoothly. Through these positive intervention efforts, more professional POs and their agencies have done a great deal to reduce recidivism among their offender clientele. The concept of a therapeutic community has engaged the courts, community leaders, and probation and parole agencies in an integrated scheme to treat different problems afflicting clients and address their diverse needs more effectively.

For juvenile offenders, many interventions, both past and present, have been attempted to reduce delinquency. The late J. Edgar Hoover believed that if we can reduce delinquency, we will ultimately reduce adult criminality. His belief was based on the questionable idea that all or most criminal offenders have delinquent pasts. Though many adult criminals are so-called late-bloomers and begin committing crimes in their early years, there is simply insufficient evidence to support Hoover's belief strongly. But this belief persists nevertheless. As a result, various intervention efforts designed to reduce delinquency among the juvenile population have been examined and evaluated. Some of these interventions will be described in these readings.

How do we know that our crime prevention efforts are successful? This is an evaluation question. Program evaluation is an increasingly popular method often used by funding organizations, especially the federal government, to create accountability and determine whether funded interventions have truly accomplished their missions or objectives. Most intervention programs are designed to attack and prevent crime at all stages of one's life. The Perry Pre-School Project was designed as an intervention to assist at-risk youths in their formative years to deter them from the conditions fostering delinquency. Other programs have come and gone, all with mixed results. Scared Straight, Hire a Gang Leader, D.A.R.E., Weed and Seed, and Project Safe Neighborhoods, for example, have targeted different groups and age levels, and under a variety of circumstances, all in an effort to deter or reduce crime and delinquency. It is beyond the scope of this collection of readings to provide descriptive information about all of these crime prevention or intervention efforts. Several articles featured in this collection, however, are program evaluations. Selections have been based on several interventions for both adults and juveniles. Their inclusion here does not mean that they are superior to other intervention programs or efforts at the community, state, or federal levels.

This collection of readings has been organized into six sections. Part I examines crime prevention generally and is designed to inform readers about what crime prevention means and how it applies to different criminal justice components. A history of crime prevention is presented, and significant historical crime prevention events and activities are described. The media has had a significant impact on crime prevention, especially drawing our attention to particular crimes and sensationalizing them. Sex crimes against children and adult sexual assaults, kidnappings, and murders; violence against and abuse of the elderly; drugs, such as Ecstasy and date-rape substances, and their intentional use to victimize others, particularly younger females; violent homicides on cruise liners; and numerous "trials of the century" involving serious offenses make us vividly aware of the impact of the media on our thoughts about crime and what can be done to prevent it. Therefore, some attention will be given to the influence of the media in depicting crime and its incidence, our fear of crime, and how we can control, minimize, or prevent it.

Part II examines law enforcement efforts to prevent crime. Several articles examine law enforcement strategies, such as geographical mapping, Compstat, hot-spot targeting, and other technology designed to reduce crime or prevent it. Greater use of technology in combating crime has been observed over the last few decades, and law enforcement agencies have put technology to good use in this respect. Technological developments have included tracking crime, focusing on crime hot spots, and identifying geographical areas where crimes are most frequent and law enforcement resources can be concentrated through crime mapping. Also, the electronic supervision of offenders with electronic wristlets or anklets and supervising offenders from outer space with global position satellite tracking suggest an unparalleled application of technological mechanisms and devices designed to thwart different types of crime and control offenders more effectively.

Part III examines how the courts have been involved in deterring offenders by focusing on sentencing and its consequences. There are many types of sentencing, and sentencing reforms have occurred at rapid rates in most U.S. jurisdictions. These sentencing systems will be described. The courts are also concerned with dispensing a wide array of punishments, designed in part to fit the crime and individual perpetrators. Some of these punishments will be presented and described.

Part IV is an examination of the broad area of corrections, including institutional corrections and community corrections, and how these respective aggregates have acted to rehabilitate and/or reintegrate offenders, thereby reducing their recidivism potential. Part V examines delinquency and its prevention. Delinquency is believed by many persons to be a forerunner of adult criminality. Thus, various delinquency prevention strategies have been proposed and used. Some of these programs are more successful at combating delinquency than other programs.

Part VI concludes with a presentation of several program evaluations of crime prevention interventions in various jurisdictions. Certain types of victims are featured, including the elderly, who are often susceptible to telemarketing fraud and other criminal practices. Sexual predators are also examined. These persons victimize children and young females most frequently. Various strategies are examined for combating these and other offenses.

Ancillaries include Part openers, general discussions of the articles included that describe their contents and relevance for crime prevention. At the end of each article, a list of questions for discussion and review is included to assist students in understanding what they have read. One favorable feature of this collection of readings is the synthesis of all bibliographies into one comprehensive bibliography at the end of the book. Thus, consistency of style in bibliographic entries and quoted materials is introduced. This comprehensive bibliography also functions as a resource for those wishing to learn more about crime prevention and its accompanying dimensions.

PART I

Crime Prevention: History and the Media

❖

Crime prevention in the United States and throughout the world is a continuing effort by many agencies and personnel to stem and control rising crime rates and cope with offending behaviors in a manner that deters criminals or rehabilitates them in ways that reduce the likelihood of recidivism. Crime prevention is a multidimensional concept, and we must recognize the fact that different agencies and organizations have established or are establishing policies and programs to prevent and control crime in their own ways.

In Part I, crime prevention is defined, including a brief discussion of various theoretical explanations of crime. Several types of deterrence are described, including general and specific deterrence. The elements of deterrence are presented, including certainty, celerity, and severity. Several types of crime prevention are discussed, including primary, secondary, and tertiary crime prevention.

Proactive crime prevention strategies involve law enforcement and each community in programs and initiatives that enable citizens to protect their property more effectively. Individuals also acquire knowledge about how they can reduce their chances of being victimized. Evidence of proactive crime prevention includes increased police visibility in high-crime areas or hot spots, intensified efforts to meet with community leaders and concerned citizens about target-hardening or making their businesses and residences more secure, and conducting more aggressive investigations when wrongdoing or law-breaking activity is suspected.

Another dimension of crime prevention pertains to processing offenders once they have been charged with one or more offenses. Prosecutors and the courts are attempting to deal more effectively with different types of offenders through legal mechanisms. State legislatures and Congress vest law enforcement agencies with powers to arrest persons for different offenses, and each statute proscribes financial and incarcerative punishments that may be imposed when criminals are caught and convicted. Various types of sentencing schemes are being used to protect the public, punish offenders, and hold them more accountable for the crimes they have committed.

Both institutional and community corrections deal with offenders who are either incarcerated in jails or prisons or who are placed on diversion, probation, or parole. Correctional clients, whether they are inmates or probationers or parolees, receive various types of treatments in the form of individual or group therapy, counseling, vocational/educational experiences, substance abuse therapy, and job-finding assistance. Depending upon their size and available funding, jails and prisons offer inmates a variety of self-help programs to enable them to improve themselves in ways that will facilitate their eventual reentry into communities. For those placed on probation and parole, they are supervised more or less closely by probation or parole officers. These officers vary in their orientations toward their jobs and what forms of assistance they will provide their clients. Their collective actions are intended to enhance offender rehabilitation and reintegration.

Juveniles who commit crime, delinquents, have a juvenile justice system that parallels the criminal justice system in most ways. Thus, most programs and practices experienced by adult offenders are also provided to youthful offenders. But some crime prevention programs and crime control efforts are specific to juveniles and are less relevant for adults.

The first essay in this collection of readings provides a general overview of crime prevention and crime control in the United States. Contemporary crime prevention and control efforts by various agencies and organizations were preceded by significant events extending back to ancient times. The earliest written codifications of criminal laws, such as the codes of Lipit-Ishtar and Hammurabi, are examined. The historical transition to more formalized crime prevention and control methods is described. In the colonial times of the 1600s and 1700s, England influenced how crime was defined and punished. The historical events that shaped early English thinking about crime and its control are presented.

The creation of the Metropolitan Police of London in 1829 was the first truly organized bureaucratic law enforcement agency, after which subsequent law enforcement organizations in the United States and other countries were patterned. Early law enforcement developments in the United States are described, together with early patrol strategies and the increased use of technology dedicated to detecting and fighting crime. Respectively, law enforcement, prosecution and the courts, and corrections are described, including their respective crime prevention and crime control initiatives. Juvenile delinquency is also examined. Various interventions that have been and are being used to combat delinquency are presented and described.

Two other essays in this section examine the role of the media in defining crime, how and why it occurs, its significance for the public, and what can be done to prevent it. Anne Seymour discusses how the media cover crimes and victimizations. As Seymour indicates, crime in the United States is big business. It attracts a great deal of attention. Seymour describes different media outlets, including television, newspapers, and the Internet. The media attempt to provide the public with every detail of crimes, especially high-profile ones. She examines the rights of victims and public's right to know about crime, listing the concerns of each. Seymour suggests various guidelines for the media to follow when covering crime and interviewing victims. She describes a victim's code of ethics as well as several significant issues for the media and courts.

Kenneth Dowler further explores the impact of the media on American society. Dowler's focus is on the public's impression of different agencies as portrayed by the media. Do the media influence how we view the effectiveness of law enforcement and the courts? Dowler illustrates how the public becomes involved and influences in various ways the punishments criminals receive. He explores the impact of the media and describes the court of public opinion as our awareness of crime is heightened.

1

"The History of Crime Prevention in the United States"

Dean John Champion

❖

INTRODUCTION

"Can crime be prevented? No. Most current crime control proposals are nonsense. The best criminological minds of our time do not have anything practical to offer" (Walker, 1992). Samuel Walker's gloomy forecast about our current crime control policies is a fair assessment of our many efforts to prevent crime. It is unlikely that we will ever develop perfect, workable crime prevention strategies that will end burglary, rape, robbery, larceny, vehicular theft, and other crimes. But on a positive note, Walker concedes that even though crime cannot be prevented, this doesn't necessarily mean that crime control is beyond our grasp. Crime prevention and its control is a continuing objective of local, state, and federal governments, and crime prevention initiatives are continuously being undertaken in almost every U.S. jurisdiction (Wilson and Petersilia, 2004).

This article is about crime prevention and its history. Crime prevention is the anticipation, recognition, and appraisal of crime risk and the initiation of some action to remove or reduce it (Marchant, 2005). Interest in crime prevention is not limited to the United States. Virtually every country in the world is interested in preventing crime and has devised one or more methods to achieve this general goal (Lab, 2004; Loveday, 2004; Maguire, Morgan, and Reiner, 2002).

The first part of this article examines crime prevention, its meaning, and evolution. The most direct and visible entity within the criminal justice system that has been given the greatest media attention is law enforcement. Law enforcement in every society follows particular mandates from citizens and their leadership. Most of these mandates are related directly or indirectly to crime prevention and control. Therefore, a brief historical account of the emergence and implementation of crime prevention and control initiatives throughout

3

the world will be presented. Although other countries have influenced crime prevention and control in the United States, England arguably has had the greatest influence over time. The relationship between English law enforcement, crime prevention and control and law enforcement systems and their evolution in the United States will be explored. This discussion is followed by a brief examination of several law enforcement crime prevention and control strategies which have been used in various U.S. jurisdictions during the past several decades.

The article next examines the role of the courts in crime prevention and control. The courts exercise considerable power through various sanctioning mechanisms. Legislatures are responsible for creating criminal laws and the courts are responsible for administering justice to those convicted of law violations. The courts are regarded as important in crime prevention and control because of the punishments judges may impose. Virtually every U.S. jurisdiction has experimented with different types of sentencing schemes designed to punish offenders for their criminal actions. No sentencing system has proved foolproof for preventing or controlling crime, however. But continuing modifications in sentencing practices and schemes are being undertaken, and often with mixed results.

The next section focuses upon corrections, particularly jails and prisons. Corrections are intended to correct criminal behavior and rehabilitate offenders. But correctional personnel are frequently overworked, understaffed, and underpaid. Correctional systems are often the last to receive governmental funding for systemic improvements. One result is extensive recidivism among those who eventually are freed from incarceration. Recidivism rates of 65 percent or higher are common, regardless of what corrections does to and for inmates while they are confined. These high recidivism rates characterize both inmates of correctional institutions and clients participating in community corrections programs. Different supervisory methods are used, often with disappointing results. Offender control strategies, which are in effect equivalent to crime control strategies, are imperfect. Both institutional and community correctional programs will be examined briefly.

Many adults have earlier careers as juvenile offenders. Juvenile delinquency, or crime committed by youths who have not yet attained the age of their majority, has been the target of scholarly study and practical interventions for over a century. While our insight into why juvenile delinquency occurs has improved, and while some of the interventions attempted have seemingly produced favorable results, we still face unacceptably high recidivism levels among our delinquent youth. Several delinquency prevention initiatives will be examined.

This reader contains a fairly broad collection of articles, essays, and reports about crime and delinquency prevention for both adults and juveniles. It follows the traditional division of the criminal justice system into law enforcement, the prosecution and courts, corrections, and the juvenile justice system. Several articles relating to crime prevention have been included in each part. The final part includes descriptions of attempted interventions with varying degrees of reported successfulness.

CRIME PREVENTION: MEANINGS AND THEORIES

Crime Prevention Defined

Crime prevention has at least two meanings. Sociologists define crime prevention as a reduction in poverty, an elimination of city slums known as breeding grounds for crime. A second meaning is architectural changes designed to make dwellings more secure against burglars or target-hardening. In the general case, crime prevention is any of several efforts designed to control criminal behavior. Crime prevention may be either direct, where environmental opportunities for crime are reduced, or indirect, where measures are used such as job training, remedial education, police surveillance, imprisonment, probation, or parole. For our purposes, crime prevention refers to all strategies or interventions designed to reduce criminal opportunity (Robert, 2003).

Theories of Crime and Crime Prevention

It is beyond the scope of this essay to investigate and report about the different theories offered to explain crime and its prevention. There are many types of crime, and for each type of crime, there are several plausible explanations for it. Theoretical schemes that attempt to explain and predict criminal behavior are loosely categorized into biological, psychological, and sociological explanations.

Biological explanations of crime explore one's physical attributes and biochemical composition. The rapid increase in the use of illegal drugs throughout the world has caused some criminologists and others to examine chemical dependencies and how they relate to criminal conduct. Most drugs are mood-altering substances. One's inhibitions are affected. Dependencies on controlled substances are frequently linked with both property crimes and assaultive behaviors as persons seek to feed and maintain their chemical dependencies (Baumer et al., 1998). Therefore, various strategies have been proposed to address the needs of chemically dependent persons and assist them in withdrawing from their drug addictions (Inciardi, 2003). Drug courts have been established to deal specifically with chemically dependent criminals and place them in rehabilitative environments known as therapeutic communities (Burdon et al., 2001; Cullen, 1997; DeLeon, 2000).

Psychological theories have attempted to link criminal behaviors to mental states or conditions. Early childhood experiences, for instance, are often linked with particular kinds of criminal conduct. As human beings grow and mature, different developmental stages have been identified as critical in forming one's personality and character. The psychological characteristics of criminals continue to be scrutinized for common elements that may explain their actions. The logic is that if we know what events are crucial in one's early development and maturational level, we might be able to impose interventions in the lives of those most likely to commit crime. Therefore, crime prevention is accomplished by attacking the psychological causes of it and interrupting the sequence of psychological events that inspire the very thoughts about committing crime (Agnew et al., 2002; Caspi et al., 1994; Krueger et al., 1994).

Sociological explanations focus upon one's socialization experiences with others, particularly one's peers. Groups are an integral part of one's experiences, and learning from others and being influenced by them in different ways are studied by sociologists and criminologists. For instance, delinquency is believed by many authorities to be a group-shared phenomenon. Because many adult criminals have earlier careers as delinquents, it makes sense to focus upon social experiences that contribute to delinquent conduct and alter them in various ways (Elliott et al., 1996). If delinquency can be prevented, then perhaps adult criminality can be prevented (Maguire, Morgan, and Reiner, 2002). Sociological theories of criminal conduct also stress the power of society as a sanctioning agent, and several interventions, including restorative justice, have been proposed as a means of encouraging persons to become law-abiding (Bazemore and Umbreit, 2001).

Crime Prevention as Crime Control

Ultimately the focus of attention of most criminal justice scholars is on controlling crime. It is believed that improving crime control will eventually reduce crime or prevent it. This is why substantial attention is given to crime control methods today throughout the criminal justice community. Since delinquency is crime committed by a juvenile, crime control strategies are broadly applicable to both adults and juveniles. Some of these strategies target adults, while other strategies are aimed at youthful offenders. More than a few strategies for crime control and prevention will be discussed in this book. These strategies will exhibit the multidimensionality of crime prevention and provide readers with an ample array of interventions that may work for either adult offenders, juvenile offenders, or both (McLaughlin and Muncie, 2001).

CRIME PREVENTION AND DETERRENCE

Deterrence

A no-nonsense approach to crime prevention is to deter persons from committing it. Deterrence is a diffuse concept and multidimensional. In the general case, deterrence refers to discouraging persons from committing crime (Braga et al., 2001; Kennedy, 1998; Levitt, 2002). Interestingly, Cesare Beccaria wrote about crime and its deterrence in 1764 in his classic work, *On Crimes and Punishments*. Beccaria was associated with originating the classical school of criminology. The classical school assumes that people are rational beings who exercise free will and choose between good and evil. Because societal progress and perpetuation are vital to nations and their continued existence, individuals must sacrifice some of their freedoms in order that all persons can pursue happiness and attain their goals. Evil actions impede societal progress and thus result in punishments. Evil acts vary in their seriousness, and therefore the severity of punishment for different evil actions should be proportionately adjusted. Beccaria believed that punishments should be swift, certain, and just, where the penalties are designed to fit the offense committed. The primary purposes of punishment, therefore, are deterrence and just deserts. Ideally, people will refrain from committing crime in order to avoid the pain of punishment. Furthermore, the punishment imposed is proportional to the amount of social and physical damage caused by the crime. In contemporary society, however, this ideal proportionality in punishment in relation to crime is seldom realized (Cullen, Fisher, and Applegate, 2000; Friedman, 1993; Maruna and Immarigeon, 2004).

Specific and General Deterrence

Beccaria's theme of deterrence has been perpetuated by contemporary scholars and modified in various ways (Nagin, 1998, 2001a). Two types of deterrence have been identified. These are specific and general deterrence. Specific deterrence refers to persons being discouraged from committing a crime because they have previously been caught and punished for an earlier offense. General deterrence refers to persons who know that others were punished for committing a crime and therefore refrain from committing the same offense for fear of being punished for it. In both instances, the fear of getting caught ideally functions as a deterrent to criminal offending. But since crime persists, it is evident that criminals continue to commit crimes despite apprehension and punishment risks (Cullen et al., 2002; Von Hirsch, 1998).

Crime prevention is also distinguished according to whether it is (1) primary; (2) secondary; or (3) tertiary. Primary crime prevention includes direct efforts to dissuade criminals from victimizing others. Primary crime prevention is similar to a preemptive strike, one which occurs before the actual criminal activity occurs. Therefore, attention is devoted to environmental design (e.g., neighborhood lighting and design, property identification); neighborhood watch programs (e.g., surveillance by citizens, citizen patrols); public education (e.g., educating the public about crime and its prevention); and social crime prevention (e.g., reducing unemployment and poverty, providing employment and/or job training assistance).

Secondary crime prevention consists of identifying certain persons most likely to engage in criminal activity and intervening in their lives to move them away from considering crime as a life alternative. Secondary crime prevention is also aimed at especially young persons, even pre-schoolers, and attempts are made to assist them to avoid the circumstances that contribute to their deviant conduct later. Early childhood intervention programs are an integral part of secondary crime prevention.

Tertiary crime prevention focuses upon persons who have been convicted of crimes and the programs created to assist them in becoming rehabilitated. Diversion is often used with minor first-offenders, where they are kept out of jails and prisons, even courts, while they perform community service or some other useful activity. Alternative dispute resolution, victim-offender reconciliation projects, restorative justice, and other similar programs are examples of various pre-trial crime control initiatives. For probationers and parolees, programming is promoted to enable them to acquire coping skills (e.g., vocational/educational training, employment assistance) or overcome their substance abuse and chemical dependencies. The main focus of tertiary crime prevention is upon offender rehabilitation and reintegration.

Critical Elements of Deterrence

Deterrence has been refined further with three critical elements: (1) certainty; (2) celerity; and (3) severity. Certainty refers to the strong likelihood that a criminal will be caught. Elaborate detection methods and forensics developments have contributed significantly to the certainty that a criminal will be identified, apprehended, and eventually punished for his/her criminal act. Celerity refers to the rapidity or speed of apprehension and punishment. If the time interval between a crime's commission and its solution is short, then the effect of a subsequent punishment is more pronounced. Severity refers to the nature of the punishment designed to fit particular crimes. For instance, the death penalty is a possible punishment for murder. It is intended to deter persons from killing one another. Knowing that you can be killed by the state if you kill another person may deter you from committing murder. But the information we have about the deterrent effects of the death penalty on homicide rates is discouraging. It is fairly clear that the death penalty fails to deter persons from committing murder (Bedau, 1992; Coleman, 1998; Van Soest et al., 2003).

EARLY FOUNDATIONS OF CRIME PREVENTION AND CONTROL

The foundations of crime prevention, control and deterrence are rooted in criminal laws of almost every society throughout the world. In remote tribal societies, criminal laws are most frequently orally articulated and understood. Ages of accountability are established, and punishments are proscribed. In industrialized, more complex social systems, criminal laws are codified and documented. The United States is a very legalistic society with elaborate court systems to hear disputes and settle them. Criminal acts are more or less clearly defined, and the nature and range of punishments are specified. But criminal laws did not originate with the United States. The earliest recorded criminal codes were established in 1868 B.C., although some historians believe similar codes existed several centuries earlier. Two ancient codes pertaining to prohibited acts and proscribed punishments are (1) the Code of Lipit-Istar (1868–1857 B.C.) and (2) the Code of Hammurabi (1792–1750 B.C.).

Code of Lipit-Ishtar (1868–1857 B.C.)

(Earliest known codifier of law in Sumeria). Perhaps the earliest codified laws pertaining to criminal acts, their prevention and punishment were contained in the Code of Lipit-Ishtar (1868–1857 B.C.). Some of these prohibited acts and their punishments are listed below:

1. If a man entered the orchard of (another) man and was seized there for stealing, he shall pay ten shekels of silver.
2. If a man cut down a tree in the garden of (another) man, he shall pay one half mina of silver.
3. If adjacent to the house of a man the bare ground of (another) man has been neglected and the owner of the house has said to the owner of the bare ground, "Because your ground has been neglected someone may break into my house: strengthen your house," and this agreement has been confirmed by him, the owner of the bare ground shall restore to the owner of the house any of his property which is lost.
4. If a man married a wife and she bore him children and those children are living, and a slave also bore children for her master (but) the father granted freedom to the slave and her children, the children of the slave shall not divide the estate with the children of their (former) master.
5. If a man's wife has not borne him children but a harlot (from) the public square has borne him children, he shall provide grain, oil and clothing for that harlot; the children which the harlot has borne him shall be his heirs, and as long as his wife lives the harlot shall not live in the house with the wife.
6. If a man rented an ox and injured the flesh at the nose ring, he shall pay one third of (its) price.
7. If a man rented an ox and damaged its eye, he shall pay one half of (its) price.
8. If a man rented an ox and broke its horn, he shall pay one fourth of (its) price.
9. If a man rented an ox and damaged its tail, he shall pay one fourth of (its) price.

The Code of Hammurabi (1792–1750 B.C., Babylon)

(Thought to be the first and most important codification of law in Babylon before the discovery of Lipit-Ishtar's code). Before the discovery of Lipit-Ishtar's code, the Code of Hammurabi (1792–1750 B.C.) was discovered in the ancient writings of Babylon. Some of these provisions are outlined below:

1. If a man charge a man with sorcery, but cannot convict him, he who is charged with sorcery shall go to the sacred river, and he shall throw himself into the river; if the river overcome him, his prosecutor shall take to himself his house. If the river show that man to be innocent and he come forth unharmed, he that charged him with sorcery shall be put to death. He who threw himself into the river shall take to himself the house of his accuser.

2. If a judge pronounce a judgment, render a decision, deliver a sealed verdict, and afterward reverse his judgment, they shall prosecute the judge for reversing the judgment which he has pronounced, and he shall pay twelve fold the damages which were (awarded) in said judgment; and publicly they shall expel him from his seat of judgment, and he shall not return, and with the judges in a case he shall not take his seat.

3. If a man steal ox or sheep, ass or pig, or boat—if it belonged to god or palace, he shall pay thirty fold; if it belonged to a common man, he shall restore tenfold. If the thief have nothing wherewith to pay, he shall be put to death.

4. If a man aid a male or a female slave of the palace, or a male or a female slave of a common man, to escape from the city, he shall be put to death.

5. If a fire break out in a man's house and a man who goes to extinguish it cast his eye on the household property of the owner of the house, and take the household property of the owner of the house, that man shall be thrown into the fire.

6. If a man owe a debt and Adad (the storm god) inundate the field or the flood carry the produce away, or, through lack of water, grain have not grown in the field, in that year he shall not make any return of grain to the creditor, he shall alter his contract-tablet and he need not pay the interest for that year.

7. If a man who is a tenant have paid the full amount of money for his rent for the year to the owner of the house, and he (the owner) say to him before "his days are full," "Vacate," the owner of the house, because he made the tenant move out of his house before "his days were full," shall lose the money which the tenant paid him.

8. If a man receive grain or silver from a merchant and do not have grain or silver to repay, but have personal property, whatever there is in his hand, when he brings it before witnesses, he shall give to the merchant. The merchant shall not refuse (it), he shall receive (it).

9. If the agent be careless and do not take a receipt for the money which he has given to the merchant, the money not receipted for shall not be placed to his account.

10. If a priestess or a nun who is not a resident in a convent open a wineshop or enter a wineshop for a drink, they shall burn that woman.

11. If the wife of a man be taken in lying with another man, they shall bind them and throw them into the water. If the husband of the woman spare the life of his wife, the king shall spare the life of his servant.

12. If a woman hate her husband and say, "Thou shalt not have me," her past shall be inquired into for any deficiency of hers; and if she have been careful and be without past sin and her husband have been going out and greatly belittling her, that woman has no blame. She shall take her dowry and go to her father's house.

13. If a man, after (the death of) his father, lie in the bosom of his mother, they shall burn both of them.

14. If a man take a wife and she bear him children and that woman die, her father may not lay claim to her dowry. Her dowry belongs to her children.

15. If a man destroy the eye of another man, they shall destroy his eye.

16. If he breaks a man's bone, they shall break his bone.

17. If a man knock out a tooth of a man of his own rank, they shall knock out his tooth.

18. If a man knock out a tooth of a common man, he shall pay one-third mana of silver.

19. If a man hire an ox and cause its death through neglect or abuse, he shall restore ox for ox to the owner of the ox.

20. If an ox when passing through the street gore a man and bring about his death, that case has no penalty.

Therefore, written codes of specific acts with accompanying specific punishments existed many centuries before the great Roman Empire. Where these laws were applicable, citizens were aware of what was prohibited and either refrained from committing these prohibited acts or committed them and suffered the consequences. Interestingly the emphasis of the punishments of both of these codes, therefore, was revenge, restitution, or victim compensation. The logical function of these codes was to deter persons from doing wrong, or whatever the society at the time regarded as behaviors or acts that should be prohibited. Prisons hadn't been invented yet, and the idea of sentencing persons to terms of months or years in places of confinement was unknown. Many centuries later, facilities would be developed in different cities and countries that would become the forerunners of contemporary corrections and our present penal systems.

ROME, CENTURIONS, AND EARLY CRIME PREVENTION INITIATIVES

Centurions and *Frumentarii*

It is well-documented that ancient Egypt and Mesopotamia had regulatory forces that maintained order and controlled law-breaking behavior (Adamson, 1991). Subsequently in early Rome, from about 100 B.C. to A.D. 200, centurions were used for crime prevention purposes. Centurions commanded units of 100 men, and these forces were used for both combat and regulating citizen conduct. During A.D. 50–100, the Romans created the first criminal investigative units called *Frumentarii*. Frumentarii: (1) supervised grain distribution to the poor; (2) oversaw message deliveries among government officials; and (3) detected crime and prosecuted offenders (Adamson, 1991). Regarding this latter function, the Frumentarii investigated crime scenes, conducted criminal interrogations, and made deals with certain criminals in exchange for information about other criminals.

The Norman Conquest and the Frankpledge System

From about 100 A.D. to A.D. 800, crime prevention developments and innovations are sketchy at best (Bailey, 1986). Of greatest interest to American crime prevention, a crude system of crime awareness and prevention was devised in early England at the time of the Norman Conquest in 1066. The frankpledge system was established, which required loyalty to the King of England and shared law and order responsibilities among the public. The frankpledge system meant that neighbors should form into small groups to assist and protect one another if they were ever victimized by criminals. These were usually civilian groups organized and administered by civilian authorities. Crime control during this period was shared among community residents. Also, these neighborhood groups were led by constables who were often favored noblemen appointed by the King. These constables were the equivalent of early police officers. Citizens performed both day watch duties and night watch duties on a rotating basis. Day and night watches were like contemporary police shift work. These watchmen were expected to yell out a "hue and a cry" in the event they saw crimes being committed or if there were community disturbances. Some of the more affluent citizens hired their own watchmen to perform crime prevention duties. These were probably the forerunners of the private police as we know them today (Adamson, 1991).

Shire-Reeves and Chancellors

During the next few centuries, English territories were divided into shires or counties, and the chief law enforcement officers of these shires were called reeves. Thus, each shire had a reeve. Combining these two terms, the term, sheriff, has been derived (shire-reeve). Shire-reeves were agents appointed by the King of England and maintained the peace. The King also appointed chancellors as his court agents to hear and settle citizen disputes, such as property boundary issues, trespass charges, and child misconduct. Between shire-reeves and chancellors, and subsequently justices of the peace originating in about A.D. 1200, order was maintained in these English jurisdictions and a system of crime control was perpetuated. These posts and the general system of justice supported by the King of England were continued for several centuries. When the American colonies were established, English practices relating to law enforcement and crime prevention were continued. This is because the new colonists simply perpetuated practices with which they were familiar.

THE AMERICAN COLONIES

As the American colonies grew and became more complex, several differences in law enforcement and judicial practices emerged compared with prior English practices. Some colonies created systems of electing sheriffs who could hire their own deputies to assist in law and crime control tasks. In other colonies, however, certain practices of law enforcement begun in early England were perpetuated in numerous colonial jurisdictions. The watchman style of using citizens on a rotating basis to maintain protective 24/7 watches over their communities was a continued crime prevention pattern.

Watchmen, Shouts, and Rattles

Most colonial communities were rural, and thus, formal crime prevention initiatives were unnecessary. More informal prevention methods were the most practical. Informal watchman monitoring in these largely rural jurisdictions is appreciated even more by the fact that between 1630 and 1790, there were only eight communities with populations of 8,000 or larger (Hageman, 1985: 16). In the colony of New York, for instance, watchmen used shouts and rattles to alert citizens of law-breakers. Watchmen were equipped with noise-making rattles and were expected to shout and shake their rattles if they observed crimes or fleeing suspects. Rattle watchmen weren't paid much. They made 48 cents per day for their efforts. Furthermore, as a punishment for their wrongdoing, offenders themselves were often sentenced to rattle watches (Richardson, 1970; Trojanowicz and Moore, 1988).

Contemporaneous Developments in England: The Bow Street Runners and Thief-Takers

In the early 1700s, jurisdictions such as Philadelphia established finite patrol areas supervised by constables who commanded squads of volunteers, drawn largely from the citizenry. These methods were copied by other colonies throughout the 1700s. During this same time period in England, Henry Fielding, an author-turned-politician, devised several new ideas about crime prevention. In 1748, he was appointed chief magistrate of Bow Street in London. He organized small groups of citizens to pursue criminals. These persons were known as thief-takers and were selected, in part, by being fleet of foot. Thief-takers received rewards from victims whenever they returned stolen merchandise taken from captured criminals. When Henry Fielding died in 1754, Sir John Fielding succeeded him and converted the thief-takers into the Bow Street Runners, a small group of paid officers who were quite successful at apprehending criminals. These activities did not go unnoticed in the colonies. Eventually, the Revolutionary War effectively separated and resolved English and American political and legal policies, although English influence on subsequent policing methods continues to the present (Peak, 1993: 9).

LAW ENFORCEMENT FROM 1800 TO THE PRESENT

The Metropolitan Police of London

The establishment of the Metropolitan Police of London in 1829 by Sir Robert Peel, the British Home Secretary, was one of the most significant developments of the early 1800s. The context within which this organization was established was in an era of police reform. Earlier, in 1792, an influential London magistrate, Patrick Colquhoun, believed that police should be used to establish and maintain order, control and prevent crime, and set an example of good conduct and moral sense for the citizenry. He also believed that existing enforcement methods, at least in London, were antiquated and improper. He believed that professionalism among officers was necessary (Lee, 1901). Unfortunately, Colquhoun didn't live to see his ideas implemented. However, strong endorsement for them came from Sir Robert Peel, a prominent government official. Despite initial hesitation from rival politicians, Peel was successful in establishing the first official law enforcement organization in England. This was the result of the Metropolitan Police Act of 1829. Under this Act, 6,000 officers were hired whose primary qualifications included the ability to read and write, be of good moral character, and be physically fit (Miller and Hess, 1994).

The general principles of the Metropolitan Police of London were:

1. To prevent crime and disorder, as an alternative to their repression by military force and severity of legal punishment.

2. To recognize always that the power of the police to fulfill their functions and duties is dependent on public approval of their existence, actions and behavior; and on their ability to secure and maintain public respect.

3. To recognize always that to secure and maintain the respect and approval of the public means also the securing of the willing cooperation of the public in the task of securing observance of the law.

4. To recognize always that the extent to which the cooperation of the public can be secured diminishes, proportionately, the necessity of the use of physical force and compulsion for achieving police objectives.

5. To seek and preserve public favor, not by pandering to public opinion, but by constantly demonstrating absolutely impartial service to law, in complete independence of policy, and without regard to the justice or injustice of the substance of individual laws, by ready offering of individual service and friendship to all members of the public without regard to their wealth or social standing; by ready exercise of courtesy and good humor; and by ready offering of individual sacrifice in protecting and preserving life.

6. To use physical force only when the exercise of persuasion, advice and warning is found to be insufficient to obtain public cooperation to an extent necessary to secure observance of law or to restore order; and to use only the minimum degree of physical force which is necessary on any particular occasion for achieving a police objective.

7. To maintain at all times a relationship with the public that gives reality to the historic tradition that the police are the public and that the public are the police; the police being only members of the public who are paid to give full-time attention to duties which are incumbent on every citizen in the interests of community welfare and existence.

8. To recognize always the need for strict adherence to police-executive functions, and to refrain from even seeming to usurp the powers of the judiciary of avenging individuals or the State, and of authoritative judging guilt and punishing the guilty.

9. To recognize always that the test of police efficiency is the absence of crime and disorder and not the visible evidence of police action in dealing with them.

Emphasized in these principles are several police-citizen initiatives, including obtaining public cooperation in observance of the law, seeking and preserving public favor, using minimal force to effect arrests of alleged criminals, and to always maintain favorable relations with the public in the process of crime control.

The Influence of the Metropolitan Police on American Law Enforcement Philosophy and Operations

Law enforcement agencies in the United States during the early 1800s were significantly influenced by Metropolitan Police of London and its principles. In fact, the New York City Police Department modeled its own organization after the Metropolitan Police of London in 1844. By the late 1850s, many other cities had patterned their law enforcement organizations after this organization. These cities included Chicago, Boston, Baltimore, Philadelphia, New Orleans, and Newark (Fosdick, 1920).

The nature of law enforcement, especially in large cities, underwent significant change because of growing urbanization and industrialization. Police organizations in city areas grew significantly. These organizations became increasingly bureaucratic, with numerous divisions and departments, each with its particular area of specialization. Local, state, and federal government law enforcement agencies expanded simultaneously. With the growth of these organizations and expanded law enforcement interests, police work gradually became more specialized.

August Vollmer and O.W. Wilson

In 1908, August Vollmer, the Chief of Police of Berkeley, California, suggested more formal professional and educational training for police officers he commanded. Relying heavily on academic specialists in various forensics areas, Vollmer initiated an informal academic regimen of police training, including investigative techniques, photography, fingerprinting, and anatomy, among other academic subject-areas. By 1917, he persuaded the University of California–Berkeley to experiment with his new criminology and law enforcement curriculum for the purpose of providing his new recruits with formal academic training.

Several of Vollmer's innovations became widely popular and adopted. For instance, he pioneered the first fully motorized police force for the purpose of developing more effective patrolling activities for his officers. Vollmer was also credited with pioneering the use of two-way radios in police cars. This innovation greatly improved crime detection and prevention activities and increased the apprehension of fleeing suspects. His police selection methods resulted in officer appointments based upon emotional, educational, and physical fitness through selection by test. He interviewed prospective recruits as a screening tool. Psychologists were also used by Vollmer for this purpose. In many respects, Vollmer is considered the father of police professionalization. Some scholars have termed this period the professionalization movement (Walker, 1992:12). One of Vollmer's students was O.W. Wilson, a former police chief in Wichita, Kansas and Chicago, Illinois. Wilson eventually became the first Dean of the School of Criminology at the University of California–Berkeley in 1950. Wilson centralized police administration and created command decision making in Berkeley. Many other cities copied Wilson's ideas during this period (Wilson and McLaren, 1977).

The Wickersham Commission

The first study of the U.S. criminal justice system on a national scale was conducted by the federal government in 1931. President Herbert Hoover appointed a National Commission on Law Observance and Enforcement, known subsequently as the Wickersham Commission, in 1929. After two years of investigation, the Wickersham Commission issued a 15-volume report. One of these volumes examined police lawlessness and concerned police abuse of authority. Another criticism was that little consistency was apparent concerning the selection, training, and administration of police recruits throughout the United States. The obvious implication was that changes in existing recruitment and training practices for subsequent police officers should be made. These were ideas for change suggested and supported by both Vollmer and Wilson. Over the next several decades, more sophisticated police selection and training methods were established in many jurisdictions and have been reasonably successful in improving the quality of officers in police departments generally.

The Law Enforcement Assistance Administration

In 1968, the Law Enforcement Assistance Administration (LEAA) was created. The LEAA was a product of the President's Crime Commission during the period 1965–1967, a time of great social unrest and civil disobedience. Because of these societal conditions, the police were playing a more prominent role in maintaining law and order. The LEAA allocated millions of dollars to researchers and police departments over the next decade for various purposes. Many experiments were conducted, including using innovative patrolling strategies in different communities. Crime prevention and crime control were key aims of LEAA activity through greater police professionalization.

The National Advisory Commission on Criminal Justice Standards and Goals

In 1973, the National Advisory Commission on Criminal Justice Standards and Goals elaborated several important goals for police departments as a part of their diverse functions. Some of these goals include:

1. Maintenance of order
2. Enforcement of the law
3. Prevention of criminal activity
4. Detection of criminal activity
5. Apprehension of criminals
6. Participation in court proceedings
7. Protection of constitutional guarantees
8. Assistance to those who cannot care for themselves or who are in danger of physical harm
9. Control of traffic
10. Resolution of day-to-day conflicts among family, friends, and neighbors
11. Creation and maintenance of a feeling of security in the community
12. Promotion and preservation of civil order (National Advisory Commission on Criminal Justice Standards and Goals, 1973:104–105).

It is clear from these goals that crime prevention and control are integral features of policing activity. These goals refer to order maintenance, conflict resolutions among community residents, and providing members of the community with a greater sense of security through the detection and prevention of criminal behavior and the apprehension of criminals.

LAW ENFORCEMENT AND CRIME PREVENTION

What sorts of crime control strategies can be implemented by law enforcement agencies? Some of the options and alternatives for police agencies include (1) greater visibility and surveillance; (2) modifications of patrol styles; (3) community policing; and (4) the establishment of awareness programs.

Greater Visibility and Surveillance

Increased police visibility and surveillance activities are believed by some scholars and practitioners to deter crime. Many of the programs promoted and supported by the LEAA were based on the idea that more money for law enforcement purposes would reduce crime. Unfortunately, despite the money provided by the LEAA, crime rates in the United States remained unchanged (Kelling, Pate, Dieckman, and Brown, 1974).

One of the most controversial studies that tested the effectiveness of preventive patrol and its influence on the crime rate occurred in 1972 in Kansas City, Missouri. This study was called the Kansas City Preventive Patrol Experiment (Kelling, 1974). Funded by a grant from the Police Foundation, the Kansas City Police Department conducted a comprehensive experiment to determine the effectiveness of routine preventive patrol (Kelling et al., 1974). The experiment varied the numbers of routine preventive patrols within fifteen of the Kansas City police beats or those habitual patrols conducted by police officers. The fifteen beats were divided into three groups of five each. In the control beats, routine preventive patrol was maintained by the usual one-car patrol. In the reactive beats, routine patrols were eliminated. Instead, police officers responded only to calls for assistance from citizens. In the proactive beats, routine preventive patrol was increased to three cars per patrol. The Kansas City Police Department randomly dispersed 1,300 police officers throughout the Southern district of the city of 500,000 according to these different beat groupings.

The duration of the experiment was from July, 1972 to September, 1973. Data were collected about crime rates during that period, citizen perceptions of police service and visibility, police response time to citizen calls, and the satisfaction of citizens with police services. The results showed that the presence or absence of police patrols had no effect on the number of residential and non-residential burglaries, auto thefts, larcenies, robberies, and vandalism. These findings were important because these crimes are usually considered deterred through preventive patrol. Furthermore, the fear among citizens about crime was unaffected. The attitudes of business persons toward crime and police services were unaffected also, as well as the level of citizen satisfaction with police services and response time. In fact, it showed that increasing or decreasing the number of police patrols in Kansas City suburbs had no effect on the amount of crime in those suburbs where the experiment was conducted.

Modifications of Patrol Styles

Several experiments have been conducted which focus upon variations in police patrol styles. In San Diego, California, the police experimented in 1977 with one-officer and two-officer patrol cars and compared their relative effectiveness of response to scenes of crime incidents (Kessler, 1985). One-officer patrol cars were usually more responsive compared with two-officer patrol cars, with an obvious savings of citizens' tax dollars.

In Flint, Michigan, experiments were conducted using police foot patrols working in tandem with patrol car units (Payne and Trojanowicz, 1985). Again, the primary benefit derived seemed to be improvements in relations between officers and citizens as well as improved officer morale rather than serious reductions in the rate of crime in the affected Flint neighborhoods. Police officers on foot patrol felt safer, felt more confident that community residents would help them if they got into trouble, felt that they were keeping up with problems in their patrol areas, and felt they were improving police-community relations (Trojanowicz and Banas, 1985a, 1985b). But was crime in Flint, Michigan, prevented or controlled as a result of the foot patrol program? The results were inconclusive.

Beat patrolling has been used as well. Police officers are assigned a regular beat where they can become closely acquainted with neighborhood residents and business persons. Obvious benefits for police-community relations include instant recognition of unfamiliar faces and potential criminals and the potential for reduced crime (Manning, 1984).

In Tampa, Florida, the Tampa Police Department experimented with golf cart patrolling during the 1980s (Smith and Taylor, 1985). Patrolling with golf carts seemed like a good idea, since golf carts were highly maneuverable and enabled police officers to access civilians more directly. However, other than improving public relations between the citizens and police who patrolled city areas on golf carts, crime prevention was not affected significantly. Subsequently, experiments have been conducted with police officers riding horses, bicycles, and scooters, and other conveyances, but little evidence suggests that these patrolling styles have caused dramatic decreases in crime in those areas where experiments have been conducted.

Community Policing

Community policing is an umbrella term encompassing any law enforcement agency or community citizen or group-initiated plan or program to enable police officers and community residents to work cooperatively in creative ways that will (1) reduce or control crime, fear of crime, and the incidence of victimizations; (2) promote mutual understanding for the purpose of enhancing police officer/citizen coproduction of community safety and security; and (3) establish a police-citizen communications network through which mutual problems may be discussed and resolved. More or less synonymous with community policing are police-community relations, the "back to the community" movement, "problem-oriented" policing, community-based policing, proactive policing, neighborhood policing, community-oriented policing, community crime and drug prevention, community-based crime prevention, citizen coproduction of community safety, the new blue line, team policing, order maintenance policing, ombudsman policing, community wellness, "grass roots" policing, and crime control policing. Many of these terms or phrases connote a cooperative or symbiotic relation between law enforcement and the community (Das, 1986).

The Establishment of Awareness Programs

Police-sponsored citizen awareness programs, particularly in crimes of theft or burglary, are helpful in assisting police in their recovery and identification of stolen property. Awareness programs include Operation Identification which involves the labeling of all valuable personal property on one's premises with an identifying number (Clarke and Hough, 1984). Police departments often furnish their citizens with devices for imprinting their Social Security numbers on valuable possessions such as television sets and stereos. If these items are subsequently stolen and recovered, they can be traced more easily to the rightful own-ers. These tactics frustrate criminals who attempt to fence their stolen goods to persons who purchase stolen property for resale.

Alexandria, Virginia, police officers work with the Police Operations Bureau to con-duct visits to new homeowners (Seiffert, 1984). They provide useful information concern-ing the neighborhood, city services, and particularly, the crime prevention responsibilities of the citizen. Homeowner's packets are provided which include emergency telephone numbers, tips on what to do if someone is breaking into the residence, and ways of making the residence less susceptible to burglars. Identification labels for valuables are also pro-vided, and a checklist is included for listing serial numbers of portable appliances and equipment that are easily stolen and prime targets of theft.

Other Programs

Numerous other programs have been implemented by law enforcement agencies to assist citizens guard against property crimes and violent victimizations. For property crimes, dif-ferent types of target-hardening have been suggested. Better locks on doors, installations of security systems wired to central monitoring sources, and a host of other crime detection devices have been recommended to those able to afford them (Graves et al., 1985). Neigh-borhood Watch programs have been implemented in high-crime areas which utilize citizens to keep an eye out for potential neighborhood intruders or suspicious activities. Voluntary citizens' neighborhood patrols have been established. These patrols assist the neighborhood generally by providing a crime watch, reporting suspicious activities to police, observing and recording license numbers of suspicious automobiles in neighborhoods, and visibly de-terring persons from burglarizing homes (Graves et al., 1985). One of the fastest growing and visible crime control programs operated at the community level is Crime Stoppers. Crime Stoppers was originated by a police officer, Greg MacAleese, in Albuquerque, New Mexico, in 1976. In 1978, he had established five programs in various cities. The Crime Stoppers program is typically nonprofit and consists of a board of directors from the com-munity. These persons set policy, coordinate fundraising, and formulate a system of rewards (Graves et al., 1985).

Law enforcement has also become quite proactive in its use of computer technology for crime fighting and prevention. In recent years police departments throughout the nation have engaged in crime mapping and the use of mathematical models in charting hot spots or high-crime areas more deserving of their attention and presence (Block, 1998; Sanow, 2003). Tracking crime by its frequency and location over time seems productive in pre-venting its occurrence in those areas designated (Maltz, Gordon, and Friedman, 1991).

THE COURTS AND CRIME PREVENTION

The courts have been both directly and indirectly involved in crime prevention and control efforts for several centuries. The primary crime prevention and control efforts exercised by the courts are through sentencing offenders for committing different types of crime. Every crime is defined and governed by a statute. Each statute has an accompanying penalty, which is either a fine, imprisonment of a specified number of months or years, or both. Judges im-pose sentences on convicted offenders. The functions of sentencing are to (1) promote respect for the law; (2) reflect the seriousness of the offense; (3) promote just punishment for the offense; (4) protect the public from convicted offenders; (5) provide educational and vocational training and other forms of rehabilitative assistance; and (6) deter future criminal conduct.

Promoting respect for the law and deterring future criminal conduct are directly connected with the crime prevention functions of the courts. The public deserves protection from dangerous persons convicted of serious crimes. Offenders without educational and/or vocational training should receive some type of assistance to enhance their subsequent reintegration into society. Rehabilitation of offenders is an indirect way of reducing crime and controlling offenders. Providing them with better means of coping by helping them to become more productive citizens should induce greater law-abiding behavior.

Sentencing, therefore, is an important court function. Through sentencing, criminals are deterred, controlled, punished, and rehabilitated. But sentencing, regardless of its severity, does not seem to fulfill the deterrence function. Over 65 percent of all sentenced offenders eventually commit new crimes. These recidivists are the primary reason that sentencing reforms occur. If a particular sentencing scheme doesn't work, then change it to a scheme that works better. Or so the thinking goes. Unfortunately, no sentencing scheme is without its critics, and all sentencing schemes are flawed in one respect or another.

The following types of sentencing schemes are used in most jurisdictions: (1) indeterminate sentencing; (2) determinate sentencing; (3) mandatory sentencing; and (4) presumptive sentencing. Indeterminate sentencing was originally used in the United States and continues to be used, despite the fact that other alternative schemes have replaced it in various jurisdictions. Indeterminate sentencing occurs where the court sets either explicit (according to statute) or implicit upper and lower limits on the amount of time to be served by the offender, and where the actual release date from prison is determined by a parole board. The judge may sentence an offender to "one to ten years," or "not more than five years," and a parole board determines when the offender may be released within the limits of those time intervals.

When judges place certain offenders on probation and allow them to remain free in their communities, some of these offenders will reoffend. In fact, about 65 percent of these persons will reoffend over time. When recidivism occurs among probationers, judges are blamed for exercising poor discretion. Parole board discretion is similar to judicial sentencing discretion. Approximately 65 percent of all paroled persons eventually are returned to prison for new crimes. When parolees recidivate, parole boards are blamed for poor decision making. Therefore, if judges and parole boards have recidivism rates of 65 percent or higher among their probationers and parolees, the indeterminate sentencing system under which offenders have been sentenced must be faulty.

One response has been to shift to a sentencing scheme that eliminates the discretionary powers of parole boards. Determinate sentencing has been viewed as an improvement over indeterminate sentencing. Determinate sentencing is a fixed term of incarceration that must be served in full, less any good time earned while in prison. Good time is the reduction in the amount of time incarcerated amounting to a certain number of days per month for each month served. If inmates obey the rules and stay out of trouble, they accumulate good time credit which accelerates their release from incarceration. In states using determinate sentencing, parole boards have no discretion in determining an inmate's early release. Prisoners serve a fixed amount of time. Prisoners may receive 15 days or more of good time credit per month for every month served. Thus, when half of their original sentences are served, they are automatically released from prison without any input from parole boards.

Judges are likewise restricted through what is termed presumptive or guidelines-based sentencing. Presumptive or guidelines-based sentencing is a specific sentence, usually expressed as a range of months, for each and every offense or offense class. The sentence must be imposed in all unexceptional cases, but when there are mitigating or aggravating circumstances, judges are permitted some latitude in shortening or lengthening sentences within specific boundaries. Presumptive sentencing is regarded as a strategy designed to remove the discretionary powers from judges to place offenders on probation or give them extraordinarily short sentences. If judges must follow guidelines, then there will be fewer probationers. If there are fewer probationers, there will be less recidivism. This simplistic thinking, though seemingly logical, is faulty. It doesn't work. When prisoners are eventually released through an accumulation of good-time credits, about 60–70 percent of them will become recidivists within a few years. Thus, their recidivism is merely prolonged.

A fourth sentencing scheme is mandatory sentencing. Mandatory sentencing is the imposition of an incarcerative sentence of a specified length, for certain crimes or certain categories of offenders, and where no option of probation, suspended sentence, or immediate parole eligibility exists. Mandatory sentences are usually imposed upon chronic or habitual offenders, those who use firearms during the commission of crimes, or who deal large quantities of drugs. One example of a mandatory sentence is Virginia Exile, an initiative passed by the Virginia legislature to provide mandatory 5-year terms of incarceration upon anyone convicted of using a firearm during the commission of a felony. The purpose of Virginia Exile is to deter persons from using dangerous weapons if they are going to commit crimes anyway. If dangerous weapons are not used, then fewer victims will suffer death or serious bodily injury. The mandatory penalty of a flat 5 years upon conviction is considered a significantly stringent deterrent to firearms use during a crime's commission (Raphael and Ludwig, 2003).

Habitual offenders who commit numerous offenses can be charged with violating an Habitual Offender Statute. If they are convicted of violating this statute, the penalty may be a life-without-the-possibility-of-parole term. Supposedly this harsh penalty will deter them from committing more crimes. Some states have Three-Strikes-and-You're-Out laws that provide for mandatory life terms for those convicted of 3 or more felonies. Other states have truth-in-sentencing provisions that dictate a fixed proportion of their sentence must be served before they become eligible for parole. Are these harsher, mandatory penalties deterrents to future criminal offending? Several critics are pessimistic and argue that they do nothing more than increase incarceration rates in prisons and jails (Boswell et al., 2002; Vitiello, 1997).

It is doubtful that any sentencing reform will generate a totally acceptable solution to the problem of sentencing offenders. It seems that no matter what is done relating to sentencing, the recidivism numbers remain virtually unchanged. Of course, it is argued persuasively that if offenders are locked up for longer periods of time, then they are not able to perpetrate crimes in their communities against innocent citizens during their incarceration. But it is presently impossible to lock up all offenders. Probably only about a fifth of all offenders who deserve incarceration can be accommodated by existing prison and jail space at any given time. This is why sound decision making is crucial during both sentencing and early release processes.

CORRECTIONS AND CRIME PREVENTION

Corrections is an umbrella term encompassing institutional and community corrections. Institutional corrections consists of prisons and jails, while community corrections oversees probationers, parolees, and other various forms of noncustodial community supervision. At the beginning of 2006 over 8.4 million persons were under some form of correctional supervision. Approximately 1/3 of these persons, or over 2.2 million, were inmates of jails and prisons, while over 6.2 million were under some form of community correctional supervision as probationers or parolees (U.S. Department of Justice, 2006).

Institutional Corrections

Jails are short-term facilities designed to hold offenders for less than one year. There are exceptions. Jail functions include (1) holding indigents, vagrants, and the mentally ill; (2) holding pretrial detainees; (3) housing witnesses in protective custody; (4) holding convicted offenders awaiting sentencing; (5) housing persons serving short-term sentences; (6) housing certain dangerous juvenile offenders; (7) holding persons on detainer warrants; (8) holding persons for probation or parole violations; (9) holding contract prisoners; (10) operating community-based programs and jail boot camps; and (11) holding mentally ill inmates pending their removal to mental hospitals. For most jurisdictions, jails are administered by county sheriffs.

In contrast, prisons are state or federally funded and operated institutions to house convicted offenders under continuous custody on a long-term basis. Compared with jails, prisons are completely self-contained and self-sufficient. The functions of prisons are (1) to provide societal protection; (2) to punish offenders; (3) to rehabilitate offenders; and (4) to reintegrate offenders.

The crime prevention/control value of prisons and jails is questionable (Barr, 1999; Kerle, 1998a). Most jails are small and ill-equipped to deal with serious inmate problems. Larger jails have better capabilities for dealing with substance abuse issues and even certain types of mental illness (Szostak and Marrow, 2001; Walsh, 2000; Wexler et al., 1992). However, most jail inmates are incarcerated for short terms and thus, any therapy they receive may be insufficient to address their particular needs fully.

Prisons are chronically overcrowded. While it is believed that prisoners should receive therapy, counseling, vocational and educational training, and other forms of therapy and assistance, the fact is that fewer than 25 percent of all prison inmates receive such assistance annually (Anderson, 1995). Vocational and educational assistance for inmates in both prisons and jails is sorely lacking, and many inmates leave these settings without ever receiving any worthwhile training (Finn, 1998a, 1998b).

Prison industries are for-profit enterprises operated within prison walls to assist prisoners in learning useful vocational skills and trades. Many citizens believe that any prisoner can have access to any job any time while confined. But only about 22 percent of all U.S. inmates are able to find work in prison industries. There simply aren't enough jobs available to accommodate all prisoners who wish to work (Garvey, 1998; Miller, 1997). The general consensus among criminal justice professionals is that prisons warehouse offenders. Under such conditions, no rehabilitation occurs. Inmates are subsequently released back into the community without new skills or needed counseling or therapy. The contribution of institutional corrections to crime prevention and control is seriously undermined, therefore.

Community Corrections

Community corrections encompasses over 6 million clients. For the majority, these consist of probationers. Less than a third are parolees. Most probation and parole programs are locally operated. There is great variation among jurisdictions concerning the types of services clients receive while on probation or parole. Various community-based correctional alternatives include programs, such as intensive probation or parole supervision, home confinement, electronic surveillance or monitoring, narcotics and drug deterrence, work furlough programs or work release, study release, day reporting centers, and probationer violation and restitution residential centers (Israel and Dawes, 2002). Also included under the community corrections umbrella are programs such as diversion, pretrial release, and pre-parole (Harris, 1999).

Probation and parole officers (PPOs) supervise clients more or less closely. PPOs have diverse functions. These functions include not only monitoring their clients' behaviors in different ways, but also furnishing them with assistance from different community agencies. The goals of community corrections programs include (1) facilitating offender reintegration; (2) fostering offender rehabilitation; (3) providing an alternative range of offender punishments; and (4) heightening offender accountability.

All offenders under probation or parole supervision sign agreements to remain law-abiding and submit to random searches by their supervising PPOs. They are subject to such searches at any time, day or night. They may be subjected to drug tests at any time. They are required to work at jobs at particular times. They must submit timely reports of their activities. They are to report if they have any contact with any law enforcement agency. About 6 percent of all probationers and parolees are intensively supervised, meaning that they have more face-to-face visits per week or month with their supervising PPOs. For most probationers and parolees, however, their supervision is minimal.

When a probationer or parolee violates one or more terms of his/her probation/parole, the violation may or may not be reported by the supervising PPO. If the violation is serious enough, or if there are frequent violations, then the matter is brought to the attention of the judge (for probationers) or the parole board (for parolees). Action will be taken to address the nature of the violation, and proceedings will be conducted to determine the outcome. Often, probation or parole violators are returned to the streets and not incarcerated. But they may be returned under more supervision. It is beyond the ability of any PPO to control the behaviors of their clients. The threat of a probation or parole violation is often a sufficient deterrent, however, and most of these persons remain law-abiding during their probation or parole terms.

It is unknown precisely how much crime prevention or control occurs while probationers or parolees are under supervision. Catching a client in the act of violating one or more probation or parole program conditions may be accidental, largely due to the lack of supervision such clients receive. For some clients, they may be arrested for new crimes. These arrests come to the attention of supervising PPOs by law enforcement agencies.

A relatively small proportion of clients is supervised by electronic monitoring and/or home confinement, and they may be obligated to adhere to curfews and other behavioral requirements. A growing number of probationers and parolees in particular states, such as Florida, are subject to surveillance by global positioning satellite tracking systems (Mercer, Brooks, and Bryant, 2000; Toombs, 1995). These nonintrusive methods of supervision seem to be effective deterrents to new criminal activity, at least while they are being used. But again, no surveillance scheme is foolproof.

JUVENILES AND DELINQUENCY PREVENTION

Juveniles Defined

Several criteria are used to classify and define juvenile offenders. In the 1899 Illinois Act that created juvenile courts, the jurisdiction of such courts would extend to all juveniles under the age of 16 who were found in violation of any state or local law or ordinance. About a fifth of all states place the upper age limit for juveniles at either 15 or 16. In most other states, the upper age limit for juveniles is 17, except for Wyoming, where the upper age limit is 18. Ordinarily, the jurisdiction of juvenile courts includes all juveniles between the ages of 7 and 18. Federal law defines juveniles as any persons who have not attained their 18th birthday (18 U.S.C., Sec. 5031, 2006).

Age Jurisdiction of Juvenile Courts

The age jurisdiction of juvenile courts over juveniles varies among the states. The federal government has no juvenile court. Common law applied in many jurisdictions provides that the minimum age of accountability is 7. Thus, it is given that youths under the age of 7 are presumed incapable of formulating criminal intent and are not responsible under the law. Most states provide lower age limits such as 12, 13, or 14 for their juvenile courts.

Delinquency and Status Offenses

Juvenile delinquents are any youths under the age of adulthood in their particular jurisdiction who commit an act that would be a crime if an adult committed it. Thus, any juvenile who commits a felony or misdemeanor would be a delinquent. Some offenses are specific only to juveniles and do not place them in the delinquency category. Such offenses are known as status offenses. These include truancy, curfew violations, runaway behavior, and underage drinking. Juvenile courts have the capacity to punish these offenders in different ways.

Regarding status offenders, juvenile courts are most interested in chronic or persistent offenders, such as those who habitually appear before juvenile court judges. Repeated juvenile court exposure by status offenders may eventually be followed by adult criminality, although there is little support for this view in the research literature. The chronicity of juvenile offending seems to be influenced by the amount of contact youths have with juvenile courts. Greater contact with juvenile courts is believed by some persons to stigmatize youths and cause them to acquire labels or stigmas as delinquents or deviants (Faulkner and Faulkner, 2004). Therefore, diversion of certain types of juvenile offenders from the juvenile justice system has been advocated and recommended to minimize stigmatization.

Deinstitutionalization of Status Offenses

One way of dealing with status offenders is to remove them from the jurisdiction of juvenile courts. This is known as the deinstitutionalization of status offenders (Trulson, Marquart, and Mullings, 2005). Because status offenders are comparatively less serious than juvenile delinquents who commit crimes, status offenders have been targeted by many state legislatures for removal from juvenile court jurisdiction. Do status offenders progress to more serious offending, such as juvenile delinquency? Do juvenile delinquents become adult offenders? This is known as career escalation. Presently, there is little agreement among professionals that either status offenders or delinquents progress toward more serious offending as they get older (Zimring, 1998). This generalization applies to both male and female offenders. One problem is that different pathways, or developmental sequences over the term of one's adolescence, are associated with serious, chronic, and violent offenders (Kempf-Leonard, Tracy, and Howell, 2001). Thus, a single trajectory or pathway cannot be used as a general forecast of career escalation, whenever it occurs. Furthermore, comparative research on career escalation among delinquent youths suggests that situational factors, such as whether youths come from abusive families and where drug and/or alcohol dependencies are evident, are more significant predictors of future, more serious offending rather than the sheer onset of status or delinquent offending (Parry et al., 2004).

With little more information than whether youths commit particular status or delinquent acts at particular ages, long-term predictions of future career escalation among these juveniles are simply unwarranted (Zimring, 1998). Arrest rates for juvenile offenders change drastically within short-term cycles of three years, rather than long-term cycles of more than three years. Also, there are different varieties of juvenile violence (McGarrell, 2005). About half of all juvenile violence is gang related. This type of violence is quite different from the violence exhibited by youths who kill their parents or other youths out of anger or frustration. In fact, researchers have been aware of these different types of violence and their origins for several decades (Irwin, 2004).

Career Escalation

The career escalation phenomenon among juveniles intensified during the 1970s and 1980s, when delinquency and crime increased appreciably (Wiesner and Windle, 2004). Correlations between rising crime and delinquency rates and the amount of status and delinquent offending led to the idea that career escalation was occurring. However, after a closer inspection of adult recidivists, a clear pattern of career escalation among juvenile offenders has not been revealed. More than anything else, domestic violence and an abusive family environment seem to be critical determinants of whether certain youths from such families will become chronic and persistent offenders (Osgood and Anderson, 2004).

Youth Violence

During the late 1980s and early 1990s, youth violence, including aggravated assault, robbery, murder, and forcible rape, increased dramatically. Concerned citizens wanted the problem confronted and eliminated. However, in 1995 a gradual downturn in juvenile violence occurred. Subsequently the amount of youth violence has either continued to decrease or has stabilized at pre-1990 levels. One contributing factor to youth violence is access to firearms. There were approximately 1,500 murder victims under age 18 in 2004. However, this compares favorably with 2,900 murder victims under age 18 during the peak year of 1993 (McDevitt, 2005). About half of all of these deaths were from firearms. Various policies and laws have been implemented to intervene in gun-related violence. Sources of illegal guns are being targeted increasingly by law enforcement agencies at local, state, and federal levels, and the penalties have been raised for illegal possession and carrying of guns as well as for persons who sell firearms to juveniles. Also, several programs have been established to treat and deal with those youthful offenders who have mental disorders and/or substance abuse problems (Bowman, 2005).

Many delinquency prevention efforts have been implemented in different jurisdictions. Often targeted are at-risk youths. At-risk youths are often those who suffer from one or more disadvantages, such as lower socioeconomic status, dysfunctional family conditions, poor school performance, learning or language disabilities, negative peer influences, and/or have low self-esteem (Brownlie et al., 2004). It is difficult to forecast which youths will become delinquent and which ones won't. For many decades, researchers have attempted to profile so-called at-risk youths by assigning to them various characteristics that seem to be associated with hardcore delinquents.

Many efforts have been initiated by juvenile courts as potentially helpful interventions involving at-risk youths. Juvenile court judges generally have sought to focus their attention on abused and neglected children. Some at-risk youths who have been placed in foster care and/or have been treated for various forms of sexual or physical abuse in their families and are considered at-risk and in need of special treatment from various social services. It has been found, for instance, that a strategy for assisting at-risk youths is to educate family and juvenile court judges in ways to improve their court practices (Fields and McNamara, 2003). Many juvenile court judges deliberately configure their court calendars to ensure that they will be assigned dependency cases and that they will remain on those cases until the children involved achieve a high degree of stability, either by being safely reunited with their families or by being placed in permanent adoptive homes (Kontos, Brotherton, and Barrios, 2003). Proper handling of cases involving these types of at-risk youths tends to decrease the likelihood that placed youths will commit delinquent acts.

Delinquency Prevention and Interventions

It is beyond the scope of this chapter to list and define each and every delinquency prevention program that has been established or operated, even in recent years. A sample of such programs will suffice, therefore, to give a fairly reasonable idea of what types of interventions have been attempted and which types of juveniles have been targeted for these interventions. Because of the great diversity of offending among juveniles, it has been necessary to devise specific types of programs to target certain juvenile offender populations. For instance, a significant amount of youth violence occurs in school settings. As a result, considerable resources have been allocated to address the problem of school violence and reduce its incidence (Patchin and Hinduja, 2005).

Some of these intervention programs target youthful sex offenders. Sex offender services and counseling are provided in various communities to assist those youths with these specific problems. Other programs target youths who engage in hate crimes (Steinberg, Brooks, and Remtulla, 2003). Such programs attempt to educate youths about the risks of gang membership as well as some of the personal and social reasons youths seek out gangs initially (Dahlgren, 2005). Even youths who are presently incarcerated in secure facilities are considered potential subjects for intervention programs. Therefore, various forms of assistance and services are made available to youthful inmates in juvenile industrial schools for their rehabilitation and reintegration.

Several programs included here are (1) the Weed and Seed Program; (2) the FAST Track Program; (3) the Juvenile Mentoring Program; and (4) Project Safe Neighborhoods. The Weed and Seed Program is a federal initiative implemented in 1994 by the U.S. Department of Justice (Justice Research and Statistics and Association, 2005). Also known as Operation Weed and Seed, the program is intended to prevent, control, and reduce violent crime, drug abuse, and gang activity in targeted high-crime neighborhoods throughout the United States. A two-pronged approach is used. Law enforcement agencies and prosecutors interact to weed out criminals who are leaders in violent crime and drug trafficking/abuse, and these agencies attempt to prevent criminals from returning to their targeted areas or neighborhoods. The seeding portion consists of bringing human services to these neighborhoods. Human services activities include prevention, intervention, treatment, and neighborhood revitalization (Barnes, 2005). A close interaction between community residents, prosecutors, and the police is sought in an effort to revitalize communities and promote public safety.

The FAST Track Program is both a rural and an urban intervention for both boys and girls of varying ethnicities. It is a long-term and comprehensive program that is designed to prevent chronic and severe conduct problems for high-risk children. It originates from the view that antisocial behavior stems from multiple factors, including the school, home, and individual (McGee and Baker, 2002). FAST Track's goals are to increase communication and bonds between these three domains, improve children's social, cognitive, and problem-solving skills, improve peer relations, and ultimately decrease disruptive behavior at home and school. FAST Track targets grades 1 through 6, but it is most intense during the 1st grade. It includes parent training, bi-weekly home visits to reinforce parenting skills, social skills training for involved youths, academic tutoring three times a week, and a curriculum is implemented which improves one's awareness skills, self-control, problem-solving skills, a positive peer climate, and teachers' classroom management skills. Program results have included better teacher-parent relations; improved interactions between parents and their children; better overall ratings by observers of a youth's classroom behavior; more appropriate discipline techniques; more maternal involvement in school activities; and greater liking of student peers by FAST Track students.

The Juvenile Mentoring Program (JUMP) is a federal program administered by the Office of Juvenile Justice and Delinquency Prevention. The three principal goals of this program are to (1) reduce juvenile delinquency and gang participation by at-risk youth; (2) improve academic performance of at-risk youth; and (3) reduce the school drop-out rate for at-risk youth (Olivero, 2005). Mentoring is a one-on-one relation between a pair of unrelated individuals, one adult and one juvenile, which takes place on a regular basis over an extended period of time. It is almost always characterized by a special bond of mutual commitment and an emotional character of respect, loyalty, and identification. JUMP is designed to reduce juvenile delinquency and gang participation, improve academic performance, and reduce school dropout rates. To achieve these purposes, JUMP brings together caring, responsible adults and at-risk young people in need of positive role models. Mentors are college students, senior citizens, federal employees, businessmen, law enforcement and fire department personnel, and other interested private citizens. Those treated range in age from 5 to 20. By 2002, JUMP was involved in attempting to keep more than 9,200 at-risk youths in 25 states in school and off the streets through one-to-one mentoring (Cain, 2002).

Project Safe Neighborhoods is a national initiative implemented to reduce violence attributable to firearms. It is also aimed at reducing gun violence among juveniles by deterring juveniles from gaining access to or possessing firearms. Persons who are banned from possessing firearms include (1) convicted felons; (2) fugitives from justice; (3) aliens in the U.S. illegally; (4) mental defectives or persons committed at any time to a mental institution; (5) persons who have given up their U.S. citizenship; (6) persons dishonorably discharged from the armed forces; (7) anyone under court order to refrain from stalking, harassing, or threatening an intimate partner or other person; and (8) anyone convicted of a misdemeanor crime involving violence or a threat with a deadly weapon. Alliances are established between various agencies of the federal government and local law enforcement agencies, schools, and other organizations. Intelligence gathering includes crime mapping, identifying hot spots which are high-crime areas of communities, tracing, and ballistics technology. Local and regional training occurs relating to the proper use of firearms for interested persons. A deterrence message is delivered by different means, in order to deter local youths from possessing firearms. This initiative is aimed at gangs, who most frequently use firearms in their illegal activities. Results thus far suggest that this initiative is having an impact on reducing the rate of firearms use among teens and particularly gangs (Project Safe Neighborhoods, 2005).

THE EFFECTIVENESS OF CRIME PREVENTION INTERVENTIONS

How do we know whether our crime prevention efforts and crime control programs work? Most programs are subsequently evaluated in terms of the general effectiveness at reducing crime or delinquency through program evaluation. Program evaluation is the process of assessing any intervention or program for the purpose of determining its effectiveness in achieving manifest goals. Program evaluation investigates the nature of organizational intervention strategies, counseling, interpersonal interactions, staff quality, expertise, and education, and the success or failure experiences of clients served by any program.

Probably the most frequently used measure of program effectiveness is recidivism. Although it is unofficial, a general estimate of an acceptable amount of recidivism associated with any intervention program is 30 percent or less. Therefore, programs that have recidivism rates of 30 percent or less associated with their clientele, either juveniles or adults, are often considered effective. This standard is purely arbitrary, however, and every program director is at liberty to choose whatever recidivism rate seems reasonable.

Recidivism rates higher than 30 percent do not mean that a particular program is unsuccessful. Also, recidivism rates among a program's clientele of less than 30 percent do not necessarily mean that a program is successful. The same intervention program may operate in one state with a recidivism rate of 42 percent, while clientele recidivism for the same program in another state may only be 15 percent. There are simply too many variables to account for these vast variations in recidivism rates. For many practitioners, the fact that a program helps at least some clientele makes that program successful, regardless of the overall rate of recidivism. In the articles to follow, many types of strategies are presented and described. Each program or intervention presented is considered on its own merits for particular target audiences. The general intent is to show the variety of programs and strategies established and implemented to make a difference so that crime prevention and control can occur.

QUESTIONS FOR REVIEW AND DISCUSSION

1. What is meant by crime prevention? What are at least two meanings of it? Discuss.
2. Differentiate between specific and general deterrence.
3. What is meant by primary, secondary, and tertiary crime prevention? Discuss each.
4. Describe two of the earliest criminal codes that have existed throughout the world. In each case, discuss their significance briefly.
5. What were some of the important goals of the Metropolitan Police of London? What was the influence of the Metropolitan Police of London upon American law enforcement? Explain.
6. How do the courts influence crime prevention? Discuss.
7. How can corrections be related to crime prevention? What sorts of interventions occur in the broad area of corrections that work toward decreasing crime in the United States?
8. Describe three different delinquency intervention programs.

2

"The News Media's Coverage of Crime and Victimization"

U.S. Department of Justice
and Anne Seymour

Adapted from U.S. Department of Justice and Anne Seymour, "The News Media's Coverage of Crime and Victimization," *National Victim Assistance Academy Textbook,* Chapter 18. Washington, DC: U.S. Department of Justice, Office of Justice Programs, National Victim Assistance Academy, 2002.

Crime in America is big news that is of significant concern to the American public. In a 1997 national survey conducted by the Roper Center in conjunction with the Newseum of Arlington, Virginia, 95 percent of 1,500 respondents said that they want to know about crime, a response rate higher than for any other topic, including local news, the environment, and world news (Center for Media and Public Affairs, 1997). Numerous studies of American news media have examined the media's coverage of crime in comparison with actual crime rates. A 1996 *U.S. News and World Report* article reported that the number of crime stories on the network evening news was quadruple the 1991 total (Office for Victims of Crime, 1996). Media reporting of crime and victimization, in both print and broadcast formats, has far-reaching effects on a number of populations and special interests.

THE CRIMINAL AND JUVENILE JUSTICE SYSTEM

Coverage of the criminal and juvenile justice system activities offers citizens an overview of the entire justice process, from law enforcement to prosecution through probation, parole, and corrections. The news media's examination of individual cases has resulted in groundswells of public opinion and action that have, in many cases, ultimately changed the way the justice system operates. In addition, the emergence of cameras in the courtroom and the *Court TV* network have expanded the American public's knowledge of the myriad intricacies that comprise our justice system.

The criminal and juvenile justice systems are also affected by their attempts to preserve the sanctity of criminal cases and, in some cases, protect victims' privacy. The espoused theory of the public's right to know often puts the media in direct conflict with system officials who believe that case confidentiality is essential to obtaining criminal convictions.

THE MEDIA PROFESSION

Since the 1980s coverage of crime and victimization has drastically changed. For instance, in 1985, footage of bodies and/or body bags on national networks elicited organized outcries from victim advocates across the nation. Today such footage is commonplace. The volatile issue of identifying victims of sexual assault in the media has been debated and analyzed from both victim advocacy and First Amendment perspectives, with little consensus from either side of the argument.

During the past 20 years or so, there has been an increase among media professionals who seek sensitivity training from crime victims and advocates so that they can accurately cover crime stories with the least amount of trauma to the victim. Today, crime victims and service providers offer training programs in newsrooms, professional journalism associations, and university-level journalism classes about media sensitivity in addressing violence and victimization. Journalists who cover crime beats are also affected by the scope and demands of their jobs. Those who cover the horror and degradation of violence on a regular basis have few outlets for the personal trauma they must endure. As such there is high demand for a protocol to debrief journalists whose assignments include regular coverage of violence.

The increase in the news media's coverage of crime and victimization has resulted in a very specialized discipline within the field of victim services: advocating for crime victims whose cases are covered by the news media. Training programs to help service providers better work with the news media who cover crime and victimization, as well as guidelines in media relations that help them enhance their professional relationships with the news media, are regularly offered at training conferences and as a component of victim service professional education.

CRIME VICTIMS

The constituency most affected by the news media's coverage of violence and victimization is crime victims. While sensitive coverage of victims' cases can be helpful, and in some cases, even healing, media coverage that is sometimes viewed as insensitive, voyeuristic, and uncaring can compound victims' emotional and psychological suffering. Most crime victims have never before dealt with the news media. They are thrust into a limelight they do not seek and do not enjoy solely because of the crimes committed against them. Many victims describe the initial assault by a perpetrator, a secondary assault from the criminal justice system, and a tertiary assault at the hands of the news media.

THE AMERICAN PUBLIC

The media play a significant role in public safety by keeping citizens apprised of:

1. increases in crime
2. trends in violence and victimization
3. efforts to prevent crime, reduce violence, and assist victims
4. measures individuals and communities can take to promote safety

In public opinion polls, the American public has offered some excellent insights into and opinions about news reporting:

1. 82 percent think that reporters are insensitive to people's pain when covering disasters and accidents.
2. 64 percent think that the news is too sensationalized.
3. 64 percent think reporters spend too much time offering their own opinions.
4. 63 percent think the news is too manipulated by special interests.
5. 60 percent think reporters too often quote sources whose names are not given in news stories.
6. 52 percent think the news is too biased.
7. 46 percent think the news is too negative.

Many of these concerns have been identified in the past by crime victims and those who serve them. *Parade Magazine* (1997) has highlighted similar concerns by leading American journalists. The media's significant focus on high-profile crimes as well as societal ills related to crime and victimization have wielded considerable influence, both positive and negative, on policies and programs relevant to criminal justice, juvenile justice, and victims' rights and services. News coverage ranging from a single report to more widespread coverage of key issues has profoundly affected the delivery of justice and victim services.

Many state laws and agency policies relevant to crime victims have been passed or strengthened as the result of media exposure. In these instances, the power of the personal story drove public policy and gave impetus to new and important subdisciplines of the victims' rights field:

1. In the early days of MADD (Mothers Against Drunk Driving), the founders of MADD effectively utilized the media to draw attention to a criminal act—driving under the influence (DUI) of alcohol and other drugs—that was not even considered a crime. As family members around the nation spoke out publicly about it, the results changed federal, state, and local policies and continue to do so today.
2. The courage of John Walsh and other parents, whose children have been abducted and/or murdered, contributed to federal and state laws during the 1980s and beyond in addressing the tragedy of missing children.

3. The brutal abduction, rape, and murder of Megan Kanka in 1994 and the ensuing media exposure about the confidentiality of sex offenders under community supervision led to the passage of Megan's Laws at the federal level in most states, which now require sex offender registries and the provision of information to communities about the location of sex offenders in their midst.

4. When mothers of victims murdered in gang violence were interviewed for a broadcast series by an independent television station in Los Angeles, their pleas for justice and understanding contributed to the U.S. Department of Justice, Office for Victims of Crime *Special Report on Victims of Gang Violence* published in 1996.

The media also provide forums for important dialogue among seemingly disparate groups. For instance, widespread attention on the use of DNA testing to clear unsolved criminal cases also focused on how DNA has been instrumental in freeing inmates who were wrongfully convicted. One poignant program brought together a sexual assault victim with the man who was freed from prison for that assault through new DNA evidence. In another instance, media attention on the lack of funding for public defense encouraged a victim advocate to address this issue at a national conference of defense attorneys from the victim's perspective—lack of funding for public defense of indigent individuals leads to delays that can be traumatic for victims.

INTERNET EFFECTS

The most rapidly growing form of media in the world today is the World Wide Web. The global virtual network that has resulted has important implications for crime victims and those who serve them. Thousands of web sites now offer information and referral services for victims of crime and victim service providers. Direct services are rapidly becoming available, as evidenced by the free confidential counseling offered online to sexual assault victims by the Brazos Rape Crisis Center in Texas. Listservs link together victim advocates and allied professionals who share interest in specific victim- and justice-related topics, simplifying the exchange of information and ideas. In some states, victim compensation claims and agency reports are filed electronically with the compensation authority.

THE PUBLIC'S RIGHT TO KNOW VERSUS
THE VICTIM'S RIGHT TO PRIVACY

The question of where a society's right to know ends and an individual's right to privacy begins is one of journalism's thorniest ethical dilemmas (Thomason and Babbili, 1988). This double-edged sword has serious implications for victims and those who serve them. While the legal aspects relevant for the First Amendment are quite clear, ethical considerations that take into account the traumatic nature of victimization and related news coverage are much more complex. Two precedent-setting cases from the U.S. Supreme Court have done much to influence the privacy of victims' rights.

In *Florida Star v. B.J.F.* (1989), a weekly newspaper in Jacksonville published a news article that identified the name of a sexual assault victim, violating its own policy of protecting the privacy of rape victims. The U.S. Supreme Court ultimately invalidated a Florida statute proscribing the newspaper publication of the identity of sexual assault victims. In making its decision, the Court balanced the state interest of protecting the privacy of assault victims against the First Amendment concerns of the free press. The Court did not focus on the privacy right of the plaintiff as much as it did on the inability of the statute to achieve its desired goal. The Court found the Florida statute unconstitutional because of its failure to protect the privacy of assault victims effectively without an impermissible intrusion on the First Amendment freedom of the press (Hughes, 1990).

The second case, *Cox Broadcasting Corporation v. Cohen* (1975), the constitutionality of a Georgia law that prohibited the identification of rape victims by the news media was questioned in a case involving a television station's reporting the name of a deceased rape victim. The Court upheld the right of news organizations to report names of victims because the commission of crime, prosecutions resulting from it, and judicial proceedings arising from the prosecutions are without question events of legitimate concern to the public and consequently fall within the responsibility of the press to report the operations of government.

CONCERNS OF CRIME VICTIMS AND SERVICE PROVIDERS

Some of the major concerns of crime victims and service providers are:

1. Interviewing at inappropriate times, such as immediately following a crime or victimization; at a funeral; in a hospital setting; and during trials when judges have issued gag orders.
2. Using euphemisms to describe victims and offenders.
3. Glamorizing the offender.
4. Exhibiting aggressive behavior toward victims, survivors, and their advocates.
5. Ignoring victims' and survivors' wishes.
6. Filming and photographing scenes with bodies, body bags, and blood.
7. Repeatedly using crime scene footage as a "lead in" to newscasts.
8. Reporting hearsay.
9. Interfering with police investigations.
10. Referring to drunk driving incidents as "accidents."
11. Failing to cover a crime at all.
12. Identifying child victims.
13. Attempting to interview survivors of homicide victims prior to official health notifications.
14. Inaccurate reporting.

GUIDELINES FOR VICTIMS WHO CHOOSE TO DEAL WITH THE MEDIA

Victims have the following rights:

1. Say "No" to an interview.
2. Select the spokesperson or advocate of your choice.
3. Select the time and location for media interviews.
4. Request a specific reporter.
5. Refuse an interview with a specific reporter even though you have granted interviews with other reporters.
6. Say "No" to an interview even though you have previously granted interviews.
7. Release a written statement through a spokesperson in lieu of an interview.
8. Exclude children from interviews.
9. Refrain from answering any questions with which you are uncomfortable or that you feel are inappropriate.
10. Know in advance the direction the story about your victimization is going to take.
11. Avoid a press conference atmosphere and speak to only one reporter at a time.
12. Demand a correction when inaccurate information is reported.
13. Ask that offensive photographs or visuals be omitted from broadcast or publication.
14. Conduct a television interview using a silhouette or a newspaper interview without having your photograph taken.
15. Completely give your side of the story related to your victimization.
16. Refrain from answering reporters' questions during trial.
17. File a formal complaint against a journalist.
18. Grieve in privacy.
19. Suggest training about media and victims for print and electronic media in your community (Seymour and Lowrance, 1988: 7–10).

GUIDELINES FOR TELEVISION TALK SHOWS AND CRIME VICTIM GUESTS

During the past 20 years, television talk shows have emerged as a powerful genre to address various issues of importance to the public. While such programs can have a powerful impact on promoting victims' rights and needs, they can also be traumatic to victim-guests, whose cases are often sensationalized. The National Center for Victims of Crime (1994) has developed guidelines for talk shows and crime victim guests. These include:

1. Television talk shows should use only those victims who have had the benefit of counseling and guidance from a trained victim counselor, professional, or advocate.

2. Crime victims should not appear in the immediate wake of their victimization, particularly if they have not had the advantage of counseling by professional victim advocates.

3. Child victims should not be guests.

4. A professionally trained victim advocate or crisis counselor should be on hand at all times.

5. Crime victims should be treated with dignity and respect at all times.

6. Crime victims should always be informed as to the format of the show.

7. If an offender is present in the studio or elsewhere in the facility, the victim should be given notice of that fact.

8. Victims should be given every opportunity to get comfortable with the set by allowing them to arrive early, even the day before the actual airing.

9. Victims should always have the right to review pictures, video/audio tapes, and graphic or other depictions that will air as a part of the show.

10. Victims should be informed in advance of their right to anonymity.

11. Victims should have the right not to have certain information disclosed about them.

12. Victims should have the right to refuse to have the program air in certain markets.

13. Victims should have the opportunity to request that disclosures that compromise their identity should be edited from the broadcast program.

14. Victims should be informed when the original show will air and if the show will be re-broadcast.

15. Victims in the viewing audience may experience a crisis reaction while watching a show about crime victimization experiences. It is strongly advised that producers provide a disclaimer at the beginning of the show cautioning viewers of the content.

CODE OF ETHICS FOR VICTIM ADVOCATES IN DEALING WITH THE NEWS MEDIA

The National Center for Victims of Crime has suggested the following code of ethics for victim advocates and the media:

I shall always:

1. Honor the victim's wishes relevant to any news media coverage of their tragedy.

2. Protect the privacy of any victims who do not wish to have contact with the news media.

3. Provide victims with guidelines on how to deal with the news media.

4. Help victims, upon request, prepare for print or broadcast media interviews.

5. Inform victims that they have the right to refuse an interview with the media.

6. Accompany crime victims, upon request, to media interviews and press conferences.

7. Review with reporters, producers, and talk show hosts exactly what questions they can and cannot ask the victim.

8. Reserve the right to end any interview if the victim shows signs of trauma during the course of an interview.

9. Discourage the participation of children in any interviews or talk shows.

I shall never:

1. Force a victim into an interview against his/her wishes.

2. Provide any information about the victim without his/her consent (Seymour and Lowrance, 1988: 15).

Advocacy for crime victims in the media has become a specialized discipline within the field of victim advocacy. Victim service providers who assume this immense responsibility must do the following:

1. Be knowledgeable about how the news media operate.

2. Be knowledgeable about victims' rights and issues in general, and about the specifics of the victim and case at hand.

3. Develop solid relationships with news media professionals who are known to be sensitive to crime victims and victims' rights issues.

4. Consider the needs and desires of the victims they represent, especially privacy concerns, as foremost among their responsibilities.

5. Be available 24 hours a day, 7 days a week for both victim and news media.

6. Be aware of and prepared to protect victims' rights in the media.

7. Be sensitive to the specific needs of the victim and/or the victim's family and friends, as well as to the parameters of the criminal investigation, criminal or juvenile justice system, and criminal or juvenile case (when applicable).

SIGNIFICANT ISSUES FOR THE MEDIA AND THE COURTS

At the National Conference of the Media and the Courts sponsored by the National Judicial College in 1996, 10 key issues affecting judges, lawyers, and reporters were identified, many of which affect victims and those who serve them. These are:

1. Encourage and establish continuing interdisciplinary educational opportunities and dialogue among judges, journalists, and lawyers to foster an understanding of each other's roles through journalism schools, law schools, and the National Judicial College.

2. Assume there is access to all court proceedings and records and place the burden of proof for closure on the entity seeking privacy. Privacy issues may overcome the presumption in appropriate cases.

3. Refrain from imposing gag orders on the news media or attorneys. Courts should seek other remedies in lieu of gag orders except in extraordinary cases.

4. Establish and/or support bench/bar/media committees that will meet regularly in every community to address issues of mutual concern.

5. Establish guidelines for trial-press management in high-profile cases. Court officials should confer and consult with media representatives to avoid unanticipated problems and understand each other's legal constraints.

6. Consider professional standards for journalists that are nonbinding.

7. Assume that cameras will be allowed in the courtroom, including the federal court system, and that such access should be limited or excluded only for strong reasons.

8. Encourage judges to explain, on the record, the reasons for their rulings.

9. Determine when and if it is appropriate to compel reporters to testify or produce notes and tapes, understanding that the media cannot serve as an arm of law enforcement.

10. Encourage media organizations to develop an ombudsman system to hear recommendations from the courts and the public where feasible.

Three guiding principles that should govern journalists include:

1. Seek truth and report it as fully as possible.
2. Act independently.
3. Minimize harm (Black, Steele, and Barney, 1995).

A MEDIA CODE OF ETHICS

Victim service providers should encourage media professionals, both print and broadcast, to adopt a code of ethics to their coverage of crime and victimization. The *St. Louis Post-Dispatch* (1992) set forth a tentative code of ethics for the media. The media should:

1. Present details about a crime in a fair, objective and balanced manner.

2. Recognize the importance of publishing or broadcasting information that can contribute to public safety, and at the same time, balance the need with the victim's need for privacy.

3. Respect the privacy of individuals who choose to refrain from dealing with the media or who choose to address the media through a spokesperson of their choice.

4. Provide a balanced perspective.

5. Never report rumors or innuendoes.

6. In crimes other than homicides, identify the victim by age and area where the crime occurs, omitting street addresses and block numbers.

7. Refrain from using information gained from private conversations with victims or their relatives.

8. Identify witnesses only when they volunteer to be named.

9. Never publish the identity of a sexual assault victim without his/her prior consent.

10. Never publish the identity of a child victim.

11. Never identify alleged or convicted incest offenders.

12. In kidnapping cases, stop identifying the victim by name once a sexual assault has been alleged.

13. Never identify the names of victims of scams that humiliate or degrade the victim without the victim's prior consent.

14. Refrain from photographing or broadcasting images that portray personal grief and/or shock resulting from a criminal act.

15. Never publish photographs or broadcast images that could place the subject in danger.

16. Refer to drunk driving incidents as crashes or crimes, not accidents.

17. Approach the coverage of all stories relating to crime and victimization in a manner that is not lurid, sensational, or intrusive to the victim and his/her family.

QUESTIONS FOR REVIEW AND DISCUSSION

1. What are some important components of the code of ethics for media?

2. What responsibilities should the media have for victims of crime?

3. What efforts should be made by judges to protect crime victims and preserve First Amendment freedoms of the press?

4. What are some major issues raised by media coverage of sensational crimes? Discuss.

3

Media Consumption and Public Attitudes Toward Crime and Justice

The Relationship Between Fear of Crime, Punitive Attitudes, and Perceived Police Effectiveness

Kenneth Dowler

Adapted from Kenneth Dowler, "Media Consumption and Public Attitudes Toward Crime and Justice: The Relationship Between Fear of Crime, Punitive Attitudes, and Perceived Police Effectiveness." *Journal of Criminal Justice and Popular Culture* 10: 109–126, 2003.

Reprinted by permission of the *Journal of Criminal Justice and Popular Culture*.

INTRODUCTION

Western society is fascinated with crime and justice. From films, books, newspapers, magazines, television broadcasts, to everyday conversations, we are constantly engaging in crime "talk." The mass media play an important role in the construction of criminality and the criminal justice system. The public's perception of victims, criminals, deviants, and law enforcement officials is largely determined by their portrayal in the mass media. Research indicates that the majority of public knowledge about crime and justice is derived from the media (Roberts and Doob, 1990; Surette, 1998). Therefore, it is imperative to examine the effects that the mass media have on attitudes toward crime and justice. The purpose of this research is to examine how the media influences audience perceptions of police effectiveness and to examine whether media consumption is related to fear of crime and punitive justice attitudes.

FEAR OF CRIME AND PUNITIVE JUSTICE ATTITUDES

Research on the effect that the media has on the public revolves around two interconnected issues. Does coverage of sensationalistic and violent crime create fear among the general public and does this fear influence criminal justice policy attitudes? Review of the research indicates that there are mixed results regarding the influence of the news media on creating an attitude of fear among the general public (Surette, 1998). In an early study, Gerbner et al. (1980) hypothesized that heavy viewing of television violence leads to fear rather than aggression. Gerbner et al. (1980) find that individuals who watch a large amount of television are more likely to feel a greater threat from crime, believe crime is more prevalent than statistics indicate, and take more precautions against crime. They find that crime portrayed on television is significantly more violent, random, and dangerous than crime in the "real" world. The researchers argue that viewers internalize these images and develop a "mean world view" or a scary image of reality. This view is characterized by "mistrust, cynicism, alienation, and perceptions of higher than average levels of threat of crime in society" (Surette, 1990: 8). Further studies on the relationship between fear and television viewing indicate a direct and strong relationship (Barille, 1984; Bryant, Carveth, and Brown, 1981; Hawkins and Pingree, 1980; Morgan, 1983; Weaver and Wakshlag, 1986; Williams, Azbrack, and Joy, 1982). Conversely, Rice and Anderson (1990) find a weak, positive association between television viewing and fear of crime, alienation and distrust. However, multiple regression analysis fails to support the hypothesis that television viewing has a direct, substantial effect on fear of crime.

In a review of the research, Heath and Gilbert (1996) find that the relationship between media presentations and crime is dependent on characteristics of the message and the audience. Presentation of large amounts of local crime news engenders increased fear among the larger public (Brillon, 1987), while the presentation of large amounts of non-local crime news has the opposite effect by making the local viewers feel safe in comparison to other areas (Liska and Baccaglini, 1990). In addition Chiricos et al. (2000) find that local and national news are related to fear of crime. The effect of local news on fear of crime is stronger for residents in high crime areas and those who experienced victimization.

In terms of audience effects, fear of victimization will depend on who is viewing the crime stories. Research indicates that residents in high crime urban areas who watch a large amount of television are more likely to be afraid of crime (Doob and MacDonald, 1979; Gerbner et al., 1980). Another important factor is whether audience members have direct victim experience or share characteristics that make them crime vulnerable. Research indicates that media sources will be more meaningful when direct experience is lacking (Gunter, 1987; Liska and Baccaglini, 1990; Skogan and Maxfield, 1981). For example, Liska and Baccaglini (1990) find that media influence was strongest for females, whites and the elderly, which are segments of the population least likely to be victimized. In another study, Chiricos et al. (1997) find that the frequency of watching television news and listening to the news on the radio is significantly related to fear. Their research indicates that television news consumption is significantly related to fear only for white females between the ages of 30 and 44. This is similar to other findings that suggest that watching crime on television has a greater effect for women and whites, who have low victim risk compared to males and non whites (Gerbner et al., 1980).

Examining the National Public Survey (NPOS), Haghighi and Sorensen (1996) find that local media attention to crime was significantly related to fear of sexual assault; getting mugged, beaten up, knifed or shot; and being burglarized while at home. Fear of crime was not significantly related to fear of car-jacking, being murdered, or being burglarized while not at home. However, they did not find the source of crime news to be a factor in fear of crime. For example, those who received their crime news from radio, newspapers or television had similar levels of worry about crime. In addition, their findings indicate that crime show viewers were more likely to worry about being sexually assaulted; getting beaten up, knifed or shot; and getting killed. However, crime-drama viewing is not related to fear of car jacking, mugging, or burglary.

Researchers argue that public fear and anxiety is inextricably connected with public pressure for solutions to crime problems. A number of research studies focus on whether media depictions of crime influence public attitudes towards criminal justice policy. They find that presentations of crime news increase public pressure for more effective policing (Garafalo, 1981a) and more punitive responses to crime (Barille, 1984; Surette, 1998). Furthermore, Surette (1998) claims that the news media feature agents of crime control as negatively ineffective and incompetent which results in support for more police, more prisons, and more money for the criminal justice system. Reith (1999) finds that for white males, crime show viewing is related to high levels of aggression towards those who break the law, and low levels against those who defend it. She also found that fear of victimization and fear of victimization based on real life experiences did not have a mediating effect on the relationship. In addition, Oliver and Armstrong (1995) find that frequent viewing and greater enjoyment of reality-based crime shows are related to holding punitive attitudes. However, frequent viewing and greater enjoyment of fictional crime shows are not related to holding punitive attitudes.

POLICE EFFECTIVENESS

Public attitudes toward police are generally positive (Huang and Vaughn, 1996). However, there are few studies that examine the media's influence on public ratings of police effectiveness. Much of the literature focuses on media portrayals of police officers and findings reveal two conflicting views. Some researchers argue that the police are presented favorably in the media, while other research suggests that the police are negatively portrayed in the media.

Presentations of police are often over-dramatized and romanticized by fictional television crime dramas while the news media portray the police as heroic, professional crime fighters (Reiner, 1985; Surette, 1998). In television crime dramas, the majority of crimes are solved and criminal suspects are successfully apprehended (Carlson, 1985; Dominick, 1973; Estep and MacDonald, 1984; Kooistra et al., 1998; Zillman and Wakshlag, 1985). Similarly, news accounts tend to exaggerate the proportion of offenses that result in arrest which projects an image that police are more effective than official statistics demonstrate (Marsh, 1991; Roshier, 1973; Sacco and Fair, 1988; Skogan and Maxfield, 1981). The favorable view of policing is partly a consequence of police's public relations strategy. Reporting of proactive police activity creates an image of the police as effective and efficient investigators of crime (Christensen, Schmidt, and Henderson, 1982). Accordingly, a positive police portrayal reinforces traditional approaches to law and order that involves increased police presence, harsher penalties and increasing police power (Sacco, 1995).

In addition, a number of researchers suggest that a symbiotic relationship exists between news media personnel and the police. It is suggested that the police and the media engage in a mutually beneficial relationship. The media needs the police to provide them with quick, reliable sources of crime information, while the police have a vested interest in maintaining a positive public image (Ericson, Baranek, and Chan, 1987; Fishman, 1981; Hall et al., 1978). However, other researchers argue that the police are not portrayed positively in the news media. For example, Surette (1998) claims that docu-dramas and news tabloid programs represent the police as heroes that fight evil, yet print and broadcast news personify the police as ineffective and incompetent. Likewise, Graber (1980) claims that the general public evaluates police performance more favorably compared with courts and corrections. Nevertheless, Graber (1980) states that the media provides little information to judge police and that the news media focus on negative criticism rather than positive or successful crime prevention efforts. In essence, most media crime is punished, but policemen are rarely the heroes (Lichter and Lichter, 1983).

Prior research suggests that public knowledge about crime and justice is largely derived from the media (Roberts and Doob, 1986; Surette, 1998). This research seeks to build on previous research by addressing three research questions:

What is the relationship between media consumption and fear of crime?

What is the relationship between media consumption and punitive attitudes?

What is the relationship between media consumption and public ratings of police effectiveness?

Police effectiveness, fear of crime and punitive attitudes are important aspects of public attitudes toward crime and justice in the United States. First, police strategies reflect departmental values, which reflect community values. Negative or positive attitudes towards the police may influence police policy making and strategy. Second, citizen attitudes toward the police may influence decisions to report crime. Third, both fear of crime and punitive attitudes may influence policy making and law making by government agencies, as public support or opposition may determine policy.

METHODS

Sample

The sample is derived from the 1995 National Opinion Survey on Crime and Justice (NOSCJ). The NOSCJ is a random telephone survey of adults (n= 1005) who reside in the continental United States. The survey is cross-sectional and samples are stratified to all U.S. counties in proportion to each county's share of the telephone households in the target area. The survey employed random digit dialing (CATI) and achieved a 62% response rate. The purpose of the NOSCJ is to provide knowledge about American attitudes toward crime and justice issues, which may lead to more informed criminal justice policy and practice. The survey examines a number of issues, such as attitudes toward courts, police, neighborhood problems, juvenile gangs, drug laws, death penalty, gun control, prisons, and worries about crime. In addition to basic demographic characteristics, NOSCJ captures information about hours of television viewing, crime show viewing and source of crime news.

Measures

Fear/Worry of Crime.   Fear of crime is measured using seven items that examine the respondent's fear/worry toward crime. Respondents are asked if they worry about sexual assault; car-jacking; getting mugged; getting beaten up, knifed or shot; getting murdered; being burglarized while at home; and being burglarized while no one is at home. Each question on worry/fear of crime has a four-category response ranging from very frequently, somewhat frequently, seldom, and never. The seven items are scaled to establish an index of fear of crime that ranges from seven (low worry) to twenty-eight (high worry). Higher scores indicate a greater amount of fear/worry about crime. Reliability analysis reveals an alpha of .86, which indicates that the scale is highly consistent.

Perception of Police Effectiveness.   Police effectiveness is measured by using seven items that examine the respondent's attitudes towards police. Three questions address respondent's confidence in police ability to protect, solve, and prevent crime. Each question has a four-category response ranging from a great deal, some, little, and none at all. Three questions address respondent's assessment of police promptness, friendliness, and fairness. Each question has a five-category response ranging from very high, high, average, low, and very low. For the scaling purposes, very low and low were combined into one category. The final question examines the respondent's belief in the use of excessive force by police in their community. The category responses range from serious problem, somewhat of a problem, minor problem, and not a problem at all. The seven items are scaled to establish an index of perceived police effectiveness that range from seven to twenty-eight. Higher scores indicate positive appraisals towards police effectiveness and lower scores indicate negative appraisals of political effectiveness. Reliability analysis reveals an alpha of .83, which indicates this scale is consistent.

Punitive Justice Attitudes.   Punitive justice attitudes are measured by using 11 items. These questions were categorical in nature and for scaling purposes they were dummy coded.
The scale ranges from 0 (punitive attitudes) to 1 (non-punitive attitudes). The scores range from 0 (highly punitive) to 11 (non-punitive) and the average score for respondents is four. The alpha level of punitive attitude scale is .72, which indicates that this scale is reliable. Nevertheless, one limitation is equating punitive attitudes with retributive attitudes. Historically, the notion of retribution meant "an eye for an eye" and emphasized "harsh" punishment. However, the concept of retribution has evolved and includes the concept of just deserts. Just deserts require that the nature of punishment be consistent with the offender's criminal conduct. The central principle of just deserts is proportionality; the severity of the punishment should be proportional to the gravity of the offense. Punitiveness is more concerned with the prevention and reduction of crime through deterrence principles (Von Hirsch, 1998). However, it is unclear whether survey respondents understand the differences between punitiveness and retribution.

Mass-Media Variables

The media variables include crime-show viewing, television hours and crime news source. Crime-show viewing is measured by asking respondents if they are frequent viewers of a television crime show. Television hours are measured by asking respondents how many hours of television they watched per week. Finally, respondents were asked the primary source of crime news. The categories include television, newspaper, radio, and friends/neighbors and are dummy coded for the analysis. Specifically, the intention is to examine the print media's effect on fear of crime, punitive justice attitudes and perceived police effectiveness.

Socio-Demographic Measures/Control Variables

A number of control variables are employed in this research to ensure that media effects are properly measured. Demographic variables such as race, gender, age, income, residence, level of education, and marital status are employed in the analysis. Race, income, residence, level of education and marital status are dummy-coded. In addition, a scale is created to measure respondent's attitudes toward problems in their neighborhood. Respondents were asked to rate the seriousness of a number of issues in their neighborhood. The issues include: trash and litter, loose dogs; unsupervised youth; graffiti; vacant houses; noise; people drunk/high in public; and abandoned cars. The scores range from eight to thirty-two. Higher scores indicate high levels of problems in the neighborhood, whereas lower scores indicate low levels of problems in the neighborhood. Reliability analysis reveals an alpha of .81, which indicates a consistent scale.

Analytic Strategy

The analytic strategy is to examine the relationship between media variables and fear of crime, perceived police effectiveness and punitive justice attitudes. The first step is to conduct univariate and bivariate analysis. The next step is to employ multivariate regression models using the ordinary least squares. Included in the models are the socio-demographic variables/control variables described above. Three models will be developed to examine the dependent variables, which will include fear of crime, punitive justice attitudes and perceived police effectiveness. The first model will examine the association between crime-show viewing, newspaper as primary source of crime news, hours of television per week and fear of crime. The control variables will include age, race, residence, marital status, income, gender, problems in neighborhood, and perception of police effectiveness.

The second model will examine the association between crime-show viewing, newspapers as primary source of crime news, hours of television viewing and punitive justice attitudes. We will employ the same control variables as step one, except that we will include fear of crime as an independent variable. The final step is to examine the association between crime-show viewing, newspapers as primary source of crime news, hours of television viewing and perceived police effectiveness. We will employ age, race, residence, marital status, income, gender, neighborhood problems, fear of crime and punitive attitudes as control variables.

RESULTS

Univariate and Bivariate Analysis

The results indicate that respondents average approximately 15 hours of television per week, while 42% of the respondents report that they are regular viewers of crime shows, and that 20% of the respondents report that newspapers are their main source of crime news.

The scaled variables were employed as both dependent and control variables. The results indicate that on a scale of seven to twenty-eight, the respondents' average score is 13.65 for fear of crime and 15 for perceived police effectiveness. On a scale of eight to thirty-two, the respondents score 11.8 for perceived problems in their neighborhood. On a scale from 0 to 11, respondents mean score is 4.09 for punitive attitudes toward crime and justice.

Socio-demographic characteristics of the sample indicate that 7.7% of the respondents are African-American, 7.7% are Hispanic and 81.4% are white; 53.1% are married; 52.1% are male; 15.9% are urban residents; the average age is 45; 58.2% are college educated; 22.1% have incomes over $60,000; 37.2% have incomes between $30,000 and $60,000; 25.8% have incomes between $15,000 and $30,000; and 14.9% have incomes lower than $15,000.

The results indicate that viewing crime shows is significantly related to fear of crime and perceived police effectiveness. Regular viewers of crime shows are more likely to fear or worry about crime. Similarly, regular crime drama viewers are more likely to hold negative attitudes toward police effectiveness. The bivariate analysis indicates that newspaper as primary source of crime news and hours of television viewing are not significantly related to fear of crime, punitive attitudes or perceived police effectiveness.

In addition, the results indicate that white, married, and low-income (15k to 30k) respondents are more likely to have punitive attitudes, whereas black, college educated, and respondents with low appraisals of police effectiveness are less likely to have punitive attitudes. The results also indicate that older respondents, males and respondents with low perception of neighborhood problems are more likely to have low fear of crime, whereas younger respondents, female, Hispanic, college-educated and respondents with low appraisals of police effectiveness are more likely to fear crime. Finally, bivariate results suggest that Hispanic, African-American, urban, and younger respondents are more likely to have negative or low appraisals of police effectiveness. Conversely, respondents with punitive attitudes, with a medium income (30k to 60k), older, white, with low perceptions of neighborhood problems are more likely to have positive or high appraisals of police effectiveness. However, there may be a number of factors that mitigate or enhance the relationships. Thus, it is necessary to conduct multivariate techniques to further address these relationships.

Multivariate Analysis

Fear of Crime.   The findings indicate that crime-show viewing is related to fear of crime. Respondents who report that they are regular viewers of crime shows are more likely to be fearful of crime. This is true even when we control for age, gender, race, income, education, marital status, perceived police effectiveness and perceived neighborhood problems. However, hours of television and newspaper as the primary source of crime news are not significantly related to fear of crime.

In this model, the strongest relationship is perceived problems in the neighborhood, followed by gender, education, regular viewing of crime shows, age, income and perceived police effectiveness. Respondents who claim that there are a high number of problems in their neighborhood are more likely to fear crime. This is not surprising, as respondents may feel unsafe in an area that they believe is conducive to crime. Female respondents are also more likely to fear crime. This is consistent with prior research that shows that females are more likely to fear or worry about crime (Garafalo, 1981b; LaGrange and Ferraro, 1989; Parker, 1993; Parker and Ray, 1990; Skogan and Maxfield, 1981; Warr, 1984). College educated respondents are more likely to be fearful of crime. This result is unanticipated, as we would assume that higher education would inform subjects about the nature of crime and justice. However, college educated respondents may feel that they have more to "lose" if they are victimized. Moreover, regular viewers of crime drama are more likely to fear crime. Television portrayal of crime and justice is largely sensational, violent and fear producing. Viewers may receive a "distorted" image of the typical crime or criminal, which may produce fear or anxiety about criminal activity. Compared to respondents with average incomes (30k to 60k), lower income respondents are more likely to fear crime. This is consistent with prior research, which reveals that low-income individuals are more likely to fear crime (Baumer, 1978; Skogan and Maxfield, 1981; Will and McGrath, 1995).

Older respondents are less likely to fear crime, which is not consistent with prior research (Baldassare, 1986; Garafalo, 1981b; Skogan and Maxfield, 1981; Yin, 1980). Finally, respondents who gave poor ratings of police performance are more likely to be fearful of crime. These respondents may believe that police are not effectively protecting the public or their community.

Punitive Justice Attitudes.   The impact of punitive attitudes on media consumption was examined. The findings indicate none of the media consumption variables are related to punitive attitudes. The strongest indicator of punitive attitudes is race, followed by education, income, fear of crime, and marital status. African-American respondents are more likely to hold non-punitive attitudes. This may be the result of inequalities of the justice system. For example, compared to whites, African-Americans are more likely to receive harsher punishments (such as the death penalty) and African-Americans are disproportionately over-represented in prisons (Reiman, 1998). Some African-Americans may feel threatened by a punitive justice model or feel that a punitive justice model reinforces discrimination and persecution of African-Americans.

In addition, respondents with college education are more likely to hold non-punitive attitudes. Those with education may be more likely to recognize the inequalities of the justice system and determine that solutions to the "crime problem" may be better served by policies of reintegration or rehabilitation. Furthermore, compared to average income respondents, low-income respondents (15,000 to 30,000) are more likely to hold punitive attitudes towards crime and justice. This is in contrast to the lowest income respondents ($15,000 or less) who hold non-punitive attitudes. One reason for the difference may be that low income ($15,000 to $30,000) respondents are more likely to bear the brunt of crime and unlike the lowest income ($15,000 or less) respondents they may feel that they have more to "lose" by victimization. As a result, low-income respondents may believe that a punitive ideology is necessary to prevent and reduce crime in the areas in which they live. Moreover, respondents with a high fear of crime are more likely to have punitive attitudes. Fear of crime may provide impetus for support of "get tough" crime policies. Finally, married respondents are more likely to have punitive attitudes. Married respondents might believe that they have more to lose if they are victimized (i.e., family and partner) and support tougher policies toward crime.

Perceived Police Effectiveness

Perceived police effectiveness on the media and various control variables was examined. The findings reveal that none of the media variables are related to respondent's perceptions of police effectiveness. A possible explanation is that there is little agreement on the role that police play on television crime dramas and news reports. Some research suggests that police are positively portrayed while others show that the police are negatively portrayed. However, the results indicate that age, perceived problems in the neighborhood, fear of crime, and race are significantly related to perceived police effectiveness. Older respondents are more likely have high ratings of police effectiveness, whereas younger respondents are more likely to have low ratings of police effectiveness. This is consistent with prior research that shows that compared to younger persons; the elderly have more favorable attitudes toward police (Garafalo, 1977; Hindelang, 1974; Thomas and Hyman, 1977).

Respondents who believe that there a high number of problems in their neighborhood are more likely to rate police effectiveness as being poor. Respondents who believe that there are a high number of problems in their neighborhood are more likely to rate police effectiveness as being poor. Respondents may believe that the local police are not properly fulfilling their role in the community. Similarly, respondents who have a high fear of crime are more likely to give poor ratings to the police. These respondents may feel that the police are not adequately protecting their communities.

Finally, African-Americans are more likely to hold low ratings of police effectiveness. This is similar to prior research which suggests that African-Americans have an antagonistic view of police (Garafalo, 1977) and that there is a "climate of distrust" between African-Americans and law enforcement (Jacob, 1971). However, other studies indicate that residence and social class mitigate the effect of race. For example, Kusow, Wilson and Martin (1998) find little support that African-Americans are less satisfied with police effectiveness. They find that both African-Americans and white suburbanites are more satisfied with police performance than African-American and white urban residents. In addition, Albrecht and Green (1977) find that low-income African-Americans living in inner cities possess the least favorable attitudes toward the police. Similarly, Parker, Onyekwuluje and Murty (1995) find that African-Americans who reside in high crime areas, and who have low incomes are more likely to have held negative attitudes toward the police. Nevertheless, controlling for income and residence we find that African-Americans are significantly more likely to hold unfavorable attitudes toward police. Waddington and Braddock (1991) find that African-Americans believe that whites receive preferential police treatment and that African-Americans are subjects of discrimination. Research indicates that there is a significant association between being black and being harassed by police (Browning et al., 1994). Other factors may include an increased awareness of police corruption, racism, brutality and racial profiling. A number of significant "social" events occurred during the 1990s. For example, the beating of Rodney King and the remarks of Mark Fuhrman elevated racism and police brutality into national issues. Finally, we have seen racial profiling or "driving while black" emerge as an important social issue.

DISCUSSION/CONCLUSION

This study reveals that regular viewers of crime shows are more likely to fear crime. Although statistically significant, the strength of this finding is minimal. In addition, there are a few limitations with regard to the measures of media consumption. First, the type of crime show that the respondent is viewing is unknown. There are numerous types of crime shows that may focus on different aspects of the criminal justice system. For example, crime shows may focus on police, courts, private investigators, defense lawyers and sometimes even the criminals. In addition, some shows are more realistic, while others routinely portray violence, and consistently misinform viewers about the nature of the criminal justice system and criminality. It would be prudent to know which dramas the respondents are viewing. Second, employing television hours watched is problematic, since there is no way of determining what type of programs the respondent is viewing. There are a number of different programs that may or may not address criminal justice issues and address them in substantially different ways. Finally, examining newspapers as the primary source of crime news suggests that only newspapers influence respondents. It would be naive to suggest that respondents are not affected by a number of sources; for example, respondents who receive their primary crime news from newspapers may also be affected by presentations of crime from other sources such as films, television and/or personal experiences.

Fear of Crime

Despite these limitations, there are some interesting results regarding fear of crime and perceived police effectiveness. Even when controlling for a number of factors, viewing crime shows is weakly related to fear of crime. Fear of crime may be "natural" reactions to the violence, brutality, and "injustice" that are broadcast to living rooms on a daily basis. Crimes on television shows and films reveal several trends. There is an overemphasis on crimes of violence and offenders are often portrayed in stereotypical ways. For example, murder and robbery dominate while property crimes are rarely presented (Surette, 1998). Offenders are often viewed as psychopaths that prey on weak and vulnerable victims. In other cases offenders are portrayed as businessmen or professionals that are shrewd, ruthless, and violent. Television crime is exciting and a rewarding endeavor, whereas victims are passive, helpless and vulnerable (Surette, 1998).

Many viewers may not understand the justice process and are unlikely to understand motivations and causes of criminal behavior. The criminal justice system is portrayed as largely ineffective, with the exception of a few "heroes" that provide justice or in some cases vengeance towards offenders (Surette, 1998). Crime shows rarely focus on mitigating issues of criminal behavior and are unlikely to portray offenders in a sympathetic or even realistic fashion. On television, crime is freely chosen and based on individual problems of the offender. Analysis of crime dramas reveals that greed, revenge and mental illness are the basic motivations for crime and offenders are often portrayed as "different" from the general population (Lichter and Lichter, 1983; Maguire, 1988). Thus, viewers may believe that all offenders are "monsters" to be feared. Consequently, heavy viewers may perceive crime as threatening, offenders as violent, brutal or ruthless and victims as helpless. These inaccurate presentations, as well as the portrayal of crime as inevitable/non-preventable may lead to an increase in the fear of crime. Nevertheless, the relationship between fear of crime and crime show viewing is statistically weak. As a result, it is important for future research to examine the relationship by employing triangulated strategies such as content analysis, experimental and survey research designs.

Police Effectiveness.　The results indicate that perception of police effectiveness is not related to media consumption. However, African-Americans and respondents who report a high number of problems in their neighborhood are more likely to give negative evaluations of police effectiveness. Therefore, direct experience may influence the respondents' attitudes toward crime problems and police response in the neighborhood. Future research should examine how the media influences these attitudes. The media may produce "feelings" that local neighborhoods are "problem filled" or dangerous. For instance, local news broadcasts may focus on highly sensational, violent and disturbing crime that occurs in the neighborhood. It may be possible that media presentation will affect attitudes toward the neighborhood.

In this sample, African-Americans are more likely to give poor ratings of police effectiveness. However, it is unclear as to why or how African-Americans gain these views. It is generally assumed that these views are the result of discrimination. Direct experience aside, the mass media may play a role in African-American attitudes toward police effectiveness. Future studies should examine how the media portrayal of the criminal justice system affects African-American attitudes toward police. The media may have a strong effect on African-American criminal justice attitudes.

In conclusion, it is speculated that the majority of the public's knowledge about crime and justice is formed through media consumption. As a result, it is imperative that we understand how the media influences public attitudes. Although there are limitations within the data set and the findings are weak, regular viewing of crime shows is related to fear of crime. However, crime show viewing is not related to punitive attitudes or perceived police effectiveness, while hours of television viewing and source of crime news are not related to fear of crime, punitive attitudes or perceived police effectiveness. Nevertheless, more research is required to determine the relationship between media consumption and attitudes toward crime and justice.

QUESTIONS FOR REVIEW AND DISCUSSION

1. What is the impact of the media on public opinion about controversial issues?

2. Is it possible for the media to cause the public to have an increased fear of crime? What are some positive and negative consequences of media coverage of how different persons have been victimized? Discuss.

3. How are police officers portrayed by the media? Do these portrayals influence how police officers perform their jobs and interact with the public? Why or why not? Discuss.

4. Is there any cause for minorities to believe that they are being targeted by the police for closer scrutiny when going about their business on city streets? Why or why not? Explain.

PART II

Law Enforcement and Crime Prevention

Law enforcement agencies are the most visible entities directly involved in crime prevention and control. Several essays are presented that describe different law enforcement initiatives designed to detect, prevent, and control crime. James Byrne and Don Hummer describe the importance of police/community partnerships in combatting crime. Following the 9/11 attack on the World Trade Center in New York City, it became all too apparent that a lack of communication between law enforcement agencies at local, state, and federal levels existed. Byrne and Hummer advocate greater efforts on the part of law enforcement agencies at all levels to devise ways to improve and coordinate their crime-fighting efforts. Also, Byrne and Hummer suggest that the police can become more proactive in working with the courts and corrections through meaningful collaborations that will assist these other agencies in maintaining better control over their clients. Thus, police agencies may play expanded roles in their crime prevention efforts through these partnerships and collaborative efforts.

Tony Aeilts directs our attention to terrorism and cybercrime, which are increasing at disturbing rates. Reinforcing the opinions of Byrne and Hummer, Aeilts suggests that greater coordination and cooperation among law enforcement agencies in combatting terrorism and cybercrime, which is so pervasive, is necessary. Furthermore, Aeilts advocates relying more on academic settings where the expertise of specialists who study crime and its causes can be integrated with law enforcement efforts to attack and prevent cybercrime. An essay by Brian Houghton and Jonathan Schachter continues Aeilts's concern about the importance of coordinating law enforcement efforts to combat crime, but Houghton and Schachter explain how terrorism extends well beyond U.S. boundaries into other countries. Therefore, they examine some of the methods of agencies that respond to the aftermath of terrorist attacks and how agencies can allocate their resources most effectively as deterrents to further terrorism.

Jon Shane describes Compstat, a relatively new crime control initiative that was pioneered in New York City during the 1990s. Compstat is a crime-mapping process that relies heavily on technology to track crime and its occurrence so that law enforcement resources can be deployed most effectively. Thus, Shane describes a system that essentially reengineers the bureaucracy of police agencies to maximize existing resources in an effort to increase public safety and lower one's fear of crime. Thomas Rich's essay describes several examples of crime mapping that have been implemented in various jurisdictions, such as New York and Chicago, although he describes the use of crime mapping in a Hartford, Connecticut, study sponsored by the National Institute of Justice. Crime mapping in Hartford was significant in maximizing Hartford's citizen crime prevention efforts as well as those of law enforcement. Greater information sharing occurred, and although Hartford's crime rate has not been significantly affected, the public's awareness of where crime occurs has been greatly improved, and crime prevention efforts in those hot spots of crime have been noticeably enhanced.

An essay about the Office of Homeland Security examines several initiatives that were implemented following 9/11, including emergency preparedness and response, infrastructure protection, and various measures to cope with the threat of chemical, biological, and nuclear threats. The Information Analysis and Infrastructure Protection Program (IAIP) is described. James Casey follows this Homeland Security discussion with an essay about the importance of task forces dedicated to investigating domestic terrorism and other types of crimes. The Federal Bureau of Investigation, Central Intelligence Agency, Drug Enforcement Administration, and other federal organizations have joined forces to gather information and deploy resources to combat possible terrorism threats. One emphasis here is upon the importance of security clearances, which mean tougher screening controls for those seeking employment in those agencies designed to protect the United States from its enemies. Further initiatives have to do with identifying persons currently residing in the United States who are most likely to engage in terrorist acts. Though not all of these individuals can be identified and investigated, substantial progress is being made in this endeavor.

Al Youngs examines the increasing importance of private law enforcement agencies and private security in crime prevention and control efforts. Youngs advocates the establishment of partnerships between the public and private police, whose collective efforts can do much to control crime.

4

"Examining the Role of the Police in Reentry Partnership Initiatives"

James M. Byrne and Don Hummer

Adapted from James M. Byrne and Don Hummer, "Examining the Role of the Police in Reentry Partnership Initiatives." *Federal Probation* 68: 62–69, 2004.

Reprinted with the permission of the Administrative Office of the U.S. Courts.

REDEFINING ROLES AND RELATIONSHIPS

The development of partnerships in law enforcement is not a new idea, but it does appear that today's police are much more likely to enter into partnerships than their predecessors, especially at the local level. One reason for this new collaborative mindset on the part of the nation's 21,143 police agencies (Maguire et al., 1998) is the adoption of community policing in many of these jurisdictions. While a review of the research on the implementation and impact of community police reforms is beyond the scope of this article (for such review see, e.g., National Research Council, 2004), it is worth noting that community policing programs do represent a fundamental shift in strategy: rather than working alone (or in teams with other officers) patrol officers are encouraged to meet and work with community groups, personnel from social services, public health, and other criminal justice agencies to address the community's crime/order maintenance problems.

As part of this new collaborative orientation, partnerships between police and a wide variety of agencies and community groups, including state and local corrections, are encouraged as an appropriate problem-solving strategy. Critics of community policing have pointed out that one consequence of such collaboration is to increase the span of control of police agencies, particularly in disadvantaged areas. With the help of these new "partners," local police can collect better and more detailed intelligence on residents, expand the scope of searches, and target both individuals (e.g., gang members, sex offenders) and "hot spot" areas (e.g., crack houses) for removal from the community. As Manning (2003) has pointed out, short-term *gains* in order-maintenance in low income, inner-city areas may be followed by long-term losses (moral, social, political) in these same communities, due to the negative consequences of incarceration on offenders, their families, and the communities in which they reside (and to which they will return). The potential for such unintended consequences must certainly be considered in the types of police-corrections partnerships highlighted in this article.

In addition to community policing reforms, sentencing reform can certainly be considered as another compelling impetus for police-corrections partnerships. Due to our reliance on incarceration as the "sanction of choice" for many crime categories (particularly drug offenders), we now have over 2 million inmates in custody in the United States. Last year, 600,000 of these inmates were released from federal, state and local facilities, a threefold increase from just 20 years ago (RAND Corporation, 2003). Due to changes in "good time" provisions, tougher parole eligibility, and the establishment of mandatory minimum sentences, one in five of these new prison releasees were max-outs, which effectively means that they returned to the community without the supervision, services, and control provided by community corrections agencies (e.g., probation, parole).

Who (if anyone) should fill this supervision, service, and control void? In many jurisdictions, the surveillance and control responsibility appears to be moving to the local police, who are likely to view prison releasees as a logical target population, especially given the "fact" that, in all likelihood, two-thirds of these offenders will be rearrested (and half will be reincarcerated) for new crimes within three years (Langan and Levin, 2002). The provision of (voluntary) services for prisoners released without parole supervision is more problematic, but it does appear that both institutional and community corrections agencies are now beginning to recognize that they also need to expand their role and responsibility vis-à-vis this group of releasees. However, it is still unclear where the money will come from to fund services for these releasees, who appear to be falling through the cracks of the current service provision network. Whatever the source, adequate funding for the mental health, housing, substance abuse, and public health problems of this subgroup of releasees appears to be a key to the success of the partnership. For reentry programs developed through federal grants and/or funds from private foundations, it will be interesting to "follow the money" as it flows to various partnership agencies, because control of the *funding* for reentry will affect the nature, duration, and orientation (surveillance, treatment, control) of the partnership.

1. An Overview of Police-Corrections Partnership Development in the United States

Parent and Snyder (1999) conducted a nationwide review of the utilization of police-corrections partnerships; in conjunction with this review, they completed site visits at 19 separate partnerships located across five states (Minnesota, Washington, Connecticut, Arizona, California). According to the profiles included in the report, five different models of police-corrections partnerships can be identified:

1. *Enchanted supervision partnerships,* in which police and probation or parole officers perform joint supervision or other joint functions related to offenders in the community....

2. *Fugitive apprehension units,* in which police and correctional agencies collaborate to locate and apprehend persons who have absconded from probation or parole supervision....

3. *Information sharing partnerships,* in which corrections and law enforcement agencies institute procedures to exchange information related to offenders...

4. *Specialized enforcement partnerships,* in which police and correctional agencies, as well as community organizations, collaborate to rid communities of particular problems, and

5. *Interagency problem-solving partnerships,* in which law enforcement and correctional agencies confer to identify problems of mutual concern and to identify and implement solutions to them (Parent and Snyder, 1999: 7)

These five models offer different strategies and problem contexts for the application of police-corrections partnerships to the myriad of issues associated with offender reentry initiatives. Unfortunately, the authors of this report were unable to provide an estimate of the number of police-corrections partnerships currently in place in the United States that utilize at least one of these models.

2. Police-Corrections Partnerships and Offender Reentry

Partnerships between law enforcement and corrections agencies appear to be an emerging strategy adopted by several federal agencies (NIJ, NIC, OJJDP) that provide funding for a wide range of offender reentry initiatives at the federal, state, and local level. In several jurisdictions, partnership development is a prerequisite for federal funding of the initiative (Taxman, Young, and Byrne, 2003a). But from where did this new-found "faith" in partnership emerge? In the absence of empirical research, it appears that program developers have turned to another source: the experience of public sector managers involved in a wide range of problem-solving scenarios. A number of recent reviews of organizational effectiveness in the public sector (see, e.g., U.S. General Accounting Office, 2004 for an overview) have emphasized the importance of the strategic use of partnerships to address issues involving multiple agencies and systems. According to the participants at a recent GAO forum on this issue, "to be a high-performing organization, . . . Agencies must effectively manage and influence relationships with organizations outside of their direct control" (GAO, 2004: 9). When viewed in this light, police-corrections partnerships represent an attempt by two independent agencies to work together to solve a common problem. In the process, the question can certainly be raised: Who is influencing whom? At their core, police-corrections partnerships can be defined by the types of roles and relationships that emerge between/among participating organizations and agencies. Below, we examine "roles and relationships" across eight "model" reentry partnership initiatives identified by The Office of Justice Programs. These eight program models certainly do not represent the full range of reentry programs currently available across the country, but they do provide a solid analytic foundation from which we can examine the problems and potential inherent in police-corrections partnerships.

Despite fundamental differences in philosophy, background, and orientation toward offenders, police-corrections partnerships have the potential to enhance public safety, streamline service provision, and achieve common goals, such as crime reduction (Parent and Snyder, 1999). They also may have unintended longer-term consequences for both offenders and communities that must be examined before we move further in this area. As described below, the Reentry Partnership Initiative (RPI) is an example of a cooperative effort to maximize law enforcement and correctional resources in a meaningful way to address a specific target issue (offender reentry). Developed by the Office of Justice Programs of the Federal Department of Justice, RPI programs form a partnership of criminal justice, social service, and community groups to develop and implement a reentry process. A key component for a successful RPI is linking local law enforcement with other agencies and actors responsible for offender reintegration. By working in conjunction with corrections personnel, and extending partnerships to include other agencies, police can enhance their presence in target neighborhoods and in the process generate support for collaborative efforts from policymakers and the general public (Parent and Snyder, 1999).

In the following section we describe the specific role of law enforcement in collaborating with representatives of corrections agencies, as well as with other key actors within the Reentry Partnership Initiative (community, treatment providers, victim, and offender). In doing so we demonstrate the pivotal role that police have in implementing a successful "shared decision-making" partnership for offender reintegration, while also highlighting potential problems inherent in this strategy.

3. Identifying the Role of Police at Each Key Phase in the Reentry Process

Local police departments have played a critical role in the development of the RPI model in several sites across the country. In an earlier review of eight "model" reentry programs completed by Taxman, Young, and Byrne (2003a), three key phases of the RPI model are described in detail: the institutional phase, the structured reentry phase, and the community reintegration phase (see figure 1). Based on their detailed reviews of reentry initiatives in eight separate jurisdictions (Maryland, Vermont, South Carolina, Missouri, Florida, Nevada, Massachusetts and Washington), we can describe and discuss the role of the police at each of these phases of reentry. We have examined similarities and differences across these eight jurisdictions in the nature, type, duration, and intensity of police involvement in each phase of the offender reentry process. It is our hope that such a review will provide critical information to program developers interested in the applicability of police-corrections partnerships to the complex problems associated with offender reentry.

THE ROLE OF POLICING DURING THE INSTITUTIONAL PHASE OF REENTRY

During the *institutional phase* of an offender reentry program, a number of decisions have to be made about offenders that involve local law enforcement, both directly and indirectly. Consider, for example, the selection of the target population for a new reentry program. Although the timing of the decision varied from jurisdiction to jurisdiction, local police departments have been involved in the selection of the RPI target population at several sites.

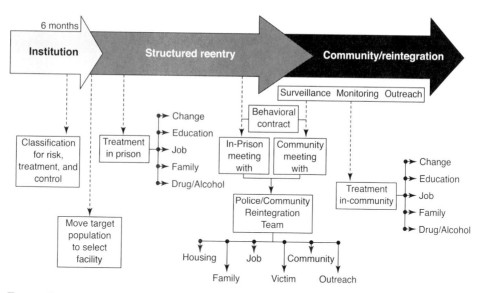

FIGURE 1
Reentry Partnership Continuum

The rationale underlying this strategy is fairly straightforward: The decision regarding whom to include and exclude from a particular reentry program should be made by the entire partnership, rather than one specific agency. By sharing decision-making vis-à-vis the targeting issue, program developers have increased the likelihood of police support for— and partial ownership of—the reentry initiative.

The dangers inherent in allowing a single agency (e.g., institutional corrections) to determine program eligibility were highlighted in the review of Las Vegas, Nevada's reentry program, in which only offenders from specific "weed and seed" areas were targeted. The police chief refused to participate in the program because of the fear that the program was tantamount to racial profiling; only high minority concentration neighborhoods were being targeted for the partnership reentry effort.

The police chief's fear was based on the possibility/likelihood that offenders reentering these targeted neighborhoods will face much closer police scrutiny (i.e., stops, surveillance, etc.) than offenders released to other areas of the city. If such "scrutiny" leads to higher rearrest, reconviction, and/or return-to-prison rates for offenders released to high minority concentration areas, then the negative consequences of this "place-based" targeting decision would be substantiated. However, no such research was conducted at this site, since the RPI program was only in its initial development stage. Rather than implement the reentry program and then monitor the comparative rearrest, reconviction, and return to prison rates of releasees citywide, the chief made a simple suggestion: expand the program beyond the initial "weed and seed" target sites, in order to "broaden" the population targeted for "potential" police profiling.

Regardless of the specific targeting decisions made across the eight reentry programs we reviewed (Taxman, Byrne, and Young, 2002), it does seem reasonable to raise the racial profiling issue and consider the implications for police-corrections partnerships. As Manning (2003: 54) recently observed,

> Racial profiling is the use of expert systems and documents that advise or encourage stopping people of a given "profile"—e.g., black teenagers; a black man in an expensive foreign car; long-haired drivers of beat-up vans; a black driver in a "white" suburban area of a city. It goes to the explicit policy-driven attempt of agencies to direct discretion and increase, for example, arrests on drug charges (Manning, 2001). Profiling of a less systematic sort is the heart of all policing—stops based on distrust, suspicion, awareness of people "out of place" in time or space, past experience, stereotyping, and other common typifications (2003: 54–55).

By targeting specific subgroups of all released offenders for inclusion in reentry programs, developers certainly increase the *awareness* of local police vis-à-vis this subgroup of returning offenders, while also changing the way police *respond* to these offenders in the community. Police in the RPI programs we visited were expected to monitor offenders' progress in the community, either by direct observations (e.g., home visits, field stops) or by utilizing any combination of community information sources (e.g., victims, volunteer guardians, treatment providers, community corrections personnel, employers). They were also expected to respond proactively to this information (e.g., increased face-to-face personal contacts, focusing on specific issues related to the victim, progress in treatment, employment, housing, etc.), based on the notion that this type of police-initiated response might be effective, especially when it focused on an individual offender's progress addressing the problems that resulted in his/her most recent incarceration (i.e., substance abuse, mental illness, employment, family problems). But despite such benevolent intentions, it is certainly possible that offender targeting represents yet another manifestation of the profiling problem. Once again it is Peter Manning (2003) who offers the most succinct summary of the research on police profiling:

> The data are overwhelming—people of color, no matter what their presence on the roads, work, or past record, are disproportionately stopped, searched, arrested, charged, and imprisoned (Meehan and Ponder, 2003a, 2003b; Walker, Spohn, and DeLone, 1996).

In addition to their role in offender targeting decisions, police may also be able to assist in other decisions made during the institutional phase of RPI, such as offender classification, institutional location, and institutional treatment. Local police have information about offenders that may be shared with institutional staff involved in offender classification and placement, such as peer/gang associations, family history and the nature of the commitment offense. In addition, police at one site (Vermont) serve on local community "restorative justice" boards that review and approve the offender's institutional treatment plan within 45 days of incarceration. While only one of the eight sites we visited includes the police in decisions regarding institutional treatment (for substance abuse, anger management, and/or other behavioral issues), it can certainly be argued that the police have a stake in offender treatment decisions. By including police in the treatment decision-making process, Vermont's RPI program developers have given police officers an opportunity to see, first-hand, how offenders change and the value of treatment interventions throughout the system.

THE ROLE OF POLICING DURING THE STRUCTURED REENTRY PHASE

The second phase of the RPI model involves *structured reentry* (see Figure 2). Police have an important role in decisions during this second phase of reentry. Typically, the structured reentry phase of RPI programs focuses on the last few months before release and the first month after release. It is during this period that an offender reintegration plan is developed and a number of basic decisions are made about when the offender will be released, whether specific release conditions will be established, where the offender will live and work, and how the offender will address his/her ongoing treatment needs. Depending on the jurisdiction we visited, police were involved in one or more of these structured reentry decision points.

Perhaps the most controversial and innovative structured reentry strategy that involves police is the use of community boards (in Vermont) to review the offender's progress in treatment and to make release recommendations. Since local police departments are represented on these boards, they will have input on release decisions and in some cases, the conditions of release. It will be interesting to track the impact of community boards on release decisions in this jurisdiction and to observe the court's response to the inevitable challenges to the authority of these community boards to essentially make early release (i.e., parole) decisions.

In several jurisdictions, the police will meet with the offender in prison to discuss his/her pending release. The purpose of this meeting is twofold: first, to explain to offenders how local policing has changed since they were initially incarcerated, due to the current

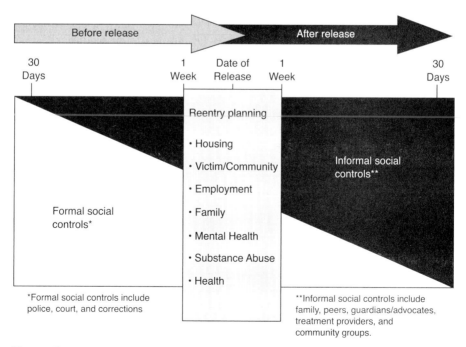

FIGURE 2
Overview of Structured Reentry Phase

emphasis on community policing (and crime prevention); and secondly, to let offenders know that the police will be watching them upon release, monitoring their progress in treatment, and that they will not be anonymous. Will one meeting between the offender and a neighborhood police officer deter the offender from criminal behavior upon release? We doubt it, but there is more involved here than an attempt to "scare" an offender straight. In Lowell, Massachusetts, for example, the police meet with the offender in conjunction with the local treatment provider, who describes the types of treatment programs available for offenders returning to this community. It is the dual message—treatment and control—that the offender hears at this meeting. Equally important, the meeting establishes an essential partnership between local police and treatment providers that will continue for the remainder of the offender's stay in the reentry program.

Another facet of the police role during the structured reentry process is the contact between the police and the offender during the first few days after the offender has been released from prison. For offenders released conditionally, police surveillance and contact serves as a supplement to probation and parole supervision. For offenders released unconditionally, police surveillance and contact represents the *only* formal offender control mechanism. As we noted earlier, since over 20 percent of offenders nationwide leave prison *without* probation or parole supervision, there does appear to be an immediate need for an expanded police role for these offenders. We anticipate that in some jurisdictions—such as the Lowell, Massachusetts, RPI (in this state, over half of prison releasees have maxed-out)—police will be in contact with local treatment providers and thus will know who is—and who is not—participating in treatment, which may affect the nature and timing of police-offender interactions. In other jurisdictions (e.g., Spokane, Washington) police will meet regularly with volunteer community "guardians," who will provide assistance to offenders immediately upon release from prison (helping with housing, transportation, etc.), placing them in a unique position to assess offender progress during reentry. In these jurisdictions, it appears that police departments have begun to fill the void created by sentencing reform generally and mandatory sentencing in particular.

Finally, one jurisdiction developed a unique strategy for improving the community surveillance and control capacity of local police. In conjunction with the State Department of Corrections, the crime analysis unit of the Lowell police department develops "profiles" of each offender released from prison and returning to the Lowell community each month, which are displayed at roll call. These profiles include the offender's most recent picture, criminal record, gang affiliations (if any), and nature of his/her last offense. This is certainly one possible strategy for reducing the anonymity of offenders returning to the community by increasing police awareness of the reentering offender population.

THE ROLE OF THE POLICE DURING THE COMMUNITY REINTEGRATION PHASE

The third phase of the RPI model is the *community reintegration* phase, which emphasizes long-term offender change, an elusive goal for the corrections system. The underlying assumption of RPI program developers is that during this final phase of reentry, there will be a transition from formal to informal social control mechanisms, such as the offender's family, peer group, faith-based community groups, employers, guardians, and other community members. The response of the police to reentry offenders during this final phase is likely to vary according to the behavior of the offender. For example, if the offender is employed and participating in treatment, then the police department's interaction with the offender will likely be minimal. However, offenders who have difficulty with the initial transition from prison to home will likely face much more intensive police intervention (both formal and informal). In Burlington, Vermont, and Spokane, Washington, for example, the police work in conjunction with local community corrections staff to conduct curfew checks on targeted offenders both by home visits and stops at targeted locations (e.g., bars, street corners). Police may also act informally by simply talking with "at-risk" offenders—those who appear to be having trouble finding a job, suitable housing, and/or receiving treatment for mental health or substance abuse problems. It appears that the police have a role in the community reintegration phase that will change over time based on the behavior of the offender and the specific features of the reentry program examined.

The Police and Institutional Corrections

When we think about the police, it is usually in the context of offender control, not offender change. But police departments in RPI jurisdictions view their role somewhat differently: they are involved in both offender control and offender change activities. In Vermont, for example, police serve on local community boards that review and approve each offender's institutional treatment plan, which was developed by the offender (in conjunction with prison program staff) within 45 days of incarceration. They are also involved in reviewing the offender's progress in treatment and in the development of a structured reentry plan. While Vermont is unique in terms of the police role in institutional treatment, the police are actively involved in pre-release planning in several jurisdictions (e.g., Massachusetts, Washington, and Maryland).

RPI programs require that police act in new ways toward the offender, not only upon release but also while incarcerated. For example, police officers at several sites actually visited the offender while in prison to discuss the police department's role in the reentry program. In the Lowell, Massachusetts program, a neighborhood police officer meets with the offender in prison about a month before the offender is scheduled to return to the officer's neighborhood. Importantly, the officer does not attend this meeting alone; he/she comes as part of a neighborhood reentry team that also includes a local treatment provider. The utilization of a police-community treatment provider "partnership" team *within* an institutional setting represents a new role for police in the institution. At the meeting, the neighborhood police officer describes how the police department has changed in recent years in this community, due in large part to two factors: (1) community policing, and (2) more cops on the street. The officer then focuses on his/her dual role as a resource person/problem-solver and community surveillance/control officer. The "message" that the offender receives is that the police are there to help the offender, but that they will do their "helping" within the broader context of public safety. In the name of public safety, police officers will *not* allow offenders to return to the community anonymously; informal surveillance of reentry offenders will occur. Massachusetts is not the only site to employ this strategy; other sites using similar approaches include Washington, Maryland, South Carolina, and Missouri.

Police will also interact with institutional corrections staff in a wide variety of activities directly related to offender reentry. First, meetings with offenders in prison must be coordinated through the state's department of corrections. Next, the development of offender profiles to be used by local police will require information to be shared by the research staffs of the releasing institution and the police department (e.g., current offenses, criminal history, institutional behavior, gang affiliations, specific release conditions). Third, the target population selected for the program should reflect police preferences. And finally, police may participate on community boards that have a direct impact on release decisions and/or the conditions of release. In Vermont, for example, offenders are expected to develop (individual) offender responsibility plans, which are reviewed by restorative justice boards comprised of a wide range of community members, including the police.

When the topic of prison release is raised, it is usually within the context of judicial and/or parole decision-making. However, it can certainly be argued that police departments should have a role in release decisions as well, in such areas as the timing of the release, the offender's location in a particular community, and the determination (where applicable) of release conditions. Once again, it is Burlington, Vermont's restorative justice model that provides the framework for this type of active police participation in the structured release process. In Vermont's RPI model, police serve on community boards that review the offender's *individual responsibility plan* approximately one month prior to the offender's proposed release date. If the offender has made progress addressing the problem/need areas identified in the plan, then the community board will likely recommend release; but if the offender has not made sufficient progress then the board would not likely support release. In essence, the local community board—with active police involvement—will be acting as a parole board at this site.

The Police and Treatment Providers

As we noted above, the role of the police in the reentry process will change not only with respect to police-offender interactions, but also in the nature and extent of police-treatment provider interactions. For many officers, this program provides them with their first opportunity to work directly and collaboratively with treatment providers. For both parties, this new partnership will likely require some intensive cross-training during the program's initial stages, because both the police and the treatment provider come from such different backgrounds and skill orientations. In such partnerships, role conflict is inevitable.

For the RPI program to be effective, this type of ongoing role conflict will have to be addressed. At one site we visited, for example, treatment staff expressed concern that offenders would not agree to participate in (voluntary) treatment programs upon release, because they believed that offenders would have trouble "trusting" the treatment providers if they arrived at the meeting together with the police. It is possible that such concerns are valid; it is also possible that they actually reflect the treatment provider's orientation toward police, not the offender's perspective. In any event, information sharing between police and treatment providers appears to be an essential feature of a reentry program where differential police surveillance and control is triggered by an offender's progress in treatment.

The Police and Community Corrections

In the eight programs we examined, we see indications of a fundamental change in the nature and extent of the interaction between police and community corrections personnel (e.g., probation/parole). In Spokane, Washington, for example, police and community supervision officers are physically located in the same "cop shops," where they often share information on offenders under community supervision. In Vermont, police and community corrections officers conduct joint "curfew checks" on reentry offenders, targeting specific locations in the community (e.g., bars) where offenders may be located. In Las Vegas,

Nevada, community supervision officers focus exclusively on the surveillance and control aspects of community supervision. Since these community supervision officers also have police "arrest" powers (and training), it could be argued that in this jurisdiction, the line between community police and community supervision officers is becoming blurred.

In Massachusetts, the Lowell police department's intelligence unit creates "posters" for each offender released to the community each month, which are hung up in the police station for officers to view at roll call. It is assumed that this information will result in an increased level of informal surveillance by police in target communities and that the results of these surveillance activities will be shared with the community supervision officers who work in this area.

In South Carolina, officers from the police and sheriff's department contact offenders immediately upon release from prison, either by phone or by home visit. The purpose of this contact is twofold: first, to demonstrate the "helping role" of police by identifying available community resources and services; and second, to reinforce the surveillance and control role of local police. It certainly appears that the role of local police is to enhance (or supplement) community supervision among conditional releasees, while taking primary responsibility for those inmates released unconditionally.

The Police and the Community

RPI programs have affected the way police departments interact with local community residents and groups, including crime victims. At two sites—Missouri and Vermont—neighborhood police officers sit on local community boards that make a wide range of decisions affecting offenders both directly and indirectly. In Washington, police departments work with volunteer "guardians," who assist offenders in a variety of areas (e.g., transportation, job preparation, housing, etc.), while also acting as another set of "eyes and ears" for the police. In Vermont and Missouri, police officers serve on restorative justice boards involved in all aspects of institutional treatment and community reintegration. As these examples illustrate, the role of the police in the community has certainly been expanded to include both informal social control strategies (e.g., the use of guardians) and the pursuit of community justice initiatives. Will such an expanded police role improve the reentry prospects of offenders or will it have potentially detrimental consequences for both the offenders and communities? At this point in the design, implementation, and evaluation process, the answer to this question is clear: we don't know. For this reason, it is critical that we examine the impact of this new wave of reentry programs on both targeted offenders (e.g., re-arrest, reconviction, reincarceration) and targeted communities (e.g., crime rates, disease rates, poverty rates).

The Police and the Victim

The police play an important role in reentry, not only in the areas of offender surveillance and control, but also in the provision of services to victims and families of victims. Victims of crime have problems and needs that are only partially addressed when the alleged offender is arrested. An examination of clearance rates (i.e., the number of reported crimes cleared by the arrest of the offender[s]) reveals that most jurisdictions do a pretty good job of making an arrest when the reported crime was a crime against a person (with clearance rates usually around 50 percent); they are not nearly as effective when it is a property crime (20 percent clearance rates). Since only a fraction of all arrested offenders are convicted and incarcerated, it is not surprising that community residents ask the police for help with the "offenders walking among us" (e.g., dispute resolution, formal and informal surveillance, active investigation). Since 9 out of 10 offenders who enter prison eventually get out, it seems logical that crime victims would ask the police for help with these offenders as well, especially when the offender has "maxed-out" of prison.

Victims of crime may need information on when the offender is being released and where he/she is planning to reside. They may want assistance in resolving ongoing disputes with the offender and his/her family and friends. They may also want increased police surveillance and protection. Finally, they may ask police assistance in filing restraining orders against the offender, especially if child protection and/or domestic violence is an issue. While getting out of prison is "good news" for the offender, it is a time of great anxiety and stress for many crime victims, friends, and family. In the past, victims could turn to community corrections for help and assistance; now, the role and responsibility appears to have moved to the police, particularly for those offenders released unconditionally from prison or jail.

The Police and the Offender

For some observers, it may seem paradoxical that police departments are now active partners in offender reentry initiatives, since these same departments were actively involved in removing these offenders from the community in the first place. To others, however, police-corrections partnerships represent an attempt to address the underlying causes of criminal behavior, by focusing on a variety of individual-level and community-level problems that have been linked to criminality.

At the individual level, offenders are often afflicted with multiple problems, including drug addiction, alcoholism, communicable disease, and mental illness. As a recent RAND *Research Brief* highlighted, "... almost 25 percent of state prisoners released by year-end 1999 were alcohol-dependent, 14 percent were mentally ill, and 12 percent were homeless at the time of arrest (2003: 1). RAND researchers go on to report that offenders released from prison have an 8 to 9 times higher prevalence rate for HIV (compared to the general population), a 9 to 10 times greater prevalence rate for Hepatitis C, a 5 times greater prevalence rate for AIDS, and a 3 to 5 times greater prevalence rate for serious mental illness (i.e., schizophrenia or other psychotic disorders). For many of these offenders, substance abuse has been a significant, long standing problem (National Commission on Correctional Health Care, 2002). Unless these individual-level problems are addressed, it seems inevitable that this month's releasees will be next month's rearrests and next year's "new" prison admissions.

Of course, the types of individual-level problems just described cannot be addressed without recognizing their broader community context (see, e.g., Sampson, Raudenbush, and Earls, 1997). Community-level problems include unemployment, income inequality, inadequate housing, homelessness, and ineffective informal social control networks (i.e., family, school, church, neighborhood). The police-corrections partnerships highlighted in this review appear to recognize the need to address problems at both the individual and community level. However, it is still unclear exactly how the "zero tolerance" policing strategies commonly associated with the "Broken Windows" version of community policing (Bratton, Wilson, Kelling, Rivers, and Cove, 2004; Kelling and Coles, 1996) will coexist with RPI program initiatives designed to provide housing, treatment, services, and support to targeted offenders. Ultimately, the success of police-corrections partnerships may hinge on the ability of local police to work simultaneously on crime prevention and crime control initiatives, and in the process, to resolve the conflicts inherent in current "broken windows" policing strategies.

A proactive, problem-solving approach is at the core of police-offender interactions in reentry jurisdiction. In the RPI model, police visit offenders in prison prior to release rather than waiting until the offender is back on the street. Utilizing the latest offender profile data, police know who is returning to their community *before* they are released. And when police interact with offenders once they return to the community it is *before* not after, a problem occurs or there is a call for service. It will likely take some time for offenders to realize that the role of the police in reentry jurisdictions has changed and that police are now involved in activities (related to housing, employment, and treatment) that can help offenders turn their lives around (Taxman, Young, and Byrne, 2003b). However, offenders must also recognize that the police will know where offenders live, which offenders are in treatment, and whether they are employed; and that they will adjust their surveillance and control activities based on this information. It remains to be seen whether the police-offender interactions associated with reentry initiatives will have their intended effect, both on individual offender change and community-level order maintenance.

CONCLUSION

The police-corrections partnerships described in this article represent an important shift in both the philosophy and practice of prisoner reentry. Given the inherent conflict associated with the interests of police and institutional corrections vis-à-vis offender reentry (after all, police remove offenders from the community and corrections send them "home" again, often to the same community), it is remarkable that these programs have emerged and appear to be successful, at least in terms of implementation. However, a number of issues related to the expanded role of police in the offender reentry process still need to be resolved, including (1) the potential for racial profiling, inherent in offender/community targeting decisions, (2) the limits of information sharing across agencies (in particular, between police and treatment providers), and (3) the impact of this expanded role for police on both offenders released from prison and jail and the communities to which they return. Similarly, both institutional and community corrections agencies will have to consider their own need for role redefinition, particularly regarding offenders who "max-out" of prison and return to the community without the surveillance, services, and control provided by traditional community corrections agencies. Police departments across the eight jurisdictions we visited appear to be filling the void created by sentencing reforms, but the long-term consequences of this expanded police role—for both offenders and the communities targeted for reentry—have yet to be evaluated.

QUESTIONS FOR REVIEW AND DISCUSSION

1. What is the role of community policing in offender rehabilitation?
2. How can the police assist in the offender's reentry into society?
3. What is meant by the "institutional phase"?
4. What is meant by "structured reentry"? Why is it important in an offender's reintegration? Discuss.
5. Distinguish between formal and informal social controls. How does each influence offender conduct? Explain.

5

Defending Against Cybercrime and Terrorism

A New Role for Universities

Tony Aeilts

Adapted from Tony Aeilts, "Defending Against Cybercrime and Terrorism: A New Role for Universities." *FBI Law Enforcement Bulletin* 74: 14–20, 2005.

Reprinted with permission from the *FBI Law Enforcement Bulletin*.

With the growth of technological access, systems, and resources, cyber-related crimes are on the rise in many communities. How will local law enforcement agencies address the growth of high-tech crime in the future? What impact will terrorism have on the nation's technological infrastructure, and how do we protect against it?

The high-tech industry is vital to the nation's economy and its future. Industries, businesses, government agencies, and private households all benefit from a healthy and well-protected technological environment. And, everyone wants reassurance that communications, financial operations, and technological infrastructure are closely guarded. The rising fear of cyber-related crime not only inhibits the use of developing technology but adversely affects national economic conditions. The FBI estimates that the average loss for a technology-oriented crime is nearly $500,000, and, further, the added cost to the consumer is $100 to $150 per computer sale (California High-Tech Task Force Committee, 1997). Other estimates indicate that losses related to high-tech crimes in the United States are $10 billion to $15 billion per year (Blumberg, 1998).

Further, 10 million Americans were victimized by identity theft in one year, with estimated losses exceeding $50 billion (Martinez, 2004), and the Federal Trade Commission reported that of the 516,740 complaints received in 2003, over 41 percent regarded identity theft (U.S. Federal Trade Commission, 2003).

Beyond the implications of cybercriminal activity, a new technological threat exists pertaining to terrorism. Since September 11, 2001, the nation has focused more on the issue of cyberterrorism because although terrorists typically have used traditional methods of physical attack (explosives, kidnappings, and hijackings), their attention may move, with increasing frequency, toward cyberterrorism. Various forms of technological infrastructure may be vulnerable to such attack; pipelines, power plants, transportation, and other hard assets rely on cybertechnology. Further, communication systems used for financial, military, police, and corporate purposes suffer from the same vulnerability. This not only includes threats against physical facilities and tangible equipment but remote cyberattacks that could disable national infrastructure as well.

DEFINING THE SCOPE OF THE PROBLEM

Headlines regarding the threat of high-tech crime have become commonplace. Cyberstalking of children, child pornography, identity theft, financial fraud, computer hacking, computer viruses, and theft of proprietary business information and intellectual property have become the prominent crime for those with even modest amounts of technological sophistication (D'Ovidio and Doyle, 2003: 10–17; Lease and Burke, 2000: 8–12; Pollock and May, 2002: 1–4; Stutler, 2000: 11–16).

Statistics related to the prevalence of high-tech crime remain unclear. Many law enforcement agencies do not clearly identify occurrences of high-tech crime. For example, a high-tech related theft of money or resources statistically is identified as a theft based upon historical definitions; the high-tech component of the crime may not be identified at all. To address this issue, the FBI and the National White Collar Crime Center implemented the Internet Fraud Complaint Center (IFCC) in 2000 (Seper, 2000: A6).

The IFCC tracks complaints it receives and coordinates with local law enforcement agencies regarding appropriate investigative jurisdiction; however, this process still does not provide consistent measurements of cybercrime.

From January 1, 2002, to December 31, 2002, the IFCC Web site received 75,063 complaints (IFCC, 2004). Additionally, the IFCC points out "that Internet usage passed the 200 million mark . . . from just 65 million in 1998" (IFCC, 2004).

This dramatic threefold increase in Internet usage in just a few years could indicate the possibility of a corresponding increase in cybercrime. Some experts argue that many ". . . victims may have serious doubts about the capacity of the police to handle computer crime incidents in an efficient, timely, and confidential manner" (Goodman, 2001:13). Business or other institutions may not report such crimes due to concerns of loss of prestige, customers, and financial status. Consequently, agencies may not adequately capture cyber-related crime statistics, and the gross impact of this type of crime, generally, may appear understated.

COORDINATING JURISDICTIONS AND SHARING RESOURCES

The difficulty of identifying the impact of cybercrime is not the only significant concern—jurisdictional issues also are problematic. When a high-tech crime occurs, it is not always clear which law enforcement jurisdiction is responsible for its investigation and prosecution.

Cyberincidents can cross regional, state, and even international jurisdictional boundaries. Crime has expanded into a virtual geographic world and traditional jurisdictions and boundaries do not apply. This virtual crime world demands cooperation and sharing of resources among agencies: ". . . although sharing information among the courts, the police, and other justice agencies at every level of government has been a goal of dedicated individuals and organizations for the past several years, the September 11 terrorist attacks have given the issue a renewed national scope. . . . The attacks they say, highlighted the lack of information exchange and underscored the importance of improved coordination among agencies (Sarker, 2002). Most law enforcement agencies simply do not have the resources to adequately deal with the myriad of potential cybercrimes (Carnevale, 2002: 12).

The ability to track criminals in multiple jurisdictions, as well as specialized knowledge of vast varieties of hardware, software, applications, foreign languages, and other related issues, requires regional, state, and national multiagency cooperation. "The most promising approach so far is a task force in which high-tech specialists from city, county, state, and federal law enforcement agencies work together and accept assistance from industry." However, one critical component is missing from that formula—the effort can and should bring high-tech resources from higher-education institutions to the forefront to assist law enforcement and national defense. "The White House's top computer security official . . . called on colleges and universities to help develop a national strategy for securing computer networks. 'I think this effort—this framework—is extremely important because it demonstrates that the issue of network security is a major concern of colleges and universities around the country,' said . . . [the] president of the American Council on Education in a statement. 'Policy makers and corporate leaders should know that the higher-education community is working together constructively to address this challenge'" (Clarke, 2002: 12).

LINKING WITH HIGHER-EDUCATION INSTITUTIONS

Higher-education resources are abundant within the realm of technology, but law enforcement agencies fundamentally underuse them. Frequently, these resources are in close proximity to many agencies but simply remain overlooked.

Specific Strategies

University High-Tech Faculty and Staff.   Law enforcement administrators should identify university faculty and staff as a significant training resource, as well as one in support of high-tech criminal investigations. Faculty members routinely conduct high-tech research, including the development and implementation of cutting-edge innovations. Their positions enable them to recognize the implications of emerging technology issues and understand potential social impacts. Their research and development often address how individuals can abuse and compromise technology, as well as find ways to protect it. "University research is crucial to developing ways to protect computer networks, in part, because businesses can't afford to spend money on long-term, high-risk research." Further, universities typically have well-developed information technology support services with cadres of highly trained staff who routinely install, repair, modify, and protect information systems. Part of their expertise comes from daily exposure to these systems on a functional level. Few local law enforcement agencies have this well-developed resource.

Additionally, institutions of higher education have high-tech classroom facilities with numerous monitors, computers, interfaces, remote projection, automated lectures, and other related capabilities, providing substantial opportunity to train multiple students, provide quality high-tech instruction, and enhance student interaction. These training resources commonly are available during academic breaks throughout the year.

An Investigative and Multiagency Protocol.   Many colleges and universities employ state-certified law enforcement agencies to protect assets of the institution. These educationally based departments can provide a critical conduit for allied law enforcement agencies and their access to university high-tech resources and personnel and serve as a mechanism to ensure investigative integrity. University police departments can monitor such issues as search and seizures, due process, and investigative protocol and provide liaison with member agencies and the district attorney. This expertise proves helpful when identifying and using nonsworn university resources in support of cybercrime investigations, and it can smooth the way toward a successful investigation.

Using a multiagency, high-tech investigation protocol can reduce potential misunderstandings about resources (departments should use personnel and other resources based upon prior agreement), protect the integrity of the investigations, and provide a system of easy reference that allows member agencies to follow a consistent and predictable process. Agencies should consider a number of factors in their protocol, including the personnel-sharing process, technological equipment and programs purchases, and grant-funding distribution.

Financial Opportunities.   Many high-tech task forces compete for a variety of state and federal grants. However, most grants require an accomplishment record indicating the importance of financial support to continue efforts to address the problem. Because many high-tech businesses have a strong interest in guarding against high-tech crime, collaborating with these organizations may produce additional financial resources. Many companies offer a variety of funding opportunities via foundations—corporate efforts to support their community. Agencies should pursue corporate high-tech support, as well as government grants.

A high-tech crime investigation partnership, in and of itself, provides a generally self-supporting mechanism. Equipment and people cost money, but the sum contribution of partnered agencies constitutes the initial formula that best would support the beginning steps of this effort. In fact, if each agency provides some limited support, such as personnel, resources, training expertise, and computer equipment, the high-tech group likely can be self-supporting. Additional funding based upon grants, foundations, and allied organizations then becomes a resource to enhance an already existing and functional program.

Stakeholders.   Together, all stakeholders should explore the various dynamics of the high-tech crime problem. Each will have a perspective unique to their needs, concerns, resources, and customers. Until such collaborative meetings occur, stakeholders will lack full awareness of their own resources and expertise. Most important, participants must gain their organization's support. Long-term approval for partnerships, protocols, and financial and personnel support is critical to the development of a realistic and substantial program. Stakeholders may vary from one region to another, but the local district attorney, college or university, area law enforcement agencies, and the FBI provide a basic formula. Businesses, which can provide information technology specialists and financial support, also should be considered an integral part of the plan.

Line-Level Personnel.   Once stakeholder organizational leaders agree to support a move toward the development of a high-tech, multiagency crime investigation group, they should identify line-level personnel who can accommodate the program's efforts. For colleges and universities, this includes their police investigators, as well as high-tech faculty and staff members. Each organizational leader should charge these individuals with the responsibilities of communicating with line-level members in partner agencies. Fundamentally, the grassroots members will form many of the long-term and functional relationships.

While it may be helpful for line-level law enforcement personnel to have extensive high-tech investigative expertise, it is *not* necessary. The preliminary development of a high-tech partnership should include those agencies with little or no high-tech expertise; an important element of this process is the development of expertise and resources over time.

A Model for the Future

The University Police Department (UPD) at California Polytechnic State University in San Luis Obispo reviewed its cybercrime issue and implemented several approaches to address the problem. First, several UPD officers received extensive training from the university's wealth of staff members and faculty with broad expertise in technology, emerging high-tech trends, and education/training abilities. The training centered on the application of computer forensics and investigative protocol as they related to high-tech crime. Next, UPD invited representatives of local law enforcement agencies to discuss the formation of a high-tech task force. The response was outstanding; representatives from departments in a four-county area attended the meeting, along with university faculty and staff.

UPD then developed an e-group site using university faculty. A list of 30 investigators from 14 agencies in 3 counties signed on to use this site as a mechanism to exchange high-tech investigation information and as a forum to solicit help with their investigations. Other meetings occurred and, subsequently, interest in a high-tech resource group grew to 46 investigators representing 5 counties in the region. Faculty members provided training and discussion ensued about joining the High-Tech Crime Investigators Association International. At that point, participation included local city police and county sheriffs' departments, state agencies, the district attorney's office, and the FBI. Additionally, the group sought participation from corporations, recognizing that they also are victims of high-tech crime and could provide high-tech expertise and resources.

Currently, this group includes about 100 members, representing dozens of agencies. Members continue to meet, communicate via the e-group site, provide high-tech training, and share investigative expertise with each other on a variety of high-tech crime investigations. This effort specifically has resulted in the successful outcome of numerous regional, multiagency, high-tech investigations with direct involvement from the forensic expertise of UPD officers and the support of high-tech faculty and staff. UPD, as an educationally oriented police agency, influenced a region and helped coordinate the high-tech resources of university police, faculty and staff, and corporations. It also provided an organized venue to coordinate the high-tech resources of regional allied agencies.

CONCLUSION

The United States is not yet adequately prepared to deal with cybercrime and terrorism. The significant cost of cybercrime, coupled with the difficulty of identifying it, is of national concern, and the law enforcement profession should align agencies and resources to address these issues. The inclusion of college and university resources in the fight against cyber-crime and the threat of terrorism may be a pivotal step. High-tech faculty, staff, and facili-ties, as well as university police departments, are a powerful combination of resources—one which exists in thousands of communities. In-depth technological expertise, high-tech classrooms, information systems support, and a built-in policing conduit all can be used to mitigate the potential impacts of high-tech crime and terrorism.

QUESTIONS FOR REVIEW AND DISCUSSION

1. What is meant by cybercrime? Why is there a growth in cybercrime? Explain.
2. What is the impact of cybercrime on U.S. citizens? How can it be prevented?
3. How is terrorism related to cybercrime?
4. How can the resources of universities coordinate with prevention efforts in combatting cybercrime?
5. Who are the stakeholders in combatting cybercrime? Discuss.
6. What type of model is proposed as a means of countering cybercrime and terrorism?

6

Coordinated Terrorist Attacks
Implications for Local Responders

Brian K. Houghton and Jonathan M. Schachter

Adapted from Brian K. Houghton and Jonathan M. Schachter, "Coordinated Terrorist Attacks: Implications for Local Responders." *FBI Law Enforcement Bulletin* 74: 11–17, 2005.
Reprinted with permission from the *FBI Law Enforcement Bulletin*.

With elections only a few days away, the terrorism threat level is at high, and law enforcement personnel are on the lookout for suspicious behavior that may indicate an imminent terrorist attack. As the morning commute gets underway, three bombs explode on a commuter train at a downtown station, killing and injuring those in the path of the blast wave and shrapnel. Law enforcement officers and emergency medical personnel respond, but, as they mobilize, four more bombs explode in another train arriving at the same station, instantly doubling the number of people dead and wounded. Soon, another bomb goes off inside a train a few miles away, requiring public safety personnel and resources there as well. The nightmare reaches its peak 5 minutes later as two more bombs blow apart a commuter train at still another downtown location, killing and injuring even more people. The emergency response community now faces mass fatalities and seemingly countless injuries at three separate sites. Though this scenario sounds like the subject of novels and Hollywood thrillers, it actually took place on March 11, 2004, in Madrid, Spain (Wright, 2004).

This type of incident, like many similar ones in recent years, has important implications for the ways in which local responders prepare for terrorist attacks of all kinds.

DEFINITIONS AND TRENDS

Coordinated terrorist assaults include elements that occur simultaneously or nearly so and are conducted by a single terrorist organization or jointly by sympathetic groups. Historically, however, the vast majority of hazardous device-based terrorist attacks have not fit this description, but have been "simple" in design, featuring only one component, such as a single placed bomb or a suicide bomber. Nevertheless, in recent years, the number of coordinated assaults has increased, especially among the terrorist groups of greatest concern to the United States. Moreover, since 1983, half of the 14 terrorist incidents with 100 or more fatalities were coordinated ones (Quillen, 2002: 293–302).

A mix of interrelated reasons makes coordinated attacks appealing to terrorist groups. Such incidents have the potential to cause greater damage than simple operations in terms of the lives, property, and geographic areas affected, as well as the psychological impact. The increased destruction lends credibility to the terrorist organization as it reflects an ability to plan and execute sophisticated operations, implies a multiplicity of personnel and supporters, and creates the impression that the group can cover many areas at the same time. This combination of perceived and actual destructive power and resultant credibility makes such attacks and the organizations that perpetrate them more "newsworthy," allowing such groups to gain public attention, one of the main goals of all terrorist campaigns.

Overall, coordinated terrorist incidents fall into three main categories: (1) parallel device attacks, where participants use more than one device simultaneously or almost simultaneously in the same location; (2) secondary attacks, where the initial assault is followed by one or more additional attacks in the same location, typically targeting responders; and (3) multiple dispersed attacks, where groups stage simultaneous or near-simultaneous ones at different locations. Depending on the type, more than one incident scene might exist, but, taken together, they constitute a single attack, with repercussions greater than those of the individual-component category. With this in mind, understanding how terrorists use coordinated assaults can assist local emergency responders in better planning, training, and organizing to respond to such incidents.

Parallel Devices

Parallel devices allow terrorists to inflict greater damage in any one incident site without having to construct or transport a single, larger one required to create similar results. In other words, rather than relying on one large bomb, terrorists can use two or more smaller, yet equally lethal, ones. The reasonable assumption that smaller devices are less vulnerable to detection raises the likelihood of the attack's execution. Moreover, regardless of the size of the bomb, even if one or more of the perpetrators is intercepted, others still may manage to complete their missions. Thus, parallel devices provide terrorists with greater assurance that they will execute at least part of their planned attack.

The use of parallel devices also allows terrorists to create multiple focus points at the incident site, thereby expanding the overall perimeter affected by the attack. With this expansion comes greater demand for both responders and resources, which can tax emergency reaction elsewhere in the jurisdiction. At the same time, this high concentration of forces in a single location potentially increases their susceptibility to secondary attacks.

The triple-suicide bombing carried out by Hamas on September 4, 1997, on the Ben-Yehuda pedestrian mall in Jerusalem can demonstrate a parallel device attack (Schmermann, 1997: A1).

In that one, three males, one dressed as a woman, each detonated a 4- to 5-pound bomb packed with nuts and bolts to create puncture, as well as blast, injuries. Five people were killed and 181 were wounded.

Attackers also employed parallel devices in the October 12, 2002, attack in Bali, which killed 202 (U.S. Department of State, 2003: 18).

The first blast, from a relatively small bomb, drew people out onto the street and was followed 10 to 15 seconds later by a much larger explosion, which caused most of the destruction. The near-simultaneous attacks increased the lethality of the bombings, which targeted mainly Western tourists.

Secondary Attacks

Secondary attacks have two or more stages of attack. The first one draws in emergency responders, regardless of the extent of deaths and injuries. In the second, the responders themselves become the target and include not only law enforcement, fire and rescue, and emergency medical personnel but civilian Good Samaritans as well.

Targeting responders serves two main purposes. First, it threatens to delay or deny treatment to victims from the first stage of the attack, increasing the likelihood of death and the severity of injuries. Second, killing, injuring, or otherwise hindering responders exacerbates the public's feelings of fear and helplessness by demonstrating the vulnerability of society's guardians. To the extent that symptoms of post-traumatic stress disorder result from both the trauma and the perceived powerlessness to influence events and outcomes, this type of attack might make such reactions more likely among responders and the public alike.

The Provisional IRA often used secondary devices (Bowcott, 1993: 2; Buck, 2002: 18).

Similarly, two bombings in 1997—one at a clinic in suburban Atlanta that provided abortions and one at an Atlanta gay nightclub—also involved the use of secondary devices (Harmon, 1999).

Multiple Dispersed Attacks

Dispersed attacks, like the other two types of coordinated assaults, seek to expand the extent and spread of damage and fear. When carried out within the same jurisdiction, they also threaten to exhaust response resources more quickly, which, as in the case of secondary attacks, could lead to delays in treatment or an increase in fear due to the perception of responders being overwhelmed.

The scope of the spread in dispersed attacks determines their impact on local responding agencies. Thus, for example, the crash of hijacked United Flight 93 near Shanksville, Pennsylvania, on September 11, 2001, taxed the responders in that and neighboring communities, but did not pull *local* responders from New York City, where they were needed to respond to the attacks on the World Trade Center. If planes were forced down in two locations on opposite sides of the same city, however, that city would have to divide its resources or rely more heavily on mutual aid.

Attacks carried out across jurisdictions or operational areas (or even across countries) create more political-strategic than local-tactical dispersion effects. The multiplicity of al-Qaeda's assaults on the U.S. embassies in Kenya and Tanzania in August 1998 (across countries) and of the ones of September 2001 (across states), for example, demonstrated to the world that al Qaeda could plan and execute highly lethal, near-simultaneous operations, hundreds of miles apart, against the world's most powerful country. In both of these cases, the group had multiple tactical targets but only one strategic target—the United States. Al-Qaeda's capability undoubtedly earned the group political capital both in terms of being taken seriously by the international community and for recruitment purposes around the world.

Al Qaeda and the groups it has inspired continue to rely on dispersed attacks, as evidenced in the May 2003 incidents in Morocco and Saudi Arabia (CNN, 2003).

These were at once dispersed across and within countries. The incidents in these two countries were dispersed in each—five simultaneous assaults in Casablanca and three simultaneous ones in Riyadh.

Other terrorist groups have carried out multiple dispersed attacks. The Hizbullah bombings of the U.S. Marine barracks and French military headquarters on October 23, 1983, killed 241 and 58, respectively (Cronin, 2003).

Almost a decade later, in the spring of 1993, the Provisional IRA executed a number of dispersed assaults, including the firebombing of two department stores, the hijacking and bombing of a pair of taxis in London, and the placing of bombs in trash cans a block apart to target those fleeing the first blast (*Daily Mail,* 1993: *The Times,* 1993).

The March 20, 1995, Aum Shinrikyo sarin gas attack on the Tokyo subway, which killed 12 and injured more than 1,000, also comprised multiple dispersed incidents (Regan, 2004).

The attackers released gas via crude dispersal mechanisms simultaneously on five different subway cars on three separate lines.

Hoaxes also can cause fear and panic in a population, and terrorists have used simultaneous multiple dispersed hoaxes to create trouble for emergency responders. In January 2004, terrorists contacted law enforcement personnel in Belfast, Northern Ireland, indicating that they had placed multiple car bombs around the city. The subsequent response to the calls strained the responder community and locked down traffic throughout the city. Given the credible threat, local law enforcement agencies had no choice but to respond.

SIMILARITIES

Probably due to ease of planning and manufacture, the individual-component portions within coordinated incidents have tended to be of the same type, such as simultaneous or subsequent pipe bombs, car bombs, or suicide bombers. Little reason exists to believe that this trend will continue, especially in light of some recent examples of mixed-type attacks.

On December 1, 2001, just yards from where the triple-suicide bombing took place in Jerusalem more than 4 years earlier, Hamas carried out a double-suicide bombing, followed approximately 20 minutes later by a car bomb (Hockstader, 2001: A1). Eleven people were killed and approximately 180 were wounded in the combined explosions. This one proves noteworthy not only because it provides an example of different means being used in the same assault but also because it demonstrates that the types of coordinated attacks can by combined. The two suicide bombers made this a parallel device attack, while the car bomb turned it into a secondary one as well. Clearly, the categories described are not mutually exclusive.

Another mixed-type and mixed-category attack is the simultaneous al-Qaeda suicide and car bombings of an Israeli-owned hotel in Mombasa, Kenya (parallel devices), which occurred at the same time as the attempted shooting down of an Israeli 757 jetliner in the same city (dispersed attacks) on November 28, 2002. While the aircraft emerged undamaged, 13 people were killed and approximately 80 were injured in the hotel bombings (Wax, 2002: A1).

IMPLICATIONS

Coordinated attacks are not a new phenomenon. However, their increasing frequency makes it worth reviewing some of the implications for local responding agencies.

Decentralize Equipment and Personnel

The potential for coordinated attacks means that local responders must have the capability to respond to multiple incidents at multiple locations. Positioning equipment and personnel in a central site might make organizational sense, but could turn into a liability in the event that attacks occur at opposite extremes of the operational area or if the equipment or personnel themselves become targets.

Resist Deploying All Resources

Agencies may find it tempting, especially in the face of a first terrorist attack, to "hyper-respond" sending everyone and everything to the incident site. But, they should resist this temptation for two reasons. First, secondary attacks could target responders and equipment. It is prudent to hold some back (though obviously not to the detriment of necessary patient care or public safety) in anticipation of such an occurrence. Second, dispersed attacks or other types of routine emergencies will demand responders elsewhere. As is the case with any mass-casualty event, rapid availability of mutual aid remains critical.

Plan, Exercise, and Train

Local responders know well the importance of prior planning and frequent and realistic training and exercises for making complex technical procedures a matter of habit. In this regard, responding to coordinated assaults is no different from reacting to any other type of emergency. Responders' actions reflect the extent to which they have prepared and trained for such occurrences. Moreover, as response to hazardous device assaults involves fire and rescue, emergency medical, law enforcement, and other agencies, all must train together for coordinated attack scenarios.

With this in mind, local agencies should add coordinated attack response "playbooks" to their emergency operations plans. Alternatively, they could include coordinated attack scenarios in other existing playbooks for similar situations. Agencies should rigorously practice the new procedures so responders at all levels become thoroughly familiar with them.

Coordinated attack response planning and training should address command-level issues as well. Emergency response agencies should consider such questions as whether to designate single or multiple incident commanders at the dispersed locations and how best to allocate and coordinate limited resources among multiple attack sites.

Protect the Force

It is difficult to know in advance whether secondary attacks will occur. An attack followed by a secondary one appears the same as a single assault *until* responders recognize that they have become the target. Therefore, responders must assume that terrorists will attempt one. This puts a premium on force protection, a role that falls primarily to law enforcement officials who can take a number of simple but crucial steps at the scene to help deter or prevent secondary attacks. These include establishing a secure perimeter far enough from the locus of the first assault to allow responders to do their jobs safely; sweeping for secondary devices; and monitoring, photographing, and interviewing bystanders, among whom might be eyewitnesses and terrorist spotters. Of importance, force protection, while essentially a law enforcement function, cannot be properly executed without the cooperation of and coordination with fire and rescue, emergency medical, and other responding agencies.

CONCLUSION

Along with the recent increase in coordinated attacks has come a corresponding rise in fatalities and injuries. Terrorists feel the need to create ever greater impact on their targeted societies, and coordinated assaults bring both added lethality and "newsworthiness." Al-Qaeda is not the only terrorist group attacking in this manner. Terrorists around the world are learning from each other's successes and adopting and refining this tactic. For emergency responders, coordinated attacks bring not only greater danger to the public they serve but also the potential that responders themselves may be targeted. To mitigate the effects of such incidents, law enforcement agencies and other local responders must incorporate coordinated attack scenarios into their planning, training, and deployment.

QUESTIONS FOR REVIEW AND DISCUSSION

1. What are parallel devices that might be used by terrorists? Provide examples.
2. What is a secondary attack? How does it compare with a multiple dispersed attack? Explain.
3. What capabilities should responders have when they have been attacked by terrorists or have been threatened by the imminent possibility of a terrorist attack?
4. Should all government resources be deployed when an attack has been made by terrorists? Why or why not? Explain.
5. Why is coordination between local, state, and federal governments important in combatting terrorism?

7

"Compstat Process"

Jon M. Shane

Adapted from Jon M. Shane, "Compstat Process." *FBI Law Enforcement Bulletin* 74: 12–21, 2004.

Reprinted with permission from the *FBI Law Enforcement Bulletin*.

Managing, directing, and controlling a modern law enforcement organization is a complex and demanding job. It is not sufficient for the chief to merely control the budget and the daily operations of the most visible segment of government; rather, he also is *expected* to control the human phenomenon known as crime (Kelling and Sousa, 2001).

How to control crime and disorder always has been a conundrum. Through the 1970s and 1980s, many criminologists posited that "collective 'root causes' like social injustice, racism, poverty [and economics] caused crime. [These implications suggested that] crime could only be prevented if *society itself* were radically changed . . . [therefore,] when it came to *preventing* (and thus reducing crime), police did not really matter."

The fact is, however, that the police *do matter* when it comes to preventing crime and keeping communities safe, despite many criminologists' academic explanations that they can do little to prevent crime and restore order. With some reorganization, law enforcement executives can put into practice one of the most innovative, deceptively simple, and economical means to controlling crime and disorder—a management process known as Compstat.

The Compstat process, pioneered by former New York City police commissioner William Bratton and his management team after he assumed command in January 1994, "is based on the principle that by controlling serious crime, police are better poised to maintain order and solve other community problems in the promotion of public safety" (McDonald, 2002).

The Compstat model stands as a classic example of how reengineering processes within a bureaucracy can produce significant public safety gains (Hammer and Champy, 1993).

The essence of the Compstat process is to "collect, analyze, and map crime data and other essential police performance measures on a regular basis and hold police managers accountable for their performance as measured by these data" (Philadelphia Police Department, 2003).

This also reflects a larger overall paradigm: accountability and discretion at all levels of the organization. By creating a management structure that keeps everyone focused on the core mission, officers and executives alike can shed the cloak of cynicism that often comes from trying to do a job whose requirements sometimes are in irreconcilable conflict (Kelling, 1995).

Most of all, "Compstat is not just for the huge departments. Any size department— 10-officer, 25-officer—can benefit from the Compstat process. The police *can* make a difference. The police *do* make a difference. The police *must* make a difference. Compstat is how" (Sanow, 2003: 4).

This article examines Compstat in detail, including its core components, the need for accurate intelligence, and four crime-reduction principles that create the framework for the Compstat process.

THE PRINCIPLES

Compstat, a strategic crime-control technique, centers around four crime-reduction principles: accurate and timely intelligence, effective tactics, rapid deployment of personnel and resources, and relentless follow-up and assessment (New York Police Department, 1994).

As an agency reengineers to support Compstat, the chief and his executive managers must set specific objectives, driven by these four principles. "This is important because establishing specific objectives sends a powerful message to all [levels of the organization]; the message indicates what the department determines worthy of focus and attention" (Bryson, 1995: 30).

Specific objectives could include reducing gang-related homicides, ATM robberies, and disorderly youth in and around a shopping mall, along with several others. For example, the New York City Police Department developed 10 specific objectives that drove its crime reductions (Henry, 2002: 227).

Once an agency sets the objectives, it can use Compstat to ensure that accountability is fixed and the desired results are achieved (Bryson, 1995).

Accurate and Timely Intelligence

Compstat, an information-driven managerial process, depends on accurate and timely intelligence. Without this, it would be seriously diluted, as would any other meaningful managerial process. The basic information necessary for prudent, informed decisions by department executives can come from a variety of sources, such as calls for service, field interview reports, prisoner debriefings, incident reports, and FBI Uniform Crime Reporting (UCR) records, with UCR reports and calls for service constituting the two most common.

Accurate intelligence reflects what actually occurred at a given time and place. Supervisory inspection and approval can authenticate accuracy. Supervisors usually review and approve all written documents before they become official records. For example, with incident reports that serve as a basis for UCR, a supervisor usually reviews and reclassifies them, when necessary, before submitting them to the FBI (e.g., reclassifying a burglary to a theft). This quality control mechanism ensures that the department possesses accurate crime reports before publishing or acting upon them.

In the case of calls for service, a field or communications supervisor compares the disposition (e.g., no cause) with the actual call classification (e.g., shots fired) and may re-classify the call if investigation determines that the initial call differs from what respond-ing officers actually discovered (e.g., a call for shots fired reclassified to youngsters playing with fireworks). Another way to ensure that the department operates on accurate intelli-gence involves independent corroboration. Officers and detectives always must indepen-dently corroborate the information they receive. The personal observations of experienced, well-trained officers will confirm or dispel information gleaned from police reports and calls for service. Independent corroboration also will confirm or dispel rumors, community rhetoric, and anecdotal information that so often become "fact" because of misunderstand-ing or misinterpretations of events or statements.

Information tends to go stale rather quickly. *Timely*, or "real-time," intelligence is the most current information available, being collected and acted upon as near to the occur-rence of the event as possible. Real-time data generation occurs when officers in the field write reports and submit them electronically, such as via wireless mobile data computers (MDC), where they are stored immediately and become instantly retrievable. This enables decision makers (e.g., commanding officers and executive staff) to view crime data as near to the time it happened as possible and respond swiftly and certainly.

Many departments do not have the capability to submit reports via MDC. They must rely on information at least a few days or, in most cases, a week old. Of course, re-sponding to week-old crime data is slightly less advantageous, particularly because the crime phenomenon is dynamic; however, agencies still can successfully deploy around such data. Crime trends and patterns rely on historical information; in fact, the more data, the better the analysis. But, for purposes of correcting daily conditions, com-manders will fare well if they reflect on that week-old information because the same criminals and the same antecedents inevitably will be present when the commanders de-ploy their counterstrategy.

Effective Tactics

"Nobody ever got in trouble because crime numbers on their watch went up . . . trouble arose only if the commanders didn't know why the numbers were up or didn't have a plan to address the problems."

(Maple and Mitchell, 1999)

Once commanders receive accurate and timely intelligence, they must develop and implement a plan of action and devise effective tactics that deal with as much of the prob-lem as possible. They cannot simply issue a directed patrol order because the likelihood of such action abating a particular problem is small. For example, when faced with drug sales emanating from a 24-hour fast-food restaurant, commanders could augment the directed patrol strategy with undercover operations, such as buy-bust initiatives and street surveil-lance, as well as inspections from the code enforcement, fire, and health departments. If the problem persisted, then they could seek civil enforcement (permanently closing the estab-lishment after identifying it as a nuisance) through the city's corporation counsel. Finally, the police department, via the municipal council, could pursue legislation to regulate 24-hour establishments more stringently, such as mandating specific closing times.

For tactics to be effective, commanders must direct specific resources toward specific problems. An array of city, county, state, and federal resources exists to help commanders accomplish their goals (see Specific Resources for Specific Problems chart).

Specific Resources for Specific Problems			
Local	**County**	**State**	**Federal**
Housing Authority	County Police	State Police	Coast Guard
Sanitation/Public Works Department	Prosecutor's/District Attorney's Office	Attorney General's Office	FBI, DEA, ATF, IRS, INS, EPA
Health and Human Services	County Sheriff's Office	Department of Corrections (DOC)	Marshal's Service
Code Enforcement	Traffic Engineering	National Guard	Customs Service
Parks and Recreation Department	Welfare (Public Assistance)	Probation Department	Social Security Administration
Public Utilities Company	Substance Abuse/ Mental Health/AIDS	Alcoholic Beverage Control (ABC)	Postal Inspectors/ Postal Service
Fire Department	Homeless Outreach	Division of Parole	Secret Service
Board of Education	Public Works Department	Department of Community Affairs	U.S. Attorney's Office
Economic Development Corp.	Division of Youth Services	Division of Motor Vehicles (DMV)	Bureau of Prisons

Whatever strategies commanders eventually devise, Compstat can provide the impetus for creative mind-mapping sessions where they can develop responses and gather and commit resources. By having commanders commit their resources, no delay arises and no excuse exists for not developing effective tactics. Compstat breeds this integrated approach, which reflects a departure from the traditional model of policing where most elements of the department operate independently.

Devising effective tactics becomes the point in the Compstat process where accountability attaches. If commanders fail to act, they risk being derelict in their duties or, worse, insubordinate. Large agencies may replace them for failing to act. However, smaller ones, with a restricted number of command-rank personnel, may use alternatives to compel commanders' participation, such as—

- holding one commander to task for a longer period of time during a Compstat meeting by asking an extensive number of probing questions to accelerate the learning curve and underline the criticality of the process;
- rewarding minimal success, at first, as a positive reinforcer until the commander becomes more deeply involved in the process and energized by the satisfaction that comes with success;
- being stern and finding other ways to communicate displeasure with performance without verbally assaulting or insulting the commander;
- working with a commander's subordinates to get the job done, in the event that the commander exhibits reluctance initially to get involved (being bypassed tends to send an urgent [and embarrassing] message);
- seeing that subordinates become invested in the process, with or without the commander, because this will motivate the commander to become involved as a way to reassert command and control;
- speaking in relatively harsh tones without demeaning the individual, addressing criticism directly to performance or behavior rather than to the personal qualities of the individual (this being the only way, for some personalities, to change the person's level of involvement); or
- demonstrating that the jurisdiction is receiving a lot of praise for its new actions to convince a commander that if he does not participate, promotion or other desirable positions will not be an option.

One final and important word about accountability—the essence of the Compstat process is *results*. Accountability must be affixed to achieve results; however, when the "dots on the map" disappear, the inevitable result is fewer crimes. In this respect, the true measure of success becomes the absence of crime. The results commanders derive emanate directly from their leadership. Strong-willed commitment from commanders to empower personnel with the authority and discretion to carry out a problem-solving effort and the fortitude to reward creative risk taking, even when mistakes occur, will yield positive gains. Commanders should give their subordinates the benefit of the doubt. If it turns out that some employees made a mistake, there will be time to hold them accountable. But, if commanders abandon them at the first accusation, and they later are exonerated, the commanders will never "wash away the smell of betrayal." They will have lost the trust of those employees *and* of those who never have been accused of making a mistake. Standing behind their subordinates is critical to morale, not just for the employees but for the enterprise as well (Guiliani, 2002).

Additionally, commanders should not consider their mistakes as failures per se. They should remember that "a mistake is just another way of doing things. The word failure carries with it finality, the absence of movement characteristic of a dead thing, to which the automatic human reaction is helpless discouragement. But, for the successful leader, [mistakes are] the beginning, the springboard to hope" (Bennis and Nanus, 1997).

Rapid Deployment of Personnel and Resources

Once commanders identify appropriate means and develop suitable strategies, they must rapidly deploy their personnel and resources. This may include adjusting work schedules, if permitted, to meet the demands. In some instances, restrictive labor agreements do not permit changing officers' work schedules as quickly or as frequently as may be needed. The least attractive solution to this problem involves paying overtime to counter the crime issue. While fine for short-term strategies, overtime funds, however, usually are scarce and limited. Moreover, appropriations probably never reach a level that an agency could sustain over a long period of time.

The split-force patrol concept offers one effective solution to restrictive labor agreements. "Under the split-force concept, one part of the patrol force is assigned to respond to calls for service, investigate crimes, and perform other assigned duties. Another part of the patrol force is held in reserve for the express purpose of conducting preventive patrol. [Instances may arise when the second portion of the patrol force must answer calls for service; however,] the primary intent is for one portion of the patrol force to be devoted exclusively to preventive patrol" (Hale, 1981; Nolan and Solomon, 1977: 58–64).

Generally, assigning two-thirds of the force to answer calls for service while one-third remains on proactive patrol provides a workable solution. "The primary advantage of split-force patrol is that it allows more attention to be devoted to preventive patrol activities and that officers are assigned this function as a *primary* responsibility." The commander now has a sufficient number of personnel unencumbered by the constant demands of the dispatcher. The proactive personnel can focus on the commander's obligations derived from Compstat, *and* the commander knows exactly who to hold accountable for the outcomes. The split-force patrol concept has received favorable results because it increases calls-for-service response productivity, enhances the arrest-related effectiveness of the patrol force, and results in improved police professionalism and accountability.

To gain the upper hand, commanders need to set their plan in motion rapidly and decisively, for the next Compstat meeting is only 1 week away. At that time, commanders will have to provide an update on their progress toward alleviating the problem.

Relentless Follow-Up and Assessment

Many who practice Compstat consider the last crime-reduction principle, relentless follow-up and assessment, the most onerous and time-consuming—also, the most important. It is foolish for commanders to design and implement an action plan and trust that others have carried it out without witnessing the results firsthand. Commanders cannot *expect* if they do not *inspect*. Periodic follow-up to orders acts as an early warning to detect problems that may arise, thereby enabling commanders to make adjustments.

Most of all, commanders must discern whether the solution met the intended goals. If not, why not? Commanders should not wait until the day before the next Compstat meeting to check with the supervisors tasked with implementing the action plan. Instead, within a few days of executing the plan, commanders should know whether the treatment has achieved the intended results (output and outcome).

If applied properly, the "output" should be linked to the "outcome." That is, if drug sales from a 24-hour fast-food restaurant are the problem, then effecting arrests and issuing summonses (output) in and around the restaurant should solve the problem (outcome). This reveals why conducting relentless follow-up and assessment proves essential: it establishes if the treatment (output) achieved the desired result (outcome). Other outcome measures include the ratio of calls handled per officer (including the possibility that excessive individual sick time might adversely affect collective performance) and response time (taking into account that at-fault and contributory accidents might adversely affect patrol car availability, also known as the serviceability factor). "Managers need to monitor decision implementation to be sure that things are progressing as planned and that the problem that triggered the decision-making process has been resolved" (Bartol and Martin, 1991: 272).

According to the New York City Police Department, some of the follow-up methods commanders can use include—

- touring the confines of their precinct (e.g., "management by walking around");
- reviewing incident reports, as well as the "Unusual Incident Report," on a daily basis;
- talking often with uniformed personnel about the issues;
- speaking frequently with the precinct detective squad supervisor and the detectives about conditions and their investigations; and
- analyzing the Compstat reports for individual performance and performance compared with other precincts, as well as trends and patterns (Guiliani and Safir, 1998).

To ensure that commanders conduct this follow-up, a scribe takes copious notes during each Compstat meeting and, at the following session, reports on what issues required attention. The affected commanders receive these notes the day after the meeting and must follow up on the outstanding issues. During the next Compstat meeting, the facilitator opens the session by asking these commanders what they have done to alleviate the problem or correct the condition. The commanders must show what they have done (the tactics, the deployment, and the investigative follow-up) to abate the matter and expound upon the results. Figure 1 summarizes Compstat's crime-reduction principles and how each successive principle flows from the preceding one.

CONCLUSION

The Compstat process creates a management structure that can help law enforcement agencies control crime and disorder in their communities.

QUESTIONS FOR REVIEW AND DISCUSSION

1. What is Compstat? How can it be used to increase public safety? Discuss.
2. What are the four guiding principles of Compstat?
3. How important is accurate and timely intelligence in fighting crime? Discuss.
4. What are some specific sources for specific problems in combatting crime?
5. Is a follow-up and assessment critical in evaluating the effectiveness of Compstat? Why or why not? Explain.
6. What are several crime reduction principles used by police departments?

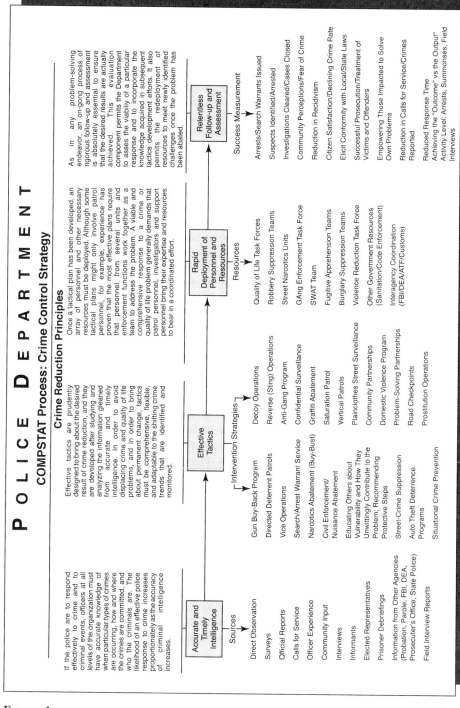

FIGURE 1

8

Crime Mapping and Analysis by Community Organizations in Hartford, Connecticut

Thomas Rich

Adapted from Thomas Rich, *Crime Mapping and Analysis by Community Organizations in Hartford, Connecticut.* Washington, DC: U.S. Department of Justice, Office of Justice Programs, March 2001.

Crime mapping has become increasingly popular among law enforcement agencies and has enjoyed high visibility at the Federal level, in the media, and among the largest police departments in the Nation, most notably those in Chicago and New York City. However, there have been few efforts to make crime mapping capabilities available to community residents and organizations, although a National Institute of Justice (NIJ)-funded project in Chicago in the late 1980s aimed at introducing mapping to community groups showed that this technology could benefit them (Block, 1998). Access to timely and complete incident-level crime information—among other obstacles—has inhibited the spread of mapping to communities.

To get the community more involved in crime prevention. Hartford, a city of 130,000 in central Connecticut, expressed an interest in providing community-based organizations with a crime mapping and analysis system. This technology—dubbed the Neighborhood Problem Solving (NPS) system—was developed and implemented in 1997 and 1998 in 14 locations throughout Hartford, including community organization headquarters, public libraries, and community policing field offices. Developed with NIJ funding, the system enables users to create a variety of maps and other reports depicting crime conditions by using a database containing the most recent 2 years of incident-level police information, including citizen-initiated calls for service, reported crimes, and arrests. Although some police departments routinely publish aggregate crime statistics and a few publish incident-level crime information on the Internet, the objective in Hartford was to extend basic mapping and crime analysis technologies beyond the law enforcement community so that neighborhood-based organizations could analyze incident-level data.

NIJ sponsored an assessment of Hartford's system by Abt Associates Inc. to determine the extent to which community organizations used it, to understand how these organizations used the software, and to assess the effect of the system on community organization effectiveness, perceptions of neighborhood safety and quality of life, and police-community relations. This discusses the findings of this research.

PROJECT ORIGIN

In November 1994, Hartford was 1 of 12 cities to receive a Comprehensive Communities Program (CCP) grant from the U.S. Department of Justice's Bureau of Justice Assistance. The Hartford CCP sought to shift the focus of city government away from the professional civil service model to a decentralized government that recognizes residents as its "customers" and attends to problems and solutions they identify. In 1988, the police department had initiated community-oriented policing with the formation of the Community Service Officer (CSO) unit. CSOs focused exclusively on problem solving within a specific neighborhood. The department also formed partnerships with other agencies, including schools, youth organizations, and other criminal justice agencies. In 1995 and 1996, Hartford established a number of CCP-supported initiatives and programs that created, in the words of one veteran community organizer, "an infrastructure" that supported the NPS system. According to this organizer, having this infrastructure in place was a necessary condition for widespread acceptance and use of the NPS system.

Citizen-based problem-solving committees, one of the most important CCP initiatives, were formed in each of Hartford's 17 neighborhoods. In many neighborhoods, these committees consisted of residents already active in the existing neighborhood citizen groups, but the committees were an entirely new group for some neighborhoods. The committees were charged with identifying and prioritizing neighborhood problems and, with the help of city agencies, implementing solutions to those problems. The city retained an independent consultant to conduct problem-solving training for the committees. The training focused on recognizing and analyzing problems, developing and implementing strategies, and assessing results. City employees were trained in community-oriented government techniques. In addition, CCP began funding the community organization United Connecticut Action for Neighborhoods in 1997 to provide additional training and technical assistance to the committees.

Beginning in 1995, the committees were eligible to receive personal computers equipped with standard business productivity software and a laser printer. Many committees immediately took advantage of this offer, although some did not apply for their computers until 2 or 3 years later. The NPS system was eventually installed on these computers. The Hartford Police Department and Abt Associates jointly administered the NPS program. The police department provided data on calls for services, crimes, and arrests to Abt Associates, which formatted the data and provided it to the community organizations. Abt Associates maintained the NPS system software, while the city of Hartford maintained the computers. Trinity College in Hartford provided the committees with e-mail and Internet accounts beginning in 1996.

SYSTEM CAPABILITIES

In 1997, representatives of the problem-solving committees, Hartford city officials involved in the city's CCP, Abt Associates staff, and representatives from the Hartford Police Department and other city service agencies held a series of meetings to determine what information—particularly automated information—would be useful (and could be provided) to the committees to support their problem-solving activities. Ideally, an information system supporting problem solving—especially one with mapping capabilities—would contain data from a variety of sources, including city, State, and Federal agencies; private and nonprofit organizations; and neighborhood-based organizations. Such data would enable maps to show a multidimensional view of crime. For example, one layer of a map display could contain a descriptive variable, such as the location of burglaries in the past month, while other layers could contain possible explanatory variables, such as demographic and social indicators or the locations of abandoned buildings or liquor establishments (Maltz, Gordon, and Friedman, 1991).

Committee representatives indicated they wanted access to a variety of information, including police, housing, and code enforcement data that could be tied to specific addresses. Unfortunately, with the exception of police calls for service, crime, and arrest data, information was either not automated or out of date by several months, although projects were under way to improve the quality of the data. By contrast, police calls for service and arrest records were entered in real time (i.e., while the call taker talks to the person calling 911 and the suspect goes through the arrest booking process), and reported crime information was typically automated about 1 week after the police officer submitted his or her completed crime report.

In light of these findings, CCP staff, the police department, and Abt Associates staff decided that the NPS system would initially focus on providing the committees with access to police calls for service, crime, and arrest data.

DATA ISSUES

Prior to participating in this project, the Hartford Police Department had a history of deploying sophisticated technologies in its crimefighting and public safety efforts. Department staff had designed and programmed advanced computer-aided dispatch, case incident reporting, and online arrest booking systems. The department has used computerized crime mapping since the early 1990s, when it participated in NIJ's Drug Market Analysis Program. Since the mid-1990s, department analysts have distributed weekly crime maps to command staff.

One important difference between a crime mapping tool developed for internal police use and one developed for use by community groups or the general public involves the issue of which data to make available to users. The NPS system provides basic "what, when, and where" information on calls for service, crimes, and arrests. No names or other personal identifying information are provided, which protects the identities of participating citizens. Community organizations are provided with the most recent 2 years of these data occurring in the organization's area of concern, which typically corresponds to one of Hartford's 17 neighborhoods. For an average-sized community organization, the 2-year timespan of data translates into about 12,000 calls for service, 7,000 crimes, and 1,000 arrests. During the study period, Abt Associates staff provided data to the community organizations every 2 weeks via e-mail or U.S. mail. Because of the 2-week delivery cycle—and because the police department entered calls for service and arrest information in real time and crime information within a week of when the officer completed the crime report—the data were roughly 10 days to 2 weeks old when delivered.

The NPS software can produce five different types of reports, each of which can be based on either calls for service, reported crimes, or arrests.

- A **detail list** shows records that meet a specified criterion (e.g., all burglaries in a neighborhood over the past year).
- A **top 10 list** shows the most frequent types of events (e.g., the 10 most frequently reported types of crime in a neighborhood over the past month).
- A **time trend graph** shows the number of events occurring over a recent set of time periods (e.g., the number of burglaries in a neighborhood by week over the past 6 months).
- An **event trend graph** shows the percentage change in the number of different types of events over a recent period (e.g., the percentage change in the number of each crime group in the most recent month compared with the previous month).
- A **pin map** shows the locations of events over a specified period (e.g., the location of all burglaries in a neighborhood over the past month). Although the report is referred to as a pin map, it is actually a graduated symbol map in which the size of the icon depicting the location is proportional to the number of events at that location.

For all reports, users can specify a desired date and time range. Standard options are available (e.g., for dates, the most recent 2 weeks, the most recent month, and the most recent year), or the user can specify any desired date and time range. Maps and graphs are produced for a specified group of calls for service, crimes, or arrests (e.g., narcotics arrests, violent crime-related calls for service, or burglary crimes). Currently, only one group can be mapped at a time. Detail lists can be sorted by date and time, by type of event, or by address. In addition, detail lists can show all events (e.g., all arrests) or only events in a certain group (e.g., only narcotics arrests).

From June 1998 to March 1999 (the end of the evaluation period), the NPS software was installed at 14 community locations in Hartford: 8 community organization headquarters, 4 community policing substations, and 2 public libraries.

SITE CHARACTERISTICS

The community organizations that received the NPS system and were trained in its use vary considerably in size, resources, and experience in community organizing and problem solving. One has approximately 15 full-time employees, most of whom are neighborhood organizers assigned to one of nine neighborhoods in Hartford. Others have one or two full-time or part-time paid staff. By contrast, the problem-solving committees are essentially groups of concerned citizens with other full-time occupations and have no paid staff or formal office space. Independent of their size and resources, the community organizations and problem-solving committees all appear to possess a strong concern about crime and public safety.

Hartford's Part I crime rate in 1997 was nearly twice the national average, even though the city, like many other cities in the Nation, experienced a significant decrease in crime in the 1990s; from 1987 to 1992, the city recorded between 20,000 and 22,000 Part I crimes per year, and by 1997, the annual total had dropped to slightly more than 12,000. Crime, however, is by no means the only issue of concern to these organizations. An organizer in one neighborhood indicated that the four issues discussed most at neighborhood meetings are (in order of importance) taxes, education, crime, and litter.

Although all community organizations with the NPS system share major crime concerns, they differ in their overall approach to addressing these problems in their neighborhoods. For example, some focus on identifying issues of concern to neighborhood residents and developing approaches to address those concerns. Other organizations focus on delivering services to neighborhood residents, such as sponsorship of job fairs or street-lighting projects. Many of the Hartford problem-solving committees work directly with police CSOs to address specific crime problems.

SYSTEM USERS

There was at least one targeted user—a person trained in the use of the system who received and processed crime data updates and whose reaction to the system was monitored—at each installation site. In many cases, these targeted users showed others in their organizations how to use the system. Having a targeted set of users distinguished this project from one that involved the installation of an NPS-like system at public kiosks or on the Internet to provide information to the general public. In general, the system in this study was designed for community organizations, and there was no attempt to encourage its use by the general public.

The four types of targeted users were:

- **Block watch organizers,** who work for a community organization and are charged with establishing new block watches and supporting existing block watches. The city of Hartford provided funding to community organizations to hire these individuals.

- **Neighborhood organizers,** who work at community organizations and undertake community organizing activities in the neighborhood to which they are assigned. In particular, neighborhood organizers support the problem-solving committees.

- **Community organization staff,** which refers to other individuals at community organizations who have a variety of responsibilities, including administration, management, grant writing, and community organizing.

- **Problem-solving committee members,** who have other full-time occupations and positions.

SYSTEM UTILIZATION

The most basic evaluation issue for the NPS system was how frequently the system was used. Across NPS sites, the frequency of system usage varied.

- **Regular users**—7 of the 14 sites used the NPS system regularly on a monthly or more frequent basis during the data collection period.
- **Irregular users**—two sites used the NPS system on several occasions but not on a regular basis during the data collection period.
- **One-time users**—four sites used the NPS system once during the data collection period.
- **Nonusers**—one site did not use the NPS system at all during the data collection period.

At the conclusion of the initial training session at each installation site, all targeted users reacted enthusiastically to the system, praising its ease of use and listing the ways in which their organization could use the system. Yet, 5 of the 14 sites either did not use the system at all or used it only once. Why did some community organizations use the system and not others?

The primary reason some sites regularly used the system was that organization leaders affiliated with the site took a personal interest in it. In contrast, the targeted users in several other neighborhoods were largely on their own and without supervisors to encourage them to use the system. In addition, several users were relatively new to the field of community organizing and naturally had a more difficult time integrating an information tool such as the NPS system into their organizing activities.

Personnel resources also influenced use patterns. Targeted users at many sites where the system was used regularly were persons whose full-time job was community organizing. At some sites where the system saw little use, however, targeted users had other full-time occupations and did not have access to volunteers, interns, or full-time organizers who could use the system. Some organizations did not regularly use the system because it was not particularly relevant to the targeted user's primary work objectives—for example, the site's primary objective was to provide job training or other services to residents. Limited accessibility to the computers equipped with the NPS system inhibited system use in two sites.

The types of maps and reports produced with the NPS system provide insight into the general types of police data and data formats community organizations in other jurisdictions might find particularly useful. Each NPS run was based on calls for service, crimes, or arrests. Significant site-by-site variations exist, however, among the regular users of the system. For example, three regular NPS users showed little interest in calls-for-service data; their sites used those data in less than 10 percent of their runs. Users at another regular-use site, however, were most interested in calls for service. Users at a third regular-use site focused most often on arrest data, reflecting a strong interest in monitoring the police response to neighborhood problems.

Four of the seven regular-use sites preferred the pin map report format. Across all sites, the pin map was the most preferred report format, and it was used in 39 percent of all NPS runs. The other report formats also showed significant use, ranging from 23 percent (the detail list) to 8 percent (the top 10 list) of all runs, thus reinforcing the notion that maps are only one method of analyzing police data and that a variety of report formats is required to provide useful information to users of police data.

Although information about the preferred data types and report formats used in Hartford may provide insight into the possible preferences of community organizations in other cities, the specific type of data displayed in the maps and reports is likely to vary depending on the issues of importance to users in those cities. Data preferences in Hartford may be representative of other urban areas, however. Narcotics-related information was the most common type of data to appear in Hartford sites' NPS pin maps, followed closely by Part I crime-related information. Together, these data constituted nearly 80 percent of all NPS pin maps. The most common Part I crime-related maps across all sites were burglaries (14 percent of all pin maps), followed by auto theft and aggravated assault (9 percent each). Overall, the interest in Hartford was serious crime, as opposed to less serious crime and quality-of-life issues. Nevertheless, there were significant variations across the regular-use sites. The percentage of maps depicting narcotics activity, for example, ranged from a low of 8 percent to a high of 81 percent. The percentage of maps depicting noncriminal activity (e.g., accidents, motor vehicle infractions) ranged from 0 to as much as 24 percent.

Just as the sites used the NPS system to varying degrees, they used it in a variety of ways and for a variety of purposes. Primary uses of the maps and reports include the activities described below.

Forming Block Watches.   Veteran block watch organizers commented that the NPS system was useful for getting people to attend block watch meetings. The block watch organizer in a neighborhood perceived as one of Hartford's safest commented that the maps and reports she showed to potential block watch members helped convince them that "there is real crime in their quiet neighborhood, so a block watch would be beneficial."

Supporting Existing Block Watches.   In several neighborhoods, block watch organizers regularly produced maps and other reports and shared them with attendees at block watch meetings. Organizers consistently commented that the maps and reports served as conversation starters for the meetings and provided valuable information. In one neighborhood, support for the block watches was highly systemized because community organization staff, together with several block watch leaders, designed and distributed a biweekly "CrimeData Update" containing NPS reports to all block watch leaders.

Supporting Neighborhood-level Organizations.   Members of citizen groups, neighborhood organizers, and other community organization staff used the NPS system to provide information to neighborhood-level organizations, much like a police crime analyst produces a set of maps for a police command staff meeting.

Raising Neighborhood Awareness.   One community organization used the NPS system to disseminate crime information to residents throughout the neighborhood on National Night Out, an annual nationwide event in which residents participate in outdoor activities designed to mark progress in "taking back the night" from drug dealers and other criminals.

Community organization staff used the NPS software to produce a two-page crime summary handout and delivered it to neighborhood block-party hosts.

Distributing Information to Law Enforcement Officials.   Several community organizations used NPS maps and reports to facilitate communication with police and prosecution officials. CSOs, for example, regularly attended neighborhood problem-solving committee meetings and were typically called on to explain and interpret the NPS output. During some of these discussions between residents and police officials, residents commented on apparent inaccuracies in the police data, highlighting what one veteran community organizer believed was the most important use of the NPS system: improving the exchange of information between the community and the police and, in particular, ensuring that the police and the community have a common understanding of neighborhood problems. In other situations, the maps and reports were used at meetings with law enforcement officials to substantiate requests for action in a hot spot or for additional police resources.

PROBLEM-SOLVING AND CRIME PREVENTION APPLICATIONS

Targeted users and the people for whom maps and other reports were produced used the NPS system to accomplish a variety of specific or general objectives. One of the most common objectives related to the NPS system was identifying and quantifying crime hot spots, including specific addresses, streets, and sections of neighborhoods. In most cases, the quantifying component was significantly more important than the identifying component because community organizers and other persons active in a neighborhood were already aware of the most problematic locations in their area. What those individuals ordinarily could not do was quantify the seriousness of the hot spot in terms of citizen complaints, reported crimes, and arrests.

Quantifying the seriousness of a hot spot serves two key purposes for community groups and neighborhood residents. First, maps and reports confirm the organizers' or residents' perception of the problem. A number of targeted users indicated that the NPS output served as a "reality check" and let residents know the problems they saw were, in fact, real. Conversely, the NPS system was also used to suggest that a problem thought to be serious was, in fact, not that serious. The second and more important purpose for quantifying problems is that community groups, armed with hard evidence of a problem, can make a stronger case both to neighborhood residents to get involved and to the police and other city agencies to provide additional resources to combat the problem. The leader of one Hartford community organization indicated that the primary value of the NPS system was using data to highlight the chronic problems in a neighborhood. He added that his organizations was often "somewhat skittish about going after a problem if the only evidence is citizen perceptions."

Although in most cases the NPS system was used to confirm and quantify known problems, targeted users noted that in some instances the system highlighted a previously unknown problem (at least to the community group or neighborhood problem-solving committee). This finding indicates what some in the Hartford Police Department hoped would be an outcome of this project—that citizens would become effective crime analysts.

Whether a property was a known or an unknown problem, community organizations used several techniques to target specific problem properties, including discussing the problem with the police CSO and other police officials, talking to the owners, and publicizing the problem in the media. In July 1998, the Connecticut Legislature provided an additional tool that the police, prosecutors, and community organizations could use to target specific properties. The Nuisance Abatement and Quality of Life Act gives the State, through the State's Attorney's office, the right to bring a civil action against any property owner whose property creates a public nuisance. The law defines a public nuisance as three or more arrests (on different dates) for a variety of crimes, including prostitution and the sale or possession of narcotics. The value of the NPS system in developing cases for the Nuisance Abatement Act is obvious, and several community organizations in Hartford used the system to identify properties covered under the Act. The organizations then notified the Connecticut attorney general's office, attaching NPS output to their letters as supporting documentation.

A number of community organization leaders in Hartford said they believed a primary use of the NPS system would be to raise awareness throughout the neighborhoods regarding crime conditions and encourage residents to focus on crime prevention. As one neighborhood organizer said, "The main use of the system is to bring the neighborhood together—getting [neighbors] to focus on an issue and mobilize around it." One community organization noted how frequently residents complained about drug activity but how infrequently they reported it to the police. As a result, the organization mounted a campaign (using NPS reports that showed how few citizen drug-related calls for service were made in the neighborhood) to encourage residents to contact the police. The number of calls for service increased substantially following this outreach effort and a number of drug arrests were made as a result.

Finally, one neighborhood organizer used the NPS system to measure the effect of a major multiyear initiative with which his organization was involved. For several years, his organization worked with Federal, State, and city officials to secure funding and garner political support to demolish a public housing development in the neighborhood. One year after the demolition, the organizer used the NPS system to address concerns that the relocation of public housing residents to other parts of the neighborhood led to crime increases. The organizer said the NPS system enabled him to be factual and precise with the organization's supporters and city policymakers about changes in the neighborhood.

OVERALL EFFECTS

How did targeted NPS users and consumers react to the NPS output? Did the maps and reports tell them anything they did not already know?

Although neighborhood activists were already aware of the most problematic properties and locations in their neighborhoods, results of the survey of regular NPS users indicated they learned much about their areas from the system. For example, 12 of 17 regular NPS users and consumers gained a much better understanding of crime conditions in their neighborhoods, and 13 of the 17 gained a much better understanding of where the crime hot spots were in their neighborhoods.

Of related interest was whether residents' perception of neighborhood safety and quality of life were affected after they viewed the NPS maps and reports; that is, did residents feel differently about their neighborhoods when they had a comprehensive database of actual and suspected criminal activity than they did when their perception of crime was based only on reports in the media and what they heard from friends and neighbors? On this issue, regular NPS users expressed a variety of viewpoints. A majority of respondents indicated that the NPS maps and reports did not affect their view of their neighborhoods: 11 of 17 regular users indicated that the level of reported crime displayed in the NPS maps and reports was about what they expected, and 9 of 17 said the NPS did not change the extent to which they felt safe. Among respondents who said the NPS system changed their view of their neighborhood, some indicated the change was positive, while others said the change was negative. Some regular users saw less crime in the maps and reports than they expected, primarily because of how the media portrayed the crime situation. However, as one community leader put it, "Some people are in denial about crime—they don't want to think about [it]," and, consequently, the maps and reports may have made them feel that the situation was worse than they previously believed.

Improving police-community interaction was an important objective for both the Hartford Police Department and many of the community organizations involved in the project. All parties hoped that providing the community with the same data that the police had would create a common frame of reference for problem identification and solving. In the end, the project can perhaps claim partial success in improving police-community relations. When asked whether the NPS system changed their organization's relationship with the police department, 6 of 17 targeted users who regularly used the system indicated that the system helped improve the relationship; the remaining 11 indicated that the system did not change the relationship. From the police perspective, CSOs working in neighborhoods where the NPS system was used most frequently were pleased to see the community have access to police data and appreciated the work that problem-solving committees and others did to identify problem areas and other crime problems.

Overall, among community organizations that regularly used the NPS system, 13 of 17 targeted users believed the NPS system was "an important source of information." The remaining four said the system was "useful once in a while." In general, community organizations appear to subscribe to the notion that "information is power." As the leader of one community organization put it, "Our effectiveness depends on our knowledge." Armed with information, community organizations will be more effective in educating neighborhood residents, interacting with the police and other city agencies, and carrying out other specific tasks and projects. In particular, several veteran community activists commented that "having the data" ensures that community groups "will have a seat at the table," meaning they can make a positive contribution to problem-solving efforts and that their voice should not be ignored by the city.

POLICY IMPLICATIONS

Community policing requires the active participation of the community, both in terms of formal and informal partnerships with the police and in initiating its own crime prevention strategies. One effective way to increase the community role in community policing is routine two-way information sharing. The NIJ-funded effort described in this article documents one approach by one police department to sharing computerized police information with the community. More police departments across the country are making crime statistics and maps available, primarily via police department Web sites, which offer a variety of data and features. Some offer static maps or statistics, while others allow users to formulate queries; some provide aggregate data, while others provide incident-level data.

The Hartford experience highlights the different ways community groups have analyzed various data. Although all regular users of the NPS system made extensive use of crime information, some placed the highest value on arrest information and others closely examined citizen calls-for-service information. The map display was generally the most popular report format but still accounted for less than half of the report runs, emphasizing that maps are only one way to look at police data. Appropriately sorted lists, graphs, and time period comparisons are also essential. In short, the Hartford experience suggests that police departments hoping to use their Web sites to provide data to the public in support of their community policing initiatives should also include extensive query capabilities and multiple report formats. New Web development tools, particularly map-based tools, allow for this versatility. In addition, data from agencies other than police departments (e.g., corrections agencies, property data, public health agencies, schools) could be included to enable users to examine possible links between these datasets and crime data.

However, it is important to note that what made the NPS system useful for community-based problem solving in Hartford was the extensive infrastructure that the city had in place to support the system, including neighborhood-based problem-solving committees, veteran community organizers, and a supportive environment in the city government and police department. Without such an infrastructure, it is probable that Hartford's NPS system not only would have been used less but would have been used for very different purposes. Specifically, instead of serving as a tool for organizing block watches, supporting neighborhood organizations, and supporting neighborhood-based problem solving, the system would have been used by individuals interested in knowing crime conditions in their area but less likely to share information from NPS with others or act on that information to effect neighborhood change. This is not to say that self-education about crime conditions is not worthwhile, but that the potential for neighborhood improvement is much greater when the primary system users are connected to organizations that operate in an environment conducive to neighborhood-based problem solving.

QUESTIONS FOR REVIEW AND DISCUSSION

1. What is meant by crime mapping? What are its purposes?
2. What is meant by Neighborhood Problem Solving (NPS)? What are some of its characteristics?
3. What are citizen-based problem-solving committees? Why are they important in fighting crime? Explain.
4. What types of users exist who might profit in different ways from using crime mapping? Describe them.
5. What are some general applications of the NPS system?
6. What are some policy implications of NPS? Discuss.

9

Homeland Security
and Emergency Preparedness

Department of Homeland Security

Adapted from the Department of Homeland Security, *Homeland Security and Emergency Preparedness*. Washington, DC: Department of Homeland Security, 2006.

The Office of Homeland Security has established several initiatives as means of protecting U.S. citizens and the country against terrorist attacks. These initiatives include (1) emergency preparedness and response; (2) information analysis and infrastructure protection; (3) border and transportation security; (4) nuclear and radiological measures; (5) chemical and biological countermeasures; and (6) system analysis and studies.

EMERGENCY PREPAREDNESS AND RESPONSE

This program thrust develops technical capabilities for minimizing the damage and recovering from any terrorist attacks that do occur and works with local, regional, state, and federal first-responders to ensure that the tools developed meet real-world needs.

National Atmospheric Release Advisory Center (NARAC): NARAC is the premier capability in the U.S. for real-time assessments of the atmospheric dispersion of radionuclides, chemical and biological agents, and particulates. In addition to its essential role in emergency response, NARAC can also be used to evaluate specific scenarios for emergency response planning. The UNC (Local Integration of NARAC with Cities) program was recently established to facilitate access to NARAC by local and state agencies to better plan for and respond to toxic releases.

Joint Conflict and Tactical Simulation (JCATS): JCATS models urban and rural conflicts involving the movement of up to tens of thousands of people, vehicles, and weapons, occurring over large areas (up to half the surface of the globe) down to encounters within buildings. In addition to evaluating military tactics, JCATS can be used to assess strategies for protecting cities, industrial sites, and critical U.S. infrastructure against terrorist attack.

Homeland Operational Planning System (HOPS): HOPS is being developed, in partnership with the California National Guard, specifically for homeland security planning and analysis. HOPS analyses provide insight into the vulnerabilities of elements of U.S. infrastructure and the likely consequences of strikes against potential terrorist targets.

INFORMATION ANALYSIS AND INFRASTRUCTURE PROTECTION

The goal of the Information Analysis and Infrastructure Protection Program (IAIP) is to comprehensively understand the threat posed by terrorists to U.S. critical infrastructure and key assets in order to inform local, regional, state, and federal protection efforts.

IAIP is critical as a threat analysis measure to evaluate nuclear, chemical, biological, cyber and explosive threats. Several programs have been conducted to analyze threats to the nation for almost 40 years and these programs provide important input to policy makers as they develop strategies for U.S. responses to events, affecting national and international security. The application of this scientific and engineering expertise toward analyzing vulnerabilities and risks of national critical infrastructure includes oil, gas, electricity, water, transportation, finance, cyber-national icons, and telecommunications. These analyses efforts have resulted in widely used methodologies for assessing risk and developing countermeasures for protection.

BORDER AND TRANSPORTATION SECURITY

Concrete-Penetrating Radar: Micropower Impulse Radar (MIR) can see many feet into concrete rubble. It was used at the World Trade Center rubble pile to search for survivors. MIR technology can also be configured for range detection or keep-out zone security applications.

Baggage Screening Technologies: Candidate technologies for improved screening of passengers and baggage are in various stages of development, including computed tomography (CT), x-ray scanning, gamma-ray imaging, neutron interrogation, and ultrasonic and thermal imaging.

Truck-Stopping Device: This simple mechanical device attaches to the back of a tanker truck and can be triggered by highway patrol officers to keep a hijacked truck from becoming a motorized missile.

NUCLEAR AND RADIOLOGICAL COUNTERMEASURES

The goal of this program is to develop, demonstrate and deploy technologies and systems to counter unconventional radiological and nuclear threats to the U.S. As a part of its mission of maintaining the U.S. nuclear deterrence, several organizations, such as the Lawrence Livermore National Laboratory (LLNL), have developed world-class expertise in nuclear science, bioscience, engineering and systems analysis.

These capabilities have been applied in support of counter-terrorism and homeland security applications for over 25 years. Long-standing efforts include LLNL's role in the Nuclear Emergency Search Teams (NEST), the Nuclear Assessment Program, and the Radiological Assistance Program.

CHEMICAL AND BIOLOGICAL COUNTERMEASURES

The mission of the Chemical and Biological National Security Program (CBNP) is to develop and field advanced strategies that dramatically improve the nation's capabilities to prevent, prepare for, detect, and respond to terrorist use of chemical or biological warfare agents. A catalyst for our early focus on civilian counterterrorism was the 1995 nerve gas attack in Tokyo's subway. LLNL began its CBNP program that year using internal investment funds and today is sponsored by the Department of Homeland Security, National Institutes of Health, U.S. Department of Agriculture, and several other defense, intelligence, and law enforcement organizations. In 2003 the Organization for Prohibition of Chemical Weapons (OPCW) certified LLNL's Forensic Science Center (FSC) to support its chemical weapons inspections.

SYSTEM ANALYSIS AND STUDIES

This program area focuses on identifying and understanding gaps in U.S. preparedness and response capabilities and the associated opportunities for technology. Systems studies are being conducted to evaluate the effectiveness of alternative approaches to mitigating the damage and disruption resulting from a full range of catastrophic terrorist threats.

> Homeland Security Analysts: Systems studies are conducted to evaluate the effectiveness of alternative approaches to early detection, interdiction, and mitigation of damage to the U.S. homeland from a range of possible threats, emphasizing weapons of mass destruction and the disruption of information systems.
>
> Vulnerability Assessment: Ongoing efforts are assessing vulnerabilities of the U.S. energy infrastructure to physical and cyber attack. For instance, the LLNL has led vulnerability assessment teams for electric and national gas utilities, refineries, and several major dams in the western states.
>
> Outreach to Operational Entities: LLNL interacts with representative state, regional, and local agencies to develop, test, and evaluate capabilities for preventing, detecting, and responding to WMD terrorism in real-world settings. Technology demonstration programs help us to obtain an operational understanding of relevant regional or city systems, including law enforcement, public health, emergency, response, and environmental protection, and facilitate the rapid deployment of new homeland security technologies.

QUESTIONS FOR REVIEW AND DISCUSSION

1. What are some measures taken by both private companies and the federal government designed to safeguard the United States against potential future attacks by terrorists?

2. What airport measures are in place to prevent terrorists from using aircraft as weapons?

3. What types of measures are being used to combat the possibility of biochemical or nuclear threats?

4. In what ways do you think the different government agencies, such as the U.S. Department of Agriculture, FBI, DEA, Border Patrol, and other agencies, can interdict the efforts of terrorists from striking on U.S. soil in future years?

5. What types of technologies are being deployed as screening devices to examine building debris from explosions or disasters? What potential uses exist for these technologies in other sectors of American society? Discuss.

10

"Managing Joint Terrorism Task Force Resources"

James Casey

Adapted from James Casey, "Managing Joint Terrorism Task Force Resources." *FBI Law Enforcement Bulletin* 73: 5–10, 2004.

Reprinted by permission of the *FBI Law Enforcement Bulletin*.

In a post-September 11 world, successful management of a joint terrorism task force (JTTF) may represent one of the most important aspects of law enforcement's unified war on terrorism. The September 11 attacks placed a high profile on FBI-sponsored JTTFs across the nation and have presented unique management issues for the FBI and participating agencies of the task forces. Organizational and strategic analysis of the threats posed by international and domestic terrorism can help law enforcement executives at all levels develop management structures and protocols for successfully operating the nation's JTTFs, proving mutually beneficial to the FBI, participating law enforcement agencies, and the country's national security effort.

HISTORY

Many of the FBI's task forces dealing with significant crime problems grew out of the agency's close working relationship with the New York City Police Department (NYPD). Both organizations have a history of innovative approaches to law enforcement and highly competent investigators willing to try new concepts. The first formal FBI task force, the Bank Robbery Task Force, primarily was staffed with FBI special agents and NYPD detectives, followed closely by participation from a host of other federal, state, and local law enforcement partners. The task force concept flourished, and, by the mid-1980s, many other formalized BFI-sponsored task forces existed, dealing with such issues as fugitives, drugs, and, eventually, terrorism. The joint task force concept is not new nor did the FBI develop it. Many levels of law enforcement successfully have used the concept for years to handle specific crime problems. All FBI-sponsored task forces, however, have two common elements that make them unique: (1) written memorandums of understanding (MOUs) between participating law enforcement agencies and (2) FBI funding to pay for participating state and local departments' expenses, such as officer overtime, vehicles, gas, cell phones, and related office costs.

Prior to September 11, the United States had 35 formal JTTFs. Shortly after the attacks, FBI Director Robert Mueller instructed all FBI field offices to immediately establish formal terrorism task forces. Today, the FBI has a JTTF in each of its 56 field offices, as well as 10 stand-alone, formalized JTTFs in its largest resident agencies. Many other field offices sponsor JTTF annexes in small- to medium-sized resident agencies, but these entities formally are attached to the respective field office. Agents and officers may reside physically in a smaller resident agency but work for the field office's JTTF. Also, shortly after September 11, Attorney General John Ashcroft ordered the U.S. Attorney's Offices (USAO) to establish antiterrorism task forces (ATTF). The mandate and mission of the ATTFs initially were unclear to many individuals in the law enforcement community, as well as to some of the USAOs, who thought that a duplication of effort at the federal law enforcement level would occur and confuse JTTF and ATTF participants. In practice, the ATTFs have evolved into senior-level working groups with scheduled policy and intelligence briefings, while the JTTFs have remained the day-to-day operational and investigative components of the law enforcement community.

STRUCTURE

Proper staffing of the task force is critical. A supervisory special agent (SSA) accomplished in counterterrorism investigations oversees the daily operations of the task force. A basic JTTF consists of a group of FBI special agents experienced in international and domestic terrorism investigations combined with other federal, state, and local law enforcement officers who bring a variety of skills to the taskforce environment. A complex mix of available resources in each jurisdiction and the historic working relationships these agencies enjoyed prior to the establishment of the task force present subtle differences within each JTTF, particularly in major U.S. cities.

Task force coordinators constitute a critical component of the JTTF. Coordinators, generally, are special agents experienced in counterterrorism who can handle administrative functions effectively. JTTF coordinators obtain MOUs for all participating agencies and manage the overtime budgets for state and local officers, acquiring automobiles, cell phones, laptop computers, and, in some cases, off-site work space for the task force. Additionally, coordinators serve as the primary line investigator liaison to all other federal, state and local officers on the JTTF. They frequently schedule emergency surveillance coverage of a subject or arrange court-authorized electronic surveillance, all of which counterterrorism investigations often use. To ensure success in the critical functions of directing operations, assigning cases, and managing liaison with other task force participants' home agencies, SSAs should delegate these administrative functions to task force coordinators.

Special agents in charge (SAC) of local FBI field offices must accommodate all law enforcement agencies in their territories that want to contribute to the counterterrorism mission. In the post-September 11 era of increased cooperation among all levels of law enforcement and, particularly, recognition that local law enforcement plays a critical role in protecting the homeland, the importance of a well-represented JTTF cannot be overstated. However, conflicts may arise when an agency contributes members to the task force on a part-time basis but, then, routinely assigns these employees to non-JTTF duties.

POSSIBLE CONFLICTS

State and local law enforcement agencies' investigative resources are limited, which becomes the primary motivation for assigning part-time task force members to the JTTF. However, a caste system can develop on a task force that includes both full-time and part-time participants. The full-time members generally are more flexible in assignments and better able to work odd hours, doing so with little or no notice. The rest of the task force may unintentionally slight part-time members ("out of sight, out of mind"), and the supervisor often may feel reluctant to give them time-sensitive assignments. The part-time members also more frequently tend to matriculate to other assignments at their home agencies, which can undermine the cohesiveness of the JTTF and breed inefficiency. Although part-time participation is possible, most task forces discourage it.

In an effective JTTF, all investigators, whether from the FBI, other federal agencies, or state and local departments, are equal partners. All investigators should be assigned substantive cases and work from the established FBI protocols for investigating terrorism, completing paperwork requirements, and using data systems. Further, to establish task force esprit de corps, supervisors should encourage JTTFs to create their own seals, patches, and jackets.

Although all law enforcement agencies interested in JTTF participation should be encouraged to join, several agencies are critical to the success of the task force. First, the task force should include the local police department where the field division's JTTF is headquartered. Generally, this is a medium- to large-sized department with detectives who have access to their agency's intelligence base as related to criminal investigative matters. This intelligence base can include formal sources, such as criminal informants, or informal relationships with business leaders and other community representatives. When a large suburban county surrounds a field office, members from that county's police or sheriff's department are important members of the task force for the same reasons. Further, the state police or highway patrol is a critical JTTF partner because of its statewide jurisdiction, databases, and access to other important state service agencies. Agents from the Bureau of Alcohol, Tobacco, Firearms and Explosives (ATF) are an important addition to the task force because of their unique skills and databases. The Bureau of Immigration and Customs Enforcement (ICE) recently transferred to the Department of Homeland Security and proves crucial to the JTTF because of the numerous immigration issues that surround many current international terrorism investigations. This list of essential participants is not exclusive but, rather, should form the basic building blocks for a successful JTTF. A wide variety of local, state, and federal agencies makes significant contributions to counterterrorism task forces across the country.

Immediate access to the National Joint Terrorism Task Force (NJTTF), located at FBI headquarters in Washington, D.C., benefits state and local law enforcement agencies participating in a local JTTF. Director Mueller set up the NJTTF as a national resource in early 2002, seeking to have representation from every federal law enforcement and intelligence agency in one location. In addition to the traditional partners, such as the Central Intelligence Agency (CIA) and FBI, the NJTTF has agents and officers from the Naval Criminal Investigative Service, Transportation Security Agency, U.S. Coast Guard, U.S. Bureau of Prisons, and approximately 50 other significant contributors to the national counterterrorism mission. While any law enforcement officer in the United States can contact the NJTTF for specialized assistance, participation on the local JTTF provides a natural seam to the NJTTF.

SECURITY CLEARANCES

Security clearances for team members and home agency managers often present a confusing issue surrounding the administration of a JTTF. Responsibility for the protection of national security information rests with the president of the United States through the director of Central Intelligence, who serves as the final authority surrounding the handling of information related to national security. Because FBI offices are repositories of national security information, a presidential executive order requires all employees, including task force officers assigned to these offices, to have a top secret (TS) security clearance. While most task force officers rarely handle TS information, they nonetheless work in a TS facility and, therefore, are required to have a TS clearance. Issuance may take 6 months to 1 year to complete because, unlike secret clearances, an investigator physically must verify all of the information concerning a candidate. According to a recent report by the Police Executive Research Forum (PERF) on terrorism, "There is a misperception that the FBI has control over the process and that local law enforcement sometimes believes that the process is an affront to their professionalism, when it is really just about following mandatory authorities" (Murphy and Plotkin, 2003).

In the aftermath of September 11, Director Mueller sought to have security clearances granted to many of the nation's state and local law enforcement leaders to assuage their fears of not getting necessary terrorist information because they lacked the proper clearance. Many law enforcement officials incorrectly believed that a great deal of information that could or should have been passed to local law enforcement was classified. Numerous local officials also were discouraged by the length of time it took for the government to process their requests for clearances. Another issue concerned the perceptions associated with different clearance levels. Again, according to PERF, "The fact that an investigator assigned to a JTTF has a top secret clearance, while the chief has only a secret clearance should not concern the chief . . . unless you are the chief. Elected and appointed local government leaders and law enforcement personnel attach significance, even status, to the higher of the two clearance levels."

The management lessons regarding clearances are three-fold. First, the issue of clearances never should cause FBI managers to be in a position of not sharing timely threat information with local law enforcement executives. Effective liaison skills, operational competence, and common sense dictate that immediate threat information needs to be passed to the appropriate law enforcement officials, working around the issue of security clearances. In other words, the threat usually can be discussed even if a sensitive source or method of how the threat was received cannot. Second, unless law enforcement executives have daily, unescorted access to FBI space or a continuing need for sources and methods information, they should acquire a secret clearance as soon as possible, not waiting unnecessarily for a TS clearance. Third, JTTF-partner executives should strive to keep their officers assigned to the task force for at least 1 year due to the time it takes those officers to acquire their own clearances. If the officer needs to be rotated or promoted, home agencies should provide as much notice as possible to the JTTF to coordinate the inclusion of another officer from the same agency and begin the clearance process.

UPDATES AND REPORTS

The very nature of the JTTF's work makes it significantly different from other task forces. It is challenging for resource-strapped agencies to justify continued task force operations when performance measures are difficult to gauge. Unlike fugitive or drug task forces, JTTFs do not have numerous arrests, search warrants, or seizures. Rather, the bulk of the work often relates to long-term surveillance, electronic court-ordered monitoring, source development, or interviews, none of which may garner significant statistics in the traditional law enforcement sense. Therefore, commanders of agencies who contribute personnel to JTTFs must be well briefed on task force operations. Successful administrators require their task force officers to provide them with weekly scheduled updates on the overall operations of the JTTF. This is particularly critical during lulls in major operations—executives must know the day-to-day duties of the JTTF, and, if a crisis occurs, they should have a firm understanding of the chain of command of other JTTF-participant agencies. The early stages of a potential terrorist incident are not the time for administrators to try to identify their counterparts among other JTTF partners.

Another information-sharing tactic is for the SAC of each FBI field office to send a personal letter to the command staff of all of the participating JTTF agencies. This monthly communication should discuss the general operations of the task force during the previous month, as well as the specific contributions made by that department's task force members. Nothing replaces effective liaison between all of the JTTF law enforcement agencies where successful chief executives communicate in a variety of formal and informal forums concerning terrorism issues in the community.

CONCLUSION

Protecting the nation's homeland from future terrorist attacks is the responsibility of all law enforcement agencies. No single police or intelligence agency exists with the expertise, personnel, knowledge of the local environment, or money to unilaterally accomplish this mission.

Unfortunately, the very nature of terrorism demonstrates that all future attacks against the homeland cannot be prevented any more than all future crimes. But, law enforcement officials can ensure that local, state, and federal agencies do all within their power and work as hard as they can to thwart future acts—the American people deserve and expect that effort from their leaders in law enforcement. Today, an effective and efficient multiple law enforcement joint terrorism task force is the most important tool for combating the complex issue of terrorism.

QUESTIONS FOR REVIEW AND DISCUSSION

1. What is the purpose of a joint terrorism task force? How did the attack on the World Trade Center towers galvanize the government into forming such a task force?

2. How important is it in the fight against terrorism for different law enforcement agencies to coordinate their efforts and not perform overlapping functions? Explain.

3. What are some potential conflicts in establishing joint task forces for combatting crimes such as terrorism?

4. What strategies can be used to maximize information-sharing among law enforcement agencies?

11

"The Future of Public/Private Partnerships"

Al Youngs

Adapted from Al Youngs, "The Future of Public/Private Partnerships." *FBI Law Enforcement Bulletin* 73: 7–10, 2004.

Reprinted by Permission from the *FBI Law Enforcement Bulletin*.

Doctors and nurses, attorneys and paralegals, parents and day care providers, presidents and aides—all people need support and assistance to accomplish their goals. Why should public law enforcement agencies be different?

Today's police departments are under monumental pressure to perform, keep crime rates low, and do it all with fewer resources. Agencies can accomplish this seemingly impossible mandate by forming supportive partnerships with private security providers.

A HISTORICAL PERSPECTIVE

Privatization of law enforcement activities is not a new concept. Perhaps, the monopolization of policing by government is an aberration (Bayley and Shearing, 2001).

Only in the last 100 to 200 years has government effectively monopolized policing, which is not uniform across all countries. In Europe, for example, France led the way in the systematic nationalization of policing in the 17th century. Nationalization followed fitfully throughout the rest of continental Europe, concentrated largely in towns and often deferring to the private authority of the landowning aristocracy. In England, policing remained largely in private hands until well into the 19th century. In the United States, where cities gradually governmentalized policing in the middle of the 19th century, private policing never really died. The constituent states did not begin to develop organized police forces until the early 20th century, and the national government did not do so until approximately a decade later.

While the 1960s characterized a period of indifference toward private security and the 1970s one of changing perceptions and some mistrust of the industry, the 1980s and 1990s most likely will be regarded as the era of collaboration and joint ventures between public law enforcement and private security. Individual and corporate citizens policed by public law enforcement also increasingly are becoming the clients of private security, as illustrated by increases in the use of corporate security and the number of gated communities (Mangan and Shanahan, 1990).

LOWER CRIME RATES, HIGHER COSTS

In the late 1990s, serious crime continued to fall in the United States, reaching a 25-year low. The potential that criminals will receive punishment and that they will serve a longer amount of time both are higher today than in the last 30 years.

The economic boom of the late 1990s, which increased wages and rates of employment, impacted the reduction of crime. But, on the other hand, criminal punishment also increased. Compared to 1996, the probability of going to prison in 1997 for murder rose 13 percent, while it increased 1 percent for rape, 7 percent for robbery, and 11 percent for aggravated assault. Once convicted, prisoners now stay incarcerated longer. Compared to the 1980s, the median sentence served by prisoners has risen for every category of serious crime except aggravated assault.

Potential criminals respond to incentives. Crime decreases when expected punishment increases, and the reverse proves true as well. To achieve an even lower crime rate, law enforcement must continue to make crime less profitable by further increasing expected punishment. But, higher arrest rates require more money for police staffing, equipment, and procedures. Higher conviction and sentencing rates require more resources for prosecution and criminal courts. The need for more prison space also increases, and, although the cost of building and maintaining more prisons is high, the cost of not doing so appears to be higher (National Center for Policy Analysis, 1999).

THE TIME FOR PRIVATIZATION

The hope of the public, as well as the goal for police departments, is to continue lowering crime rates. However, achieving this requires more policing and more cost precisely when law enforcement agencies face serious recruitment problems, additional equipment costs, a decrease in tax revenues, and legislative restrictions denying access to any surpluses. "Many municipalities and counties lack the necessary funds due to legislated limits on taxation and spending, inadequate bonding, capacities and voters' reluctance to approve special bonding obligations or other spending measures" (Smith, 1991).

Fortunately, privatization of certain police department functions has proven a powerful solution to the problem. The steady decline of governments' capital resources and their increasingly urgent search for ways to continue providing the services that citizens demand without raising taxes are driving the privatization trend. Some federal agencies have saved as much as 50 percent by hiring contractors to provide services.

Police in today's environment typically spend less than 20 percent of their time on crime-related matters. In California, a police officer my cost $100,000 a year, taking into account salary, benefits, and such overhead expenses as squad cars. Faced with rising calls for service, this proves expensive for tasks, such as transporting prisoners, providing court security, conducting traffic control, and serving summonses. The real trend in the future will be contracting out the functions of public police that do not involve crimes or emergencies.

For example, the Fresno, California, Sheriff's Department reaped savings by outsourcing its transport of prisoners. The total cost for the department to transport a prisoner from San Diego to Fresno was $284 using a private firm. The same trip using sheriff's department personnel and equipment would cost three times as much.

Police departments in 18 states currently use, or plan to use, private security guards to fill support roles. One firm provides security for six major public transit systems around the country, transports prisoners, maintains booking and security for a juvenile assessment center, and supplies security for court houses in 40 states. Other public-private partnerships exist coast to coast (Moore, 1996).

Just as corporations outsource many services to enable them to concentrate on core competencies, the use of private firms by law enforcement agencies frees them to concentrate their efforts on duties that only trained police officers can, and should, do. Over the past several decades, privatization in law enforcement has grown to such an extent that virtually every function, including security, jails, prisons, and court-related services, is being contracted out somewhere in the United States. Using private security on site at businesses, sporting venues, and malls is no new trend. But, agencies can outsource other duties that do not require the authority to make arrests or use deadly force. Such tasks include directing traffic, guarding prisoners, assisting at crime scenes, transporting prisoners, processing reports, and investigating accidents (West, 1993).

THE APPROACH TO PUBLIC-PRIVATE PARTNERSHIPS

Public-private partnerships can provide many benefits, especially in terms of pairing law enforcement with a private security provider to save public monies. Agencies should consider several recommendations when determining whether to use this type of partnership (Benson, 1996).

- Services with the potential to be priced should be considered as candidates for private provision or user charges.
- To save money and help police officers become more available to perform the tasks that only they can conduct, agencies should privatize tasks that do not require the full range of skills of police officers.
- Private companies should provide such services as response to burglary alarms, and people with alarm systems should pay for the services that they demand.
- Private security can prove effective in a distinct geographic area; therefore, owners of apartment complexes should consider private policing. Further, agencies should encourage competition between apartment complexes to provide safer environments. Requiring publication of apartments' safety experience helps renters make informed decisions.
- Agencies should consider any relatively low-skill or specialized high-skill services as a candidate for transfer to private security.

- Departments should ensure that the cost of monitoring contractor compliance and performance should not exceed the savings from privatization.
- Agencies should request that their state legislatures consider whether the current legal status and regulations pertaining to private security are appropriate in view of the expanded role expected from them, such as emergency vehicle status and expanded powers of arrest.
- Problem-oriented policing offers the prospect of improved police-private partnerships in dealing with specific crime problems.
- The community policing approach offers hope for improving police performance and the community's sense of participation. Like privatization, community policing helps society better determine the use of its scarce police resources. Further, it brings the police "back" to constituents. Successful community policing satisfies the desires of the community (Blackstone and Hakim, 1996).

ONE COMMUNITY'S EXPERIENCE

Lakewood, Colorado, offers an example of the benefits of outsourcing law enforcement tasks to private firms. Lakewood boasts a population of 145,000 within the metropolitan Denver area. Its progressive approach to public-private partnerships in law enforcement is demonstrated by its track record—the city has contracted with outside firms for police department assistance for nearly 10 years. As a result, the Lakewood Police Department considers the public-private partnership beneficial. It helps in terms of deployment, as well as economically. "Paying a private security officer an hourly rate to guard a prisoner or a crime scene frees up police officers. Police don't have to call in an officer on overtime or pull someone off patrol duty."

Lakewood's current privatization efforts include the use of trained citizen volunteers for police administrative work, such as fingerprinting citizens and issuing parking tickets to violators of handicapped parking. Graduates of its citizen police academy volunteer with the Lakewood Police Department and serve as a surveillance unit regarding specific crimes, such as graffiti. Civilian investigative technicians conduct follow-up, question victims and suspects, and prepare affidavits.

Further, the Lakewood Police Department contracts with a private security firm to guard prisoners hospitalized in facilities in the Denver metropolitan area and to provide assistance in protecting crime scenes. These private security officers are specially selected for crime-scene detail based on their background and experience, and they often attend Lakewood Police Department roll calls for training (similarly, members of the Lakewood Police Department attend the security roll calls). These private security firm officers know the rules of evidence, and, in fact, many are certified police officers in the state of Colorado. They provide 24-hour assistance and typically respond with officers within 4 hours of the department's request. In addition, for security purposes, background investigations have been completed on each of these officers.

In Lakewood, the cost of an off-duty police agent is $37 per hour, including vehicle. Many crime scenes take an average of 2 days to process. Because 24-hour protection is required, using private security at $29 per hour for this assignment, a savings of nearly 22 percent, makes economic sense. Furthermore, the partnership has strengthened the lines of communication and trust between police and private security personnel. "In this partnership, everyone's a winner. The police department is a winner in that we are providing essential services at a reduced cost. Through the private portion of it; it's good for business; it employs people; it's good for our economy" (Ruffin, 1999).

Such moves to privatization are substantiated by the numbers. Private security guards outnumber public law enforcement officers by 3 to 1 nationally, and 4 to 1 in California. The trend is not confined to the United States; Canada, the United Kingdom, and Australia have approximately twice as many private guards as public police (Ruffin, 1999).

CONCLUSION

Today, law enforcement agencies have fewer resources to accomplish their goals. Departments can form partnerships with private security firms to save money, as well as to free trained police officers to conduct duties that only they should address.

Public law enforcement entities can gain more efficient use of funds and personnel in public-private partnerships, in addition to extending their reach and effectiveness. Properly defined and managed, a partnership with a private enterprise can make the job of police officers more effective and rewarding and the results reported to voters more positive in the long run.

QUESTIONS FOR REVIEW AND DISCUSSION

1. What is privatization of policing?
2. Who are those who make up private security? Discuss.
3. How can private security corporations work cooperatively with police agencies in preventing crime? Discuss.
4. Describe the Lakewood, Colorado, experience of outsourcing law enforcement tasks to private security.

PART III

The Courts and Crime Prevention

This section examines how prosecution and the courts deal with crime prevention and control. The opening essay by J.W. Barbrey and Keith Clement describes different state sentencing schemes. The variation in sentencing methods used by the states shows how legislatures and the courts have implemented sentencing reforms to heighten offender accountability and impose innovative sanctions intended as deterrents to future criminal activity. Several types of sentencing are described, including indeterminate and determinate sentencing, presumptive or guidelines-based sentencing, and mandatory sentencing. Sentencing enhancements, truth-in-sentencing provisions, and habitual offender statutes are examined and their deterrent value is assessed. These authors also describe various sentencing reforms and the reasons for these reforms. No sentencing scheme is perfect, as these authors note. But one consistent theme is that sentencing in the United States has become tougher and more punitive. The question of whether crime prevention has occurred as the result of these sentencing reforms is debated.

Barry Ruback examines the impact of economic sanctions on crime and its control. Ruback suggests that in jurisdictions such as Philadelphia, economic sanctions have functioned well to bring about modest reductions in certain types of offending. Asset forfeiture, fines, victim compensation and restitution, and other economic sanctions seem to work well with particular kinds of offenders. Ruback also describes those most likely to be targeted for different types of economic sanctions and explores the consequences of such sanctions for these offenders.

Harry Mika and his associates have examined crime prevention from the view of victims. Victim participation in sanctions against criminals has been sporadic, and numerous interjurisdictional variations exist. One increasingly popular method for involving victims in the sanctioning process is restorative justice, which is defined, discussed, and criticized. This essay is followed by an article by Nicholas Turner and Daniel Wilhelm, who suggest that the politics of criminal justice may be changing. These authors explore public attitudes, legislative concerns, crime trends, and fiscal concerns as factors that are increasingly modifying how crime is viewed and confronted. It is evident from Turner and Wilhelm's discussion that more than a few states have changed their sentencing policies and have established several alternatives as means of punishing offenders. Some of the reasons for these political shifts in how crime is defined and punished are described and discussed.

12

"State Sentencing Schemes, Part I and II"

J. W. Barbrey and Keith E. Clement

Adapted from J. W. Barbrey and Keith E. Clement, "State Sentencing Schemes, Part I." *American Jails* 15: 27–37, 2001; J. W. Barbrey and Keith E. Clement, "State Sentencing Schemes, Part II." *American Jails* 15: 23–28, 2001.

Reprinted with the permission of the American Jail Association.

There has been a considerable amount of research into the evolution of criminal sentencing in the United States. Friedman (1993), Morris and Rothman (1995), and Walker (1998a) took a historical approach, tracing the major developments in the United States from the Colonial period to the twentieth century. The theoretical roots of criminal sanctions have been explored (Akers, 1994; Besci, 1999; Frankel, 1972; Hart, 1968; Packer, 1968; Stumpf and Culver, 1998), while some have concentrated on rehabilitation and indeterminate sentencing (i.e., Morris, 1974). In the past few decades, others (Clear, 1984; Cole, 1999; Griset, 1991; Messinger and Johnson, 1977; Wicharaya, 1995) traced the development of determinate sentencing, as it quickly replaced the indeterminate model. Many, including Austin (1996), Benekos and Merlo (1995), Clarke and Homel (1997), Engen and Steen (2000), Frankel (1972), Hegelin (1994), Lanagan (1998), Oliss (1995), Turner et al. (1995), and Walker (1998b) have all evaluated individual reforms in great detail, drawing conclusions about anticipated effects and recommending additional reforms.

Although the origins of recent sentencing reforms have been identified and described, these efforts typically describe reforms at a single point in time. For example, Clarke and Homel (1997), Ditton and Wilson (1999), and Wicharaya (1995) all take a snapshot of what states are doing at an instant. Their studies are current through the mid-1990s. Although they note when states adopted particular reforms, and describe sentencing reform history, they do not look at patterns of policy adoption.

We contribute to the body of knowledge about sentencing policies in two major ways. First, our research is current through 2000. Our analysis includes all of the major determinate sentencing reforms, plus two additional reforms from the last six years that do not necessarily fall into the determinate mold. Second and most significantly, we trace the adoption rates of each major reform over time. Our original intention was to determine whether any noticeable patterns in adoption rates existed.

Our findings indicate a clear pattern of "waves" of reform. Waves are a useful heuristic tool to understand the evolution of state sentencing reforms. We offer three types of reforms: first wave, bridge, and second wave. What does the "waves of reform" theoretical framework have to offer criminal justice researchers? It offers insight into types of policy tools developed by states in pursuance of effective sentencing and penal policy. After we understand the objectives that state legislators are trying to accomplish through sentencing reform, we can understand why these policies are adopted.

THE DEMISE OF INDETERMINATE SENTENCING

Imprisonment by the turn of the twentieth century was generally rehabilitative, because the overriding goal was to send reformed offenders back into society. A series of piecemeal reforms swept through the noisy, over-crowded, filthy state prison systems beginning in the mid-1800s. Parole, pardons, probation, and "good time" credits were used to reduce overcrowding and the amount of punishment, while also providing some measure of control over prisoner behavior (BJA, 1996; Friedman, 1993; Morris and Rothman, 1995; Morris and Tonry, 1990; Walker, 1998a). Other policy makers still wanted a better "means by which the duration and severity of imprisonment may in all cases be modified by the conduct and character of the prisoners" (Walker, 1998a: 96). This last reformative demand evolved into indeterminate sentencing, first codified in 1877 for New York's Elmira Reformatory (Griset, 1991; Morris and Rothman, 1995; Walker, 1998a).

The basic idea of indeterminate sentencing was that a judge would not set a fixed prison term at the time of sentencing. Offenders would remain incarcerated until they were "cured" of their bad behaviors; then they would be returned to society. Typically, judges would give a minimum sentence, determined by state law, according to the type of offense. However, the *maximum* term was not set at the time of sentencing. At the end of the minimum term, a prison board would review the behavior of the offender, and then they would determine whether (or when) the prisoner was fit for release. Those capable of changing their bad habits could receive leniency, while those not able were fated to lengthy terms (Frankel, 1972; Friedman, 1993; Lanagan, 1998; Walker, 1998a).

During the 1960s, public concern over the denial of bail to poor defendants arose from the civil rights movement. Although "release on recognizance" and other reforms did reduce the number of defendants being held in jail for trial (Stumpf and Culver, 1998; Walker, 1998b), their implementation coincided with a dramatic increase in felony crimes, during the period of domestic turbulence in the United States between 1963–1973. Numerous studies showed that the treatment and diversion programs of the 1960s and 1970s did not reduce recidivism. Multiple prison uprisings highlighted the fact that previous reforms had never removed brutal and racist prison conditions. Inmates, liberal activists, and academics complained that indeterminate sentencing led to disparities in prison terms between blacks and whites (Auerhahn, 1999; Clear, 1984; Tsoudis, 2000).

Civil rights groups felt that treatment programs allowed state-sanctioned intimidation. The welfare programs of the Johnson and Nixon administrations seemed ineffectual in reducing crime. The American public was tired of riots and protests and wanted law and order. Political leaders started proposing "get tough on crime" policies (Lanagan, 1998; Wicharaya, 1995).

Conservatives began to loudly insist that any leniency, whether it be in the form of treatment programs, pretrial release, probation, or short sentences, all turned dangerous criminals loose on unsuspecting communities. Incapacitation proponents believed that the lengths of prison sentences were related to a corresponding reduction in the crime rate. To ensure that punishments were severe and certain, various strategies were employed to limit the lenient discretion of liberal judges, who utilized statutes that were "soft on crime" (Lanagan, 1998; Walker, 1998b; Wicharaya, 1995). The Twentieth Century Fund's Task Force on Criminal Sentencing (1976) and a report from the Committee for the Study of Incarceration (1976) both called for a shift toward determinate sentencing in order to ensure longer periods of incarceration (BJA, 1996).

New policies started to emphasize deterrence and the use of incarceration, not for rehabilitation, but for punishment. A paradigm shift in penology had occurred, and policy makers frustrated with the inability of indeterminate sentencing to reduce crime began a wave of reforms that quickly spread across the country.

THE NEW SENTENCING REFORMS

Determinate Sentencing and Abolition of Parole

Determinate sentences and policies that abolish early parole release were among the first of a slew of early sentencing reforms. Determinate sentencing deals with two perceived weaknesses of indeterminate sentences and rehabilitation. Justice is to be served by informing the inmates how many years to expect in prison, instead of allowing them to languish in jail for indeterminate periods of time. Judicial discretion is reduced, because the new statutory scheme is not as broad as the wide spread between minimum and maximum terms meted out under indeterminate sentences. Corrections officials retain discretion in awarding "good time" or credits for good behavior.

Some states introduced determinate sentencing without the use of guidelines or commissions. For examples, in 1977 Indiana replaced true indeterminate sentencing with determinate "flat," or fixed, sentences that allowed good time credits. Courts were given discretion in determining whether to incarcerate and the length of sentences. Discretion was shifted to the courts and prosecutors away from the parole boards (BJA, 1996).

Although not having "guidelines" per se, Indiana classifies felonies and misdemeanors into categories (class A, B, C, etc.) and gives specific sentence term ranges for each class. The statutes also provide a specific number of years that can be subtracted or added for mitigating or aggravating factors (Indiana Code 35-50-2-3 thru 35-50-2-7, 2000).

Voluntary Guidelines

Voluntary (or "advisory") guidelines were the first experiment with sentencing reform in states not yet willing to take a determinate route. They originated in 1974 as a pilot study funded by the National Institute of Justice, intended to gauge the feasibility of sentencing guidelines. Initially limited to five cities between 1975 and 1980, they spread to seven states by the early 1980s, including Florida and Massachusetts (BJA, 1996).

As the name implies, judges were given the prevalent sentencing norms (i.e., a historical description of past sentencing practices) for certain offenses and were encouraged to consider and apply the guidelines when sentencing offenders. However, judges had complete discretion in deciding whether to abide by those norms (Parent et al., 1996; Wicharaya, 1995). Early assessments showed that the voluntary guidelines tended to be poorly developed and executed, primarily because judges ignored them (BJA, 1996).

Virginia has voluntary guidelines that were adopted statewide in 1991, after a one-year pilot program conducted in six court districts. The guidelines were intended to reduce sentencing disparities. Judges make two sets of decisions when using the guidelines:(1) should the individual be imprisoned and for what length of time, and (2) should individuals not imprisoned be sent to a local jail or should they be released on probation. The guidelines are updated every year, and reflect the sentencing practices of the past five years, showing recommendations for eight felony categories, including homicide, assault, robbery, and drug offenses (BJA, 1996).

Presumptive Guidelines

A second type of guidelines was "presumptive" sentencing. Presumptive guidelines have three elements. First, a legislatively created sentencing entity, usually an expert sentencing commission, adopts sentences authorized by sentencing guidelines. Second, judges are expected to hand down sentences within the ranges in the guidelines, or provide written justification for their deviation. Third, the guidelines provide for some form of review of the departure, either by commission or appeal (Parent et al., 1996).

Guidelines can take the form of a prescribed minimum-maximum sentence range for different categories, or classes of crimes. Usually, a list of mitigating and aggravating factors is also provided within the state's revised statutes that allow prosecutors and judges to add or subtract years from the sentence range midpoint. Factors may include previous convictions, characteristics of the victim, or circumstances of the particular crime (BJA, 1996).

> When an offense involves specific aggravating or mitigating factors, the judge may impose a sentence above or below the presumptive sentence (middle term) within predetermined upper or lower limits. Any deviation from the permissible range and from the recommended dispositional criteria for incarceration requires reasoned justification. (Wicharaya, 1995: 43)

Michigan's 1998 guidelines classified over 700 criminal offenses into nine classes. They included sentence calculation methods for multiple offenses, attempted offenses, habitual offenders, and 19 other offense variables (Lyons, 1997). Colorado also divides felony offenses into six categories, with specific numbers of years or months to be added or subtracted from each category depending on the circumstances of the crime. Aggravating factors in Colorado include causing death or serious bodily injury, using a firearm, the defendant was free on bail or parole when committing the crime, sexual assault of a child by a caregiver, or intent to distribute drugs (Colorado Revised Statutes Sec. 16-11-309).

The guidelines structure can also be a sentencing grid chart or matrix (Engen and Steen, 2000). Potential danger to the community, chance of recidivism, availability of prison space, and other factors influence the matrix upon which judges make their sentencing decisions. The most common form of matrix system is a two-variable grid, incorporating the recommendations of the 1976 Committee for the Study of Incarceration (BJA, 1996). Kansas has an example of this form of presumptive guidelines for felonies.

> The sentencing guidelines grid is a two-dimensional crime severity and criminal history classification tool. The grid's vertical axis is the crime severity scale which classifies current crimes of conviction. The grid's horizontal axis is the criminal history scale which classifies criminal histories. The sentencing guidelines grid for non-drug crimes as provided in this section defines presumptive punishments for felony convictions, subject to judicial discretion to deviate for substantial and compelling reasons and impose a different sentence in recognition of aggravating and mitigating factors as provided in this act. (Kansas Statute No. 21-4704, 2000)

Many competing objectives of sentencing are reflected in sentencing guidelines. Primary objectives under guidelines were just punishment, deterrence, incapacitation, and rehabilitation (Oliss, 1995). Secondary objectives include crime reduction, population management, and equity, or reducing disparity in criminal sentences (United States Sentencing Commission, 1984).

Mandatory Minimums

Mandatory minimum statutes provided for automatic imprisonment after a conviction for specific offenses under specific circumstances, with fixed minimum and maximum terms. Some statutes allowed discretionary parole within the period between the minimum and maximum, while others prohibited parole until a proportion of the sentence was served (Engen and Steen, 2000; Wicharaya, 1995).

In typical mandatory minimum statutes, prison terms must be at least a prescribed number of months. Imprisonment is not automatic in some states with mandatory minimums, because judges have discretion when deciding to use incarceration or another punishment, such as probation or community service. Nevertheless, when imprisonment is chosen, the minimum term is required. Mandatory minimums are often reserved for serious felony crimes, such as murder, rape, aggravated robbery or arson, certain drug offenses, or crimes involving the use of a firearm (Wicharaya, 1995).

California alone has enacted at least 200 mandatory minimum or term enhancement laws since 1979 (Ross, 1995). For example, California provides mandatory minimums for first-degree murder if the offense was due to the defendant's knowledge of the victim's sexual orientation, gender, or physical disability (CA Penal Code Section 187-199). Massachusetts uses minimums for convictions for assault and battery against certain public officials, the mentally handicapped, and emergency personnel (Mass. General Laws Sec. 265).

Many states use mandatory minimums for crimes against children. In Arizona, first-degree murder of a child requires a 20-year sentence, while sex offenses against victims under the age of 12 require life imprisonment (with a 35-year minimum) before the offender becomes eligible for parole (Lyons, 1997).

Sentence Enhancements and Habitual Offenders

Enhancements can be divided into three categories: criminal history, victim status, and conduct (Ross, 1995). Criminal history enhancements cover repeat offenders. Victim status enhancements include hate crimes or racially motivated crimes. Conduct enhancements are the most numerous, and include "use a gun, go to prison" laws. Enhancements cover many violent crimes and can add significant time onto base terms (Clement, 1998).

Habitual offender laws are another commonly adopted reform, and may appear as separate general habitual offender statutes that apply to all offenses, or as enhancements tied to other crime classification categories. Many states illustrate the first model, where the number of previous convictions forms the basis of an independent sentencing scheme (Hegelin, 1994). A 1970 Texas law puts all three-time felons in prison for 25 years to life, and West Virginia incarcerates three-time felons for life without the possibility of parole (Hegelin, 1994).

The second model increases penalties for multiple felonies by giving sentence enhancements to a base sentence on the basis of prior convictions. For example, an offender convicted of grand theft with two previous convictions would receive 5 years for the immediate offense, and then additional 3-year enhancements for each prior conviction (BJA, 1996). Similarly in South Dakota, those convicted of a second or third offense would have their primary sentence increased by being sentenced under the next class of felony *above* the current offense (South Dakota Code Sec. 22-7-7). Indiana allows the sentences of habitual offenders to be increased up to *three* times the statutory term, not to exceed 30 years; however, if there were two prior violent felony convictions, then the maximum term could be life imprisonment (Indiana Code Sec. 35-50-2-8 and 35-50-2-8.5).

Three Strikes (TS) Laws

Three-strikes was unique because it entailed longer prison sentences. The original concept was a mandatory life sentence for a limited group of criminals, who had the propensity to be involved in a larger percent of crimes, and who were convicted of a third serious offense (Hegelin, 1994). TS is based on the assumption that repeat offenders of serious offenses should be removed from society for long periods of time (National Institute of Justice, 1997). There were multiple versions of TS, including "second-strike" variants. All of them limit the possibility of offenders receiving anything other than a prison sentence (BJA, 1996).

The idea first gained popularity on the west coast, after the highly publicized murder of Polly Klass. Her killer was Richard Allen Davis, a recent parolee with an extensive criminal record (Walker, 1998b). While legislative intent is often similar, wide variation exists between state versions of TS. Some states had provisions that might double or triple the sentences normally received for the same crime on the first offense. California had a common version that required a sentence between 25 years to life for those convicted of a violent felony who had two previous felony convictions. Georgia required a mandatory minimum life term for a second violent felony conviction.

Additionally, differences between "strikeable offenses," penalty enhancements, and whether strikes must be "violent" or "serious" felonies exist between state versions (Clarke and Homel, 1997). While differences exist in the nuances of the law, similarites exist as well. More than half of TS states have abolished parole, early release, and limited good time credits (Clarke and Homel, 1997).

Typically, three specific changes in penal policy occur from TS. First, offenders must serve their time in state prisons rather than in local jails, drug rehabilitation, or state hospitals (Cameron, 1997). Time spent in county jails is not applied towards the prison sentence. With increased trial rates, some individuals may spend considerable time in jail awaiting sentencing. Second, three strikes increases prison sentences by requiring term enhancements for second, third, and fourth strikes. Longer prison stays decrease bed turnover in institutions and drive up further demand. Finally, the calculation of good time credits has been significantly reduced. Good time laws stipulate that sentences be reduced a certain amount for each month or year of the sentence, as long as the inmates' conduct is good (Shover and Einstadter, 1988).

Truth in Sentencing (TIS)

Truth in Sentencing Laws originated from the Violent Crime Control and Law Enforcement Act of 1994. The act offered prison construction grants in exchange for the restriction on the possibility of early release (Ditton and Wilson, 1999). "Previous policies which reduced the amount of time an offender served on a sentence, such as good-time, earned-time, and parole board release are restricted or eliminated under truth-in-sentencing laws" (Ditton and Wilson, 1999: 3). TIS mandates that participating states require persons convicted of many violent crimes to serve not less than 85 percent of the sentence. By 1998, 27 states participated in this program. Another 14 states have adopted TIS laws requiring certain offenders to serve a specific percentage of their sentences. In 1998, approximately $550 million for 10,000 new state prison beds will be available to states under VOI-TIS federal grant programs (Austin, 1997). TIS is a very broad policy, applying to many offenders each year, leaving little flexibility for committed states to sentence eligible offenders. TIS laws require offenders to serve a substantial portion of their sentence and reduce the discrepancy between the sentence imposed and actual time served in prison (Ditton and Wilson, 1999).

Victims' Rights

Prior to the victims' rights movement, victim participation and statements were considered prejudicial to offenders' rights to a fair trial and sentence. However, this perception has changed and now most states recognize a right of victims to input their preferences into both the trial and sentencing phases of the criminal justice process.

In 1982, a task force appointed by the Reagan administration recommended that victims of crime, like those accused of crimes, should have certain rights. Since the mid-1980s, a victims' rights movement has been gaining momentum (KlassKids, 2001), persuading "state legislatures to pass bills enabling victims of violent crimes (or their survivors) to address the court before a sentence is handed down" (Stumpf and Culver, 1992: 122). Twenty-seven states amended their constitutions to allow victims (or their families) greater participation in the trial and sentencing phases of offenders. In April 1996, three members of the U.S. Congress proposed a victims' rights amendment to the U.S. Constitution. Two months later, President Clinton endorsed it (KlassKids, 2001).

Louisiana has provisions within its revised statutes and amended its constitution. Victims complete a "notification and registration" form that is included in the case files of prosecuting attorneys, and must be attached to prisoner files kept by the state correctional department. This ensures that victims can be contacted during all phases of the criminal justice process. Prosecutors must consult with victims on the disposition of case and must treat them with care during interviews and trials. Victims have the right to review presentence and postsentence reports, may submit "impact statements" during trials, and must be informed of the sentences allowable by state statute. A Crime Victims Services Bureau informs victims of pending appeals, parole and pardon hearings, and release dates (Louisiana Rev. Statutes 46:1844).

Megan's Laws

In 1994, the federal Jacob Wetterling Act was passed, requiring all those convicted of sex crimes to register with their local police department after release from prison. That same year in New Jersey, seven-year-old Megan Kanka was raped and murdered by a neighbor, who was a twice-convicted sex offender. New Jersey teenager Amanda Wengert had been killed two months earlier under similar circumstances. The fathers of the two girls persuaded NJ lawmakers and Governor Christine Todd Whitman to pass a series of new statutes in 1994. They collectively became known as "Megan's Law." President Clinton signed a federal version of Megan's Law in 1996 (Township of Evesham, 2001).

The purpose of Megan-type laws was to force state and federal law enforcement agencies to give communities any available information about released sex offenders. It was hoped that new public awareness would aid law enforcement investigations, allow communities to protect their children, and deter sex offenders from committing future crimes. In New Jersey, county prosecutors use guidelines from the state Attorney General and a 12-member council to evaluate the risk posed by particular offenders. If a risk is found, schools, community organizations, and neighbors are notified of the offender's presence and are given his/her description (Township of Evesham, 2001).

States provide access to the information differently. Twenty states offer access to sex offender registration systems over the Internet. The information can include the offender's photograph, a description, a list of the offender's crimes, and even his/her home address. In 16 of these states, law enforcement agencies offer the information on their Web sites, while the four others (Illinois, New Hampshire, Oklahoma, and Washington) provide the information through private organizations (Hillis, 1995).

A few state courts have prevented the data from being published on the Internet due to privacy and safety concerns. Some states limit access to registries by requiring individuals to visit their local police departments to see the data. Requests for information must be about specific individuals or persons living at specific addresses (Hillis, 1995).

METHODOLOGY

In order to analyze state sentencing schemes and reforms, we conducted a state-by-state survey using a variety of primary sources (state codes and statutes) and secondary sources (government documents and scholarly works).

A State Sentencing Survey Instrument was used to determine the basic sentencing schemes of all 50 states, paying particular attention to the year in which states adopted each reform.

From the Internet, we scanned state statutes, lookin at how laws (or reforms) were worded, the details of state criminal procedures, and the mechanisms by which laws were intended to be effective criminal justice and/or sentencing reforms. We also compared or used a large variety of government documents, research in briefs, and other sources from the U.S. Department of Justice, National Institute of Justice, National Council on State Legislatures, and various state publications, both published and electronic. The objective was an accurate and clear historical account of current state sentencing practices.

From this painstaking research, we compiled approximately 200 pages of state statutes and other secondary government information.

Limitations of State Level Research and Methodology

While coding data, not all of our decisions were easy ones. It was difficult to tell whether some laws were clearly new sentencing reforms, and different sources sometimes offered conflicting and further confirming evidence may have been hard to find. Competing sources defined important terms differently or statute wording was ambiguous and interpreted in multiple ways. In order to reduce the probability of incorrectly classifying state laws, we incorporated all recent major policy research on reforms included in the study. This is why the source for each piece of information used is carefully cited, including where the contradictions exist.

For purposes of analysis, if we could not verify the adoption date of laws, whether unavailable or due to conflicting sources, they were left out of the analysis. The only variable affected by this problem is habitual offender laws. Four states (Michigan, Georgia, Utah, and Virginia) were identified with habitual offender laws as early as the 1920s. However, these laws were extremely narrow in focus, and each of these states has modified its habitual offender laws since. The character of the earliest habitual offender laws is different than the first wave laws. These four states were treated as having habitual offender laws, but no adoption date was provided.

FINDINGS

Our first step of analysis was to examine the frequency of reforms adopted annually over the study period (1963 through May 2000). The data indicates that state sentencing reforms are very common. Over the study period, the ten policy variables were adopted 328 times by respective states. States adopted an average of 6.5 sentencing reforms each.

What makes the number of reforms most impressive is that many criminal justice and sentencing reforms are not even included in this study. Specific sentence enhancements (not related to habitual offenders), expanded firearms laws, drug laws, and juvenile offender laws are examples of policies we did not include. Due to the scope of criminal justice policies in these specific areas, we were unable to include the wide range of changes in criminal codes. Drug laws and juvenile justice in particular have separate and distinct bodies of literature. Clearly though, states have been very busy modifying their sentencing systems. If we take these additional policies into consideration, there has been a huge level of sentencing policy activity in the last three decades.

All the policies we reviewed are not randomly distributed, as Figure 1 shows.

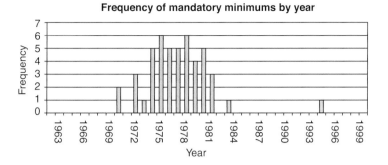

FIGURE 1

FIRST WAVE

Sentencing reforms were infrequent from 1963 to 1973, consistent with the uniformity of state indeterminate sentences through this time. Colorado and North Carolina's habitual of-fender laws were the only study variables adopted prior to 1971, the same year as the ad-vent of mandatory minimum laws in Vermont and Wisconsin. Several years of minimal adoption appear through 1975, with reforms limited to habitual offender and mandatory minimum laws. However, after a few years of trickling policy adoptions, we see a gather-ing head of steam towards a first wave of reforms.

The innovation of several other policies around this time shows a growing level of state activity in criminal justice matters. In 1976, abolition of parole (Maine) and determi-nate sentencing (Colorado and Maine) appear. From 1976 through 1983, seven or more re-forms were adopted annually. The first wave peaks in 1977. Table 1 describes the details of the 19 reforms adopted this year.

Habitual Offender Laws

The first adopted reform in the state reform survey was habitual offender laws. The patterns of adoption for habitual offenders are very interesting. While all 50 states have some form

Table 1 Breakdown of Reforms Adopted in 1977		
Reform Type	Percentage	Count
Determinate Sentences	16%	3
Habitual Offender Laws	42%	8
Discretionary Parole Release Abolished	16%	3
Mandatory Minimums	26%	5
Total		**19**

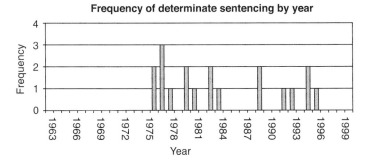

FIGURE 2

of habitual offender laws, at least 4 states have had them since the 1920s or 1930s. But generally, these laws were very narrowly tailored and did not cover many widely charged offenses. Modern habitual offender laws are broader, allowing for more chargeable offenses and wider discretion for prosecutors to apply habitual offender laws.

Of the 46 states with habitual offender laws included in the analysis, most of the changes were adopted during the first wave. Contributing to the first wave apex in 1977 was the year of highest habitual offender adoption, accounting for 42 percent of that year's total reforms. Thrity-six states adopted habitual offender laws between 1963 and 1991, all prior to the second wave generation of habitual offender laws. Figure 2 illustrates the adoption patterns of habitual offender laws.

Between 1992 and 1998, nine states passed this new generation of habitual offender laws. While four of these laws were passed in 1993 alone, three others were adopted well after the end of the Three Strikes brief window of policy adoption. It is interesting to note that none of the states that recently adopted habitual offender statutes also has Three Strikes Laws. During the heyday of the Three Strikes movement, some states decided instead to update their habitual offender laws.

Mandatory Minimums

Mandatory minimums were also an important source of first wave reforms. In 1977, they accounted for 26 percent of reforms adopted. Most mandatory minimum laws were adopted before 1982, with 43 states adopting them between 1973 and 1982 (See Figure 3). Arizona adopted them in 1995, and three other states do not yet have them.

There are four important aspects of the first wave sentencing reforms. First, the first wave reforms were early policy innovations. They were relatively crude (not as direct or as punitive as many modern reforms), and reflect transitional philosophical values.

Second, each typically consists of a single policy tool. While broadly tailored to various classes of offenders or criminal conduct, these earlier reforms are not comprehensive in scope. That is, they affect either prison admissions or departure rates. For instance, early habitual offender and mandatory minimum laws applied to few categories of offenders exhibiting narrow categories of behaviors.

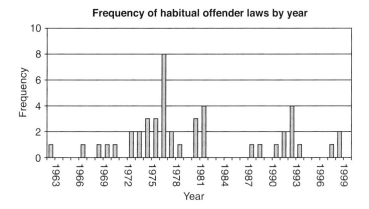

FIGURE 3

Third, first wave reforms are designed to directly address the inadequacies of indeterminate sentences. In this sense, we are talking about single tools or approaches to solving one of two specific perceived problems of indeterminate sentences. People convicted of certain crimes were required to go to prison, increasing prison admissions rates.

Fourth, they typically offer admissions and departure policies, but not both. For example, early habitual offender laws and abolished parole release affect only departure rates. If offenders' early release options are reduced through structured sentences, one presumes inmates serve longer terms than previously available with unstructured sentencing.

Under mandatory minimums, if the qualifications are met, and the laws are not discretionary, prison admissions are affected. However, by stipulating mandatory terms of incarceration, the potential exists for mandatory minimums to also affect departure rates. Forcing offenders to serve mandatory additional five-year terms for example, of using firearms in the commission of a crime, means offenders spend longer terms in prison. When reforms affect both admissions and departure rates, they offer a much better opportunity to create negative policy implications like expanding prison populations and overcrowding. In any case, some mandatory minimum laws are the exception to the typical early sentencing reforms, which usually focus on either changing admissions or departure rates.

BRIDGE REFORMS

What we call "bridge" policies address multiple sentencing goals, use combinations of sentencing tools, and were adopted over a longer amount of time. These policies have been adopted over most of the study period, in essence forming a bridge between first and second wave reforms. They are more complex than the simplistic first wave reforms.

Determinate Sentences

Nineteen states are identified as having determinate sentencing as an important component of their basic sentencing structure. The first adoption of a determinate sentencing law was in Colorado in 1976, followed by three more states in 1977. In other words, about 20 percent of the total adoption rate of determinate sentencing states was achieved within the first year of the initial adoption.

However, coding states for their basic sentencing scheme can be a very tough prospect. Several states today rely on a combination of both indeterminate and determinate sentencing. For instance, by and large, New York is considered an "indeterminate" state. Nevertheless, under the 1998 Jenna's Law, first-time violent offenders and repeat offenders are sentenced under determinate sentences and mandatory minimum laws (Lindsmith Center, 2000).

Other than New York's Jenna's Law and Ohio's recent reforms that included determinate sentences, most activity with this reform took place between 1976–1984 and 1989–1995 (see Figure 4). This is why determinate sentence reform is considered a bridge reform, in addition to changing both admissions and departure rates. All instances of determinate sentence adoption occurred within this period of time, except for Ohio and New York respectively.

Abolition of Discretionary Parole Release

Eighteen states abolished discretionary parole release over 22 years. More than other reforms, this reform seems to occur in one state at a time instead of multiple states enacting it in one year. Abolition or parole release first appeared in Maine, the same year determinate sentencing was adopted. There was a lull in policies abolishing parole between 1984 and 1989, in between the two waves. Yet, this reform spans both waves, with 11 adoptions between 1976 and 1990, and 7 more from 1992 to 1998.

Sentencing Guidelines

The advent of guidelines reform followed quickly upon the introduction of determinate sentences. The first states to adopt any form of sentencing guidelines were Utah (1978), Colorado (1979), and Minnesota (1980). Almost two thirds of states that adopted guidelines did so prior to 1992, with a second round of eight states adopting guidelines between 1992 and 1998.

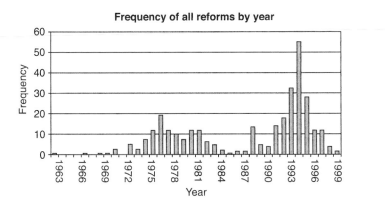

FIGURE 4

Today, 22 states have some form of sentencing guidelines. Of all states with sentencing guidelines, they are almost evenly split between voluntary or presumptive sentencing guidelines. Twelve states have presumptive guidelines and ten states have voluntary guidelines. There does not appear to be a relationship between voluntary or presumptive guidelines and the adoption of sentencing commissions.

Sentencing Commissions

Sentencing commissions are even more popular than sentencing guidelines, with 25 states identified with them by 1998. All guidelines states except Colorado and Rhode Island also have a commission. Five states have no guidelines, yet have a sentencing commission (including Illinois, Massachusetts, Montana, Nevada, and New York).

Although the specific details of state reforms vary, the fundamental assumptions and combinations of sentencing tools in bridge reforms are similar respective to each policy.

Determinate sentences reflect incapacitation, retribution, and deterrence in a stricter, structured form of sentencing. Sentencing guidelines can reflect any of the competing sentencing goals, but typically reflect a combination of deterrence and equality in formulating sentencing matrices.

Sentencing commissions accomplish many penal goals. For instance, the appellate review of terms handed out by judges focuses on the equity of various sentences. The annual review and modification of the state sentencing schema can increase presumptive terms for perceived weaknesses in the sentencing structure. States seem to find utility in having a sentencing commission to promulgate and monitor penal policies. Because of the politically insulating factors associated with having a separate expert policy formulation entity, it appears a wise move when an independent commission is able to develop and oversee the implementation of state criminal justice and penal policies.

Bridge policies usually affect both prison admissions and departure policies. Determinate sentencing mandates prison terms for an increased amount of criminal offenses, yet also affects departure rates by either severely reducing or abolishing parole. When the threshold for incarceration is set lower in sentencing guideline matrices, meaning more offenses are classified as imprisonment sanctions, admissions rates can explode.

SECOND WAVE REFORMS

We witness the growing punitive nature of sentencing reforms after a brief lull in adoptions from 1986–1988. Between one and three reforms were adopted annually in this period; Delaware adopted guidelines in 1987 and several other states adopted victims' rights legislation. In 1989, there was a quick spike in reform adoption with regards to victims' rights laws, determinate sentencing, guidelines, and commissions. While a moderate level of reform activity was going on through 1991, it did not begin to rise quickly until 1992 when 14 reforms were adopted.

We place the start of the "second wave" in 1992 with the acceleration of reform adoption, and ending in 1998, after which we see sentence reforms drop precipitously. The peak of the second wave was in 1995, when 55 reforms were adopted. Although no state implemented victims' rights laws during the peak year of 1995, 15 states implemented victims'

Table 2   Breakdown of 1995 Reforms

Reform Type	Percentage	Count
Mandatory Minimums	2%	1
Abolished Discretionary Parole	4%	2
Determinate Sentences	4%	2
Sentencing Commissions	7%	4
Three Strikes Law	18%	10
Megan's Law	29%	16
Truth In Sentencing	36%	20
Total		**55**

rights laws in 1994 and 1996 combined. Table 2 lists a breakdown of reforms adopted at the apex of second wave.

A presumption exists that a tougher approach to crime spawns new generations of stricter, more punitive policies aimed at reducing crime. The "second wave" of reform evolved as policy-makers began using combinations of "first-wave" crime-fighting tools together with newly developed sentencing approaches.

Truth in Sentencing (TIS)

There were several states that were ahead of the curve when adopting these policies. Indiana (1979), Washington (1984), and Delaware (1989) were all credited with adoption of early versions. However, most TIS Laws, particularly federally conforming versions, were adopted in the second wave of reforms.

Of the 1995 second wave apex, 36 percent of the total reforms that year stem from the clear spike in TIS laws in 1995, with 20 states implementing it in that year alone. Forty-one states have adopted some variation of TIS Law by 1998, and of these, 37 were adopted between 1992–1998. Of all TIS Laws in effect, 33 states have either a federally conforming version or stricter. This leaves 9 states with TIS schemes in place, but not meeting the federal 85 percent minimum sentence time served provisions.

Three Strikes (TS) Laws

An interesting note when comparing TS policy adoption to patterns of other policies is the sheer speed of adoption. After Washington implemented it in 1993, 23 states and the federal government followed almost immediately. This policy was diffused and innovated between 1993 and 1995. All states adoped it within a brief three-year period. Of the 1995 second wave apex, 18 percent of the reforms were Three Strikes.

Victims' Rights Amendments

Victims' Rights was intermittently adopted prior to 1992. Thirty-two states enacted victims' rights laws between 1992 and 1998. It was clearly a second wave reform, with only seven occurring prior to 1992. The biggest year for victims' rights laws was 1996, with more than 25 percent of the total. It was interesting to note that no victims' rights legislation was adopted in 1995, the apex year of the second wave of reforms. However, victims' rights were adopted in six states in 1992, so it was partially responsible for triggering the second wave.

Megan's Laws

All 50 states have statutes resembling Megan's Law. Colorado, Idaho, Louisiana, Massachusetts, Washington, and West Virginia had laws requiring public notification prior to New Jersey, and therefore did not enact a new law after 1994. Nevertheless, Megan's Law and its variants are clearly a second wave reform, with six occurring between 1981 and 1994, and the remaining 46 occurring after 1994.

Megan's Law alone accounted for 29 percent (16 occurrences) of the 1995 second wave apex. Because Megan's Law was so heavily adopted in 1995, we were concerned that this one-year spike would create an artificial apex, or somehow distort our wave. Consequently, we recalculated Figure 1, excluding this variable from the frequency distribution of reforms. We found that although Megan's Law contributed to the overall height of the 1995 spike, the removal of the variable did not affect the overall wave pattern.

CONCLUSION

It is quite evident that sentencing reforms in general have become stricter and more punitive. New generations of tougher sentencing laws are a factor in massive prison population growth in most American states. While the purpose guiding first wave reforms was a remedying of perceived shortcomings of rehabilitation and inderminate sentences, the second wave reflects a different set of priorities and processes. As states struggled to reduce crime and protect their citizens, there was an increasing federal interest in uniform state sentencing practices. State policymakers began developing sophisticated sentencing tools to better deal with respective crime problems.

So the question becomes, how do states decide which sentencing policies or reforms best reflect their needs? With so many sentencing reforms, laws, and practices to choose from, how are these policies selected? What objectives are political officials trying to accomplish with sentencing reform adoption? What factors or processes are responsible for the adoption of so many reforms within a relatively short period of time?

The driving question becomes, why do states adopt sentencing reforms in the first place?

Federalization

The federal government has an interest in uniform state sentencing practices to limit discrepancies and inequality in state sentencing practices. Some states are self-motivated by reforms adopted by the federal government. In other words, federal adoption of sentencing reforms is good enough justification for some states to follow suit and adopt similar reforms. In other circumstances, the national government places coercive pressure on states to adopt similar reforms. It should serve as little surprise that the federal government has already adopted most of the reforms included in this study.

Getting states to go along with Truth in Sentencing, Guidelines, or Megan's Law is easier with a carrot-and-stick approach. For example, states are encouraged to adopt TIS to recoup prison construction costs through a federal matching grant. By states voluntarily accepting the federal government's 85 percent sentence provision, more uniform sentencing practices are introduced to some states. Megan's Law, by contrast, is an outright federal mandate on states to adopt sex offender registration and tracking laws! In addition to the increasing influence of federal sentencing practices upon states, we also see evidence of hybridizaiton of state sentencing reforms.

Hybridization in the Second Wave

Hybridization is going on as states adopt combinations of earlier sentencing tools to reduce crime and develop new policies. States are using the same sentencing tools, but in different configurations. Whether states have passed reforms or not, each has developed its own way of fighting crime. The difference between states with or without TS and TIS is less than we think. States are prepared to deal with career criminals with their preexisting statutes.

There are two important components to hybridization: (1) the wide diffusion of similar sentencing tools used in different combinations, and (2) the tendency of states to have similar results (growing prison populations) despite any individual variation between state sentencing schemes. In other words, career offenders are sentenced tough in all states, whether the state has TS, TIS, guidelines, or none of the above. If the distinctions between sentencing schemes are further blurred, criminal justice researchers face substantial methodological concerns.

Legislative intent behind different reforms looks similar. TIS and TS both target the same offenders, those with the greatest propensity to commit crimes of violence. In this vein, both TS and TIS reforms incorporate aspects of the first wave. Three Strikes laws are a combination of habitual offender statutes, mandatory minimums, criminal history sentencing enhancements, abolition of parole, and reduction of "good time" credits. The rubric of Truth in Sentencing is a composite of determinate sentences, enhanced penalties for violent crimes, the abolishment of parole, and reduction in "good time" credits. These combinations of tools form more lethal sentencing practices.

Texas is the perfect example of hybridization of state sentencing practices. Violent offenders in Texas are classified into "Aggravated" and "Non-Aggravated" by their offense of record at prison admission. Aggravated violent offenders must serve half of their sentences in actual time before becoming eligible for parole; offenders with sentences greater than 60 years must serve a minimum of 30 years before parole eligibility; and other offenders must serve 35 or 40 years depending on the severity of the charge before becoming eligible for parole, Non-Aggravated violent felons must accrue "good time" and "actual credits" equal to a minimum of one-fourth of their sentences (Fabelo, 2000). This provision incorporates a harsh habitual offender law, with mandatory minimums, in a guidelines-type format.

Furthermore, Fabelo (2000) concludes that if present policies continue, Texas' aggravated violent offenders entering prison today will serve 89.1 percent of their terms, and non-aggravated violent offenders will serve 66.5 percent. Violent offenders are not releasable on good time credits alone. If offenders are not paroled, they serve their full sentences. Texas judges are granted leeway on applying these statutes to the most deserving offenders, but at the same time are not constrained by nondiscretionary sentencing reforms. When the state sentences a first-time offender to a relatively long period of time, then lets him out having served one-fourth as served, the offender should try diligently to stay out of further trouble.

On one hand, they do not have Three Strikes, Sentencing guidelines, or Truth in Sentencing. On the other hand, they have sentencing provisions that utilize the important and effective components of these three major reforms although technically having none of these three reforms, Texas has the ability to "truthfully" sentence, along TIS lines, by denying parole and making offenders serve their entire sentence. But Texas does not conform to federal TIS because it only enforces a 50 percent threshold. Also, Texas has tough habitual offender laws that function as effectively as either TS or TIS. Policies that abolish parole, an important theme of TIS, are now accomplished through different laws enacted in Texas.

Clearly, substantive and methodological concerns exist with comparing states on the basis of adoption of various sentencing reforms. If some states control habitual offenders with Three Strikes and other states control them with other sentencing tools, we lose the ability to compare states on the basis of simple policy adoption. Instead, we must understand more fully the nature of specific reforms, which when used in various configurations, yield similar types of sentencing outcomes. Hybridization is the effect of similarity between a variety of earlier first wave reforms and new composite second wave reforms. In this way, our waves of sentencing reform is a useful construct for both criminal justice scholars and practitioners.

QUESTIONS FOR REVIEW AND DISCUSSION

1. Why do states change their sentencing laws? Explain.

2. Is there any particular sentencing law that seems to be better than the rest of the sentencing laws? Why or why not? Explain.

3. What is meant by truth-in-sentencing? How is it applicable to the states?

4. How has the federal government influenced state sentencing practices?

5. Do mandatory sentences, such as three-strikes and habitual offender statutes, deter criminals from committing serious offenses? Why or why not? Discuss.

6. What type of sentencing scheme does your particular state follow? Has your state used other sentencing schemes in past years?

7. Why were citizens and legislators so critical of indeterminate sentencing? Discuss.

8. What problems for corrections are created when sentencing laws are changed and mandatory minimum sentences are established? Discuss.

13

The Imposition of Economic Sanctions in Philadelphia

Costs, Fines, and Restitution

R. Barry Ruback

Adapted from R. Barry Ruback, "The Imposition of Economic Sanctions in Philadelphia: Costs, Fines, and Restitution." *Federal Probation* 68: 21–26, 2004.

Reprinted with permission by the Administrative Office of the U.S. Courts.

Other than traffic offenses, economic sanctions have been used relatively infrequently in the United States, in large part because of the country's heavy reliance on incarceration. Moreover, financial penalties are considered to have no effect on wealthy defendants, for whom the amounts are assumed to be inconsequential, and to be unfair to poor defendants, for whom the additional monetary burdens are assumed to be overwhelming.

Despite these arguments for not using economic sanctions, there are three reasons why they are being imposed more frequently than in the past. First, the costs of criminal justice operations are becoming so high that offenders are now expected to pay at least part of those costs. Second, concern for victims has increased and will continue to increase, causing restitution to be awarded more frequently. Third, there are pressures for alternatives to prison because of the high cost of incarceration, the limited number of spaces available in some prison systems, and the belief of some people that long periods of incarceration are unjustifiable on grounds of just deserts and are ineffective in deterring future crime.

PURPOSE, IMPOSITION, AND PAYMENT OF ECONOMIC SANCTIONS

This study uses data from Philadelphia during the period 1994–2000 to examine the imposition of three types of economic sanctions: fines, costs, and restitution. Although research typically focuses on only one of these economic sanctions, in actual cases they are usually not used in isolation. That is, sentencing often involves multiple economic sanctions used in conjunction with probation and sometimes incarceration.

Fines.   Fines are monetary penalties paid by the offender to the state. Fines have several advantages over other types of penalties (Hillsman, 1990). They are obviously punitive. They can be tailored to the seriousness of the particular crime and to the specific individual's criminal history and resources. They are also flexible, since they can serve as sole penalties or can be combined with other sanctions, ranging from treatment to incarceration. Moreover, they allow the offender to remain in the community, work, and avoid the stigma and social costs of incarceration (Gordon and Glaser, 1991).

Within a jurisdiction, judges usually apply the "going rate" for fines, such that all violators of a particular offense are obligated to pay similar amounts (Hillsman and Greene, 1992). Because judges tend to use this going rate for fines, however, they do not adjust the seriousness of the penalty to the particular defendant (Hillsman and Greene, 1992). And, since this going rate is usually low (in order to accommodate the poorest offenders), fines have little penalty value for affluent offenders. Typically, judges' adjustments to fines are at the back end, rather than at the initial sentencing. That is, judges might sometimes excuse the remaining unpaid portion or simply let the probation period expire without enforcing the fine (Hillsman and Greene, 1992).

Costs.   Costs refer to money paid by the offender to the state to partially cover the expenses of prosecution, confinement, and community supervision. In some cases, these funds also support expenditures such as victim/witness assistance and victim compensation. Generally, the amount of costs imposed is a standard rate for each count. Thus, the only question in these courts is whether to impose costs, not how much.

Olson and Ramker (2001) found that judges in rural areas were significantly more likely than judges in urban areas to impose probation fees, probably because rural judges are likely to be more responsive than urban judges to their communities and more concerned with the imposition of justice in individual cases than with the processing of large numbers of cases (see also Weisheit, Wells, and Falcone, 1995). These researchers also found that higher amounts of probation fees were paid in rural areas, probably because judges in rural areas were concerned that offenders pay something, whereas judges in urban areas were concerned that fees should be imposed and enforced only if they were set at a level high enough to justify the time and expense of collection.

Restitution.   Restitution refers to a convicted offender's court-ordered obligation to compensate victims for their losses resulting from the crime. Most often, restitution involves an offender making monthly payments to cover the costs of damaged or stolen property, although these monies may also be ordered to cover medical expenses and lost wages (Harland, 1981). Restitution is widely supported because it both addresses victims' needs for compensation and meets the criminal justice system goals of punishment and rehabilitation. Today, every state has a law addressing restitution, and 29 states mandate restitution unless the judge gives compelling reasons for not doing so (Office for Victims of Crime, 1998, p. 356), consistent with the call made by the President's Task Force on Victims of Crime (1982).

In one study of restitution, Outlaw and Ruback (1999) examined adult probation cases from Allegheny County (Pittsburgh), Pennsylvania in which restitution was or could have been a condition of probation. Results indicated that judges ordered restitution most often when damages were easy to quantify and that offenders were most likely to pay the restitution when they were able to pay and when the victim was a business. Restitution payment was negatively related to rearrest, and this effect was especially strong among married persons, who were more integrated into the community. This finding is consistent with an experimental study in which juveniles randomly assigned to formal restitution programs had lower recidivism than juveniles randomly assigned to other dispositions (Ervin & Schneider, 1990).

Restitution programs have generally not been seen as successful because (1) there is a reluctance to impose restitution on offenders who are assumed not to be able to pay it, (2) payment on restitution orders typically follows other financial obligations (e.g., costs, fines), and (3) there is often ambiguity about who is responsible for monitoring, collecting, disbursing, and enforcing restitution payments (Office for Victims of Crime, 1998, p. 358). Thus, it is not surprising that collection rates of restitution are low, ranging in two national studies from 45 percent (Smith, Davis, and Hillenbrand, 1989) to 54 percent (Cohen, 1995).

Multiple Economic Sanctions.   Opposite predictions could be made about the relationship among these three different types of economic sanctions. On the one hand, one could hypothesize that they would all be positively related, in that judges might believe that if offenders can pay one, they can pay them all. On the other hand, one could hypothesize that they would all be negatively related; that is, an increase in one type of economic sanction would result in lower amounts of other types of economic sanctions. Such a pattern would be evidence that judges recognize offenders' limited financial resources and consider offenders' ability to pay in setting the amounts of economic sanctions.

A study of probation fees in Illinois found support for both hypotheses. Olson and Ramker (2001) found that probationers ordered to pay both fines and probation fees had lower average monthly fees than did probationers ordered to pay only fees. However, Olson and Ramker found that there was no trade-off between fees and other penalties when those other conditions were non-economic (e.g., treatment, community service). They also found that probation fees were more likely to be imposed and more likely to be paid if fines were also imposed, a pattern that suggests the imposition of some economic sanctions is positively related to ability to pay.

A study in Pennsylvania also suggests that there is no clear pattern to the imposition of economic sanctions. In this study of four medium-sized urban counties (Ruback, Shaffer, & Logue, 2004), the imposition of fines was negatively related to the imposition of restitution. The imposition of costs was positively related to the imposition of fines but unrelated to the imposition of restitution. When these sanctions were imposed, the amounts of fines, costs, and restitution were positively related.

In their analysis of economic sanctions in misdemeanor cases in Los Angeles, Gordon and Glaser (1991) found that the amount of financial penalties imposed (restitution, fines, cost of probation supervision) was affected by the type of crime (assaults, burglaries, drug crimes, DUI, or theft). Compared to drug offenders, offenders convicted of burglary, DUI, and theft received significantly higher financial penalties, a result that suggests judges did not believe financial penalties were appropriate for drug offenders. Finally, they found that the predictors of the different types of economic sanctions were the same, a result that suggests judges treated restitution, fines, and costs similarly.

The present research was designed to examine the relationship among costs, fines, and restitution in Philadelphia, the fifth most populous city in the United States and a city with one of the country's highest violent crime rates (Federal Bureau of Investigation, 2003, Table 6, p. 39). This research is an improvement over prior studies in that it had a large sample of both misdemeanor and felony cases and that it examined cases over a seven-year period.

STATUTORY CHANGES IN PENNSYLVANIA

Aside from looking at the relationship among three types of economic sanctions, we were also interested in looking at the effect of the 1995 statutory change making restitution mandatory. In 1995 Pennsylvania made mandatory the paying of restitution to victims whose property was stolen or damaged or who suffered personal injury as a direct result of a crime (18 Pa. C.S.A. §1106). Moreover, judges were to impose full restitution regardless of the offender's financial resources. Consistent with results in four medium-sized urban counties in the state, we expected an increase in the imposition of restitution after the statutory change and either no effect or a decrease in the imposition of fines and costs. In 1998, Pennsylvania enacted a second statutory change regarding restitution. Under this law, 50 percent of all payments by an offender had to be directed to restitution for victims. We expected this change to result in slightly higher rates of imposition of restitution, as judges would be more likely to believe that ordered restitution would reach victims.

Method

Data for the years 1994–2000 were taken from computer files maintained by Philadelphia. Cases were sampled on the basis of crimes that were considered to be "restitution eligible," that is, cases with an identifiable victim (an individual, a business, or a state agency). This classification excludes DUI and drug offenses. Also excluded are cases determined to have no identifiable victim, based on crimes listed in Title 18 (Crimes and Offenses) of Pennsylvania Consolidated Statutes Annotated.

Description of the Sample

For each case there were 20 items of information. The first, the variable on which cases were selected for inclusion in the study, was the major charge. Under this selection procedure, there were 108 crimes for the years 1994 through 2000. Of the 84,970 cases in the data set, 84,185 (99 percent) were accounted for by 33 crimes with at least 50 cases. The remaining 75 types of crime accounted for 778 cases, and 13 cases were missing this information. Across crime types, three dummy variables were created to capture the nature of these crimes: (a) attempted vs. completed, (b) conspiracy vs. no conspiracy, and (c) violent vs. property.

The data contained information about whether or not there was a private criminal complaint, whether the court was a municipal court (which handles misdemeanors) or Court of Common Pleas (which is a court of general jurisdiction), the date of arrest, the type of attorney (coded as public defender or court-appointed attorney versus a private attorney), the date of sentencing, the amount of fines imposed, the amount of restitution imposed, whether costs were imposed, whether probation was imposed, the starting date of probation, the expiration date of probation, the actual termination date of probation if it were different from the expiration date, the gender of the offender, the race/ethnicity of the offender, the method of case termination, the reason a case would still be open after the expiration date, the date of rearrest (if any), and the number of days between the date of sentencing and rearrest.

There were a total of 84,970 cases in the data set, broken down by year as follows: 12,146 in 1994; 12,210 in 1995; 12,683 in 1996; 12,445 in 1997; 12,704 in 1998; 12,017 in 1999; and 10,765 in 2000. Of these cases, 54,812 were felony cases processed in Common Pleas Court and 30,151 were misdemeanor cases processed in Municipal Court (7 cases did not have information about which court was involved).

Most of the offenders were black. The remaining offenders were white (21 percent), latino (5 percent), other (2 percent), or missing (1 percent). Most offenders committed property crimes, and most did not have a private attorney.

The 5,415 cases in which the state was the victim were analyzed separately because they differed substantially from cases in which the victim was a private individual or business. Most important, there were gender differences. Women committed 14 percent of the crimes where the state was not the victim, but 83 percent of the crimes in which the state was the victim. Blacks committed 71 percent of the crimes in which private individuals or businesses were the victim, but 83 percent of the crimes in which the state was the victim. The analyses were limited to those individuals who were 16 years or older.

Results

Three types of economic sanctions were investigated: restitution, fines, and costs. The results are presented in two parts, relating first to the imposition of each sanction overall, and specifically by year. Second, there is a multivariate analysis of the imposition of each type of sanction.

Change over Time

One of the issues we were interested in was whether the imposition and payment of restitution changed over time, and, if so, what factors might be related to this change. Although there was an increase over time in the proportion of cases in which restitution was imposed in cases in which private individuals/businesses were the victims, there was a decrease in the proportion of cases in which costs and fines were imposed.

Although there was a significant increase in the average amount of restitution ordered, there has not been a comparable increase in the average fine ordered. A pre/post test of the impact of the 1995 mandatory statute indicated a significant increase in the percentage of cases in which restitution was ordered, from 16 percent (for the year 1994) to 22 percent (for the years 1996–2000), χ^2 (1,72760) = 239.95, $p < .001$ (Yates' correction). A pre/post test of the impact of the 1998 statute indicated a small but significant increase in the percentage of cases in which restitution was ordered, from 21 percent (for the years 1996 and 1997) to 24 percent (for the years 1999–2000), χ^2 (1,47910) = 72.09, $p < 0.001$ (Yates' correction).

Individual and Business Victim Cases

Cases in which individuals and businesses were victims were analyzed in terms of the imposition of economic sanctions, the payment of economic sanctions, and the effect of economic sanctions on recidivism.

Imposition of Economic Sanctions.   Restitution was significantly more likely to be ordered for younger individuals, for whites, for individuals who had private attorneys, for cases in Common Pleas court, for cases after the 1995 statute was imposed, for probation cases, and for cases in which costs were imposed, and were significantly less likely to be imposed for cases in which fines were imposed. Fines were significantly more likely to be imposed for males, for older individuals, for whites, for offenders with private attorneys, in Municipal Court, when costs were also imposed and were significantly less likely to be imposed when restitution was imposed. Costs were more significantly more likely to be imposed for older offenders, for black offenders, for cases after the 1995 statute, for offenders who had private attorneys, in Municipal Court, when fines were also imposed, and when restitution was also imposed. Overall, then, costs were positively related to both restitution and fines; restitution and fines were negatively related. This pattern suggests, consistent with Olsen and Ramker's finding, that judges make trade-offs when imposing restitution and fines, requiring offenders to pay one or the other. However, if judges impose either restitution or fines, they are also likely to impose costs.

State Victim Cases

The 5,415 cases in which the state was the victim were analyzed separately from the other cases because they differed in substantial ways from cases in which private individuals or businesses were the victims. Ten different property crimes were included in this category (e.g., tax violations, medicaid fraud, food stamp fraud), but public assistance violations accounted for 5,295 (98 percent) of the cases. As noted earlier, offenders in this category of state victim crimes were primarily female and black. Restitution was imposed in 4,494 cases (83 percent). The range of restitution orders was from $15 to more than $100,000 (M = $4,382; Mdn = $3,000; Mode = $2,500). Fines were imposed in only 53 cases (1 percent). The range of fines was from $50 to more than $100,000 (M = $6,406; Mdn = $750; Mode = $500). Costs were imposed in 1,880 cases (35 percent).

Restitution was significantly more likely to be ordered for welfare cases, for individuals who had private attorneys, and for cases after the 1995 statute was imposed and was significantly less likely for male offenders, for cases in which fines were imposed, and for cases in which costs were imposed. Fines were significantly more likely to be imposed when costs were also imposed and were significantly less likely to be imposed when the offender was black, for welfare cases, in Common Pleas Court, and when restitution was imposed. Costs were significantly more likely to be imposed for male offenders, for offenders who had private attorneys, in Common Pleas Court, and when fines were also imposed, and were significantly less likely after the mandatory statute and for welfare fraud cases. Overall, then, fines and costs were positively related; restitution was negatively related to both fines and costs.

DISCUSSION

This study examined three types of economic sanctions—costs, fines, and restitution—for both misdemeanors and felonies and for both private individual/business victims and the State as victim.

Summary of the Findings

Overall we found that restitution was more likely to be imposed for property crime whereas fines and costs were more likely to be imposed for nonproperty crimes (most of which were violent). One of the clear findings from this study was that the 1995 statute making restitution mandatory had an effect: both restitution imposition rates and restitution amounts ordered were higher after the statute than before. Contrary to our expectation, restitution was awarded to the State at a higher rate than to private victims, and this difference was even more pronounced after the statutory change making restitution mandatory.

The increase in imposition rates for crimes against private individuals and businesses after the statute was probably not greater for three reasons. First, despite the mandatory nature of the statute, it may be that in practice restitution is ordered only if the victims request it. It is likely that victims are not aware that they must make this request. Second, most of the offenders are probably poor and the odds are low that they would be able to make payments. Third, the amounts of money involved are relatively small, and judges, prosecutors, and probation officers may not believe that the money that could be recovered is worth their involvement.

In contrast to private victims, offenders of most crimes in which the State is the victim were ordered to pay restitution, and the increase after the statutory change was even more dramatic. This effect of greater benefit to the State than to private individuals and businesses probably represents an unintended consequence, in which the State was simply better able to meet the legal and practical requirements of receiving restitution. Specifically, with the State, there was no possibility of victim participation or victim responsibility, the state agencies involved asked for restitution, the exact amounts of loss were known and easily quantified (see Outlaw & Ruback, 1999), the offenders in the non-welfare fraud cases probably did have money (since they were relatively more likely to have private attorneys) and therefore there was a greater probability of payment, and the average amounts of money involved were relatively large.

This study also found no simple relationship among the three different types of economic sanctions examined here. On the one hand, judges appeared to make tradeoffs between restitution and fines for both individual/business victims and the State as victim. Thus, when the statute required higher rates of restitution, judges appeared to balance that increase with a decrease in the imposition of fines. On the other hand, however, the relationship between fines and costs was positive for both individual/business victims and the State as victim. That is, if judges imposed fines, they were also likely to impose costs.

Taken together, these patterns suggest that judges might be looking at offenders' ability to pay these sanctions. When the choice lies between restitution to victims and fines paid to the government, judges follow the mandatory law and impose restitution. However, when payments are due to the State and County governments through fines and fees, judges impose both or do not impose either.

This explanation is consistent with results from an anonymous statewide survey concerning the imposition of restitution, which was sent to all criminal court judges in the State in September 2001. Of the 147 judges responding, 17 identified their county as Philadelphia. Typical of these judges' views of restitution was the statement of one: "Except in fraud and theft/burglary cases, we rarely see requests for restitution. Most of our offenders are too poor to pay anything substantial." Another judge wrote, "You can't get blood out of a stone. When you have rapes, aggravated assaults, gun-point robberies of those with no skills who have never held a job, what good is restitution? They will be in jail for five to ten years and have no assets. It's the exception, not the rule, in the major cases in a large city."

More quantitative responses were also consistent with the view that most offenders in Philadelphia could not afford to pay restitution. A set of t-tests comparing the responses of these 17 judges from Philadelphia to the remaining judges indicated several significant differences. Compared to the judges in the rest of the state, Philadelphia judges were more likely to take type of offense into account, more likely to lower fines in order to reduce the total economic sanctions, less likely to say they impose restitution for violent victims, more likely to say collecting restitution is a problem, more likely to impose indirect criminal contempt charges for failing to pay, more likely to believe that too much time elapses before payment is made, more likely to believe that there is inadequate contact with offenders, more likely to believe that inadequate priority is given to warrants, and more likely to believe that offenders think nothing serious will happen to them.

These responses suggest that judges in large cities impose economic sanctions differently than do judges in suburban and rural areas. Future research should examine how tradeoffs in economic sanctions are made in different types of counties for different types of crime, and whether the tradeoffs between economic sanctions and incarceration differ in urban and rural counties.

QUESTIONS FOR REVIEW AND DISCUSSION

1. What are fines? What are their functions relative to offenders? Discuss.
2. When restitution was made mandatory in Pennsylvania, how were criminals affected?
3. What input do victims have in whether restitution is ordered?
4. Indigent offenders may not be able to pay fines and make restitution. What alternatives can judges impose in these cases?

14

Listening to Victims

A Critique of Restorative Justice Policy and Practice in the United States

Harry Mika, Mary Achilles, Ellen Halbert,
Lorraine Stutzman Amstutz, and Howard Zehr

Adapted from Harry Mika, Mary Achilles, Ellen Halbert, Lorraine Stutzman Amstutz, and Howard Zehr, "Listening to Victims: A Critique of Restorative Justice Policy and Practice in the United States." *Federal Probation* 68: 32–38, 2004.

Reprinted by permission from the Administrative Office of the U.S. Courts.

For at least the past 25 years, the victim role in criminal justice has been debated in theory and contested in practice. Of particular significance to proponents of restorative justice is Christie's (1977) assertion that conflict is the "property" of the victim. Normatively then, victims should assume a central role in justice responses to crime and anti-social behavior. But empirically, have they? Elias (1992, 1993) rather emphatically makes the case that they *have not:* the use and abuse of victims, he claims, is the stock and trade of the U.S. justice system. A very different response to the prospect or the reality of a central victim role suggests just as emphatically that they *should not.* A recent iteration of this view (Ashworth, 2002) argues several familiar "points of principle" that would circumscribe or circumvent a victim role, including the limited legitimate interest of victims in compensation and reparation, and the "risk" that victim participation and prejudice threatens proportionality (the direct and unfettered link of the sentence to the seriousness of the offence) and undermines the independence of tribunals, courts and conferences. More critical considerations range from the impact of research and policy initiatives on the status of victims within the criminal justice system (Lamb, 1996; Mawby and Walklake, 1994) to focused consideration of advantages of informal versus conventional justice responses for victims of crime (Strang, 2002). This paper, and the research it describes, seeks to address the conjecture about the victim role in restorative justice policy and practice in the United States. Minimally, it attempts to encumber the debate with evidence, by taking the elemental step of *listening* to what victims and their advocates have to say.

PROJECT BACKGROUND

This paper details the activities and outcomes of the *Listening Project,* a collaboration of professionals active in the victim community and the field of restorative justice in the United States. Funded through the Center on Crime, Communities & Culture of the Open Society Institute, the project was housed in the Institute for Justice and Peacebuilding at Eastern Mennonite University from 1999–2002, and thereafter in the Office on Crime and Justice of the Mennonite Central Committee US.

The *Listening Project* was specifically designed to confront the significant deficiencies of restorative justice practice pertaining to victim participation and impacts for victims, their advocates and victim services generally. A core project objective was to collaboratively propose an action plan to create more responsive restorative justice programs and beneficial outcomes for victims. A number of strategies for gathering the input of victims and their advocates, and for facilitating dialogue between victims, victim services and restorative justice personnel were undertaken, divided into two phases.

Phase I of the *Listening Project* sought to enhance and amplify the voices of victims, victim advocates and victim services. Teams representing victim and restorative justice advocates traveled to seven states during 1999–2000 (Vermont, Ohio, Washington, Texas, Missouri, Wisconsin and Florida) to listen and record the ideas and concerns of victims, victim service workers, and victim advocates regarding victim needs, the victim experience of justice, and impressions of restorative justice in general. One hundred twenty individuals were involved in these listening sessions across the seven states.

Where Phase I of the *Listening Project* emphasized listening and documentation, Phase II was an intense and structured dialogue between representatives of the listening sites, victim, their advocates, victim services personnel, and restorative justice practitioners. Held over two days in early 2001, this meeting critiqued and amplified preliminary findings of the study, identifying major areas of agreement and concern regarding restorative justice, and creating an agenda for reconsidering and enhancing the victim role and benefits from restorative justice initiatives.

ORGANIZATION OF THE RESEARCH

The following pages seek to capture the range of opinions and observations expressed in the listening sessions of project personnel with victims, their advocates, and victim service workers during Phase I of the study, as well as the deliberations of the Phase II discussions. A number of data sources have been incorporated here. Prominent among these are the full transcripts of the listening events from which a significant amount of direct feedback about restorative justice has been derived. Additionally, meeting facilitators also reflected on what they heard and experienced, and more than 75 percent of the participants of the listening events completed brief surveys to assist with the evaluation of the project. Those additional observations have been included. Finally, detailed notes from the general meeting and dialogue of Phase II have in large measure shaped the presentation in the final sections of the report. This material both clarifies and adds to information gathered during the listening sessions, and proposes the contours of an agenda for restorative justice to increase its responsiveness to concerns of the victim community.

These data provide a comprehensive and generally consistent appraisal of contemporary restorative justice policy and practices, largely from the perspectives of victims, their advocates and victim services. It is important to note that the very nature of this exercise—explicitly, to appraise and critique—is prone to result in *cautious reflection and emphasis of shortcomings.* The reader might therefore leave with a somewhat distorted view, perhaps an overly negative view, of the impact of restorative justice on the victim community. That consequence is certainly unintended *and* largely unsupported by much of the data. No artificial effort was made to balance this likely outcome, such as attempting to elicit more positive feedback regarding restorative justice. While some participants in this project voiced the need for some type of audit of existing restorative justice programs, and indeed this has been articulated as a recommendation, the project itself was not designed for this purpose.

The findings and conclusions of the *Listening Project* are distributed among seven interrelated sections. *Impressions of Restorative Justice* reflects on the definition of the concept, its values, priorities and promises, and expectations for restorative justice in the victim community. *Experiences with Restorative Justice* describes encounters with restorative justice processes, practices and programs. *Impediments and Challenges to Restorative Justice* details difficulties with implementing and operationalizing core values and practices, including reflections on uncertain prospects. *Architecture of Responsive Restorative Justice* considers the fundamental features of good practice, including consistency of policy, objectives, processes and outcomes. *Summary Reflections on Restorative Justice* explores the broader context of concerns with restorative justice policy, practice and potential. *The Working Agenda for Restorative Justice* enumerates a variety of strategies, short and longer term, for increasing the responsiveness and impact of restorative practices. The initiative and responsibility for such strategies are divided between the victim and restorative justice communities. Finally, *A Conclusion, A Beginning* features five themes that captured the most deliberations among project participants in charting a collaborative way forward.

IMPRESSIONS OF RESTORATIVE JUSTICE

There are mixed sentiments about what restorative justice has come to represent. For some, restorative justice promotes a balanced view of crime as an event affecting a number of different people. A justice practice should therefore encourage the direct involvement of these parties, such as promoting needed dialogue between victim and offender. Where the contemporary justice system does not work well for victims and others, restorative justice promotes needed change. Restorative justice acknowledges that crime is personal: Adherents of this view often suggest that assisting victims, addressing their needs and helping them through their problems, and allowing and encouraging victims to participate in processes and outcomes that affect them, are primary aims of restorative justice. For some victims, working with offenders has been an essential element of their own healing journey.

But the idea of an offender-oriented restorative justice colors other impressions of its practice. Very often, restorative justice not only reflects offender needs—making amends, and changing and rehabilitating offenders—but also is *driven* by such needs.

Restorative justice may be offender initiated, and may be oriented to an offender time-line. Such needs and practices may not be compatible with victim needs, however. Where offenders are provided with help to change their lives, but victims are not provided help to deal with their trauma, victims feel betrayed by the offender orientation of restorative justice.

Restorative justice may also promote unrealistic or unreasonable goals. Where restorative justice appears to go hand-in-hand with expectations for reduced offender penalties, victims may perceive restorative justice as a way out for offenders whose primary motivation might be to avoid responsibility or pain. It is often the expectation of restorative justice programs that offenders will offer genuine apologies for what they have done. But where offenders are not sorry for what they have done, victims may feel harmed again for this failure of justice. Similarly, restorative justice appears to imply that victims are in some sense obligated to assist offenders. This distorts the hope of victims to assist *themselves* through restorative justice processes. Victim participation for the purpose of offender rehabilitation may be at least an unreasonable burden, if not outright objectionable. Ideas that restorative justice is a panacea are immodest, and without merit. Restorative justice is relatively untried and untested—where is the compelling proof that it works?

For some, restorative justice has not captured the central realities of crime and trauma from a victim's point of view. Restorative justice is the current flavor of the month, and while it may be politically astute to promote ideas of "victim involvement" and "victim centered," these appear to be merely afterthoughts and perhaps manipulations of victims. The definitions of restorative justice are overly broad and confusing, and provide this open invitation for opportunism. For example, some mediation groups appear to have turned their attention to violent crime largely due to the financial incentives for this type of programming. The "cookie cutter" approach to restorative justice, despite even profound differences in the circumstances from one jurisdiction to another, reveals a real lack of responsiveness to *local* needs, and a lack of basic political savvy as well.

EXPERIENCES WITH RESTORATIVE JUSTICE

The view is widely shared that restorative justice may promote offender diversion, court docket relief, easing of jail and prison crowding, and even justice system respite from demands of victims. However, restorative justice provides little victim relief. While that objective appears to be a very low priority, there is nonetheless significant pressure and even coercion to have victims and victim services join the restorative justice bandwagon. Too often, funding for victim programs hangs in the balance; the "choice" may involve a direct affiliation with restorative justice programming, or the prospect of no programming at all. In the view of some from the victim community, it appears that resources set aside in these times for restorative justice have exceeded, and may have even reduced, resources made available for victim services.

The issue of victim input in restorative justice has unfortunately been limited to consideration of victim participation in a particular conference or process. But victims are routinely excluded from participation in program planning. In some communities, surrogates are used to assume the role of victims on some reconciliation panels. Very often, training about victims, victim trauma and victim needs involves no victims or victim advocates. But regardless, restorative justice personnel are quick to expect or demand that victims become advocates for restorative justice.

Many in the victim community feel that while there is significant advocacy and "talk" about restorative justice, and though it may be enshrined as the new justice policy, there is too little pragmatic action taken and few changes are being made, while lines of authority and responsibility for program development remain obscured. Victim advocates and victim services personnel often have difficulty enlisting restorative justice experts to answer questions or to assist with training needs. Too often, prominent restorative justice practitioners have waded unsuccessfully into highly visible cases, without proper (and available) consultation and skills, producing in their wake a backlash against restorative justice in the victim community as well as negative results for victims.

With respect to meaningful impact on victim needs, some feel that restorative justice is little different from the justice status quo. For victims, it remains tone deaf to their aspirations.

IMPEDIMENTS AND CHALLENGES TO RESTORATIVE JUSTICE

A number of assumptions, practices and prospects appear to impede the realization of restorative justice goals. Where restorative justice has come to mean making something go away or bringing something back, the idea of "restoring" for victims falls on its face. Such language, if not the sentiment behind the language, is at least confusing and often offensive to victims. For many in the victim community, one type of programmatic response—face-to-face meetings between the victim and offender (mediation)—is synonymous with restorative justice. This narrow conception of restorative justice seemingly *excludes* many victims, where offenders are not identified, or offenders refuse to participate in such a process, or where it is inappropriate for such a meeting between victim and offender to take place at all. The technique of mediation also presumes a "dispute" and a "relationship" between victim and offender, and for many victims, this trivializes the nature of deep harms and the character of their relationship to offenders.

Further, where financial restitution remains the primary objective of mediation practice, it is questionable whether mediation is at all appropriate for personal crimes involving violence. Domestic violence and sexual assault are certainly ill suited to an intervention with restitution as its centerpiece. Restorative justice presumes to be a rational, contemplative process in response to events (crimes). But are criminal events rational, involving as they might individuals (offenders) whose damaging and violent choices, coupled with drug, alcohol and mental problems, defy rationality to begin with? Such circumstances continue to raise fundamental safety concerns about restorative justice processes in the eyes of victims.

Where restorative justice functions as an adjunct or extension of the formal justice system, there are significant questions about who the "official" or "real" victim is. The needs of those who are harmed by offenders who have not been identified or arrested are going to be ignored. The emphasis of restorative justice on how crime affects the community tends, in the view of some, to again marginalize those immediately affected by crime, distorting and diverting justice responses to victim needs. Not unlike conventional justice programming and policy, restorative justice uses victims to promote and rationalize its agenda. Indeed, the very credibility of restorative justice is thought by its proponents to hinge upon victim involvement. Despite the rhetoric, the experience of the victim community is only too familiar. While victim needs and aspirations are important political fodder for various cases, such needs and aspirations seldom find resolution in meaningful and sustained victim enfranchisement in justice.

And what of the prospects of restorative justice? In some jurisdictions, where limited and routine victim services represent begrudging concessions from the formal justice system to begin with, there appears to be no room for the development of restorative options. Without credible evaluation of restorative justice programs, there will continue to be resistance to their blanket implementation and reluctance in the victim community to embrace them. "Turf" disputes about the ownership of restorative justice ideas and programs will deflect from their impact and potential. In a relatively short period of time, some perceive that restorative justice has become overly professionalized, undermining its professed goals of inclusiveness and accessibility.

ARCHITECTURE OF RESPONSIVE RESTORATIVE JUSTICE

The victim community offers numerous suggestions for how restorative justice policy and practice might be responsive to its needs and aspirations. These are targeted to key dimensions of restorative justice, including its philosophy, policy and practices, and even to broader social concerns.

A number of key assumptions or tenets should guide restorative justice programming. Not only should victim involvement be reflected in the processes themselves, but the planning and programming of restorative justice should have a distinct victim imprint as well. Restorative justice should be an available option for victims, but it clearly is not suited for every victim, or even for every offender. When restorative processes are appropriate, and at the direction and initiation of the victim, direct dialogue with the offender should be a possibility. Some victims may choose restorative justice processes to seek levels of closure and peace: These victims should receive adequate information about what these possibilities might entail, and then be given the support to pursue these outcomes. Restorative justice might look well beyond the narrow view of conventional justice regarding who the "real" victim is, to those harms and their victims where no offender refuses to participate in restorative justice processes. Justice for these victims must involve responses that are detached from offender-dependent processes.

Restorative justice must be mindful that victim interests and needs must be clearly articulated and supported *before* they are presumed to be included with those of offenders and communities in the name of justice. *If* victim interests and needs are valuable to the articulation of restorative justice, its proponents should have a vested interest in advocating for the support of victims. Over time, those needs and interests will change, and restorative justice might itself be flexible and dynamic in order to remain responsive to victims. Restorative justice has set for itself an ambitious set of goals and objectives. But from the view of the victim community, it is minimally expected that restorative justice will promote healing for those affected by crime, respect and empathy for victims, tolerance, trust and hope among participants in justice, accountability from offenders, and uniformity, fairness and quality in its processes.

On a very practical level, restorative justice programming and processes must accommodate victim needs. For example, victims should be provided with complete information about processes and possible outcomes, both positive and negative, as a matter of course. Whenever possible, restorative justice processes should encourage the involvement of advocates and family members of victims (as well as family members of offenders).

Processes and outcomes that include restitution must involve efforts to fairly represent the financial situation of the victim (not only that of the offender), including the predicament and challenges caused by a criminal event. Restorative justice processes must guarantee rights to victims, such as confidentiality, the ability to choose to become involved or to cease involvement, the option of reconsidering an outcome, and the ability to give voice to their own needs and aspirations (in lieu of being side-stepped by surrogate voices, such as prosecution). Under all circumstances, restorative justice processes must provide a safe environment for victims, and its objectives must be premised on offender accountability to victims and victim respect.

Restorative justice might address larger social needs that directly serve the interests of the victim community. For example, restorative justice should be educational in nature, informing not only offenders but also the public about victim trauma. Education about the impact of crime (including the needs of victims), education about offenders and their situations for the victim community, and general education and awareness about restorative justice for justice professionals serve important needs and address glaring deficiencies. It is logical that restorative justice would concern itself particularly with children and their early, formative education regarding issues of respect and accountability. Minimally, the currency and popularity of restorative justice suggests opportunities for forging new coalitions between victim services and justice personnel generally, and for encouraging community support of crime victims.

SUMMARY REFLECTIONS ON RESTORATIVE JUSTICE

A variety of participants in this study, including representatives from the victim community and restorative justice personnel, share an overlay of irony and even skepticism toward these deliberations, when the *longer view* or broader context is taken into consideration; namely, what has been promised versus what has been experienced. These cold and sober realities are essential considerations in developing a comprehensive understanding of restorative justice in this time and place, and for developing an agenda for justice practice that is responsive to victims' needs and aspirations.

Much of the feedback from the victim community about their experience of justice involves injustice, disrespect, exclusion, lack of empathy, and irrelevance. Victim input often emphasizes the failure of conventional justice to respond to personal and severe trauma, while on the other hand seeking to limit restorative justice practices to relatively minor offences. Many in the victim community are leery of the promises and record of restorative justice; they remain skeptical that the conventional system of justice will ever "deliver" for victims. Yet conventional justice participants, while acknowledging that their forays into restorative justice produce little victim impact (as they are offender-oriented initiatives), remain quite defensive about what they see as the generally improved availability of victim services over time.

The victim community is itself diverse, with often complicated relations between and among victims, victim advocates and victim services. Restorative justice generally seeks to engage a monolith "victim" that may not exist in the first place. The victim community often questions the pragmatic differences for their interests and needs between flavors of justice. Victims and their advocates who observe the slow and minimal development of victim services (including the limitations of victim rights) over time often presume that restorative justice will fare no better. Similarly, the poor treatment of victims in conventional justice approaches may well be replicated in restorative justice programming, particularly where restorative justice is a mere adjunct or extension of the conventional system of justice. It follows for some that negative reactions to restorative justice are related to other elements of the bigger picture, such as the incomplete implementation of victim rights, lack of enforcement of such rights, inadequate victim services generally, and the marginality of victims in conventional justice processes.

While "victim input" and "collaboration" are allegedly key ingredients of restorative justice, the precise manner in which these operate remains mysterious. Victims talk, yet no one is listening: Such a ritual may be therapeutic for some interests, but certainly not for the victim community. In the many contexts where promoting or implementing *any* change in justice practices is a struggle, the needed coalitions and alliances may well be beyond the capacity of restorative justice, itself a fractious collection of interests and personalities.

Some in the victim community wonder aloud if victim involvement in restorative justice is a booby prize, a minor accommodation where full participation in justice, victim rights and enforcement of rights, and a full complement of victim services are unlikely scenarios and outcomes under the conventional justice regime. Further, there is concern for a backlash against victim services from restorative justice initiatives irrespective of what they do or do not offer victims. If millions of justice dollars are pumped into new programming that involves little or no victim involvement, participation and control, might this be interpreted as a *lack* of victim need, or interest, or competence?

As noted, a brief survey was sent to all participants in the listening sessions in seven states, with more than 75 percent responding. Regarding the *process* of the *Listening Project,* a considerable majority of respondents agreed that the location of the meeting was comfortable and safe, adequate time was reserved for the meeting, they felt at ease with other participants, the group included those who should have been there, and they had the opportunity to express their views openly and be listened to, including their frustrations with restorative justice. Regarding the *outcomes* of the meeting, a considerable majority agreed that the event had met their expectations, they were taken seriously by other participants, questions and concerns were addressed by the facilitators, and the meeting had raised awareness about both restorative justice generally, and victim needs and victim experiences in restorative justice processes. However, beyond the positive appraisal of the process and short-term outcomes of the *Listening Project* by participants in seven states, the survey data suggests that perhaps the most important conclusion to be drawn concerns the very salience of *listening.*

WORKING AGENDA FOR RESTORATIVE JUSTICE

The final sections of this paper present an overview of a two-day, intensive deliberation of the foregoing input of the victim community during listening events in seven states, and proposed agendas or action steps that might be pursued independently or collaboratively by the victim community and restorative justice advocates in the United States. These agendas and action steps are acknowledged to be only the beginning of a longer conversation that will be needed to work out many crucial details of these proposals, through more discussion and debate.

Reactions to the Input of Listening Events

A relatively wide range of responses characterize the reaction to the summary input of the listening events among the victim community and restorative justice advocates assembled for the Phase II palaver. These included general comments, interests and issues that emerged or were prodded by the input, and efforts to account for (to mitigate or to support) the findings.

In general, input varied among the seven venues where listening events were held. A number of reasons for this seemed probable, including group size and composition, specific backgrounds and direct experiences with restorative justice programming among the states represented (ranging from fairly extensive, to almost none), how tightly or loosely the specific session was organized, who comprised the listening team, and whether the listening event was coupled to a larger dialogue or discussion (such as a listening event held in conjunction with a conference or statewide meeting). Clearly, restorative justice was unfamiliar to some participants in the listening sessions, and they were responding to either what they had heard about restorative justice generally, or the local reputation of restorative justice programs and services. In addition to providing input for restorative justice personnel on the needs and experiences of the victim community, the listening events also functioned for some participants as learning opportunities about restorative justice: This appears to have been variable among the sites as well.

The findings sparked additional discussion of the very *idea* of restorative justice. Restorative justice itself was assumed to be a monolith, undifferentiated in its philosophy and practice. It was clear, however, that there was no common, working definition of restorative justice, nor a shared understanding (or agreement) about its benefits. Restorative justice, it was cautioned, does not reflect a systemic approach to victim communities of interest or to victim services. Training in restorative justice is not uniform.

Some thought the findings painted a false dichotomy between advocates of restorative justice and advocates for victims, since some of the latter are themselves passionate about restorative justice. Further, many victim advocates are hopeful and highly motivated to explore *choices* for victims. Among victim advocates, some feel the conventional justice system is unlikely to be any more responsive to victim needs than it is presently, and restorative justice is worth serious consideration for this reason alone. Other advocates feel the victim movement has made significant strides already, and restorative justice is a distraction or nuisance.

The presentation of input from the listening sessions during the two-day discussion was itself a flash point for discussion and debate. Some were concerned that the summary was too negative in its substance and tone, feeling that a more positive and hopeful spin on restorative justice would be more appropriate. Some recalled specific dialogue leaning to a more positive tone that did not seem to be reflected in the summary overview. Others argued that the depiction of victim input relative to restorative justice was accurate, confirming hunches and experiences, and truthful (albeit an uncomfortable truth for restorative justice advocates). Participants also expressed concern about the lack of deliberate efforts to differentiate among distinct interests and needs in the victim community *vis a vis* restorative justice. Mentioned specifically were victims of domestic violence and victims of specific ethnic and religious groups.

A number of common or synthesizing themes generated broad agreement among participants in the group discussion, as they reflected upon the summary input from the listening meetings. For example, victim services often appear to be merely an afterthought to the development, scope, and control and ownership of restorative justice initiatives. This lack of inclusion and lack of coalition building fires significant disappointment in restorative justice policy and practice. These failings also clarify to a significant degree the fault line that exists presently between restorative justice and victim services. Practically, it is manifest in competition for funding and political power, and lack of relevance. It breeds suspicion, skepticism and confusion in the victim community, or worse, reckless restorative justice programming further harms victims.

Participants agreed that the dialogue between restorative justice adherents and the victim community has just begun, and its continuation is vital. It is critically important to develop definitions of restorative justice philosophy, practice and programs that are consistent. Victim-sensitive language is often missing in restorative justice literatures. Similarly, education about restorative justice, including the principles and values upon which it is premised, is vital. Restorative justice might parlay its currency, its political ascendancy and influence, to advocate on behalf of victim interests and needs. Options for victims of violent crime remain desperately needed. And without question, restorative justice must remain vigilant and mindful of its duty to attempt to repair relationships that have been damaged with the victim community.

An Agenda for Restorative Justice

After careful deliberation on the findings of the listening events and the subsequent analysis and synthesis by a broad representation of study participants, proposals emerged for preliminary and interrelated action steps targeted to restorative justice advocates and the victim community. These are presented in summary format. While their detailed exposition, ranking of priority and a timeline for action are absent here, such gaps are highly suggestive of the future work and opportunity that remains, some of which have been underway since 2002.

Overall, participants recommended that *restorative justice practitioners and advocates* take leadership roles and responsibility for the following 10 tasks:

- Continue to engage the victim community and establish ongoing dialogue in all states, including initiatives to conduct local "listening" with the victim community.
- Carefully reconsider the "cookie cutter" approach to a diverse victim community; in particular, reconsider the prospects (opportunities and limits) of restorative justice approaches to victims of domestic violence and sexual assault.
- Re-examine existing restorative justice programming, including the nature of victim participation and consultation, and effectiveness of programs relative to victim needs.
- Pursue matters of peer accountability, appropriate roles, and standards of practice and qualifications of practitioners to maximize positive impact on the victim community and minimize unintended consequences and harms.
- Mandate training for restorative justice practitioners in victim sensitivity, including education on victim trauma. Training (as well as other forms of technical intervention and assistance) should provide a springboard for collaboration with the victim community and should include meaningful sponsorship by the local victim community, including planning and delivery roles.
- Advocacy for restorative justice programming must go hand-in-hand with rigorous evaluation and demonstrable proof of beneficial possibilities for the victims of crime with minimal risk of further harms. The victim community must be consulted in determining the appropriate evaluation standards and measures of success and harm to be used. The restorative justice community

must develop a sensitivity and genuine interest in feedback from the victim community on program impact.

- Renew and invigorate efforts to address the minimal requisite of responsive programming, namely, listening and responding to victim needs.
- Work in partnership with the victim community, not in competition, to advocate for the requisite justice resources to respond to victim needs.
- Advocate for victim involvement, control and leadership of programming that intends to address victim needs.
- Carefully delineate between and define restorative justice philosophy and practice, and remain mindful of the need to be very clear about why justice programming should involve victims, and who program initiatives are designed to serve.

A series of action steps are also proposed *for the victim community,* including its practitioners and advocates, suggesting pivotal and catalytic roles in the following six areas:

- Develop guidelines and standards for programming in the victim community, including restorative justice initiatives that seek to ensure and maximize victim input and impact, and minimize further harm to victims.
- Advocate for restorative justice where it is responsive to and a reflex of victim needs.
- Encourage training and education in the victim community on the philosophy and practice of restorative justice. Take an active and leadership role in training (and other technical interventions and assistance) for restorative justice advocates and practitioners that enables them to work effectively, responsively, and responsibly with the victim community.
- Maintain a high profile in deliberations of programs that affect victims. Participate in efforts to promote state-wide and national dialogue about responsive justice approaches to the harms and obligations that flow from crime, as well as local listening initiatives.
- Continually assess, document, and articulate the concerns and needs of victims. Advocate for what victims want, even in new and uncomfortable areas.
- Become more vocal and involved in defining the community role in justice (specifically, the community role in restorative justice), careful to differentiate between what individual victims need, and the larger context of societal harms and needs.

To reiterate, while these items are nominally assigned to either the restorative justice or victim communities of interest and practice, they are nonetheless highly interdependent. At the end of the day, the commonality of this multifaceted agenda is most likely to produce the desired result of effective and responsive justice for victims.

A CONCLUSION, A BEGINNING

Five broad areas or themes stood out in the deliberations as opportunities for collaboration between restorative justice advocates and practitioners, victims, victim services personnel, and victim advocates. These ideas involved considerably more discussion than the foregoing action points and proposals, and there was a clear and convincing sense of urgency and primacy to these proposals in particular.

First, participants advocated *structured community dialogue,* the purposes of which are to define terminology, identify program models and promising practices, develop appropriate evaluation criteria, and determine the bases and design of meaningful collaboration between the restorative justice and victim communities. In essence, this action step involves the logical extension of the *Listening Project* to a more focused effort to resolve differences and find areas of mutual concern and agreement. Additional themes or topics that might be involved in this structured community dialogue include philosophical issues pertaining to the practice of restorative justice, program viability (resources, timelines and outcomes), funding concerns and resource limitations, unintended consequences, myths and misconceptions in these communities about the other, and specific applications of restorative justice to types of crimes and types of victim needs. Such dialogue might also involve specific identification of restorative justice program initiatives that are failing victims, difficulties in assessing victim needs, and the like. Structured community dialogue might take place at several different levels, in local communities, state-wide, or nationally (for example, requiring dialogue involving victim participation in decisions about state and/or federal funding of restorative justice programs).

In response to the need for consideration (prospectively in program planning, or retrospectively in program evaluation) of program impact, a second proposal involves deliberate *program feedback.* One strategy for providing program feedback might be to make available "teams" comprised of representatives of the victim and restorative justice communities to consult with local areas, at their invitation, about restorative justice programming. In essence, team members with national exposure in their respective areas of expertise (for example, victim services programming or restorative justice program evaluation) would attempt to provide timely and cost-effective input to local initiatives. Such feedback might include assisting local programs in developing suitable options, while advocating for more universal standards of good practice. A complementary mechanism to promote "feedback" would be the development of assessment tools or instruments designed to facilitate self-evaluations.

A third proposal calls for *publication.* A consortium, representing a collaboration of both victim and restorative justice communities, might produce a series of monographs, targeted to the interests and needs of specific groups. These might include the courts and policy makers, as well as the victim community and restorative justice advocates and practitioners. Perhaps the most vital publication need is a tool for practitioners to be used in the field as a guideline to standards, best practices, and "how to" strategies for facilitating local dialogue, program planning, development and implementation, evaluation, and the like.

In response to those articulating training and education needs in virtually every aspect of the *Listening Project* deliberations, a fourth proposal is a collaborative approach to *training* that would become the norm. Experts in the respective victim and restorative justice communities would participate together in all aspects and types of training at the local, state and national levels, including various training opportunities at academies and national conferences. Collaborative training objectives would include mutually clarifying restorative justice goals and values, working through elicitive training models and techniques, exploring myths and perceptions between the victim and restorative justice communities, and the like.

Finally, consistent with the above proposals but acknowledging complexities, the *articulation of standards* was identified by participants as especially worthy of a collaborative approach. Absent such standards of practice, efforts to evaluate restorative justice programs are thought to be meaningless. Time and again, participants expressed concerns about poor and unresponsive practices, even injurious practices, and the very prevalent ambiguities that exist presently about what constitutes restorative programming. The *Listening Project* has suggested a wide range of possible standards for consideration and implementation, ranging from conditions of victim participation to qualifications of restorative justice practitioners. Efforts to collaboratively propose standards are the next step, as well as further deliberations about ensuring compliance with minimal standards, and the roles of program audits and evaluations in promoting best practice. Strategies for arriving at acceptable standards (successive rounds of structured community dialogue), the possibility of segmenting standards (identifying minimum, preferred and exemplary standards), and the importance of considering the diversity of community settings, needs of victims, and local resources in proposing relevant standards represent only some of the many aspects of this critical piece of remaining work.

The publication of a paper on the *Listening Project* should in no way suggest that these critical discussions, deliberations and debate are settled. Far from it, this paper seeks to document an important and challenging conversation that is only in a fledgling stage of *listening*. It is a conversation in need of amplification, replication, and dogged persistence, certainly in the United States, but perhaps elsewhere as well. The concluding section of this paper signals only a transition to another phase, an invitation to collaboratively and respectfully pursue mutual interests in justice for victims.

QUESTIONS FOR REVIEW AND DISCUSSION

1. What is restorative justice? How is the *Listening Project* related to restorative justice? Explain.

2. What are some criticisms of restorative justice? Are these criticisms justified? Why or why not? Explain.

3. What is meant by victim input? How much input does a victim have in restorative justice?

4. Can both individuals and communities be considered victims? Why or why not? Discuss.

5. What is meant by structured community dialogue? What are its purposes?

15

"Are the Politics of Criminal Justice Changing?"

Nicholas R. Turner and Daniel F. Wilhelm

Adapted from Nicholas R. Turner and Daniel F. Wilhelm, "Are the Politics of Criminal Justice Changing?" *Corrections Today* 64: 74–76, 2002.

Reprinted with permission of the American Correctional Association.

For those who are either deeply involved in or merely observers of American criminal justice policy, a pattern has emerged within the past two years that is unmistakable. Had someone predicted it at the close of the 1990s, the forecast would have strained credulity. After two decades of an unabated race to implement tough-on-crime policies (mandatory minimums, three strikes and truth-in-sentencing legislation), sentencing and correctional initiatives in 2001 and 2002 have taken on a decidedly different cast. Across the country, state legislatures have repealed mandatory minimums, reduced sentences and expanded treatment options on an unprecedented scale.

RECENT POLICY INITIATIVES

In 2001 and 2002, 15 states took legislative or administrative action to ameliorate the effects of stringent sentencing laws. Of these, Connecticut, Indiana and North Dakota repealed mandatory minimum sentences relating to some nonviolent offenses. Mississippi pared back truth-in-sentencing requirements and joined Louisiana, Texas and Virginia in expanding the number of inmates eligible for early release and loosening release rates. Iowa granted judges greater discretion in sentencing certain felony offenders. Alabama and New Mexico eased habitual offender laws. Wisconsin passed a law allowing some successfully rehabilitated offenders to petition a court, with the prosecution's consent, to reduce their sentences. And Hawaii, Idaho, Oregon and Washington enhanced treatment options for nonviolent drug offenders.

Louisiana provided one of the most interesting examples. The state faced skyrocketing prison populations and corrections spending since the early 1990s. From 1995 to 2001, the state's incarcerated population jumped from 25,260 to approximately 36,000, and corrections spending rose by 45 percent from 1994 to 1999. Since 1998, Louisiana has led the nation in incarceration rates, with a rate nearly 40 percent higher than the national average. In response, last year, the state passed legislation that removed mandatory sentences for certain nonviolent offenses and cut many drug sentences in half. The former 10- to 60-year penalty for possession of 28 grams of cocaine, for example, was reduced to a sentence of five to 30 years. The Legislature also limited the application of the state's three strikes law. The changes were estimated to generate some $60 million in prison operations savings, some of which will finance drug courts and other alternatives to incarceration. After three years during which the incarceration rate grew at an average rate of 43 per 100,000 citizens, in 2001—the year the legislation was enacted—Louisiana's rate dropped from 801 to 800.

Hawaii's elected officials have pursued a different approach to reform. Taking a lesson from California voters, who passed a treatment in lieu of incarceration referendum at the end of 2000, Hawaii passed legislation this year mandating drug treatment for nonviolent drug possessors. The law states that "Hawaii's criminal justice system requires a major shift in philosophy to address the needs of drug offenders by requiring nonviolent drug possession offenders to participate in community-based supervision and treatment, instead of incarceration."

The law, which became effective July 1, requires that any first-time offender convicted of possession or use of a controlled substance who does not have a prior conviction for a violent felony in the past five years be sentenced to probation to undergo drug treatment. Treatment is broadly defined to include any drug or substance abuse services provided outside a correctional facility. If an offender fails to complete treatment and is unamenable to further treatment, he or she may be returned to court and subject to the sentences otherwise applicable to the offense. The statute also provides that parole and probation are not to be revoked for first violations involving possession or use of controlled substances. The state has allocated $2.2 million for treatment expansion to serve some 200 offenders initially eligible under the law, although observers agree that more funding will be necessary.

FACTORS LEADING TO POLICY CHANGES

There are three factors that seem to be behind the changing criminal justice landscape in statehouses across the country. First, the widespread and uniform drop in crime from 1994 through 2000 has lessened the expectation that policy-makers must address public safety concerns in the ways they did in the 1980s and 1990s. Second, and related, public perceptions about crime, safety and policy responses have shifted dramatically. Finally, the acute budget crisis this past year and next has put pressure on government officials to look for savings and to be smarter about spending.

Decrease in Crime.   This decline is reflected in both violent crimes and property crimes. From 1973 to the early 1990s, violent crime rates fluctuated in the United States. But between 1993 and 2000, the rate of all violent crimes and property offenses measured by the

Bureau of Justice Statistics fell drastically. Violent crimes decreased by 44.1 percent. Homicides, not included in the previous figure, dropped by 61 percent. Property crimes declined by 44.2 percent. These reductions are probably partially responsible for changing public attitudes toward crime and incarceration.

Changing Public Attitudes.   Americans are not as concerned about crime as they were several years ago. A 1994 survey by the Pew Research Center for the People and Press showed that 29 percent of respondents thought that crime was the most important problem facing their communities. By 2001, only 12 percent gave the same answer. Similarly, a 1994 Harris poll found that 37 percent of respondents considered crime and violence to be among the most important issues for the government to address. In 2000, that figure had dropped to 11 percent.

Public attitudes about incarceration are changing as well. A recent opinion poll by Peter D. Hart Research Associates showed that the public is questioning whether harsh prison sentences are the best way to punish nonviolent offenders. In 1994, 48 percent of Americans surveyed said that they favored addressing the underlying causes of crime, while 42 percent preferred deterrence through stricter sentencing. The Hart poll, conducted late last year, found a substantial change in public opinion, with 65 percent of respondents preferring to address root causes of crime and only 32 percent opting for harsher sentencing. The survey specifically found a change in attitudes toward mandatory sentencing. In 1995, a 55 percent majority of those surveyed said that mandatory sentences were a good idea, while 38 percent said that judges should be able to determine a defendant's appropriate sentence. The 2001 Hart report found those numbers reversed: Only 38 percent responded that mandatory sentences were a good idea, while a plurality of 45 percent said they preferred judicial discretion.

The Hart survey also documents acceptance of alternatives to incarceration for nonviolent drug offenders. With regard to simple drug possessors, 76 percent of the survey's 1,056 national telephone respondents said that they favored "supervised mandatory drug treatment and community service rather than incarceration." Seventy-one percent were in favor of applying the same treatment-based approach to small-scale drug dealers.

The Hart data have been corroborated by a public referendum in California. In November 2000, 61 percent of the state's voters approved Proposition 36, which mandates treatment instead of incarceration for certain nonviolent drug offenders. The California Legislature has predicted that implementing the proposition will save at least $100 million to $150 million per year in prison costs and will avoid prison construction costs of $400 million to $450 million. Heartened by this success, the Campaign for New Drug Policies, a political advocacy group, is targeting Ohio (and until recently, Florida and Michigan) for similar ballot initiatives this year.

Fiscal Pressures.   Critics of the tough on crime direction of sentencing reform of the 1980s and 1990s long argued that spendthrift lawmakers driven by political gain and fear of appearing "soft" ignored the fiscal ramifications of new policy. Tough-on-crime advocates asserted that no price was too high for initiatives that would protect public safety. There is little debate about who won the argument: During the past two decades of the 20th century, America's incarcerated population grew more than 281 percent, finally approaching 2 million, while expenditures for state and local corrections increased 601 percent, according to the Bureau of Justice Statistics.

Those same calls for fiscal probity that fell on deaf ears during times of economic expansion, rainy day funds and ballooning revenues now carry more weight in a dramatically new environment. In April, 43 states had reported budget gaps due to either lower than expected revenues or spending overruns. The aggregate state budget shortfall was $27.3 billion. By June, the aggregate state budget shortfall rose to $37.2 billion. Aggregate state balances—a combination of general-fund ending balances and rainy day fund balances—were down in 37 states. Remarkably, 26 states collected less revenue in fiscal year 2002 than in 2001. Spending cuts had been considered or implemented in 40 states. The prognosis for 2003 looks worse. The National Conference of State Legislatures estimates that the fiscal year 2003 aggregate budget shortfall will be at least $58 billion, with 13 states reporting budget gaps exceeding 10 percent of their total state budgets.

Perhaps nowhere was the impact of the fiscal crisis more plainly stated than in Louisiana. As state Rep. Danny Martiny (R), chairman of the House Criminal Justice Committee, explained to the media after reform legislation passed, "[T]he people expect us to be tough on crime and they expect us to lock everybody up and throw away the key. And that's great as long as you've got a jail and you've got the finances. But we've come to a point where we just can't afford to keep doing it." State Sen. Charles Jones (D), the architect of the legislation, told reporters that Louisiana had "lost control of the prison population," adding, "We cannot continue to spend $600 million on prisons," according to the Associated Press.

IS THE POLICY SHIFT A TREND OR AN ABERRATION?

That 15 states in two years enacted policies to mitigate the effects of previous tough on crime initiatives is noteworthy. The more interesting question, however, is whether this is the extent of the reform or there is more to come. Certainly, advocacy groups, from the Sentencing Project to the Drug Policy Alliance (backers of Proposition 36 and similar drug policy reforms) are hopeful that the constellation of forces motivating change continues to impact the political process.

From Alabama to Wisconsin, and Idaho to Nebraska, government leaders have supported nascent efforts to examine current sentencing structures and to see if their states can be not just tough, but in the words of Alabama Attorney General Bill Pryor, as stated in the *Birmingham News,* both "tough and smart" when it comes to sentencing. Whether government leaders capture the moment and succeed in this ambition will depend largely on their ability to deal with three challenges.

The era of dropping crime rates may be coming to an end. According to the FBI's Uniform Crime Reporting program (crime reported to the police), crime rose by 2 percent in 2001 and 2000 levels, with the most pronounced increases occurring in the West and in property crimes. BJS' *National Crime Victimization Survey* states that crime rates are at their lowest level since the survey was started in 1973. In 2001, the survey indicated that violent crime dropped 10 percent and property crime, 6 percent. The important thing to remember, regardless of which indicator is followed, is that the unprecedented reduction in crime will not last forever. When it begins to rise in a sustained way, will the public begin to feel vulnerable once again and become less tolerant?

Solving an acute fiscal problem with long-term solutions is difficult. Changing sentencing laws can save money in the long term by affecting admissions flows and lengths of stay, if that is the desired outcome. However, unless the change in policy is dramatic, savings may not be substantial immediately. For legislators and executives confronting today's deficits and shortfalls, the prevailing interest is often saving money today. This makes it difficult to focus on policy solutions that—while they make sense—do not bring immediate relief.

A shift in the politics of criminal justice does not mean that politics as we know it has dropped out of the equation. Across the country, elected officials remain keenly sensitive to the accusation that they are taking any steps—including engaging in any reforms—that could be interpreted as, or portrayed by political opponents as, soft on crime. For recent confirmation that the charge still packs a wallop, especially in primary campaigns in which a political party's more orthodox members turn out, one need only look to Kansas. This past fall, in the state's Republican primary for attorney general, state Sen. David Adkins (R) was repeatedly attacked by his opponent for support of the 2000 legislation designed to reduce the flow of technical probation and post-release supervision violators into the state's correctional facilities. In 2000, technical violators accounted for more than 71 percent of new admissions to Kansas' prisons and the system was facing a looming corrections population and budget crisis. The legislation reduced the periods of supervision for certain low-level drug and property offenders, instituted mandatory graduated sanctions for probation violators and identified a target population of offenders for community corrections. It helped to forestall successfully, at least temporarily, the need to construct and operate a new prison in Kansas. Adkins, by the way, lost the primary.

The challenges are indeed daunting. And the question remains whether additional states will be able to leverage correctional and budgetary crises to explore reform or whether the opportunity for change ebbs with each uptick in crime, every demand for an instant solution and each successful political characterization of reform as a threat to public safety.

QUESTIONS FOR REVIEW AND DISCUSSION

1. What are three factors that indicate changing criminal justice policy toward punishing offenders? Discuss each.

2. Have public attitudes toward punishment and particular types of offenders changed in recent years to influence legislators and the need for change? Why or why not? Explain.

3. Do Americans seem as concerned about crime today as they did during the 1990s? Why or why not?

4. What evidence suggests greater public acceptance of community programs that are designed to promote offender reintegration and reentry?

5. Though the crime rate during the early 2000s has declined, do officials believe this trend will continue in future years? Why or why not? Explain.

PART IV

Corrections and Crime Prevention

The role of corrections in crime prevention is often either unrecognized or understated. Corrections is often an abstraction, something lurking in the background, largely because citizens are not often aware of the presence or location of jails and prisons in their communities, and usually do not know which persons among them are under probation or parole supervision. But the impact of both institutional and community corrections on crime prevention and control is extremely important. This part is divided into two logical subparts: institutional corrections and community corrections. Institutional corrections encompass jails and prisons, and the articles included focus upon inmates and initiatives by corrections officials and others to address their needs in ways that will facilitate their rehabilitation and eventual reintegration back into society. The community corrections articles focus on probationers and parolees. These articles pertain to what probation and parole agencies do to supervise these offenders and assist them in becoming productive citizens in their communities.

The opening essay by George Parks and his associates examines an experimental meditation project that was established and operated at the North Rehabilitation Facility in King County, Washington, north of Seattle. Described is the meditation course offered by local volunteers, who are drawn from the educational community. Inmates are taught a new code of moral conduct and receive practical training to develop their minds through meditation. The 10-day meditation course is described and its consequences for inmate recidivism are discussed. The costs of operating the program compared with its benefits are assessed.

One highly correlated variable with criminal conduct is substance abuse. Many persons entering prisons and jails have substance abuse problems. William Burdon and his associates describe various initiatives attempted in different states, such as California, to provide therapeutic communities for convicted substance abusers. Conventional incarceration methods do not seem to be effective at deterring drug-dependent offenders from recidivating. During the past few decades, greater attention has been given to offender treatments rather than punishments through the use of therapeutic communities. This concept is defined and discussed. Various agencies and community organizations are involved in substance abuse treatment programs, and the viability of the therapeutic community is greatly dependent upon cooperation from these multiple sources for successful offender treatment. The implications for offender rehabilitation and possible recidivism are described.

Another concomitant of criminal activity is a lack of education. Many criminals are high school dropouts or have unsuccessful educational experiences. Sharon Abel describes an adult basic/secondary educational program in a Wisconsin detention center. Her essay details the efforts of educators in Sheboygan County, Wisconsin, to provide jail inmates with basic educational skills to assist them in reintegrating into society. Improving their educational level does much to make them more marketable to employers, and this furthers their reintegrative potential. Their recidivism is therefore minimized as one result.

Over two-thirds of all offenders under some form of correctional supervision are supervised by probation and parole agencies. In 2005, over 6 million offenders were free in their communities under varying degrees of supervision by probation or parole officers. For parolees, the matter of reentry is troublesome. Kristofer Bucklen, Gary Zajac, and Kathleen Gnall discuss several problems parolees experience that eventually lead to the revocation of their parole programs. This Canadian study is significant because it focuses upon parole violators and the nature of offending that led to the revocation of their parole. Several types of parole violators are described, and different parolee needs are depicted. Several solutions for assisting parole violators are described. David Allender also examines the problem of offender reentry, this time from the perspective of U.S. parolees. Allender describes Project RIO (Reintegration of Offenders), which consists of a multistage helping program to provide vocational/educational training, life skills, medical care, and other forms of assistance, both psychological and social, to parolees. Allender also discusses the role of police and their collaboration with probation and parole agencies in fostering a rehabilitative and reintegrative milieu for offenders.

Melissa Hook and Anne Seymour address the matter of prisoner reentry as well, although their focus is upon community safety. There is a delicate balance between the offender need for a proper rehabilitative environment within the community and public safety needs. Hook and Seymour discuss prisoner reentry in the context of community involvement in the reentry process. Their essay tracks offenders and victims from a crime's commission through sentencing, incarceration, and eventual release through parole. They discuss the importance of community volunteers in offender reintegration as well as victim input through victim impact statements. Several solutions for enhancing offender reentry in ways that promote offender rehabilitation while simultaneously ensuring public safety and welfare are discussed.

One of the problems with offender reentry is both probationer and parolee resistance to assistance from their supervising agencies. Those most in need of assistance often reject it. Thus, rehabilitative and reintegrative efforts of various agencies are frustrated by the offender-clients themselves. William Elliott's essay addresses this issue and examines various sources of offender resistance to agency assistance. One of the most resisted forms of assistance is offender counseling. Elliott describes this resistance and offers several reasons for why it occurs. He then provides several practical solutions for overcoming offender resistance to counseling. One method he describes is reversal of responsibility. Also discussed are redirection and reframing. These "3R's," therefore, are regarded as potential strategies counselors may use to overcome offender resistance to counseling assistance.

16

"The University of Washington Vipassana Meditation Research Project at the North Rehabilitation Facility"

George A. Parks, G. Alan Marlatt, Sarah W. Bowen,
Tiara M. Dillworth, Katie Witkiewitz, Mary Larimer, Arthur Blume,
Tracy L. Simpson, Heather Lonczak, Laura Marie MacPherson,
David Murphy, and Lucia Meijer

Adapted from George A. Parks et al., "The University of Washington Vipassana Meditation Research Project." *American Jails* 17: 13–17, 2003.

Reprinted by permission of the American Jail Association.

In November 1997, the King County North Rehabilitation Facility (NRF) cautiously opened its doors to a meditation program for inmates. NRF, located just north of Seattle, Washington, was already committed to a rich menu of offender change programs and services. Most of the 272 "long-term" inmates at NRF were recidivists characterized by significant involvement with alcohol and other drugs, and often, with one or more co-occurring mental disorders as well.

Today, meditation often has esoteric or "new age" connotations, but the meditation course initiated at NRF, Vipassana meditation, is not a religious or mystical practice, not a relaxation technique, or an escape from reality. Vipassana meditation, as taught by instructor S.N. Goenka and assistant teachers under his direction, is a systematic process of mental training and ethical conduct in which sustained self-observation leads to increased awareness, self-control, and inner balance (Hart, 1987).

The Vipassana meditation course is offered free of charge by well-qualified volunteer teachers and course assistants in communities all over North America and throughout the world. To be successful in a correctional context, it takes a serious commitment from both the inmate and the penal institution. The Vipassana meditation course requires ten continuous days of intensive meditation training in a self-contained area segregated from the main jail population in which inmates and volunteer teachers observe a rigorous schedule of eleven hours per day of meditation practice and a code of moral conduct, and inmates are taught a method of mind training they can practice the rest of their lives.

After considerable planning and preparation, Vipassana meditation courses were held at NRF every three to four months from November 1997 through August 2002 using multipurpose program space. In total, 20 courses were conducted at the facility. Total start-up costs were minimal, and the largest ongoing expense was for additional hours of security coverage for the ten-day period of the course. The Vipassana meditation courses at NRF were successfully implemented due to model collaboration between security, program, and food services personnel. A vegetarian menu for courses was developed that required no additional staffing to prepare and serve. Program classroom and office space was modified for rapid conversion to residential use by meditating inmates. Procedures for course set-up (security clearing and training volunteers, notifying health services and classification units, risk management protocols, inmate orientation, etc.) became routine over time.

In order to evaluate the outcome of the Vipassana program on post-release criminal behavior, the NRF Programs Manager completed the Vipassana Recidivism Study (Murphy, 2002) which included data collected from courses one through eight. The study consisted of a two-year criminal history preprogram review and a two-year recidivism postprogram review. The sample size of Vipassana course completers for this study was small (n=75), and NRF did not have the resources to review recidivism data outside King County. Nonetheless, this study provided valuable baseline information that led to the awarding of a two-year research grant from the National Institutes of Health to the University of Washington to study the effects of the Vipassana meditation program at NRF on alcohol and drug relapse and recidivism.

Final outcome results from the recidivism study (Murphy, 2002) revealed that approximately half (56 percent) of the inmates completing a Vipassana course at NRF recidivated as measured by returning to King County Jail (KCJ) custody within two years, compared with a 75 percent rate of recidivism in a NRF General Population Study (Murphy, 2000; n=437). Moreover, the average number of bookings for Vipassana course completers declined from 2.9 preprogram to 1.5 postprogram. Fifty-four percent of women who completed the course returned to KCJ, as compared to 57 percent of men. This is remarkable given that the criminal histories and presenting problems were more severe for women than men admitted to NRF.

Using the encouraging results from NRF Vipassana Recidivism Study (Murphy, 2002) and their experience studying meditation, alcohol problems, and criminal conduct (Marlatt and Kristeller, 1998; Parks and Marlatt 1999), a team of researchers at the University of Washington (G. Alan Marlatt, Ph.D., principal investigator) received funding in October of 1999 to conduct a two-year study on the effects of the Vipassana meditation course at NRF on alcohol and drug relapse, psychosocial functioning, and recidivism.

The University of Washington (UW)-NRF Vipassana Research Project was funded by the National Institute on Alcohol Abuse and Alcoholism (under the National Institute of Health), in association with the Fetzer Foundation of Kalamazoo, Michigan. From the start, the UW-NRF Vipassana Research Project involved close collaboration among University of Washington researchers, North Rehabilitation Facility staff, the Vipassana community, and the NRF residents who volunteered their time to take part in the study.

The UW research team began collecting data before the men's course held in January 2000 and continued through the last Vipassana course held at NRF, a women's course completed in August 2002. In total, nine courses were included in the research study, five men's courses and four women's courses. The research was designed to systematically compare Treatment as Usual (TAU) at NRF with Treatment as Usual plus taking the Vipassana meditation course (TAU+V). TAU included a rich array of rehabilitation programs, such as chemical dependency treatment, alcohol and other drug education, mental health services, cognitive-behavioral programs, adult basic education and GED testing, acupuncture, housing case management, and vocational programs.

For research design and ethical reasons, a randomized clinical trial (with a no-treatment control group) was not possible, so the study used a quasi-experimental design in which Vipassana meditation course completers were compared as a group to all NRF residents who did not take the course, but who completed the same precourse and postcourse assessments. When the 3- and 6-month follow-up assessments are collected, the Vipassana meditation course completers will be matched to those NRF residents most similar to them who resided at the jail at the same time, but who did not take the Vipassana course. These case-matched pairs will provide comparative outcome data for the final research report. Data collection for the project is ongoing and this article a series of statistical analyses (analysis of variance or ANOVA) were used to determine differences between the Vipassana meditation course completers (TAU+V) and the treatment as usual control group (TAU) on alcohol and drug use, psychosocial outcomes, and recidivism between precourse assessment and three-month follow-up. The results reported here are preliminary in several ways. First, they represent a subset of the entire NRF study sample that has completed both the precourse and three-month assessments. Additional research participants will complete questionnaires at three-month and six-month follow-up assessments before final results can be analyzed. Second, the results reported were calculated before case matching could take place. Final published results will include only Vipassana meditation course completers and their case-matched controls. Last, all dependent measures have not yet been analyzed and, therefore, reported results in this paper are partial.

Given these limitations, the following results provide support for the reports with preliminary results. Overall, the preliminary data are suggestive of a clear trend favoring the Vipassana meditation course completers, although TAU at NRF was also shown to have significant positive effects.

The data collection for the study began with a precourse assessment, occurring within one week of the beginning of each Vipassana meditation course, which asked residents about the last 90 days they lived in the community before their current incarceration. A postcourse assessment, occurring within one week after each of the nine courses ended, was completed by research participants who were still detained at NRF during that time. To complete the longitudinal study, former NRF inmates filled out two additional follow-up assessment questionnaires at three and six months after their release from NRF. They were assessed at follow-up whether they were living in the community or in jail at the time of each assessment. Research participants were paid five dollars for assessments completed while incarcerated and 30 dollars for assessments completed while residing in the community.

UW-NRF VIPASSANA RESEARCH PROJECT PRELIMINARY RESULTS

The preliminary results of the UW-NRF Vipassana Research Project reported here compare Vipassana meditation course completers (n=29) with the TAU control group (n=59) on a variety of measures at 90 days prior to incarceration and at the three-month follow-up after release into the community. Of 306 inmates who consented to participate in the study, 88 participants completed precourse, postcourse, and three-month follow-up assessments. The following analyses refer to this subsample. Statistical tests demonstrated that there were no significant differences between the TAU+V and TAU groups on drug or alcohol use, psychosocial measures, or NRF program participation at the baseline assessment.

A series of statistical analyses (analysis of variance or ANOVA) were used to determine differences between the Vipassana meditation course completers (TAU+V) and the treatment as usual control group (TAU) on alcohol and drug use, psychosocial outcomes, and recidivism between precourse assessment and three-month follow-up. The results reported here are preliminary in several ways. First, they represent a subset of the entire NRF study sample that has completed both the precourse and three-month assessments. Additional research participants will complete questionnaires at three-month and six-month follow-up assessments before final results can be analyzed. Second, the results reported were calculated before case matching could take place. Final published results will include only Vipassana meditation course completers and their case-matched controls. Last, all dependent measures have not yet been analyzed and, therefore, reported results in this paper are partial.

Given these limitations, the following results provide support for the overall positive impact at the three-month follow-up assessment for TAU at NRF, and more strongly for TAU plus the Vipassana meditation course (TAU+V). The rehabilitation programs offered at NRF had an overall positive impact in general on all inmates participating in the study. Data analyses revealed significant reductions at three-month follow-up on tobacco use, peak drinking episodes, alcohol-related problems, and weekly heroin use for both groups in the study. On the psychosocial measures, psychoticism was significantly lower in both groups.

However, several of the study's results favor the Vipassana group over the TAU group. Vipassana completers experienced fewer adverse drinking-related consequences and demonstrated greater perceived control over their drinking behavior. Together, these results suggest that the Vipassana participants were being more thoughtful about when, where, and how they were consuming alcoholic beverages. In addition, they used significantly less marijuana, crack, and powder cocaine in the three months following release. Drug abuse severity scores for the use of all illicit substances of the Vipassana meditators were also significantly lower at the three-month follow-up, reflecting not only less drug use, but less drug-related negative consequences. Since many of the offenses committed by NRF inmates were alcohol or drug related, these results may also contribute to reduced recidivism.

Regarding psychosocial measures, the levels of depression and thought suppression in the Vipassana course completers were significantly lower than in the TAU group. While not statistically significant, hostility and anxiety were also lower for the Vipassana group. Finally, Vipassana meditators scored significantly higher on their level of optimism, indicating they were more hopeful about their future.

The study found no significant differences between the groups for recidivism based on the number of days incarcerated or new charges at the three-month follow-up, although Washington State-wide arrest data have yet to be analyzed. Participants in both groups had an average of less than one recidivism event within the three-month follow-up window compared with the two-year time frame in Murphy's study (2002). Consequently, there was not enough variation in criminal conduct to detect any difference between the two groups. Statewide arrest data and recidivism at six months will be analyzed to determine if any group differences exist for the final report of the study.

Given the present trend toward increased incarceration of individuals who have problems with alcohol and substance abuse, often co-occurring with mental disorders and physical health problems, there is a growing need for the availability and implementation of effective, low cost substance abuse treatment interventions for jail-based correctional populations. Jail-based substance abuse treatment programs offer an opportunity for inmates to change long-standing habitual behavioral problems such as psychological functioning, addictive behavior, and criminal conduct.

The preliminary results of the UW-NRF Vipassana Research Project as well as the NRF Vipassana Recidivism Report (Murphy, 2002) are noteworthy because of the potential ability of a mindfulness practice, as taught in the 10-day Vipassana meditation course, to significantly impact problem behaviors such as alcohol and drug abuse which are often associated with reoffense. The preliminary results suggest that a 10-day Vipassana meditation course offered in jails or prisons could provide a relatively low cost and effective rehabilitation program for some substance abusing offenders. (Additional information regarding the research can be obtained by contacting the first author.)

NRF closed its doors after 21 years on October 31, 2002. Its deteriorated pre-WWII structures could no longer be used or replaced. Fortunately, NRF is not the only correctional facility in North America that has offered Vipassana courses. In addition to courses at the North Rehabilitation Facility, one course has been conducted in the San Francisco San Bruno facility and two were completed at the W.E. Donaldson Prison in Bessemer, Alabama. Other correctional facilities are in the planning phase.

QUESTIONS FOR DISCUSSION AND REVIEW

1. What is the Meditation Research Project? What are some of its key elements?
2. How much recidivism was observed at the NRF? What factors explained it? Discuss.
3. What are co-occurring disorders?
4. How was the successfulness of the meditation program evaluated?

17

Prison-Based Therapeutic Community Substance Abuse Programs

Implementation and Operational Issues

William M. Burdon, David Farabee, Michael L. Prendergast,
Nena P. Messina, and Jerome Cartier

Adapted from William M. Burdon, David Farabee, Michael L. Prendergast, Mena P. Messina, and Jerome Cartier, "Prison-Based Therapeutic Community Substance Abuse Programs: Implementation and Operational Issues." *Federal Probation* 66: 3–8, 2002.

Since the 1980s, attempts to break the cycle of drug use and crime have included providing treatment to substance-abusing offenders at various stages of the criminal justice system, including in prison. Although a variety of approaches to treating substance-abusing inmates have been developed, the therapeutic community (TC) is the treatment modality that has received the most attention from researchers and policy makers.

Therapeutic communities in prisons have several distinctive characteristics: (1) they present an alternative concept of inmates that is usually much more positive than prevailing beliefs; (2) their activities embody positive values, help to promote positive social relationships, and start a process of socialization that encourages a more responsible and productive way of life; (3) their staff, some of whom are recovering addicts and former inmates, provide positive role models; and (4) they provide transition from institutional to community existence, with treatment occurring just prior to release and with continuity of care in the community (Pan, Scarpitti, Inciardi, and Lockwood, 1993). Because prison environments stress security and custody, the designs of prison-based TCs are modified versions of the community-based TC model. However, the goals of prison-based TCs remain the same as community-based TCs, and they are generally designed to operate in much the same way (Inciardi, 1996; Wexler and Love, 1994).

Evaluations of prison-based TC programs that have been conducted in several states and within the federal prison system have provided empirical support for the development of these programs throughout the nation. An early study that had a substantial impact on policy was the evaluation of the "Stay'n Out" prison TC in New York (Wexler, Falkin, Lipton, and Rosenblum, 1992), which found that the TC was more effective than one treatment or other types of less intensive treatment in reducing recidivism, and that longer time in TC treatment was associated with lower recidivism rates after release to parole. The positive findings from this evaluation became the foundation for federal and state initiatives to support the expansion of prison-based TCs during the 1990s.

The Stay'n Out evaluation did not examine the impact of aftercare on outcomes by program graduates following release to parole, but more recent evaluations have assessed the provision of aftercare in connection with other prison-based TCs. These studies have provided consistent evidence that adding aftercare to prison-based TC treatment for graduates paroled into the community significantly improves clients' behavior while under parole supervision (Field, 1984, 1989; Knight, Simpson, and Hiller, 1999; Martin, Butzin, Saum, and Inciardi, 1999; Prendergast, Wellisch, and Wong, 1996; Wexler, Blackmore, and Lipton, 1991; Wexler, De Leon, Kressel, and Peters, 1999; Wexler, Melnick, Lowe, and Peters, 1999b) and thus increases the likelihood of positive outcomes (i.e., reduced recidivism and relapse to drug use).

It should be noted that most of these studies did not employ a true experimental design in which study-eligible inmates were randomly assigned to either a treatment or a non-treatment condition. Therefore, it is possible that some of the presumed effects of these programs may have been the result of self-selection bias, that is, systematic differences between inmates who opted for, and remained in, treatment and those who did not. However, a recent evaluation of treatment programs within the Federal Bureau of Prisons found that inmates who had completed treatment in one of the federal prison programs were significantly less likely to relapse to drug use or experience new arrests in the six months following release than were inmates in a comparison group, even after controlling for individual- and system-level selection factors (Pelissier et al., 2000).

THE CALIFORNIA INITIATIVE

California has more individuals under correctional supervision (i.e., prison and parole) than any other state (Bureau of Justice Statistics, 2001a,b). As of September 30, 2001, there were 161,497 inmates in California's 33 prisons (California Department of Corrections [CDC], 2001a). Of these, 45,219 (28 percent) were incarcerated for an offense involving drugs, at an unusual cost of approximately $1.2 billion (CDC, 2001b). Another 21 percent were incarcerated for a property offense, which in many cases was related to drug use (Lowe, 1995). As of September 30, 2001, there were 119,636 individuals on parole in California. Of these, 38 percent had been incarcerated for a drug offense and 26 percent had been incarcerated for a property offense (CDC, 2001a). Furthermore, according to CDC (2000), 67 percent of the individuals entering the state's prison system in 1999 were parole violators; 55.5 percent of these were returned to custody for a drug-related offense.

In response to the large number of prisoners and parolees with substance abuse problems, and in an attempt to reduce recidivism rates, the California legislature has appropriated approximately $94 million toward the expansion of prison-based substance abuse programs based on the TC model of treatment. As a result, since 1997, the number of prison-based TC beds within the California state prison system has increased from 500 in 3 programs at 3 prisons to 7,650 in 32 programs at 17 institutions. Additional expansions are planned to further increase these numbers to approximately 38 programs providing substance abuse treatment to approximately 9,000 inmates at 19 institutions (CDC, 2001c). The initiative is operated by CDC's Office of Substance Abuse Programs (OSAP). The treatment is provided by contracted treatment providers with experience in TC treatment for correctional populations.

The selection of the TC as the model of treatment for these programs was based largely on the positive results that emerged from the evaluation studies (cited above) of prison-based TCs in other parts of the country and, more specifically, the results of an evaluation of the Amity TC in San Diego, California (Wexler, 1996). Also, as a result of those evaluation findings, the California initiative includes a major aftercare component for graduates from the prison-based TC programs that provides funding for up to six months of continued treatment (residential or outpatient services) in the community following release to parole.

The TC substance abuse programs (SAPs) in the California state prison system provide between 6 and 24 months of treatment at the end of inmates' prison terms. Combined, these programs cover all levels of security classification (Minimum to Maximum) and male and female inmates. With few exceptions, participation in these programs is mandatory for inmates who have a documented history of substance use or abuse (based on a review of inmate files) and who do not meet established exclusionary criteria for entrance into a TC SAP (e.g., documented in-prison gang affiliations, being housed in a Security Housing Unit within the previous 12 months for assault or weapons possession, Immigration and Naturalization Service holds). Also, most of the TC SAPs are not fully separated from the general inmate populations of the institutions within which they are located. Outside of their designated housing unit and the 20 hours per week of programming activities in which they are required to participate, TC SAP inmates remain integrated with the general population inmates of the facility in which they are located.

Inmates who successfully parole from these prison-based TC SAPs have the option of participating in up to six months of continued treatment in the community. Unlike prison-based treatment, participation in aftercare is voluntary, and failure to enter community-based treatment in accordance with the established aftercare plan does not constitute a parole violation.

As part of the ongoing expansion of these prison-based TC SAPs, UCLA Integrated Substance Abuse Programs (ISAP) is conducting process evaluations of 17 of these programs (located in 10 institutions and totaling approximately 4,900 beds). ISAP (previously known as the Drug Abuse Research Center [DARC]) has an extensive background in corrections-based treatment research, including some of the earliest studies done on prison-based treatment of drug-involved offenders (Anglin, 1988; McGlothlin, Anglin, and Wilson, 1977; Hall, Baldwin, and Prendergast, 2001; Hser, Anglin, and Powers, 1993; Hser, Hoffman, Grella, and Anglin, 2001; Prendergast, Hall, Wellisch, and Baldwin, 1999). The main purpose of these process evaluations is to (1) document the goals and objectives of CDC's drug treatment programs and any additional goals and objectives of each provider, (2) assess the degree to which the providers are able to implement these goals and objectives in their programs, (3) determine the degree to which the provider conforms to the therapeutic community model of treatment, and (4) collect descriptive data on SAP participants. The process evaluations use data drawn from program documents; observations of programming activities; interviews with program administrators, treatment and corrections staff, and OSAP personnel; periodic focus groups with treatment staff, custody staff, and inmates assigned to each program; and standardized program assessment instruments. Client-level information is derived from the records of the in-prison treatment providers and from an intake assessment instrument administered by the providers at the time clients enter the TC SAPs.

IMPLEMENTATION AND OPERATIONAL ISSUES

The process evaluations have revealed a number of macro-level issues that are relevant to the implementation and ongoing operations of prison-based TC substance abuse treatment programs in general; that is, these issues are not unique to California. The first three issues (collaboration and communication, supportive organizational culture, sufficient resources) represent system-related issues, while the remaining four issues (screening, assessment, and referral; treatment curriculum, incentives and rewards; and coerced treatment) represent treatment-related issues. Many, if not most, states that establish or expand TC substance abuse treatment for inmates face the same, or similar, issues (Farabee et al., 1999; Harrison and Martin, 2000; Moore and Mears, 2001). Thus, these issues will be discussed in terms of their importance as key elements in developing and sustaining effective TC substance abuse treatment programs in correctional environments.

Collaboration and Communication.   Any initiative that is aimed at implementing and/or expanding substance abuse treatment in a correctional environment represents an effort to bring together two systems (i.e., corrections and treatment) that have conflicting core philosophies regarding substance use and abuse. Correctional systems view drug use as a crime. As such, their goals are based on philosophies of punishment and incarceration. The focus of a correctional system is on the crime that was committed and the sanctions to punish the offender and deter him/her from engaging in subsequent criminal activity. Treatment is secondary. On the other hand, substance abuse treatment systems view drug use as a chronic, but treatable disorder. The focus of the treatment provider is on treating the person for his/her substance abuse problem with the goal of reducing the drug use and improving the mental and physical health of the person (Prendergast and Burdon, 2001). Furthermore, the reality of the relationship between these two systems is that the treatment system operates *within* the correctional system, with the latter typically serving in the role of contractor. As such, the correctional system can be viewed as a "superordinate" system within which the "subordinate" treatment system operates.

This organizational reality, combined with the conflicting philosophies of the two systems, places constraints on what treatment providers are able to accomplish in their attempt to provide effective substance abuse treatment services to inmate populations. Most important, the goals and philosophies of the subordinate treatment system do not have as much influence as those of the superordinate correctional system. Because of this, effective and open communication and collaboration between the two become critical. Both systems need to be committed to developing and maintaining an inter-organizational "culture of disclosure" (Prendergast and Burdon, 2001). That is, they need to develop a common set of goals and they need to share system-, program-, and client-level information in an atmosphere of openness and mutual understanding and trust. However, it is ultimately incumbent upon the larger controlling superordinate system (i.e., the correctional system) to ensure the presence of an environment within which this level of communication and collaboration can occur. To the extent that this does not occur, the ability of treatment providers to operate prison-based TC SAPs as intended and to create a culture that is conducive to therapeutic change is negatively impacted.

Supportive Organizational Culture.   Developing and sustaining an environment that facilitates and supports effective communication and collaboration among treatment and correctional staff is difficult at best. Most departments of corrections are, by nature, highly bureaucratic organizations that require personnel to operate in accordance with written policy and procedure manuals and/or legislative code. This fact, combined with the underlying philosophies and objectives of correctional systems, supports and reinforces a well-developed and firmly entrenched organizational culture that emphasizes safety, security, and strict conformance to established policies and procedures. For the most part, such an organizational culture does not facilitate or support the presence of a system, such as a substance abuse treatment program, that has different philosophies and objectives. Yet, in order for substance abuse treatment programs to operate with any degree of effectiveness, there must be some degree of meaningful *integration* of the criminal justice and treatment systems. For this to occur, the organizational culture must be altered in a way that facilitates the work of treatment programs, while ensuring the continued safety and security of the inmates, staff, and public. While it is not realistic to expect that treatment programs operating within a correctional environment should be exempt from departmental and institutional policies and procedures, it is also not realistic to expect treatment programs, especially those that are designed as TC treatment programs, to operate effectively in a prison environment that is not designed for and does not support the existence and operation of such programs.

Altering an organizational culture requires time. In a correctional environment, it is also likely to require changes or additions to existing policies, procedures, and possibly even legislative penal code. Most important, however, and given the paramilitary nature of correctional systems, change must be initiated at the top of the organizational hierarchy and directed downward to line staff. Thus, the commitment and continued support of correctional management at both the departmental level (e.g., department director, deputy directors) and institutional level (e.g., wardens, deputy wardens, associate wardens) are required for treatment programs to exist and operate effectively within the prison environment.

To this end, departmental and institutional management can facilitate the successful implementation of treatment programs by issuing regular written and verbal statements of support for them. Also, efforts should be made to incorporate policies and procedures into existing departmental operations manuals and (if necessary) penal code that facilitate the ongoing operation of these programs, while ensuring the continued safety and security of staff (custody and treatment) and inmates. Over time, such efforts may result in a shift in the organizational culture to one characterized by strong support for the presence of substance abuse programs. Without this commitment and support from correctional management and the resulting change in organizational culture, treatment programs will not be able, and should not be expected, to operate at their full potential.

Sufficient Resources.   As important as open communication and collaboration and the existence of a supportive organizational culture are to the existence and effectiveness of prison-based treatment programs, the continued availability of sufficient resources (primarily financial resources) properly directed at these services is essential to ensuring treatment effectiveness. Indeed, most discussions of the elements of an integrated system of care address the issue of resources (Field, 1998; Greenley, 1992; Rose, Zweben, and Stoffel, 1999; Taxman, 1998). While departments of corrections understandably want to control costs, commitment of insufficient financial resources, especially in the form of funds for salaries, will likely prevent the recruitment and retention of experienced and qualified treatment staff, resulting in persistent staff turnover.

Paying treatment staff salaries that are competitive with the local markets from which they are recruited may not suffice. Even for individuals who have previous experience as substance abuse treatment counselors, working in a prison environment is often a far more stressful experience than they may expect. More often than not, new counselors will have little or no experience working with prisoners or in a prison setting, and many may not even be familiar with the TC model of treatment. Indeed, because of the shortage of experienced staff for prison programs, it is not unusual for the minimum requirements for entry-level counselors in prison-based treatment programs to omit requirements that they be certified to provide substance abuse treatment in a criminal justice setting, or even have any previous experience as a substance abuse treatment counselor. In most cases, these requisites are obtained after the counselors have been hired and have begun working with client populations, generally through organized training and certification courses that they are required to attend within a prescribed period of time. In addition, most (if not all) new counselors are subjected to long periods at the beginning of their employment (usually the first 2–3 months) during which they are "tested" by the inmates and struggle to establish their personal boundaries of interaction. Also, unlike previous experiences that they may have had in substance abuse treatment settings, their counseling methods and interpersonal interactions (both formal and informal) with inmates may be severely restricted and closely watched by both their supervisors and custody staff to ensure that they do not become overfamiliar with the inmates.

In short, many individuals who come to work in prison-based treatment programs are unprepared for the realities of working with inmates in a prison environment. In addition, low pay, combined with a highly stressful working environment, quickly diminish whatever altruistic motivations most counselors had when they were hired. Many of them may fail to develop appropriate boundaries of interaction with SAP participants, "burn-out" within a short period, and end up being terminated or resigning.

The difficulty treatment providers have in recruiting and (more important) retaining experienced counseling staff negatively impacts almost every aspect of a treatment program's operations. Most important, frequent staff turnover prevents inmates from developing therapeutic bonds with counselors and becoming engaged in the treatment process. Sufficient resources in the form of higher pay scales that reflect the uniqueness of working in a correctional environment, higher prerequisites for newly hired treatment staff (e.g., previous experience working with inmate populations, certification to provide counseling services in a correctional environment), and adequate administrative support for counseling staff are among the keys to minimizing staff turnover. The presence of a stable and experienced treatment staff who are properly supported administratively will, in turn, result in a more stable and consistent treatment curriculum, which will further engage clients in the treatment process.

Screening, Assessment, and Referral.   Therapeutic community treatment is the most intensive form of substance abuse treatment available. It is also the most costly to deliver. In addition, not all substance-abusing offenders are alike in terms of their characteristics or needs. As these characteristics and needs vary, so too do individuals' needs for specific types of substance abuse treatment. Simply put, not all substance-abusing offenders are in need of TC treatment. This clearly demonstrates the need for a scientifically valid and reliable method of identifying substance-abusing offenders, assessing their specific treatment needs, and matching them to an appropriate modality and intensity of treatment.

Given the bureaucratic nature of correctional systems and their philosophical foundations of punishment and incarceration, entrenched organizational cultures, and pressures to conform to existing policies and procedures, many correctional systems may opt instead to identify and assign inmates to treatment programs based on reviews of inmates' criminal files by department personnel for any history of drug use or drug-related criminal activity. Indeed, in correctional systems characterized by a less than supportive organizational culture, decisions to place inmates into treatment programs may be based less on whether they have a substance abuse problem than on other factors relating to such things as institutional management and security concerns. When this occurs, inmates who could or should be placed into these programs (i.e., those with substance abuse disorders) may be *excluded,* whereas inmates who may not be amenable to or appropriate for treatment programs may be *included* (e.g., those who have severe mental illness or are dangerous sex offenders). This, in turn, directly impacts the treatment providers' ability to provide efficient and effective treatment services to those who are most in need of them. Also, inmates with minimal substance abuse involvement may be referred to intensive TC treatment, which they may not need. The use of scientifically valid and reliable methods of screening inmates for substance abuse problems and assessing their specific needs will aid in ensuring that each inmate is referred to the proper modality and intensity of treatment. This will further enhance the effectiveness of existing programs by not populating them with inmates who do not have serious substance abuse problems or who are not amenable to treatment.

Treatment Curriculum.   "Community as method" refers to that portion of TC philosophy that calls for a full immersion of the client into a community environment and culture that is designed to change the "whole person." In correctional environments where treatment programs are not fully segregated from the general inmate population, inmates participating in the treatment curricula remain exposed to the prison subculture and its negative social and environmental forces, which may weaken or negate whatever benefits they receive during programming activities. This is especially true in the case of mandated treatment programs, where problem recognition and motivation for change among many treatment participants may be lacking, at least initially. In addition, SAP participants, most of whom have become indoctrinated into the prison subculture, with its taboos on self-disclosure and sharing of personal information, have difficulty discussing personal issues in group settings, which is a basic component of most TC treatment curricula.

To counteract the negative influence that exposure to the prison subculture has on participants in treatment, it is important that treatment curricula be structured, rigorous, and void of repetitiveness. In addition, the early phases of treatment are important because of their potential effect on a client's motivation for change and willingness to engage in the treatment process. In community-based treatment, increasing the number of individual counseling sessions during the first month of treatment has been shown to significantly improve client retention (De Leon, 1993). Clearly, given the higher proportions of involuntary clients in correctional treatment programs, the initial phase of treatment should emphasize problem recognition and willingness to change before introducing the tools to do so. Also, one-on-one counseling in the early phases of the treatment may serve as a useful tool for gradually introducing inmate participants to and engaging them in the TC treatment process, which relies more on group dynamics and community.

Incentives and Rewards in Treatment. By their nature, correctional environments enforce compliance with institutional rules and codes of conduct through negative reinforcement—the contingent delivery of punishment to individuals who violate these rules and codes of conduct. Seldom, if ever, do inmates receive positive reinforcement for engaging in pro-social behavior (i.e., complying with institutional rules and codes of conduct). Similarly, the TC model specifies disciplinary actions that should be taken in response to TC rule violations (De Leon, 2000), but says little about rewarding *specific* acts of positive behavior (e.g., punctuality, participation, timely completion of tasks). Rather, reinforcement for positive behavior takes the form of moving the client to more advanced stages of the TC program and conferring on him/her additional privileges. As such, this type of reinforcement "tends to be intermittent and, in contrast to sanctions, less specific, not immediately experienced, and based on a subjective evaluation of a client's progress in treatment" (Burdon, Roll, Prendergast, and Rawson, 2001, p. 78).

Where participation in prison-based TC treatment programs is mandated for inmates meeting established criteria, the emphasis on punishments and disincentives in the treatment process acts to compound the resentment and resistance that inmates feel and exhibit as a result of being coerced into treatment. Incentives and rewards would likely alleviate much of this resentment and resistance and may even increase motivation to participate in treatment. However, at some institutions, the ability of treatment providers to develop and implement incentive or reward systems may be limited by departmental and institutional policies and procedures that forbid the granting of special privileges, rewards, or other incentives to specific groups of inmates (e.g., those participating in a treatment program). In sum, the ability of treatment providers to implement effective systems of incentives and rewards in the treatment process may be restricted due to the priority that the penal philosophy takes over the treatment philosophy within the context of a prison-based treatment program.

Coercion alone is rarely sufficient to promote engagement in treatment. Overcoming inmates' resentment over having been mandated into treatment and their resulting resistance to participating in treatment requires that programs and institutions not only remove disincentives, but also incorporate incentives, when possible, that would serve as meaningful inducements to participating in the treatment process. Gendreau, in his 1996 review of effective correctional programs, recommended that positive reinforcers outnumber punishers by at least 4 to 1. Possible incentives for treatment participation could include such things as improved living quarters and enhanced vocational or employment opportunities, or, where allowed, early release.

Coerced Treatment. Much of the growth in criminal justice treatment (both in California and nationally) is based on the widely accepted dictum that involuntary substance abuse clients tend to do as well as, or better than, voluntary clients (Farabee, Prendergast, and Anglin, 1998; Leukefeld and Tims, 1988; Simpson and Friend, 1988). However, these studies were based on community-based treatment samples. As mentioned above, coerced participation in prison-based treatment programs breeds a high degree of resentment and resistance among many of the inmates forced into these programs. Some inmates desire to change their behavior and welcome the opportunity to participate. Other inmates may, over time, *develop* a desire to remain and participate. However, a substantial portion of the inmates coerced into treatment remain resentful, refuse to participate, and, in many cases, actively disrupt the programs and the existing community culture. Furthermore, despite their continued disruptive behavior and the negative impact that it has on providers' ability to deliver effective programming, efforts to remove these disruptive inmates from the programs in a timely fashion often prove elusive due to correctional department policies and procedures governing the movement and classification of inmates in the prison environment.

One possible strategy to overcome this resentment and resistance and to expedite the development of a TC culture would be to limit admissions during a program's first year or so to a relatively small number of inmates who volunteer for treatment. Once a treatment milieu is established, issues such as program size and the presence of involuntary inmates may prove more tractable. Also, motivation for treatment should be a consideration for prison-based treatment referral and admission. Ideally, the majority of clients referred to prison-based programs (particularly new programs) should be inmates with at least a modicum of desire to change their behavior through the assistance of a treatment program.

SUMMARY

Since prison-based TCs first appeared in the 1980s, numerous evaluations have been conducted at both the state and federal levels that have provided empirical support for the effectiveness of these programs in reducing recidivism and relapse to drug use, especially when combined with continuity of care in the community following release to parole. Other studies have focused on the so-called "black box" of treatment (i.e., the treatment process) in an effort to identify relevant factors that predict success among participants in TC treatment programs (e.g., Simpson, 2001; Simpson and Knight, 2001). However, few have focused on the system- and treatment-level process issues relating to the implementation and ongoing operations of TCs in correctional environments and how these issues impact the ability of treatment providers to effectively provide treatment services to inmate populations.

It is also important to note that most (if not all) of the issues discussed in this paper have application beyond prison-based TCs and should be considered in any initiative that seeks to implement or expand substance abuse treatment in correctional settings. In addition, although these issues may appear to address different aspects of treatment program operations, they are not mutually exclusive. Indeed, to maximize the operational effectiveness of substance abuse treatment programs in correctional environments, they should be considered in their entirety.

QUESTIONS FOR REVIEW AND DISCUSSION

1. What is a therapeutic community? How is it useful in offender treatment for substance abuse? Explain.
2. How did the UCLA Integrated Substance Abuse Programs (ISAP) conduct process evaluations of different therapeutic programs?
3. Why is it important in TC to have a supportive organizational culture?
4. What is meant by the "community as method"?
5. How important is it when dealing with prisoners with substance abuse problems to keep them segregated from the general prison population? Discuss.
6. How is the successfulness of TC often measured?

18

"Adult Basic/Secondary Education Program for the Incarcerated in Sheboygan County, Wisconsin"

Sharon Abel

Adapted from Sharon Abel, "Adult Basic/Secondary Education Program for the Incarcerated in Sheboygan County, Wisconsin." *American Jails* 14: 57–61, 2001.

Reprinted with permission from the American Jail Association.

On any given day the diversity in my Sheboygan County Detention Center classroom includes but is not limited to diversity of age, gender, physical and cognitive ability, race, ethnicity, criminal record, socioeconomic status and background, employment status and history, religion, gang involvement, alcohol/drug use, and sexual orientation. Differences in color and language are more obvious but no less obtrusive or distracting to the learning process than a student whispering to the teacher, "That guy over there has Hepatitis B. Can I get it from him if he sneezes on my keyboard or coughs in my direction?" The types of differences and the ranges within types are increasing (Hickman, 1998, p. 56). The jail population reflects the "New Faces on Main Street" (Wisconsin Public Television video).

The need to keep the peace among people who outside of jail likely would avoid communicating altogether tends to be more challenging than the whole idea of working with criminal offenders. Criminal records cannot be ignored; but too much focus on preliminary hearings, alternatives to revocations, and sentencings does distract from studying for High School Equivalency Diplomas and preparing for college level courses. The irresponsible behaviors (such as laziness and procrastination) of criminal-thinking individuals; the victim stance taken by most inmates; and the egocentrism of most people, incarcerated or otherwise, consistently drain me as I work to motivate the unmotivated, marginally motivated, and those with less than noble motives. Keeping all that in mind, looking back at my nine years of teaching experience in the Sheboygan County Jail/Detention Center, the most intense moments have resulted from tension and hostilities between inmates/students.

The similarities among my students are generally not tendencies that will contribute positively to a teaching/learning environment. Some of the traits they are likely to share are history of failure; nonreflective, impulsive behavior; desire for immediate results; external locus of control; egocentrism; socially inappropriate life experiences; functionally illiterate; absence of or misplaced self-esteem; high and multidrug usage; criminal thinking (Montross and Montross, 1997, pp. 179–185); cognitive deficits; defensive or negative attitude; difficulty controlling anger (Gathright, 1999, p. 143); and learning disabilities (Steurer, 2000).

Reflecting on my challenge, I approached this research project looking for *easy-to-apply strategies* on how I, the instructor, can better meet the needs of the diverse populations and individuals in the Adult Basic/Secondary Education Program for the Incarcerated in Sheboygan County, Wisconsin.

SETTING THE TONE FOR SUCCESS

"Enthusiastic, motivated and prepared teachers equal student success and job satisfaction" (Nolen, 1999, p. 110). To repeatedly return to a negative, high-stress environment like a jail (Moynahan, 1999) with a positive attitude is not an easy task to muster. To remain sincerely positive and enthusiastic when surrounded by negativism, cynicism, and sarcasm of inmates, officers, administrators, support staff, attorneys, agents, and the like is even more difficult to accomplish. The saving grace here is, from my experience, no matter how negative the environment in the cellblocks or pods or even the hallways en route to the educational programming room, in the end the teacher sets the tone for the jail classroom. In order for students' internal negative attitudes to pervade the learning environment, verbalization and confirmation in a gripe session need to occur. As long as damaging cynical and sarcastic comments are isolated, kept to a minimum, and immediately called on by the instructor or fellow students, the overall teaching/learning environment has a good chance of remaining vital as long as the instructor has set a positive tone.

The instructor's personal tone can be enhanced by the use of music. Music "primes the brain's neural pathways" (Rosebrough, 1999, p. 2). Plastering the walls with posters filled with motivating phrases is another idea. Push the positives and reduce the negatives in the classroom. Eliminate embarrassment, unrealistic deadlines, sarcasm, and excuses. "Brain research tells us that fear and frustration can lead to a hopelessness in the learner that actually causes the brain to downshift in a physiological sense" (Rosebrough, 1999, p. 3). Instructors need to realize that what is challenging to one student is frustrating to another; they can improve the classroom tone by learning to be sensitive to students as individuals. "To teach for success, you need to (evaluate) ask tough questions about your own teaching and you need to (test) ask tough questions that reveal how well your students can perform" (Shrawder, 1999, p. 1).

STARTING SUCCESSFULLY

Many inmates lack formal education and are stymied by the forms they are required to fill out (Gunn, 1999, p. 76) during intake. Some have trouble spelling their own names correctly. This is a critical juncture in creating a healthy rapport between instructor and student. Depending upon the individual student's receptiveness to outside assistance, the instructor might choose at this time to suggest a peer tutor from among the group. The teacher benefits from being aware of who has befriended whom when suggesting a peer tutor. This may or may not be the time to attempt a connection between those who have self-segregated. To avoid conflicts and bruised egos, the teacher needs to be acutely sensitive to the relationships—positive, negative, and apathetic—in the classroom and back in the cellblocks or pods. A formal peer tutoring program is not essential; however, it can be instrumental in making instruction more effective for students, and inmate aides are offered a rare status in a jail setting (Steurer, 2000, p. 167).

Byron Kuster explains the importance of reducing the fear of the unknown and the fear of failure right away in the beginning with a thorough orientation. He suggests the following methods be part of the adult correctional education orientation to increase educational effectiveness:

- Compel each student to determine his/her education and employment goals and why accomplishing those goals is personally important.
- Collaborate with each student to determine realistic goals for the duration of his/her length of stay in the county facilities.
- Collaboratively break down the goals into manageable weekly and daily goals, so that each student can be held accountable for his/her productivity (1998 June, pp. 67–71).

The key to Mr. Kuster's suggestions is the personalization. Even within the productive chaos of a lab-style classroom, teacher and student experience important one-on-one time.

To bring unity, even if only temporary, to a diverse group, a shared task or focus can help in building bridges. To gather everyone together, the teacher could get the attention of each individual and facilitate a group activity. Morton H. Kaplan of Columbia College, Chicago, states: "One thing I know for sure—we lose an audience . . . any audience . . . in the first five to ten minutes of a presentation. Sometimes it takes less than that" (1999 April, p. 2). The first five minutes are critical; they serve as the sales pitch for the balance of the lesson. Mr. Kaplan suggests the following strategies for "building momentum" and captivating an audience:

- Use riddles to mystify them.
- Play communication games.
- Give fun quizzes.
- Ask questions that require thought to answer.
- Make them laugh.
- Lead them into ethical discussions.

- Tell success stories of former students.
- Expect creativity.

INSTRUCTIONAL STRATEGIES FOR DIVERSE POPULATIONS AND INDIVIDUALS

Counselors and probation/parole agents can be great resources, mentors, or both for new correctional educators. Some suggestions offered by counselors on how to keep groups on track are the following:

- Structure everything. Have an agenda.
- Lay down certain rules which must be followed (such as no violence or threats of violence).
- Teach participants how to negotiate for what they want done in the group.
- Confront participants immediately if they are out of line.
- In all situations challenge them to focus on their own responsibility. "That's where they can make a positive difference" (White, 1998, p. 20).

Humor can be an element of effective communication in the classroom. It can help arouse student interest, thus motivating students and boosting attention and comprehension. However, one should remember, humor should be part of instruction "only when students feel liked by their teacher and safe in their learning environment." Trust should precede humor. Otherwise, any benefits that may be derived through humor are not worth the risks (Civikly-Powell, 1999, pp. 5–8).

To establish a high-trust environment the instructor can employ these skills:

- Demonstrate good listening habits.
- Serve as a role model.
- Be an initiator.
- Be open to feedback.
- Be willing to make personal changes.
- Deal with fears of public speaking and encourage others to speak.
- Facilitate, rather than direct, discussions (Cascio, 2000b, p. 43).

Correctional educators need to be creative (Caramanis, 1999). The instructor's creativity with lesson plans is essential to bring the diversified group together. An instructor might facilitate a group essay by asking his/her students to dictate responses to "A mother is . . . A father is . . . A family is . . . A neighbor is . . . A city is . . . " (Wright, 1965, p. 115). Another teacher might solicit verbal, written, or both responses to John F. Kennedy's Inaugural Address (1961 January 20): ". . . the torch has been passed to a new generation of Americans . . . unwilling to witness or permit the slow undoing of those human rights to which this nation has always been committed. . . ." He/she might then ask the students to apply the speech to their generation(s). More than likely at least one or two of the generations represented in the class were born after Kennedy's inauguration, and in the jail setting it is likely at least one if not two generations represented in the class were born before his inauguration. Such topics can promote critical thinking and discussion. The group may find itself dividing or bonding across lines of age rather than lines of race.

DELIVERY METHODS

Controversy continues regarding tutorial or lab-style instruction versus group instruction (Rosica and Wall, 1997, pp. 187–190). Frederic M. Muse in volume 49 of the *Journal of Correctional Education* states: "Individualized instruction represents the preferred method of instruction for at-risk, troubled, and underachieving youth" (p. 78). Since some of my students are juveniles-adjudicated-as-adults and many of my adult students have the maturity level of children, Mr. Muse's opinion applies to my circumstances. A combination of approaches is most likely best in order to serve all learning styles.

HELP IS AVAILABLE

Correctional educators who enjoy their work can serve as a cheerleading squad for a lonely jail teacher. Dennis Zaro, prerelease teacher at a California State prison, writes:

> You can tell the character of a person by the manner they treat those who have no impact on their destiny. Truly inspired, dedicated, effective correctional educators are magnanimous human beings. While they work within the confines of bureaucratic institutions whose primary consideration is "safety and security," they strive to provide educational opportunities for students whose achievements have little or no relevance to the objectives of the institution. Correctional educators work within a "school" overshadowed by a larger institution, which does not prioritize student learning. (2000 March, p. 191)

Mr. Zaro suggests watching for future articles in *The Journal of Correctional Education* that will focus on teaching strategies for immediate implementation, strategies that do not require purchase orders or large-scale program adoption (2000 March, p. 193).

The Civil Rights Act of 1964 created the Community Relations Service (CRS) under the U.S. Department of Justice. CRS staff are available to assist state and local government officials and criminal justice staff to reduce problems based on discrimination. CRS offers free training on issues such as racial conflicts, disparity in treatment, and cultural competency (Kerla, 1998, p. 173).

Conflict Resolution Training is available through the American Correctional Association. Such training focuses on "how to prevent and effectively resolve conflicts, which can destroy morale, impede teamwork and decrease effectiveness" (Shuford and Spencer, 1999, p. 104).

QUESTIONS FOR REVIEW AND DISCUSSION

1. What are some difficulties in establishing learning programs for inmates in detention centers?
2. What are some teaching strategies for encouraging law-abiding behavior?
3. What are some problems with the diversity of inmates in jails?
4. What is the importance of establishing trust while attempting to teach vocational/educational skills to jail inmates? Discuss.

19

"Understanding and Responding to the Needs of Parole Violators"

Kristofer Bret Bucklen, Gary Zajac, and Kathleen Gnall

Adapted from Kristofer Bret Bucklen, Gary Zajac, and Kathleen Gnall, "Understanding and Responding to the Needs of Parole Violators." *Corrections Today* 66: 84–87, 105, 2004.

Reprinted by permission of the American Correctional Association.

According to national statistics, the number of offenders reincarcerated for violating parole increased more than sevenfold during the past two decades (Travis and Lawrence, 2002).

In 1980, state prisons admitted approximately 27,000 parole violators, representing 17 percent of total prison admissions. By 2000, state prisons admitted approximately 200,000 parole violators annually, representing 35 percent of total prison admissions. During this same period, new court commitments as a percentage of admissions declined from 81 percent to 60 percent. In addition, the growth in parole violator admissions during the past two decades was so sharp that such admissions to state prisons in 2000 approximates the total number of offenders admitted to state prisons in 1980.

The Bureau of Justice Statistics estimates that parolees are currently responsible for between 10 percent and 12 percent of all arrests for serious crimes in the United States (Petersilia, 2003).

Further, in 1999, 22 percent of those in state prisons reported being on parole at the time they committed the crime that landed them in prison. It is now well-documented that the high parole revocation rate is one of the major contributing factors to the growing U.S. prison population (Travis and Lawrence, 2002).

In her recent book, *When Prisoners Come Home*, Joan Petersilia notes that the United States spends a great deal of money to incarcerate nearly 300,000 parole violators nationwide and that leaving parolees unattended and without services is not only bad policy, but also dangerous, leaving many victims in its wake (Petersilia, 2003).

The problem, according to researchers at the Urban Institute, however, is that "we do not know much about the underlying behavior of parole violators" (Travis and Lawrence, 2002).

In Pennsylvania, parole violator admissions have increased by 55 percent during the past six years. To put it in perspective, the growth rate of Pennsylvania's initial court commitments during the past six years was only 37 percent. This 55 percent increase in parole violator admissions is primarily due to a 68 percent increase in technical parole violator admissions. Altogether, one-third of the Pennsylvania Department of Corrections' total admissions are now a result of parole violations.

THE PAROLE VIOLATOR SURVEY

In response to concerns that parole violators are becoming a driving force behind increasing prison admissions, the Pennsylvania DOC recently conducted a needs assessment of its parole violator population. The primary objective of the assessment was to explore what was happening in inmates' lives while they were out on parole that may have contributed to their return to prison. In exploring the needs of parole violators, the DOC placed primary emphasis on examining the dynamic psychological antecedents of recidivism, as interpreted through the self-reported experiences of parole violators. This study builds on a similar Canadian study developed in the late 1990s. The Canadian authors best summarize the utility of such a needs assessment in stating that "previous work has shown that a variety of measures can predict recidivism but does little to elucidate what actually happens when an experienced offender reoffends after release from prison. . . . In contrast, this study proceeds from the perspective that criminal actions are the result of ongoing psychological processes, and that they can be understood better in this context" (Zamble and Quinsey, 1997).

Thus, this study is an attempt to redirect attention from the general determinants of recidivism to an investigation into the individual processes of recidivism. Findings from this study are intended to inform more effective treatment approaches for offenders and better prepare them for the challenges they will face upon release.

To assess the needs of parole violators, the Pennsylvania DOC conducted a survey of technical and convicted parole violators who returned to incarceration in 12 state correctional institutions. Nearly 600 parole violators were surveyed during a two-month period early last year, representing approximately 75 percent of the DOC's total parole violator admissions during that time period. The surveys were administered to parole violators as soon as possible after their return to prison to elicit fresh recollections of the events surrounding the violation. The in-depth survey, developed by DOC staff, included questions concerning living arrangements, finances, employment, leisure activities, marital/family relationships, alcohol/drug use, community supervision experience, and thoughts and emotions while last on parole. At the end of the data collection period, a total of 542 surveys was completed.

After initial results from the survey were compiled and analyzed, reoccurring themes were further explored by conducting focus groups of parole violators at four of the participating institutions. Results from the survey were also matched with other data sources for three purposes: to look for reoccurring themes across multiple data sources, expand the data pool of information gathered on parole violators and examine the consistency of respondents' answers as a measure of reliability.

RESULTS

One of the first considerations when interpreting the survey results was whether technical parole violators and convicted parole violators represent two significantly different populations with unique needs. This study revealed compelling evidence to suggest that technical parole violators and convicted parole violators are statistically very similar populations. An analysis of Level of Service Inventory-Revised (LSI-R) scores indicated a similar distribution of risk levels for technical parole violators and convicted parole violators (see Figure 1). Further, an analysis of survey answers revealed only two differences between technical parole violators and convicted parole violators. Convicted parole violators indicated that money management issues more strongly contributed to their failure while on parole, and technical parole violators were more likely to report trouble finding a place to live upon release from prison. Other than these two marginally significant differences, answers to all of the remaining questions on the survey did not differ by parole violation status.

Findings from this study can be divided among four primary domains: social network and living arrangements, employment and financial situation, alcohol or other drug use, and thoughts and emotions. For the most part, parole violators reported positive information regarding their social network and living arrangements. Only 20 percent of respondents indicated that they were not prepared by prison to meet their post-release living needs. Eighty-two percent indicated that they had few difficulties finding a place to live after release. In addition, nearly three-fourths of parole violators indicated that they lived in low crime neighborhoods while last on parole, although this may be more a function of individual perception of the level of neighborhood crime. Positive findings on living arrangements were further reaffirmed through discussions with parole violators in focus groups.

For the most part, parole violators also reported maintaining a solid support network of family and friends to turn to for help or support. Eighty-nine percent of those in a relationship (wife, girlfriend, etc.) reported that the relationship was working out mostly good to excellent. Further, 85 percent indicated that they had at least one friend who they could

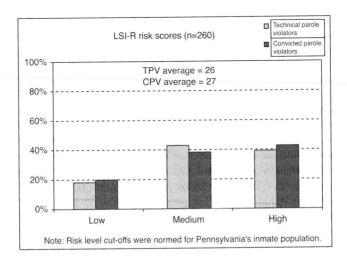

FIGURE 1

turn to for help, 89 percent indicated that they could turn to their partner/spouse for help, and 89 percent indicated that they could turn to their families for help. From both the survey results and the focus groups, parole violators also reported spending the majority of their leisure time with family members.

The study revealed no clear pattern concerning the extent of the parole violators' criminal associations, other than that older offenders appear to maintain less criminal associations than the younger ones. While 83 percent indicated that at least one of their family members or friends had been arrested in the past, the survey and focus group findings were unclear as to the extent of the association parole violators maintained with criminal family members and friends. Some evidence from both the survey and the focus groups indicates that maintaining criminal associations does not seem to be a significant problem for many parole violators and especially for older ones. Given that pro-criminal/antisocial association is a well-documented criminogenic risk factor, this finding begs the question as to whether parole visitors reported honestly or consistently across time about their level of criminal associations. By matching the survey results to criminal association subscales on two other needs-assessment instruments, it was determined that parole violators indeed seem to report consistently across several measures about their level of criminal association, with an estimated potential deception rate between 12 percent and 19 percent (Andrews and Bonta, 1997).

For the most part, parole violators reported encouraging information concerning employment. Eighty-two percent of parole violators indicated that they were legally employed while last on parole. Seventy-six percent indicated that legal employment was their primary source of income. Only 17 percent indicated that it was difficult to get a job when last released from prison. In focus groups, parole violators reiterated the theme that it was not difficult to find a job. A common complaint, however, was that the types of available jobs were unsuitable and provided insufficient income to make ends meet. To a certain degree, this represents a legitimate concern for the types of employment that parolees are eligible to obtain upon release from prison. On the other hand, the weight of the evidence gathered from this study suggests that many parole violators hold unrealistic job expectations and simply refuse to take low-end jobs or work their way up from the bottom.

Further, parole violators indicated significant financial management difficulties. Financial management problems only exacerbated the quandary of trying to make ends meet while holding low-paying jobs. Seventy-seven percent of parole violators indicated that they had some sort of debt while last on parole, with a median debt of more than $4,500. Parole violators reported that money management issues were among the strongest problems contributing to their failure on parole and that prison prepared them very little or not at all to deal with their financial situations upon release. Interestingly, while those who indicated illegal activities as a primary source of income reported a significantly larger monthly income than those who indicated legal employment as a primary source of income, both groups reported being equally unable to make ends meet. This suggests that even when provided with an adequate income, many parole violators lack the financial discipline and money management skills to save and pay for necessities.

Survey results and focus group findings indicated that a significant proportion of parole violators regularly used alcohol or other drugs while last on parole. Fifty-seven percent indicated that they drank or used drugs while last on parole an average of three days a week. Also, 54 percent reported that they started drinking or using drugs longer than a month before receiving their most recent violation, indicating that substance abuse problems were not unique to the last days before receiving a parole violation. However, those who had previously participated in prison substance abuse treatment programming indicated that they were significantly better prepared to deal with substance abuse problems. This suggests that in-prison substance abuse treatment seems to have a significant impact on parole violators' perceptions of positive treatment effects.

From the focus groups, the most evident trend in the domain of alcohol or other drug use was that there appears to be a dichotomy between parole violators with high alcohol or other drug needs and those with low alcohol or other drug needs. For some violators, alcohol or other drug use represented a major obstacle that significantly contributed to their failure on parole. These individuals represent the true addicts. On the other hand, many parole violators reported drinking or using other drugs while last on parole, but their violation did not appear to be the immediate result of their substance use. Instead, for these individuals, substance use represented one of many symptoms of a more profound problem of antisocial values, attitudes and beliefs.

Parole violators indicated that emotional problems, such as stress, depression, frustration and worry, contributed more to their failure on parole than any other potential contributor, including alcohol and other drug use, employment, living arrangements and relationship problems. The majority of parole violators recalled that the moments leading up to their violation were characterized by a variety of confusing and dysphoric emotional experiences. This immediately raises the question of whether parole violations are directly caused by unpleasant emotional experiences or by other factors. Given that every person experiences negative emotions at some point in life and that most do not resort to criminal behavior when experiencing such an occurrence, it seemed unlikely that the presence of a dysphoric emotional experience would directly cause an individual to violate parole. Indeed, further examination of the data and follow-ups in focus groups revealed three other important factors.

First, many parole violators held unrealistic expectations about what life would be like outside of prison. Throughout the survey, respondents reported confidence in their ability to easily find and keep high-paying jobs, avoid risky situations and people, maintain friction-free relationships, and generally be successful on parole. While 89 percent of parole violators reported that they were mostly or completely confident that they would succeed while last out on parole, by the very nature of this study all of the respondents failed on parole. It becomes difficult for parole violators to manage negative emotional experiences when they are expecting that life outside of prison will be easy and that most things will go right for them.

Second, the majority of parole violators indicated strong antisocial attitudes. Most reported believing that more positives than negatives would result from their particular violation such as earning respect, getting money or experiencing excitement. When they did discuss negative consequences, parole violators primarily spoke in terms of negative consequences to themselves and tended to diminish the negative consequences to others. One-third of parole violators reported that they often did not care or did not care at all about what others thought of them while they were last on parole. These types of antisocial attitudes make it easier for parole violators to respond in a criminal manner when faced with negative emotional experiences. A core concern for parole violators is not that they experience dysphoric emotions but that they are unequipped to respond pro-socially.

Third, the most prevalent theme identified throughout this entire study is that parole violators indicated poor self-management, self-control and problem-solving skills in the face of emotional instability or the daily obstacles of life. The Canadian parole violators study came to a similar conclusion, referring to this as a lack of "coping skills" (Zamble and Quinsey, 1997). Poor self-management or coping skills are particularly evidenced by four specific traits: impulsivity, failure to generate alternative courses of action, failure to recognize consequences of actions and keeping problems to oneself or failing to take avoidance steps. Forty-five percent of parole violators said that they did not consider alternatives to the sequence of events that led to their parole violation. One-third said that there was never a point in the sequence of events leading to their violation in which they could have stopped or forgotten the whole thing. Forty percent said they reached a point before their violation where they felt they were not in control anymore. Forty-four percent did not worry at all about the possibility of getting caught before participating in the act that eventually led to their parole violation. Seventy-seven percent did not tell anyone that they were having thoughts about acting out the events that led to their parole violation. When asked in focus groups what they would do differently when next released from prison, many of the parole violators were able to describe their problems but could not articulate a strategy for addressing them. Also in focus groups, many violators relayed stories of being tripped up by a multitude of events or experiences, such as a family illness or death, and subsequently violating a condition of parole.

POLICY IMPLICATIONS FOR TREATING PAROLE VIOLATORS

The results of this study support four specific policy implications for treating parole violator populations. First and foremost, programming for parole violators should specifically focus on cognitive-behavioral treatment that involves coping strategies, behavior rehearsal and relapse prevention components. Previous research has established that cognitive-behavioral programming is an effective model of treatment for offenders (Andrews and Bonta, 1994). Programming for parole violators should not focus on eliminating negative emotional experiences, but should instead focus on reinforcing pro-social behavioral reactions to negative emotional experiences. Treatment should emphasize that every person will undoubtedly and unavoidably experience unpleasant emotional experiences at some point in life. When these uncontrollable experiences occur, an individual is only able to control his or her behavioral response. Rehearsing problem-solving techniques and pro-social behaviors should be a primary treatment target.

Also, re-entry programming should focus more attention on teaching parole violators specific and transferable life skills such as financial responsibility and money management techniques. Money management is a particularly important subset of self-management that seems to present significant obstacles for parole violators and, therefore, should be a primary target for prison release preparation. Many parole violators need to learn and rehearse the skills necessary to manage monthly bills and debt repayments, given the salaries that they are realistically able to obtain.

In addition, due to severity of alcohol and other drug problems experienced by a certain proportion of parole violators, it is important that correctional systems continue to reinforce intensive alcohol and other drug treatment programs that are known to be effective such as therapeutic communities. Conversely, treatment staff should not make the assumption that all parole violators who drank or used drugs while last on parole have a significant substance abuse problem and must primarily receive intensive alcohol and other drug treatment. In fact, it is perhaps more appropriate that parole violators with low alcohol and other drug needs primarily receive a core cognitive-behavioral program that focuses on general attitudinal and behavioral skills that are transferable across various domains, including employment, alcohol and other drug use, and relationships.

Finally, programming should encourage parole violators to stay "rooted in reality" and maintain realistic post-release expectations. Parole violators must come to understand that life outside of prison will not often be easy and that a criminal record can make life all the more difficult. For instance, employability training should prepare parole violators for the real possibility that they may need to start off working a low-end job and gradually work up to a promotion or better job. In-prison treatment for parole violators will be effective to the degree that it is able to simulate a real world environment within the artificial environment of prison. Again, role-playing is a particularly useful tool for simulating such an environment and preparing parole violators for realistic life expectations.

FUTURE STEPS

The Pennsylvania DOC has learned a great deal from the results of its parole violator study. In fact, staff are designing a pilot program for parole violators that will address each of the major policy implications identified in the study. More specifically, the proposed program will include a core cognitive-behavioral component that will focus on teaching parole violators generally transferable self-management and problem-solving skills. A thorough assessment of individual needs will then be used to tailor individual treatment plans and place parole violators in issue-specific treatment groups according to their assessed needs. This model, based on Pennsylvania's detailed analysis of the process of recidivism and assessment of the needs of parole violators, is expected to better prepare parole violators for re-release and will hopefully serve to reduce future parole violator admissions to Pennsylvania's prisons.

QUESTIONS FOR REVIEW AND DISCUSSION

1. In what ways can parolees violate their parole conditions?
2. Should all parole violators be returned to prison? Why or why not?
3. Are all parole violations serious? Why or why not? Give some examples.
4. What types of assistance for parolees do the authors recommend? What do you think? Discuss.

20

Offender Reentry
A Returning or Reformed Criminal?

David M. Allender

Adapted From David M. Allender, "Offender Reentry: A Returning or Reformed Criminal?" *FBI Law Enforcement Bulletin* 73: 1–10, 2004.

Reprinted by permission of the *FBI Law Enforcement Bulletin.*

Perhaps the most vexing problem facing the criminal justice system in the United States today is how to deal with offenders who have "paid their debt to society" and are released from a structured correctional setting back into the community. Rarely does society lock up a person and "throw away the key." Instead, 95 percent of all offenders sent to state prison facilities will be released and returned to the civilian population (Hughes and Wilson, 2002).

How to address this situation has more important consequences for society than the ongoing debate about whether a prison sentence should be punitive or treatment oriented. While incarcerated, the offender, at the very least, is "warehoused" away for the protection of the general public. Upon release, however, the community will be confronted, based on policy decisions made and implemented, by either a returning criminal or a reformed offender.

AMERICAN PENOLOGY

Concern for the real purpose behind a court-imposed sentence in response to a criminal offense is not a new feature on the American political landscape. Rather, the debate goes back to the earliest period of this country's existence. A brief look at the history of penology in this country can confirm this observation. In 1787, Benjamin Franklin's Philadelphia, Pennsylvania, home was the site for the first meeting of the Philadelphia Society for Alleviating the Miseries of Public Prisons (PSAMPP). At the time of this gathering, local jails—basically holding pens that made no attempt to separate prisoners by age, sex, or offense—housed the majority of incarcerated persons. Upon adjudication of their cases, most of those convicted received sentences that entailed some form of corporal punishment or hard labor and removal from the jail population. PSAMPP members felt that this treatment of offenders was misguided and, by design, failed to correct the unacceptable behavior on the part of the prisoner. As a solution, they lobbied the government of Pennsylvania to construct Eastern State Penitentiary, a facility that opened in 1829 as the first modern-day prison. Behind its drive to build Eastern State, PSAMPP had as its goal: "The Penitentiary would not simply punish, but move the criminal toward spiritual reflection and change. The method was a Quaker-inspired system of isolation from other prisoners, with labor" (Eastern State Penitentiary, 2004).

To inspire their changes, Pennsylvania, at the time, built possibly the most expensive building in the United States. Equipped with central heat and running water when the White House still used wood-burning stoves and latrines, the penitentiary represented an attempt to positively affect the lives of inmates. In reality, PSAMPP's well-intentioned effort at reform led to the creation of the first "supermax" facility in the world. For 23 hours a day, inmates were confined in individual cells that had small, private exercise yards that they could or had to go into for 1 hour per day. Staff members passed food to the inmates through a slot in the cell door. Inmates had no contact with each other, and the staff restricted conversation with them to the amount necessary to operate the prison. When prisoners had to move around inside the institution, they wore hoods over their heads and faces. Eventually, inmates could exercise in a common yard together, but, for many years, they had to wear a hood with eyeholes to limit familiarity within the inmate community. In addition, the institution restricted reading material to the Bible. All of these measures were put in place to help inmates meditate and reflect on the errors they had made. PSAMPP members felt that upon reflection on their transgressions, inmates would become enlightened, which would lead to a resolve to make positive changes in their lifestyles and behaviors. Eastern State modified these practices over the years as new theories on penology altered the beliefs of those working in the field of corrections. The facility itself served as a penitentiary for 142 years, finally closing in 1971.

The history of Eastern State Penitentiary illustrates how American society, in over 200 years, has failed to reach an agreement on what it hopes to accomplish by sentencing offenders to prison. Given this historical background, it is time to make use of modern research methods to identify and implement strategies that show promise in successfully reintegrating offenders into society as productive members.

RECIDIVISM IDENTIFIED

Recent research by the Bureau of Justice Statistics helps to demonstrate the need to develop effective measures designed to assist recently released inmates (Langan and Levin, 2002). The study examined prisoners released from 15 states, which returned a total of 272,111 of their charges to free society in 1994. This number represented approximately two-thirds of all inmates freed from custody that year. The researchers focused on four factors that they felt identified recidivism: "rearrest, reconviction, resentence to prison, and return to prison with or without a new sentence." Their findings proved disturbing. Within 2 years, 67.5 percent of released inmates were charged with a new crime, 46.9 percent were found guilty of their latest charge, and 25.4 percent were sent to a correctional facility in response to their new offense. Violations of release conditions (technical violations, not new offenses) led to additional incarceration time for many inmates released in 1994. Considering all of the factors, a total of 51.8 percent of the inmates released in 1994 were back in prison by 1997. This human tragedy is felt not only by the inmates, their families, and friends but by society as a whole. The most obvious cost of this failure to gain compliance with societies' mores lies in the extraordinary expense of incarceration, $49,007,000 by all levels of government in 1999. The victims of these offenders, however, pay a price not so readily apparent. The study estimated that before returning to prison, these offenders committed approximately 744,000 crimes between 1994 and 1997 (Gifford, 2002; Langan and Levin, 2002).

CHANGES IN SENTENCING

By the middle of the 20th century, most states had a parole board responsible for administering an early release policy. Courts generally gave out sentences for a range of years. For example, a felony conviction for a nonviolent theft might be 2 to 4 years, instead of a set time, such as 30 months. Parole board members held the power to decide whether an inmate went free after 2 years of imprisonment or had to serve the equivalent of 4 years. The system, by its very nature, was subjective and prone to abuse. Public displeasure led to reforms and a switch to determinate sentencing, with an equally applicable formula that allowed for early release based on "good time" earned by the inmate. A deficiency for the new procedure was a loss of postrelease control formerly held by the parole boards. When the board granted release, it set terms that parole officers administered. With the advent of determinate sentencing, however, more inmates began serving their entire sentences, then were released without control or assistance. An unintended consequence of this procedure has been a dramatic reduction in funds available for parole officers with a resultant proportionate decrease in the control of ex-inmates at a time when appropriate direction could have a positive impact on their lives.

Truth-in-sentencing laws, which several states have adopted, have further complicated issues surrounding offender reentry. In many jurisdictions, violent criminals must serve at least 85 percent of their court-imposed sentences before being considered for parole or release (Travis, 2000). Other states, such as Indiana, make use of determinate sentences where inmates know that if they do not commit any transgressions while incarcerated, they will be released after serving 50 percent of their original sentences. These states consider the released inmates as having served their time and do not subject them to any additional monitoring or control. But, these are individuals who, based on prior behaviors, society has a strong interest in, either for rehabilitation or close supervision. In attempting to ensure punishment and fairness, legislative bodies have made decisions that did not take into account the fact that once these individuals have served their time, they will be released into the same neighborhoods they came from to again prey upon the citizens who live there.

One researcher, addressing the topic of how to deal with reentry, said, "The answer to the question, 'If not parole, then what?' is typically, 'More prison.' Yet asking a different question—'How should we manage the reentry of large numbers of people who have been imprisoned for a long time?'—might elicit a different answer" (Travis, 2000). He continued with what has become a common theme in enlightened discussions on the topic of reentry, "They all come back" (Travis, 2000). He suggested reassigning some of the functions formerly performed by parole boards. Among the items to consider is a body charged with controlling the actions of inmates after release, as well as monitoring their behavior prior to release to ensure that they have received the tools to become successful when they return to free society. While this approach would seem to conflict with the sentencing reforms enacted in response to complaints concerning the old parole structure, the number of former inmates being rearrested so quickly after their release confirms the need for fine-tuning the system.

REENTRY BY OFFENSE CATEGORY

Many Americans are slowly starting to realize that offenders need help to succeed and not reoffend upon their release from correctional facilities. Society long has recognized its responsibility to care for delinquent youths because they are too immature to make decisions for themselves. Due to this, special programs exist in a number of jurisdictions to work with juvenile offenders before and after their release. Now, the general public has begun to realize that many adult offenders lack the social skills necessary to become successful, contributing members of their communities. To help these individuals, many people have recognized the need to provide training and alternatives for those being released.

Citizens have demanded that at least two widely different classes of offenders incur special attention upon their release from incarceration. Interest in both groups has drawn considerable political attention, but for different reasons. An educated electorate voicing concern to appropriate legislative bodies can lead to the establishment of reentry programs. Depending upon the type of inmate targeted and the focus of the interest group, a reentry initiative developed in this manner may or may not offer the best chance for rehabilitation.

Sex offenders became the first to draw extensive public attention. Fear that released offenders would again prey upon those members of society least able to protect themselves led to several measures, including the National Sex Offender Registry. Also, in *Kansas v. Hendricks,* the U.S. Supreme Court ruled that institutions may hold sexual offenders beyond their court-imposed sentence if they can demonstrate that inmates have displayed a mental condition that indicates their likelihood of committing new offenses upon their release (117 U.S. 2072). Other efforts have occurred to ensure released inmates are tracked and given either treatment or additional punishment, whichever professionals deem as the more appropriate for their condition.

A second category of offenders warranting special consideration in the eyes of the public includes those sentenced for what some perceived as "minor" drug crimes. Based on information in the media and high-profile movies, many members of the community seem to believe that large numbers of incarcerated drug offenders have as their only *real* crime an addiction to an illegal substance. While some persons undoubtedly have been imprisoned for usage amounts of drugs, most of those serving time for simple drug possession offenses, in fact, were actively involved in some manner with the trafficking of illegal substances. Numerous ways exist for a known drug dealer to end up charged with possession instead of dealing. The most common occurs when prosecutors, with police encouragement, allow a person to plead guilty to possession after selling drugs to a cooperating individual or informant. In such cases, a trade-off for the law enforcement community occurs—the identity of the witness, often an undercover officer, remains unknown, thereby protecting the witness and allowing the police to use that person again. Drug couriers that risk arrest for the profit gained by moving another's drugs from one point to another are among those convicted of simple possession. Others facing these charges include those caught in "whisper" stops where the informant or undercover officer arrange a drug deal and police intercept the dealer before the individual can reach the meeting spot. These few examples illustrate why the public and researchers need to become better informed about conditions in the drug enforcement field before accepting, at face value, that courts have imprisoned a large population of offenders for drug addictions.

Public concern has led to an acceptance of the need for drug treatment and for the increasing requirement for appropriate programs. Many offenders incarcerated for crimes not related to drugs either abuse or are addicted to an illegal substance. Effective screening by correctional personnel can identify those most in need of and receptive to treatment as a step to securing them placement in proper programs. The limited funding available for treatment programs, which occurs because no one can prove that criminal activity did not happen due to a specific intervention effort, drives the rationale behind referring only the best candidates for treatment. In contrast, by their very nature, enforcement programs generated numbers of arrests and citizen contacts. Fiscal agents endeavoring to make effective use of available funds understandably are more comfortable with efforts that produce a verifiable result, usually numbers, as opposed to a successful outcome that remains difficult to prove.

PROJECT RIO

Institutions have employed a wide variety of programs and ideas in recent times to either force ex-inmates to conform to societal norms or assist them in making the transition from prison to freedom. One such program is Project RIO, a state-funded and locally controlled effort in Texas.

In June 1998, the National Institute of Justice evaluated and reported on this effort. Under the formal title of ReIntegration of Offenders, the project began in Texas during 1985 as an effort to reduce the recidivism rate for inmates released by state correctional facilities. A quick look at the number of offenders Texas must deal with can effectively illustrate the scope of the problem. In December 1996, for example, Texas correctional institutions housed more than 132,000 inmates. Members of the Texas legislature agreed with the premise that without gainful employment and other steps to reintegrate them into society, ex-inmates likely will reoffend and a large percentage will return to prison. They approved funding for Project RIO in 1984 with implementation in 1985. Elected officials took an enlightened stance when they mandated that to receive funds, several agencies would have to collaborate on the effort. The Institutional and Parole Division of the Texas Department of Criminal Justice and the Texas Workforce Commission, the state employment agency established in 1935 that successfully serves the entire state, equally share direction of the project. The size of the RIO agency— 100 paid staff located in 62 sites serving 92 cities and towns—demonstrates the extent of the commitment. Moreover, itinerant service providers travel to towns where large numbers of parolees reside to provide service for rural areas (U.S. Department of Justice, 1998).

Inmates are introduced to RIO in a variety of ways. Upon entry into a correctional facility, each offender must complete an orientation process. During this introduction, project staff members provide new inmates with a brochure describing how Project RIO works and how it can benefit them. As an example, the school that provides vocational and technical training inside the prisons requires inmates who participate in any course to enroll in the project. Staff members from RIO make periodic attempts to recruit inmates through oral or video presentations and by bringing potential employers to the facilities. While processing out of institutions, inmates must attend a 30-minute orientation on RIO. Even if inmates fail to take advantage of the opportunities provided by the project upon release, they still can sign up later. This late sign-up often occurs because the ex-offender's parole officer makes a referral or a current or past participant in RIO assures the parolee that the program works.

Once inmates or parolees decide to take advantage of the benefits connected with Project RIO, they receive services tailored to fit their needs. Finding a job begins with a week of life-skills and job-search training. Program specialists then attempt to match ex-offenders with available positions and make calls to appropriate employers within the network of 12,000 companies that already have hired RIO participants. Project counselors realize the need to take a holistic approach to the problems and conditions that the ex-inmates face. For this reason, they provide ex-offenders with information on and assistance in obtaining community services, housing, medical care, and other resources for handling problematic issues. An important component of the program involves ongoing monitoring of the ex-offender's work performance and behavior, with timely intervention by parole or Project RIO workers before a problem reaches the level that will require reincarceration of the individual.

Overall then, how successful is the effort at keeping offenders from returning to prison? As the study of offenders released around the country during 1994 showed, by 1997, 51.8 percent had returned to prison. This represents an enormous drain on public resources and a waste of potential contributions those imprisoned might make to society. Texas A&M University evaluated RIO in 1992 and judged the program a success. Evaluators studied 1,200 inmates released that year and found that those who chose to participate in RIO had lower rates for both arrest and reincarceration. University researchers identified a number of factors that they believed had an effect on the ex-offender's ability to assimilate back into society. The study then grouped subjects into categories of high, average, and low risk to obtain as much information as possible on the effectiveness. As might be expected, high-risk subjects had the most chance of being rearrested. This held true regardless of status with RIO, but project subjects faired significantly better than non-RIO individuals, 48 percent as opposed to 57 percent. Although the difference in rearrest rates for average-risk, 30 percent versus 32 percent, and low-risk, 16 percent versus 19 percent, ex-offenders did not vary widely. In both categories, RIO participants did better than their counterparts not in the program.

Texas A&M University followed new cases filed against ex-offenders to conclusion and determined that Project RIO also had influenced the rate of incarceration for ex-offenders. Those individuals in the high-risk category were rearrested at a much higher rate than the other categories and, correspondingly, were imprisoned in a much greater percent. RIO enrollees returned to prison less often than those who chose not to enter the program. Among those considered high risk, 23 percent from RIO as opposed to 38 percent non-RIO, went back into prison. In the average-risk ranking, the tally was 8 percent RIO versus 11 percent non-RIO. Non-significant difference occurred for re-imprisonment among those studied who ranked as low risk.

The Texas A&M study not only indicated the success of the RIO effort but also identified both the scope of its work and the extent of its positive influence on the lives of the participants. Between 1995 and 1998, over 100,000 released inmates voluntarily partici- pated in RIO, which found jobs for 69 percent of those in need. Of those who chose not to enter the project, only 36 percent obtained gainful employment. Obviously, more ex- offenders working and paying taxes as opposed to serving time in prison can result in a pos- itive impact on society (Byrne, Taxman, and Young, 2003).

NEW PARTNERSHIPS

Community policing is changing the manner in which many law enforcement agencies around the nation do business. Instead of being what many authors a couple of decades ago characterized as an army of occupation stationed in America's inner cities, police in many areas are emerging as true partners for citizens and other service providers. A number of factors have influenced this change, including a better-educated police work force and a need for all parties to cooperate so they could stretch limited resources and achieve their goals. Operating largely under the federal government umbrella, grant providers, in actual- ity, have been responsible for changing the face of American policing.

A report prepared for the National Institute of Justice by the University of Maryland documented eight communities using local police as an ingredient in ongoing reentry ini- tiatives. The information contained in the report may usher in a new phase of law enforce- ment activity (Byrne, Taxman, and Young, 2003).

The research identified five steps in the reentry process: (1) program eligibility, (2) institutional treatment plans, (3) structured prerelease planning, (4) structured reentry, and (5) community reintegration strategies. The authors felt that the last three phases were equally dangerous for an offender's successful reentry. In all of the areas, police have the knowledge and ability to make meaningful contributions. While offenders are incarcerated, police, an often overlooked intelligence resource, can supply information on their families, associates, gang affiliations, and neighborhood problems they likely will encounter. Rather than relying on a "cookie-cutter" approach, examining information of this type would prove valuable in the development of treatment and prerelease plans most likely to aid inmates.

During the structured reentry phase, programs often use police as a deterrent for of- fenders should they violate the terms of their release agreements. This approach differs in a significant way from older methods of policing. First, law enforcement officers meet face- to-face with offenders and tell them frankly what the community expects and what the con- sequences will be if they fail to meet expectations. Second, officers serve as a resource to help offenders who may have problems achieving what authorities expect. In some juris- dictions, police work closely with probation and parole agencies, even participating in home visits and curfew checks, to ensure that offenders meet the requirements of their release agreements. Last, police in some jurisdictions sit on boards that determine whether offend- ers have achieved a successful outcome. This probably represents the most controversial use of police in the reentry process because of the appearance, real or imagined, that the law en- forcement community is not really an impartial voice in the decision-making process.

In years past, inmates normally were released under the supervision of either a parole or probation department. Changes in sentencing procedures have greatly increased the number of prisoners released unconditionally into communities across the country. Police are the only enforcement agents for those released unconditionally. Where the goal of incarceration is simply to punish criminal behavior, traditional policing methods (if ex-inmates reoffend, they are rearrested and suffer new consequences) would be an acceptable governmental response. The information now available, however, shows that the recently released most likely will fail without help. The law enforcement community may be forced to expand its range of services to assist ex-offenders unless some other group comes forward to fill the void.

During the community reintegration phase, officers work to lessen the friction that always accompanies change. When offenders return to their neighborhoods, they form only part of the equation. Family members often must rearrange their lives to accommodate another person in the household. Victims still may be a part of the community and require reassurance that they will not be victimized anew. Community groups need to know that any future transgressions will be dealt with quickly. Police often are the focal point for all of these entities. If offenders make a successful transition, the involvement of the police will be limited to positive interactions with both the offenders and the community.

CONCLUSION

Offender reentry is a pressing issue for society. Governmental resources have been severely taxed as legislatures have criminalized more and more behaviors. Determinate sentencing, coupled with mandatory minimum time requirements, has resulted in longer stays for offenders. Many treatment and educational programs have not been able to keep pace with the demand. Unconditional release, for those having completed a determinate sentence, has resulted in many offenders being returned to the environments that initially contributed to their abhorrent behavior. Without new tools to assist them in avoiding pitfalls, ex-offenders are likely to repeat previous negative actions, which could lead to their reincarceration. This, in turn, causes multiple injuries to society, including the cost of the crime itself, the need for appropriate housing for the offender, the loss of productivity that could be expected had the person not reoffended, and the harm to the family structure of victim and offender. The magnitude of the problem defies a quick-fix answer.

New ways of thinking are a necessary step to reducing the recidivism rate. Project RIO is a shining example of what can be done when effective partnerships are formed and conditions allow them to function in the proper manner. Moreover, finding the role for law enforcement to work with other team members in reentry would benefit everyone concerned. With its emphasis on problem solving, community policing is changing the face of law enforcement around the country. Not everyone, however, agrees with using police officers in this way, and some agencies may be reluctant to incorporate them for fear of having their own work overshadowed. But, by establishing guidelines for law enforcement involvement, cooperating partners could ensure that their needs are met and police officers would better understand what is expected of them. Using law enforcement personnel could reduce costs and lessen the workload of some overworked agencies. Officers would benefit from working in these programs because they would be placed in close contact with those who, statistically, are the most likely to commit new crimes. Although it is heartening to see that steps are being taken to improve programs available for those leaving correctional facilities, more work still needs to be done to help offenders reform, rather than return to their criminal ways.

QUESTIONS FOR REVIEW AND DISCUSSION

1. Why is offender reentry a problem for society? Discuss.

2. What were some early conditions under which inmates in prisons were maintained? What was the Philadelphia Society for Alleviating the Miseries of Public Prisons? What were its goals?

3. How is recidivism defined? How have changes in sentencing laws influenced recidivism, if at all? Discuss.

4. How are social skills, vocational/educational skills, and positive attitudes among parolees important to their successful reentry into society?

5. What is Project RIO? What are its components or characteristics? Was it successful? Why or why not?

6. Which types of offenders need more help than other types of offenders when reentering society following incarceration? Why?

7. What is meant by structured reentry?

21

"Offender Reentry Requires Attention to Victim Safety"

Melissa Hook
and Anne Seymour

Adapted from Melissa Hook and Anne Seymour, "Offender Reentry Requires Attention to Victim Safety." *APPA Perspectives* 27: 24–29, 2003.

Criminals and juvenile justice professionals do not dispute the fact that crime victims' needs and concerns should be considered when an offender is released from incarceration or detention. Furthermore, key public safety stakeholders, in collaboration with the U.S. Department of Justice, are currently monitoring and successfully integrating the half million offenders leaving custody each year.

However, the primary focus of reentry initiatives is on offenders and their needs. Professionals who work with crime victims assert that "whatever it takes" to promote successful offender reentry must include provisions to ensure the safety and address the concerns of crime victims. Offender release brings up critical issues regarding core victim rights, including notification, restitution, protection, and participation, and these should be addressed through reentry initiatives. Victim-sensitive pre-release and post-release strategies that correlate with practices to improve the offender's potential for successful return to the community should be an integral part of the reentry process.

COMMUNITY PARTICIPATION IN REENTRY PARTNERSHIPS

One of the goals of these reentry alliances is the creation of model programs that generate collaborative efforts among local professionals and volunteers from the public and private sector that can enhance opportunities for successful offender reintegration. The health of neighborhoods and communities—including the well-being of victims—depends on the effective supervision and tangible support of the newly released offenders. An essential ingredient in any formula that tries to improve reentry options is a concerned, educated and engaged community.

Study Affirms Need for Community Participation

In 2000, the Victims' Issues Committee of the American Probation and Parole Association (APPA) conducted a study to determine the extent to which victims' concerns are included in reentry initiatives. One of the goals of the project was to identify the ideal partners in a reentry initiative that could best address the safety and well-being of victims and the community.

The APPA study on the victim component of offender reentry found that the education and involvement of community members who are victim-centered and who can reflect victim concerns are much-needed components in reentry partnerships. In *The Victim's Role in Offender Reentry: A Community Response Manual,* Seymour stresses that:

> *"The Successful reentry of offenders into the community is neither a linear process, nor one that can be accomplished by a single agency. It requires collaboration and commitment from literally anyone concerned about community safety."*

Crime Victim Participation

An equally vital component in the formation of reentry protocols is input from crime victims. Their experience of crime, its aftermath, and its long-term effects informs many aspects of any reentry program. Seymour writes:

> *"The inclusion and consideration of crime victims' rights and needs in offender management that has emerged over the past decade does provide a strong foundation for reentry partnerships. It offers an important framework for justice professionals to prevent crime and the revictimization of people who have already been hurt by crime. They can voluntarily contribute to policy development; serve as advisors to create new programs and approaches that hold offenders accountable and reduce recidivism; participate in victim/offender programming; and strengthen the core of community action that is necessary for success."*

A VICTIM'S PERSPECTIVE

Few victims remain unaffected by the thought of their offender's return to the community. A survivor of a horrendous kidnapping, sexual assault, and attempted murder describes her state of mind anticipating her rapist's upcoming release. Looking back on her experience, she recalls that:

> I have survived the experience of working with the criminal justice system to see my offender caught, tried, and sentenced. Today, I am faced with yet another challenge, one which, at the moment, seems the most difficult to face: the reality of my offender's release. I actually began contemplating this event the moment the sentence was handed down. My thoughts went something like this: "I have this many years to live my life. Better make the best of it." The thought that follows is: "Let's not think about this right now, as I have so many years to be free from the constant fear of being stalked and possibly killed by this person."

CONCERN BEGINS AT THE TIME OF SENTENCING

A survivor's concerns about offender reentry begin long before the offender is even considered for release, perhaps even at the moment of sentencing. However, the process of addressing the issue is often one that is avoided, perhaps because of the emotional scars it re-opens and the difficult work and planning it requires.

OFFENDER AWARENESS OF VICTIM CONCERNS

The survivor quoted above, who now works as a victim advocate and a leader in restorative justice, believes that correctional agencies should address victim-related reentry issues with offenders through the use of victim impact panels and focus groups. They need to explore such questions as the following:

- Do offenders fantasize about or plan to seek revenge against those they have harmed?
- If so, in what way?
- What are their intentions toward their victims upon release?

System Must Address Both Offender and Victim

Far too often these questions are displaced by the criminal justice system's concerns over the offenders' successful readjustment in the outside world after years of incarceration. Clearly those challenges may be daunting. Will the families accept them? Will they find a job and a place to live? Will they abuse alcohol or other drugs? Will they reoffend?

Peter Michaud, the Director of Victim Services at the New Hampshire Department of Corrections, poses a different, more fundamental question:

> Why do we have a justice system? Not because of crime. We have a justice system because someone has been hurt by a crime. We need to take into account the harm that has been done to a victim and help that hurt. To be truly effective in our criminal justice effort, we have to include the fact that a crime has harmed someone.

WHAT CONSTITUTES THE COMMUNITY?

While many people tend to think of community as a physical place and space, it is just as often created by relationships that people build, beginning with one-on-one and emerging into groups of varying sizes that share a common bond and mutual interests. The community as reentry partner exhibits a mindset that is responsive to the concerns of returning offenders and victims and is proactive in its efforts to promote local safety and well-being. Joseph Lehman, Commissioner of Corrections in Washington State, observes: "The community truly feels a stake in the processes and outcomes of justice, successful programs for offenders and victims are an attainable goal. It is only with this sense of ownership that reentry partnerships can succeed."

Seymour divides community relevant to reentry collaborations into key components:

- The victims and the offenders, both of whom may be isolated from traditional communities like families and friends. They often experience shame, blame, and guilt as well as a lack of acceptance and understanding.
- The justice system that is united by profession and a desire to do the work of public safety better.
- The local communities and neighborhoods into which offenders will be released, and possibly the home of the victim(s) (in interfamilial cases when family reunification is a goal).

CAN THE COMMUNITY HAVE A ROLE IN DETERMINING AND MEETING VICTIMS' NEEDS?

Despite obvious concerns over privacy and confidentiality, most justice and victim assistance professionals wholeheartedly embrace the concept of an increased community role in victim assistance. But as Reggie Wilkinson, Director of the Ohio Department of Rehabilitation and Corrections, points out: "Flexibility is necessary. It is important to find out who needs help and who wants help." Denise Giles, Director of Victim Services for the Maine Department of Corrections, concurs: "Community support and involvement should be the victim's choice."

Expanding on the idea of community partnerships, Michaud expresses the need for "a process in place in the community that assures that victims and survivors are safe when their offenders reenter and includes an understanding of their safety needs from the victims' perspective."

HOW CAN COMMUNITIES HELP VICTIMS?

In *The Victim's Role in Offender Reentry: A Community Response Manual,* Seymour explores ways in which reentry support team members might initiate assistance to victims when their offenders begin the pre-release phase of reentry and what measures they may take to provide support throughout the process. The "reentry support team member" in this case signifies volunteers who are trained to provide supportive services to victims.

Good Neighboring

The concept of victim support has its foundation in the age-old concept of listening, expressing concern and providing assistance, if requested from someone in need. Ellen Halbert, Director of the Victim/Witness Division of the District Attorney's office in Travis County, Texas, and Editor of the Crime Victims Report, believes that existing good neighbor policies can contribute significantly to meeting victims' needs relevant to offender reentry. She says:

> Community members can provide enormous emotional support by a regular phone call to victims to find out what they need. Neighbors can offer to keep an eye out for them; they can assist in fixing window and door locks and adding lights to the outside of the house. They can,

as a neighborhood, work out a safety plan for the victim, identify people that victims can call if they are afraid, and establish people who will touch base regularly with the victim. They can create an aura of safety around a victim by helping them stay connected with the neighborhood.

Understand Victims' Needs

Giles stresses: The greatest help communities can provide to victims when their offenders reenter is to acknowledge crime victims in the community and to educate the public as to victims' needs.

For example, Giles has helped implement community forums through town meetings in Maine that address the release of sex offenders into the community. Continuing training and technical assistance about victim trauma and victims' needs, for community members as well as justice professionals, are a critical component.

SERVICE AVAILABILITY AND ACCESSIBILITY

Community members can also be aware of and educated about the range of victim assistance and social services available in the community. They can work with victims to identify basic needs that can be met by community volunteers, such as the following:

- Providing food and shelter, transportation, and child care;
- Developing a list with contact information (24-hours-a-day, seven-days-a-week) of family members, friends and neighbors who can be called on to provide support and assistance;
- Coordinating neighborhood watch or "cocooning" activities if a victim has safety concerns
- Ensuring that local law enforcement agencies—including police, probation and parole—are aware of the victim's status and concerns; and
- Encouraging increased surveillance on offenders who may pose a threat to a victim's safety.

Public Awareness

Public awareness of victims' rights issues related to offender reentry efforts can be raised by the following measures:

- The community can actively disseminate information that educates members about victims' rights, needs and services.
- Crime victims should be informed of their rights and services that are available when their offenders reenter the community.
- The public must be made aware of victim vulnerability during the offender reentry period to be of assistance.
- The media should be educated about the importance of reentry efforts as they affect both offenders and victims in order to better understand and convey to the public the importance of successful reentries.

The development of a public awareness plan can include the following elements:

1. Slogans that emphasize victims' needs;
2. The observance of national commemorative months and weeks that honor victims and those who serve them;
3. List-serves, user groups or web-based message boards that maintain regular contact with key community volunteers; and
4. Publication of regular newsletters for partnership members.

Community members can also write articles and submit opinion pieces to print and broadcast news media—including letters-to-the-editor, opinion/editorial columns and broadcast editorials—that highlight the victim component of offender reentry.

Advocacy

In the United States today, there are over 30,000 laws that define and protect victims' rights. Constitutional amendments in 32 states often strengthen victims' basic statutory rights and, in some states, provide for measures of compliance. However, many laws on the books are not enforced uniformly, and victims sometimes have few remedies available to enforce their rights. Community members can support the review of and, if needed, revisions in existing state victims' rights laws.

COMMUNITY SUPPORT FOR VICTIMS' RIGHTS AT THE TIME OF REENTRY

Reentry partnerships should examine existing victims' rights laws related to their safety and participation throughout reentry processes. Compliance is a major concern to ensure that measures are in place to facilitate uniform implementation of victims' rights and to provide remedies to victims whose rights have been ignored or violated.

When community reentry support team members have knowledge of victims' rights that are relevant to offender release, the likelihood that those rights are respected and enforced is greater.

While an understanding of victims' rights is essential for improved enforcement, how and when that information is acted upon depends on individual victims and their wishes. Some victims will choose not to be informed, involved, or related in any way to the offender reentry process.

Seymour describes several ways that community reentry volunteers can enhance the delivery of core victims' rights. First of all, they can request and attend training programs co-sponsored by correctional agencies and victim service providers that address victims' rights relevant to reentry programs and how such rights can be implemented in a multidisciplinary manner.

The following victims' rights comprise the core programs and community responses addressing victim-related reentry issues:

1. Notification;
2. Protection;

3. Victim Impact Statements; and
4. Restitution.

NOTIFICATION

The victims' right to notification is critical to involving victims throughout the entire justice process and to informing them of rights and services that are available to them. Often called "the threshold right" from which all other victims' rights and services emanate, victim notification takes on added importance within the context of offender reentry (see D. Beatty, speech at the "Automated Statewide Victim Notification Conference," Louisville, KY [1999]). The most notable victims rights relevant to reentry are the following:

- Victims' rights to notification of the offender's status and location;
- Rights to participate in hearings and events relevant to the offender's case status; and
- Rights of notification relevant to receiving restitution and information that can contribute to a victim's sense of safety and security.

Community reentry volunteers can learn enough about notification so that they can provide advice and referrals to victims at any point in the reentry process. It may be helpful to some victims to offer to serve as the recipient of "dual notification" so that a "cocoon of support" can be immediately provided. Volunteers can assist in the following ways:

- Offering to accompany victims and to attend hearings relevant to the offender's status;
- Providing translation services to victims who do not speak English or reading notification information to victims who are illiterate;
- Serving as a conduit of information between institutional, community corrections, and victim assistance professionals when the victim needs support or services; and
- Providing input from victims developed while providing assistance and support during notification.

PROTECTION

Everyone has the right to feel safe and to be safe, but return to safety may be an arduous journey for those who have experienced criminal victimization. Therefore, the right to have knowledge of the case status and the status and location of the offender can be keys to a victim's sense of well-being. When and how information is conveyed concerning the release of an offender, his or her state of mind, and his or her impending whereabouts can be critical to the ability of a victim of violent crime to address the real or perceived likelihood of revictimization.

Generally, victims are subject to two principal types of fear:

1. Actual fear that results from the experience of the crime, longstanding feelings of intimidation and terror developed in a relationship where there is a history of

violent behavior, and threats from the offender or his or her acquaintance following the crime.

2. Perceived fear when the trauma of victimization causes victims to feel fearful. The fear may be more widespread and include not only the offender, but also the justice system, and the people and things that remind them of the crime—even when there has been no direct or implied threat.

Victims May Not Voice Fears

Victims often do not express their feeling of fear—actual or perceived—so it is important to make a practice of asking them if they have concerns for their safety, and work with the victim to address them.

Volunteers Important to Safety Plan

In a successful reentry partnership, community volunteers can be the "backbone" of efforts to promote victim safety. Volunteers can learn about victim trauma and how it affects feelings of safety so they are able to communicate appropriately with them. They can help victims document their safety concerns and communicate them to supervision and surveillance officers. In some cases, the safety concerns can be addressed in the offender's conditions of supervision. Furthermore, reentry volunteers can help document violations of conditions of supervision that affect victim safety so that they are addressed immediately.

Developing Safety Plans

Many victims can benefit from assistance in developing safety plans. They may require a "safe harbor" when they are afraid to be in their homes or places of employment, or they may need help in relocating altogether due to threats of intimidation, harassment, or harm. Sometimes creating a cocoon of support of neighbors and friends will help victims feel safe and prevent further revictimization while validating their safety and security concerns. A reentry volunteer can offer to be a 24/7 on-call support person for victims who experience crises and serve as liaison to the agency with responsibility for supervising the offender.

Victim Impact Statement

True justice takes into consideration exactly how people are hurt by crime—physically, financially and emotionally. One of the most powerful tools for defining victim impact in the cadre of victims' rights and services is the victim impact statement (VIS). Whether it is a written description or one that is delivered orally—in person or by audiotape or video—the VIS describes the physical, financial, and emotional effects a crime has on an individual victim and his or her family.

Use of VIS in Justice System

The VIS is used by probation agencies in preparing pre-sentence investigation (PSI) reports for the court, and for judicial consideration at the time of sentencing. Paroling and correctional authorities use the VIS as they make decisions regarding the classification of incarcerated offenders or the release of the offender from custody. The VIS is particularly useful when correctional agencies prepare offenders for reintegration into the community. The VIS assists in the identification of offenders' counseling needs, treatment needs and issues related to accountability and understanding the impact of crime. The information garnered from the VIS can help in developing an offender's reentry case plan, and provide reentry team members with crucial insights into victims' needs and concerns.

Community/Neighborhood Impact Statements

Community/neighborhood impact statements (CNIS) can inform and empower local residents in areas affected by crime and offer them opportunities to convey the impact of crime on the neighborhood to community policing or community probation officers. Particularly in neighborhoods where the distribution of illicit drugs and violent crime are chronic, the CNIS is an important tool for airing individual and neighborhood concerns: focusing the attention of residents on the extent of the problem and uniting them in a common effort to actively address group victimization and the toll it take on their well-being. For example, the CNIS can ask for input from community members in a neighborhood to which an offender is being released about their specific concerns and the type of information they need to feel safe. Participating in the creation of a CNIS can also generate opportunities for neighborhood involvement in both victim- and offender-related programs and issues.

RESTITUTION

Restitution is one of the only ways that crime victims can hold offenders directly responsible for the harm that they have caused. Courts in all 50 states are mandated by law to order offenders at sentencing to reimburse victims for financial losses incurred as a result of their criminal behavior. Because only a few states have prison industry programs in which offenders can accumulate enough wages to substantially reduce the amount of restitution owed, offenders generally initiate payments to victims when they are released from incarceration. The inclusion of a restitution payment program that determines amounts and timing of payments should be an integral part of offender reentry planning (when restitution has been ordered).

Assistance to Victims with Restitution Issues

Community reentry volunteers can ensure that victims with whom they are working have written information that explains their restitution rights and how to enforce them. When victims have not been provided the opportunity to request restitution, or if restitution has not been ordered in cases involving pecuniary losses, volunteers can serve as a liaison to the corrections or reentry partnership authority to facilitate restitution.

Restitution Enforcement

When restitution has been ordered and the offender has rejoined the community, reentry volunteers can serve as a liaison between the victim, supervising officer, and offender in responding to delinquent or nonexistent restitution payments. They can also organize or serve on a restitution-specific advisory committee for reentry that cultivates a culture in the business community that supports offender accountability to victims for their financial obligations. Employers engaged in this process can offer employment to offenders that includes an agreed upon payment of restitution that is automatically deducted from wages. Reentry volunteers can also support offenders by offering classes in budgeting and money management, and providing regular reminders to offenders with whom they work about the importance of paying restitution obligations on time and in full.

COMMUNITIES MUST PAY ATTENTION

As the nation prepares for the release of a half million offenders annually over the next decade, measures must be taken to address core victims' rights relevant to offender reentry. Safety and well-being are critical issues to victims whose offenders are being released or preparing to be released. The neighborhoods and communities in which victims live can provide assistance to them in several principal ways:

- Support;
- Advocacy;
- Liaison services; and
- Public awareness.

Members of the community can positively affect outcomes for victims and offenders at the time of reentry through the following measures:

- Reacting with sensitivity to victim trauma and how it affects feelings of safety;
- Providing assistance with safety concerns;
- Developing awareness of notification rights and their importance; and
- Recognizing and supporting both victims and offenders in adhering to restitution orders.

The vital role of the community is highlighted throughout the APPA manual, and Hook emphasizes:

> If victims and offenders understand that people in their communities are paying attention—that the community has a vested interest in making sure that the reentry process goes smoothly—it could change the whole dynamic. Victims would be less vulnerable, offenders would be more responsible, and the community would be looking out for its own people, actively engaged in maintaining a safer and healthier culture.

QUESTIONS FOR REVIEW AND DISCUSSION

1. How much emphasis should be placed on an offender's right to be rehabilitated within the community? Discuss.
2. How much attention should victims receive whenever their victimizers are about to be paroled back into the community? Explain.

3. How can communities develop greater awareness of the needs of victims? How are these needs offset by the need to place offenders in a therapeutic community environment that will enable them to become rehabilitated? Discuss.

4. How can restitution to victims by offenders be enforced? What community mechanisms can be used to improve the ability of offenders to make restitution?

5. What rights do victims have regarding notification of an offender's early release from prison? Should victims be allowed to participate in parole hearings? Why or why not? Explain.

6. What are victim impact statements? Are they useful in deterring offenders from committing future crimes? Why or why not? Explain.

22

Managing Offender Resistance to Counseling

The '3 R's'

William N. Elliott

Adapted from William N. Elliott, "Managing Offender Resistance to Counseling: The '3 R's.'" *Federal Probation* 66: 43–49, 2002.

Reprinted with permission by the Administrative Office of the U.S. Courts.

It is the rare correctional counselor who, upon the conclusion of a counseling group, is not left feeling battle-weary, disillusioned and unsure of his or her competence. Offenders are often highly resistant to counseling interventions and seek to avoid the sometimes painful process of self-examination at all cost! They will exhibit a wide range of combative behavior intended to distract, derail, and otherwise discourage the counselor from conducting effective treatment. Offenders have devised elaborate strategies intended to wrest control of the counseling process and engage in tactics designed to evade the assumption of personal responsibility for their criminal conduct. When all else fails, of course, offenders will engage the counselor in an overt and often heated struggle for power and control which can exact an enormous emotional toll from the counselor.

Walters (2001) contends that the most important issue in managing offender resistance to treatment is the *avoidance* of extended debates with offenders. If the counselor chooses to enter into verbal combat with a resistant offender, the latter only escalates his or her efforts to win the debate. This is attributable to the "win at all cost" mentality which characterizes criminal offenders and substance abusers, as well as the desire to "save face" in front of peers. Unfortunately, correctional counselors often tend to respond to offenders' opposition to treatment interventions by directly and forcefully challenging them. Such a confrontational approach invariably results in the very power struggle which it is so important to avoid.

How, then, does the counselor effectively address offenders' opposition to treatment without becoming entangled in a struggle for control of the therapeutic process? The purpose of this article is to introduce the "3R's" of managing resistance to treatment: *redirection, reframing,* and *reversal of responsibility.* These interventions enable the counselor to call attention to an offender's behavior without provoking a conflictual and unproductive interaction. However, before presenting the "3R's" by way of description and illustration, it is necessary to examine in greater detail the problems inherent in the direct confrontation of offender resistance.

CONFRONTATION

Most models of counseling and treatment emphasize nonconfrontational and nonadversarial methods. Similarly, research has consistently revealed that confrontation arouses defenses and activates resistance. Confrontation sometimes deteriorates into a means of attack and an attempt to tear someone down. Such a misuse of confrontation forces the recipient into a corner out of which he or she must emerge fighting in a desperate attempt to save face. Goldring (1997) suggests that confrontational interventions are only effective when they catch a person by surprise and expose dramatic discrepancies between professed and overt behavior. Indeed, Fautek (2001) conceives of confrontation as a special form of constructive criticism containing a healthy mixture of observation and suggestion.

However, the current author has seldom used, or seen other clinicians use, confrontation in such a therapeutic manner. More times than not, the author and others have resorted to confrontational approaches in an ill-fated attempt to outwit an offender who has artfully dodged personal responsibility for his or her criminal thinking or behavior. In short, the treatment agent becomes immersed in a power struggle in which he or she is mismatched.

THE 3R'S OF MANAGING OFFENDER RESISTANCE

For nearly two decades the author has endeavored to simultaneously challenge incipient criminal thinking on the part of offenders in treatment, and avert or quickly withdraw from futile and endless struggles for control. The author has enjoyed considerable success in the use of three management strategies derived from his experience in a positive peer culture/guided group interaction program for juvenile offenders. All three strategies represent *indirect* approaches to the management of treatment resistance and the avoidance of power struggles in the process.

Redirection

Offender resistance is often the by-product of a criminal thinking pattern identified by Walters (1998) as the *power orientation.* This particular cognitive pattern is a derivative of two criminal thinking errors, the *zero-state* and the *power thrust,* originally described by Yochelson and Samenow (2000). In both cases, the authors are referring to an offender's attempt to regain a sense of control over his or her environment following a perceived loss of same. In psychoeducational classes or counseling groups, offenders are frequently exposed to information and criticism which is often ego-dystonic or otherwise unpalatable. One way offenders can combat or avoid such information is to distract or divert the clinician from the task at hand. If successful with such a (power orientation-based) ploy, the offender is able to avoid the hard work associated with self-examination.

Redirection quite simply involves the counselor's effort to return the focus of attention to the issue or task at hand. The first, and most obvious, way to redirect offenders' attention is by *ignoring* resistance. Indeed, as long as the offender's remark or action is mild and unlikely to cause any substantial harm, the counselor is advised to let it go unaddressed. This is especially true if an offender gossips with staff members in an attempt to derail the treatment specialist from his or her agenda. Ignoring a potentially disruptive remark will serve to maintain the flow of interaction within the class or group, and preclude the inevitable power struggle surrounding a limit-setting intervention by the therapist.

Another form of redirection is *undefocusing,* defined by Stanchfield (2001) as a continuous reference to the issue at hand. Defocusing entails offenders' efforts to shift the counselor's attention from his or her agenda. Through skillful utilization of undefocusing, the clinician remains undaunted by such manipulative ploys and thus adheres to his or her lesson plan. For example, consider the following interaction between a substance abuse counselor and an offender during a drug education class.

Counselor: "Okay, let's continue our discussion of the basic steps in developing a relapse prevention plan."

Offender: "Hey, Mr. Blackburn, did you see on the news that marijuana can ease the suffering of cancer and AIDS patients: How come you never tell about the positive effects of drugs?"

Counselor: "You raise an interesting question, Mr. Collins. However, it is not relevant to our discussion of relapse prevention."

Offender: "Yeah, but it has something to do with illegal drugs. Isn't that what this class is all about?"

Counselor: "The issue you bring up may be important to consider at some other time, but right now we need to make sure that everyone has a solid understanding of relapse prevention."

Notice that the counselor is patient and polite in addressing the offender, but is unwavering in his redirection to the agenda for this particular class meeting. The counselor recognizes, but does not directly confront, the attempt by the offender to defocus; a power struggle is thus averted.

Undefocusing is also useful when an offender attempts to engage the counselor in an argument. Offenders are likely to become argumentative when they are challenged, criticized, or held accountable. The argument invariably turns to the counselor's performance of his or her duties, with the offender citing examples of the staff member's unfairness or ineptitude. It is imperative that the therapist redirect the offender to his or her *own* treatment, as illustrated in the following dialogue between a counselor and a member of a group of female offenders:

Offender: "Miss Reynolds, you keep talking about the need to show tolerance and respect to each other. But some of the officers in my dorm treat us like we're numbers—not people. I'm afraid I'm just going to click on one of them some day."

Counselor: "Then perhaps the group needs to give you some more help with stress management and anger control. Aren't they two key aspects of your treatment plan?"

Observe how the counselor virtually ignores the offender's reference to staff. It is absolutely essential to help an offender maintain focus on *his or her* contribution to interpersonal conflict, rather than allow the offender to become defocused and waste time and energy trying to change the behavior of people over whom he or she has no control.

Nearly every correctional treatment specialist who conducts counseling with offenders is faced with at least one group member who loves to tell "war stories." Although these autobiographical sketches, whether true of otherwise, can be interesting and engrossing, they are seldom relevant to treatment and, in many cases, are intended to distract from the group process. Undefocusing can be very helpful in redirecting the offender to the task of *meaningful* self-disclosure and self-examination. By so doing the clinician is essentially saying to the offender (and group as a whole), "This is not story telling hour; we have *real* work to do!"

Redirection is also facilitative in identifying parallels between offenders' current behavior and prior criminal conduct. Offenders often espouse the view that they can't "work on" therapeutic issues while incarcerated because prison is an "artificial environment." The reality, however, is that offenders bring their core conflicts into the therapeutic process, whether the issue surrounds interpersonal relationships or attitudes toward authority. Therefore, whenever an offender describes how he or she behaved irresponsibly in the past, the astute therapist will redirect the individual to the way he or she behaves in the counseling group. Following is an example of such an interaction employed by a counselor working with inmates in a residential substance abuse program:

Offender: "Back when I was shooting up and robbing people, I didn't care about anything except getting my next hit on the pipe. Now that I'm clean and sober, I see how selfish I used to be."

Counselor: "Would you like to get some feedback from the other guys (group members) regarding how you continue to hurt others and show signs of selfishness?"

By redirecting the offenders' attention to the present, the counselor reminds the offender that treatment is a continuous process and suggests that parallels between past and current antisociality continue to exist. Notice, also, that the counselor redirects the offender to other group members, who can share many more firsthand observations of the offender's behavior than the counselor. The strategic activation of the group process is itself a highly effective means of pre-empting a power struggle between the counselor and the offender receiving feedback.

Time and time again, the author has found the examination of *current* interpersonal conflicts and other psychological issues to be considerably more useful than reviewing historical events. Indeed, historical explorations are not only unhelpful, but often serve to *detract* from the task of understanding *current* attitudes and behaviors. The correctional counselor is thus encouraged whenever possible, to redirect the offender from "then and there" to "here and now."

Reframing

Many correctional counselors make their work with treatment-resistant offenders more difficult than is necessary by ignoring straight-forward and relatively simple interventions. For example, when an offender denies that he has exhibited evidence of an antisocial thought or behavior, some clinicians will forcefully and relentlessly confront the offender, thereby prompting a futile and exhaustive power struggle. If, on the other hand, the therapist were to succinctly and nonconfrontationally reframe the offender's denial as a lack of readiness to engage in the change process, the offender has the option of simply agreeing or disagreeing with the therapist's observation. Reframing, then, represents the second of the "3R's" of managing resistance. This intervention entails asking offenders to adopt a perspective different from the one they currently embrace. In the following paragraphs, the author describes four methods whereby resistance can be reframed so as to highlight the offender's need for treatment without provoking a power struggle. Examples of each type of reframing are provided.

One of the simplest, but nevertheless potent, ways in which denial and resistance can be reframed is to address an offender's semantics. Words mean very different things to chronic offenders than to most people. For example, the word "respect" to many offenders means that other people stay out of his or her way. Likewise, offenders often consider a "friend" to be someone who will do or say whatever the offender wants. Offenders will also choose specific words in order to trivialize violent or otherwise irresponsible behavior. For instance, perpetrators of domestic abuse may refer to their violence toward women as a "little problem." In any of these cases, it is incumbent upon the therapist to reframe the offender's words such that the covert (true meaning) is made overt. Consider the following excerpt from a group counseling session with sex offenders:

Rapist: "Yeah, I'll admit that I got a little rough with the lady. But it's not like she had to go to the hospital or anything."

Counselor: "Can you clarify exactly what you mean by 'getting a little rough'"?

Rapist: "Well, you know, I mean she ended up with a few bruises and maybe a black eye, that sort of thing."

Counselor: "That's interesting. According to the police report, your victim had two black eyes, showed evidence that she'd been choked, and sustained several cuts and abrasions which became infected because she had *not* been taken to the hospital."

Rapist: "Yeah, well, what do you want me to say"?

Counselor: "What do the rest of you guys (group members) think about Mr. Chambers' use of the expression, 'I got a little rough with the lady'"?

In this vignette, the counselor successfully reframes the offender's initial statement in terms of the true severity of the physical injuries inflicted by the rapist. Notice, too, that the counselor astutely challenges the offender's semantics by relabeling "the lady" as "your victim." Moreover, the counselor wisely chooses to redirect the offender's resistance to the group, thus avoiding what was intended by the offender to become a power struggle.

Another way of reframing is to put a negative spin on a statement which an offender intends to be perceived as positive. For example, many offenders believe that they should be treated with respect by all who enter their path. Such an entitlement-based belief can easily be challenged by staff members whose remarks are found to be harsh or discourteous. Consider the following scenario:

Offender: "Can you guys (other group members) believe that I got a shot (disciplinary report) just because I told that rookie (first year correctional officer) to call me 'Mister?' Just because she wears a badge doesn't mean she can't give me the respect I'm due."

Counselor: "Is that all you said"?

Offender: "Pretty much, I just told her that she needed to treat us guys with respect if she wanted to get any."

Counselor: "So basically, you told the officer how to act . . . how to do her job. Is that right"?

Offender: "No man, I just asked her for some respect."

Counselor: "You asked, or did you demand"?

Offender: "I don't know. She might have taken it like a demand."

In this dialogue, there are actually two examples of reframing. First, the counselor suggested that the offender was essentially telling the officer how to do her job. Second, he relabeled the offender's use of the word "asked" as a "demand." In both instances, the counselor reframed the offender's statement to the officer as disrespectful—the very way he claimed to have been treated by the officer! The offender's statement is thus cast in a very different light than the one initially presented by the offender.

A third means by which therapists can reframe offenders' opposition to treatment is to reinterpret such resistance in a positive context. For example, correctional treatment specialists are bombarded by offenders who want to blame their criminality on peer pressure, poor parenting, poverty, and so forth. A therapist's stance which regards such a disadvantage as an "opportunity" or a "challenge" can help break through the offender's denial. Indeed, changing the attribution for one's criminality from a "recipe for failure" to an "opportunity for growth through adversity" can increase the probability of future success. Offenders should be asked which interpretation, positive or negative, is most likely to enable them to achieve their goals, avoid conflicts with others, and feel the way they want to feel. Consider the following illustration:

Offender: "I can't believe I let that asshole [peer] punk me."

Counselor: "What do you mean?"

Offender: "He got into my locker and took some coffee without asking me. Hell, I would have given it to him if he told me he needed some."

Counselor: "So, you feel like he got over on you?"

Offender: "Yeah, plus I haven't said anything to him about it."

Counselor: "Why not"?

Offender: "Cause I'm afraid that we'll get into a fight and I'll end up going to the hole" [disciplinary segregation].

Counselor: "It sounds to me like you're thinking about long-term goals instead of letting your feelings run your life. That's a real step forward, isn't it"?

Offender: "Yeah, I guess so. I mean, I do want to get closer to home and I've already got 16 months of clear conduct. I don't want to blow it now."

Counselor: "So getting close to home so you can visit with your family is more important to you than settling a score over some coffee. Is that right"?

Offender: "Yeah, I guess so."

In this scenario, the counselor first seeks to clarify what the offender means by the word "punk." Before a statement can be reframed, the counselor must understand the precise meaning of an offender's statement to himself. The counselor then reinterprets the offender's decision not to retaliate as evidence that he is delaying immediate gratification and, instead, focusing on what is most important to him. This use of reframing is essentially an exercise in values clarification: The antisocial value (not permitting inmates to "get over") is put side by side with a prosocial value (securing family contact). The offender is then asked to determine which value is pre-eminent.

Much of the therapist's work with offenders involves explicating criminal thinking errors and highlighting an offender's choice to be irresponsible. Accordingly, the final method of reframing to be examined is the identification of the criminal thinking pattern(s) implicit in an offender's resistance, and then pointing out its destructiveness for both the offender and others. For example, if an offender is describing random acts of kindness he has performed prior to incarceration, this manifestation of *sentimentality* is labeled as such. The offender is then challenged to explore the pain he has inflicted on others, and to dispense with the idea that doing good deeds is somehow compensatory for committing crimes. Elliott and Walters (1997) offer additional strategies for the therapeutic management of criminal thinking patterns exhibited by offenders undergoing treatment.

Elliott (1984) has articulated a four-step process whereby offenders' resistance is reframed in terms of problem behaviors typically found among juvenile offenders participating in positive peer culture/guided group interaction programs. This device is easily modifiable for use in highlighting specific criminal thinking patterns manifested by offenders in other venues. The process is intended to expedite the identification and confrontation of problematic behaviors or cognitive distortions as they occur in counseling or psychoeducational groups. Perhaps more importantly, adherence to the four steps described below will effectively preclude lengthy and often bitter power struggles between the counselor and the offender whose behavior is being challenged.

Step 1.   The counselor simply acknowledges that an offender's statement or action is indicative of criminal thinking. The criterion for such an assessment is whether or not the offender or someone else is or could be harmed in any way by the verbalization or gesture.

Step 2.   The statement or action is labeled (reframed) in terms of the underlying criminal thinking pattern. The author recommends that Walters' (2001) classification system be utilized because of the solid theoretical foundation upon which it is built as well as its economy (i.e., only eight cognitive patterns). However, some counselors might opt to employ Yochelson and Samenow's (2000) array of 52 criminal thinking errors. Regardless of the system adopted, the idea is to label the cognitive error as such.

Step 3.   The counselor articulates his or her rationale for reframing an offender's behavior as evidence of the identified thinking pattern or error. This statement of rationale should be cogent and succinct, and limited to a description of the specific way in which the offender's statement or action is or could be harmful to self or others. Whereas the application of a label (Step 2) simply calls the offender's attention to his or her criminal thinking, the rationale statement pinpoints the self-defeating and/or socially destructive nature of same.

Step 4.   The offender is asked whether or not he or she recognizes and accepts ownership of the criminal thinking pattern identified in Step 2 and clarified in Step 3.

This is a *yes or no* question; there is no need for any prolonged, contentious response on the part of the offender. By the same token, neither the counselor nor other offenders should debate the inmate's decision to accept or reject the confrontation. The intent is simply to make the offender aware of his or her criminal thinking patterns as they are evidenced. Hopefully, after repeated confrontation regarding the same or similar patterns, he or she will move toward accepting responsibility for same.

Following is an example wherein the four-step process for exposing criminal thinking patterns is applied following the issuance of certificates to offenders who just completed a drug education class:

Offender: "Hey, Miss Weaver. Is this (certificate) all we get!"

Counselor: "What do you mean, Mr. Johnson?"

Offender: "This certificate isn't worth the paper it's written on. The Parole Board isn't going to pay any attention to this."

Counselor: "Are you aware of a criminal thinking pattern you're displaying?" (Step 1)

Offender: "I'm just making an observation."

Counselor: "Could it be that you're engaging in entitlement based thinking?" (Step 2)

Offender: "How do you mean?"

Counselor: "What I heard was that you felt that you were entitled to something more than what you received. In other words, it was as though you were deprived of something which you were owed. In the past when you've felt that way, you have robbed people to get what you want." (Step 3)

Offender: "I don't see that at all. I just want something to show for my effort."

Counselor: "You don't see your statement as an example of entitlement?" (Step 4)

Offender: "No, I really don't, but I'll look into it."

Counselor: "Good."

The entire four-step process, if executed in the manner depicted in the preceding example, should require no more than sixty seconds. The counselor is admonished to approach all four steps in a calm, matter-of-fact, and utterly non-defensive manner. Again, the purpose of these steps, like all approaches to reframing, is to clarify the nature of resistance and encourage self-examination.

Reversal of Responsibility

The excuses and justifications verbalized by offenders to explain their criminality are prime targets for early counseling and treatment efforts. Offenders frequently attribute their antisocial behavior to unfairness or societal injustice, or they may blame the victims of their crimes and/or others in order to minimize the seriousness of their criminal conduct. Such external projections of blame are referred by Walters (1990) as "mollification," and by Yochelson and Samenow (2000) as "the victim stance." Walters contends that, regardless of the form it assumes, mollification must be challenged; otherwise, the offender will continue to externalize responsibility for his or her criminality rather than engage in honest self-examination.

Unfortunately for the counselor, the confrontation of deeply entrenched criminal thinking patterns, such as mollification or the victim stance, is a daunting therapeutic task. Offenders cling tenaciously to their self-serving neutralizations and rationalizations, and will shift from one justification system to another in order to evade personal responsibility for the harm they have caused to others. Accordingly, they become highly defensive and fiercely resistant when directly challenged by treatment staff. It has been the author's experience that spiraling and inherently counterproductive power struggles are inevitable consequences of a counselor's well-intentioned confrontation of an offender's display of mollification. Moreover, the intensity of the offender's resistance to assuming personal responsibility for his or her antisocial behavior is often so great that redirection and reframing prove ineffective as interventions. At this juncture, it is necessary to employ the most complex yet powerful of the "3R's," reversal of responsibility.

Reversal of responsibility, hereafter referred to simply as *reversals,* requires the counselor to reflect an offender's words or actions back to him or her in such a manner that the offender must assume personal responsibility for them. Virtually anything an offender does or says represents reversal material, but the third "R" is especially useful in responding to an offender's externalization of blame for his or her current life situation. For example, consider the following dialogue between a correctional counselor and a prison inmate:

Offender: "You know I wouldn't be here (juvenile correctional facility) if both my parents weren't alcoholics."

Counselor: "So you're suggesting that everybody who has parents with problems gets into trouble?"

Offender: "Well, not exactly. I'm just saying that I didn't get an even break."

Counselor: "I see. So, in other words, you had no choice but to break the law. Is that what you're saying?"

Offender: "No, I'm not saying that I didn't have any choice, just that it was a lot harder on me than on other kids."

Counselor: "I get it: in order to live a responsible life, you've got to have an easy life."

Offender: "No! That's not what I mean at all. I . . . I . . . don't know what I mean."

Notice how the counselor's reversals placed the inmate in such a bind that he could not escape the personal responsibility for his dilemma. Observe, too, that the reversals were presented matter-of-factly and non-sarcastically. This intervention is only effective when applied in a manner which is respectful and non-offensive especially when the offender's mollification assumes the form of complaining about the counselor or other staff as depicted below:

Offender: "Hey, Mr. Gregory (balding drug treatment specialist), you need to hand out some shades. That sun shining off your head is blinding us (inmates in drug education class)."

Counselor: "You know, Terry, it will be really great when you feel good enough about yourself that you don't have to put others down."

In this brief exchange, the counselor takes the wind out of the offender's sail, but does so in a way which is neither harsh nor humiliating. The counselor manages to retain his own sense of dignity and self-respect while according the same consideration to the offender.

Moreover, the reversal is potentially therapeutic, in that it identifies a critical treatment issue (self-esteem) and promotes self-examination. Obviously, the counselor's reversal in this case served to preclude an emotionally charged and fruitless power struggle.

Reversals represent an indirect method of challenging resistance rather than directly disputing or criticizing an offender's comment or action. For example, the counselor might say, "What did that behavior get you?" instead of, "Your behavior only succeeded in making your situation worse." The former statement challenges the offender to consider the motives for and consequences of his behavior, whereas the latter response only serves to discourage the offender and place him on the defensive. By asking the simple and straightforward question, "What did that behavior get for you?", the counselor holds a mirror up to the offender so that he can examine the self-serving yet self-defeating nature of his behavior. Indeed, one way to conceive of reversals is to regard them as efforts to clarify an individual's choice points and their consequences.

There is an infinite array of reversal strategies, all of which are intended to focus the offender's attention on what *he or she* is doing to contribute to a current predicament. The counselor's job is not to deny the contribution of other people, but to remind the offender that he or she has no control over the actions of others. Such an approach preempts a needless debate and struggle for power by suggesting that even though outside forces may play a role in an offender's misfortune, the offender is ultimately responsible for his or her behavior. For instance, consider the following brief interaction:

Sex Offender: "I was molested by my step-father and uncle. I guess I was destined to do the same thing to somebody else."

Counselor: "I understand that you experienced adversity while growing up. However, what does that have to do with making a decision to harm children now?"

Notice that the counselor does not actively dispute the offender's mollification statement, thereby averting an argument or debate. Instead, the counselor acknowledges the adversity experienced by the offender as a child, but challenges him to assume full responsibility for his choice as an adult. The strategic employment of reversals can, therefore, enable the counselor to successfully target mollification without becoming embroiled in a power struggle with an offender.

The effective use of reversals is informed by at least three caveats. First, under no circumstance should a reversal contain or imply any ridicule, anger, or sarcasm. Second, reversals are not to be confused with the popular notion of "reverse psychology," which is occasionally humorous but often condescending. Finally, like any treatment strategy, this intervention requires considerable practice before one can become proficient in its application.

CONCLUSION

The author has introduced three strategies through which correctional counselors can effectively manage offender resistance to treatment without becoming mired in a circular, contentious, and altogether useless power struggle. Indeed, the "3R's" effectively challenge primary issues, such as mollification and other criminal thinking patterns, but do so without leading the counselor to a beleaguering and demoralizing verbal conflict with an offender. Redirection, reframing, and reversal of responsibility all serve the purpose of continuously presenting offenders with feedback that counters their tendency to discount or deny the injury they have brought to both themselves and others.

The successful application of the "3Rs's" is contingent upon the counselor's recognition that he or she must *not* try to convince an offender to change his or her thinking or behavior. Any attempt in that regard will most certainly degenerate into a power struggle because the offender will fervently endeavor to convince the counselor that change is unnecessary or unattainable. In fact, it is *not* the counselor's job to make *any* decisions for an offender; rather, the counselor simply supplies the offender with information and affords him or her the opportunity for self-examination and change. One might even argue that, to an offender who is resistant to treatment, the counselor's best reply is simply this: "It's your life, and it's your choice to look into the mirror."

QUESTIONS FOR REVIEW AND DISCUSSION

1. What are the "3R's" of managing offender resistance? Discuss each.
2. Why do you think that offenders might be resistant to counseling? Discuss.
3. How can counselors overcome offender resistance to counseling?
4. How is effective counseling related to reducing subsequent recidivism among released offenders? Explain.
5. What is meant by the "reversal of responsibility"?

PART V

Juvenile Delinquency and Its Prevention

❖

Juvenile delinquency and its prevention has captured the attention of the public for over a century. Many studies have been conducted to explain why delinquency occurs and how it can be prevented. Several direct delinquency prevention efforts are discussed in this part. The part opens with an essay by Nancy Rodriguez. Rodriguez investigates the influence and relevance of restorative justice as a tool to successfully intervene in the lives of youthful offenders. Restorative justice is defined and examined as it is presently practiced in Maricopa County, Arizona. One important finding resulting from Rodriguez's research is that not all youths are equally qualified to participate in restorative justice programs. For some youths, restorative justice simply doesn't work. She describes ways that the most suitable juveniles can be targeted and assisted. The effectiveness of restorative justice in Maricopa County is assessed, and the potential for its use in other jurisdictions is examined.

James Gray describes an increasingly popular form of administering juvenile justice with his examination of peer courts. Also known as youth courts, these courts have proliferated in the United States at such a rate that by 2005, there were over 1,200 of them operating in various jurisdictions. The idea of being judged and punished by one's peers is not especially novel; for adolescents, peer courts have proved to be remarkably successful. The emphasis of peer courts is on offenders accepting responsibility for the delinquency they have committed, and restitution is the most frequently used punishment. Subsequently, some of those found guilty by peer courts may join future peer courts as judges against other peers. The successfulness of the peer court experience is examined and discussed.

Barbara Burns and her associates examine delinquent offenders in need of treatment and various services, with special focus on young children who are defined as being at risk. At-risk youth are those who often are brought up in homes with substantial marital instability and lack of cohesiveness. Also, lower socioeconomic status contributes to one's at-risk definition. Such children often don't do well in school and fail to adapt and adjust. Normal social relationships do not occur. Thus, Burns and her associates describe various treatments that can be applied to help them overcome or deal with their disabilities and/or problems. Burns et al.'s extensive review of interventions includes social welfare resources, the service sector, mental health services, and educational services and school interventions. Specific intervention programs are described for various jurisdictions, including Michigan, Minnesota, Sacramento County, California, and Toronto, Ontario, Canada. Several solutions to early childhood problems are suggested.

Kathy Elton and Kerrie Naylor address one of several important status offenses: truancy. Their examination of truancy as a pervasive issue includes an inspection of a truancy intervention program established in the Jordan School District near Salt Lake City, Utah.

Program elements are described as well as outcomes. Their pilot program appeared to have several positive results for decreasing truancy, at least in the jurisdiction they examined.

In the concluding essay for this part, Kristin Parsons Winokur, Ted Tollett, and Sherry Jackson investigate ways youth intervention programs can be evaluated. They describe PAM (Program Accountability Measures) analysis, which focuses on the effectiveness of day treatment for juveniles as well as commitment programs. Their investigation and report, which took place in Florida, describes various ways program effectiveness can be classified or categorized. They also include measures of program costs as potential ways of assessing program effectiveness. Their examination includes evaluations of day treatment programs, sex offender programs, wilderness camps, halfway houses, boot camps, and group treatment homes. Comparisons are made between male and female juvenile clientele, with females faring much better in terms of lower rates of recidivism compared with male clients. Close program monitoring is recommended.

23

Restorative Justice, Communities, and Delinquency
Whom Do We Reintegrate?

Nancy Rodriguez

Adapted from Nancy Rodriguez, "Restorative Justice, Communities, and Delinquency: Whom Do We Reintegrate?" *Criminology and Public Policy* 1: 103–130, 2005.

Reprinted by permission from the American Society of Criminology.

Criminal justice systems have created and implemented various programs based on the ideals of restorative justice. A fundamental component of restorative justice is the community's capacity to successfully reintegrate offenders back into their communities (Bazemore, 1999; Clear and Karp, 1999, 2000; Karp, 2001). Within this theoretical framework, community characteristics become especially important given the direct role community members play in restorative justice programs. Although researchers have proposed that structural characteristics have an important impact on restorative justice and community justice programs, no prior research has incorporated community-level measures to the study of such programs. This lack of research is especially surprising given that community characteristics remain significant predictors of crime, delinquency, and recidivism (Bursik and Grasmick, 1993; Eliott et al., 1996; Gottfredson et al., 1991; Hoffman, 2001; Rountree et al., 1994; Sampson and Groves, 1989) and have been shown to be relevant in decision-making processes within the justice system (Bortner et al., 2000; Bridges and Crutchfield, 1988; Bridges et al., 1993; Britt, 2000; Frazier and Lee, 1992; Hawkins, 1993, 1999; Myers and Talarico, 1987; Peterson and Hagan, 1984; Sampson and Laub, 1993; Secret and Johnson, 1997; Wilson, 1987, 1996). Given that restorative justice and community justice programs alike rely on the established relationships found within communities to bring "justice" to neighborhoods, examining community factors that are reflective of a community's capacity to provide such justice is central to a comprehensive understanding of restorative justice program processes and effectiveness.

This study relies on multilevel linear modeling to analyze how individual and community indicators influence restorative justice processes and impact. Juvenile court data from a restorative justice program in a metropolitan county in Arizona are used to explore the individual and community characteristics (e.g., heterogeneity, percent unemployed, percent Spanish-speaking households, and crime rate) of juveniles selected for restorative justice participation. To identify the impact of restorative justice on offenders, this study also compares the levels of recidivism between juveniles in the restorative justice program and juveniles on standard probation.

RESTORATIVE JUSTICE AND JUVENILE DELINQUENCY

Restorative justice can be characterized by dialogue (i.e., among a victim, an offender, and community members), relationship building, and the communication of moral values (Presser and Van Voorhis, 2002). The dialogue consists of open discussions on the harm caused by the offense and the designation of an appropriate resolution that reflects the values of the community (Clear and Karp, 1999). The inclusion of community members in restorative justice processes empowers the entire community in that it allows local citizens to represent their neighborhood's values and norms (Clear and Karp, 1999, 2000; Karp, 2001). Consistent with the ideals of community justice, restorative justice programs must ensure that communities have the capacity to recommend and provide resolutions for criminal behavior. Existing ties between individuals and the ability to develop well-defined skills that offenders need to successfully reintegrate into their communities are some indicators of this capacity (Clear and Karp, 1999; Karp and Clear, 2002b; Karp et al., 2002; Morris, 2002). In theory, the collaborative effort between community members and criminal justice agencies produces an effective mechanism of crime reduction that may also lead to the solving of other community/neighborhood problems.

Within juvenile courts, restorative justice programs hold juveniles accountable for their delinquent acts, aim to develop juvenile competencies, and protect the community (Bazemore and Griffiths, 1997; Bazemore and Maloney, 1994; Hayes and Daly, 2003; Umbreit and Stacy, 1996; Umbreit and Zehr, 1996). Juveniles are held responsible for their acts and released back into their communities having received needed services such as counseling, educational, and/or vocational training (Bazemore, 1992; Bazemore and Umbreit, 2001). Juveniles are then reintegrated into communities ready to contribute to the overall well-being of their community.

Juvenile delinquency cases have been processed through several types of restorative justice programs including victim-offender mediation programs, community reparative boards, circle sentencing, and family group conferencing (Bazemore and Griffiths, 1997; Bazemore and Umbreit, 2001; Maxwell and Morris, 1993; McElrea, 1996; Melton, 1995; Umbreit, 2000; Umbreit et al., 2001). Although these programs represent the most common restorative justice programs for juveniles, modifications to programs have been encouraged to ensure that restorative justice meets the unique needs of particular communities (Bazemore and Umbreit, 2001). The various types of programs share the common features of community participation and the localization of the resolution process (Bazemore and Griffiths, 1997; Bazemore and Umbreit, 2001; Melton, 1995; Umbreit, 1994, 1995; Umbreit and Coates, 1993; Umbreit et al., 2001).

To date, studies have produced mixed findings on the impact of restorative justice programs on recidivism. While some studies show lower rates of recidivism among juveniles in restorative justice programs than offenders in comparison groups, such differences fail to achieve statistically significant levels (McCold and Wachtel, 1998; Niemeyer and Shichor, 1996; Umbreit, 1994, 1993). Other studies fail altogether in showing lower rates of recidivism among juveniles in victim-offender programs (Roy, 1993). More recent studies have produced more favorable findings regarding the impact of restorative justice programs on recidivism (Hayes and Daly, 2003).

Given the important role of community characteristics in court decision-making processes and crime, the inclusion of community factors in evaluating a restorative justice framework is appropriate. In fact, proponents of restorative justice and community justice have identified how community characteristics influence the reintegration processes. Braithwaite (1989) indicates that "systematically blocked legitimate opportunities" make structural economic dimensions (e.g., urbanization and high residential mobility) instrumental in the shaming process (p. 97). Braithwaite acknowledges the possible use of measures at the individual *and* community level in studies of offender reintegration. In fact, he notes it is appropriate to create and use aggregate (community) measures from individual-level data in such studies.

Clear and Karp's (1999) notion of community context within a community justice framework emphasizes the role of social class (i.e., disadvantaged neighborhoods vs. economically and socially prosperous communities) in the reintegration process. Within this framework, it is recognized that community context (e.g., high rates of poverty, unemployment, single-parent households) cannot be ignored given the particular association such measures have with crime. Clear and Karp identify urban change and segregation as the two most important structural factors that affect the quality of life. Further, they argue that community justice will *not* succeed unless such community dimensions are addressed. It is possible that those communities plagued by structural factors that limit the legitimate opportunities of community members are the areas where community justice may have the most impact on the overall quality of life (Clear and Karp, 1999).

LOCALIZING RESTORATIVE JUSTICE: THE MARICOPA COUNTY COMMUNITY JUSTICE COMMITTEES

Consistent with the efforts of other criminal justice agencies to develop restorative justice programs, the Maricopa County Arizona Juvenile Probation Department created Community Justice Committees (CJC) in 1995 to deal with an increasing juvenile crime rate. The purpose of this program is to divert juvenile offenders from formal court processing and bring those cases to communities for resolution. A specific intent of the committees is to work with the juveniles, family members, and the community in an attempt to develop juveniles' skills, restore a sense of community that was destroyed by the delinquent offense, and ultimately, hold juveniles accountable for their actions. The committees follow a family group conferencing model in that victims, family members, and communities actively respond to the delinquent offense in search of appropriate resolutions for offenders (Bazemore and Umbreit, 2001; Maxwell and Morris, 1993, 1997; McElrea, 1996; Morris et al., 1993; Umbreit, 2000).

Juvenile probation officers are responsible for overseeing the committees that include two to four community members (i.e., volunteers), the victim(s), family members, and the juvenile offender. The recruitment of volunteers is handled by the Maricopa County Juvenile Probation Department. The Department solicits volunteers who are then assigned to one of the CJCs and work alongside the CJC probation officer. Volunteers take part in training that includes a review of the restorative justice model and the "balanced approach," which has been adopted by the juvenile court. Volunteers are responsible for reviewing the case file of participating juveniles with the juvenile and parents/guardians. During the conference, volunteers discuss the case with other panel members and determine an appropriate resolution to be met by the juvenile. The resolutions may be to include any of the following tasks: (1) restitution to the victim, (2) community service, (3) fine, (4) counseling, and (5) educational sessions. Juvenile offenders are given between 60 and 90 days to successfully complete the terms recommended by the committees.

Volunteers are also responsible for representing their neighborhoods in the conference process. Most often, volunteers (i.e., community members) may reside in the same neighborhoods as the juvenile offenders. To ensure that the restorative justice program reaches varying neighborhoods and communities, conferences are held in different locations throughout the county.

The placement of juveniles into the restorative justice program is based on a decision-making process that involves juvenile probation staff and the Maricopa County Attorney's Office. Officials from both agencies review all juvenile referrals and select those cases in which formal prosecution will be deferred if the juvenile is willing to participate in the diversion program. Upon selection, juveniles must accept responsibility for the delinquent offense and agree to have their cases processed through the restorative justice program. Juvenile court personnel attempt to target first- or second-time offenders and exclude sex offenders and violent felony offenders from program participation. In cases in which a juvenile fails to successfully complete the terms designated by the resolution, a formal petition for the original delinquent offense is filed by the County Attorney's Office.

THE PRESENT STUDY

Using 1999 through 2001 official juvenile court data, I examine the selection process and the impact of the restorative justice program on recidivism in Maricopa County, Arizona. The lack of studies that have incorporated individual- *and* community-based characteristics of offenders to examine restorative justice programs has been previously documented (Kurki, 2000). Virtually no information exists on the types of communities where restorative justice programs have made the greatest impact. By capturing how community characteristics such as racial/ethnic heterogeneity, unemployment, and delinquency rates impact the reintegration of juvenile offenders, this study will be able to empirically establish whether restorative justice efforts are most often localized in particular communities and whether recidivism of program participants varies by community type.

Prior research has documented the relationship between communities and juvenile court processing. For example, geographic location of juvenile courts has been shown to have an impact on the assessment of juveniles' needs (Sanborn, 1994). Researchers have proposed that studies of juvenile courts should also examine the economic and social conditions that surround juvenile courts (Crutchfield et al., 1994; Feld, 1999; Hagan, 1994). In fact, some researchers have noted that the incorporation of such indicators may be most appropriate in early juvenile court processes (Bortner et al., 2000). An examination of deferred prosecution (an initial decision-making process) that includes individual *and* community characteristics is consistent with the recommendations presented in prior studies of juvenile court processes. To date, no prior study has examined the selection process of juveniles in restorative justice programs. Interestingly, the selection process serves as an indicator of what particular juveniles are deemed most appropriate by court officials for reintegration. Identifying how individual and community indicators influence restorative justice processes can provide an empirical test of claims that propose these programs select offenders *least* in need of community support and treatment (Kurki, 2000).

The inclusion of community-based data to assess recidivism of juveniles in a restorative justice program is theoretically appropriate given the critical role of communities in the reintegration process. Moreover, community-level measures such as urbanism, poverty level, and ethnic composition of communities have been shown to be important predictors of crime and delinquency (Bursik, 1988; Hawkins, 1993, 1999; Osgood and Chambers, 2000; Wilson, 1987, 1996). Although the role of community characteristics in the reintegration process is certainly essential, studies in this area have yet to empirically analyze such measures. An examination of community characteristics can reveal whether restorative justice programs tend to be concentrated in specific communities (e.g., predominantly white versus racially/ethnic heterogeneous communities) and whether such communities have the "capacity" (e.g., high unemployment versus low unemployment areas) to successfully reintegrate juvenile offenders. One possible assumption is that the more homogeneous a community, the easier the reintegration of offenders given the common values and norms of community members. Conversely, the more heterogeneous (e.g., economically, culturally, and racially/ethnically) a community, the more challenging the reintegration process given such differences.

The incorporation of community characteristics to the study of restorative justice has *both* pragmatic and theoretical relevance. Such an inclusion will not only reveal how juvenile court officials use community factors in the selection of juveniles for reintegration but also whether program impact varies *across* communities. Consequently, this study examines the following research questions:

1. Is there a relationship among individual-level characteristics (e.g., race/ethnicity, gender), community-level characteristics (e.g., ethnic heterogeneity, unemployment rate, juvenile crime rate), and the decision to select juvenile offenders for participation in a restorative justice program?

2. Is there a relationship between participating in a restorative justice program and recidivism, and the effects of individual- and community-level characteristics?

DATA AND METHODOLOGY

Data for this study come from the Maricopa County Juvenile On-Line Tracking System database. These data capture information on juveniles' court processing from the time the juvenile is referred to the juvenile court until court disposition. To examine the selection of juveniles to the restorative justice program and program impact on recidivism, all juvenile referrals eligible for diversion from January 1999 through June 2001 were examined (N = 7,264). The first dependent variable, *CJC* (CJC = 1; other diversion program = 0), is measured by comparing those juveniles selected for the CJC program with offenders not selected for the program. Juveniles not selected for participation in the CJC program have their cases diverted through standard diversion mechanisms (e.g., paper citation, standard diversion program). The second dependent variable of interest, *recidivism* (yes = 1; no = 0), was constructed by following offenders in both groups for a 24-month period after successfully completing program requirements.

An extensive meta-analysis of 35 restorative justice programs (i.e., 27 victim-offender meditation programs and 8 conferencing programs) revealed that restorative justice programs were far more effective in reducing crime than were traditional correctional supervision mechanisms (Latimer et al., 2001). Similarly, Nugent et al. (2001) reanalyzed data from four studies of victim-offender mediation programs and found that juveniles who participated in such programs were far less likely to recidivate than were juveniles in the comparison groups.

Restorative justice assumes a *community responsibility* for criminal activity, while addressing the harm caused by the offender. However, community aspects can facilitate *or* hinder offenders' reintegration processes. Community characteristics such as crime, racial/ethnic composition, and economic resources can directly influence this reintegration process. For example, a juvenile offender from a community characterized by similar norms and values may have an easier time reintegrating (e.g., remaining crime free) in their community than an offender from a socially disorganized community (Braithwaite, 1989; McElrea, 1996). Unfortunately, little is known regarding how community aspects influence restorative justice processes or how they impact future crime and delinquency.

THE INFLUENCE OF COMMUNITIES IN DECISION-MAKING PROCESSES, DELINQUENCY, AND COMMUNITY JUSTICE

Community characteristics have been widely used by researchers in studies of adult and juvenile courts to explain the decision-making processes of court officials (Bridges and Crutchfield, 1988; Britt, 2000; Myers and Talarico, 1987; Peterson and Hagan, 1984; Secret and Johnson, 1997). Most of these studies have incorporated community-level data in an effort to explain the more severe punishment received by minority offenders. For example, the perceived "dangerousness" of racial/ethic groups who are viewed responsible for street-level crime may lead to more severe punishment (or formal social control) of minority offenders, especially when their communities are characterized by high levels of unemployment, crime, and racial/ethnic heterogeneity (Blalock, 1957; Bridges and Crutchfield, 1988; Frisbie and Neidert, 1977). In studies of juvenile court processing, community-level data such as crime, unemployment, and poverty rate have been shown to significantly influence detention, adjudication, and disposition decisions of white and non-white juvenile offenders (Bridges et al., 1993; Frazier and Lee, 1992; Sampson and Laub, 1993; Secret and Johnson, 1997). For instance, non-white juvenile offenders have typically been held longer in detention and have suffered harsher dispositions when processed by the juvenile justice system at different points.

An extensive body of research has also examined the role of community characteristics on crime and delinquency. Community characteristics have primarily explained the connection between race and crime, as well as offending differences within and between communities. Researchers have found direct and indirect relationships between crime and community components, including residential instability, family disruption, ethnic heterogeneity, poverty, and urbanism (Bursik, 1988; Hagan, 1992; Hawkins, 1993, 1999; Osgood and Chambers, 2000; Wilson, 1987, 1996). Characterized as features of social or community disorganization, these structural dimensions have been shown to mediate the relationship between individual offenders and criminal activity.

The data in this particular study are limited to those juveniles that completed the diversion programs and exclude those who failed to comply with the terms of diversion (non-completers).

At the individual level, both extralegal and legal variables are included in the analyses. Demographic indicators consist of *gender* (boys = 1; girls = 0), *race/ethnicity* (dummy coded variables for Hispanic/Latinos and blacks with whites as the omitted category), and *age* at time of court referral. Legal variables include the most serious *offense at referral* (i.e., property, status, and public order with person as the omitted category) and the number of *prior offenses* in juveniles' official court records. Controls for *school status* (enrolled in school = 1; not enrolled in school = 0) at the time of court referral and the *year* when the case was processed are also included.

To incorporate Braithwaite's (1989) and Clear and Karp's (1999) ideas regarding the role of community and structural factors in reintegrative processes, four community measures are analyzed by taking juveniles' residential zip codes at time of referral and linking them to zip code data from the 2000 Census (U.S. Bureau of the Census, 2000, Summary Tape File 1 and 3) (N = 110). A measure of *racial and ethnic heterogeneity* (Blau, 1977), where higher values indicate greater racial/ethnic heterogeneity, was computed based on racial/ethnic proportions of the population for each zip code.

Unemployment includes the percent of all residents in the labor force who reported being unemployed. A cultural indicator, *Spanish-speaking households*, was also analyzed. Spanish-speaking households represent the percent of households who reported Spanish as the primary language spoken in the home. This measure enables a test of whether language barriers present unique challenges to restorative justice and, more directly, to juveniles from predominately Spanish-speaking neighborhoods. *Delinquency* consists of the number of all delinquency referrals within each zip code reported to the juvenile court during the year 2000. These data were provided by the Maricopa County Juvenile Probation Department.

Given the nested nature of the data (i.e., individuals within zip codes), hierarchical linear modeling is used to analyze the data. As both dependent variables in this study are dichotomous, hierarchical generalized linear models (HGLM) are used to estimate the impact of individual- (Level 1) and community-level (Level 2) data on the outcomes (Raudenbush and Bryk, 2002).

Table 1 presents the dependent and independent variables used in the analyses along with the corresponding coding scheme.

TABLE 1   Description of Variables

Variable	Code
Independent Variables	
Individual-Level Data (N = 7,264)	
Sex	Boys = 1; Girls = 0
Race/ethnicity	Separate dummy variables for race/ethnicity; Whites are reference category
White	
Black	
Hispanic/Latino	
Age	Age at time of referral
School Status	Attending School = 1; Not Attending = 0
Referral	Separate offense dummy variables; Person offenses are reference category
Person	
Property	
Status	
Public order	
Prior offenses	Number of prior delinquent referrals
Year	Separate year dummy variables; cases processed during 1999 are reference category
1999	
2000	
2001	
Community-Level Data (N = 110)	
Heterogeneity	Racial/ethnic Heterogeneity measure
Unemployment Rate	Rate of all labor force classified as unemployed
Spanish-Speaking Households	Rate of households with Spanish as the primary language spoken at home
Delinquency	Delinquency referrals
Dependent Variables	
CJC	CJC = 1; Other Diversion Program = 0
Recidivism	Yes = 1; No = 0

FINDINGS

Before a review of the findings from the multivariate analyses, descriptive statistics by group (i.e., CJC vs. the other diversion group) shows that 62% of juveniles in the restorative justice program were boys, a higher percentage than in the other diversion group (i.e., comparison group). The average age for juveniles in both groups was 14 years old. The restorative justice group contained a smaller proportion of Hispanic/Latinos than did the other diversion group, but the representation of blacks was fairly consistent across both groups. Most cases in the restorative justice program involved property offenders (63%), whereas status offenders comprised the largest proportion of juveniles in the other diversion group (65%). Juveniles in both groups had, on average, at least one prior court referral. More than three fourths of juveniles in both groups were attending school at the time they were referred to juvenile court. Interestingly, the rate of recidivism did not substantially vary across both groups (28.3% versus 31.2%).

Data on Level 2 measures (i.e., community-level data) by group indicate that the average rate of racial/ethnic heterogeneity across communities of restorative justice participants was lower than those communities of juveniles in the comparison group. The unemployment measure shows that an average of 5% of community members in the restorative justice group versus 6% in the comparison group were unemployed. Also, on average, 19% of households in communities of restorative justice participants reported Spanish as the primary language spoken at home, a lower percentage than the comparison group (28%). The crime measure shows that the average number of delinquency referrals across communities of restorative justice participants was lower than those communities of juveniles in the other diversion program.

SELECTION PROCESS

To determine whether the mean selection rate of juveniles into the restorative justice program varied across communities, a one-way analysis of variance (ANOVA) model was estimated. The significant random effects intercept indicates that the rate of selection varies across zip codes (significant at $p < 0.05$). It is possible that the variation is simply caused by the unequal distribution of important individual-level characteristics across communities. To control for this, a random-coefficient model including only the individual-level measures was estimated. Findings show that property offenders were more likely to be selected by juvenile court officials for the restorative justice program. In particular, property offenders were 1.9 times (exp [0.638]) more likely to be selected than were person offenders. On the other hand, status offenders were 0.04 times (exp [−3.270]) less likely than were person offenders to be selected. Black juvenile offenders were 0.73 times (exp [−0.321]) less likely than were white offenders to be selected. Variance components indicate that the probability of being selected varied across communities (based on the significant intercept) even after controlling for individual characteristics. Additionally, the age, status offenses, total priors, and year coefficients showed statistically significant variance, which indicates that their effects on selection process varied across communities (i.e., zip codes). This result suggests that juvenile court personnel used these indicators differently across communities in selecting juveniles for restorative justice participation.

In an effort to explain why the mean selection rate varied across communities, community measures were included in the prediction model. Of the four community-level indicators, three significantly influenced the selection process. The rate of unemployed residents, Spanish-speaking households, and racial/ethnic heterogeneity significantly influenced the mean rate of selection, while controlling for individual characteristics. The unemployment rate of communities has a positive effect on the selection process, which indicates that juveniles from communities with a higher percentage of unemployed residents were more likely to be selected for the program. On the other hand, the effect of the proportion of Spanish-speaking households and racial/ethnic heterogeneity is negative, which reveals that juveniles from communities characterized by Spanish-speaking households and racial/ethnic heterogeneity were *less* likely to be selected for the restorative justice program. Level 1 estimates were similar to the estimates. Interestingly, after the inclusion of the community-level data, Hispanic/Latino offenders were significantly less likely to be selected for program participation than were white offenders.

RECIDIVISM

A second set of HGLM models was estimated to assess the effects of the restorative justice program on recidivism and to determine if restorative justice was more effective in some communities than in others.

The one-way ANOVA model confirmed that the mean rate of recidivism varied across zip codes (i.e., random effects intercept significant at $p < 0.05$). As with the selection model, to determine if the variation was simply caused by the unequal distribution of important individual-level characteristics across communities, a random-coefficient model including only the individual-level measures was estimated. Fixed-effects indicate that restorative justice participation decreased recidivism. Specifically, juveniles who took part in the restorative justice program were 0.81 times (exp $[-0.205]$) less likely to recidivate than were juveniles in other diversion programs. Variance components indicate that the mean level of recidivism still varied across communities (based on the significant intercept) after controlling for individual-level characteristics. However, the variance of the restorative justice coefficient did *not* vary across communities. Hence, restorative justice participation had the same effect in reducing recidivism across all communities. Had the variance of the restorative justice program been significant, the inclusion of Level 2 measures would be warranted in an attempt to explain the variation of program effects across communities. Given the interest in examining restorative justice impact on recidivism and, consequently, to determine whether recidivism effects varied across communities, findings from the incorporation of Level 2 effects are excluded from this presentation. Other significant individual-level indicators of recidivism included sex, age, property offense, status offense, and prior offenses. Boys, status offense, and juveniles with more extensive delinquency records were more likely to recidivate. Yet, older juveniles and property offenders were less likely to recidivate.

DISCUSSION

Community differences have been identified as important aspects of community justice and offenders' reintegration (Braithwaite, 1989; Clear and Karp, 1999). However, minimal attention has been given to how community characteristics influence restorative justice and community justice programs. Incorporating community characteristics to studies of restorative justice expands information of the reintegration process in several ways. First, identifying the individual and community measures that guide juvenile court officials in their selection of juveniles for program participation reveals the types of juvenile offenders and communities perceived to be most in need of a reintegrative process versus those more appropriate for traditional juvenile court supervision programs. Second, by incorporating community characteristics to the examination of program impact (e.g., reducing recidivism), it can be determined whether program impact varies across communities.

The current findings on selection process reveal that both individual and community characteristics influence the decisions made by juvenile court officials. Some researchers have hypothesized that programs tend to target predominantly minority juveniles, whereas others have alluded to the targeting of predominantly white juveniles. Findings here show that race/ethnicity plays a significant role in the selection decision. Both black and Hispanic/Latino juveniles were *less* likely than were white offenders to be selected for placement in a restorative justice program. This race/ethnic effect found here may not be viewed as evidence of racial disparity given that all offenders in this study were selected for diversion processes (vs. formal court processing). However, although all offenders were given an opportunity to not have their cases formally processed in juvenile court, the opportunity to take part in the reintegration process was certainly influenced by race/ethnicity, and it reveals that white juvenile offenders are most likely served and treated by this restorative justice program.

The effect of legal variables shows that property offenders were more likely than were person offenders to be selected for program participation. Such a selection process may be a product of two different mechanisms. First, program policy dictates that sex offenders and violent felony offenders should be excluded from participating in the restorative justice program. Not surprisingly, the probability of selecting juveniles with a person offense is relatively low. Second, offenses in which a victim is *directly* involved may be perceived by court officials as more fitting for the reintegration process. Victims conveying the monetary loss and other harms may be elements highly sought by officials seeking restorative justice cases. Victim's presence clearly enables the desired dialogue among offender, victim, and community members that is central to the reintegration process.

Although community context plays a central role in the restorative justice process, prior studies have only described the types of communities that may facilitate or challenge the reintegration process. The lack of inclusion of community measures in prior community justice and restorative justice studies made it difficult to ascertain which types of communities were more likely to have a reintegrative process in their communities relative to other communities. Findings from this study expand prior research in this area by empirically demonstrating that juveniles from communities characterized by higher levels of unemployment were more likely to be selected for restorative justice participation; yet, juveniles from communities characterized by higher levels of Spanish-speaking households and racial/ethnic heterogeneity were *less* likely to be selected.

Interestingly, the decision to select restorative justice participants may be related to a preceding decision-making process. That is, before juvenile court officials decide on the appropriateness of a juvenile for restorative justice participation, they may first attribute the delinquent act to something and/or someone. One possibility is that court officials seek to reintegrate juveniles from socially disorganized communities, for example, those communities characterized by high unemployment. Juveniles from these communities may be perceived most in need of the reintegration process. Other community characteristics such as racial/ethnic heterogeneity may be viewed by court officials as indicators of areas with high crime rates and perceive juveniles from such communities as more responsible for their delinquent act *and* less appropriate (i.e., less deserving) for reintegration, which supports the assumption that the more racially/ethnically mixed a community, the more challenging the reintegration process becomes. Most studies examining the effects of race/ethnic composition in decision-making processes have focused on white and black populations. According to Census 2000 data, Hispanic/Latinos comprise 25% of the population in Maricopa County, whereas blacks make up only 4% of the population. Findings on the role of racial/ethnic composition found here stress the importance of examining groups other than blacks in studies of racial threat and disparate treatment.

Another explanation for the effect of community characteristics in the selection process of juveniles may be more practical in nature. Although it is unlikely that court officials are aware of *specific* community measures (e.g., racial/ethnic heterogeneity and unemployment rate at the zip code level), they may certainly be able to identify those communities that can facilitate a reintegrative process. For example, communities characterized by high unemployment may have a higher concentration of community members that can participate in the restorative justice program. Court officials' decisions to select offenders may be indirectly influenced by the ability to have community members (i.e., volunteers) and parents from those communities take part in the committees.

Communities characterized by a high percentage of Spanish-speaking households may present a challenge to juvenile court officials. Court officials may be less likely to select juveniles from those communities given the difficulty in obtaining community members and family members who speak English and wish to participate in the program. The language barrier, which can be overcome with the presence of a translator, requires additional resources from the court that may not be readily available or affordable.

Prior studies of restorative justice programs have produced mixed findings on the impact such programs have on recidivism. Findings from this study indicate that juveniles who participated in the restorative justice program were less likely to recidivate than were offenders in standard supervision programs. The lack of variation in the effect of restorative justice participation across communities indicates that the program reduces the likelihood of recidivism for all offenders regardless of their community characteristics. Although community variation occurred in the selection process and community characteristics were significant predictors of who was selected, these aspects did not play a significant role in the effectiveness of the program. In the end, regardless of whether the selection decision made by court officials is attributed to their perception of juveniles, communities, or mere artifacts of program capacity (e.g., availability of volunteers), lower recidivism by restorative justice participants was exhibited across all communities.

Findings from this study have theoretical and practical importance. First, the inclusion of community measures in this study enabled an empirical test of how particular community characteristics influence the reintegration process. By identifying the influence that community measures such as unemployment, racial/ethnic heterogeneity, and Spanish-speaking households have in the selection of juveniles for reintegration, a direct empirical relationship can be substantiated between restorative justice and communities. Second, the focus on the decision-making process of juvenile court officials vested in implementing and overseeing the reintegration process has been neglected in prior studies. It is important to recognize that juvenile court officials, before the implementation of any evaluation design (e.g., randomization, matched design), identify those appropriate for reintegration. These decisions have a direct influence on where community justice is likely to be "nested." Third, identifying that certain communities are less likely to take part in reintegrative processes provides valuable information regarding the perceived appropriateness of correctional supervision. Findings here demonstrate that certain communities are less likely to be granted access to reintegrative processes and more likely to be exposed to traditional correctional supervision mechanisms. The difference in access to restorative justice programs provides insight on how court officials allocate court resources and where restorative justice programs may be expanded. Lastly, the reduction in recidivism experienced by restorative justice participants provides support for the expansion of community-based programs that seek to incorporate community members and victims in the justice process.

This study has empirically substantiated the important impact individual and community characteristics play in restorative justice. However, several limitations of this study should be noted. Data on parents' marital status and/or living arrangements were not available for the juvenile population under study. Given the important role families play in the restorative justice process, the omission of such measures necessarily ignores parents' role in restorative justice. Second, findings from this study are only representative of white, black, and Hispanic/Latino juveniles. Although other racial/ethnic groups are processed through the program, their numbers were relatively small and therefore excluded from these analyses. Thus, findings of this study cannot represent the experiences of Native-American, Asian, or other racial/ethnic offenders. Third, because drug offenders were excluded from this study, it is unknown whether restorative justice can be effective in dealing with substance abuse as proposed by some (Braithwaite, 2001). Fourth, this study included only cases where juvenile offenders successfully completed the terms of diversion. It is possible that terminated cases (e.g., dropouts) experienced different recidivism outcomes than those presented here. Lastly, many juvenile risk factors (e.g., psychological, social, educational) were not available for examination in these analyses. It is certainly possible that these excluded data have a direct or indirect influence on the selection decision and recidivism outcome. In sum, although these limitations do not enable full generalization of these findings, this study has significantly advanced existing knowledge of restorative justice by addressing the role community characteristics play in reintegration programs.

CONCLUSION

This research set out to incorporate community measures to the study of restorative justice processes. By using official juvenile data and Census data, this study found that individual- (e.g., race/ethnicity) and community-level (e.g., unemployment rate, racial/ethnic heterogeneity, proportion of Spanish-speaking households) characteristics significantly influenced the selection of offenders to a restorative justice program. When examining restorative justice impact, findings of recidivism show that offenders who took part in the restorative justice program were significantly less likely to recidivate than were offenders in the comparison group. Moreover, the effect of restorative justice on recidivism did not vary across communities. Hence, all offenders in the restorative justice program, regardless of their community's characteristics, were less likely to recidivate.

Findings from this study present several directions for future research. First, studies of restorative justice must continue to examine the processes that guide the placement of juveniles into programs. Examining how court officials perceive offenders and communities when reintegration policies are involved is important because the selection decision is the first formal step in the reintegration process. As such, future research should examine front-end processes of restorative justice programs and address whether court officials (e.g., probation officers) consider individual juvenile attributes, which may be indirectly correlated with community characteristics, *or* whether they consider their experiences and knowledge of those communities when making decisions. Few studies have relied on interview data of court personnel to assess decision-making processes. Studies based on interviews with court officials can provide insight to how both individual and community characteristics influence juvenile court processes and outcomes. Second, studies should incorporate multiple community measures to explore how restorative justice and, in general, community justice is shaped by community characteristics. In particular, racial/ethnic composition should be considered in future studies regardless of whether community justice programs are nested in homogeneous or heterogeneous communities. The "dynamic" nature of communities, especially the role that the growing Hispanic/Latino population plays in communities, should be recognized and addressed in future studies. Third, studies must continue to explore the important role of individual characteristics in examining restorative justice programs. Although a few researchers have identified the types of offenders most likely to succeed in the reintegration process, future research should examine whether particular offenders are most likely to succeed in restorative justice programs. Further, studies must examine the possible interactive effects between individual- and community-level data to expand our understanding of the restorative justice process.

QUESTIONS FOR REVIEW AND DISCUSSION

1. How does Maricopa County, Arizona, use restorative justice for delinquent youth?
2. What is a deferred prosecution, and how does it further client reintegration?
3. How are delinquents selected for inclusion in restorative justice programs?
4. Is there any evidence that minority youths are being targeted for restorative justice programs compared with other youths? Discuss.
5. How do courts determine which youths are most likely to benefit from restorative justice programming?
6. What appears to be the relation between recidivism and participating in restorative justice, at least in this study? Explain.

24

"The Peer Court Experience"

James P. Gray

Adapted from James P. Gray, "The Peer Court Experience." *APPA Perspectives* 27: 30–33, 2003.

Reprinted with permission from the American Probation and Parole Association.

Without question, numbers of things with our young people are not going well in our society today. Even worse, in several well-publicized situations our local government organizations have not only been unresponsive, but sometimes they have been a part of the problem. However, our citizens, parents and taxpayers should be aware that many things are going right, too. One of those successful and helpful programs is peer court *(also known as youth court or teen court)*.

We started our peer court in Orange County, California in 1994. The purpose was to provide an institutional means for our young people to focus upon ethics, individual responsibility, the long-range importance in their lives of getting accurate information and making intelligent decisions based upon it, and the fact that they are important role models for others, especially their younger siblings.

Orange County's Peer Court is a diversion program that presents real juvenile court cases that are carefully screened by the probation department to high school "jurors." The juvenile subject must admit the truth of the charged offense and, along with his/her parents, waive their rights to confidentiality. They personally appear at a high school outside of their own school district (so that no one present knows them) with at least one parent. A jury of students at the host high school is impaneled after short questioning to determine if they can be fair and impartial. A probation officer reads a statement of facts about the case, and then the subject and parent are sworn and given an opportunity to make a statement about themselves, their backgrounds, the offense, or anything they feel would be important for the jury to know about the situation. A sitting county judge presides over each of the sessions, and also asks questions; however the program is designed for most of the questioning to be done by the high school jurors. After enough questions are asked to enable the jurors to feel that they have received sufficient information, the jury retires along with a volunteer adult attorney advisor to deliberate and reach a recommended sentence to give to the judge. The attorney advisor tries to keep the jury focused, but does not participate in the deliberations.

When the jury returns, the judge reviews the recommendations and tries to incorporate them into the sentence. If the juvenile subject completes the sentence within four months, the underlying offense is dismissed. The only sanction for a failure to complete the sentence is to refer the underlying offense back to the district attorney for prosecution. Obviously, the district attorney must exercise appropriate discretion in making this decision; however, that office has stated that it will consider the subject's failure of the diversion program as a "factor in aggravation" in whether or not to proceed. We stress that these are serious matters. Even though juvenile records are still sealed for most purposes, there are always exceptions and the risks of having a criminal conviction should not be taken lightly.

Peer court sentences can include virtually anything except incarceration or the payment of a fine. They frequently include community service, such as picking up trash in a park, graffiti removal, and/or working with the sick, injured or elderly at local medical institutions; individual and/or family counseling; restitution to the victims of the offense; completion of alcohol and/or other drug abuse programs; writing letters of apology to the victims of the offense and/or parents, or essays about what they have learned from this experience; being ordered to attend school regularly, and attend all classes; and participating as a juror at a future peer court session.

One of the critical issues in our program is the screening and selection of the offenses. Many of them are shoplifting or other petty thefts, receiving stolen property, graffiti or other vandalism, trespass, "simple" alcohol, marijuana or other drug offenses, and driving a motor vehicle without a license and/or taking a parent's car without permission. We never accept cases involving dangerous weapons, and only rarely do we accept offenses dealing with violence. Exceptions to this have been cases like a juvenile male who assaulted another male because he had insulted his girlfriend, as long as there were no injuries.

Without a doubt it would be less costly and time consuming to have the Probation Department implement a diversion program without peer court. However, even though we

Who Administers Youth Court

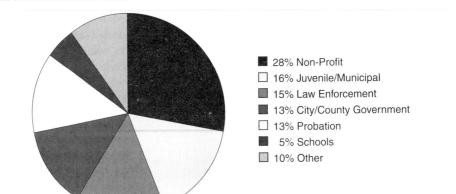

- 28% Non-Profit
- 16% Juvenile/Municipal
- 15% Law Enforcement
- 13% City/County Government
- 13% Probation
- 5% Schools
- 10% Other

have a history of success with the individual juvenile subjects and their parents, the real impact of our program is to pursue those "teachable moments" not only with the subjects themselves, but also with the jurors and other high school students in the audience. (A total of 4174 young people either participated in or observed our Peer Court in the 2001–2002 school year.) For example, when our jurors ask a parent one of our "sample" questions like "Why don't you know who your child's friends are?" both the parents as well as all of the young people in the audience start to focus upon the fact that young people actually expect a parent to parent. We have had jurors ask the subjects if they want their younger siblings to smoke marijuana. When they say "no," people focus on the fact that if the older sibling smokes, no matter what is said, the younger sibling will probably follow the lead of the older. As a result, the students realize that they are mentors for their younger brothers and sisters, and the examples they set are important. These are valuable lessons that are often not learned elsewhere.

Peer court makes distinctions between a friend and an acquaintance. We ask questions like, "Would friends request a person to shoplift an item and give it to them?" "Does it matter who you choose as friends?" "If your friends tend to ditch classes, smoke marijuana or shoplift, how successful do you think they will be in later life?" "If you hang out with them, what are the chances that you will end up doing the same things, with the same results?" On the other hand, "If you surround yourselves with friends who work and study hard and are successful, don't you think that this will increase your chances of being successful as well?" Other questions are asked like "Don't you realize that if you do something positive that this will have a gratifying effect upon the people who love you, and that the same thing is also true in reverse?" "How do think your parents are feeling having strangers tell you how they should raise you," and "How disappointed do you think they feel that you are in trouble?" "Did you ever think about this before you shoplifted that tape cassette from the store?" These questions are particularly probative when the parents sitting next to their child are in tears.

Petty theft is a big problem with young people. We frequently ask the subjects if they have ever had something stolen from them. If so, we ask how they felt when the theft was first discovered. And then we will say something like, "Tell the truth—didn't you want to throttle the person who took that item from you? Do you think your victim felt any differently? Is that what you want to inflict upon other people?" We also ask the subject if he/she is a thief. Yes it is true that they stole something on that particular occasion, but did their parents raise them to be a thief? After a few more questions, we center the discussion onto the fact that it really is easy to steal, and most often it can be done without anyone discovering who did it. However, people like us don't do that. Why? Not because of possible punishment, but because "I am better than that!" Even though no one else will know, I myself will, and that is not who I am. Numbers of times, our judge has had placed a $20 dollar bill at the back of the assembly hall, saying that it is that judge's money. If anyone takes it that would, of course, be stealing, but this time there will be no legal consequences. Nevertheless, we expect that our students there are better than that. So far, the money has always been there at the end of each session.

We focus upon other matters of behavior by our young people as well, such as courtesy and respect. For example, we are still old fashioned enough to believe that a man does not sit down before first helping his mother to be seated. If one of our male subjects sits down first, we take the time to make both mother and son stand up again and do it the respectful way. Or our judges will make the comment that they are sorry the subject does not take these proceedings more seriously—because if they did, they would tuck in their shirt, or wear more appropriate attire, etc. before coming to our peer court session.

We also have some problem areas. When the subject, or even the subject's parent, does not take our proceeding seriously, saying, for example, that this is a waste of time, or that our sanctions are not appropriate, we simply will agree with them, saying that this program is not meant for them. Then we refer the matter back to the district attorney for prosecution. In addition, although this can get touchy, if a parent appears to be inappropriately defending the subject and enabling the anti-social behavior to continue, we have been known to ask the parent to depart, and require the subjects to defend their conduct themselves. Similarly, if a subject fails our program and the district attorney does not prosecute, that word gets out among the students quickly and our program loses credibility. As a result, if the subjects say in any way that they are not guilty of the offense, or do not think it can be proved, we send it back. As we tell them, we are not running a railroad. That means that neither the probation department nor the district attorney can send us cases for which proof is lacking. If they do that, they will undercut our credibility and our program.

We always try to end our sessions on a positive note. In appropriate cases, we tell the subjects that we believe this never will happen again, and that there is simply no reason why they cannot enjoy happy, successful and satisfying lives. We schedule four cases in a two-hour session. By the time we have handled the four hearings, at least two of the juries have usually returned with their recommended sanctions, and then by the time we have handled those sentencings, the other two juries have returned. We also encourage an "open forum" atmosphere in which the young people ask questions of the judge. Many questions show a heightened interest in the judicial process.

Once everything has been completed and the students are dismissed, the subjects and their parents have a conference with our probation officer in which logistical questions are answered, and court documents are signed. During this time, our judges often speak privately with the subjects and parents, giving encouragement and recommendations. This has been found to furnish positive reinforcement to all of the parties.

We are now holding sessions in 13 of our county's high schools. We have deeply benefited from the efforts of our team, which is comprised of members of the Orange County Constitutional Rights Foundation, Department of Education, Probation Department, District Attorney's Office and Superior Court. Most of the participants are volunteers, including all of our judges, on-scene probation officers, host high school officials, attorney advisors, and student ROTC bailiffs. Each of our high schools has been adopted by a law firm, which graciously supplies young attorneys to act as our advisors.

The results of our program have been gratifying. For example, the no-show rate for the sessions has consistently been below ten percent. Of the 207 subjects who went through the peer court sessions in the 2001–2002 school year, only 12 failed to complete the ordered sentences and their cases were referred back to the district attorney for prosecution. Obviously, if the "success" rate were 100 percent, we would not be taking serious enough cases. So we are pleased with those results.

In addition, since the educational component is one of the major reasons for the program, we are pleased with the statistics taken from a survey of 516 of the students who participated as jurors, bailiffs or observers. After observing the sessions, 74 percent of the participants and 60 percent of the observers agreed that peer court is an effective way to reduce youth crime; 83 percent of the participants and 70 percent of the observers agreed that peer court is an effective way for students to learn about the legal system; 80 percent of the participants and 60 percent of the observers agreed that peer court is an excellent alternative to the formal court/juvenile justice system; and 74 percent of the participants and 56 percent of the observers agreed that peer Court is an effective way to keep youth from committing other crimes in the future. In addition to these statistics, there are numerous individual comments on the surveys about consequences and individual responsibility and pride.

Preliminarily, of course, this survey verifies the old maxim that people who get involved in a program get more out of it. However, youth crime is a difficult area in which to get positive results. Combining the results of this survey with our observations tells us that our peer court program is contributing to an ethical dialogue and focus that otherwise appear to be lacking. It is one thing for adults to admonish our young people, and another for them to hear it from their peers. In addition, the program is assisting our young people in developing sophistication about life that is hard to develop or define. For example, in one of our cases that involved the shoplifting of some cough syrup, one of the jurors asked the subject if he was addicted to the alcohol in the syrup. After a few more questions, it became apparent that the answer was yes. In another case, where one of the shoplifting subjects stated that his career objective was to become a firefighter, after recommending that this offender perform a suitable number of hours picking up trash at a county park, the jurors recommended that he serve the remainder of his community service at a fire station. In each session, we see further examples of the increased sophistication of our student jurors, and it is a rewarding sight to see.

One of the biggest pitfalls in these sessions is the adults becoming too dominant. The program is designed for peers to listen to the problems of their peers, and to render peer justice. To the degree that the judges begin to preach, or to take too much control, then we undercut our own program. However, the probation department does give judges some access to confidential information not possessed by the jurors, such as prior arrests, truancy, parental problems, etc. So when the questioning begins to lag, or starts to go in an inappropriate direction, it is the responsibility of the judge to bring the discussion back on track. The trick is not to overdo it.

The involvement of the Department of Education has brought an added benefit. They have put together a curriculum package that teaches about government, the justice system, advocacy, and the importance of acquiring accurate information, and then incorporates our peer courts into the curriculum as a field trip and practical learning experience. This allows the peer court concept to be extended beyond our 13 high schools, and adds some real life experience to the educational process. In addition, at some time in the future, we hope to create several video programs of simulated peer court sessions, which also can be used for instructional purposes.

Nationally, the youth/peer/teen court movement is strong. According to the National Youth Court Center website (http://www.youthcourt.net) as of the end of July 2003, there were close to 900 youth court programs in 46 states and the District of Columbia. Most of them are diversion programs like ours. Otherwise, there are many differences among the programs. A few have their juries decide guilt or innocence, and many use youth prosecuting and defense attorneys and judges. Most youth courts hold their session in courtrooms; however, we have chosen to hold ours in the schools. In doing that, we give away a little of the sanctity of the courtroom, but gain a great deal in student attendance. In my view, it is clearly worth the trade. We also feel that those programs that use youth attorneys sometimes

---

Youth Court Provides the Community

- An early intervention and prevention program

- An option on the continuum of juvenile services

- A way to hold juvenile offenders accountable

- A means for educating youth on the legal and judicial system/Builds competencies

- A meaningful forum for youth to practice and enhance skills

- An avenue for building ties between youth and their community

---

result in the best attorney carrying the day, instead of focusing upon and emphasizing the subject's responsibility for his/her actions.

We are proud of our peer court program. If anyone would like to have some further information, please feel free to contact Mr. Greg Ronald at the Orange County Probation Department at (714) 935-6647, or Ms. Gwen Vieau at the Constitutional Rights Foundation of Orange County at (949) 440-6757, ext. 137, or at gvieau@crfoc.com. We have found that the concept of young people delivering justice to their peers works. Our young people are confronting and addressing the impact of their behavior upon their victims, their families and themselves, and along the way are learning critical citizenship, knowledge and skills. We believe that something good is happening here and thought you would like to hear about it.

QUESTIONS FOR REVIEW AND DISCUSSION

1. What are peer courts? Who administers them?
2. How are youths screened for participation in youth courts? Are the most eligible youths selected? Why or why not? Explain.
3. What is Orange County's Peer Court? Describe it.
4. What are some valuable services that peer courts provide the community?
5. In what ways is it more important for delinquent youths to be judged by their peers rather than adults? Explain.

25

"Treatment, Services, and Intervention Programs for Child Delinquents"

Barbara J. Burns, James C. Howell, Janet K. Wiig, Leena K. Augimeri, Brendan C. Welsh, Rolf Loeber, and David Petechuk

Adapted from Barbara J. Burns et al., *Treatment, Services, and Intervention Programs for Child Delinquents*. Washington, DC: U.S. Department of Justice, 2003.

Compared with juveniles who start offending in adolescence, child delinquents (age 12 and younger) are two to three times more likely to become tomorrow's serious and violent offenders. This propensity, however, can be minimized. These children are potentially identifiable either before they begin committing crimes or at the very early stages of criminality—times when interventions are most likely to succeed. Therefore, treatment, services, and intervention programs that target these very young offenders offer an exceptional opportunity to reduce the overall level of crime in a community.

Although much can be done to prevent child delinquency from escalating into chronic criminality, the most successful interventions to date have been isolated and unintegrated with other ongoing interventions. In fact, only a few well-organized, integrated programs designed to reduce child delinquency exist in North America today.

The Study Group on Very Young Offenders (the Study Group), a group of 39 experts on child delinquency and child psychopathology convened by the Office of Juvenile Justice and Delinquency Prevention (OJJDP), has concluded that juveniles who commit serious and violent offenses most often have shown persistent disruptive behavior in early childhood and committed minor delinquent acts when quite young. Therefore, comprehensive intervention programs should encompass children who persistently behave in disruptive ways and child delinquents, in addition to young juvenile offenders who have committed serious and violent crimes. Focusing on children who persistently behave disruptively and child delinquents has the following advantages:

- If early interventions are successful, both groups are less likely to become chronically delinquent if they are exposed to additional risk factors that typically emerge during adolescence.
- If early interventions are successful, both groups are less likely to suffer from the many negative social and personal consequences of persistent misbehavior.
- Both persistent disruptive behavior and delinquency can be reduced at an early age through effective interventions.

Child delinquents who become serious and violent offenders consume significant funds and resources from the juvenile justice system, schools, mental health agencies, and other child welfare and child protection agencies. Nevertheless, many children, especially those who behave disruptively, are not receiving the services they need to avoid lives marked by serious delinquency and criminal offending. More intervention programs fostering cooperation among families, schools, and communities need to be devised, implemented, and evaluated.

TREATMENT APPROACHES

A growing body of research has focused on the treatment of juvenile offenders and juveniles with conduct disorder. An examination of 200 studies published between 1950 and 1995 found that the most effective interventions for serious and violent juvenile offenders were interpersonal skills training, individual counseling, and behavioral programs (Lipsey and Wilson, 1998). Another review of 82 studies of interventions for children and adolescents with conduct problems found strong evidence for several effective treatments, including delinquency prevention and parent-child treatment programs for preschool-age children and problem-solving skills training and anger-coping therapy for school-age children (see, e.g., Brestan and Eyberg, 1998).

Examples of effective interventions include the parent training programs based on Patterson and Gullion's *Living with Children* (1968), which are designed to teach adults how to monitor child problem and prosocial behaviors, reward behavior incompatible with problem behavior, and ignore or apply negative consequences to problem behavior. Another example of effective interventions is the parent-training program developed by Webster-Stratton and Hammond (1997), which involves groups of parents in therapist-led discussions of videotaped lessons.

Far less evidence of efficacy is available for psychopharmacology than psychosocial treatments; the results of studies are often conflicting. For example, one study found that lithium effectively reduced aggressiveness in juveniles (Campbell and Cueva, 1995), whereas two other studies did not produce this result (Klein, 1991; Rifkin et al., 1997) and one found only limited benefits from lithium treatment (Burns, Hoagwood, and Mrazek, 1999). Other medications for children with conduct disorder are also being studied, including methylphenidate, dextroamphetamine, carbamazepine, and chlonidine.

Controlled research on institutional care (e.g., psychiatric hospitalization, residential treatment centers, and group homes) for children with conduct disorder is limited, and the findings are less than encouraging. To some extent, this result may be linked to the finding that interactions among delinquent juveniles are prone to promote friendships and alliances among them and intensify delinquent behavior rather than reduce it (Dishion, McCord, and Poulin, 1999). Several older clinical trials demonstrated that community care was at least as effective as inpatient treatment. A recent study that compared inpatient treatment with multisystemic therapy (MST) found that this community-based alternative treatment was more effective at the 4-month follow-up (Schoenwald et al., 2000). A series of controlled studies (Burns et al., 2000) with older delinquents involved in MST found multiple positive outcomes (e.g., fewer arrests, less time in incarceration).

SERVICE SECTORS

In its effort to document information about services for child delinquents age 12 and younger, the Study Group was concerned with two primary issues: access to services and patterns of service use among juveniles who seek help. As opposed to focusing only on juveniles who have committed offenses, the Study Group focused on juveniles with conduct disorder or who exhibited conduct disorder symptoms. This approach stemmed partly from the fact that mental health services and treatment programs typically describe juveniles by diagnosis and do not identify delinquent status. Symptoms or a diagnosis of conduct disorder functions as a proxy for early-onset offending.

Although conduct problems usually are apparent and children (in most circumstances) are identified for some type of service, it is not known exactly which service sectors are most used and, perhaps more important, whether effective treatment is provided. Although much research has focused on the onset, prognosis, course, and outcome of conduct disorder in children, seldom has research explored the link between conduct disorder and offending and the services and interventions used to address them. It is apparent, however, that the most effective interventions for younger children focus on parents and are home- or school-based. This section offers a brief overview of the four service sectors most commonly used to help juveniles with conduct disorder symptoms or a conduct disorder diagnosis: mental health, education, child welfare, and juvenile justice.

Mental Health

Early-onset offenders have frequently developed multiple mental health problems early in life. These juveniles, however, often are not identified until they have had some contact with the police or the court. In general, a large proportion of juveniles with any type of psychiatric disorder do not receive specialized mental health services. It is unclear whether the same is true specifically for juveniles with conduct problems. Considerable evidence suggests, however, that conduct disorder is highly prevalent among juveniles referred to mental health services (Kazdin, 1985; Lock and Strauss, 1994). Conduct disorder accounts for 30 to 50 percent of psychiatric referrals among juveniles, making it the most frequent reason for referral in this age group. Although the juvenile justice system can serve as a gateway into professional mental health services, this is not always the case. For example, one study found that juveniles with a court contact and those with delinquent behavior but no court contact were about equally likely to have sought help for their behavioral problems and to have received professional mental health treatment (Stouthamer-Loeber, Loeber, and Thomas, 1992).

In some juveniles, the early onset of delinquency is associated with attention deficit/hyperactivity disorder (ADHD). The Multimodal Treatment Study of Children With Attention Deficit/Hyperactivity Disorder (MTA Cooperative Group, 1999a), compared combinations of medication and behavioral treatments (including parent management training, use of a behavioral aide in the classroom, and child behavioral treatment in a summer program) with a standard community treatment (e.g., a pediatrician prescribing stimulant medication for children with ADHD).

For ADHD, medication worked better than the combined behavioral treatments. Children receiving both behavioral treatment and medication responded better than those receiving behavioral treatments alone, whereas behavioral treatments combined with medication worked no better than medication alone. Families whose children received behavioral treatment, with or without medication, were more satisfied with their children's treatment than families whose children received only medical treatment; behavioral treatment improved juveniles' acceptance of and compliance with medical treatment; and combined treatment was associated with a lower dose of medication (MTA Cooperative Group, 1999b). In other words, one type of treatment (e.g., behavioral) appears to enhance family compliance with other treatment components (e.g., medication). Although the evidence base for pharmacological interventions with children and adolescents is less developed for juveniles with conduct disorder than for those with ADHD, the results highlight the importance of combining multiple components into clinically successful treatment programs that involve both children and their families.

Education

The Study Group found that school systems can play an important role in identifying a child's need for mental health services and providing such services. For example, juveniles and parents most often contact teachers about emotional and behavioral problems. In a North Carolina study, 71.5 percent of juveniles with serious emotional disturbances received services from schools, compared with much smaller proportions of help from other service sectors (Burns et al., 1995). However the adequacy of school-based mental health services has been questioned, largely because school personnel, such as guidance counselors, have limited mental health training. School interventions that seek to change the social context of schools and improve academic and social skills of students have a more holistic appeal and success rate.

Child Welfare

Child welfare services, especially the foster care segment, may also serve as a major gateway into the mental health-care system. The child welfare system provides children and adolescents with financial coverage for mental health care through Medicaid. In addition, children and adolescents enter the child welfare system primarily because of maltreatment such as child abuse and neglect, conditions associated with a higher risk of psychiatric problems and delinquency. For example, recent reviews of child welfare studies suggest that between one-half and two-thirds of children reentering foster care have behavior problems warranting mental health services (Landsverk and Garland, 1999). Two studies of computerized Medicaid program claims found substantially greater use of mental health services by children in foster care than by children in the overall Medicaid population

(Takayama, Bergman, and Connell, 1994). Nevertheless, little is known about how the child welfare system identifies child delinquents and potential child delinquents and refers them to mental health services. These children are a critical population for early intervention because of their exposure to trauma and other risk factors and their consequent externalizing (or acting out) behavior. By using the results of additional research, the child welfare system could serve as an early warning system for identifying children who demonstrate conduct problems and are at an increased risk of entering the juvenile justice system during their adolescence.

Juvenile Justice

Conduct disorder is characterized by externalizing behaviors as opposed to internalizing behaviors. It is not surprising, then, that this disorder is found more often among juveniles referred to the juvenile justice system than in the general population (Otto et al., 1992). In one review of nine studies the prevalence rates of conduct disorder for juveniles in the juvenile justice system ranged from 10 to 90 percent, and rates were higher for incarcerated juveniles than for those residing in the community (Cocozza, 1992). Mental health and substance use disorders are pervasive among incarcerated juveniles. For example, among 697 juveniles in detention in Cook County, IL., 80 percent had at least one mental health or substance use disorder; 20 percent had an affective disorder, 24 percent an anxiety disorder, 44 percent a substance use disorder, and 44 percent a disruptive behavior disorder (Teplin, Northwestern University Medical School, personal communication, 1997). The limited attention given to providing mental health services to incarcerated juveniles raises questions about whether the lack of studies in this area is also associated with a failure to provide needed services.

SERVICE USE PATTERNS

Despite the need for more research, the outlook for the treatment of juvenile offenders in general is more encouraging now than it was 10 years ago. Several strategies for a comprehensive approach involving community actions have shown promise for juveniles who exhibit conduct disorder symptoms. In addition, three recent studies have shed light on patterns of service use and may have implications for future intervention programs. The Great Smoky Mountains Study (GSMS), conducted in 11 counties of western North Carolina, examined access to services. The Patterns of Care (POC) Study in San Diego County, CA, provided information on service use patterns for juveniles and families seeking treatment. (The POC study consists of an annual count of youth involved in service delivery systems and a longitudinal survey of youth who received services.) The Cost of Services in Medicaid Study in southwestern Pennsylvania examined service use and costs for juveniles with conduct disorder and juveniles with oppositional defiant disorder.

As expected, the studies found that education was the service sector most likely to intervene and that the mental health sector provided services to a significant proportion of juveniles who exhibited conduct disorder symptoms. Institutional placement (in a psychiatric hospital or detention center) remained a significant form of treatment for children who exhibited conduct disorder symptoms. Unexpectedly, the juvenile justice system had limited contact with juveniles who exhibited severe antisocial behavior, and when there was contact, the rate of mental health services intervention was extremely low. In the GSMS, the major finding was that youth with a significant history of serious antisocial behavior were not identified by the justice system, suggesting an important potential role of police in detection and referral.

If appropriate services are not available through the police or courts, a well-defined mechanism for obtaining timely help is needed. The first step toward obtaining effective treatment is gaining access to services. However, although the early detection of emotional and behavioral problems has long been a public health goal, the common delay between symptom onset and help-seeking is apparent. For example, in the child welfare sector, it appears that a child's first access to mental health services is often triggered by foster care placement. A further issue is how widely available effective interventions are to such youth once they gain access to treatment in typical mental health settings.

SCHOOL INTERVENTIONS

Research shows that school interventions that change the social context of schools and the school experiences of children can reduce and prevent the delinquent behavior of children younger than 13. Several approaches to school interventions have yielded positive results. These approaches include classroom- and schoolwide behavior management programs; social competence promotion curriculums; conflict resolution and violence prevention curriculums; bullying prevention efforts; and multicomponent classroom-based programs that help teachers and parents manage, socialize, and educate students and improve their cognitive, social, and emotional competencies. Research also shows that community-based activities such as afterschool recreation and mentoring programs can reduce child delinquency (Jones and Offord, 1989).

Several classroom and school behavior management programs have positively influenced children's behavior. For example, evaluations of the Good Behavior game showed that proactive behavior management in the classroom can reduce aggressive behavior and promote positive long-term effects on the most aggressive elementary school children (Kellam and Rebok, 1992; Kellam et al, 1994). Murphy and colleagues (1983) found that programs that effectively manage behavior on the playground can reduce aggressive behavior. By providing structured activities and timeout procedures for elementary school children, teacher's aides were able to reduce disruptive and aggressive behavior during recreational periods. Mayer and Butterworth (1979) have shown that schoolwide behavior management and consultation programs in urban elementary schools can increase the safety of students and enhance learning and healthy social interactions.

Curriculums that seek to promote social competence teach prosocial norms and enhance children's problem-solving and social interaction skills. Several of these curriculums have been successfully used to reduce aggressive behavior and, in some cases, child delinquency. Examples include PATHS (Greenberg and Kusche, 1993), the Social Relations Intervention (Lochman et al., 1993), the Metropolitan Area Child Study (Eron et al., forthcoming), the Social Competence Promotion Program for Young Adolescents (Weissberg, Barton, and Shriver, 1997), and the Montreal Longitudinal Experiment Study (Tremblay et al., 1990). Although variations exist regarding the specific content, number of sessions, and ages targeted by these programs, social competence promotion programs with sufficient intensity and duration consistently have been found to reduce aggressive and other antisocial behaviors of children younger than 13.

Conflict resolution, violence prevention curriculums, and antibullying programs also focus on problem-solving and social interaction skills. In addition, they seek to educate children about the causes and destructive consequences of violence and bullying (Olweus, 1991). The Second Step curriculum for elementary school students and the Responding in Peaceful and Positive Ways curriculum for middle school students have successfully reduced aggressive behavior in children (Grossman et al., 1997). Social competence and violence prevention curriculums can be combined with other intervention components into multicomponent approaches, as illustrated by Fast Track (Conduct Problems Prevention Research Group, 1999a, 1999b), the Child Development Project, and the Seattle Social Development Project (SSDP).

Multicomponent classroom-based programs seek to reduce misbehaving (both inside and outside the classroom) and strengthen academic achievement. Fast Track, the Child Development Program, and SSDP have shown positive effects in reducing early behavior problems (Battistich et al., 1997; Conduct Problems Prevention Research Group, 1999a, 1999b; Hawkins et al., 1999). Each of these programs included classroom- and family-focused components. Positive effects of the Fast Track intervention on the disruptive-oppositional behavior of first-graders were evident immediately after the program concluded. Today, those children are being tracked to determine whether the ongoing intervention will continue to influence their behavior. The Child Development Program used proactive behavior management and cooperative learning strategies with elementary school students. The program successfully reduced antisocial behavior (including interpersonal aggression and weapon carrying) among children in a high-implementation subgroup. In the classroom, SSDP combined proactive behavior management strategies with interactive instructional methods, cooperative learning, and cognitive and social skills instruction for students. Effects of the program on children's antisocial behavior were shown during the intervention, immediately after its completion (at the end of elementary school), and when the students turned 18 (6 years after the intervention ended) (Hawkins et al., 1999).

These results clearly document the important role that schools can play in the prevention of child delinquency. This role is particularly important in light of research findings that indicate that children whose academic performance is poor face a greater risk of becoming involved in child delinquency than other children (Herrenkohl et al., 2001). Through the school and classroom management policies and practices that they adopt, and through the instructional methods and curriculums that teachers choose to use in the classroom, schools can promote or inhibit offending behavior among students. Good schools are a fundamental component in preventing delinquency.

From the perspective of preventing child delinquency, good schools are schools with explicit, consistent, and contingent (and fairly applied) expectations for behavior. Good schools use interactive and cooperative methods of instruction that actively involve students in their own learning. Good schools empower parents to support the learning process and to practice more effective child management skills. Good schools offer elementary and middle school children curriculums that promote the development of social and emotional competencies and the development of norms against violence, aggression, and offending.

Schools that do these things promote academic attainment and reduce the risk for antisocial behavior among their students. Federal, State, and local efforts should focus on encouraging schools to assess their current practices in these areas and to adopt practices, programs, and approaches shown to reduce offending behavior. Currently, 94 percent of the resources intended to combat violent offending are used after violent offenses have occurred. To adequately prevent youthful offending, more resources should be made available to ensure that schools use methods and programs that will help them effectively educate and socialize children.

JUVENILE JUSTICE PROGRAMS

Most children with a conduct disorder diagnosis or who exhibit conduct disorder symptoms do not enter the juvenile justice system before age 12. Nevertheless, the likelihood that many of these juveniles will eventually come in contact with the system during their adolescence is a clear incentive for earlier justice system involvement. This section summarizes the status of the juvenile justice system's involvement with child delinquency and describes several promising programs.

The juvenile court system typically gives child delinquents more opportunities to reform than it gives to older offenders, which explains why juvenile courts do not normally adjudicate very young, first-time offenders. When confronted with child delinquents (even if they are repeat or serious offenders), juvenile courts must deal with legal issues surrounding the handling of these children in a system that does not really anticipate their presence. Traditionally, the courts have been expected to intervene only when families, service agencies, and schools fail to give children the help they need. Children exhibiting problem behaviors often have not been served adequately by child welfare, social services, child protective services, mental health agencies and public schools (Office of Juvenile Justice and Delinquency Prevention, 1995). Because their needs have not been met elsewhere, the juvenile court has long been a "dumping ground" for children with a wide variety of problem behaviors (Kupperstein, 1971).

The juvenile court's intervention in child delinquency has been affected by policy changes during the 1970s and 1980s—e.g., the Federal Juvenile Justice and Delinquency Prevention (JJDP) Act of 1974—which have increased the diversion of status offenders, nonoffenders, and child delinquents from juvenile court processing. In the view of many judges, this diversion has meant a lost opportunity to help children (Holden and Kapler, 1995). Despite policy changes, however, the juvenile courts continue to handle many status offenders, nonoffenders, and child delinquents. Yet the policies of the past 25 years have restricted the development of programs for these children. A fairly strong principle seems to be commonly held—that very young children should not be subject to dispositions normally reserved for older or more serious offenders. However, dispositions specifically tailored to address the unique circumstances of child delinquents are scant. The juvenile justice system has no special facilities for these young offenders, and few programs are designed specifically for them. Nevertheless, among these few programs, the Study Group has identified some promising interventions for child delinquents.

Michigan Early Offender Program

Established in 1985 by a Michigan probate court, the Early Offender Program (EOP) provides specialized, intensive, in-home interventions for children age 13 or younger at the time of their first adjudication and who have had two or more prior police contacts. Interventions include individualized treatment plans, therapy groups, school preparation assistance, and short-term detention of up to 10 days. Comparisons with a control group showed that EOP participants had lower recidivism rates, fewer new adjudications per recidivist, and fewer and briefer out-of-home placements. In general, both parents and children reported positive changes in family situations, peer relations, and school performance and conduct after participating in EOP (e.g., Howitt and Moore, 1991).

Minnesota Delinquents Under 10 Program

The Delinquents Under 10 Program in Hennepin County, MN, involves several county departments (Children and Family Services, Economic Assistance, Community Health, and County Attorney's Office). A screening team reviews police reports and then determines appropriate dispositions for children. Interventions include an admonishment letter to parents from the county attorney, referrals to child protective services and other agencies, diversion programs, and targeted early interventions for children deemed to be at the highest risk for future delinquency (Hennepin County Attorney's Office, 1995). For each targeted child, a specific wraparound network is created. Networks include the following elements:

- A community-based organization to conduct indepth assessments, improve behavior and school attendance, and provide extracurricular activities.
- An integrated service delivery team made up of county staff who coordinate service delivery and help children and family members access services.
- A critical support person or mentor.
- A corporate sponsor that funds extracurricular activities.

Sacramento County Community Intervention Program

Sacramento County, CA, welfare authorities found that families of most young (ages 9 to 12) children arrested in the county had been investigated for both neglect and physical abuse. In addition, children who were reported as abused or neglected were six to seven times more likely than other children to be arrested for delinquent behavior (Brooks and Petit, 1997; Child Welfare League of America, 1997). Based on this data, the Community Intervention Program (CIP) for child delinquents was developed (Brooks and Petit, 1997). The intervention begins when law enforcement officers notify the probation department that a child between ages 9 and 12 has been arrested. The court intake screener than refers the children who have instances of family abuse or neglect to CIP. Next, a community intervention specialist conducts a crisis assessment and provides initial crisis intervention services to the child and family. The intervention specialist then conducts an indepth assessment, which includes physical and mental health, substance abuse, school functioning, economic strengths/needs, vocational strengths/needs, family functioning, and social functioning. The intervention specialist coordinates all services, which are community based and family focused and may vary in intensity over time to match the needs of the child and family. Intervention services include individual and family counseling and abuse and neglect risk monitoring.

Toronto Under 12 Outreach Project

The Under 12 Outreach Project in Toronto, Canada, is a fully developed intervention program that combines social learning and behavioral system approaches. The multisystemic approach uses interventions that target children, parents, schools, and communities, as required. Interventions include skills training, cognitive problem solving, self-control strategies, cognitive self-instruction, family management skills training, and parent training. These interventions are organized in eight major program components, such as a 12-week afterschool structured group session, a 12-week parent training group, in-home academic tutoring, school advocacy, teacher consultations, and individual befriending, which connects juveniles with volunteers who help them join recreational facilities in their community.

A COMPREHENSIVE MODEL

Based on the initial experiences of these community-based efforts and a recognition of the multiple causes of child delinquency, the need for a comprehensive model emerges to guide new efforts. Historically, interagency coordination and collaboration in service delivery to children have been less than impressive (Knitzer, 1982; Nelson, Rutherford, and Wolford, 1996). Undoubtedly, children with serious behavioral disturbances need to receive several different services simultaneously in a continuum of care that involves multiple human services agencies. A comprehensive wraparound model is needed to integrate interventions for children who have committed delinquent acts or are at risk of delinquency. The model should integrate prevention, early intervention, graduated sanctions, and aftercare in a comprehensive approach that enables communities to address child delinquency more effectively (Wilson and Howell, 1993).

Mechanisms for a Comprehensive Approach

The Study Group has identified three crucial mechanisms for coordinating and fully integrating a continuum of care and sanctions for child delinquents:

Governing Body.   The Study Group recommends that communities and governments create a governing body, or interagency council, that includes (at a minimum) representatives from all human services organizations and agencies related to juvenile justice that provide services to child delinquents and their families. These agencies include child welfare, education, health and human services, housing and human development, juvenile justice, and mental health. The council must have the authority to convene the agencies and to direct their work toward developing a comprehensive strategy for dealing with child delinquency.

Comprehensive Assessment and Case Management.   The Study Group believes that an effort must be made for comprehensive assessments of referred child delinquents at the front end of the juvenile justice system. One option is to use a single mechanism, such as a community assessment center, to perform risk and needs assessments for a wide range of agencies, thus providing a single point of entry and immediate and comprehensive assessments. These "one-stop shops" could help integrate multidisciplinary perspectives, enhance coordination of efforts, and reduce service duplication. However, to ensure that child delinquents have access to available services and that the services are effectively delivered, it is also critical to implement integrated case management, tracking of children through the system, periodic reassessment, and monitoring of service provisions (Oldenettel and Wordes, 1999).

Interagency Coordination and Collaboration.   Although juvenile justice, mental health, child welfare, and education services may have the same clients, these agencies often work at cross-purposes or duplicate services. The Study Group recommends developing wraparound services to target children and families in a flexible and individualized manner tailored to their strengths and needs (Goldman, 1999). Although promising and effective wraparound models have been developed for children with emotional disturbances and their families, the best method of addressing child delinquency within the juvenile justice system has not been determined. One program, the 8% Early Intervention Program in Orange County, CA, ensures coordinated service delivery by operating under the authority of the probation department and using contractual arrangements for services (Schumacher and Kurz, 1999).

Prevention

Any program that targets children and child delinquents should include a strong prevention component with a focus on discouraging gang involvement. Often, the most dysfunctional adolescents in urban areas are recruited into gangs (Lancot and Le Blanc, 1996). Prior delinquency and antisocial behavior also predict gang membership (e.g., Hill et al., 1999). A successful program in Montreal, Canada, combined parent training with individual social skills training for aggressive-hyperactive boys ages 7 to 9 and found that, when compared with a control group, significantly fewer boys in the treatment group joined a gang (Tremblay, et al., 1990).

Early intervention is paramount in preventing delinquency and gang involvement, especially for disruptive children. One approach programs can take is improving parenting skills to better manage impulsive, oppositional, and defiant children. Another approach targets parents at high risk for abusing and neglecting their children. An example of this approach is the Children's Research Center's innovative method for identifying the relative degree of risk for continued abuse or neglect among families that have a substantiated abuse or neglect referral (Children's Research Center, 1993). With this method, children are classified according to risk levels, which are then used to determine services. Community policing should also be part of early intervention. For example, a program in New Haven, CT, brings police officers and mental health professionals together to provide each with training, consultation, and support and to offer interdisciplinary interventions to child victims, witnesses, and perpetrators of violent crime (Marans and Berkman, 1997).

Graduated Sanctions

Child delinquency intervention efforts need to be linked to a system of graduated sanctions—a continuum of treatment alternatives that includes immediate intervention, intermediate sanctions, community-based correctional sanctions, and secure corrections (Howell, 1995). One such program, the 8% Early Intervention Program, focuses on juveniles younger than 15 who, although they represent only 8 percent of the total probation caseload, are of greatest concern to the community because they account for more than half of all repeat offenders among juvenile probationers and because they are at risk of becoming chronic, serious, and violent juvenile offenders (Schumacher and Kurz, 1999). The following problems serve as criteria for inclusion in the 8% Program:

- Significant family problems (e.g., abuse/neglect).
- Significant school problems (e.g., truancy, suspension).
- A pattern of individual problems (drug and/or alcohol use).
- Predelinquent behavior patterns (e.g., running away or gang associations).

The 8% Program targets these juveniles upon court referral. Cases are identified during screening at probation intake and verified through a comprehensive risks and needs assessment process. A youth and family resource center provides well-coordinated, intensive, and multisystemic intervention services that focus on strengthening the family unit, improving school attendance and academic performance, teaching and modeling prosocial behavior and values, and ensuring easy access to intervention resources.

A LESSON LEARNED FROM INNOVATIONS IN CANADA

Legislation and policy developments that focus on child delinquency do not always work as expected. Programs and policies sometimes lack coordination, proper data collection, adequate monitoring and feedback, and ongoing analysis. Nonetheless, a review of such practices can prompt policymakers to develop new and improved approaches. Canada's near two-decade-old approach to child delinquency is a case in point.

The Canadian Young Offenders Act of 1984 effectively decriminalized children younger than 12 by making them exempt from the juvenile justice system. The rationale was that these children would be better served through provincial and territorial child welfare and mental health services. However, several surveys of Canada's 10 provinces and 3 territories revealed that the legislation did not lead to a systemic development of multifaceted interventions tailored to children's unique needs.

Nevertheless, the surveys influenced the Earlscourt Child and Family Centre to make several recommendations, which the Study Group believes may offer guidance to jurisdictions in the United States and Europe. Canada has already taken the first step toward improving services by developing early assessment and centralized services protocols in Toronto. The following recommendations made to the Canadian government emphasize early identification and intervention.

The Study Group found that the best intervention and service programs provide a treatment-oriented, nonpunitive framework that emphasizes early identification and intervention.

When considering intervention program development, it is important to recognize the fact that no single system—juvenile justice, education, mental health, or child welfare—can reduce child delinquency on its own. The Study Group's survey of juvenile justice practitioners found that they were unanimous about the need for integration among agencies (Loeber and Farrington, 2001). However, providing multiple services for troubled children in a comprehensive, integrated manner has proven difficult. Several pioneering programs provide models of consistent coordination among agencies concerned with children. Such integrated efforts will give communities the opportunity to identify children who either have committed delinquent acts or are at risk of delinquency and then help communities target individualized interventions for these children and their families. Should this effort occur on a large scale, the potential for significantly reducing the overall level of crime in a community will increase. As a result, the future expenditure of associated tax dollars will likely decrease.

Children Committing Offenses Act (CCOA).   To ensure accountability and meet community standards of public safety, the Canadian CCOA would mandate that services to child delinquents be based on an assessment of their risk for further offending. The Act would provide clear direction to police regarding their responsibilities in tracking children and would ensure services according to established protocols. The Act would also provide for the placement of specially designated police liaison officers who are trained to intervene with delinquent children, coordinate with community agencies, and participate in community teams (Augimeri, Goldberg, and Koegl, 1999). This Act may inspire similar legislation in other countries.

National Information Center on Very Young Offenders.   This proposed center would encourage, monitor, and evaluate interventions for children younger than 12. It would track the incidence of offending and act as a clearinghouse for interventions. To meet prevention goals, the center would facilitate a nationally sustained parent education program to promote parenting skills and would offer technical assistance to communities. It would also focus on antibullying and antistealing campaigns targeting both the entire school population and children most at risk of offending.

Community Teams for Children Under 12 Committing Offenses.   In this initiative, community teams of representatives from police departments, child welfare programs, schools, mental health agencies, and other organizations would be mandated to provide services for children who commit offenses and their families and for teachers, children's peers, and communities in general. The teams would conduct needs and risk assessments and would assign interventions according to offense severity. Within this framework, multifaceted interventions would be tailored to individual children and their families. Temporary placement options would range from secure mental health facilities to treatment in foster homes.

SUMMARY AND CONCLUSION

Because persistent disruptive behavior and child delinquency are predictors of later serious and violent offending, the Study Group suggests that efforts to reduce serious delinquency should focus on children who exhibit persistent disruptive behavior in addition to child delinquents and serious juvenile offenders. Little evidence supports the idea that harsher sanctions in the juvenile justice system reduce child delinquency. Instead, effective interventions to reduce both persistent disruptive behavior and child delinquency have been developed.

QUESTIONS FOR REVIEW AND DISCUSSION

1. Who are child delinquents? Why is it important to examine programs that deal with preventing the conditions that eventually lead to delinquency among them? Discuss.
2. What are some of the treatment interventions that have been described?
3. Do early-onset youthful offenders tend to have multiple mental health issues? How does conduct disorder relate to poor mental health? Explain.
4. How do child welfare services intervene to make a difference in the lives of early-onset youths?
5. What can schools do to prevent or minimize the occurrence of delinquent conduct?
6. What are three state- or county-level programs that have experimented with interventions relating to early-onset delinquent conduct? What are some of their program characteristics and treatment methods?
7. How important are graduated sanctions in dealing with youthful offenders?
8. What helpful information about delinquency interventions has been gleaned from Canada's delinquency prevention programming? Discuss.

26

Truancy Mediation
A Collaborative Approach to Truancy Intervention

Kathy Elton and Kerrie Naylor

Adapted from Kathy Elton and Kerrie Naylor, "Truancy Mediation: A Collaborative Approach to Truancy Intervention." *APPA Perspectives* 25: 34–36, 2001.

Reprinted by permission from the American Probation and Parole Association.

Truancy continues to be a major concern facing juvenile courts, schools and society. Statistics show that youth who are not in school during the day are at high risk for delinquency and are likely to be engaged in criminal activity (OJJDP, 1997). "Many research studies have revealed that truant students are more likely to join gangs, use drugs and alcohol and engage in other criminal and violent activity than students that stay in school" (OJJDP, p. 1, 1999). Justice officials, administrators, teachers, parents, police officers and legislators struggle with the issue of truancy and are consistently trying new policies and program interventions aimed at keeping students in school. The purpose of this article is to describe a pilot truancy mediation program, discuss how it works, and examine its effectiveness in reducing truancy problems in secondary schools thereby diverting youth from the juvenile justice system. Precautions for those considering this type of intervention are also outlined.

AN ALTERNATIVE APPROACH TO TRUANCY INTERVENTIONS

Mediation, as a dispute resolution process, has many advantages over the formal court process:

1. Mediation is informal and confidential;
2. Mediation proceeds more quickly than the formal court process;

3. The final agreement is not imposed upon the parties by a judge but instead designed in their own best interests by the parties involved; and

4. Mediation is non-adversarial since the solution is designed by both parties and has the potential to preserve the relationship once the process has concluded (Administrative Office of the U.S. Courts, 1998).

The advantages of alternative dispute resolution processes extend to all forms of mediation programs, including truancy mediation (BEST Conference, 1999).

Mediation, as a truancy intervention program, places the focus on student decision-making, goal-setting and performing to certain standards autonomously. Providing students with the freedom to choose from a variety of options, the choice of taking the responsibility to act independently, and the prerogative of setting goals to accomplish higher level tasks lead to the probability of student success and increased motivation (Baumrind, 1967; Coopersmith, 1969; Felker, 1974; Purkey, 1970). The mediation process allows the student to explore optional activities, be autonomous in making decisions about his or her life, and be a willing participant in the process.

Truancy mediation also gives the parties involved the opportunity to enhance discussion about the "core issues" or real reasons the student is not coming to school. The symptoms of truancy are often buried beneath other problems such as substance abuse, neglect, family dysfunctions or other social problems.

COLLABORATIVE PILOT PROGRAM IN PLACE

During the 1998–1999 and 1999–2000 school years, Jordan School District and the Administrative Office of the Courts in Utah collaborated in an interagency, pilot, truancy mediation intervention program. The program was implemented as an intervention, hoping to divert truancy cases from entering the juvenile court system. Mediation, as an intervention program for resolving truancy, incorporates aspects of motivation theory (Naylor, 1983) and aspects of alternative dispute resolution theory making it a viable alternative to solving traditional truancy problems and concerns. Mediation utilizes the presence and skills of a neutral third party who promotes cooperation between disputing parties and provides the parties the opportunity to resolve their differences without court intervention. The mediator helps identify the interests of the parties involved, facilitates discussion of those interests in a productive way, assists the parties in creating possible solutions to the conflict, and helps test the feasibility of those solutions until the parties in dispute can agree on an outcome that serves the interests of all involved.

In the Jordan School District, students in the schools participating in the truancy mediation pilot program were given the option of participating in truancy mediation before they were formally referred to juvenile court for habitual truancy. The student, the student's parents and a team from the school (usually consisting of an assistant principal, a counselor and the attendance secretary) participated in the mediation session. The mediators in the program were trained community volunteers recruited and supervised by the Administrative Office of the courts. The mediator's role was to equalize the power at the table by being a third party neutral who ensured that all parties felt comfortable discussing the truancy issue. The mediator also encouraged dialogue around options which helped to solve the truancy problem.

An illustration of this type of intervention for resolving truancy problems is exemplified in the following story:

> A ninth grade girl was having problems attending her classes and getting to school on time. The traditional interventions of conferences, phone calls home, detention, contracts, suspension and counseling were implemented. The assistant principal was not having any success convincing the student to come to school.

Truancy mediation was discussed with the student as an option before a court referral would be made. The student and parent agreed to the idea. As the student, her mother and the school officials discussed the problem at the mediation table, it came to their attention that the young lady was having the most problems in two of her classes. As the dialogue continued, it was revealed that this student was classified as special education and the two classes she was struggling in were her mainstreamed classes. This was not necessarily new or surprising information to the group, but the student was very honest in her disclosure to the mediator that the problem was that both of the teachers in these classes had a procedure whereby class assignments were corrected during class time by exchanging papers with peers in the class. The student shared with the mediator that she was a poor speller and that other classmates would make comments when they would correct her papers. This was very embarrassing to her, so she had stopped attending those classes or would always turn her work in late so that the teacher would have to correct it. The special education team leader, who was part of the mediation team from the school, offered to meet with the two teachers and the student and talk about the student's need for accommodations in the classes. The young lady appeared relieved and agreed that she would be more committed to attending those classes if she did not have to fear embarrassment in them.

The next issue which came to the attention of the mediation team was the fact that this student's parents were in the middle of a difficult divorce. The student felt comfortable sharing her feelings about the situation with the mediator and said that she would be willing to meet with the school psychologist on a regular basis to help her cope with the stresses at home. The student committed that with the changes in the school and support of the school, she could improve her attendance.

PROGRAM OUTCOMES

The pilot truancy mediation program in Jordan School District proved to be very successful during the 1998–1999 and 1999–2000 school years. In the first year there were 19 cases referred from one pilot school, and all but two of the youth improved their attendance. During the second year there were 75 cases referred to the mediation program, and only 16 of the cases resulted in a referral to juvenile court. This intervention kept 59 students out of the court system due to their improved attendance. As a group, the students who participated in the mediation intervention were missing 32.2 percent of their classes per week prior to the mediation session. After mediation, the students absences were reduced to a composite of only 19.7 percent of their class periods per week. Students improved their attendance an average of 12.5 percent after mediation.

Other positive outcomes noted in the pilot program were:

1. The mediation program created a "team approach" to resolving the truancy problem rather than an adversarial approach;

2. Relationships between the student and school staff were formed and/or strengthened as well as relationships between the school and the parents were strengthened;

3. The mediation process offered an opportunity for those involved to discuss the "core issues" involved in the truancy problem (i.e. drug use or parent-child conflict);

4. The agreements were individualized to meet the needs of the students and the school;

5. The students were empowered to "buy in" to their agreements;

6. Community mediators were brought into the school and viewed the school as more willing to help and assist students;

7. The process forced an "equalization of power" at the table for negotiating agreements;

8. Administrators in the schools were more likely to pursue truancy cases, rather than let the students "fall through the cracks" because court processes are so laborious; and

9. If the student violated the mediated agreement, he/she was fast-tracked through the court process.

Parents, students and administrators commented on the effectiveness of the program when they completed surveys following the mediation sessions. The overall evaluation surveys indicated that all parties felt that the student was held accountable for his/her behavior. Over 95 percent expressed that they were satisfied with the agreement reached in mediation. Parties agreed that during the mediation process, they were able to freely express their thoughts and feelings. Some of the parent comments included:

- "It was nice to have someone try and come up with some solutions, rather than just giving up."
- "It was comfortable knowing that the school personnel were here to listen and help the student, along with the mediator to help with communication."
- "I appreciate having a choice of mediation or court. The school was very helpful and accommodating and went above and beyond what I had expected of them."

PROGRAM PRECAUTIONS

Since this is still a pilot program, we suggest some of the following precautions to schools and districts interested in learning more about the program:

1. The program has to be voluntary for families and schools. It is very important that those involved see the potential benefits of the program and go to the table willingly. Schools must view the program as a way to help the student and not just another "hoop to jump through" before taking the student to court.

2. Trained volunteer mediators from the community should be utilized in the program. In our pilot program, all volunteer mediators have had 32 hours of basic

mediation training and have attended a 90 minute orientation on truancy medi-ation. The volunteers have also observed two other mediation sessions in the schools as well as co-mediated until the coordinator of the program feels the volunteer is ready to be placed on the roster for truancy mediation.

3. Schools who participate in this program must have a philosophy conducive to me-diation which involves family, student and school as equal partners in problem solving. The trained volunteer mediator is truly a "third party neutral" and assures that all parties at the table are equal in status. The volunteer brings credibility to the intervention by being skilled at conflict resolution processes and is able to guarantee that all parties' ideas are adequately expressed and taken seriously.

4. School personnel need to be open to a variety of options for students' successes and have the attitude that students should be given a chance. The approach within the mediation session must be that students do not have to "earn what they need, but rather they are given a chance with the expectation that their at-tendance improve in order to keep what has been negotiated.

5. The school district and court promoting the program must agree to fast-track students to truancy court if students do not honor the mediated agreement. The schools need to be rewarded for taking the extra time and effort to mediate with the students and families. Fast-tracking the students to court if they do not im-prove their attendance helps the schools feel the time spent in mediation is worthwhile. Also, court officials see the mediation process as an attempt to get to the "roots of the problem" and acknowledge that all alternatives have been exhausted leaving truancy court as the appropriate "next step."

QUESTIONS FOR REVIEW AND DISCUSSION

1. What is truancy? Why is it a problem?
2. Are truant youths more likely to engage in juvenile delinquency? Why or why not? Explain.
3. How can mediation function as an intervention in preventing truancy? Discuss.
4. Describe the mediation project conducted in the Jordan, Utah, school district.
5. What were some positive outcomes of the mediation project?
6. What are some general guidelines for schools participating in similar mediation projects in future years? Discuss.

27

What Works in Juvenile Justice Outcome Measurement?

A Comparison of Predicted Success to Observed Performance

Kristin Parsons Winokur, Ted Tollett,
and Sherry Jackson

Adapted from Kristin Parsons Winokur, Ted Tollett, and Sherry Jackson, "What Works in Juvenile Justice Outcome Measurement? A Comparison of Predicted Success to Observed Performance." *Federal Probation* 66: 50–55, 2002.

Reprinted by permission of the Administrative Office of the U.S. Courts.

In the current environment of increased demands for accountability and outcome measurement, it is essential to develop sound empirical models for evaluating the effectiveness of juvenile justice programs. Since Martinson's (1974) indictment of rehabilitation, many researchers have revisited the question of "what works" in the juvenile justice system (Steele, Austin, and Krisberg, 1989; Rivers and Trotti, 1989; Andrews, Zinger, Hoge, Bonta, Gendreau and Cullen, 1990; Gottfredson and Baron, 1992; Wilson and Howell, 1993; Greenwood and Turner, 1993). Most studies, however, have employed simplistic methods of comparing programs on the basis of aggregate recidivism outcomes, with no consideration of the types of offenders served by the program or the cost to operate the program. This study presents an innovative program evaluation methodology that accounts for programmatic differences in the underlying risk factors of the population of youths served relative to program cost-effectiveness. The authors were part of a team of researchers who developed what is now referred to as the Program Accountability Measures (PAM) analysis. This outcome-based model has been used to evaluate juvenile day treatment and commitment programs in Florida. We discuss here the development of this methodology and present outcome findings by program model, gender composition of program, and program security level.

MODEL DEVELOPMENT

The PAM methodology was begun in the early 1980s and initially consisted of a comparison of non-residential and residential juvenile commitment programs in terms of rates of recommitments and successful program completion. Later a measure of program cost was incorporated into the model and an overall cost-effectiveness summary score was calculated for each program. These preliminary versions of the model were in themselves rather innovative in light of the fact that 47 percent of states surveyed in a recent study do not track even basic recidivism outcomes for the programs serving juvenile offenders in the state (Florida Department of Juvenile Justice (FDJJ), 1999). Part of the difficulty encountered in conducting statewide accountability studies of juvenile justice programs is the fact that many states do not operate centralized juvenile justice systems. As such, uniform program data are not available and the comparison of program indicators obtained from decentralized information systems is often plagued by validity and reliability problems. Findings from a recent national survey of juvenile justice specialists indicate that difficulties with evaluation of juvenile justice programs are widespread (Justice Research and Statistics Association, 1999). In this survey of evaluation practices, only 5 percent of state juvenile justice specialists responded that they are satisfied with their state's evaluation methods. Among the top reasons respondents cited for dissatisfaction were difficulties comparing across programs without common performance measures, and the fact that the large diversity of programs makes it difficult to develop standard evaluation outcome measures. The most common approach to evaluation reported in the survey responses was program monitoring.

We sought to develop a model based upon common performance and outcome measures to evaluate Florida's day treatment and residential program effectiveness. Florida has one of the largest juvenile justice systems in the nation, with a current roster of nearly 300 residential programs and over 6,200 beds. A wide variety of program models are utilized, including family-style group homes, wilderness camps, halfway houses, boot camps, specialized mental health programs, specialized sex offender programs, and maximum security "juvenile prisons." Juvenile programs in Florida include both non-residential, day-treatment programs and residential commitment facilities. Residential programs are currently classified into four security levels: low-risk, moderate-risk, high-risk, and maximum-risk programs. Approximately 80 percent of Florida's programs are contracted, with the majority contracted to non-profit providers.

Despite the challenge inherent in comparing outcomes within and between a large field of widely varying programs, growing legislative pressure for accountability and efficient use of resources requires the development of a technique to equitably evaluate and compare outcomes for the state's many juvenile justice programs. Florida's program models and security levels make side-by-side recidivism rate comparisons impractical and inequitable. Not surprisingly, tremendous variation exists in the characteristics and backgrounds of the youth committed to the various programs. If programs were ranked strictly on recidivism, low-risk wilderness camps serving minor offenders, for instance, would *always* fare better than high-risk programs serving youth with serious offending histories. In fact, even among facilities with similar treatment models, the youths served have divergent socio-demographic backgrounds and relative risks for recidivism.

Working from previous versions of the model that compared programs using a summation of basic youth offense factors and cost measures, we refined the methodology by using statistical analyses to standardize across all programs and control for the individual characteristics of youths served in the program. Seeking an accountability model that would allow for the comparison of programs both within and between security levels and program models, we developed a measure that would estimate the difference between a program's expected success rate, given the clientele served, and the program's actual performance, or observed success rate. More specifically, the PAM model calculates how well a program is *expected* to do based on the program youths' risk of reoffending (expected success) and compares this to how well the program youths actually performed (observed success). This ensures that programs serving more difficult youth are not held to inequitable standards due to the higher re-offense risk of the youth they serve, and provides a realistic measure of program effectiveness for those programs serving less challenging youth. While this standardized measure evaluates overall program effectiveness in terms of recidivism outcomes, it does not account for program differences in *cost-effectiveness*. Of equal importance to legislative decisions about juvenile justice budget allocations are cost/benefit comparisons of programs. Therefore, we also incorporated into the model a mean cost differential factor that compares the program's average cost per successful completion to the statewide average cost.

DATA SOURCES

The PAM analyses presented here include effectiveness comparisons for all day treatment and residential programs serving youths in Florida during the two-year period between July 1, 1998 and June 30, 2000. Seeking to improve validity and reliability through increased sample sizes, we chose to examine a two-year period rather than one-year snapshot. Using the JJIS database, we determined that a total of 17,762 youths were released from 186 programs during this time. Demographic, offense history, and subsequent juvenile court recidivism data were obtained from JJIS. Recidivism was defined as any juvenile adjudication, adjudication withheld, or adult conviction for an offense that occurred within one year of a youth's release from a program to the community or a conditional release program. For those youths who reached 18 years of age during the follow-up period or had a case handled in adult court, recidivism data were obtained from FCIC and DOC.

CALCULATING THE PAM SCORE

A PAM score is calculated for each program to provide a program rank based on its effectiveness and cost relative to other programs. The score is derived from a formula based on: (1) program youths' reoffending, and (2) average cost per youth completing the program. Program effectiveness is defined as the difference between a program's predicted success and its actual success. To determine predicted success, we initially used logistic regression analyses to predict the likelihood of reoffending based on youths' risk factors. Four factors were identified as statistically significant predictors of reoffending for the youths served in Florida's programs. These factors include: age at release from program, age at first offense, number of prior adjudications and gender. Males were much more likely than females to receive a subsequent adjudication, adjudication withheld or adult conviction following program release. Younger offenders were more likely to reoffend than older youths, and the more prior adjudications a youth had, the greater the odds the youth would reoffend upon release. Having identified the four significant predictors of recidivism at the individual level, we used Hierarchical Linear Modeling (HLM) to calculate the probability of success (no subsequent adjudications or convictions), plus or minus a margin of error (i.e., the 99 percent confidence interval), for the 186 programs that released 15 or more youths between fiscal years 1998–99 and 1999–2000. Expected success is then compared to how well program youths actually performed, or the *observed success rate.* The difference between a programs' expected success rate and its actual success rate provides a measure of the crime reduction effect the program achieved.

Cost-effectiveness is measured by comparing the program's mean cost per completion to the statewide average. Cost figures are limited to FDJJ expenditures for the program and do not include other sources of funding, either governmental or private. A program's total expenditures for the two-year period of the analyses are summed and divided by the number of youths completing the program during this time. This figure is then compared to the average cost per completion statewide, which was $23,555.

The PAM score is calculated as the sum of the program effectiveness measure weighted by a factor of two-thirds and the program cost-effectiveness measure weighted by a factor of one-third. Program and cost-effectiveness categories were created to facilitate the comparison of programs across security levels and program models. The categories are defined as:

Program Effectiveness Categories
- *Effective Programs:* These programs are defined as having an observed success rate above the expected success range.
- *Average Programs:* These programs are defined as having an observed success rate within the expected success range.
- *Below-Average Programs:* These programs are defined as having an observed success rate below the expected success range.

Cost-Effectiveness Categories
- *Low-Cost Programs:* One-third of the programs were grouped into this category on the basis of having a cost per completion below $15,690.
- *Moderate-Cost Programs:* One-third of the programs were grouped into this category on the basis of having a cost per completion between $15,690 and $26,999.
- *High-Cost Programs:* One-third of the programs were grouped into this category on the basis of having a cost per completion of about $26,999.

FINDINGS

We present findings from the analysis of all 186 programs according to program model, gender composition, and security level. This presentation is intended to serve as a demonstration of the type of analysis permitted by the PAM model. However, it is important to note that we use the PAM model in Florida not as a mechanism for comparing program models, but rather to evaluate the performance of *individual* commitment programs by comparing expected outcomes to observed performance within each program. The PAM analysis also permits the ranking of individual facilities relative to all other commitment programs in the state.

Mirroring the population breakdown of security levels among Florida's juvenile commitment programs, most of the 186 programs evaluated in the analyses presented here are moderate-risk facilities (46 percent). The sample consists of equal proportions (20 percent) of minimum-risk day treatment programs and high-risk residential programs. The low-risk security level represents 12 percent of the sample, while maximum-risk juvenile prisons comprise the smallest percentage (3 percent) of the sample and population of commitment programs in Florida. Most juvenile correctional facilities in Florida serve male offenders (66 percent). Notably, however, the minimum-risk day treatment facilities are typically co-ed programs.

There are a number of program models or treatment approaches used within Florida's juvenile justice system. We compare the most common models used in terms of program and cost-effectiveness (as such, due to omission of least common models, sample size may be somewhat reduced). The following is a general overview of each program model presented:

- *Day Treatment Programs:* These facilities represent the least restrictive portion of the juvenile commitment continuum. They are day schools that provide education and rehabilitative programming to committed youth who continue to live at home. The most common day treatment program in Florida is based on an experiential learning model developed by the private provider Associated Marine Institutes. These programs provide instruction and hands-on training in marine-based activities.

- *Group Treatment Homes:* Group treatment homes are generally small programs located in a neighborhood setting. The facility typically consists of a house with enough bedrooms to accommodate up to twelve youth. The treatment focus is on social skill acquisition and education to assist in the youth's reentry into the home community. Although some homes provide onsite education, the majority of facilities allow youth to attend local public schools. Rehabilitation focuses on family involvement and community-oriented experiences.

- *Wilderness Camps:* These are adventure-based programs in rustic settings. Wilderness camps emphasize self-sufficiency through experiential learning and include private providers such as Outward Bound. Activities include shelter construction, community service projects, ropes courses, canoe trips, challenge courses, and counseling. These camps typically serve between 18 to 40 youths at one time.

- *Sex Offender Programs:* This model specifically targets only youths adjudicated on sexual offenses. These programs provide a range of care, counseling and treatment based on standards established by the Association for the Treatment of Sexual Abusers or the National Adolescent Perpetrator Network.

- *Halfway Houses:* Halfway house programs typically serve 15–30 youths in a moderate-risk security setting. These programs provide 24-hour awake staff supervision and many are hardware-secure, as well. Education is provided onsite. Some halfway house programs permit limited community access, though generally youth confined in halfway houses do not leave the facility grounds.

Programming includes substance abuse counseling, individual and family counseling, and sexual development services.

- *Boot Camps:* The military-based boot camp programs utilize a highly structured, impact incarceration approach delivered by trained drill instructors. An initial verbal confrontation period is used to break down resistance to authority and treatment, and to firmly establish the boot camp expectations for the youth or "recruit." The programs emphasize "changing criminal thought processes," education, work, physical training, and counseling in a regimented environment.

- *Youth Academies/Youth Development Centers:* These program models are designed to provide between six and twelve months of secure residential treatment to serious offenders. Services include diagnostic evaluations, substance abuse intervention, mental health services, sexual dysfunction interventions, gang-related behavior interventions, vocational services, self-sufficiency planning, and behavior modification aimed at curbing misconduct.

- *Juvenile Prisons:* Commitment facilities classified under this program model are physically secure residential programs with a designated length of stay ranging from 18 to 36 months. The prisons are maximum-custody hardware-secure with perimeter security fencing and locking doors. The facilities are required to provide single-cell occupancy, except that youth may be housed together during prerelease transition. Placement in a program at this level is prompted by a demonstrated need to protect the public. Youth remain in these programs during their entire stay except in emergency situations and are provided all services on-site. They are not allowed home visits or involvement in the community.

Among the programs evaluated here, the greatest percentage (39 percent) fall into the halfway house model. Day treatment programs (22 percent), wilderness camps (11 percent), and youth academies/centers (10 percent) were the next most common treatment approaches employed by the programs included in the study.

As outlined earlier, program effectiveness scores are grouped into three categories. Overall, the results indicate that the majority (61 percent) of commitment programs in Florida are performing as would be expected given the youth served. That is, most programs are average in program effectiveness. Only 16 percent of the programs evaluated perform better than expected, while nearly one-quarter of the facilities actually perform below average in terms of recidivism outcomes.

The results indicate that minimum security day treatment programs appear to have the largest number of programs performing better than expected, after controlling for the individual risk factors of the youths served. The program effectiveness of day treatment programs is nearly double that of programs in the next most effective security level, high-risk residential programs. In fact, only 5 percent of all day treatment programs fall into the below average effectiveness category, while among residential programs, between 26 percent and 32 percent of all programs are ranked below average in effectiveness.

In addition to recidivism outcomes, day treatment programs are, on average, less costly than residential programs. More than three-quarters of day treatment programs are ranked as low-cost facilities, compared to between 0 percent and 41 percent for residential programs. Fewer than 10 percent of the minimum-security programs are high-cost facilities while 100 percent of the juvenile prisons are grouped into this cost category. Not surprisingly, as security level increases, average facility costs also generally increase. The findings reveal that on average, programs that perform better than expected in terms of recidivism also tend to cost more to operate.

Nearly 80 percent of the programs performing below average are moderate- to low-cost facilities. It is interesting to note that of the programs performing above average and doing so with relatively low operating costs, all are classified within the day treatment program model. This suggests that the community-based approach offers not only the greatest effectiveness when controlling for youths' individual risk factors, but also does it at minimal cost.

A breakdown of program effectiveness in terms of varying program models or treatment approaches reveals once again that most programs are performing within the average effectiveness range. However, there are some notable differences among program models and the above/below average effectiveness classification. Sex offender programs, day treatment programs, and boot camps have the greatest percentage of facilities categorized as above average effectiveness, after controlling for youths' likelihood to recidivate given individual risk factors. The program models most likely to demonstrate average or below average performance are also those programs that are among the most numerous: halfway houses, wilderness camps, group treatment homes, and high-risk youth academies. Together, these four program models comprise 65 percent of Florida's juvenile commitment programs.

Our final analyses examine program effectiveness in terms of treatment models and the gender composition of youth served. The effectiveness of program models varies by gender. Group treatment homes appear to be a more effective model for female offenders than males. In fact the majority of male group treatment homes perform worse than expected, while none of the female group treatment homes are below average in effectiveness. This finding suggests that delinquent girls may respond better to the less secure, community-oriented treatment approach offered within this program model. Similarly, despite the existence of a very large number of halfway houses serving males, not a single male halfway house performed better than predicted and nearly half are classified as below average. Among halfway houses serving females, on the other hand, one-third are in the above average category and none are in the below average category, suggesting that the halfway house treatment model, as it is implemented in Florida, may be more effective with female youth. Because the majority of day treatment programs are co-ed, too small a number of exclusively male or exclusively female programs exist to draw meaningful conclusions. Similarly, the small number of female boot camps and female wilderness programs prevents meaningful comparisons with the male versions of these programs. A female juvenile prison was recently opened in Florida, and is one of the only facilities of its type in the nation. However, this program has yet to be evaluated using the PAM model, because insufficient time has elapsed since the program opened to allow for the required one-year recidivism follow-up.

Programs serving females, in general, perform better with regard to expected recidivism than programs serving males, even after controlling for the influence of gender on youths' individual likelihood to reoffend. The factors underlying the generally strong performance of female juvenile commitment programs are not clear. However, the Florida Department of Juvenile Justice has made enhancement of gender-specific programming a priority for a number of years, an effort spearheaded by a very active "Girls Initiative" statewide workgroup. In addition, the Department obtained Challenge Grant funding to conduct an extensive four-year empirical investigation into the characteristics, needs, and backgrounds of girls incarcerated in the "deep end" of the juvenile justice system. The findings of the study have been widely disseminated among juvenile justice professionals at all levels throughout the state. It is possible that this emphasis and prioritization of girls' programming has had a significant impact on the effectiveness of facilities serving female juvenile offenders.

SUMMARY AND DISCUSSION

The primary intent and greatest value of the Program Accountability Measures model is its cost-benefit approach to comparing individual juvenile commitment facilities. Programs are held accountable to the level of performance anticipated for the youth they serve, rather than to a static statewide recidivism target. The PAM approach solves a major problem faced by evaluators of juvenile justice programs, namely, the difficulty of comparing across program models, security levels, and other factors that may impact the relative likelihood of reoffending of the youth served by individual facilities. The PAM analysis allows evaluators to take an important step beyond simple recidivism measures and program monitoring. It is indeed possible for a program with a high number of recidivists to be ranked as more effective than other programs with fewer recidivists. Once the underlying risk factors of the youth served are held constant, however, it becomes clear to what extent the program performed better than predicted.

Program monitoring, the most common method of program evaluation, can yield valuable information about facility safety and contract compliance; however, it cannot predict—and is not intended to predict—program outcomes. In fact, a recent comparison between program monitoring performance and PAM-based program effectiveness in Florida revealed that monitoring outcomes are unrelated to effectiveness. While this may seem counterintuitive, many possible explanations exist. Most important, perhaps, is that the factors that contribute to successful juvenile rehabilitation are still not fully understood, and therefore cannot be written into even the most carefully crafted contract or thoughtfully written operational policies. Additionally, ensuring the delivery of services such as counseling and education does not necessarily ensure the quality of those services. The effectiveness of interventions within program models may actually be higher related to factors too intangible to be measured by even careful contract monitoring. Quality of management and its impact upon the culture within a program, the nature of staff-to-client interactions, staff turnover, and the level of dedication of key staff members may be more predictive of treatment success than objective measures such as program model, monitoring outcomes, and funding levels.

The statistical approach of the PAM model offers evaluators, policymakers, and funding sources an important new option to measure and reward the intangible factors that contribute to successful outcomes. Currently in Florida, private providers' past PAM performance is one measure used to score proposals to operate new juvenile justice programs. Poor past performance decreases the likelihood that a provider will be awarded new contracts. PAM scores have also been used to identify programs that warrant in-depth study. For example, a particularly high-performing boot camp was targeted for intensive study in the hopes that other boot camp operators could benefit from qualitative information regarding the facility's operations. More recently, a high-risk program for younger juvenile offenders was selected for in-depth analysis using that Correctional Program Assessment Inventory (CPAI), given the programs' consistently poor performance compared to the expected recidivism of the youth served.

The Program Accountability Measures approach represents a major step forward in juvenile justice program evaluation. Increased demands for accountability in human services demand advanced outcome measurement and cost-effectiveness. While program monitoring continues to be a necessary and useful evaluation technique, the statistically-controlled recidivism measures employed here offer a roadmap to comprehensive, accurate evaluation of whether juvenile commitment programs accomplish their primary mission: reduction of re-offending among the youth they serve.

QUESTIONS FOR REVIEW AND DISCUSSION

1. What is meant by Program Accountability Measures analysis? What are some of its features?

2. How are Florida's day treatment programs evaluated? Discuss.

3. How are PAM scores calculated? What are the criteria that influence one's amenability to treatment?

4. Program and cost effectiveness are often compared. Why is so much interest focused upon the cost of interventions such as the one discussed here?

5. Describe four treatment program models.

6. What are halfway houses? What sorts of services do they seem to provide for offenders?

7. How is accountability related to recidivism? Discuss.

PART VI

Crime Prevention Programs for Selected Offenses: Program Evaluation and Policy Implications

❖

There are many types of crime. In fact, a discussion of all types of crime and ways of preventing all forms of crime and delinquent behavior is well beyond the scope of this collection of readings. In this concluding part, several specific types of crime will be highlighted for discussion as examples. A useful feature is a discussion of program evaluation and several ways of determining whether particular programs are effective. How do we know that certain interventions work? There are several answers to this question, none of which is clear-cut. This part is divided into several sections. The first section deals with program evaluation itself and examines how specific programs are assessed in terms of their effectiveness. The meaning of program effectiveness is examined.

In the sections that follow, several types of interventions used with probationers are examined and discussed. Offenders with special needs are defined and described. Several court strategies for sanctioning offenders are examined. Some of these court sanctions work better than others. Several programs for prison and jail inmates will be presented and discussed. For those released back into their communities, specific programs for parolees will be described. Several youth interventions will be described and assessed. The last section of this part focuses on specific targets of crime, including the elderly and those most vulnerable to sexual assault. Several types of crime are described that impact these different categories of victims.

Richard Rosenfeld, Robert Fornango, and Eric Baumer examine three different intervention programs used by law enforcement agencies to combat crime. They examine the effectiveness of Compstat, Ceasefire, and Exile as interventions attempted in different jurisdictions. Compstat originated in New York, while Ceasefire targeted delinquent gangs in Boston. Exile is a Virginia-based program that attempts to deter criminals from using firearms during a crime's commission. Are these various initiatives effective at deterring violence? The authors are somewhat pessimistic about the program evaluations of Compstat and Ceasefire and their effectiveness in curbing violence. However, Exile is a program that has decreased gun-related homicide slightly. A conservative interpretation of these results is recommended, and the authors note that although their own analyses of these programs are inconclusive, more research is needed before these programs can be regarded as successful or unsuccessful.

Jeanne Stinchcomb's essay is especially important, in that a foundation is clearly articulated for program evaluations of many types. Stinchcomb describes several classification strategies for evaluating whether programs are effective. This analysis and description should prove useful for agencies that wish to make evaluations of their own programs.

Edward Szostak and Marisa Beeble describe a jail diversion program whereby inmates with mental health issues are diverted to social services rather than incarcerated. All too often, jails and prisons have become repositories for the mentally ill in society. Such individuals come to the attention of law enforcement easily and are often incarcerated rather than treated for the mental illnesses they have. Without treatment, these persons are subsequently released, only to become rearrested and jailed again. This is like a revolving door. These authors suggest several screening strategies that can keep offenders with mental health issues out of jails and in hospitals where their mental health needs can be properly addressed.

Offenders on probation or parole are subject to many forms of supervision. One supervisory method that became quite popular in the mid-1980s is electronic monitoring (EM). EM utilizes electronic anklets or wristlets that emit electronic signals that can be intercepted by paroling or probation agencies and personnel. Ralph and Robert Gable discuss EM and its positive and negative effects. EM doesn't control behavior. Rather, it serves as a means of identifying an offender's whereabouts at particular times. These authors believe that for the right types of offenders, EM can inspire prosocial behaviors and thus reduce their recidivism.

Because much crime committed is gang-related, several initiatives have been established to reduce the likelihood that probationers and parolees will continue their gang affiliations when released into their communities. PROGRESS (Proactive Gang Resistance Enforcement, Suppression, and Supervision) is a program described by Greg Hagenbucher. Teams of probation/parole officers target especially high-risk offenders, or those most likely to have gang ties, for more intensive supervision and monitoring. One aim of PROGRESS is to ensure program compliance. Evidence is presented by Hagenbucher that PROGRESS is successful in achieving this objective and minimizing recidivism.

Probationers represent a broad array of offenders and it is impossible to characterize them accurately. What works to deter some probationers from further offending may not work with other types of probationers. Robin Campbell and Robert Victor Wolf describe problem-solving probation and review the efforts of problem-solving probation programs in four different communities where experiments with this intervention were conducted with various probationer samples. Problem-solving probation initially focuses on the factors and conditions that contribute to probationer/parolee program violations, and then the steps needed to reduce their recidivism by solving some or all their problems. Programs in several cities are described, including Operation Night Light in Boston; a reparative board program in Vermont; the use of community justice officers who work with youthful offenders in Deschutes County, Oregon; and a beat supervision program in Maricopa County, Arizona. The relative successfulness of each of these programs is discussed and their implications for applications in other jurisdictions are examined.

Mark Cohen and his associates have investigated citizen willingness to pay for particular crime control programs. Citizen support for crime control programs is important. Using a cost-benefit analysis, Cohen et al. have shown that the public regards each crime differently and is thus more or less willing to pay for a specific crime's deterrence or prevention. Socioeconomic status and other factors are associated with citizen willingness to pay and whether certain types of intervention programs will be well-received by the public.

David Karp and Kevin Drakulich describe the Vermont Reparative Board, which is a three-pronged effort directed at probationers that utilizes the balanced approach and emphasizes both community and restorative justice principles, including public safety, offender accountability, and victim reparation or restitution. When offenders are sentenced, some of them are ordered to appear before reparative boards, which are frequently staffed by trained community volunteers. Victim participation in reparative board discussions, which are conducted over several weeks, is strongly encouraged. Compared with traditional probationer treatment and supervision, recidivism among participating probationers was greatly reduced. The implications for reparative boards in other jurisdictions are discussed. Continuing with the theme of restitution is the work of John Gillis, who discusses the importance of restitution in heightening offender accountability and responsibility. Different forms of restitution are presented as well as a discussion of various issues.

Shelley Johnson Listwan and her associates have written about those in correctional settings with different types of personality disorders. Having mental disorders is closely associated with poor institutional adjustment. Thus, programming efforts of institutional officials with these particularly affected inmates are frustrated. Listwan et al. discuss ways of detecting who has psychiatric disorders and what can be done to treat them within institutional settings. Elizabeth Anderson and Theresa Hilliard describe several different kinds of special-needs offenders. Special-needs offenders include not only the mentally ill as discussed by Listwan et al., but also the elderly, the terminally ill, patients with communicable diseases, persons with physical disabilities, and those who are developmentally disabled. Different strategies for coping with special-needs offenders are examined as well as the potential problems they create for administrative staff. Interestingly, more than a few institutionalized offenders have co-occurring disorders. They may be mentally ill and have substance abuse problems, or some other combination of two or more problems. Stanley Sacks and Frank Pearson have written an essay about co-occurring substance abuse and mental disorders among offenders and the specific problems these co-occurring disorders may pose for supervising officials.

Anne Morrison Piehl's essay closely examines whether parole is effective. Her essay is based on a report prepared for the Urban Institute and looks at parole effectiveness in the United States between 1980 and 2003. There is substantial recidivism among parolees, and Piehl rightly questions parole effectiveness and whether supervision of parolees matters. She discusses possible answers to this question and suggests various solutions for improving parole supervision effectiveness. James Byrne and Faye Taxman examine eight model programs that pertain to parolee reentry. Several important reentry trends are examined. Thus, they elaborate on Anne Piehl's concern that contemporary parole supervision practices are questionably effective. One important concept examined by Byrne and Taxman is structured reentry, which is the process whereby the offender makes the transition from prison to the community. Specific offender reentry strategies are recommended and discussed.

Francis Cullen, John Eck, and Christopher Lowenkamp examine the phenomenon of environmental corrections, which seeks to reduce the opportunities probationers and parolees have for committing crime. They recommend that probation and parole agencies must rethink existing parole/probation supervision strategies, steering away from "scare tactics," to more prosocial, positive actions that will enable offenders to become more effectively rehabilitated and reintegrated.

Juvenile offenders may be amenable to mediation programs such as restorative justice or alternative dispute resolution. Robert Smith and Victor Lombardo describe a juvenile mediation program that was the basis of experiments in several West Virginia counties during the late 1990s. Eligibility requirements for entry into this program are discussed and several program objectives are outlined. The use of volunteer mediators assists youths in acquiring remorse, and contractual agreements between youths and program officials help juveniles to remain focused on program goals. The juvenile mediation program is reported as successful, with a 70 percent success rate among participating youths. Kurt Siedschlaw and Beth Wiersma describe a Work Ethic Camp (WEC), which is a more formalized approach to changing youthful offender thinking. The WEC is selective and only includes low-risk non-felony youths who participate in a 120-day exercise. A cognitive approach is used to change a youth's thinking. Thus, it is unlike a boot camp, despite having several similarities. The anticipated outcome of the WEC is a new appreciation among youths for work experiences and an acquisition of positive work ethics. The results of this program are described.

The elderly are especially vulnerable as crime victims. Some statistical information is presented by Patsy Klaus about crimes against persons 65 and older. Kelly Dedel Johnson's essay examines financial crimes against the elderly, such as different types of fraud. She provides an excellent discussion of several responses different agencies have taken to reduce elderly victimization. One type of crime that often targets the elderly but also applies to a broad range of unsuspecting citizens is telemarketing fraud. The U.S. Department of Justice, Criminal Division discusses telemarketing fraud, including its several variations. A follow-up article by the Criminal Division of the U. S. Department of Justice describes other types of fraudulent schemes and how to recognize them. Information is provided about how they can be detected and what persons can do to avoid being victimized.

A growing concern of the American public is the sex offender. Several high-profile sex offense cases, several involving children, have been covered heavily by the media. Because of extensive media coverage of sex offenders and television programs such as *Nancy Grace*, the public has become increasingly outraged over sex offenders and is supportive of harsh punishments. One belief among citizens is that sex offenders are highly likely to recidivate. Thus, according to this belief, they should be penalized more severely than persons who commit nonsexual crimes. Lisa Sample and Timothy Bray focus on sex offenders in their essay and attempt to answer the question of whether sex offenders pose a pervasive danger to others. They discuss both the criminal and subsequent civil penalties that may accrue to persons convicted of various sex offenses. Their analysis of sex offense data obtained from the Illinois State Police for the period 1990–1997 has provided a substantial database for their study. Their conclusion, as it pertains to Illinois sex offenders, is that sex offending compared with other types of offending has low recidivism rates. Thus, on the basis of their Illinois data, they question whether sex offenders generally are overpenalized. They question whether the media have created an irrational fear among the public about the potential dangerousness of sex offenders in general, based on high-profile sex offense cases they have chosen to cover in their televised reports.

Tempe, Arizona, officials have written about sexual assault. In an essay about sexual assault, the City of Tempe identifies various myths and facts about sexual assault. While their statistical information to some extent challenges the tentative conclusions about sex offenders made by Sample and Bray, rapists and other types of sex offenders are vividly described. Proactive solutions are identified so that those most likely to be victimized by rapists can avoid these crimes. One important contribution of this essay is a victim's bill of rights. All too often, the focus of attention is upon punishing offenders rather than consoling victims. Victims have rights as well, and many of these rights are articulated. This part concludes with an essay prepared for the Massachusetts Department of Public Health by Michelle Harris and Mark Bergeron-Naper. Harris and Bergeron-Naper describe several different sexual assault prevention programs that were implemented during the 1997–1998 period. These projects are described, including their individual components and aims. The common theme of these projects was that they were peer-driven. Groups of adolescent peers met at different times and discussed sexual assault prevention. The programs were believed to be beneficial as potential deterrents to adolescent sexual victimization.

28

"Did Ceasefire, Compstat, and Exile Reduce Homicide?"

Richard Rosenfeld, Robert Fornango,
and Eric Baumer

Adapted from Richard Rosenfeld, Robert Fornango, and Eric Baumer, "Did *Ceasefire, Compstat*, and *Exile* Reduce Homicide?" *Criminology and Public Policy* 4: 419–450, 2005.

Reprinted by permission from the American Society of Criminology.

As crime rates in the United States plummeted in the 1990s, it was inevitable that police and other public officials would claim credit for the decline. How could they resist? Rates of violent crime, especially in the large cities, were falling to levels not seen since the 1960s (Rosenfeld, 2004). Falling crime rates are good news for politicians, and for good reason: "The potential political payoff is huge," a columnist wrote during New York's crime decline. "If the crime numbers continue their precipitous fall, no one will be able to beat Mr. Guliani when he comes up for re-election. . . " (Herbert, 1995). In his 1996 State of the Union address, President Clinton embraced the nation's crime drop and declared: "At last, we have begun to find a way to reduce crime" (Krauss, 1996). A few months later, Clinton greeted the release of FBI crime figures with the claim: "Because of our tough and smart decision to put more cops on the street and get kids, guns and drugs off the street, we are now beginning to reverse the trend in violent crime" (Butterfield, 1996: A1).

President Clinton joined local officials around the country during the 1990s in what one journalist called "a chorus of self-congratulation" (Krauss, 1996). In city after city, officials attributed the falling crime rates, in whole or part, to a new program or policy they had instituted. Austin's mayor linked crime reductions to community and problem-oriented policing. Buffalo's police commissioner attributed the decrease to more aggressive enforcement, targeting career criminals, and a youth curfew. In Chicago, the addition of new officers and community policing were credited (the claims for Austin, Buffalo, and Chicago are described in *Law Enforcement News*, 1997). Detroit's police chief highlighted his efforts to "improve the image of the police with the community and get as many people involved as possible" (Butterfield, 1995: 10). The Mayor of East St. Louis attributed the crime drop in his blighted city to more officers, new equipment, and antidrug and antigang-targeted patrols (Gillerman, 1996). Houston's chief cited computerized crime analysis, more officers, storefront stations in crime hotspots, and an antigang taskforce (Butterfield, 1995: 10). In Los Angeles, officials credited hot-spot and community policing, but they also cited neighborhood crime prevention, a gang truce, and an earthquake as reasons for the crime drop (Feldman, 1994).

Criminologists generally greeted such claims-making with skepticism and countered with alternative explanations for the crime drop, most featuring some combination of withered drug markets, the booming economy, mass incarceration, or the "little brother syndrome" (younger adolescents were turned off by the drug use and violence of older adolescents) (Lardner, 1997; see also Butterfield, 1996, 1998; Lacayo, 1996). Some criminologists acknowledged they had no idea why crime rates were decreasing and limited their public commentary to airy proclamations such as "I think we can now say a trend has been established" and "Something broad is happening" (Butterfield, 1996). Overviews of the crime drop published as it was coming to an end contained elaborate statistical descriptions of the trends but remarkably little in the way of explanatory research on either the crime-reduction claims advanced by public officials or the counterclaims of the "experts" (Blumstein and Wallman, 2000; Cook and Laub, 2002: Rosenfeld, 2002, 2004). "The academic world," one critic observed, "has not distinguished itself in this field of inquiry" (Lardner, 1997: 54).

Evaluating the impact of policy initiatives on crime trends is challenging under the best of circumstances; it is even more difficult to isolate whatever additional difference policy may have made when crime rates are already on the decline. Furthermore, most crime-control policies are not designed for valid evaluation, and those with built-in evaluation designs usually are intended to prevent the criminal behavior of individuals rather than reduce the crime rates of populations. An individualistic bias pervades criminology. In the midst of the 1990s crime decline, the significant advances in criminology were in the study of individual developmental patterns of delinquency and other problem behaviors (Farrington, 2003); analysis of aggregate crime trends remained on the periphery of the field (LaFree, 1998).

In this article, we seek to advance the study of policy impacts on crime trends through an assessment of homicide trends in three cities with widely publicized local law enforcement initiatives: Boston's *Operation Ceasefire*, New York's *Compstat*, and Richmond, Virginia's *Project Exile*. Each program has been credited with reducing rates of serious violent crime, including homicide, and each has been subject to some form of outcome evaluation. However, to our knowledge, the crime-reduction effects of the three programs have never been evaluated with comparable data and methods, and the existing evaluations either lack systematic comparisons with crime trends in other cities or fail to control for other influences on crime trends, both of which are critical for separating the change in crime trends associated with policy interventions from changes caused by other factors. We use piecewise linear growth models to evaluate homicide trends in the three cities during, before, and in the case of Boston, after the intervention periods. Our models control for a broad range of other influences on homicide trends and are fit to data from all U.S. cities with a 1990 population greater than 175,000 (N = 95).

Let us be very clear about our objectives. We do not claim to evaluate the three interventions *per se*; we have neither the data nor the methods for doing so. Rather, we evaluate homicide trends in the three cities in and around the respective intervention periods and draw inferences from that evaluation about the accuracy of claims that the interventions reduced homicide. Those inferences cannot be as strong as many program proponents or critics would like, but they should be preferred over the baseless success claims and counterclaims and handful of disparate empirical investigations that have characterized evaluations of the three policing initiatives to date.

THE INITIATIVES

Ceasefire, Compstat, and *Exile* arguably are the most important local law enforcement initiatives intended to reduce serious criminal violence launched during the 1990s. Certainly, they are the best known. In this section, we describe each of the programs, their intended outcomes, claims asserting their success, and prior research on their crime-reduction effects.

Background and Program Logic

Ceasefire, Compstat, and *Exile* were launched against a backdrop of sharply escalating violent crime rates during the late 1980s and early 1990s. Homicides in Boston among youth aged 24 years and under more than tripled between 1987 and 1990 and remained above 1980s levels and through the mid-1990s (Kennedy et al., 2001: 1) New York registered a record 2,245 homicides in 1990, well above the previous record of 1,826 set in 1981, prompting one seasoned journalist to warn: "If there are 2,000 murders this year, get ready for 4,000. New York is dying" (quoted in Karmen, 2000: 7). Richmond consistently ranked among the top ten U.S. cities in homicides per capita during the late 1980s and early 1990s; in 1994, it ranked number two, behind New Orleans, with a homicide rate of 80 per 100,000 residents (authors' calculations from the FBI's *Uniform Crime Reports*).

Although the three initiatives were similarly situated in a context of rising violent crime, they differed in problem diagnosis, design, and strategy. From 1996 to 1999, Boston's *Operation Ceasefire* focused on firearm violence involving youth gangs. *Ceasefire's* central objective was to deter youth firearm violence through direct communication to gang youth that firearm possession and use would not be tolerated, and all available levers would be pulled to ensure swift and tough punishment of violators. The dual strategy of "retail deterrence" and "pulling levers" was implemented in a series of meetings with gang members involving police, youth workers, probation and parole officials, the U.S. attorney, and the local district attorney. "We're here because of the shooting," they would say. "We're not going to leave until it stops. And until it does, nobody is going to so much as jaywalk, nor make any money, nor have any fun" (Kennedy et al., 2001: 27–28). The gang members were told to spread the word on the street. Youth workers also took the message directly to other gang youth. "Stop the Violence" posters were put up throughout areas with high levels of gang violence. Other posters described the sanctions, including federal charges and sentences, applied to recalcitrant gang members: "They were warned," the posters said. "They didn't listen (Kennedy et al., 2001: 28–41; see also Kennedy, 1998).

A different kind of "retail deterrence" through aggressive order maintenance policing is at the heart of New York's *Compstat*. Begun in 1994 with the installation of William Bratton as police commissioner and continuing to the present, *Compstat* sought to restore order on the streets and accountability for crime in the police department. The police were no longer to tolerate minor offenses; they were to make arrests for vagrancy, vandalism, littering, minor drug possession, prostitution, public drunkenness and urination, aggressive panhandling, and harassment by "squeegee pests." The logic of the approach is taken from the so-called broken windows theory of crime causation: Minor crimes and disorder invite more serious offending by signaling that the police and community have lost control of the streets (Kelling and Bratton, 1998; Kelling and Coles, 1996; Wilson and Kelling, 1982). Aggressively restoring order reverses the message, thereby deterring more serious crime. In addition, frequent arrests for minor offenses on occasion net bigger fish, such as persons wanted on warrant for serious crimes or who are illegally carrying firearms or large quantities of drugs for sale. Other enforcement changes were introduced under Bratton, including "buy and bust" offensives against drug sellers and anti-gun patrols, but for Bratton the "linchpin strategy" was aggressive order maintenance policing (Bratton and Knobler, 1998: 228).

The other component of the New York strategy is to hold commanders accountable for the crime rates in their precincts. At regular meetings in the "war room" at police headquarters, top administrators grill commanders on their knowledge of crime patterns and on their crime-reduction activities and plans (Karmen, 2000: 92–94). A deterrence logic underlies this approach as well, now directed at police officials rather than at offenders: You are directly responsible for what happens under your command. If you fail, there will be consequences.

In practice it is nearly impossible to separate the two components of *Compstat* for evaluation purposes. Even in principle disagreement exists concerning which one should be credited for New York's crime decline during the 1990s. Bratton believes order maintenance policing was the "key" to falling crime rates. Mayor Giuliani, on the other hand, maintained that police reorganization and greater accountability were primarily responsible (Karmen, 2000: 94–96, 120). Critics contend that order maintenance policing in New York departed markedly from the "broken windows" model, and that whatever effect it may have had on crime was because of aggressive stop-and-frisk tactics aimed primarily at racial and ethnic minorities (Fagan and Davies, 2001). In any event, our analysis is limited to the question of whether New York homicide trends differ significantly from those of other cities after *Compstat* was initiated. We cannot determine which aspect of *Compstat* (or *Ceasefire* or *Exile*) may have been responsible for observed differences in the trends.

A more traditional deterrence logic underlies Richmond, Virginia's *Project Exile*, which was formally initiated in February of 1997. *Exile* entails sentence enhancements through federal prosecution for violent or drug crimes involving firearms. Federal sentences for such crimes generally are longer than those in state courts, bail is denied more often, and sentences are served in federal prisons likely to be located out of state (Raphael and Ludwig, 2003: 254). By increasing the expected penalty for firearm-related offenses, the program is intended to deter firearm carrying and criminal use. By sentencing more violent offenders to longer prison sentences, the program also is intended to reduce crime by incapacitating violent felons. It is unclear whether deterrence or incapacitation is the primary objective of *Exile's* sentence enhancements. However, the broad "outreach" campaign accompanying the program is intended explicitly to deter criminal use of firearms. *Exile* is advertised extensively in print and electronic media and on city buses and business cards carrying the blunt and bleak warning that "An illegal gun will get you five years in federal prison," the mandatory minimum sentence for federal "felon-in-possession" cases (http://www.vahv.org/Exile). There is, then, something of a "retail" component to *Project Exile's* practice of deterrence, if not as precisely targeted to particular groups and neighborhoods as was the case in Boston's *Operation Ceasefire*.

Prior Outcome Evaluations

The most important obstacle in the way of rigorous outcome assessments of the three programs is that each of them was implemented city-wide, leaving thereby no like situated areas without the intervention that might serve as within-city controls. A second obstacle to reliable evaluation is that the different aspects of each program were implemented more-or-less at the same time, so that even if a "program effect" was found, it would not be obvious which program component should be credited (sentence length? advertising? change in enforcement? change in command accountability? which levers?). Not surprisingly, then, those few outcome evaluations that have been conducted take the form of single-case time-series investigations with limited comparisons with crime trends in other cities.

New York.   The single exception is Kelling and Sousa's (2001) study of violent crime trends during the 1990s in New York's 76 police precincts. Controlling for changes in borough-level unemployment, age composition, and a measure of drug involvement, they find an association between decreases in violent crime and increases in "broken windows" policing, as measured by misdemeanor arrests. Kelling and Sousa (2001) interpret this result as evidence for a key plank of Bratton's policing reforms and against so-called root cause explanations of New York's crime drop and crime in general. Although the coincidence of rising misdemeanor arrest rates and falling violent crime rates across New York City precincts is compelling, Kelling and Sousa (2001) do not control for several additional factors commonly associated with violent crime (e.g., poverty, family structure, immigration trends) and fail to consider the possibility of reciprocal causation between their policing measure and violent crime: Decreases in violent felonies may enable the police to devote greater attention to less serious offenses, which results in increases in misdemeanor arrests.

Other assessments of *Compstat* are less sanguine but also less conclusive about its crime-reducing consequences. Several investigators have pointed out that New York's sharp decline in homicide and other violent crimes during the 1990s was not unique; San Diego, San Antonio, Houston, San Francisco, Los Angeles, and other large cities that had not implemented similar policing reforms also registered very sizable declines (Harcourt, 2001: 90–94; Joanes, 2000). In an early assessment, Fagan et al. (1998) observed that nongun homicides had begun to fall in New York well before the *Compstat* reforms were implemented in 1994. They also find, however, that the drop in firearm homicides is more consistent with the timing of *Compstat* and conclude that the policing changes may have contributed to that decline. Even a harsh critic of broken windows policing concedes that it "contributed in some degree to the decline in crime in New York City" (Harcourt, 2001: 103). Finally, the most comprehensive assessment of the sources of New York's crime drop concludes that changes in policing likely accounted for some decrease, along with a booming economy, escalation in imprisonment, shrinking drug markets, favorable demographic trends, and possible changes in the values of adolescents and young adults. However, the author could draw no conclusions regarding the size of the policing effect (Karmen, 2000: 262–266; see, also Conklin, 2003).

In summary, most independent assessments of the policing changes under Bratton conclude that they probably reduced levels of violent crime in New York over and above the effects of other factors. The most definitive of the studies (Kelling and Sousa, 2001) does not compare New York crimes trends with those in other cities. The others place New York trends in the context of those elsewhere, but they do not employ comprehensive samples of comparison cities or control for other determinants of violent crime.

Boston.   The Harvard researchers who participated in the development of *Operation Ceasefire* compared the timing and magnitude of violent crime trends in Boston with those in other New England cities and a national sample of large cities (Braga et al., 2001; Kennedy et al., 2001; Piehl et al., 2003). In a two-part investigation, the researchers first performed a time-series analysis of monthly youth firearm homicides, gun assaults, and shots fired calls in Boston before and during the intervention period, controlling for changes in unemployment, size of the youth population, adult homicide victimization trends, index crime trends, and youth drug activity as measured by arrests. The results indicate a reduction in firearm violence, net of the controls, coinciding with the implementation of *Ceasefire*.

In the second part of the study, the researchers compared Boston monthly youth homicide trends with those in 29 other New England cities and 39 large U.S. cities, which they adjusted for linear and nonlinear trends in each series, monthly effects, an autoregressive component, and an intervention component in each series. They found three cities in addition to Boston with significant values on the intervention component, but either the direction or precise timing of those effects differ from Boston's. The Harvard team concluded that *Ceasefire* was associated with a significant reduction in youth firearm violence. Their conclusion would be more persuasive had they included additional controls in both the within- and between-cities analyses they conducted. Nonetheless, their findings are consistent with claims of a program effect.

Richmond.   Richmond's *Project Exile* has been subject to a single published outcome evaluation. Raphael and Ludwig (2003) evaluate claims that *Exile* significantly reduced firearm homicides in Richmond by comparing Richmond gun homicide trends during the 1980s and 1990s, Richmond trends with those in other cities, and adult and juvenile homicide arrest rates in Richmond. The first comparison shows that Richmond gun homicide rates had increased markedly during the 1980s, peaking in the early 1990s. Raphael and Ludwig (2003) conclude that Richmond's gun homicide decline during the 1990s was to be expected as part of a general regression to the mean common across U.S. cities with high homicide rates. They conclude from their comparison of Richmond's gun homicide trends with those of other cities that the proportional drop in Richmond's rates through the 1990s was not unusual. What was unusual was Richmond's gun homicide rate in 1997, the year *Exile* began. Raphael and Ludwig (2003) suggest that 1997 was subject to "transitory" influences because it broke a two-year "trend" that began in 1995 and resumed in 1998. Therefore, they dropped 1997 from their trend analyses. "Using this unusual year as the base for calculating the change," they maintain, "is bound to inflate the apparent impact of the program" (Raphael and Ludwig, 2003: 258).

To control for unmeasured influences on Richmond homicide trends, Raphael and Ludwig (2003) compare trends in juvenile and adult homicide arrest rates. The logic of the comparison is that juveniles are not subject to *Exile* provisions (or not to the same extent as adult criminals) but are affected by other factors driving homicide rates. They find that juvenile homicide arrests increased slightly from 1995/1996 to 1998 (again, 1997 is omitted), but adult arrests increased even more over the same period. In other large urban counties, adult homicide arrests declined at a greater rate than did juvenile homicide arrests. Neither finding is consistent with the idea that *Exile* reduced homicide among Richmond adults.

In summary, Raphael and Ludwig (2003) find little evidence to support claims that Richmond's *Project Exile* reduced firearm or overall homicide rates. We regard their evaluation as suggestive but far from the final word on *Exile's* effects. We reserve our specific criticisms until we present the findings from current analysis.

The results of the outcome evaluations of *Compstat, Ceasefire,* and *Exile* are mixed. Evaluations of *Compstat* and *Ceasefire* support claims that the interventions resulted in reductions in homicide. The single published study of *Project Exile* concludes that it had little apparent effect on Richmond firearm homicide rates. It is difficult to compare findings across the evaluations of the three interventions, because they targeted differing population groups and homicide types, and because they are based on distinct sources of data and methods of analysis.

We use the same data sources and methods to evaluate all three interventions. The logic of our approach assumes that an effective intervention will produce a reduction in homicide that (1) differs significantly from corresponding changes in comparison cities; (2) occurs during or after but not before the intervention period; (3) occurs in the specific type of homicide targeted by the intervention; and (4) is independent of other influences. By the same logic, an ineffective intervention will produce a reduction in homicide that does not differ significantly from changes in comparison sites or occurs before the intervention or does not occur in the homicides targeted by the intervention or is brought about by conditions other than the intervention. To be deemed "effective" (or not ineffective), an intervention must meet all four conditions. To be found ineffective, it must fail to meet only one of them.

ANALYTICAL STRATEGY

To assess the effects of the three interventions, we apply growth-curve models to homicide trends in Boston, New York, and Richmond. We estimate each city's homicide trend as a function of a baseline model of covariates fit to data for the 95 largest U.S. cities. An intervention's effectiveness is indicated by a reduction in homicide during the intervention period that is significantly greater than the average reduction for the sample. Our strategy cannot conclusively rule out other possible explanations for observed differences in homicide trends between cities with and without the interventions. However, the *absence* of such differences would place a particularly strong onus on program defenders to demonstrate that an observed homicide reduction resulted from a particular intervention.

Data

The homicide data for the analysis were obtained from the Supplementary Homicide Reports (SHR) for the 95 U.S. cities with a 1990 population of 175,000 or more over the period 1992–2001. The data correspond to the distinct type of homicide targeted by each intervention. Boston's *Ceasefire* was designed to reduce firearm homicides among the "gang age" population of adolescents and young adults. The policing strategies in New York were intended to reduce homicides (and other crimes) of all types, regardless of weapon or age of the offender. Richmond's *Exile* specifically targeted firearm homicides. Accordingly, the analysis of *Ceasefire* was carried out with SHR data on victims of firearm homicide ages 15–24, the *Compstat* analysis with data on total homicide victimizations, and the *Exile* analysis with data on all firearm homicide victimizations. The SHR data were missing for 62 of the 950 city-years in the analysis. Estimated values for the missing data were obtained from within-city regressions of observed values on a period variable (1992 = 0).

To obtain unbiased estimates of the effects of the interventions on homicide rates, we created baseline models incorporating well-established covariates of homicide (Land et al., 1990; Messner and Rosenfeld, 1998). Measures of social and economic disadvantage and population density were obtained from the 1990 Census and the 2000 Census, The density measure was logged to reduce skewness, and all measures were interpolated between census years and extrapolated to 2001. The disadvantage measure was derived from a principal components analysis of several highly intercorrelated variables: percent of families with children under age 18 headed by a female, percent black, median family income (logged), the male unemployment rate, the poverty rate, and the Gini coefficient of income inequality. This measure of economic and social disadvantage corresponds closely to that in Land et al. (1990).

Prior research has found that homicide trends are negatively related to trends in incarceration and police density (Levitt, 2002; Marvell and Moody, 1997; Spelman, 2000). We incorporated in our analysis the yearly state incarceration rate corresponding to each of the 95 cities, obtained from the Bureau of Justice Statistics, and an annual indicator of police per 100,000 city residents, computed from the number of sworn full-time officers reported in the Law Enforcement Management and Administration Statistics (LEMAS) surveys.

Finally, several studies have shown a connection between homicide trends and crack cocaine markets in U.S. cities (Baumer et al., 1998; Blumstein, 1995; Cork, 1999; Ousey and Lee, 2002). We developed a city-level proxy measure of the level of cocaine use among arrestees from the 20 cities in our sample for which yearly Drug Use Forecasting (DUF) and Arrestee Drug Abuse Monitoring (ADAM) data were available between 1990 and 2000. The proportion of arrestees testing positive for cocaine reported by DUF-ADAM was regressed on a composite measure of socio-economic disadvantage, the percentage of city residents living in the same house for five or more years, and the percentage of the population residing in owner-occupied housing. The fit statistics indicated that the model could serve as suitable proxy for city-level variation in cocaine involvement. The predicted values from the equation were used to estimate the extent of cocaine use in cities for which the DUF-ADAM data were unavailable.

Method

The primary research question is whether the three intervention sites experienced greater declines in homicide than other cities during the intervention period after adjusting for between-city differences in other determinants. The analytic strategy must therefore provide estimates of both the within-city trajectories in homicide and between-city differences in those trajectories. We use growth-curve analysis to obtain these estimates. Growth-curve analysis estimates the homicide trends for each city and compares the intercept and slope parameters across cities. Traditionally, such trends are estimated as a polynomial function of time, with single parameters for the linear trend and change in the growth rate. Because our interest lies with the trends during the intervention periods, we estimate the linear components as a series of piecewise trends. The piecewise strategy estimates a linear trend component for successive subperiods of the series, in effect allowing the slope to "bend" at predetermined points. Two linear components are specified in the piecewise models for New York and Richmond, corresponding to the pre-intervention, and intervention periods. Three linear components are specified for Boston, corresponding to the pre-intervention, and post-intervention periods.

RESULTS

Average homicide trends were examined for the 95 cities in our sample as well as trends in the three intervention sites: Boston, New York, and Richmond. Homicide rates declined in the largest U.S. cities during the 1990s to about 13 per 100,000 population at the end of the decade from 20 per 100,000 at the beginning. Homicide rates in Boston fell from roughly 15 per 100,000 during the early 1990s to about 6 per 100,000 at the end of the decade, only to rise again to 11 per 100,000 in 2001. In New York, they plunged to about 8 per 100,000 from 27 per 100,000 over the same period. Richmond homicide rates roller-coastered through 1997, reaching a peak of 80 per 100,000 in 1994, before falling to about 36 per 100,000 at the end of the decade. Homicide rates dropped substantially in the three cities during their respective intervention periods, but it remains to be seen whether these declines were significantly greater than those observed elsewhere after adjusting for relevant correlates of crime trends.

To examine whether the observed homicide declines in Boston, New York, and Richmond were significantly greater than those observed in other large cities, we applied piecewise linear growth-curve models to the trend in the type of homicide targeted by each intervention.

Boston

Results for the trend in youth firearm homicide rates targeted by Boston's *Ceasefire* were examined. The average youth firearm homicide rate for the sample exhibits no significant change during the pre-intervention period ($\beta = -0.015$). It dropped significantly during the intervention period ($\beta = -0.015$, $p < 0.01$), but that change becomes nonsignificant once the covariates are introduced in the conditional model. Boston's youth firearm homicide rate exhibits a greater decrease than the sample average during the intervention period, in both the unconditional and conditional specifications. Although neither difference is statistically significant, the difference between Boston and the sample average in the conditional model just misses the most permissive significance threshold ($p = 0.101$). Finally, the Boston trend did not deviate significantly from the sample average during the post-intervention period in either model.

Boston's youth firearm homicide rate dropped an estimated 25% per year during the 1996–1999 intervention period, compared with a decline of 14% in the average rate during the same period. After adjusting the changes for the effects of the covariates, Boston's youth firearm homicide rate fell an estimated 30% per year during the intervention period, and the average rate dropped 16%. Although the estimated decline in Boston's rate was nearly double that of the sample average in the conditional model, the difference is not statistically significant, even by a permissive standard of $p < 0.10$. The lack of statistical significance reflects Boston's low youth firearm homicide counts during the intervention period (ranging from 21 in 1996 to 10 in 1999). Relatively small year-to-year changes in the number of youth firearm homicides in Boston resulted in large percentage changes. Therefore, the prudent conclusion regarding *Ceasefire's* impact is that it is statistically indeterminate given the small number of youth firearm homicides in Boston.

It is possible that the age range used to define the youth firearm homicide rate in our analysis is too narrow. In supplementary analysis, we reestimated the Boston models using a broadened victim age range of 11–24. Widening the age range of victims adds only three homicides in Boston during the entire 1992–2001 period. Not surprisingly, the supplementary estimation results differ only slightly from the original results, with a marginally significant p-value for the "Boston effect" in the conditional model of 0.092. This result does not alter the substantive conclusion that *Ceasefire's* impact on youth firearm homicides in Boston is difficult to discern given the small number of incidents.

New York

The New York homicide trend did not deviate significantly from the sample average during the 1992–1993 pre-intervention period. The New York rate fell more sharply than the sample average during the intervention period, although the difference is only marginally significant at $p < .10$. However, when the covariates are introduced in the conditional model, the difference between the New York and the average homicide trend becomes nonsignificant. Thus, after adjusting for measured differences between New York and other large cities, the magnitude of the decline in homicide in New York between 1994 and 2001 seems not to have been atypical.

It is possible that *Compstat* had a greater effect on New York's firearm homicide rate than the total homicide rate, as Fagan et al. (1998) have suggested. However, substituting the firearm homicide rate for the total rate in the conditional model yields no significant deviation of New York's firearm homicide trend from the sample average during the intervention period (results not shown).

Consistent with prior research (Marvell and Moody, 1997), the growth in incarceration during the 1990s is consistently related to the homicide trends examined in this study. We cannot rule out entirely the possibility that *Compstat*, and perhaps *Ceasefire* and *Exile*, had an indirect effect on homicide through incarceration. Conceivably, the programs increased state prison sentences that, in turn, reduced homicide rates.

More research is necessary to determine how much of the growth in New York's state prison population was caused by the policing changes under *Compstat*. New York's imprisonment rate grew steadily through the 1980s and 1990s, with no evident acceleration after 1994 (Karmen, 2000: 147). Moreover, the proportion of New York City felony arrests resulting in a prison sentence peaked in 1993, the year before *Compstat* was introduced, and declined thereafter (Karmen, 2000: 155–156). A growing felony arrest rate could still have produced an increase in the size of the prison population, even after the imprisonment-to-arrest ratio began to decline. However, *Compstat* could not have contributed to the growth in New York's prison population that occurred before 1994, and it is not likely that it was responsible for all of the growth after 1994.

Richmond

The Richmond story differs from those in Boston and New York. The unconditional model shows that Richmond's firearm homicide rate fell by nearly 16% per year after *Exile* was introduced in 1997, but that decrease is not significantly greater than the almost 10% average reduction in firearm homicide for the sample. However, after controlling for other factors, Richmond's firearm homicide rate exhibits a 22% yearly decline, whereas the average reduction for the sample remains about 10% per year. That difference is statistically significant ($p < 0.05$).

This finding differs from those obtained by Raphael and Ludwig (2003) in their evaluation of *Exile*, which concluded that the intervention had little effect on Richmond's firearm homicide rate. The discrepancy may be from the use of a longer firearm homicide series in the current study. Raphael and Ludwig (2003) analyzed firearm homicide rates through 1999, whereas the series used in this study extends the intervention period two additional years to 2001. Raphael and Ludwig (2003) also omitted the year 1997 from their analysis, on the ground that the unusually high rate of firearm homicide in Richmond that year constitutes an unreliable base on which to gauge the effectiveness of *Exile*. We question this analytical decision. It is not evident why 1997 should be dropped from the Richmond data and not, for example, 1994, when the homicide rate spiked to 80 per 100,000.

Compared with other large cities, Richmond's high level of homicide is "unusual" in general and not just in 1997.

Nonetheless, it is true that assessments that include 1997, the year *Exile* was introduced, are more apt to find a program effect than those from which 1997 is excluded. We therefore omitted 1997 from our analysis and replaced it with the 1996–1998 average firearm homicide count. Reestimating the conditional model on the revised series reveals a marginally significant downward departure of Richmond's firearm homicide trend from the sample average during the intervention period ($p < 0.10$; results not shown). We also respecified the conditional model by including the 1992 and 1997 firearm homicide rates as additional covariates in the pre-intervention and intervention estimations, respectively. Controlling for between-city differences in initial levels of firearm homicide helps to account for possible selection bias associated with the location of crime control interventions in high-crime cities and minimizes omitted variable bias by capturing unmeasured influences on homicide. Not substantively meaningful differences emerge from the reanalysis; in fact, the "Richmond effect" become somewhat stronger with the initial firearm homicide rates in the model (results available on request).

It would have been instructive had Raphael and Ludwig (2003) also compared their results with and without *Exile's* first year in the analysis. However, the primary reason for the difference between the current results and those from the Raphael and Ludwig (2003) study probably is the inclusion of other determinants of homicide trends in our analysis. We find a significant divergence between Richmond's firearm homicide trend and that for other large cities only after introducing the covariates in the conditional model. Raphael and Ludwig (2003) acknowledge the importance of controlling for other influences on firearm homicide when examining the impact of *Exile* (p. 270):

> The most important concern with our analysis is whether we are able to distinguish the effects of Project Exile from those of other unmeasured factors that drive crime trends over time at the local level. Our comparison of Richmond homicide trends to those of other cities is intended to

address this concern. However, such comparisons may be invalid because of unobserved differences among cities in policing, age structure, and other factors likely to influence homicide rates.

Their comparison of juvenile and adult homicide arrest trends is intended to identify the effects of unmeasured factors on Richmond's trend in firearm homicide rates, on the assumption that juveniles are not subject to the threat of federal imprisonment for using a gun in crime, but are affected by other influences on firearm violence. But juveniles are not threatened by state imprisonment either, and we find a significant effect of state incarceration rates on firearm homicide trends. Raphael and Ludwig's (2003) use of juveniles as a "control group" does not effectively eliminate the effect of incarceration and perhaps other influences on Richmond's trend in firearm homicide.

In summary, we find evidence consistent with an intervention effect on homicide trends for Richmond's *Project Exile*. Richmond's firearm homicide rate fell more rapidly than the average firearm homicide rate among large U.S. cities, with other influences controlled. We cannot rule out the possibility that unmeasured factors are responsible for Richmond's drop in firearm homicides after *Exile* was introduced in 1997. However, they apparently do not include changes over time in police size, drug involvement, or incarceration rates, all prime candidates for explaining the decline in big-city homicide rates during the 1990s (Rosenfeld, 2004). Nor do they include between-city differences in resource deprivation, population density, or unmeasured factors correlated with the initial (1997) level of firearm homicide. Furthermore, unmeasured factors that may be responsible for Richmond's homicide reduction must have come into play after and not before *Exile* was initiated, because Richmond's firearm homicide trend before 1997 did not deviate significantly from the sample average. These results, although not definitive, amount to a fairly strong circumstantial case for *Exile's* impact, and shift the burden of proof back to critics to identify factors not captured in our models that may explain Richmond's sizeable drop in firearm homicide after 1997.

Confidence in the Results

We do not find evidence supportive of a program impact on homicide trends for Boston's *Operation Ceasefire* or New York's *Compstat*. In both instances, the homicide trends during the intervention did not diverge significantly from the sample average, although the Boston results are marginally significant when the age range of the target group is expanded to encompass 11–24 year-olds. Our methods may lack sufficient power to detect *Ceasefire's* effect on youth firearm homicide, although in the nature of the case, it is difficult to identify with high confidence program effects on low base-rate events. This point is illustrated nicely by comparing the confidence intervals around the point estimates of the divergence of the Boston, New York, and Richmond homicide trends from those of other large cities during the respective intervention periods.

Despite the relatively large point estimate, we cannot confidently conclude that a nonzero difference exists between Boston's youth firearm homicide trend and those of other large cities. The Richmond results inspire somewhat greater confidence in the *existence* of a difference between Richmond's firearm homicide trend and the average trend for the sample, although the difference may have been quite small. We are more confident still in the results for New York, which are in line with earlier criticisms that factors other than *Compstat* were responsible for New York's homicide drop during the 1990s (Eck and Maguire, 2000; Karmen, 2000).

DISCUSSION

The decade of the 1990s was a period of marked innovation in policing practices in American cities. As new policies and procedures were introduced, crime rates began to fall across the country, which resulted in claims that the enforcement changes were responsible for the crime drop. Criminologists generally met such claims with skepticism, but they could not point to a substantial body of research of their own that refuted them. Their criticisms often came off as harping or nit-picking, which prompted some practitioners to boast that they would defeat not just crime but criminology. A reporter quipped in 1995 that New York's Police Commissioner William Bratton would not be satisfied "until every last criminologist surrenders" (quoted in Karmen, 2000: 75).

Researchers failed to provide the public or policy makers with clearly articulated standards for judging the credibility of local officials' success claims. The standards are easy enough to identify; they are found in every textbook on social research methods. Before an intervention can be deemed effective in reducing crime, the observed reductions must be plausibly linked to the characteristics of the intervention. Second, the observed reductions must have occurred where and when the intervention was present and not where and when the intervention was absent. Third, the observed reductions must be shown to have exceeded the expected rate of crime decline, the change that would have taken place absent the intervention, what the textbooks term "history." These criteria constitute the minimum threshold, the prima facie case, for granting credence to claims that an intervention has reduced crime. Insisting that they are met is, or should be, the research community's first response to official claims-making and the basis on which the public is advised whether to take the claims seriously.

Criminologists also must impose these minimum methodological standards on themselves. It is not the research community's responsibility to make the prima facie case for a program's effectiveness; that is the burden of program proponents. The researcher's job is to subject the case to systematic empirical evaluation. What is remarkable about the criminological research community's response to the success stories told by local officials during the 1990s crime drop is how little research went into it. Even widely publicized innovations such as *Ceasefire, Compstat,* and *Exile* attracted no more than a handful of outcome evaluations. And the evaluations that were conducted are not easily compared with one another, because they employed different empirical methods and data.

These considerations prompted this investigation. Our intention has been to empirically assess claims made regarding reductions in homicide associated with *Ceasefire, Compstat,* and *Exile* and to offer a model for how such investigations might be undertaken in the future. We do not claim to have presented the last word on either the specific interventions or a general analytic strategy. On the contrary, given the paucity of existing research, our effort must be viewed as a point of departure for ongoing evaluation of the impact of local law enforcement interventions on crime rates.

Few commonly accepted standards exist for undertaking statistical evaluations of crime-control interventions using observational data and econometric methods, even though these are the data and methods we are stuck with for evaluating large-scale initiative such as those addressed in this study. We propose that such evaluations meet the same requirements we would impose on program officials: the evaluation strategy must systematically compare observed crime reductions with those that would have occurred without the intervention. That in turn requires comparisons with other places and controls for other influences based on nationally representative samples, especially when evaluating widely known programs such as *Ceasefire*, *Compstat*, and *Exile*. Statistical models should be applied that efficiently estimate differences across places in crime trends before, during, and when possible after the intervention. We have chosen piecewise growth models and hierarchical methods for these purposes, but other approaches are defensible. What no longer can be defended are isolated evaluations of significant crime-control initiatives that cannot be compared with one another and do not even begin to rule out competing explanations.

This is no mere academic requirement. Current federal crime control policy in the form of *Project Safe Neighborhoods* (PSN) was inspired by the presumed success of Richmond's *Exile* and has been implemented in every federal judicial district in the country. PSN's goal is "to reduce the violent crime rate in our communities," and it promises "accountability" by "measuring success based on 'outcome' rather than 'output'" (http://www.projectsafeneighborhoods.gov). PSN's impact on violent crime remains to be seen. But it establishes a rationale and national platform for greater cooperation among program planners to ensure coordinated interventions and among researchers to devise common evaluation criteria. We should expect to see greater uniformity and generalizability in the resulting evaluations than have characterized the research on the great policing initiatives of the 1990s.

QUESTIONS FOR REVIEW AND DISCUSSION

1. What was the target of Boston's *Operation Ceasefire*? In what respects was it designed to be a crime deterrent?

2. What is *Compstat*? What types of persons were affected by *Compstat*? What were the program's objectives?

3. What are the key elements of Virginia's *Project Exile?* Was it successful? How were potential criminals deterred from using dangerous weapons in committing offenses?

4. Did any or all of these programs succeed in reducing homicides in their respective cities? Why or why not? Discuss.

5. In what respects are the findings from this research controversial? Do they conflict with the conclusions drawn by supporters of the programs evaluated? If so, how?

29

How Do We Know If It Works?
Evaluation Strategies for Making Evidence-Based Decisions

Jeanne B. Stinchcomb

Adapted from Jeanne B. Stinchcomb, "How Do We Know If It Works?: Evaluation Strategies for Making Evidence-Based Decisions." *American Jails* 18: 17–24, 2004.

Reprinted by permission of the American Jail Association.

From staff to inmate programming, every correctional initiative requires fiscal resources. But funding for anything beyond mandated basics is often an extravagant indulgence in today's post-9/11 era of budget cutbacks and "doing more with less." Even worse, at the same time that revenues have been declining, jails have been confronted with escalating populations of inmates with chronic illnesses, infectious diseases, mental health problems, and geriatric disabilities.

With demands increasing and abilities to meet them diminishing, many jail administrators face making painful fiscal choices between institutional security, health care, and inmate programming. Given the necessity of security and health care, reduced programming is often the only realistic alternative. Both jails and prisons throughout the country have therefore experienced a sharp reduction in educational, vocational, and life skills programming (Weedon, 2004: 6).

MAKING WISE INVESTMENTS—THE "MISSING LINK"

Within such a no-growth environment, fundamental safety-and-security expenditures inevitably take precedence. As a result, whenever scarce resources are devoted to programmatic luxuries, it is essential to assure that such resources are invested wisely. In the past, decisions to fund correctional initiatives have been based on everything from experience to popularity. But the wastefulness of continuing to support unproductive or unproven programs is no longer an option. A critical question therefore becomes whether fiscal expenditures are justified by research evidence. If they ever did, jail administrators today no longer can afford to make uninformed choices about initiating or continuing costly programs. But before informed choices can be made, evaluation must be integrated into program planning and practice. Few employers would advocate keeping staff on the payroll without periodic standardized performance evaluations. Yet major criminal justice policies are commonly implemented without giving thought to how their effectiveness will be measured (Stinchcomb, 2005).

In the past when evaluations were conducted at all, they were often half-hearted, *ad hoc* efforts—more an afterthought than a decision-making ingredient. Yet regardless of the subject, the best decisions are clearly based on a foundation of good information. No one, for example, would consider buying a new car or a major home appliance without doing their homework in advance—comparing costs, features, and performance effectiveness. However, programmatic decisions in corrections have often been conducted without the benefit of such insight. But this is a new era—when resources are fewer at the same time that demands for accountability are greater and competitive pressure is forthcoming from the private sector. Surviving in such an environment demands a more objective, evidence-based decision-making process. Economically and administratively, the use of evaluation research can no longer afford to continue as the missing link in correctional decision making (MacKenzie, 2000: 463).

WHAT DO WE NEED TO KNOW TO MAKE BETTER DECISIONS?

Making informed, evidence-based decisions means identifying what information decision-makers need to know. Then the challenge is determining how to find it out efficiently, economically, and in a timely manner, without taking shortcuts that sacrifice the integrity of the evaluation and the credibility of the findings. When evaluating any intervention, it is always tempting to focus on the bottom line. After devoting considerable time, effort, and resources to a program, it is natural to want to know what was or was not actually achieved. This is what is known as an outcome or summative evaluation because its focus is on the final product(s).

Like behavioral change in general, outcome measures can be either intermediate or long-term. For example, a parent faced with a chid who refuses to share toys might employ any number of interventions, from punishment to psychological counseling. In the short term, effectiveness can be measured first-hand by changes in the child's behavior when playing with others. But the long-term (and more important) results can only be assessed by following the child into adulthood and determining whether selfishness prevailed or values of sharing and reciprocity were successfully instilled. In terms of evaluation research, this translates into:

1. *Intermediate outcomes: What were the direct post-intervention accomplishments?* These measures indicate whether the program improved the knowledge, skills and/or capabilities of the participants—i.e., did they learn more than they

knew previously? Have they developed new behaviors? Are they doing things differently? These short-term outcomes are termed "intermediate" because they fall in between initial intervention and ultimate impact.

2. *Long-term impact: What was the ultimate result?* These measures indicate whether any of the initial results translated into long-term improvements—i.e., was the knowledge or skill resulting from a staff training program applied on the job? If so, did it have any effect on the organization? Did the knowledge or skill resulting from an inmate anger management program result in fewer disciplinary infractions? If so, did the inmate's changed behavior continue upon release? A causal chain of evaluation research illustration is presented below.

Initial Intervention -----> Intermediate Intervention -----> Long-Term Impact

MEASURING INTERMEDIATE AND LONG-TERM CHANGE

Intermediate and long-term outcomes could also be distinguished on the basis of what the intervention is trying to achieve—that is, whether the emphasis is on *micro-level individual change* (intermediate outcomes) or *macro-level social or organizational change* (long-term impact). Returning to the anger management example, is the purpose to reduce disciplinary infractions while the offender is in jail? Or is it to avoid anger-related behavior upon release? While evaluation strategies might ideally seek to measure both, when a choice must be made, it should primarily be driven by the intent of the program. For example, the parents concerned about their child's selfishness may be equally concerned with helping the child develop into a benevolent, caring adult. Promoting sharing behavior in childhood is an essential first step. But this intermediate accomplishment does not guarantee long-term results. Intermediate outcomes are therefore necessary but insufficient to achieve a long-lasting impact.

ESTABLISHING INDICATORS OF SUCCESS—BE CAREFUL WHAT YOU PROMISE!

The selfish child example also illustrates a basic principle of evaluation research—i.e., the need to specifically identify the results that the intervention is designed to produce. In the case of correctional interventions, that means determining just how ambitious the program should aim to be. While it may be intuitively appealing to establish extremely challenging, long-term outcomes, accountability considerations might argue for more conservative goals. At some point, anticipated ambitions must be measured against actual results.

This raises further questions about the extent to which a brief intervention can legitimately be held accountable for the subsequent success or failure of comprehensive long-range results. Moreover, even if the program were successful in stimulating broader change, it would be a challenge to determine the extent to which it was responsible for desired outcomes. For example, was the anger management program the primary cause of reduced disciplinary actions? Or did a new management policy discourage officers from taking disciplinary action without exhausting all alternatives? Was the program responsible for lower recidivism upon release? Or did a change in post-release follow-up services cause fewer recommitments?

SUMMATIVE (OUTCOME) AND FORMATIVE (PROCESS) MEASURES

A summative assessment provides an indication of the program's effectiveness. As such, it represents the bottom line. In turn, a formative evaluation indicates what aspects of the program were responsible for its ultimate success or failure. As the term itself indicates, formative evaluations identify what elements formed the nature of the intervention. While product is the focus of a summative outcome assessment, it is process that is the target of a formative evaluation. These differing evaluation perspectives are illustrated as follows:

Differing Evaluation Perspectives

Process (Formatted)		Outcome (Summative)
Planning		Outcome
Objectives	Curriculum	
Process		Short-term
Instructors	Participants	Long-term
Is it working efficiently according to our operational plans?		Is it producing effective results according to our outcome expectations?

FORMATIVE (PROCESS) MEASURES: WHAT WAS DONE?

While focusing on bottom-line outcomes such as recidivism is appealing, these summative measures represent only one means of evaluation. Moreover, as we saw with the anger management example, long-term outcomes cannot be interpreted in isolation. In fact, outcome results raise almost as many questions as they answer. For example, if findings indicate that the program did not accomplish its objectives, the next question is, Why not? It is of little use to know that a program failed to achieve what it set out to do. Far more valuable information is obtained in the process of learning *why*? From the opposite perspective, while it is obviously encouraging to learn that a program did, in fact, achieve its intended outcomes, for replication purposes, it is still critical to know why— i.e., what was it about the program that contributed to its effectiveness?

It is therefore essential to document the precise features of the intervention—including qualifications of the instructors, content of the curriculum, and nature of the participants. Such qualifications of the instructors, content of the curriculum, and nature of the participants, and such qualitative, process-oriented research, describes program content, delivery, and contextual factors. These, in turn, can either reinforce or reduce the ability to achieve goals. Program planners may know exactly what was intended. But in the process of developing and delivering the program, things can break down. Messages might get garbled. Anticipated resources might not be available. Or the program might simply lose sight of its original intent and go off in a different direction over time.

A process assessment can determine if what was originally conceived on paper is what is, in fact, occurring in practice. Not only can this help to explain outcome results, but it may also point out the uselessness of even proceeding with an outcome evaluation (Stinchcomb, 2001: 58). After all, if the program is not being conducted according to what was intended, what basis do we have for believing that the changes we expected would occur? When a process evaluation shows little similarity between what was intended and what was implemented, there is no point in looking further to see if expected results actually occurred (Blount, 2003: 80). If they did, it was not because of what was offered.

SUMMATIVE (OUTCOME) MEASURES—WHAT WAS ACCOMPLISHED?

When planning a road trip, we identify a destination, consult a map, and select a route. A process evaluation of our trip would tell us whether the route we selected was the best way to get there, by whatever criteria we define as the best—i.e., fastest, least troublesome, or most scenic. If it wasn't, the process assessment would help us determine what to change in order to improve the experience on our next trip. On the other hand, a summative evaluation would determine whether we actually arrived intact at our destination, or did we detour so far off the planned route that we never quite got there, or got there so late, we had to turn around immediately.

In terms of outcomes, change-oriented programs can be evaluated from any one of four perspectives shown below. Depending on the level of sophistication, they can range from individual reactions to learning, behavior, and ultimately, results (Basarab and Root, 1992; Kirkpatrick, 1998).

Evaluation	Methodology	Comments
Reaction	How participants felt about the program, e.g., post-intervention opinion surveys that document participant perceptions.	It is one thing for participants to like a program—or even feel confident that they got something of value from it. Yet we all know that perceptions do not always equate with reality. That brings us to learning outcomes.
Learning	What new knowledge, skills, or abilities obtained from the program—e.g., pre/post tests documenting to what extent they actually comprehended program content.	Here we have a level of documentation that indicates regardless of how participants felt about the program whether they did or did not learn anything as a result of it.
Behavior	Whether participants use newly acquired knowledge, skills, or abilities on the job or in their personal life—e.g., follow-up measures documenting behavioral changes.	It is one thing to acquire new learning and another to put it to use. At this level of assessment, we are not only interested in whether they can pass the test, but whether they can actually apply what was learned.
Results	Long-term impact of the program—e.g., follow-up assessments documenting significant macro-level changes (i.e., safer community; improved organization) that can be attributed to the altered behavior of participants.	Here we are not just concerned with how the intervention has been applied individually, but more significantly what long-term outcomes it has produced.

Obviously these techniques are listed from low-to-high in terms of how costly, time-consuming, and scientifically respectable they are. For example, their validity ranges from very subjective participant "satisfaction indicators" to more objective pre/post test scores, to the real proof-of-the-pudding with regard to long-term, post-intervention change. These approaches can also be matched with the formative and summative evaluation strategies discussed previously and arranged on hierarchy from least-to-most-sophisticated. An evaluation hierarchy might be:

1. Impact Evaluation
   (Results)
2. Outcome Evaluation
   (Behavior)
3. Outcome Evaluation
   (Learning)
4. Process Evaluation
   (Reaction)

SELECTING EVALUATION STRATEGIES—FROM REACTIONS TO RESULTS

When correctional programs have been subjected to assessment, they have generally tended to rely on reaction evaluations. But such strategies are based more on anecdotal information than empirical evidence. It is not until evaluation methodology reaches the level of learning and/or behavior that either actual outcomes or long-term impact can be documented. Ideally, an outcome or impact evaluation includes a control group. That is, a matched group of people who did not participate in the program would be identified, their evaluation results would be compared with the participants, and any differences between them would be presumably credited to the intervention. This can be costly and difficult. But causality cannot be attributed to the intervention without a control group, which helps to rule out alternative explanations of the results.

The selection of evaluation strategies will be driven to some extent by available resources. But more important, it should be based on the program's goals and objectives. That is why it is important to avoid promising anything for which you are not willing to be held accountable. For example, learning outcomes, behavioral outcomes, and impact measures for a hypothetical anger management program for jail inmates are shown below. Which are the most valid measures of whether the program is really working? Which are you willing to be held accountable for?

Learning Outcome	Behavioral Outcome	Short-Term Outcome	Long-Term Impact
Gain an honest insight into your ability to control your anger	Commit to facing potential for anger and to strengthening your defense against it	Feel better about your determination to control your anger	Improve self-esteem

Recognize the personal consequences of your uncontrolled anger and its impact on others	Develop greater empathy for the victims of your anger, including yourself	Improved self-respect for others	Enhanced family and work relationships
Determine the types of circumstances that are most likely to trigger your anger	Recognize in advance when you are about to confront an anger-induced situation	Avoid situations that are likely to induce your anger	Involvement in fewer anger-inducing situations
Learn the skills needed to employ socially acceptable alternative methods for dealing with your anger	Practice socially acceptable options when confronted with emotionally charged situations	Improved self-control; fewer violent expressions of anger	Less anger-related institutional and post-release misconduct

As noted earlier, when correctional programs are evaluated, it is often limited to a formative process assessment. This generally takes the form of a satisfaction survey that participants fill out upon the completion of the course. Much like the forms used by college students to evaluate their professors at the end of the term, participants are asked a series of questions relating to how the course was presented, how well the material was taught, whether all objectives were covered, and so on. Such instruments may even ask questions that appear to be outcome- or impact-related, such as whether participants believe that they now have greater empathy for their victims, can avoid anger-generating situations, have more self-control, or feel better about themselves.

But even the addition of such seemingly behavioral items does not make a formative evaluation summative. In other words, it does not address the outcomes or impact of the program. That is because we do not know for sure if each participant is answering truthfully, rather than in a socially desirable manner. Moreover, even if participants are sincere about changing and are as truthful as possible, we have no way of knowing through a formative evaluation whether intent actually translated into behavior. Thus, formative evaluations are often known as satisfaction indicators, since all they essentially tell us is how satisfied the participant was with the program. They do not tell us anything about what was learned, whether that learning changed behavior, or whether their changed behavior had any short- or long-term impact. In other words, they do not tell us whether we accomplished what we set out to do. For that, we need a summative evaluation.

Why then aren't all programs subjected to the rigors of an evaluation that assesses at least outcomes, if not impact as well? After all, such evaluations tell us whether it's working and enable us to make informed, evidence-based decisions, therefore applying increasingly scarce resources to the most promising prospects. But while it makes logical fiscal sense to conduct more rigorous assessments with greater integrity, the higher up we go on the evaluation hierarchy, the more sophisticated, labor-intensive, and thus, more costly the process becomes.

For instance, for *learning outcomes*, one objective example is (1) pre/post knowledge testing of participants and a comparison/control group. One advantage of this example is relatively high validity—changes in post-test scores can more confidently be attributed to the program, since many other possible explanations for findings, or new policies, are controlled. Two disadvantages of this example are (1) the challenges of identifying a control or comparison group and administering the test to them; and (2) the time and costs of developing and administering the test.

A second objective example is the pre/post knowledge testing of participants alone. A major advantage is moderate validity, or no comparison/control group to account for extraneous variables, but before-and-after knowledge of participants is documented. However, two disadvantages include (1) test resistance among the participants; (2) the time and cost of developing and administering the test.

A subjective example is a post-training opinion survey of how much participants believe they enhanced their learning of key topics. Two advantages are that (1) they are relatively easy to develop and administer, and (2) they are unlikely to face opposition from participants. Two disadvantages are (1) there is an absence of validity—no way to empirically confirm that participants actually comprehend what they report learning; and (2) enjoyment may be mistaken by participants for learning.

Like everything else in life, making evaluation decisions involves trade-offs. Both summative (learning/behavioral) and outcome (short-/long-term) approaches have strengths and weaknesses. For example, those that are the easiest and least costly to administer also tend to be the least empirically valid. Additionally some measures are objective, representing factual, concrete measures that can be independently observed. Others are more subjective, reflecting softer indicators based on the self-impressions or personal opinions of participants or observers. As with all other fiscal decisions that must be made by correctional administrators, the task then becomes weighing the advantages against the disadvantages and making the optimal decision that time and resources will permit.

For *behavioral outcomes*, one objective example might be an independent on-site follow-up to determine the extent to which the participants' behavior changed upon release. Two advantages of this type of outcome are that (1) it documents higher-level outcomes that have more relevance than cognitive learning, and (2) it provides subsequent feedback on actual application of classroom learning. Three disadvantages, however, are that (1) they are time-consuming and costly; (2) without valid information about the pretraining behaviors of participants, or a comparison/control group, findings are anecdotal; and (3) there may be resistance from participants.

For *short-term impact*, an objective example is an independent on-site follow-up to determine the extent to which participants' behavior changed upon release. Two advantages are that (1) it documents macro-level outcomes that have greater impact than cognitive learning or behavioral outcomes; and (2) it provides feedback on the actual impact of learning. However, three disadvantages are that (1) it is time-consuming and costly, depending upon how extensive the measures are and how difficult they are to obtain; (2) the difficulty of establishing causality, i.e., ruling out alternative explanations of either success or failure; and (3) there may be resistance by participants. A subjective example may be a survey or telephone follow-up to determine the extent to which participants believe the goals were met. Two advantages are that it (1) documents macro-oriented outcomes that have greater impact than cognitive learning or behavioral outcomes, and (2) provides feedback on the actual impact of learning. However, three disadvantages of this subjective example are that (1) it has low validity—there is no way to confirm that change actually occurred in the manner reported; (2) findings are anecdotal opinions; and (3) surveys/telephone calls may have low return rates.

OPERATIONAL CONSIDERATIONS

Although influenced by time, resources, and many additional constraints, evaluation strategies should primarily be driven by the goals and objectives of the intervention. What was intended to be accomplished? More specifically, what evidence is needed to determine if intentions were actually achieved? It is, after all, one thing to develop an intervention with highly ambitious aspirations. But it is quite another thing to realistically measure such aspirations and be held accountable for the extent to which they were accomplished. Yet without such evidence, we have no basis for making the informed decisions that are increasingly essential as fiscal resources are progressively diminishing. Now the challenge is to make evidence-based decisions so that less is needed to do more.

QUESTIONS FOR REVIEW AND DISCUSSION

1. What are evidence-based decisions, and why are they important?
2. Compare and contrast summative and process measures. What are the characteristics of each?
3. What are the differences between learning and behavioral outcomes? What are some advantages and disadvantages of each?
4. What is the importance of evaluating outcomes in terms of both their short-term and long-range consequences? Discuss.

30

"Mental Health Jail Diversion"

Edward W. Szostak
and Marisa L. Beeble

Adapted from Edward W. Szostak and Marisa L. Beeble, "Mental Health Jail Diversion." *American Jails* 17: 35–41, 2003.

Reprinted by permission from the American Jail Association.

Today, jails and prisons nationwide are faced with the dilemma of how to handle over-crowding subsequent to the increased rates of incarceration of individuals with mental illnesses and/or co-occurring substance abuse disorders (Bureau of Justice Assistance, 2000b). It is estimated that between six and eight percent of the population housed in jails meet the diagnostic criteria for a serious mental illness (National GAINS Center, 1994; Walsh, 1998; Wolff, 1998), while 50 percent of the jail population manifest symptoms of other mental illnesses (Walsh, 2000). Furthermore, 60 to 80 percent of jail inmates with mental health needs are those with co-occurring mental health and substance abuse disorders (National GAINS Center, 1994).

The increased rates of incarceration of individuals with mental illnesses have been at-tributed to a number of factors, such as deinstitutionalization, a lack of community-based services, and more rigid efforts put forth toward community safety (Lamb, Weinberger, and Gross, 1999). Many researchers agree that deinstitutionalization has been the lead in trans-forming a formalized mental health system into an unfastened network of mental health, so-cial service, corrections, and justice professionals (Wolff, 1998). This ultimately resulted in the transference of individuals with mental illnesses/co-occurring disorders from state psy-chiatric hospitals to jails, a process referred to as transinstitutionalization (Barr, 1999).

Not only has transinstitutionalization caused over-crowding in jails and prisons, but it has also resulted in the unjust detainment of offenders with mental health and/or substance abuse needs. Although many jails provide mental health services, they are not adequately equipped to treat mental illnesses or substance abuse disorders (Morris, Steadman, and

Veysey, 1997). The primary concern of a jail is to ensure the safety and security of inmates, staff, and the community, not to provide quality mental health care. Jail administrators and correctional officers often do not have the necessary staffing or training to monitor and provide services for this population (Walsh and Holt, 1999). Therefore, when an inmate with mental health needs begins to illustrate symptomology or act out, they are often placed in "lock down" or segregated from others, causing exacerbated symptoms (Conly, 1999). Servicing this population results in amplified costs, liability, and the need for increased staffing (Wolff, 1998).

As a result of these issues, many correctional facility staff and mental health advocates have indicated a parallel level of understanding related to the need for an intervention to serve this population outside the jail. This mutual understanding between corrections and mental health professionals has begun to lay the foundation for the creation of diversion programs nationwide. Following is the story of how Albany County, New York, was able to bridge the gap between the criminal justice and mental health systems and how this effort evolved into the Mental Health Jail Diversion Project (MHJDP).

Albany County, located in eastern upstate New York, has a population of 305,548 and consists of urban, suburban, and rural areas. Within this county resides the Albany County Correctional Facility (ACCF), the fifth largest jail in the state, which has a capacity to serve 1,026. ACCF serves the entire county, providing detention for arrested individuals as ordered by local justice courts, superior courts, federal courts, and parole (Szostak and Marrow, 2001).

In 1999, ACCF experienced the unfortunate death of an inmate diagnosed with schizophrenia, after an altercation with correctional staff that attempted to restrain him to control his violent behavior. His death was ruled "positional asphyxiation."

Albany County Department of Mental Health (ACDMH) and the correctional facility became the recipient of criticism in the media by mental health advocates, including Joseph Glazer Esq., President/CEO of the Mental health Association in New York State (MHANYS).

Well over a year after the death, Sheriff James L. Campbell notified Edward W. Szostak, superintendent of the ACCF at the time, of an upcoming scheduled meeting with Joseph Glazer. On the day of the meeting, Joseph Glazer, along with another attorney and a newspaper reporter, arrived at the ACCF for the meeting. Sheriff Campbell was unable to attend, leaving the meeting in the hands of Superintendent Szostak. Approaching the meeting with much uncertainty, the superintendent was surprised to find the outcome very productive and beneficial. The discussion did not center on the prior death case, rather ways in which we all could improve the system to better serve the needs of individuals with mental illnesses and/or co-occurring substance abuse disorders. Superintendent Szostak informed the group of some of the innovative projects that were currently taking place in the correctional facility, such as the OPTIONS committee that has met monthly since its inception in 1997. The OPTIONS committee, comprised of a diverse group of departmental directors and managers from appropriate disciplines, manages the integration of existing health, mental health, substance abuse, and social service systems to promote more positive outcomes for clients.

Mr. Glazer and his guests were impressed with the stated mission and drive of the OPTIONS committee to seek methods to improve the systems throughout the county for all inmates with medical, mental health, or substance abuse disorders. Mr. Glazer asked Superintendent Szostak if he would be willing to work with MHANYS on ways to improve the criminal justice system to divert individuals with mental illness into more appropriate treatment services. Without hesitation, Superintendent Szostak agreed and pledged his support toward achieving this common goal. The meeting ended with understanding, mutual respect, and an aim to work collaboratively across agency boundaries.

Several months later, Mr. Glazer notified the sheriff and jail superintendent that MHANYS had applied for and received a federally funded grant for the planning and development of a project that would divert individuals with mental illnesses out of the criminal justice system to effective community-based treatment services. This $300,000 two-year Community Action Grant was sponsored by the Substance Abuse and Mental Health Service Administration (SAMHSA), and consisted of two phases. Phase I, the consensus-building phase, intended to identify and bring together public and private mental health, criminal justice, law enforcement, substance abuse, and judicial segments of the community. Phase II, the implementation stage, was designed to assist stakeholders in identifying, finalizing, and implementing the steps necessary for program development and integration into the community. Throughout both Phase I and II, a systemic third party evaluation by Dr. Patricia O'Connor, project evaluator, is in place to assess the level of consensus that was achieved and also the extent to which the implementation stage is consistent with the group's intent.

MENTAL HEALTH JAIL DIVERSION PROJECT OF ALBANY COUNTY PHASE I—CONSENSUS BUILDING

During the consensus-building phase, Project Director at the time Colette Robinson helped to bring stakeholders together and was successful in developing a jail diversion committee, which was comprised of key representatives from the following agencies and organizations within the county:

- Albany County Consumer Advocacy Board
- Albany County Correctional Facility
- Albany County Department of Mental Health
- Albany County Department of Social Services
- Albany County District Attorney's Office
- Albany County Executive's Office
- Albany County Probation Department
- Albany County Public Defender's Office
- Capital District Psychiatric Center
- Catholic Charities
- ClearView Center
- Community Living Associates Program
- Consumer Representatives/Family Members
- Homeless and Travelers Aid Society
- Local clergy
- Local community members and advocates
- Local law enforcement agencies
- Mental Health Association of the Capital Region
- Mental Health Legal Services

- National Alliance for the Mentally Ill
- National GAINS Center
- NYS Defenders Association
- NYS Office of Mental Health
- Rehabilitation Support Services

The preexistence of the OPTIONS committee and ACDMH's jail diversion initiative helped to facilitate access to relevant stakeholders. During Phase I, Joseph Glazer and Superintendent Szostak remained active in trying to spread the word throughout the county regarding the jail diversion efforts by presenting to groups such as the New York State Sheriffs' Association Jail Administrators. Superintendent Szostak was able to facilitate access to criminal justice professionals and gain credibility in their eyes in regard to offenders with mental illnesses. Shortly following, Superintendent Szostak announced that his retirement as jail superintendent would take place midyear 2002, and Joseph Glazer took the opportunity to hire Mr. Szostak as a consultant for the project. Project staff continued to work throughout this phase to gain community support, while also identifying what type of jail diversion program would best fit the needs of Albany County and how to ensure a smooth transition into the county.

PROJECT MODEL

During the consensus-building phase, stakeholders identified a deferred prosecution model, presently used in Connecticut and Arizona, to be ideal for the structure of Albany County. This exemplary model, recognized by SAMHSA, was selected for its efficacy to produce sustainable outcomes and meet the needs of the county's judicial system structure. Specifically this model has been proven to

- reduce the incidence and length of incarceration of persons with mental illnesses or co-occurring disorders,
- increase cost-effectiveness of treatment,
- improve treatment outcomes by engaging clients in treatment planning, and
- reduce the costs associated with incarceration by more than half (Solnit, 2000).

This model also incorporates six key elements recognized by researchers to be essential for program success. These six components are strong, effective project coordination, regularly scheduled meetings of key stakeholders, a boundary spanner (a liaison to manage interactions between different systems), early identification of detainees with mental health needs, nontraditional case management, and integrated services (Veysey, Steadman, Salasin, and Wells, 1995).

PHASE II—IMPLEMENTATION

During the implementation stage, which is currently underway, program staff and stakeholders have been working to ensure that all activities related to program development reflect fidelity to the exemplary model selected for replication. During this phase, new project staff were hired, including a new project director, Nicole Chaffin, a local project manager, Marisa Beeble, and a jail diversion coordinator (boundary spanner role), Louis Meunier.

The Mental Health Association of the Capital Region, housing the local project manager, and the Homeless and Travelers Aid Society, housing the jail diversion coordinator, were selected to make this project operational within the county.

Working closely with community stakeholders, project staff have developed the necessary resources and tools to ensure that the process of implementation is effective and that it incorporates the common mission of all involved parties. Throughout this stage, attention has been given to developing a project flow chart, outlining referral protocols, creating policies and procedures, addressing release of information and confidentiality issues, heightening community awareness, project advertisement, and identifying sustainable funding. Working closely with the project evaluator, Dr. Patricia O'Connor, and jail diversion coordinator, Louis Meunier, Local Project Manager Marisa Beeble constructed a statistical database to be used to track outcome data. This outcome data will be used to measure project success and may be used to support project replication in other areas within New York State.

INTERAGENCY COLLABORATION

Collaboration and continued commitment from a number of community organizations, consumers, and criminal justice professionals have become the foundation of this project. Recognizing this, stakeholders continue to meet on a regular basis to ensure adherence to the model, continue to maintain communication between all players, and continue to enhance program processes. The coordination of stakeholders and use of distinctive case management allow for an integrated service system to serve our clients in a manner which minimizes service gaps within the community. Using the Single Point of Access (SPOA) through ACDMH's county coordination, we are able to ensure our clients receive assistance with housing, employment services, substance abuse treatment, and outpatient or inpatient mental health treatment, as appropriate.

This concerted effort of the MHJDP includes the following project partners: Albany County Department of Mental Health, Homeless and Travelers Aid Society, Rehabilitation Support Services, The Mental Health Association in New York State, Inc., and The Mental Health Association of the Capital Region, Inc.

THE PROCESS OF DIVERSION IN ALBANY COUNTY

When a person known, or suspected, to be living with mental illness is arrested and has no history of violence, the individual is referred to our jail diversion coordinator (JDC). Various referral sources include judges, public defenders, legal counsel, family members, along with mental health, law enforcement, and correctional professionals. In response to a referral, our JDC meets with the potential client to assess symptoms, legal circumstances, and willingness to comply with a monitored treatment plan which, together, determines program eligibility.

Available to our JDC are ACDMH clinical professionals who provide mental health evaluations, in both the court and correctional settings. Following this, the JDC consults with ACDMH on diagnosis and treatment options and makes the recommendation to the court. With the court's authorization, the JDC and client collaborate on an individualized treatment plan. The court then defers the disposition of the case, and the client is released contingent upon compliance with treatment and court expectations. The individual is then linked to the appropriate treatment and services including mental health and substance abuse treatment, housing and employment assistance, and any other needed services. Throughout the process, the JDC monitors compliance and reports back to the court as needed. Successful completion of the program may result in a reduction or dismissal of the pending charges.

At the same time this process is initialized, a process is also occurring behind the scenes. The Jail Diversion Committee, led by Marisa Beeble, develops and maintains the relationships and agreements needed for our JDC to access the necessary community-based services. The committee also troubleshoots any problems which arise related to accessing services and/or other obstacles the JDC may encounter. The consistent communication between the local project manager and jail diversion coordinator allows for the integration of these processes.

BENEFITS TO OUR CLIENTS, OUR LOCAL JAIL, AND OUR COMMUNITY

This project allows for more appropriate, effective, and humane treatment for people living with mental illnesses in Albany County.

Some of the benefits to this population include the following:

- Access to comprehensive, integrated, and participatory treatment and service planning
- Linkages to community-based services and supports
- Individualized case management to assist with coordinating treatment services
- Possible avoidance of a criminal conviction and other barriers to employment
- Improved quality of life that parallels successful treatment

Jails are not designed to be mental health facilities; rather they provide safety and security to our community. Jail diversion provides an outlet for jail administrators by

- reducing additional liability to the county;
- freeing up jail beds, to be utilized for more serious offenders;
- reducing increased medical and mental health treatment costs associated with incarceration;
- reducing costs associated with additional supervision required for inmates at risk; and
- allowing staff to focus their attention on more serious criminal offenders to ensure safety and security within the facility.

Additionally, our community realizes benefits from the Jail Diversion Project, including

- a substantial cost savings related to the reduction in the average length of incarceration for individuals diverted, compared with those not diverted;
- increased efficient use of resources and services in the community, by the successful engagement of clients in treatment;
- additional alternative sentencing options for our judicial system; and
- reduced homelessness and dependence on social services.

OUTCOMES AND FUTURE INTENTIONS

Since the project's inception, the MHJDP has successfully diverted eight individuals. This three-month period has thus far yielded very successful results by engaging our clients into treatment services they may have otherwise not been able to access. Many of our clients have successfully secured jobs, housing, and regained control of their illnesses. In the afore-mentioned project benefits, diversion has successfully reduced the average length of incar-ceration of a client from 215 days to 25 days, based on project outcome data, as of March 2003. We expect to serve 25 clients by the end of September 2003, and funds permitting, to serve 75 clients in the following year.

Additionally, although not yet accounted for, we expect our clients to have a lower rate of recidivism than those individuals who do not participate in the diversion program. We will attempt to demonstrate reduced rates of recidivism by tracking individuals for a minimum of three months following successful completion of the program, and then com-paring these individuals to the average number of reoffenses of an individual with mental illness.

With future financial support, this project will expand its capacity to engage the re-maining fourteen points of entry into the criminal justice system in Albany County, further facilitate the integration of services for persons with mental illness, and ensure the collec-tion of reliable and valid outcome data to be used as a basis for project replication in other areas within New York State. Thus far six counties, including Fulton, Montgomery, Gene-see, Chautauqua, Dutchess, and Westchester, have indicated interest in implementing this model into their local justice system to improve the lives of individuals living with mental illness who have committed nonviolent offenses. It is our goal to promote both the expan-sion of the MHJDP throughout our state and the continuation of community collaboration across agency boundaries.

QUESTIONS FOR REVIEW AND DISCUSSION

1. What is jail diversion?
2. What are some outcomes of jail diversion for reducing the number of jail inmates?
3. How important is interagency collaboration in dealing with mental health dis-orders detected among jail inmates? Discuss.
4. How were inmates of Albany County positively impacted by the jail diversion program?

31

Electronic Monitoring
Positive Intervention Strategies

Ralph Kirkland Gable
and Robert S. Gable

Adapted from Ralph Kirkland Gable and Robert S. Gable, "Electronic Monitoring: Positive Intervention Strategies." *Federal Probation* 66: 21–25, 2005.

Used with the permission of the Administrative Office of the U.S. Courts.

The Supervised Release of business executive Martha Stewart from Alderson Federal Prison Camp in March, 2005, brought unprecedented attention to the use of electronic monitoring. Ms. Stewart and other CEOs who have been electronically monitored (e.g., Diana Brooks of Sotheby's) are non-violent offenders who appear to present little threat to the community. Electronic monitoring in such cases is not a matter of public safety, nor is such monitoring required to facilitate the integration of these offenders into society. Rather, the monitoring serves as a socially expedient intermediate sanction that is more punitive than traditional probation, but less harsh than incarceration.

The punitive aspect of electronic monitoring (EM) is primarily a result of a more rigorously enforced compliance with the conditions of community supervision. Violations can be more easily documented with EM than with traditional procedures, and sanctions can then be applied. The intention of the designers of the original prototype system was not, however, to enhance compliance but to help offenders gain self-esteem and socially valued skills (Gable, 1986). The present paper is a brief critique of current and future users of EM as a mobile communication technology.

In 1964, Ralph Schwitzgebel at Harvard University designed and patented (#3,478,344) with William S. Hurd a prototype electronic monitoring system in Cambridge, Massachusetts (*Harvard Law Review,* 1966; Schwitzgebel, Pahnke, and Hurd, 1964). Juvenile offenders were monitored within prescribed geographical areas where repeater stations were located. When an individual's transceiver activated the repeater station, his location was indicated on a lighted map at the base station. A few years later, Ralph Schwitzgebel's twin brother (Robert Schwitzgebel), a professor at UCLA and later at Claremont Graduate University, licensed an FCC-experimental radio station that supported a modified prototype system capable of sending tactile signals and of permitting two-way coded communication (Schwitzgebel, 1969; Schwitzgebel and Bird, 1970). Both of these radio-frequency transmitter/receiver systems were relatively expensive and electronically primitive by contemporary standards. As Mainprize (1966: 6) noted, "Schwitzgebel's efforts to promote EM fell upon the shores of economic and technical impracticality."

In 1983, district judge Jack Love, a former federal public defender, was thinking of a way to keep someone from going to jail and persuaded Michael Goss, a computer salesperson, to develop a system to monitor five offenders in Albuquerque, New Mexico (Ford and Schmidt, 1985). A second system was implemented by Thomas Moody in Key Largo, Florida. By 1987, 21 states had reportedly begun EM programs, with more than 900 offenders being monitored (Schmidt, 1988).

In the following 15 years, the number of persons in the United States supervised outside jail facilities by EM had greatly increased, with estimates ranging from 12,000 to 75,000 (Cohn, 2003; *Sourcebook*, 2005). Roughly estimated, about 20 percent of community-based supervision in the United States now involves electronic monitoring, and equipment is provided by approximately 20 private companies. Similarly, in England and Wales, about 20 percent of 5,000 offenders who started pre- or post-release supervision in 2004 were electronically monitored (National Probation Service, 2005); in Sweden approximately 25 percent of 15,000 prisoners were placed on electronic monitoring in 1998 (Cohn, 2000).

Two changes are generally credited with the rapid growth of EM in the 1980s. The first change was the expansion of the prisoner population as a result of mandatory minimal prison terms, especially for low-level drug offenses. This led to prison overcrowding and subsequent judicial mandates to limit prison intake. The second change was expansion of a technological infrastructure for information processing. Analog telephone networks were replaced by digital networks; this replacement permitted easier integration with more powerful and lower-cost microprocessors. In terms of number of units presently deployed, EM can be judged a success. In terms of social benefit, the assessment is less certain.

EVALUATION OF PROGRAM EFFECTIVENESS

The efficacy of EM, as a form of intensive supervision, can be measured in many ways. The most common outcome variables include recidivism, revocations, and recorded infractions. The appropriate use of any of these variables obviously depends on the reason that the offender originally entered the criminal justice system. EM is most commonly used with the following types of offenses (Lilly, Ball, Curry and McMullen, 1993; Connelly, 1999):

- Drug possession
- DUI

- Driving without a license or with a suspended license
- Assaults and battery involving domestic affairs
- Petty theft, or theft without injury
- Welfare or housing fraud
- Credit card fraud or embezzlement

Selection criteria have, in some studies, also limited EM participants to persons with positive attributes such as strong family support (Roy, 1997) or individuals who are employed or attend school and can pay an income-based fee for participation (e.g., San Mateo County, 2005).

Despite the common assertion that EM is primarily used with offenders who would otherwise be imprisoned, evidence suggests that there has been "net-widening" to include low-risk offenders who would not normally be incarcerated (Bonta, Wallace-Capretta, and Rooney, 1999; Jackson, DeKeijser, and Michon, 1995; John Howard Society, 2000). Thus, the low recidivism rate of some programs is not a result of the deterrent power of EM, but merely a reflection of the low-risk profile of the participants—a "Martha Stewart" effect.

Because the risk profiles of offender participants differ, as well as the variables measured and the nature of the supervision accompanying EM, no clear and consistent pattern of benefit has emerged. For example, a qualitative assessment of a home-confinement program in Florida concluded that, despite some technical problems, EM was "generally successful" as an alternative to incarceration (Papy and Nimer, 1991). A study of 126 monitored drug offenders in Los Angeles compared to a matched group of 200 drug offenders who were not monitored showed significantly fewer major violations for the monitored group during monitoring as well as 90 days subsequent to monitoring (Glaser and Watts, 1992). A study of a home detention program in Indiana by Roy (1997) reported that about 75 percent of the offenders did not recidivate after one year.

In contrast, Finn and Muirhead-Steves (2002) found no significant difference in the number of rearrests after three years between electronically monitored offenders and a control group. No significant differences were observed in a one-year evaluation by Petersilia and Turner (1992) between probationers in an EM program and probationers in an intensive supervision program. Similarly, a two-year comparison of the reconviction rate of regular probationers in the U.K. with 261 offenders under electronic house arrest found no difference between the two groups (Sugg, Moore, and Howard, 2001).

A carefully designed one-year follow-up study in Canada that compared 262 male offenders in EM programs with unmonitored inmates and probationers concluded that, after controlling for offender risk and needs, "EM does not have a post-program impact on criminal behavior" (Bonta, Wallace-Capretta, and Rooney, 1999: 25). A comprehensive meta-analysis of 381 articles and abstracts on the effectiveness of EM with moderate to high-risk offenders has been published by Renzema and Mayo-Wilson (2005). They found no convincing evidence that EM is more effective in reducing the rate of offending than other prison diversion programs. These reviewers concluded that:

> It is hardly surprising that recidivism has not been reliably reduced by an intervention that is typically quite short, applied in a standard fashion, and applied to a diverse group of offenders

for whom it may or may not have any relevance to their motives for offending. Extant EM programs seem akin to giving aspirin to a mixed group of hospital patients and then wondering why their underlying diseases have not been cured. (Renzema and Mayo-Wilson, 2005: [in press].

MONITORING WITH GRADUATED SANCTIONS

Electronic monitoring would appear, at least initially, to be a technology well suited for correctional interventions that apply sanctions of gradually increasing severity. Such graduated sanctions are typically administered as a structured, incremental response to non-compliant behavior of a parolee or probationer. As an integral part of this strategy, a comprehensive classification system was developed for assessing the probability of re-offending by adjudicated youth (Wilson and Howell, 1993). The classification system is accompanied by a conceptual matrix that guides agencies in making disposition decisions. Suggested sanctions include brief work assignments, daily attendance at self-help groups, curfew restrictions, more frequent drug testing, short jail stays, as well as home confinement with monitoring.

The sanctions are aversive events intended to punish and eliminate unwanted behavior. Behavioral scientists have carefully studied the effects of punishment for more than 35 years (e.g., Skinner, 1969), and the basic principles are firmly established. Laboratory experiments have demonstrated that the most effective aversive stimuli are certain, severe, and immediately related to the unwanted behavior. Community EM programs that are designed to maximize the specific deterrent effects of punishment generally attempt to follow these principles. However, two practical and persistent difficulties limit effectiveness:

1) *Technical constraints.* Technical problems with EM are inevitable, particularly in a commercial market where equipment suppliers try to get a competitive edge by equipment innovations. A possible violation in the form of an "alert" or "exception event" can be triggered by equipment malfunctions such as a telephone's advanced calling features being activated by a family member, failure of a field monitoring unit to pick up a transmitter signal, or a computer crash. Other system glitches can occur when a backlog develops in the process of verifying exception events by the monitoring center, or when a staff member fails to enter into the computer an approved change in an offender's schedule.

Receivers are sometimes placed in a residence in order to warn a potential crime victim (who is typically involved in a domestic violence situation) that an offender has come within a defined and prohibited geographical radius. Such false alarms are troublesome for potential victims as well as police and offenders. Erez and Ibarra (2004: 18) noted that false alarms in the EM program initially caused unnecessary fear among potential victims. Later, when the alarms "became routine," irritation was expressed.

2) *Judgments made by program staff.* Even if EM technology were infallible, immediate and unequivocal sanctions could not be reasonably applied. Consider, for example, the very common situation of a parolee associating with ex-convicts. Will an immediate sanction actually be administered? Or, if an offender fails to show up for an appointment, will a severe sanction be automatically applied? Probably not, at least for the first few times, because we know that some degree of relapse is almost inevitable. Assuming that the program

staff agrees on a grace period after an exception event, will the offender be told in advance or be left to guess and gossip about it? Issuing threats without follow-through sends a mixed message that mitigates the effectiveness of punishment routines.

On the other hand, a program that unerringly punishes offenders for technical violations cannot be expected to reduce recidivism rates because EM is likely to identify more violations than traditional supervision (Crowe et al., 2002). Imposing the punishment trilogy of "certainty," "severity," "immediacy" on the normal ebb and flow of human relationships is simply unrealistic and negates the common-sense judgment of program staff.

An essential tenet of learning theory is that *punishment does not change behavior; it temporarily suppresses it.* A person may conform to rules to avoid punishment, but once the threat of punishment is removed, the original behavior is likely to reoccur. Drivers typically slow down when they observe a police car behind them; they resume their previous speed when the police car turns to a different road. Similarly, a higher rate of criminal activity has been observed when intensive supervision is ended (MacKenzie and De Li, 2002). Erwin (1990: 72) reported that among probationers who completed the electronic monitoring program "there is a pattern of return to drugs and crime among a significant number of cases soon after they are transferred off the ISP [intensive supervision program] caseload to regular probation supervision." In a meta-analysis involving 66,500 offenders receiving intermediate sanctions (e.g., E.M., fines, restitution), Smith, Goggin, and Gendreau (2002) found no reduction in recidivism after completing a minimum of six months of supervision.

The process of applying increasingly severe sanctions, if empirically-established behavioral principles are followed, may also have undesirable side-effects. It prompts anger and resentment. When offenders are released from a correctional facility, they want "freedom," and typically view (perhaps unreasonably) parole conditions that include sanctions or mandatory treatment as more hoops, hurdles, and hassles to overcome. The degree of frustration and hostility expressed by offenders varies, but a visit from a probation officer is seldom a welcomed occasion. A first-hand account of the work of an EM officer in England (Jones, 2005: 585) suggests that his job lacks the glamour that a corrections professional might want:

> Getting a PID [personal identification device] to register can simply mean waiting outside the property from perhaps the relative safety of the vehicle. However, even this can have an element of risk, for instance, having personally had my car (a company vehicle) attacked on many occasions, including, urinated on from upstairs windows, youths surrounding the car on mass, tires been let down, as well as even on numerous occasions being approached in my vehicle by local prostitutes touting for business.

Punishment *does* have a legitimate role in rehabilitation, but only as a *temporary* means of suppressing behavior that is dangerous to self or others. While the dangerous behavior is being suppressed, or immediately thereafter, desired behavior should be rewarded. Monitoring appears to reduce recidivism only when it is paired with a treatment program (cf., Bonta et al., 1999). Without a treatment-only control group, the possibility that the treatment itself might account for any observed improvement cannot be ruled out. Indeed, it could be that the coercive nature of EM with sanctions might actually reduce whatever treatment effectiveness existed. In summary, a substantial and creditable body of knowledge indicates that a program having *sanctions-only* will result in high compliance in the short term but does not improve compliance in the long term.

Few, if any, programs have used EM *primarily or exclusively* as a positive reinforcement tool. The following section of this paper outlines what we believe can be the effective use of electronic monitoring without (or with only minimal) negative sanctions.

POSITIVE MONITORING

Electronic monitoring should place public safety as a priority. Because incapacitation and punishment are short-term solutions to a long-term problem, public safety will substantially improve if decision-makers devise policies based on non-incarceration strategies such as positive reinforcement. The 678-page report of the Reentry Policy Council (2004: 398) recommended that "community supervision officials should develop a system of graduated positive reinforcements that help to imprint pro-social behaviors and attitudes." Outlined below are a few well-established incentive-oriented principles that can be used with EM.

Reward small steps. Offenders want and deserve recognition for improvements, even if their present behavior is only a small improvement and does not meet a normally expected standard. When a child is learning to walk, or an adult learning to play a musical instrument, he or she is given praise for what—by adult or professional standards—would be a very inadequate performance. As the behavior improves, the standard is raised. The reason for the reward should be made clear to the recipient, and it should occur relatively rapidly and frequently at the outset of the rehabilitation program.

Vary the value of the incentives. Positive consequences should vary in economic or symbolic value. Possible options include letters of commendation, verbal praise, reduction of fines, complimentary tickets to sports or music events, and sobriety anniversary celebrations. The more unexpected and specific the consequence is to the individual's personal interests, the better. An inexpensive gift that shows that the offender was recognized as a human struggling to "make it" in a seemingly indifferent or hostile world is better than a group-oriented formality. One of the most dramatic surprises given to a probationer during the original EM project in Cambridge (MA) was being driven to his work (as a gas station attendant) for two days in a donated limousine. He was the "big man" of the neighborhood. Financial limitations and agency rules mean that correctional personnel must be creative in designing appropriate incentives. Tangible rewards might be distributed at a day reporting center where activities such as drug testing—clearly distinguished from any EM program— normally take place.

Behavioral contracts are *not* an effective way to shape or maintain behavior. There are at least two reasons to avoid contracts or promises as a type of incentive. First, contracts give the offender the option of breaking the contract, possibly in a moment of impulsive anger that everyone later regrets. Second, if the conditions of the contract cannot be fulfilled for legitimate reasons, the corrections agent must either ignore the violation or punish the offender. Neither of these reactions is satisfactory because it justifies the offender's predisposition to view correctional authorities as malicious, arbitrary, duplicitous, or simply inept.

Vary the timing of the incentives. The element of surprise is helpful. Routines may be desirable in matters of maintenance (e.g., paychecks, dinner time), but fixed schedules are not the most effective way to motivate behavior. Consider the example of a virtually use-less behavior-change gratuity—the Christmas bonus. Because Christmas bonuses are usu-ally given during the same week every year, the gift is no longer a surprise. In fact, employees occasionally complain that they did not get as large a bonus as they expected. Employee motivation and goodwill would be better fostered if the same expenditure, in goods or money, were spent over the course of the entire year, immediately contingent on desirable employee performance.

In terms of social learning theory (cf., Akers and Sellers, 2004), incentives should be given on a "variable ratio/variable ratio schedule" (differing amounts/differing times). The initial EM project used variable schedules of reinforcement to shape prompt attendance of delinquent youth at paid tape-recorded interviews. At the beginning, the youth would arrive as much as 3 hours late or 3 hours early, occasionally resulting in potential violence between gangs or ethnic groups. An interviewee might receive a $5 bonus for being "only" 45 minutes late, then no bonus for being 5 minutes early, followed by a pair of highly-desired baseball tickets when he was 10 minutes late but gave a good interview (Schwitzgebel, 1965). The tim-ing, contingency, and value of the bonuses were unpredictable, but always given in a manner that would not diminish the self-respect of the recipient or make him feel obligated to accept.

The typical shelf-life of a positive EM intervention should be less than one year, ex-cluding aftercare. This follows the general treatment guidelines of Cullen and Gendreau (1989), who recommended interventions of at least 100 hours over a 3- to 4-month period ending in one year. Frequent interaction at the beginning of supervision should be tapered off toward the end as the behavior becomes maintained by more natural, long-term incen-tives. A monitoring transmitter might be conceptualized as a "social prosthetic device" sim-ilar to a walker that is down-graded to a crutch, then to a cane, and finally abandoned.

Develop two-way communication. Mobile technologies have the capacity to allow program staff to give incentives based on real-time documented behavior such as attendance at a drug treatment class. The 1969 tactile EM system referenced previously allowed pro-gram staff to contact offenders unobtrusively while they were in a GED (general educa-tional development) class. Some of the two-way signaling at that time was little more than high-tec frivolity, but it was enjoyed by both parties. Messages should be brief and sporadic as well as unpredictable.

Contemporary embodiments of communication technology, such as cell phones and laptops, have become very important to young adult friendships and social identity. These should be used as a medium for reinforcing behavior. A London-based educational project has used pocket PCs and cell phones with picture messaging to send reminders and in-structions to at-risk youth (Attwell and Savill-Smith, 2004). When a communication tool becomes the source of unexpected rewards of sufficiently high perceived value, the device seldom gets inexplicably "lost."

Actively intervene. Careful observation of an individual's criminal pattern often re-veals a unique sequence of preparatory behaviors. Intervening early in the sequence of in-tended criminal behavior (e.g., when an offender gets on the bus to go downtown) is more effective than later in the sequence (e.g., when the offender enters the game arcade). House detention can, of course, prevent the entire sequence of behavior, but it is overly restrictive and does not allow common social activities such as grocery shopping or going to a movie at night. If the offender has a bad feeling about what is going to happen, this is the time for the offender to contact program personnel or a sponsor. Twelve-step programs, for example, often encourage participants to contact their sponsors in advance of a potential setback.

Rewarding desired behavior *before* unwanted behavior occurs is critical to success. The probationer will not make contact if he or she will be punished. To the contrary, EM participants should be able to signal staff when they are doing something unusually "good." Of course, these reports need to be checked for accuracy, but verifying positive reports or the "tall tales" of offenders is much more appealing to staff than checking-out violations.

CONCLUSION

The basic proposition of this paper is that electronic monitoring and other mobile technologies should be used to positively reinforce pro-social behavior. Unfortunately, during the past four decades electronic monitoring migrated into programs that are generally sanction-oriented and of questionable long-term value. Missing from the formal structure of most electronic monitoring programs are concepts such as "networks of support," "humor," "affection," and "hope."

The past does not have to determine the future. Advances in context-aware technology (e.g., global positioning systems, sensor-enabled telephones) will certainly provide opportunities for increased surveillance and information acquisition. As program designers, we can drift toward a callous authoritarianism in which individuals are motivated by fear, or we can design cooperative groups that are motivated by surprisingly pleasant experiences. The criminal justice system may be the least likely place to develop an inspiring pro-social communication network. But it is also the place where unexpected generosity can most easily change lives.

QUESTIONS FOR REVIEW AND DISCUSSION

1. What is meant by electronic monitoring?
2. When was electronic monitoring first used and under what circumstances?
3. What is the primary purpose of EM? Does EM appear to be successful?
4. Does EM control one's behavior? Why or why not? Explain.
5. How can public safety be assured when offenders are on EM? What safeguards are in place?
6. In what ways does EM heighten prosocial behavior among offenders?

32

"PROGRESS: An Enhanced Supervision Program for High-Risk Criminal Offenders"

Greg Hagenbucher

Adapted from Greg Hagenbucher, "PROGRESS: An Enhanced Supervision Program for High-Risk Criminal Offenders." *FBI Law Enforcement Bulletin* 72: 20–24, 2004.

Reprinted by permission of the *FBI Law Enforcement Bulletin*.

Overall, a relatively small number of offenders commit the majority of crimes in the United States. Or to illustrate this numerically, 100 different individuals do not commit 100 different crimes; instead more like 20 people perpetrate that number of offenses. Because a significant number of previously convicted criminals repeat their illegal acts following incarceration, does a method or means exist whereby government entities can deter such recidivism? Can local agencies take action? While most corrections departments place formidable rules of supervision on criminal offenders in their care and custody, the methods they use may well determine whether offenders return to their criminal behavior. Can improved and intensified monitoring of these individuals on probation/parole reduce criminal activity and, thereby, recidivism?

PROGRAM DEVELOPMENT

The Wausau, Wisconsin Police Department and the Wisconsin Department of Corrections (DOC)/Division of Community Corrections in Marathon County believed that a concerted effort to ensure compliance with rules of supervision could result in reduced criminal activity and recidivism. To this end, these two agencies formed a partnership to develop a program to help increase rule compliance. Developed specifically to work with high-risk offenders, or those deemed by the DOC to require the most supervision, such as gang members, violent criminals, and sex offenders, the two agencies called their effort Proactive Gang Resistance Enforcement, Suppression, and Supervision, or more simply, by the acronym PROGRESS.

The agencies designed the program to allow probation/parole agents to conduct systematic home visits on high-risk offenders during the hours of least expectation. They felt that to ensure effective placement, supervision, and compliance, offenders needed rules, limits, structure, and consistency. Home visits could afford the agencies the opportunity to determine or detect risk factors before offenders violated their rules of supervision. The program had two basic objectives: (1) for offenders to become aware of the increased certainty of detection of rule violations, and (2) for offenders to experience the immediate consequences of such violations. In short, the agencies wished to stress the *certainty* of punishment, not the severity. They hoped that these objectives would cause offenders to, ultimately, voluntarily comply with the rules of supervision or at least react with a greater degree of compliance.

PROGRAM IMPLEMENTATION

The process of conducting home visits on high-risk offenders necessitated a creative, flexible, and adaptable partnership between the DOC and the police department. This included defining each partner's goals and objectives, identifying and securing resources, establishing procedures and gaining support from such other entities as the district attorney's office, the sheriff's department, and the city council. Moreover, because the process required DOC probation/parole agents and Wausau Police Department officers to work nonstandard hours, the agencies had to recruit experienced agents and officers possessing traits best suited for the task, such as good communication skills, resourcefulness, and the ability to make decisions on their own.

Probation/parole agents always led the home visits with the police officers available as support and to provide safety and immediate action if custodial detention or criminal activity was discovered. First-time home visits were comprehensive and thus more time-consuming than follow-up visits. During first-time visits, probation/parole agents discussed the rules of supervision not only with the offender but also with other occupants of the home, when applicable. They performed a walk-through of the residence to ensure that the living situations complied with these rules and recorded such items as the number and location of exits plus the location and sleeping arrangements for the offender and other occupants. This process allowed agents to meet the offender's family or other occupants, thereby enabling them to assess the offender's environment and to offer support and assistance.

Which offenders the agents visited and when they contacted them varied, depending on the rules of supervision. Regardless, agents always completely documented all home visits. They recorded information such as the time of contact and those present at the home. At those visits when the offender was not available, agents left notice of their presence and any instructions for the offender.

PROGRAM RESULTS

Working at least once a week and averaging about 30 visits per night, the PROGRESS team conducted nearly 130 nights of home visits during the 2 years of operation (October 1999 through September 2001). The team worked approximately 1,150 hours, averaging about 5 hours a night. It made nearly 2,500 offender contacts in about 4,000 home visits and slightly more than 1,100 contacts with offenders' families or friends. The team found roughly 200 offenders in violation of supervision.

The majority of violations involved alcohol and curfew infractions, followed by contact with unauthorized persons. Violations per contact by year demonstrated a reduction of 43 percent from October 1999 through September 2000, which showed a rate of 1 per 13 visits, compared with October 2000 through September 2001, which revealed a violation rate of 1 per 26 visits. Interestingly the beginning quarter (October through December 1999) reported a ratio of 1 violation per every 7 visits, while the ending quarter (July through September 2001) recorded a ratio of 1 violation per every 39 visits.

Not all violations of supervision resulted in custodial arrests. About 20 individuals on high-risk supervision had their probation/parole revoked as a direct result of violations or crimes discovered during home visits. About 15 people received formal alternatives to revocation (i.e., not ending their probation/parole but imposing new, more stringent rules of supervision). Police arrests for discovery of criminal violations or outstanding warrants showed a fairly consistent decrease during the program. In over 20 cases, officers arrested friends and family members for encouraging offenders to violate their rules of supervision.

PROGRAM EVALUATION

The PROGRESS program achieved its ultimate goal of increasing rule compliance. The program's objectives of offenders becoming aware of the increased certainty of rule violation detection along with experiencing the immediate consequences for such violations contributed greatly to the program's success. Statistics indicated a steady decline in the number of rule compliance violations, which decreased from 14 percent in the first year to 3 percent the second. The program has proven successful in other areas as well, such as the reduction in arrests by law enforcement officers for criminal offenses detected during home visits and the increase in the number of offender contacts initiated. The number of police arrests declined from a high of 12 during the first quarter to 2 for the last quarter. The program attributed the increase in the number of offender contacts initiated to the decreases in rule violations. Although rule violations are time consuming, the decrease in the number of violations allowed additional time for home visits. Finally, the program worked so well in the first year of monitoring high-risk gang and violent crime offenders that the DOC added high-risk sex offenders to the list of homes to visit.

Besides these quantitative outcomes, some unexpected benefits occurred as well. For example, the media presented several excellent articles about the program. In addition, the program garnered positive responses from the offenders involved, as well as their families. Perhaps most notable, many offenders exhibited a much higher level of interaction with agents and officers, even to the point of helping in investigations.

The PROGRESS program also had a positive effect on the relationship between the DOC and the police department. The partnership enabled each agency's members to discover the importance of the other's operations, encouraging flexibility, creativity, trust, and respect. Improved information-sharing helped officers investigate and solve crimes and provided probation/parole agents with information on high-risk offenders' known associates. Both agencies benefitted greatly from the exchange of information and the atmosphere of cooperation. In the final analysis, the program's success resulted primarily from the dedication of the personnel involved and the close collaboration between the DOC and the Wausau Police Department.

CONCLUSION

Recognizing that only a few individuals commit the majority of crimes represents a well-known problem, but finding ways to combat this has been a challenge. Too often the law enforcement and the corrections sides of the equation have not joined together to pursue workable partnerships. The Wausau Police Department and the Wisconsin Department of Corrections/Division of Community Corrections in Marathon County, however, developed a program that demonstrated PROGRESS in this area.

The Proactive Gang and Resistance Enforcement, Suppression, and Supervision program revealed how law enforcement officers and probation/parole agents can form a team that not only punishes offenders who violate their rules of supervision, but also helps offenders attempting to change their past criminal behavior and become productive members of society. Such efforts deserve the support of communities searching for strategies to help reduce crime by decreasing recidivism.

QUESTIONS FOR DISCUSSION AND REVIEW

1. What is meant by PROGRESS? What were its goals or objectives?
2. How did probation/parole officer home visits deter offenders from law violations and increase compliance with their program rules?
3. What were the measurable effects of the program? How much did PROGRESS decrease the rate and/or number of rule violations and crimes committed by clients under supervision?
4. What was the role of law enforcement in the PROGRESS program? Was it an effective role? Why or why not? Explain.
5. How were the different agencies (e.g., law enforcement, probation/parole) benefitted by PROGRESS?
6. Do you think it is possible to establish programs like PROGRESS in your own community?

33

Problem-Solving Probation

Overview of Four
Community-Based Experiments

Robin Campbell
and Robert Victor Wolf

Adapted from Robin Campbell and Robert Victor Wolf, "Problem-Solving Probation: Overview of Four Community-Based Experiments." *APPA Perspectives* 26: 26–34, 2002.

Reprinted by permission from the American Probation and Parole Association.

INTRODUCTION

Probation was introduced to the United States in 1841, when a wealthy shoemaker named John Augustus asked a Boston judge to release a man charged with public drunkenness into his custody. Augustus brought the man home, had him sign a temperance pledge and three weeks later returned the man to court sober.

It would be hard to recognize probation today based on this simple, homespun beginning. At the end of 1999, there were more than 3.7 million people on probation in the United States, making it by far the most common sanction for criminal offenders. And while Augustus, known as "the father of American probation," worked only with drunks and minor offenders, 51 percent of probationers today have been convicted of felonies, according to the Bureau of Justice Statistics.

Modern probation departments are also having trouble replicating Augustus' early success with rehabilitation: Today, nearly one of every five adults charged with a violent felony is already on probation, according to a panel of probation experts convened by University of Pennsylvania professor John J. DiIulio Jr. and the Manhattan Institute. This has led to widespread public dissatisfaction with probation, and even admissions from probation leaders themselves that such dissatisfaction "has often been fully justified." (*See "Transforming Probation Through Leadership: The 'Broken Windows' Model," Manhattan Institute, 2000*).

Faced with huge caseloads, high recidivism rates and public disaffection, probation and correction departments around the country are trying to re-connect with the spirit of innovation that inspired Augustus 160 years ago. In some places, virtually everything is up for re-examination, from job descriptions and department structure to the very principles underlying their work.

This exploration within the field of probation mirrors efforts taking place across the criminal justice system as police, prosecutors, defense attorneys and courts try to address a number of interrelated problems, including:

- declining public confidence in the effectiveness of the criminal justice system;
- concerns about "revolving-door justice"—offenders being processed through the system again and again;
- the growing volume of cases in the system, which makes it difficult to give individualized attention to particular victims or offenders; and
- the sense that players in the criminal justice system have become nothing more than processors, handling cases without regard to larger results like improving public safety, reducing recidivism or rehabilitating offenders.

One way the criminal justice system has begun to respond to these problems is by shrinking their operations to a more human scale. Large, centralized court systems are creating small, neighborhood-based community courts that focus on low-level crimes, like prostitution and public drinking, which undermine a community's quality of life. Prosecutors are taking some of their deputies out of the courtroom and placing them in neighborhood offices, where they partner with community members to develop innovative solutions to safety problems. Police are working more closely with average citizens and developing new programs that go beyond solving crimes to preventing crime before it happens. And probation departments are doing all of the above—opening neighborhood offices, partnering with the community and focusing on prevention.

"Community justice" has become the shorthand term used to describe these problem-solving efforts. Community justice tries to make the justice system more effective by re-establishing links between criminal justice players and the communities they serve. Guided by the philosophy of community justice, criminal justice agencies are asking some basic questions: What makes community residents feel unsafe? What resources can the community itself bring to bear on its own problems? How can criminal justice agencies—working with citizens, other government agencies and community organizations—address these problems in a way that produces lasting improvements? Community justice ultimately seeks to transform the very way people think about crime—not as cases to be processed but as problems to be solved.

CHANGING THE JOB DESCRIPTION

While the four experiments described in the following pages are inspired by probation's historical ideal, they also represent new strains of thinking. One key ingredient all the programs emphasize is a role for the community. Inspired both by Augustus' early hands-on experiments and by the principles of community justice, which call for creating partnerships between criminal justice agencies and ordinary citizens, these programs have sought to incorporate neighborhood residents and their concerns into their work. They do this in a number of ways:

- by placing probation officers in neighborhood offices, where they meet regularly with members of civic and merchant organizations to discuss their concerns about crime and their ideas for reintegrating offenders into the neighborhood;

- by partnering with local organizations and other government agencies to develop better referral networks and support systems for probationers in the community;

- by relying more extensively on community residents, including the relatives, neighbors and employers of probationers, to monitor and control the behavior of their clients; and

- by giving community residents a part in actually supervising or working with probationers.

These experiments are finding that increased contact between probation departments and communities benefits everyone involved. Since probation officers—even those assigned to a community-based office—can't monitor their clients every minute of the day, neighbors, employers, relatives and anyone who comes in contact with probationers can serve as an extra set of eyes and ears. And community members are far more likely to report a problem or a violation if the probation officer is a friendly and trusted player in the community than an unknown stranger behind a desk in a central office far away.

Probation officers are also in a much better position to make appropriate referrals and help re-integrate their clients into a community if they're familiar with the neighborhood's resources. It isn't always enough to know the name of a local job-training program; a personal relationship with the director of the program, as well as with potential local employers, can make the difference between a referral that fails (because the program is full, or isn't geared to a probationer's particular needs, or because employers aren't willing to hire ex-offenders) and a referral that ultimately results in a probationer who is productively employed.

In addition, probation officers need to know a community and its citizens well, or they simply won't be able to address local safety problems. Probation officers who engage the community can find out where communities feel unsafe and what local problems are the community's top priority. If crowds hanging out at a local corner instill fear in residents, probation officers can require their probationers to stay away from the area and not contribute to the problem. And if garbage in empty lots is a chief concern, probation officers can place probationers on clean-up crews.

The community benefits from this relationship in a number of ways. First and foremost, the community's concerns become incorporated into the development of probation strategies; this can give residents greater confidence in the criminal justice system and add to their sense of safety. Also, giving the community an active role in the re-integration of offenders gives citizens a personal stake in ensuring that, on the one hand, probationers follow the rules laid down by the court, and, on the other hand, probationers are given a meaningful second chance to lead productive lives as law-abiding citizens. In this way, safety and offender rehabilitation go hand in hand.

MARICOPA COUNTY: BEAT SUPERVISION

Maricopa County, Arizona, brought these principles into play in 1996 when the county's Adult Probation Department established an experimental satellite office in a neighborhood known as Coronado. The county is part of metropolitan Phoenix and covers more than 9,000 square miles, making it larger in area than many states. But Coronado is only two square miles—a manageable size for an experiment in what is sometimes called "beat supervision."

Beat supervision borrows from the model of a cop on the beat, who is assigned to a particular neighborhood and over time gets to know the community, its inhabitants and its problems. Similarly, a "beat" probation officer works in a community office and is assigned probationers from the surrounding neighborhood rather than to a randomly selected roster of probationers from across the whole county. By introducing the beat model, probation officials in Maricopa hoped to tighten supervision of probationers and more effectively reintegrate them into the community.

The experiment was motivated by several factors. In the first place, a member of the probation staff had recently returned from a vacation in Madison, Wisconsin, with tales of that city's success with beat supervision. Secondly, the Phoenix Police Department had recently launched a community policing effort in Coronado, making it a natural location for an experiment in community-based probation.

"The police officers were already well known to the community and respected and associated with community safety, so by riding on their coattails, that eased affairs. It helped create the perception on the part of the public that we are part of law enforcement also," said Leslie Ebratt, Maricopa County's Adult Probation Officer Supervisor.

This white paper offers a window into how probation departments are using community justice to improve the way they do business. The paper describes in detail four distinct efforts to reform probation and examines the lessons learned from these early experiments. Since community justice calls upon criminal justice agencies to adapt to local conditions, it's no surprise that the four programs are as varied as the jurisdictions they cover: a statewide program in Vermont gives hundreds of community volunteers the authority to determine and supervise the conditions of probation; a partnership between probation and police officers in Boston focuses on gang violence in a crime-ridden urban neighborhood; a top-to-bottom restructuring of the probation department in Deschutes County, Oregon, emphasizes crime prevention; and an experiment in "beat supervision" in Maricopa County, Arizona, places probation officers in direct and regular contact with the community.

While very different, the four programs are united in a shared commitment to making probation more effective. By building connections with local communities, focusing attention on broader goals like crime prevention and offender rehabilitation, and striving for ways to give probation staff more resources and lower caseloads, these programs seek to build renewed confidence in probation—both among the departments' own workers and the public at large.

PROBATION'S ORIGINAL PROMISE

In many respects, these four experiments are an attempt to fulfill probation's original promise as a tool for rehabilitating offenders. When probation was first conceived by Augustus in the 19th century, probation officers were expected to take an active interest in the details of offenders' lives to help them reform their ways and ensure their successful reintegration into society.

Unfortunately, many probation departments adhere to this vision on paper—in their charters and mission statements, for instance—but have given up on actually pursuing these ideals in practice. Huge caseloads, inadequate funding and lack of accountability have turned probation officers, especially in large urban jurisdictions, into little more than deskbound bureaucrats. The average New York City probation officer has 240 cases, according to Michael Jacobson, former commissioner of probation for New York City and professor of criminology at John Jay College in New York. And in some urban jurisdictions, like Los Angeles County, caseloads can rise as high as 1,000 per officer.

Clearly, probation officers with caseloads that high don't have time to get to know individual probationers or the communities in which they live. When confronted with so many cases, probation officers try to prioritize offenders, giving what time they have to the most serious and potentially dangerous clients on their list while devoting few resources to the rest. This means that, at best, a handful of probationers may get the necessary referrals and support to guide them on the path of reform while the vast majority live in the community with virtually no supervision.

By and large, high caseloads have not translated into large budgets for probation departments. With incarceration drawing the lion's share of correctional dollars— $20,000 to $50,000 annually per prisoner compared to only about $200 per probationer—probation departments are forced to be creative. In New York City, where about 90,000 people are on probation, low-risk offenders are expected to report periodically to computerized kiosks. "With so little money being spent on probation, you have to make some choices," Jacobson said. "We decided to focus on the highest risk people and give them intensive supervision. But that means tens of thousands of people whom we deemed lower risk report to a machine. No one would call it an ideal situation."

And even when they do make referrals to supportive services like drug treatment and job training, most probation officers lack the time, training and resources to monitor outcomes. Are probationers staying in drug treatment and getting sober? Are they completing job-training programs and finding employment? Even more important: Are probationers complying with court mandates, including curfews and the all-important requirement that they avoid further trouble with the law? These questions relate directly to the public's concerns about safety and offender supervision and rehabilitation—but few busy probation departments have the time or resources to answer them.

PROTECTING THE PUBLIC

"It's been amazing to me that when you ask your probation and parole staff to give you examples of what they do that protects the public, they're baffled," said a participant in a U.S. Department of Justice roundtable of probation leaders (see *"Rethinking Probation: Community Supervision, Community Safety," Office of Justice Programs, U.S. Department of Justice, December 1998*). And yet protecting the public is exactly what probation departments need to do if they are to earn the public's support. It is precisely the potential dangers— periodically brought to the fore by news coverage of probationers who re-offend—that lead politicians and community leaders to criticize probation as "soft on crime" and call for its abolition. "There isn't another arm of government in which policy is based so much on in-dividual incidents," Jacobson said. "When someone on probation does a horrible thing, it doesn't matter that for the last 9,999 cases nothing horrible happened."

The image of probation as a failure is reinforced by the numbers. Roughly half of all probationers fail to fulfill the terms of their probation sentence, and in any given year hun-dreds of thousands of probationers fail to report in. Even more disturbing: About two-thirds of all probationers are re-arrested for committing a different crime within three years of their sentence. In 1991, the nearly 162,000 probationers who went to jail for new offenses were responsible for at least 6,400 murders, 7,400 rapes, 10,400 assaults and 17,000 rob-beries, according to the Manhattan Institute.

Despite these alarming statistics, the nation remains heavily reliant on probation as an alternative to incarceration: at the end of 1999, there were 3.7 million adults on proba-tion, which was more than twice the 1.8 million in prison. And growth in the probation pop-ulation—about 3.8 percent a year since 1990, according to the Bureau of Justice Statistics—is expected to continue.

Furthermore, an active community organization in Coronado, the Greater Coronado Neighborhood Association, had recently received a grant from the Department of Justice for an anti-gang initiative and was looking for partners. This last point was especially for-tuitous, although the group had to be persuaded that partnering with probation officers was a good idea.

"The neighborhood was terrified," says Kate Wells, a Coronado resident who was ac-tive in the neighborhood association at the time. The organization was afraid that opening a probation office in Coronado would harm the neighborhood by drawing criminals from other parts of the county. This fear needed to be confronted even though Coronado, with ap-proximately 250 probationers among 10,000 local residents, had a higher than average pro-bationer population. "It took three or four months to realize that [the probationers] were our neighbors," Wells recalled.

AN ASSET TO THE COMMUNITY

Not long after probation officers moved into space provided by the neighborhood associa-tion in September 1996, the Coronado probation officers had an opportunity to demonstrate how they could in fact be an asset to the community. When the roof of the building was se-verely damaged in a storm, the probation officers in Coronado organized approximately 40 probationers to replace it. Guided by the probation officers, the probationers also repainted the building's exterior and landscaped the grounds, leaving the place far more attractive than when they moved in. "They set off on the right foot right from the start," recalled Wells. "They did a tremendous amount of work."

"Part of what we're trying to do in the neighborhood is enhance the community in general," explained Leslie Ebratt, Maricopa County's Adult Probation Officer Supervisor. "We believe that by doing so, we reduce crime. Not just crime committed potentially by our offender population; we make it less of an environment to support crime in general." In this way, beat supervision in Maricopa tries to do more than just monitor probationers more closely; it also tries to advance public safety in any way it can.

Now, four years after the storefront probation office opened, members of the Coronado community know they can come there for help. For example, a block watch captain asked the probation officers for help with a campaign to get speed bumps at a dangerous intersection. "We got together as many probationers as we could to go door to door to get petitions signed," Ebratt said.

Community service has changed the way area residents perceive offenders; and it has also given offenders a sense of pride to see the positive impact they can have on their own neighborhood, Ms. Ebratt said.

Of course, Coronado's community-based probation officers also learn more about their probationers through closer observation and contact with their families and neighbors. Ebratt recalled a case in which a probation officer got to know the wife of a probationer after several visits to their home. This familiarity gave the wife courage enough to page the officer one day when her husband became verbally abusive toward her. Although the probation officer was ill at the time, he contacted a local community-based police officer with whom he had developed a working relationship. When the police subsequently visited the probationer's home, they discovered that the man had a gun, a violation of his probation. After consulting with the probation officer, it was decided that the man posed a threat to his wife's safety and he was arrested. "By being in the neighborhood and knowing more intimately what's going on with the individual we can intervene when problems arise before those problems develop into new crimes," Ebratt said.

BOSTON: OPERATION NIGHT LIGHT

In May 1992, during the funeral of a reputed gang member at the Morningstar Baptist Church in the Mattapan section of Boston, gunfire broke out and someone was stabbed when members of a rival gang infiltrated the ceremony. The incident, captured on videotape by a local television station, horrified the city, which since the late 1980s had been gripped by an epidemic of gang violence that would peak the following year, with 98 adult and 16 juvenile homicides, according to statistics supplied by the Massachusetts Probation Service. "Things were out of control on the street," said Bernard Fitzgerald, chief probation officer for Boston's Dorchester region. "We weren't enforcing the conditions of probation and we couldn't effectively do it without the cooperation of the police, given the rate of violence."

A few weeks after the Morningstar melee, an Anti-Gang Unit detective named Bob Merner and two probation officers, Bill Stewart and Rick Skinner, talked informally about ways to stop the violence. Research suggested that probationers were responsible for as much as 20 percent of serious crime. Stewart and Skinner thought they could make a dent in this by, among other things, making sure probationers were complying with curfews that were a condition of their sentences. They wanted to "put a little more of a net over [probationers] than we would normally have," explained Ronald Corbett, deputy commissioner of the Massachusetts Probation Department.

Probation officers already had the authority to arrest offenders who violated conditions of their probation, but they didn't feel comfortable making arrests because, for one thing, they didn't carry weapons. In a marriage of convenience, they turned to the Police Department for help. And out of that partnership, a new approach to community supervision of probationers was born.

NIGHT RIDE

On November 12, 1992, at 8:45 p.m., Stewart, Skinner and two other probation officers joined Detective Merner and two more policemen for their first night ride, with Stewart and Skinner following the crowded police cruiser in Stewart's 1985 Chrysler LeBaron station wagon.

Within five minutes, Stewart recalls, a report of a shooting came across the radio and the police cruiser sped away. By the time the station wagon arrived at the site, the yellow police tape had already been hung, so Stewart and Skinner stayed back. Then Skinner was called inside; the shooting victim, a young man lying on the pavement with a bullet in his chest, was one of his probationers.

Stewart, meanwhile, still watching from outside the tape, spied one of his own probationers among a group of kids standing nearby. By now it was approximately 9:30 p.m., so he walked up to the boy and, surprising him, asked why he wasn't at home, complying with his curfew.

"That's not fair," he said the boy replied. "Probation don't ride in no police car!"

Stewart suddenly understood that the boy counted on police and probation not to work together so he could take advantage of the system. "On that statement," he says, "Night Light was born."

Operation Night Light, as it came to be called, was a formal partnership between the Boston Police Department and the Office of the Commissioner of Probation for Massachusetts.

The most obvious advantage of this partnership was that it gave probation officers access to more information about their probationers' lifestyles—information that could help them catch violations, pick up early signals that a probationer may be going astray and make more appropriate and timely referrals to supportive services. Police officers benefited, too. By becoming more familiar with probationers' comings and goings, their favorite hangouts and their associates, police officers had more and better information to work with when developing crime-fighting strategies.

OFFERING YOUTH AN ALTERNATIVE

The creators of Operation Night Light understood, however, that getting tougher on crime wasn't by itself enough. "If you're going to do suppression of youth violence, you have to have something to offer as an alternative," explained Fitzgerald. To provide such alternatives, Operation Night Light turned to the community for help.

Historically, Boston's poor and minority communities, where much of the city's violence was concentrated, have been wary of law enforcement personnel. Yet the events at Morningstar had shocked community leaders as much as anyone else, and this gave police and probation officials a rare opportunity to seek common ground with them. The Ten Point Coalition was a consortium of African-American churches—including Morningstar—that had mobilized in response to the gang epidemic. After the incident at Morningstar, the coalition and law enforcement decided to work together.

Mark Scott, director of the Ella J. Baker House, a social service organization affiliated with the Ten Point Coalition, has been a long-time advocate for youth involved in the courts. Scott still serves as a youth advocate, but the Ella J. Baker House now conducts fatherhood and cultural literacy programs for juvenile probationers in connection with Operation Night Light.

"Initially our relations with the probation officers were antagonistic," Scott said of the days before Operation Night Light. "We viewed them as cops. They viewed us as advocates for bad kids. But over time, we began to understand them as allies." He and his former antagonists now work together to maximize each child's access to guidance and support. "We try to team up with probation officers to put two adults in [the probationer's] life," he explained.

VERMONT: STARTING WITH THE PUBLIC

Between 1984 and 1994, the population of Vermont's state prisons increased by 133 percent. Yet during that same decade prison bed space in the state grew by only 79 percent. Faced with the expensive prospect of building more prisons, Vermont's Department of Corrections began looking for alternative ways to deal with crime.

In what was an unusual decision at that time, the department turned to the public for guidance. In January 1993, it hired John Doble Research Associates Inc., a New York-based research firm, to conduct three, two-hour focus groups in the cities of Brattleboro, St. Johnsbury and Burlington. In May 1994, it followed up with a statewide telephone survey. The results of this research were startling. Only 37 percent of respondents approved of the state's existing corrections procedure. "We were rated lower than Jimmy Carter was rated at the height of the Iran hostage crisis," recalled John Perry, director of planning at the Vermont Department of Corrections. An astonishing 75 percent thought the entire system needed reforming.

According to Perry, people were emphatic about what they wanted in an ideal system: They wanted to be safe from violent predators, they wanted accountability from nonviolent offenders, and they favored options that allowed average citizens to participate in the judicial process themselves. When presented with specific proposals, the public was similarly unambiguous. "When we gave them the concept of the reparative board," says Perry, "92 percent thought it was a hell of a good idea."

Reparative boards became more than just a popular idea in 1994, when the state overhauled its entire sentencing structure. Under this new state policy, low-risk non-violent offenders, such as shoplifters, vandals and check forgers, are given the option of meeting with a reparative board, a group of community volunteers who develop and monitor 90-day probation sentences that require offenders to make up for the harm their actions may have caused.

The Reparative Probation Program is an alternative to regular probation, which in Vermont "can be pretty onerous," sometimes, albeit rarely, lasting a lifetime, Perry said. Those who participate avoid regular probation if they successfully complete what the board asks them to do within 90 days.

REPAIRING THE DAMAGE

Reparative boards usually have three to six members at any given session and usually meet on a weekly or biweekly basis. Sessions, which can last anywhere from 30 minutes to two hours for the most complicated cases, are open to the public, and friends or relatives of the victim and the offender are encouraged to attend. If the victim is present, he or she has an opportunity to talk about the impact the crime has had on his or her life. The offender than tells his or her side of the story. Board members ask questions, talk about how the offense has hurt the community at large and negotiate a contract that describes steps the offender must take to repair the harm caused by the offense.

"The theory is offenders have offended us and they owe us a debt. And the way they repay the debt is not by costing us tax dollars, but repaying the debt, by fixing what was broken, restoring what was damaged," Perry said.

Barbara Leslie, coordinator of three reparative boards in Burlington, Vermont, offered the example of a 24-year-old woman who appeared before a panel for stealing three checks worth about $800.

"When she came to us, we found she was in an abusive relationship, in the middle of getting a divorce, and she had issues with substance abuse she was denying," Ms. Leslie said.

The board had her write a letter of apology to the victim and, because she was unemployed and didn't have money, ordered her to perform extra hours of community service in lieu of paying back the $800—but only after the victim okayed the terms.

"We try to put the victims at the center of everything and ask the offenders to spend a fair amount of time thinking about the victims," Ms. Leslie said.

FROM WRECK TO REPARATION

Alan Taplow, a retired purchasing manager who sits on a reparative board in Barre, Vermont, described the case of a young man who, after being evicted from a party at about 3 a.m., drove his car into a trash hauling bin, knocking over a propane gas tank and creating a dangerous, potentially explosive situation. He was rescued from the wreck by two police officers, charged with driving under the influence, and, in addition to receiving various fines, given the option of participating in a reparative board. The contract he worked out with the board included the following:

- To understand the impact of his crime, the man was asked to research and write at least five pages of reflections on the experience, including what he learned about police work relating to drunken driving and the work of the Fire Department in similar emergency situations.
- To make amends to the victims, he agreed to write letters of apology to the Police and Fire Department personnel directly involved in and endangered by the incident. He was also asked to write letters to the people evacuated from their homes while the propane was being cleared.
- For community service, the man, a landscape designer and stone worker, was required to work with town selectmen to plan and implement a project to beautify the village square.
- Finally, to learn ways not to re-offend, he agreed to undergo alcohol assessment and comply with any resulting recommendations for treatment.

The young man reappeared in front of the board three months later, having completed all of his contract save for the landscape project. Because the ground was too cold, the board granted him an extension until spring.

Reparative boards now handle more than 30 percent of the state's probation case load, with at least 350 citizens on more than 50 boards throughout the state. "We have towns demanding that they get a board," Perry said. "We are expanding as fast as we can."

With the creation of the reparative boards, the state's probation officers' jobs also changed. In addition to supervising directly those offenders who don't go through the boards, they support the reparative boards in a variety of ways: helping track down victims, building a referral network for offenders and coordinating communication between the boards and the court. Officers are also expected to meet with the community to cultivate support for and involvement in the reparative boards.

In theory, with the boards' supervising so many low-level offenders, probation officers should have more time to focus on high-risk cases involving felony or violent offenders. But that hasn't happened yet. While the reparative boards are siphoning off some of the work normally performed by probation officers, the officers' regular caseloads continue to rise. Niel Christiansen, corrections services manager for the Burlington Court Reparative Services Office, said that due to the increasing popularity of probation as a sanction, the caseloads of officers on his staff have doubled to about 200 over the last five years, thus keeping probation officers as busy as ever. And yet, while many probation officers are still frustrated with their heavy caseloads, many are also deriving new satisfaction from working more closely with community and victims. "When you're working only with one party to a situation, you tend to hear that perspective. Reaching out to victims helps balance it, and that's a good thing," Christiansen said.

DESCHUTES COUNTY: REINVENTING A DEPARTMENT

Deschutes County, near the center of the state of Oregon, is one of the fastest growing counties in the United States. Not long ago, loggers and environmentalists sparred here over the fate of the spotted owl. Now the region's rural past is giving way to an increasingly urban future. Deschutes County today is home to burgeoning high-tech and service industries; yet it is still not uncommon for children living on area farms to shoot sage rats as part of their morning chores before heading off to school.

Given these conditions, the county's decision to integrate community-based probation into a comprehensive redesign of its judicial services was a preemptive one. "[The change] was not problem centered," said Dennis Maloney, director of the Deschutes County Department of Community Justice. "It was, I would call it, foresight centered."

Maloney, an advocate of restorative justice, a philosophy that emphasizes repairing the damage done by crime to individual victims and communities, was speaking on a panel in Washington, D.C., in 1996 when he was invited to lunch by U.S. Attorney General Janet Reno, who was attending the event. During the meal, the attorney general expressed an interest in restorative justice, but was troubled by its purely reactive stance. "Shouldn't we have a national crime policy that calls for as much emphasis on prevention?" Maloney said she asked him. She then proposed a slightly revised concept: community justice, which combines restorative justice with community development efforts aimed at crime prevention.

Several months later, Deschutes County received a grant from the National Institute of Corrections to create a pilot community justice program. State laws tied the county's hands in making changes to its adult probation program. But its juvenile division was radically restructured. Under the new system, juvenile probation officers were reassigned into three teams: the Accountability Team, which interacts with offenders and the courts, the Community Outreach Team, which works with the community to develop service projects for both probationers and at-risk youth, and the Restorative Team, which offers mediation in lieu of court for low-level offenses and also tries to ensure that offenders pay back their victims for the harm they've done.

Within this new model, many of the traditional boundaries of probation fell away and probation officers, now renamed "community justice officers," began treating juvenile probation as part of a larger effort to eliminate crime before it began. No longer would they be simply probation supervisors; they were now community problem-solvers and probation was but one of their tools.

Community-based probation was integrated throughout the new system in a variety of ways. The Restoration Team, for example, drafts agreements between offenders and victims requiring offenders to make up for their actions by, say, working for their victims until any cost incurred as a result of the offense has been reimbursed. Offenders on probation may be assigned to the Restorative Community Work Service, which requires them to work on projects that the Community Outreach Team and the local stakeholders have jointly developed; these community service projects—like helping build a house for low-income family—are designed both to pay back the community as well as give offenders a sense of accomplishment. In some cases, offenders may even be eligible for a program called Fresh Start, which pays them a minimum wage ($6.50 in Oregon) until they earn enough to repay their crime victim.

PREVENTION PROJECTS

"The best way to work with crime in the community is to work on prevention projects," said Ken Mathers, a ten-year veteran of Deschutes County's Juvenile Probation Department and now team leader of the Community Outreach Team. "The second part of the job is working with offenders and connecting them with the community."

An example of how Mathers combines both approaches occurred in the summer of 1999 when the Community Outreach Team organized a fundraiser to sustain a popular summer music and food festival in the city of Bend called Munch & Music. "One person from their board came to our department and said 'This is drug and alcohol free, and we believe it's crime prevention. Can you help us out?'" recalled Mathers, explaining how he became involved in such an unusual project. After agreeing that it would benefit the community, the Outreach Team recruited over 100 volunteers, including 50 kids—of whom only a few were from the corrections system—to do everything from selling tickets and distributing food to performing for the audience. A group from the Youth Investment Program, a four-month incarcerative program, even performed a play at the event. "These are kids who are sort of the thugs around town, and here they're dressed up in drama gear," said Mathers. "Several months ago people would say these kids are thugs, now what they're saying is that these kids have some amazing skills."

Projects such as the Munch & Music fundraiser illustrate how Deschutes County's community justice officers have moved beyond simply trying to monitor offender behavior to prevent criminal behavior in the first place. By working with the community to create meaningful activities for both offenders and kids at risk of offending, they are working to provide alternatives to criminal activity. "Crime prevention occurs whenever we can connect a kid with a community," said Mathers. "The more connected kids are, the more preventative that is."

MEASURING SUCCESS

As the four initiatives described in this article continue their ongoing experiments with community justice, they are struggling with ways to measure the effectiveness of their programs.

In Boston, Operation Night Light, which was eventually extended to adult as well as juvenile probation, has pointed to significant drops in local crime. While Operation Night Light cannot by itself be credited with this success because it was not the only anti-crime initiative undertaken in Boston during the 1990s, the numbers are impressive. There were only 31 fatalities in the city in 1999, only one of which involved a victim 16 and under compared to 98 adult and 16 juvenile homicides in 1993. Also in 1999, according to Bernard Fitzgerald, chief probation officer for Boston's Dorchester region, the city saw only 8,636 criminal complaints compared to previous annual rates of anywhere from 12,000 to 15,000.

Maricopa County has also produced some encouraging numbers. Among Coronado probationers ordered to do community service, 71 percent complied, compared to only 28 percent in a comparison group, said Leslie Ebratt, the adult probation officer supervisor in Maricopa County. Likewise, 70 percent of Coronado offenders who owed restitution to victims made payments, compared to only 44 percent in the comparison group.

Vermont uses public opinion as a measure of its success. The state continues to poll citizen satisfaction with the corrections system and it is beginning to see evidence that satisfaction is rising. From the 1994 low of only 37 percent approval for the system, the number of positive assessments of the state's corrections system has risen to 44 percent—a small but encouraging sign of changing public perceptions, according to Perry, the state Corrections Department's director of planning. Also, compliance with board-imposed sanctions has been at nearly 85 percent.

Meanwhile, Deschutes County has tracked the responses of offenders to their new programs. "A lot of community work service is really kind of mundane activity," Maloney said. "Offenders don't like that kind of work. They think it's demeaning and they know that there's not much value to it. But when you have them build child abuse centers, parks, things of very high value, offenders show up at a high rate. And they will often work longer than ordered."

The enthusiasm expressed by "Brian," a young man who spent four months in Deschutes County's Youth Investment Program, working every other week to build a house with Habitat for Humanity, supports Maloney's assertion. "It was a great feeling knowing that we were helping these people," he said. "It was kind of a way to pay back for the things we had done and at the same time give us a feeling of respect." That serious crime among juvenile offenders like Brian has fallen 27 percent in the two years since Deschutes County's new program was launched further supports this impression.

Job satisfaction among probation officers is also an important indicator. "I used to measure a good week's progress by how many files I processed," recalled Mathers, of Deschutes County, who confessed that he was pursuing a career change before the department overhaul. "You'd always stack your files up as you finished them and say 'I'm done with that,' almost like a brick layer. With [the new system], the measurement's completely different. We may get a call from a citizen we don't even remember meeting and they're complimenting us on how we're working with youth or how we've beautified an area. That type of reward far surpasses stacking up the files."

OBSTACLES

Large organizations, and government agencies in particular, tend to be resistant to change. Thus it should come as no surprise that planners in Boston, Deschutes County, Maricopa County and Vermont encountered obstacles as they tried to implement their experimental programs.

"The biggest obstacle that we met was people's shackling to tradition," explained Maloney of Deschutes County. He pointed out that many of the people who had trouble giving up the old ways couldn't explain why they should be retained.

Vermont encountered challenges in several areas. Defense attorneys, for example, initially discouraged their clients from submitting to the reparative boards because of the unpredictable nature of each individual board. "A defense lawyer's job is to get the best deal he can for his client, so what they want to do is nail down the deal," explained Perry, the director of planning. "The whole point of the reparative board is you don't know what's going to happen because the community is going to figure it out." This resistance was eventually overcome by experience, as Vermont's defense attorneys discovered that in practice the reparative boards were not unduly onerous on their clients.

Another obstacle they faced in Vermont was the reluctance of some community volunteers to bring victims into the process. Ms. Leslie said that in her area it's been "challenging" finding enough volunteers to do victim outreach because of the complex emotions involved. "People don't like to deal with victims," she said.

One of Operation Night Light's major challenges was to overcome distrust between Boston's probation officers and police, who were accustomed to working separately and inclined to protect their "turf." "It was a new way of doing business at first, and many of our officers were skeptical," recalled the state probation department's deputy commissioner, Corbett.

In Oregon, the Department of Community Justice fostered public support through a media campaign that showed offenders working on community service projects. "The media and the public never cared about what went on in my office," one officer told Maloney after the officer organized juvenile probationers to build bunk beds for poor families and photographs of the work appeared in the local paper. "Now we're getting cheered."

The power of public opinion was evident in Boston, too. "The pioneers got such good press that it didn't take too long to get a lot more people involved," said Corbett. Today, Operation Night Light is so well accepted that incentives for officers to work nights and weekends have been written into the Probation Department's contract and nearly 45 percent of the work force have signed up to participate. Said Corbett, "The change has taken root and is part of the DNA of the organization now."

RESOURCES

Given the early results and public acclaim that these community justice experiments have generated, many probation departments across the country are eager to pursue change. At the same time, many complain that they simply don't have enough money to experiment.

Vermont, Deschutes County and Maricopa County relied on outside grants to kick-start their programs, but the simple fact is that probation has been underfunded for decades and there's no reason to think the situation will soon change. The problem is, in part, probation's lousy reputation. "Probation gets funded exceptionally poorly, so it can't possibly do the job it's supposed to do; so then legislators say, 'You're not doing your job right, so why should we give you more money?'" Jacobson said. "Another problem is that prison and the death penalty dominate the debate about crime in this country, even though twice as many people are on probation. People just don't want to talk about probation. There's periodically talk in the field about abandoning the word 'probation' because it has such a negative connotation."

Faced with such a grim funding picture, it's clear that probation departments can't depend on an influx of new cash to pay for innovation. They will have to find a way to make adjustments with the resources they have. There is some good news, however: Some experimental probation programs have been able to offset higher costs through new efficiencies.

In Coronado, for example, community-based probation officers have been able to maintain the same caseload, approximately 60 per officer, as the county's traditional probation officers. This is possible, said Leslie Ebratt, because the time community-based staff save by not driving to remote areas can be applied to their new responsibilities. After Operation Night Light was established in Boston, probationer behavior improved, allowing probation officers there to become more efficient as well, according to Bill Stewart. In the early days, he says by way of example, probation officers went into the field three times a week. Now they have to go only once a week.

Oregon has looked for creative solutions to help pay for the cost of adding crime prevention to its probation officers' responsibilities. For its Youth Investment Program, for example, a four-month incarceration program followed by at least six months of "aftercare," the county negotiated an agreement with the state granting it the equivalent of what it would cost to house the offenders in a state facility. Half of that money is earmarked for youth-crime prevention.

Perhaps the most cost-efficient thing about the Vermont program is that the boards are staffed by community volunteers. "Our idea," said Lynne Walther, a restorative justice consultant who helped design the reparative boards, "is that the community will do most of the time-consuming work."

Each of these programs' experience suggests that financial considerations need not be an obstacle to launching a problem-solving experiment. Moreover, some are optimistic that problem-solving probation will ultimately attract more money as it proves, over time, its effectiveness.

CONCLUSION

The willingness of probation leaders to admit that probation needs an overhaul has spawned innovation and experimentation—with or without increased financial support or resources. As the four programs profiled above demonstrate, change is in the air.

But much more can be done. These four experiments affect only a small fraction of the nearly four million people on probation. And while the task of reforming probation may seem daunting, the potential rewards are vast. As members of John DiIulio's task force wrote, "Probation is at once the most troubled and the most promising part of America's criminal justice system."

Probation's promise is in its potential to reach millions of offenders and keep them on the path of reform; to strengthen communities by involving ordinary citizens in the supervision and rehabilitation of probationers in their midst; to partner with a broad array of agencies in and out of the criminal justice system; and to experiment with new ways of solving problems. Whether it's called "community-focused probation," "problem-solving probation" or "broken-windows probation," these new approaches have the potential to reverse the public's negative impression of probation and have a far-reaching impact on crime rates and a community's sense of safety—and ultimately, help probation live up to the vision laid down by John Augustus so many years ago.

QUESTIONS FOR REVIEW AND DISCUSSION

1. What are the major aims of probation? Do these aims seem to be realized by probationer recidivism and other official records? Why or why not? Explain.

2. What do probation officer caseloads have to do with their effectiveness in performing their jobs?

3. What was the "beat supervision" program in Maricopa County, Arizona? What were some of its key elements?

4. What is Operation Night Light? Who was targeted by this program? Was it successful?

5. What are reparative boards? How is Vermont's reparative board designed to prevent crime? Discuss.

6. How are crime prevention projects related to working collaboratively with offenders in reintegrative and rehabilitative efforts? Explain.

7. What are the major obstacles organizations encounter when attempting to establish crime prevention programs? Discuss.

34

"Willingness-to-Pay for Crime Control Programs"

Mark A. Cohen, Roland T. Rust, Sara Steen,
and Simon T. Tidd

Adapted from Mark A. Cohen et al., "Willingness-to-Pay for Crime Control Programs."
Criminology 42: 89–109, 2004.

Reprinted by permission from the American Society of Criminology.

INTRODUCTION

Cost-benefit analysis is a well-developed methodology that has become an important component of regulatory and policy development for many government agencies. Since the early 1980s, federal government regulatory agencies have been required to conduct cost-benefit analyses on major regulatory initiatives—requirements adopted by Executive Order and implemented by the Office of Management and Budget.

Recent Congressional proposals would mandate similar requirements. Such analyses have thus become a routine tool in the development of environmental, health and safety regulations. Unlike regulatory programs, however, criminal justice programs have rarely been examined using the cost-benefit framework, in large part because there has not been enough data to do so.

This study provides new estimates on the cost of crime that can assist criminal justice researchers and policy analysts in comparing the costs of criminal justice policies to their crime control benefits. While tallying the costs of a criminal justice program is relatively straightforward, estimating the benefits is often much more difficult. Unlike criminal justice costs, which involve buying goods and services, hiring employees and so on, the benefits of criminal justice programs involve many nonmarket goods such as reduced pain and suffering to crime victims and reduced fear to the public. Those nonmarket goods are valuable but more difficult to quantify. Indeed, we know they are valuable because people are willing to pay to avoid being victimized and to avoid that fear.

Prior methodologies for estimating the cost of crime have relied largely on estimating the costs of various components of crime—victim medical fees, lost wages, police and prison expenditures, and even intangible items such as pain, suffering and lost quality of life to victims—and totaling those figures. Cohen (1988) developed a methodology for estimating the cost of individual crimes based partly on jury awards for pain, suffering and reduced quality of life, an approach later used in a study commissioned by the National Academy of Sciences (Cohen, Miller, and Rossman, 1994) and in subsequent NIJ-funded research (Miller, Cohen, and Wiersema, 1996). While jury awards are one way to capture some of the intangible costs of crime that previous approaches had ignored, the method is not entirely appropriate for use in cost-benefit analysis. Conceptually, when deciding whether to fund a program, we want to know how much the public expects to benefit—hence how much they would be willing to pay. Thus, economists generally prefer *ex ante* measures of "willingness-to-pay" (WTP) when conducting cost-benefit analysis (Cook and Graham, 1977) as opposed to the *ex post* analysis of victim costs and jury awards used in previous studies.

This paper reports on a new approach to valuing crime based on the WTP concept, using the "contingent valuation" (CV) methodology developed in the environmental economics literature. The methodology has been used extensively to place dollar values on nonmarket goods such as improvements in air quality, saving endangered species and reducing the risk of early death—social benefits that do not have direct market analogs. There have been literally hundreds of CV studies, meta-analyses and textbooks written on the subject. Although used in many different policy contexts, contingent valuation has not generally been employed in criminal justice research. One exception is Cook and Ludwig (2000) and Ludwig and Cook (2001), who use the CV method to estimate the amount that the average household would be willing to pay to reduce the gun violence of criminals and juvenile delinquents. Similarly, Zarkin, Cates, and Bala (2000) report on a pilot study in which they use the CV method to value drug treatment programs. We employ a similar methodology to study the public's willingness to pay to prevent the crimes of burglary, armed robbery, assault, rape or sexual assault, and murder.

Overall, we find crime costs to be significantly higher than previous estimates that did not use the CV methodology. As Nagin (2001a, 2001b) noted, the prior estimates of Cohen (1988) and Miller, Cohen, and Wiersema (1996) are based on the cost to an individual victim—and thus ignore the external social costs associated with crime that those who are not victims endure, in particular, the reduced quality of life to neighborhoods, nonvictims and society in general. Because our survey asked people to consider a program that reduces crime by 10 percent in their community, respondents might reasonably consider the external benefits to nonvictims (including themselves).

The next section of the paper describes our survey design process and interview methodology. The third section presents our main survey results on the public's willingness to pay for crime control programs. The fourth section provides further insights into the nature and robustness of our results and examines how willingness to pay varies by demographic characteristics. The fifth section compares these estimates to previous estimates of the cost of crime. Concluding remarks are reserved for the final section.

Survey Design and Methodology

In designing this study we closely followed guidelines established by a distinguished panel of social scientists (Arrow et al., 1993) commissioned by the National Oceanic and Atmospheric Administration (NOAA) to assess the contingent valuation methodology. This panel was brought together because NOAA had drafted regulations calling for the use of the methodology when estimating natural resource damages in legal proceedings involving compensation for damaged public property. The panel concluded that CV is a valid approach and provided a set of guidelines for concluding a reliable survey.

The survey instrument was drafted using an extensive design process including consultation with a panel of experts, three professionally selected and moderated focus groups designed to be demographically representative, 12 hour-long cognitive interviews and professional interviewer training and monitoring. The survey design process is described in detail in Cohen, Rust, and Steen (2002).

Most of the NOAA panel recommendations were followed. One that was not is noteworthy. Arrow et al. (1993) caution CV researchers to describe the program under consideration thoroughly. However, their report is primarily concerned with environmental amenities and programs designed to mitigate environmental harm. Thus, for example, researchers might be interested not only in the value of saving a particular endangered species, but also in the value of "no mining" versus "no logging" options that protect habitat. We are not interested in one particular crime control policy. We are interested instead in valuing crimes themselves.

In the focus groups we used to pretest questions, one of the key concerns expressed was that survey respondents would not be able to separate their desire for reduced crime from the way it is reduced. For example, though everyone might agree that fewer assaults would be a good thing, there would be significant disagreement over whether a policy mandating life in prison for third-time offenders should be implemented if it were shown to deter assaults. In evaluating preliminary survey questions, some focus group participants noted that they had trouble separating their cynicism for the ability of the government to effectively control crime from their own willingness to pay. The final survey was therefore worded carefully to ensure that a crime control policy was not specified. Instead, respondents were told that a crime prevention strategy had worked last year and that the program had community support.

Respondents were asked if they would be willing to vote for a proposal requiring each household in their community to pay a certain amount to be used to prevent one in ten crimes in their community. They were then randomly given three of five crimes; the order of the questions was randomized to avoid any systematic bias associated with "anchoring" to the first crime. The crimes were (1) burglary, (2) serious assault, (3) armed robbery, (4) rape or sexual assault and (5) murder. Given the time limitations of our survey, we identified five of the most commonly understood and important crimes. However, the crimes were not defined for the respondents, and no information was provided on the prevalence, risk of victimization, average tangible losses or severity of injuries normally associated with the violent offenses. Instead, respondents were asked to respond based on their understanding of these crimes.

Our approach thus attempts to measure individual willingness to pay based on actual levels of fear and concern in the community—not on what people might pay if they fully understood the risks and consequences of victimization. The text of the survey follows:

> "Now I want to ask you how much of your own money you would be willing to pay to reduce certain crimes. In each case, I am going to ask you to vote 'yes' or 'no' to a proposal that would require your household and each household in your community to pay money to prevent crime in your community. Remember that any money you agree to spend on crime prevention is your money that could otherwise be used for your own food, clothing or whatever you need . . .

Last year, a new crime prevention program supported by your community successfully prevented one in every ten [INSERT CRIME] from occurring in your community. Would you be willing to pay [INSERT AMOUNT] per year to continue this program?"

The amounts inserted into the text were randomized between $25 and $225 (in $25 intervals). The maximum annual cost of $225 was selected based on focus group discussions in which participants indicated $200 would be the most they would consider paying for such programs. Once an amount was chosen for a particular respondent, the same amount was used for all three crime types for that respondent. After the first question was finished, the following was read:

"Now please disregard the crime prevention strategy that we just discussed and think of this. Last year, a new crime prevention program supported by your community successfully prevented one in every ten [INSERT CRIME] from occurring in your community. Would you be willing to pay [INSERT AMOUNT] per year to continue this program?"

The process described above was then repeated for the second and third crimes. The respondent was specifically asked to disregard the earlier question in order to eliminate any "income effects" associated with the earlier response. That is, a respondent might be willing to pay $200 per year to prevent murders and assaults individually, for example, but might not be willing to pay $400 combined to prevent both. To determine whether we could add the three bid levels together, or if there were any income effects associated with adding their responses, we asked a final follow-up question at the end of the third crime type:

"I realize that I asked you to evaluate each crime prevention strategy individually. However, now I'd like you to think of adding all of the money you have spent on each strategy together. You said that you'd pay up to [INSERT AMOUNT] to prevent one in ten [INSERT CRIME], up to [INSERT AMOUNT] to prevent one in ten [INSERT CRIME], and up to [INSERT AMOUNT] to prevent one in ten [INSERT CRIME] in your community. Now, if I were to add all that up it comes to [INSERT AMOUNT]. Would you be willing to pay this amount out of your own pocket to prevent all of the crimes we have just talked about?"

Telephone interviews were conducted with a sample that is representative of the entire U.S. population of adults (those aged 18 or older). A random digit dial sample of 4,966 telephone numbers yielded a total of 3,055 estimated "eligible" numbers (excluding business, disconnected numbers, fax lines and so on) and a total of 2,228 actual households we contacted. Of these, 1,300 completed interviews. Depending on the definition used, the "response rate" ranged from 43 percent (1,300/3,055) to 58 percent (1,300/2,228).

The data are weighted to adjust for probabilities of selection and to adjust for nonresponse on age, sex, education and race. Results of this study can be projected to the English-speaking population 18 years of age or older living in households in the fifty United States and the District of Columbia.

The survey was designed with numerous checks to ensure that respondents understood the questions, could respond with some rationality and consistency, and were not biased by the wording of previous questions. We also tested for (and rejected) any potential interviewer bias, temporal changes in responses and potential bias due to external media attention on crime issues that might have occurred around the time of the survey.

Willingness-to-Pay Estimates

Respondents were willing to pay different amounts to prevent each type of crime. At the lowest bid level ($25), 75 percent were willing to pay to prevent murder, 69 percent for rape or sexual assault, 60 percent for serious assaults, 56 percent for armed robbery and burglary. At the highest bid level ($225), 59 percent were willing to pay to prevent rape and sexual assault, 46 percent for murder, 41 percent for robbery, 35 percent for assault and 27 percent for burglary. To be conservative, we have recoded all "don't know" and "refused" responses as "no."

The percentage of individuals willing to pay for crime prevention generally declined with each bid level increase. In some cases, however, it increased. Such apparently inconsistent percentages can generally be explained by sampling error, because the maximum of the 95 percent confidence interval of the smaller bid level almost always exceeds the minimum of the confidence interval of the next larger bid level.

To convert these yes/no responses to a WTP estimate, several steps are required (see Haab and McConnell, 1997, for complete details on our methodology). First, the method assumes that WTP decreases monotonically as the bid level increases. As noted, despite an overall downward trend there are several "local" fluctuations where WTP increases between adjacent bid levels. At these points the responses for the adjacent bid levels are consolidated, effectively smoothing the function downward as the bid range is expanded to encompass both bid levels. Next, a choice must be made as to what dollar value to affix to a given bid range. A lower bound estimate is based on the actual bid level, and is conservative in its assumption that we know only that respondents would be willing to pay "at least" X dollars. An upper bound estimate is based on the upper end of the bid range and assumes that we don't know that individuals wouldn't pay up to the next bid level. The third approach, and the one followed here, is to assign the mid-point as the dollar value.

The third step is to calculate the probability density function (PDF) at each bid level. The PDF measures the marginal increase in the percentage of people unwilling to pay at a given bid level. For example, while 40.4 percent are unwilling to pay $175 or more for murder, 54.4 percent are unwilling to pay $200 or more. Thus, the PDF for murder at the $200 bid level is 14.0 percent (54.4 percent minus 40.4 percent). The final step requires multiplying the PDF by the corresponding dollar figure—mid-point of the range—and summing across all categories, yielding an estimate of the willingness-to-pay.

The mean WTP ranges from $104 annually per household for a 10-percent reduction in burglary to $146 for a 10-percent reduction in murder. The 95 percent confidence intervals around these estimates are generally plus or minus 10–20 percent.

These figures can be converted into an implied "cost per crime" based on the number of crimes and households in the United States. To construct these cost estimates, we first estimated the number of crimes that a 10-percent reduction implies. For example, we estimate that a 10-percent reduction in burglaries would prevent 426,123 burglaries. Because the average household is willing to pay $104 for a program that reduces burglaries by 10 percent and there are 103 million households in the United States, collectively $10.7 billion would be spent on such a program ($104 × 103 million = $10.7 billion). Dividing this figure by the 426,123 crimes averted yields WTP per crime of $25,000. Similar calculations yield estimates for serious assaults ($70,000), armed robbery ($232,000), rape and sexual assaults ($237,000) and murder ($9.7 million). Note that these figures do not mean that the average household would be willing or able to pay $200,000+ to avert being an armed robbery victim. Instead, they mean that (a) the average household would be willing to pay $110 to reduce their local community rate of armed robbery by 10 percent, and (b) the collective WTP in the United States to prevent one armed robbery at the margin is $200,000. This is no different than saying the average citizen cannot afford to buy a new police car, for example, but would be willing to pay $10 towards a police car knowing that their safety is increased.

Detailed Analysis of Responses

In this section, we analyze the willingness-to-pay responses in more detail to assess the extent to which they vary by the demographic characteristics of respondents. We also consider whether methodological or other survey-specific factors might have biased the responses.

In all cases, WTP decreases with the bid level. For example, the coefficient on the bid amount is -0.005 for armed robbery ($p < .01$). That is, respondents demand less crime prevention as the cost of crime prevention increases. We tried both curvilinear and piecewise linear specifications of the bid levels. However, we could not reject the hypothesis that willingness-to-pay is linear over our range of $25 to $225.

WTP is higher for blacks, with burglary and armed robbery being statistically significant. This is consistent with the apparent higher victimization risk facing blacks. We also find that WTP decreases with age (with three crimes being statistically significant) and is lower for low-income individuals (and statistically significant in four out of the five crimes). That low-income individuals in households with annual income less than $35,000 would be willing to pay less is not entirely surprising. Although low-income individuals generally have higher risks of victimization, ability to pay and other priorities apparently override any potential concern due to this higher risk. This raises potential distributional equity concerns if policymakers use WTP estimates yet also want to use crime reduction policies as a form of wealth redistribution. One way this could be done is to adjust the estimates based on the "median" income or higher income household WTP. In our case, this would slightly increase the cost of crime estimates.

Although not reported here, additional variables were also included in similar logistic regression equations. First, numerous checks of the data were made to determine whether we introduced bias in our survey design. One common concern with CV studies is often termed "anchoring," whereby responses depend on either earlier questions or the actual bid level. To control for this problem, we randomly rotated the order of the crimes to each respondent. Further analysis revealed that there was no ordering effect. For example, if we restrict the data to the first crime given to each respondent, there is no statistically significant difference in the estimated WTP between the first crime scenario and the second or third. We also tested to see if any particular ordering significantly changed the results and found that it did not.

Earlier in the survey, respondents were asked other questions about their preferred sentences for various criminal offenses. In half of the surveys, respondents were provided information about the cost of a year in prison ($25,000); in the other half, they did not. We found no evidence of any statistically significant differences in willingness-to-pay responses based on whether this prison cost information was provided.

Respondents were also asked another set of questions in which they had to allocate tax dollars among various crime prevention programs or to offer residents a tax rebate. Half of respondents were asked to allocate $100 per resident, the other half, $1,000. There was some evidence of anchoring for the crime of rape/sexual assault. Respondents asked to allocate $1,000 were more likely to be willing to spend their own money to reduce rape and sexual assault than those who were asked to allocate $100. Because this problem did not arise in any of the other four crime categories, we do not know if this was a chance occurrence or evidence of anchoring. We have some doubt about the anchoring hypothesis, however, because we showed that rape/sexual assault is the least sensitive crime to income.

We also observed considerable consistency across other questions in our survey. For example, we included a variable to measure the percentage of the $100 or $1000 that the respondent preferred to be given back to residents as a tax rebate. Presumably, respondents who preferred to allocate a larger percentage of tax dollars to a rebate instead of additional crime prevention programs would be less willing to pay for additional crime prevention programs out of their own pockets. Indeed, a variable measuring the percentage of taxes allocated to a rebate was the most highly significant variable explaining the yes/no vote in the WTP logistic regressions.

Finally, note that these figures are based on a 10-percent reduction in one crime type. Due to wealth constraints and diminishing marginal utility, it is not clear that respondents would pay the same amount per crime for larger reductions. As detailed earlier, the survey specifically instructed respondents to view each of the three (out of five) crimes they were asked about independently and to ignore any money they indicated they would be willing to pay for the earlier crime type. However, after the third crime, they were asked if they would be willing to pay the sum of the three amounts they settled on for all three (or two if they were only willing to pay for two) programs. In response, 81.0 percent said they would be willing to pay the sum of all three, 16.2 percent said no and 2.8 percent said they did not know. The percentage of yes respondents did not vary by either the total bid amount or income of the respondent. Thus, at the bid levels introduced in this survey (ranging from $25 to $250 per year), we did not find significant income or wealth effects.

The CV findings were compared to prior estimates of victim costs in Miller, Cohen, and Wiersema (1996) and criminal justice-related costs in Cohen (1998), inflated to 2000 dollars. In all cases, the estimates from the contingent valuation survey are higher than the prior estimates, ranging from 1.5 to 10 times higher. The estimates for serious assaults, rape and sexual assault, and murder are between 1.5 and 3 times higher. Armed robbery and burglary are about 5 to 10 times higher. Note that the estimate for murder ($8.5 to $11 million) is at the upper end of the range of Viscusi's (1998) most recent range for the value of a statistical life, between $3 million and $9 million. To put these figures into perspective, if we simply multiplied the total number of crimes by these cost estimates, they would imply a total social burden of $625 billion for these five crimes (compared, using prior estimates, to about $215 billion). This represents about $6,000 per household or about 10 percent of average household income in 2000. A 10-percent reduction in these crimes would be valued at about $600—or 1 percent of household income.

Theoretically, some economists have argued that the WTP estimates should be smaller because they are based on *ex ante* estimates and their willingness to *pay,* compared to prior estimates that are *ex post* compensation (willingness to *accept*) measures (see, for example, Cook and Graham, 1977). At this point, we can only conjecture why the implied WTP estimates are significantly higher than previous cost of crime estimates. Part of the reason might simply be due to lack of information by survey respondents about the magnitude and severity of current crime rates. Thus, for example, if the typical survey respondent overestimated their risk of being a crime victim, they would tend to overstate their willingness to pay to prevent crime. Even if true, however, it is not clear that the WTP estimates should be ignored if they relate to fear of crime and public well-being.

A study by Anderson (1999) estimates and aggregates many of these external costs, including the cost of the criminal justice system, private security costs, the opportunity cost of time spent by people in locking homes and other prevention measures. Anderson estimates the aggregate burden of crime to be between $1.1 and $1.7 trillion, compared to the $450 billion of victim costs estimated by Miller, Cohen, and Wiersema (1996)—about three to four times the victim costs. Thus, the per crime figures estimated here are plausible and consistent with the Anderson (1999) study and the Nagin (2001a, 2001b) critique of earlier crime cost estimates.

The fact that crime costs are 1.5 to 10 times previous estimates is of more than academic interest. As Cohen (1988) showed, early cost-benefit analyses in the criminal justice arena calculated the cost of crime using the amount of out-of-pocket losses to victims. In one example, Cohen (1988) described a prior cost-benefit analysis of an early release program that concluded, based on an extensive study of the recidivism rate of prisoners let out early, that reduced prison costs saved taxpayers more than the added cost of new crimes. However, once the monetary value of pain, suffering and reduced quality of life to victims was included in the cost of these new crimes, the cost-benefit ratio switched sides and the early release program was shown to be a failure. The higher cost estimates found in this study further raise the threshold for such early release programs (that is, the benefits in terms of crime prevention would have to be higher than previously thought to meet or exceed the cost of increased crime). On the other side of the equation, costs involved in crime prevention strategies would be more readily justifiable given these higher estimates of the social costs of crime. This could also significantly alter previous findings. For example, Levitt (1997) found that increased hiring of police reduces crime. However, based on the cost of hiring a sworn officer and the monetary value of crimes averted, he concluded that only in one of his model specifications did the benefits unequivocally exceed the costs. Thus, while Levitt was particularly cautious about drawing policy conclusions from his analysis, the case for more police officers would be significantly strengthened if these new crime cost estimates were substituted in his cost-benefit ratios.

CONCLUSION AND FUTURE RESEARCH

This study has demonstrated the applicability of the contingent valuation method of valuing nonmarket goods to the criminal justice arena. In our nationally representative sample of 1,300 U.S. residents, we found that the typical household would be willing to pay between $100 and $150 per year for crime prevention programs that reduced specific crimes by 10 percent in their communities, with the amount increasing with crime seriousness (for example, $104 for burglaries, compared to $146 for murders). In the aggregate, these amounts imply a marginal willingness-to-pay to prevent crime of about $25,000 per burglary, $70,000 per serious assault, $232,000 per armed robbery, $237,000 per rape and sexual assault, and $9.7 million per murder. This compares to an estimate of about $200 per year that Cook and Ludwig (2000) and Ludwig and Cook (2001) estimate the average household would be willing to pay to reduce gun violence caused by criminals and juvenile delinquents by 30 percent, which translates into about $1 million per injury. Our estimates of $232,000 for armed robbery and $9.7 million for murder are very consistent with their estimate of $1 million per nonfatal gunshot injury.

These figures—based on a WTP approach—are between 1.5 and 10 times higher than prior estimates of the cost of crime to victims. By focusing exclusively on costs to victims of crime and the criminal justice system, previous studies have ignored other social costs of crime. Such costs include prevention expenditures for personal security, averting behavior by potential victims (for example, taking taxis instead of walking home and avoiding certain neighborhoods), third-party costs of insurance (for example, parking lot owners insuring against claims by victims that there was inadequate lighting) and government welfare programs. There are other, nonmonetary costs of crime that may also factor into individuals' willingness to pay for crime prevention, such as general concerns about community safety. It seems likely that our estimates reflect in part willingness to pay for the ability to live in safe communities. We find that people value more than just the reduced costs of victimization—they are also willing to pay for reductions in these other social costs of crime.

WTP appears to vary by both income and demographic characteristics. Lower income respondents generally were willing to pay less for equivalent crime reductions despite being generally more at risk. However, all else being equal, blacks are generally willing to pay more than whites to reduce the incidence of crimes for which they face a higher risk of victimization. Given these preliminary findings, future studies should focus on the relationship between risk of victimization and willingness-to-pay.

The results of our pilot study of willingness-to-pay provide support for continuing this line of research. Respondents appeared to be able to distinguish between crime types and to vary their willingness-to-pay accordingly. Preliminary estimates of the cost per crime using this methodology appear to be reasonable—and considerably higher than previous estimates that focused primarily on victim costs and not on other costs to the community.

The estimates derived in this study are based on the public's willingness to pay for crime reductions. It is well known, however, that the public often misunderstands the actual risk (or consequences) of victimization. Thus, we might have obtained different results if the survey explicitly described the risks of victimization (and respondents fully understood those risks). Which approach is better is a philosophical question. People respond to perceived risks. They decide whether to walk home at night or take a cab, whether to install a burglar alarm, and whether to vote for a candidate promising to spend more (or less) on crime control programs based on perceived risks and fears. Our approach is therefore to learn from the public what value it puts on these perceived risks. The alternative approach of attempting to value actual risks also has merit in the policy arena and is one direction that future research should explore.

QUESTIONS FOR REVIEW AND DISCUSSION

1. How much are persons willing to pay for crime prevention? Discuss.
2. What is meant by cost-benefit analysis? How was it used here to determine the amount citizens would pay to prevent crime?
3. What crimes were used as examples in this study? Are these fairly typical of the types of crimes of most concern to citizens? Why or why not? Explain.
4. Does willingness to pay to prevent crime vary by socioeconomic status? Why or why not? Discuss.

35

Minor Crime in a Quaint Setting

Practices, Outcomes, and Limits
of Vermont Reparative Boards

David R. Karp
and Kevin M. Drakulich

Adapted from David R. Karp and Kevin M. Drakulich, "Minor Crime in a Quaint Setting: Practices, Outcomes, and Limits of Vermont Reparative Boards." *Criminology and Public Policy* 4: 655-686, 2004.

Reprinted by permission from the American Society of Criminology.

When Americans think of crime-ridden places, Vermont is not the first location that comes to mind. It is not in such "quaint settings" that we expect to find important criminal justice innovation. Yet criminologists, practitioners, and policy makers have taken notice of Vermont's Reparative Probation. This is despite the fact that this program focuses on minor offenders in a state with relatively little crime. In 1999, the program received the Ford Foundation's Innovations in Government Award. Since its inception in 1995, criminal justice agencies have launched literally hundreds of "community board" programs across the United States. Most have adopted the Reparative Probation model. Schiff et al. (2001) estimate that the United States had 227 board programs serving juvenile offenders in 2001. Their survey did not seek information about programs for adult offenders or those outside the United States.

Although several evaluations of U.S. and international community and restorative justice programs have been published (see Braithwaite, 2002 for a review), we report on the first formal independent evaluation of outcomes of a probation-based community board model and of Vermont Reparative Probation in particular. This article draws on the technical evaluation (Karp, Sprayregan, and Drakulich, 2002), funded by a grant from Vermont's Department of Corrections (VDOC), from which we highlight the major findings and focus on their policy implications.

Reparative probation may be seen as an alternative probation model, designed to offset the public's dissatisfaction with traditional probation. "As a brand name, probation is unfortunately irretrievably associated in the public consciousness with a lack of accountability and a reactive agenda" (Maloney et al., 2001: 29). Rather than focus on enforcement of restrictive conditions, the program described here invites participating decision makers to seek outcomes that provide concrete benefits to victims, offenders, and the communities in which they live.

The reparative board model is similar to other restorative practices because it invites dialogue between key stakeholders to negotiate restorative agreements. It differs in that it most often hears cases that are victimless (such as drunk driving and underage drinking) or those where victims choose not to participate. It also differs by including a standing pool of citizen volunteers that would not typically participate in other conferencing models.

Interest in the philosophy of community justice, especially as an alternative to the traditional adversarial model, has grown quickly in the past decade, generating a variety of programs that stress victim and community involvement (Clear and Karp, 1999; Karp and Clear, 2002a). Karp and Clear (2000) argue that through system accessibility, community involvement, and reparative and reintegrative processes, criminal justice systems can achieve restoration, social integration, community capacity, and community satisfaction. Although McCold (2004) finds community justice and restorative justice to be competing philosophies, with the former concerned less with addressing victims' needs and incorporating healing dialogue than restorative justice, Reparative Probation may be considered to be a community justice and restorative justice program implementing restorative principles by focusing on dialogue between key stakeholders (victims, offenders, affected members of the community) and reparation of individual and community harm. It also emphasizes community justice principles such as citizen volunteer involvement, decentralized, community-level decision making, and offender reintegration.

VERMONT'S REPARATIVE PROBATION PROGRAM

Although Vermont's reparative boards exemplify community and restorative justice philosophies, it should be noted that Vermont's program was developed independently of these academic traditions by policy makers within VDOC in response to rapid increases in incarceration that were overwhelming the system (Perry and Gorczyk, 1997). Their use of the term "reparative" was not an attempt to distinguish themselves from restorative practices; rather it was conceived before staff were aware of restorative justice principles and programs. Despite this independent development, Reparative Probation is consistent with both community and restorative justice. According to VDOC, their goals include "providing public safety, offender accountability, and victim reparation," all compatible with the ideas of restorative justice, as well as "building healthy communities, empowered to control their own justice processes and dispute resolution strategies," which is compatible with the larger community justice philosophy (Perry and Gorczyk, 1997: 30).

Michael Dooley (1996: 32), a member of the Reparative Probation development team at VDOC, notes that "the central feature of the program is the offender's face-to-face public meeting with representatives of the community." John Gorczyk, Commissioner of VDOC, and John Perry, Director of Planning, at the time of the program's inception argued that the primary customer of their services is not the offender, as corrections officials might typically claim. Instead, they argued it was the public, and its members ought to be included in correctional planning and programming (Perry and Gorczyk, 1997). After extensive "market research" to evaluate their customers' needs," they shifted their management goals:

> We began to recognize that we are not simply in the prison business, and we are not simply in the probation business. We are in the business of providing public safety, offender accountability, and victim reparation. We are also in the business of building healthy communities, empowered to control their own justice processes and dispute resolution strategies. (Perry and Gorczyk, 1997: 30)

As part of their research, VDOC examined Vermont public support for the creation of reparative boards and found it "overwhelmingly endorsed the concept of Community Boards participating in sentencing. The questions dealing with this idea got responses of 92 percent, 93 percent, 95 percent positive ratings" (Perry and Gorczyk, 1997: 29). Karp et al. (2004) argue that stakeholder (offender, victim, community volunteer) participation in the justice system enhances that decision-making process, leading to greater satisfaction among the stakeholders and better outcomes for each. Ultimately, this community involvement builds community capacity.

Vermont's reparative boards may be classified as one variation of restorative justice programming and are often contrasted with victim offender mediation, conferencing, and circle programs (Bazemore and Umbreit, 2001: Roche, 2003). Board programs have been variously titled Community Reparative Boards in Vermont, Neighborhood Accountability Boards in California, Youth Aid Panels in Pennsylvania, Community Justice Councils in Michigan, Community Councils in Toronto, Youth Offender Panels in England and Wales, and Community Panels in New Zealand. Roche (2003) notes that board models vary significantly: Some are youth only, some serve as a pretrial diversion, some have no authority to enforce agreements, and so on.

Under the community justice model, a partnership is formed between the justice system and the local community. "The justice system follows community leadership while monitoring community process" (Pranis, 1998: 42). Thus citizens are actively involved in core decision making. The citizen role in Reparative Probation is unique among probation volunteer programs. Typically, volunteers serve as one-to-one mentors, but they have no authority over sanctions (Shields et al., 1983). In Vermont, volunteers have parameters, just as judges have sentencing guidelines, but their decisions about the sanctions are not merely recommendations to the court and are put into effect without judicial review.

In addition to the authority of board members in negotiating reparative contracts, an indirect measure of their decision-making authority is the variety of ways volunteers serve the program. The primary role for board members is to sit on boards, meeting with offenders and victims, and negotiating contracts. Most volunteers serve in this capacity. In addition, we find several other programmatic roles for volunteers. They serve as victim liaisons, in charge of contacting victims and ushering them through the process. They also serve as victim impact panel coordinators, community service coordinators, intake assistants, and caseworker assistants.

Reparative Probation can be summarized as follows. Upon conviction of a minor nonviolent offense, larceny or drunk driving, for example, the judge has the option to sentence the offender to probation with the condition that he or she appears before a local reparative board, although this stipulation is entirely at the judge's discretion. VDOC has established criteria for program eligibility based on offense severity and offense history. Essentially, these criteria eliminate the very minor probation cases, in which judges place offenders, but ask nothing of them except to be law-abiding. They also eliminate more serious probation cases that require greater supervision by probation officers, risk assessment, and formalized treatment protocols. Offenders are adults, although the program accepts individuals as young as age 16. Thus, there is some overlap with a similar board program administered by a separate state agency for juveniles. The latter program accepts offenders through age 18 (O'Brien et al., 2002).

A board composed of trained citizen volunteers convenes with the offender to discuss the impact of the offense and find a restorative resolution. Victims (when applicable) and other affected parties, such as the offender's family, are invited to participate by providing impact statements and attending reparative board meetings with offenders. Boards meet with offenders whether or not victims choose to participate, and most victims, as will be reported below, do not participate. Board meetings vary in length, but average between 35 and 40 minutes (Karp, 2001). The outcome of the meeting is a negotiated agreement, signed by the offender, specifying a set of tasks to be accomplished during a 90-day probationary period. All participants in the meeting, especially offenders and victims, are encouraged to actively contribute to the decision-making process, and the contract is arrived at by consensus. Typically, offenders will return to the board for a mid-term review and a final closure meeting before discharge. Offenders who fail to comply are in violation of probation and returned to the court.

The board members receive training and try to accomplish four goals in each case. First, they wish to engage the offender in tasks that will help him or her better understand the harmful consequences of the crime to victims and the community. This may entail asking the offender to listen to the victim's account. It may mean asking the offender to write an essay describing the harm that was done. Second, the board seeks to identify ways the offender can repair the harm to victims. Third, they try to engage the offender in making amends to the community. Restitution to the victim, community service, and letters of apology may be negotiated. Fourth, the board works with the offender to find a strategy to reduce the likelihood of reoffending. This might include a wide variety of educational and counseling opportunities.

Board meetings are held on a weekly basis, with a board typically hearing two new cases, with some additional follow-up and closure meetings. They are typically held in an informal conference room in a town hall, public library, or probation office. Attention is given to the seating of victims and offenders prior to the meeting such as having victims wait in a separate room or office. Boards vary in their formality, but all are much less formal than the courtroom setting. Boards usually consist of four or five members of the community where the crime was committed. Meetings begin with introductions, proceed through a general review of the incident and become task-oriented as they strategize over terms of the agreement. Boards can ask nonmembers, such as offenders, to leave the meeting for a period of private deliberation. Although this was a common practice at the program's inception, it has now been largely abandoned, and decision making is conducted as openly and collectively as possible.

VDOC probation officers serve as case managers who are responsible for paperwork as well as preparation and follow-up work with probationers as they complete reparative tasks. Some VDOC staff are specifically charged with developing community resources, such as community service opportunities for offenders. Staff, and in some places, board volunteers, received specialized training to become victim liaisons, learning how to contact victims, collect victim impact statements, and prepare them for participation in board meet-ings. VDOC staff are responsible for providing oversight, ensuring that boards operate within their mandate, and operate equivalently across the state (Karp and Walther, 2001).

Board members are volunteers recruited through advertisements and word-of-mouth. They must observe a board before committing to membership, and they receive ongoing training as members. A survey of board members found that 74% had served for longer than one year, 40% having served for more than two years (Karp et al., 2004). Members are di-verse in age, but they tend to be older (86% are over age 40); roughly equally divided be-tween men and women (45% male); overwhelmingly white (97% white), as is the state and correctional populations; diverse economically, but disproportionately well educated (73% with college or graduate degrees); diverse religiously with equal proportions religious and nonreligious; and diverse politically (38% liberal, 38% moderate, 21% conservative).

METHODOLOGY

Objective

This study evaluates the effectiveness of Reparative Probation in realizing identified pro-gram goals. This study does *not* provide comparative results between program participants and a control group, such as cases in a traditional probation program. Wherever possible, results are compared with those found in other restorative justice programs.

Identifying Program Goals

Working closely with VDOC staff, the evaluation team developed a list of theoretical out-comes that program staff believed to be central goals of the program. This process of out-come identification is in keeping with the philosophy of participant-driven evaluation (Bazemore and Stinchcomb, 2000).

In this study, four outcomes are evaluated. Table 1 identifies the four program goals and evaluation indicators. From these, our research team developed specific measures.

Sample

We evaluate a sample of reparative cases that terminated in the year 2000. Termination may occur because the offender has successfully completed probation or committed a violation that returns him or her to court. These cases may have begun earlier, i.e., in 1999, but they must have finished by the end of 2000. As VDOC data collection procedures have evolved and improved since the beginning of the program, as have training procedures for board members, we focused attention on a recent set of cases. Focusing on year 2000 cases also enabled us to examine recidivism data for one year after termination.

In 2000, 1,902 cases were terminated. Of these 379 cases involved "deferred sen-tences" where all paperwork was destroyed after termination. All deferred cases were eliminated from our study (thus reducing the N to 1523), and we make no inferences about the deferred subgroup of reparative probationers. As this program and restorative justice more generally is concerned with victim participation, we included all 43 cases in which VDOC records indicated that victims had attended the board hearing. Then, based on an estimate for adequate statistical power, we extracted a random sample of 205

TABLE 1   Vermont Reparative Probation Goals and Indicators

Program Goals	Outcome Indicators
Communities are involved	• Offenders and supporters participate • Victims and supporters participate • Community volunteers participate
Victims' needs are addressed	• Victims' needs are addressed adequately by the reparative process
Communities are restored	• Community harm is repaired • Community is satisfied
Offenders are responsible	• Offenders understand impact • Offenders acknowledge responsibility • Offenders make amends • Offenders build social ties • Offenders are law-abiding

cases for study. One of these cases, on close analysis, was discovered to have been misclassified as a reparative case and was deleted from the sample. In two other pairs of cases, the same offender was listed twice, so they were combined, yielding a sample of 202 cases. The final sample is composed of 245 cases after adding the victim participation case.

Data Collection

Data collection involved four separate efforts: data retrieval from administrative databases and administrative personnel interviews, a content analysis of case files, a victim survey, and a community service site survey. Occasionally, we cite data from other studies of Vermont Reparative Probation to inform key outcomes dimensions.

Administrative Databases, Personnel Interviews and Case Files.   A review of administrative databases supplemented by personnel interviews provided some of the most general information about the program, including the numbers of boards and volunteers over time, as well as general descriptions of the reparative and regular probation populations. The case files were collected and coded for each case in our sample. Case file analysis helped correct inaccuracies in VDOC databases, such as correcting for cases designed as having victims when there were none, and those designated as victimless, but they were not.

Victim Survey.   Victims were interviewed by telephone. The victim survey was designed to collect simple, critical information rather than an in-depth study of the victim experience with reparative probation. Of the 89 cases with direct victims, 40 completed the victim survey (45%). Of these, 20 attended the reparative board meeting and 20 did not attend. Although the evaluation team attempted to retrieve missing information wherever possible, many victims could not be contacted because case files were incomplete, inaccurate, or out-dated. Although this response rate is not high, our refusal rate was low, with a few explaining that they did not have the time to participate, the crime happened too long ago to recall details, or it was an insignificant event. Although using the termination date allows the selection of a group of cases known to be completed, this does result, in some cases, in a few years between the crime, the meeting, and the interview with the victim. The victims were interviewed in the summer of 2001, and a few of the offenders were sentenced as early as 1997, with some meetings occurring as early as 1998.

Community Service Site Survey.   For each offender assigned community service, we identified information about their placement and conducted a telephone survey of service sites. We were able to complete 82 service surveys for the 158 offenders who completed or partially completed community service (52%). This low response rate is primarily a result of inadequate service site information. The most common problem faced by the evaluators was that service hours were recorded, but the placements were not identified in the case files. Fifteen sites could not be contacted despite several attempts by telephone. Finally, contacts at a few sites listed were unaware of the program and claimed not to have put probationers to work.

FINDINGS

Before reporting the evaluation results, we compare the Vermont Reparative Probation population with other Vermont probationers.

First, reparative probationers represent about 20% of all Vermont probationers. Reparative probationers are more likely to be younger and less well educated (because many are still high school aged). Both probationer populations are overwhelmingly white, and this is representative of Vermont as a whole. Both groups are disproportionately male, but there are comparatively more females in the reparative population. Both groups are also disproportionately misdemeanants, with reparative probationers more likely to have committed lesser offenses.

Outcome #1—Community Involvement

Community Volunteer Participation.   Board members' participation is a central feature of reparative probation. Although program record-keeping in this area was often incomplete, the numbers suggest increases in all categories, including more board members and other volunteers, and more hours volunteered by board members and others. As the program gains more referrals, and as volunteer participation increases, boards subdivide to handle cases in more localized settings. Over the course of 2000, 11 more boards were formed, serving ten more communities.

Victim Participation.   Many cases can be considered victimless, such as underage drinking or drunk driving (without an accident involving others). In our analysis, we include theft and fraud as crimes with victims—even if it was shoplifting a CD from WalMart—as long as we could identify an individual who could participate in the program as a harmed party, such as a store manager. Our review of police reports indicates that 89 of the 245 cases had victims. Of these, 40 participated in the board meetings. Because we included in our sample all known cases with victim participation, in order to estimate victim participation rates for the entire Year 2000 case population, we relied on VDOC estimates for the number of total cases with direct victims. Of the 1523 cases in the total population, 391 cases (26%) had direct victims. Our finding that 40 victims participated in all Year 2000 board meetings, therefore, yields a participation rate of 10%.

This evaluation was not designed to analyze why victims participate or fail to participate in the program. However, that 90% of victims fail to participate is a troubling finding. Our data offer some insight into only two of several possible explanations. First, many were simply not contacted by VDOC. Second, many were commercial victims of shoplifting and have little interest in participation. The second is understandable; the first required remediation. VDOC administrative records indicate that 26% of Year 2000 cases had victims, whereas our own analysis of police reports discovered more cases with victims than those designated by VDOC. Among those victims we surveyed, several indicated that they had not heard of the program and would have participated had they been invited.

Outcome #2—Victims' Needs

Meeting the needs of victims is central to the mission of restorative justice programs. We consider both emotional and material needs of victims, considering objective data relevant to victims and subjective reports by victims about their experience with the program. Due to the small number of victims overall and our difficulties locating contact information for many of them, our victim survey sample size is small. We were able to speak with 20 of the 40 victims who participated in a board meeting and 20 of the 49 victims who did not. However, given the importance of victims in this program, we present the following findings, but caution against generalizing.

A first victim concern regards their *participation* in the process. The survey data reveal a number of comments by victims indicating that they would have participated in the board meeting, but they were never informed about it. Of the 20 who did participate, no one was dissatisfied by their level of participation or by the support they received by the board. Four victims were very dissatisfied, however, because they believed the offender did not come to understand how the crime affected them and failed to accept responsibility for the offense. Comments associated with dissatisfaction referred to the behavior of the offender during the meeting, such as him or her "not getting it," "just giving lip service," or "the offender wasn't sorry." Although it is rare for victims to participate in board meetings, when they do, the experience appears to be favorable for the majority of them.

Although some participating and nonparticipating victims were dissatisfied by the reparative contract, most were either satisfied or very satisfied. Only three nonparticipating victims believed the "reparative board process as a whole" was not helpful to them. Otherwise, both groups believed it to be either somewhat or very helpful. Only one person (a nonparticipating victim), in fact, thought the program should be discontinued. Interestingly, we did not find any statistically significant differences in satisfaction levels of victims who participated and those who did not participate in board meetings. This finding, when considered alongside the dissatisfaction of several victims who were not contacted to participate, might suggest that the option of participation is more important to victims than actual participation.

Whether or not victims attend the board meeting, having offenders apologize to them is a common reparative task. Our analysis of reparative contracts reveals that 46 (52%) of the

89 cases with direct crime victims included apology letters. We did not find a difference in the likelihood of receiving an apology between those victims who participated in the board meeting and those who did not participate. Qualitative comments from our victim survey indicate that some victims received a verbal apology during the meeting. Some others, however, noted frustration that they did not receive one or received one that they believed to be insincere.

Another victim concern is *restitution* for material losses such as stolen or damaged property. Our analysis of administrative data and our victim survey produced mixed results on restitution. The data indicate that restitution was ordered by the board in 32 of the 40 (80%) reparative cases where material harm was identified and outstanding at the time of the board meeting. It is notable that victims participated in four of the eight meetings where such restitution was not included. Looking at restitution completion 8–20 months after termination, 19 of the victims had received full restitution. Although boards are reasonably responsive to victims' material needs, many offenders do not pay their financial obligations. In our victim survey, we expected to find a correlation between offender payment and victim satisfaction that their material needs were addressed. However, six victims indicated that these needs were not well addressed despite full payment by the offender. We also found that victim participation in the board meeting did not increase either satisfaction with material outcomes or the likelihood of payment by the offender.

Outcome #3—Community Restoration

Here, we examine attempts made to ameliorate the community consequences of crime through community service and community satisfaction with these efforts. Data were gathered for the total number of cases that included community service tasks, and for subgroups of cases that are victimless, cases where victims participated, and cases where victims did not participate.

Community Harm.   More than half of offenders were assigned community service as part of their reparative contracts, and most of these completed their service requirement. Some probationers were assigned service by the court prior to their appearance before the board even though this conflicts with program design, but boards had the latitude to alter these assignments. In addition to service, we also found evidence that boards negotiate donations to charities. Although rare, donations may be viewed as community restitution analogous to victim restitution.

Our community service site survey finds that almost all activities involve unskilled manual labor, such as yard work, cleaning, photocopying, or sorting food or clothes. Twelve percent of the service activities called on some social skills, and these primarily had to do with organizing youth recreational activities, such as at a Boys and Girls Club. Both the supervision of offenders while they conducted their service and whether offenders worked with nonprobation volunteers varied greatly. We did not find satisfaction to be related to either level of supervision or service with nonprobationer volunteers, as agencies appeared satisfied with the service program whatever their arrangement.

In the restorative model, this service does not serve as punishment for the offender; rather it is a way for the offender to restore the community. In light of this goal, the service might be more meaningful to both the offender and the community when it is linked to the offense, which can happen in a variety of ways (Karp, 2001). The most direct link is when the service repairs harm caused by the offense, such as when the offender cleans graffiti that he or she painted on public property. A direct link is also made when the service addresses problems associated with the offense, such as when a drunk driver gives a public presentation to a school driver education class. This was found in very few of the service assignments. Less direct, but still linked, is service that is selected by the victim, but we were not able to measure this. A weak and indirect link to the offense is that the offender completes the service in the town where the offense occurred, which usually was the case.

Community Satisfaction.   Community satisfaction can be measured in a number of ways. In addition to Vermonters in general, board members and community work service sites both symbolically represent the community in the board process. The board members serve as representatives of the community, whereas service sites present the opportunity for offenders to repair community harms. For this reason, their satisfaction with the process can also be thought of as a measure of community satisfaction with the process.

The survey of community service sites indicates widespread satisfaction with probationer service. Most were somewhat or very satisfied with offender service in general, and all of the sites would like to continue receiving probationers for service. Only 60% of the sites remembered the particular offender in our sample, but of them, all were somewhat or very satisfied by the work of the specific offender. In general, all of the respondents believed probationers' service was somewhat or highly beneficial to the community. Almost all believed the work was also somewhat or highly beneficial to the offender. No one type of service was found to be significantly more beneficial to the offender or the community than the others.

Agency comments generally reflected the satisfaction statistics. Respondents thought reparative probation "was a great program." Some agencies reported hiring or wanting to hire offenders who volunteered for them. The few negative comments revealed that agencies sometimes have difficulty with offenders failing to show up for assigned service, not working very hard, or causing friction with nonprobationer volunteers (in one case, a sexual harassment complaint was filed). In addition, agencies would like to see more communication with VDOC.

Karp et al. (2004) reported that board members were also satisfied with their participation in the program, and they largely reported that it increased their sense of membership in the community. A survey of Vermont residents found that very few were aware that the program existed, but upon having it explained to them, almost all favored its use (John Doble Research Associates and Greene, 2000).

Outcome #4—Offender Responsibility

Offenders' Understanding of the Impact of Their Offenses.   Boards frequently negotiate contract tasks designed to educate the offender about harm. We identified these tasks by examining contracts. Tasks that are primarily designed to benefit others (such as apology letters to victims) were not included, but it could be argued that they might also help the offender gain understanding about the harm. Most cases had contract tasks specifically designed for offender understanding of harm. Of these, the most frequently assigned task was an essay or research paper, followed by attending a victim impact panel. The essays might ask offenders to reflect on the harm, on why the law they broke exists, or to gather data, such as the total medical costs of drunk-driving accidents for the state. A small fraction of cases asked an offender to present such material publicly either as a letter to a newspaper or through public speaking. Many boards made use of a program called ENCARE, a national volunteer program offered by emergency room nurses to educate the public about trauma prevention (with a particular focus on drunk driving). Occasionally, boards will ask offenders to engage in other activities, such as victim-offender mediation, to watch a particular video or discuss the crime with a family member or respected community member.

Making Amends.   In this study, we use several measures to determine if victim and community restoration took place, as reported above. As a global measure, although indirect, we report here the extent to which offenders complete their contracts. We find that 81% of offenders successfully completed reparative probation. Undoubtedly, some contracts were modified over the probation period, but as a rule, offenders cannot be successfully terminated unless they have abided by contract terms. The only exception to this is restitution. Because the program was designed as a 90-day program, and many offenders do not have the means to pay restitution within that time period, offenders are successfully terminated when they complete all other contract tasks. They are then placed on "administrative probation" until restitution is completed.

Building Social Ties.   Reparative contracts include tasks designed to help the offender "learn not to reoffend." This focus on reintegration specifies that board members consider offender needs. Although not trained in assessment or treatment, board members try to find ways that offenders can better connect with the conventional community. Tasks were categorized as competency tasks when they had no discernable benefits to anyone other than the offender. We provide no evaluation here of the quality of these tasks in relation to "what works" in correctional rehabilitation (Cullen and Gendreau, 2000), and informal interviews with VDOC staff suggest they do not regard these tasks as a significant component of the program and have chosen to dedicate their correctional treatment resources to more serious offenders. Finally, we exclude community service as a competency task even while we believe it may be a vital means of reintegration (Bazemore and Karp, 2004).

Our analysis of contracts finds that most had tasks to develop competencies. We found only one case in this sample where a service assignment was specifically designed to help the offender become better integrated, and not to serve as a response to community harm. In this case, the offender was asked to organize a neighborhood block party. The most common competency assignment was driver safety, such as placement in a program called CRASH designed for DWI offenders. Many were referred to counseling for substance abuse or mental health. Some were referred to alcohol or substance abuse screening, which is merely an assessment, with no requirement for follow-through if a problem is identified. A small number of the offenders were asked to engage in some form of future planning, such as writing a 5-year-plan, or were required to seek further education, such as getting a GED. A few were assigned to a specific competency class, such as anger management or decision making, or referred to job training. One task was hard to classify—indeed, we think it contradicts the restorative philosophy—but we include it here as competency development through deterrence. A few offenders were required to tour a prison, presumably so they can be "scared straight."

In some categories, we have no measure for assessing offender need relative to the tasks assigned; thus, we cannot evaluate where the program is effectively addressing all offender needs. With regard to education, among the offenders who did not have a high school degree (38% of the sample), only 25% of them were assigned education-related tasks such as obtaining a GED. With regard to alcohol/substance abuse, 49% of cases were alcohol or drug-related, such as drunk driving, underage drinking, or drug possession. Seventy-five percent of these cases were assigned relevant competency tasks, such as screening, treatment, or driver safety.

Recidivism.   Although restorative justice programs have not been designed to specifically reduce recidivism, any program concerned with offender reintegration must naturally be concerned with this dimension. Restorative programs should not increase recidivism over traditional alternatives. However, Latimer et al.'s (2001) meta-analysis suggests that restorative programs do have a statistically significant effect on recidivism—reducing it over traditional sentencing options. Unfortunately, this study cannot compare reparative probation recidivism rates with traditional probation recidivism rates.

As recidivism is often defined in a variety of ways, we chose a definition that best describes offender reoffense within the time period allowable in this study. We used the following definition of recidivism. A recidivist is any probationer who committed a crime within one year of their reparative board meeting. In cases where the board meeting date was missing, we used the date the offender was sentenced to reparative probation (ten cases). A crime is defined by a conviction or plea of guilt; thus, we include only those rearrests that led to a conviction. We used the rearrest date to define the time of offense commission.

Our study reveals that about one third of reparative probationers were rearrested within one year of their board meeting (with no substantive differences across the three subgroups), although very few were rearrested for violent offenses. Of those rearrested, most were for DWI and various other driving offenses. Typically, these were for driving with a suspended license—licenses that were suspended most likely for a prior DWI. Other rearrests were for drinking infractions, such as underage drinking.

PROGRAM COMPARISONS & POLICY IMPLICATIONS

We turn now to consider the policy implications of our findings, comparing them to research on boards in the United Kingdom and New Zealand. We also draw conclusions about the effectiveness of restorative community justice, reparative boards as a restorative practice, and the problems and promise of implementing such a program in other settings, such as the "big city."

Although VDOC staff identified program goals independently of the community and restorative justice literature, Reparative Probation seeks to implement many of the values and principles of those justice philosophies (Bazemore, 2000; Braithwaite, 2002; Clear and Karp, 1999). Many of these goals are shared by other correctional agencies, such as Colorado Division of Probation Services, for example. Such program goals may represent the future of probation in the United States and are consistent with the platform of the American Probation and Parole Association (APPA, 2003). However, most agencies currently remain offender-focused, little concerned about the impact of their programming on victims or the community. Others have implemented change, but they are not collecting data that will measure the impact. Because the community and restorative agendas are new, data collection and reporting are themselves an indication of policy shift.

The question, of course, is whether these data present a positive picture. We will briefly discuss the results along the dimensions of community involvement, victims' needs, community restoration, and offender responsibility. Where possible, we have made comparisons with other relevant studies.

This report finds substantial *community involvement* and limited *victim involvement* in the program. Rarely do probation programs offer volunteers the opportunity to determine sanctions like they do when serving on reparative boards. Although most volunteers serve as board members, some specialize by working with victims, assisting caseworkers, and co-ordinating with various community organizations to develop community service opportunities. Recruitment of volunteers increased over the study period, as did the number of hours contributed by volunteers. The number of boards also increased, in order to serve more communities. Vermont Reparative Probation is clearly an affirmation that volunteers can be recruited to serve in core programmatic roles, including those that involve substantial decision-making authority.

That said, there are still important questions to ask about the increased involvement of volunteers in the criminal justice system. Vermont does not use volunteers as a substitute for probation officers, and it is not likely that volunteers can ever be as well trained or accountable as paid, professional probation staff. This raises the second potential problem with boards of volunteer citizens: composition. Reparative probation is, of course, not the only way members of the local community are included in the justice process. Composition and cross-sectional representation have long been debated with regard to juries (for example, see Vanderzell, 1966). Reparative boards, consisting only of volunteers, are likely to be less representative and more homogenous than juries. More importantly, offenders have the ability to contest the inclusion of jury members, and they have no similar rights with regard to the boards.

Even if composition is less important in the relatively homogenous state of Vermont, this may be a larger issue in other locations. Crawford and Newburn (2003: 90) note that for Youth Offender Panels in England and Wales, "Local areas experience difficulty in recruiting a representative body of community panel members." In the United States, those brought before the justice system are disproportionately young, poor, and ethnic and racial minorities. In a more diverse setting, we would be very concerned if board members were predominantly, for example, older, wealthy, and white. Most importantly, board members need to represent the local community in which offenders reside, operating at a neighborhood level, rather than by municipal, county, or jurisdiction levels.

In New Zealand, Maxwell et al. (1999) describe a board model that operates in two communities, one serving offenders of primarily European descent with primarily European board members, and the other with Maori offenders with primarily Maori board members. In the United States, Albany County (NY) Probation Department's Accountability Board sees offenders from one neighborhood and relies on a pool of members from the same neighborhood (Arbor Hill). In contrast to Vermont boards, this is an urban, predominantly African-American board, representing a low-income community. Research will need to focus on the effects of composition on board decisions and outcomes for offenders in diverse settings.

Probably the most problematic results we found in this evaluation have to do with victim participation. It is here where programmatic intent diverges substantially from practice. Although a majority of reparative cases are victimless, when cases with direct victims are heard, they participated by attending a board meeting only 10% of the time. Further inquiry is necessary to better determine the causes for such low participation rates, but reasons may include the failure to identify and contact victims, and victim disinterest due to time delays, the low severity of cases, and unfamiliarity with the process.

Although considered a restorative justice model, boards tend to be much more offender driven than other restorative practices, and recruitment of victims is less of a programmatic necessity. Maxwell et al. (1999: 58) note that, "in a fully restorative process,
decisions would be made by the people who are most directly affected by the offending
rather than by nominated representatives of the community or state." They found that the
New Zealand boards had victim participation rates of 58% (European) and 2% (Maori). In
the Youth Offender Panels in Great Britain, Newburn et al. (2002) found that only 13% of
victims attended board meetings, which is notably similar to the Vermont outcome. However, they note that victim participation varied by jurisdiction and identify several strategies
for increasing participation.

VDOC has taken several steps to address this issue. First, VDOC has provided increased training and guidelines for soliciting victim participation. Second, they are seeking
to implement "restorative sentencing." Here, the courts may refer cases to a restorative
process before sentencing, so that the process can help determine the sentence. This differs
from the current practice of receiving cases only after adjudication and may increase victim
participation by having board meetings more quickly follow arrest and enhance victims' interest in the outcome. Third, VDOC is working closely with Community Justice Centers to
increase the number of cases sent to boards through court diversion, bypassing the courts entirely, again reducing time delays. Finally, VDOC has provided training in conferencing to
both staff and volunteers. This restorative model is likely to be better suited to eliciting victim participation. Several cases have been conferenced successfully as an alternative to board
referral, but there is no systematic effort to replace boards with conferencing or to delineate
which cases would go to boards and which would go to a conference. Follow-up research on
these practices will help determine their potential roles in increasing victim participation.

In terms *of addressing victims' needs,* the results are mixed. Although limited contact
information prevented us from contacting many victims, we spoke with victims who did and
did not participate in the program. Most victims who did participate were satisfied by their
participation, felt supported by the board, and believed the offender accepted at least some responsibility for the offense. More generally, we did not find significant differences in attitudes
or outcomes for those who did and did not participate. Most victims received apology letters.
And victims with material harm still outstanding at the time of the board meeting were likely
to get restitution included in the reparative contract. Victims tended to like the reparative contracts, felt the program was helpful to them, and believed the program should continue.

Like other restorative programs, reparative boards focus on repairing harm to victims.
The findings here are consistent with those found in New Zealand and Great Britain
(Maxwell et al., 1999; Newburn et al., 2002). Many victims want the opportunity to confront offenders about the harm they caused and would like to receive recompense. Those
who participate tend to be satisfied by the experience, and those who receive apologies and
restitution welcome it, especially when they perceive the apologies to be sincere and the
restitution is paid in full. Frustration surfaces most often when victims are not given the opportunity to participate and when they believe offenders lack remorse.

A common strategy of *community restoration* is community service. Sixty-five percent of offenders were assigned community service as part of their contracts, and most of
these offenders fully completed their assigned hours. A survey of service sites revealed that

almost all were satisfied with the work performed and all of them wanted to continue receiving offenders from the program. The biggest problem with the community service assignments is the lack of a strong link between the offense and the service. Although the service is symbolically linked to the community by largely occurring in the town where the offense occurred, this is not a strong or obvious link, and the result may be a task that offenders might experience as more punitive than restorative. Through the process of the meeting, boards have the opportunity to assign community service with different meanings attached than courts are usually able to do, but if the only link is the town, then the boards have failed to capitalize on this opportunity.

Both the New Zealand boards and Great Britain boards made similarly high use of community service, but Newburn et at. (2002: 29) also note that, "trying to tailor the reparation to the offence . . . [was] regarded as extremely difficult." Neither board study surveyed agencies that received offenders for service, but one study of community service work by offenders in Scotland (McIvor, 1993) reports similarly high levels of satisfaction among agencies. McIvor also found that when problems occurred, they most often had to do with poor attendance, lack of motivation, and antisocial behavior. Almost all of the Scottish agencies were willing to continue offering placements, just as was found in Vermont.

In terms of *offender accountability and responsibility,* Reparative Probation seeks to ensure that offenders are accountable for their actions by repairing harm and seeks to educate offenders about their responsibilities as community members. Offender responsibility is defined by their understanding of the harm they caused, gaining skills/competencies that will help them be productive citizens, successfully completing the contract, and law-abiding behavior. In general, most offenders are successful and law-abiding.

Most offenders are assigned tasks in their contracts to help them gain a better understanding of the harm. Typically, these include writing essays, attending victim impact panels, or a drunk-driving impact course. Offenders are also frequently assigned competency-building tasks. These tend to include driver education, treatment/counseling, or a drug or alcohol screening. Such activities are also commonly employed in other board programs (Maxwell et al., 1999; Newburn et al., 2002). Most offenders successfully complete these tasks.

Competency building is one of the most theoretically exciting but practically disappointing parts of the program. In theory, community members may have more diverse social networks than probation officers that could facilitate offender reintegration. Yet the tasks typically assigned in contracts are relatively superficial, poorly linked to effective correctional treatment programs that identify and address offender needs, and are not likely to foster attachments between offenders and board members or between offenders and positive role models in the community. Levrant et al. (1999) sensibly propose a marriage of restorative practices with effective offender treatment programming. In principle, the two are not incompatible, but in Vermont, limited resources have precluded the Department of Corrections from providing extensive services to minor offenders. Board members may effectively serve as mentors to probationers. For example, they may rotate responsibility for in-depth mentoring even if this meant hearing fewer cases or recruiting more volunteers.

Most offenders (81%) successfully completed the program, and this is similar to completion rates in other board programs (Maxwell et al., 1999; Newburn et al., 2002). With regard to recidivism, 31% of offenders were rearrested within one year of the board meeting. The majority of rearrests were for DWI or other driving offenses. Very few were rearrested for violent crimes. Maxwell et al.'s (1999) study of New Zealand boards found recidivism rates (reconviction at one year) of 14% for one program and 30% for a second. Newburn et al. (2002) found a rate of 22%. These rates may be lowered by pairing restorative decision making with effective correctional treatment. One example of this comes from Winnipeg's Restorative Resolutions program, which does not include victim or community participation, but it emphasizes offender contracts that repair harm and reduce risk. Bonta et al. (1998) found a 5% reconviction rate at one year.

Concluding Speculations

The focus on Reparative Probation in Vermont has been on relatively minor crimes. A key question for policy is whether the Vermont model can be generalized. We conclude by considering the potential application of reparative boards beyond low-level offenses and beyond quaint settings.

At face value, focusing on restoration and reintegration is appropriate for more serious offenses and offenders. Braithwaite (2002) argues, for example, that restorative justice may be effective in more serious cases, and the evidence from the Australian conferencing research supports this (Strang et al., 1999) as does Umbreit's (2003) research on victim offender mediation in cases of serious violence. However, more serious offenders will typically require correctional interventions that board members are little trained to assess or recommend, and given the low rate of victim participation, we hesitate to recommend the participation of victims of more serious offenses without more careful assessment of boards' effectiveness in working with such victims. Perhaps the most conducive niche for restorative boards in more serious cases is with reentry. Here, both victims and community members have an abiding interest in the behavior of the offender. VDOC has recently begun to implement a similar board model for such cases. "Offender reentry panels" will seek input from victims, correctional staff, and treatment providers, and they will meet with offenders to craft contracts that offenders must complete while incarcerated and during the supervised release period (Vermont Department of Corrections, 2003).

The 2000 Census indicates that Vermont has 0.2% of the U.S. population and none of the 100 largest cities. Vermont has far fewer racial and ethnic minorities and immigrants than the rest of the United States. Vermont has more high school and college graduates, more homeowners, and greater residential stability. Although the income level in Vermont is comparable with the rest of the country, the poverty rate is much lower. All these census characteristics appear throughout criminological, community, and urban studies literatures as positive factors. Because Vermont may be the ideal setting for reparative boards, we much wonder if they work as well in the other settings in which they operate. The most difficult arena would be the most crime-prone areas: urban areas with concentrated poverty. The simple answer is that without an increase in other social services notoriously deficient or absent in these areas, it is not likely to work as well as in Vermont. It may also be distinctly more difficult to recruit a volunteer pool, engage the participation of victims, and find necessary opportunities for offender integration. But this criticism presumes that the reparative board model can only thrive in areas of well-developed social capital. It is also possible that reparative boards are one viable mechanism for building that capital.

QUESTIONS FOR REVIEW AND DISCUSSION

1. What are reparative boards? Describe the Vermont Reparative Board.
2. What are the purposes of reparative boards? Discuss.
3. How are offenders screened for participation in the Vermont Reparative Board program?
4. What is the nature of victim participation in reparative boards? Is it necessary that victims participate in reparative board discussions? Discuss.
5. What are several responsibilities of offenders when accepting the terms of reparative board recommendations? Explain.
6. How does the Vermont Reparative Board compare with reparative boards in other jurisdictions and countries?

36

Restitution
Making It Work

John W. Gillis

Adapted from John W. Gillis, *Restitution: Making It Work.* Washington, DC: U.S. Department of Justice, 2002.

INTRODUCTION

Many crime victims are awarded restitution at the sentencing of an offender but fail to receive any money. Others are paid only a small portion of the restitution ordered. A recent study of restitution collection in Colorado found that convicted offenders ordered to pay their victims more than $26 million in 1996 still owe more than $20 million. Even though many restitution orders will never be fully paid, states are taking various legislative approaches to improve the collection of restitution.

STATUS OF THE LAW

All states have statutory provisions relating to the collection of restitution. States have addressed this issue by laying the groundwork for collecting restitution at sentencing and enforcing restitution orders during the payment period.

LAYING THE GROUNDWORK FOR COLLECTING RESTITUTION

Courts can take many steps well before collection efforts begin that may make enforcing restitution orders much easier. The sentencing court can lay the groundwork for collecting restitution by thoroughly investigating the assets of convicted offenders, preserving those assets, and routinely entering income deduction orders.

Investigating the Assets of Convicted Offenders

Many states have attempted to improve the collection of restitution by providing for a thorough investigation of the assets of convicted offenders, either before or after restitution is ordered. A complete investigation of a defendant's assets can help the court craft a workable payment plan, which should decrease the likelihood of default. If the defendant later defaults on any payments, the court can use this information to help determine whether the failure to pay restitution is willful.

A list of a defendant's assets also can assist the victim or other entities in their collection efforts. In California, a victim is entitled to see a defendant's disclosures identifying all assets, income, and liabilities or certain other documents concerning financial information. Until all restitution is paid, Kansas gives a crime victim the right to any information regarding the offender's financial assets, income, or employment that is in the possession of the district court, parole board, or any community correctional service program.

Preserving the Assets of Convicted Offenders

In some cases, defendants may conceal assets or may even waste assets in an attempt to avoid paying restitution. Pennsylvania allows the prosecutor to seek a restraining order or injunction when the criminal complaint is filed or the offender is indicted to preserve assets that may be used later to pay restitution. Before entering such an order, the court must hold a hearing to find a substantial probability that the commonwealth will prevail in the action, the restitution order will exceed $10,000, the property to be preserved appears necessary to satisfy any restitution order, and the failure to enter the restraining order or injunction will result in the property being made unavailable. Under certain circumstances, a temporary emergency restraining order can be issued "without notice or opportunity for a hearing, whether or not a complaint, information, indictment[,] or petition alleging delinquency has been filed."

California takes another approach. By state law, it is a separate offense to dispose of property to avoid paying restitution; the offense is usually a misdemeanor but may be a felony.

Entering Income Deduction Orders

The routine entry of income deduction orders—or garnishment orders—can streamline the process of collecting restitution. California and Florida both provide for automatic entry of an income deduction order at the time restitution is ordered. In California, this order is enforceable only when a defendant defaults on restitution payments, but in Florida, the order is effective immediately.

ENFORCING RESTITUTION ORDERS

States have enacted various provisions to enforce the collection of restitution orders when a defendant defaults in payment. These provisions are described below.

Improved Monitoring of Restitution Payments

A first step in any effort to improve the collection of restitution must be a system for monitoring a defendant's compliance with the restitution order. Wisconsin requires its Department of Justice to establish a separate account for each person in custody or under supervision who has been ordered to make restitution. The court is to order a 5 percent surcharge to support the administrative expenses that result from such a system. In New Jersey, the Victims of Crime Compensation Board is charged with developing a system to track and dispense restitution and other offender payments, financed by a $3 offender assessment deposited into the Criminal Disposition and Revenue Collection Fund.

In Michigan, the probation or parole officer is required to review, twice a year, every case in which restitution was ordered to ensure that payments are being made as ordered. The officer must also perform a final review at least 60 days before the expiration of an offender's probation or parole. If an offender is not paying restitution, the officer must file a written report with the court. Similarly, in Utah, the Corrections Department is responsible for collecting restitution and must file a violation report with the court if a defendant fails to pay.

Accurate information regarding payment must be shared between agencies that play a role in collecting restitution. In Iowa, for example, if probation is revoked for failure to pay restitution, the probation department is to forward the restitution plan, payment balance, and other pertinent information to the corrections department. In Massachusetts, when an offender is ordered to pay restitution to a victim, "the victim has the right to receive . . . a copy of the schedule of restitution payments and the name and telephone number of the probation officer . . . responsible for supervising the defendant's payments."

Single System for Collecting Restitution and Other Court-Ordered Payments

Some states have attempted to improve the collection of restitution and other court-ordered payments—such as court fees—through a single system. Washington was an early leader in this area, devising a system for collecting an offender's legal financial obligation that combines into one debt the restitution, statutorily imposed crime victim compensation fees, court costs, court-appointed attorney fees, and other costs assessed by the court against an offender. When moneys are collected from the offender for the legal financial obligation, restitution is to be paid first. Other states, including Alabama and New Jersey, also address collecting such costs through a single entity.

Attachment of State Payments to the Defendant

Some states allow by statute various state payments, which ordinarily would first go to the defendant, to be used to satisfy restitution orders. For example, Maryland and Wisconsin laws allow a defendant's lottery prize to be used to pay restitution. Iowa requires that any witness fees paid to an inmate be applied toward restitution. In Tennessee, 15 percent of the amount raised by the sale of inmate arts and crafts must be applied to restitution. Several states provide that whenever a prisoner is awarded damages in a civil suit, the award must be used to pay restitution.

In Montana, any time a prisoner accumulates more than $200 in his or her prison inmate trust account, the excess is forfeited and used to pay any outstanding restitution. Similarly, Iowa law requires its director of corrections to deduct restitution payments, according to the inmate's restitution plan, from the inmate's account, which consists of money received by the inmate from any source.

In some states, a defendant's bond may be used to satisfy a restitution order. Under an Illinois appellate court ruling, courts may order that bond proceeds be applied to restitution even when someone other than the defendant provided the money.

Wages from Prison Work Programs

By law, many prison work programs must direct a portion of the offender's wages to the payment of restitution. Some statutes apply only to programs within the prison, others to programs run by private industry using prison labor, and still others to work-release programs. Because California law requires a deduction from prison wages for the payment of restitution, a California appellate court has ruled that trial courts may presume the payment of restitution from prison wages unless evidence shows that a defendant would be ineligible.

Often, statutes prioritize how an inmate's work program wages should be allocated to pay any restitution and other payments an inmate is required to make. For example, Louisiana law provides that wages from its prison industries program will be paid in the following order: (1) federal and state taxes and Social Security deductions, (2) 30 percent of the remainder after tax and Social Security deductions to the victims of crimes committed by the offender to the extent of their loss and thereafter to any state compensation fund, (3) 20 percent of the remainder after tax and Social Security deductions to the Department of Corrections, and (4) 40 percent of the remainder after tax and Social Security deductions to the inmate's spouse and children. If an inmate has no spouse or children, this portion shall be paid to any victims of crimes committed by the offender to the extent of their loss and thereafter to any state compensation fund. The amount remaining is deposited into the inmate's personal fund.

Revoking Probation or Parole

States generally provide that probation or parole may be revoked for failure to pay restitution. The offender's failure must be willful. Because this can be hard to prove, the remedy is not widely invoked. However, in some cases, courts were able to determine that a defendant's failure to pay was intentional. For example, in one case in Illinois, a defendant had accepted a plea agreement under which he was to pay $5 a month. When he did not make the first $5 payment, the court found that his failure to pay was willful because he had given every indication that he was able to pay that amount. Such willful failure to pay was sufficient to revoke the defendant's conditional discharge.

A California defendant had her probation revoked after she had been given numerous chances to pay restitution and had lied to the court regarding a loan application for money to pay restitution. In sentencing the defendant to prison, the trial court judge noted the defendant was not put in prison "for nonpayment of a debt. That's against our constitution. But this defendant is totally failing to comply with the orders of the court." The appellate court upheld the trial court judge's ruling.

Extending Probation or Parole

Some states permit the extension of probation or parole when restitution remains unpaid at the time supervision is to expire. Because restitution is a sentencing condition, extending a defendant's probation or parole enables the criminal justice system to exercise continued jurisdiction over that sentence.

Arkansas law provides that if a defendant fails to make all restitution payments at the time probation ends, the court has authority to continue and extend probation. Under Arizona law, probation may be extended up to 3 additional years for a felony and 1 year for a misdemeanor to allow an offender time to satisfy the requirements of a restitution order. In Kentucky, parole is to be extended until restitution is paid in full.

In contrast, Washington provides for continuing jurisdiction as long as restitution remains outstanding; there is no need to specifically extend supervision.

Using State Entities or Private Collection Agencies to Collect Restitution

Several states have amended their laws to allow restitution orders, particularly orders in default, to be referred to private collection agencies. Some states add the collection fee to the amount due from the defendant, and others deduct this fee from the amount paid by the defendant. Under Alabama law, district attorneys are authorized to establish special restitution recovery divisions. On written notification that a defendant has defaulted in payment of restitution, the division may collect or enforce such orders. A collection fee of 30 percent of the outstanding amount is added to the debt. The district attorney's office is authorized to retain 75 percent of that collection fee, with the remaining 25 percent to be used by the circuit court for operating expenses. The district attorney's office is authorized to contract with a private collection agency to collect outstanding debts.

Kansas has taken a different approach to restitution collection. Under Kansas law, the attorney general is authorized to contract with certain entities to collect restitution and other court costs. The list of approved collection agencies is then published for use by courts and victims. Collection entities receive a fee of up to 33 percent of the amount collected, which is to be deducted from, not added to, the amount owed by the defendant. Meanwhile, at least three states—California, Iowa, and Virgina—allow the restitution debt to be referred to the state taxation authorities for collection.

Converting Restitution Orders to Civil Judgments

Most states allow restitution orders to be converted to civil judgments, especially when restitution remains unpaid at the end of the defendant's probation or parole. In some states, a restitution order is automatically entered as a civil judgment, whereas in others, the victim is authorized to have an order entered as a civil judgment. Kansas places an additional burden on the victim, requiring the victim to pay court costs for entering such a judgment. In some states, the conversion to a civil judgment happens immediately; in others, the conversion or entry takes place only when a defendant defaults on the payment.

CURRENT ISSUES

Lack of Data

Data are generally lacking on the amount of restitution ordered and collected. In the few states that have data on the gross amount of restitution collected, insufficient information is available on the percentage of restitution collected. Until the information is available, states will continue to be hampered in their efforts to improve restitution collection.

Victim Enforcement of Restitution Orders Converted to Civil Judgments

As noted, most states provide for unpaid restitution orders to be converted to and enforced as civil judgments. However, few crime victims understand the means available to enforce such judgments. The California Victim Compensation and Government Claims Board, formerly the California State Board of Control, has attempted to address the problem by developing a simple brochure for crime victims. The brochure describes procedures for converting a restitution order to a civil judgment and investigating the assets of the defendant.

CONCLUSION

State legislatures and criminal justice experts alike have recognized that holding a convicted offender financially responsible for the harm caused by the crime is a proper criminal sanction. They also recognize the importance of restitution in promoting the recovery of the crime victim. However, until the process of collecting restitution improves, these twin benefits cannot be fully realized. This process must begin before the restitution is ordered, with a thorough investigation of the defendant's assets and earning abilities and the court's ability to preserve those assets when necessary. At the same time, a state must have a system in place to monitor compliance with restitution orders and the means to enforce the orders. With increased focus on all aspects of collection, states have the potential to make restitution orders far more meaningful.

QUESTIONS FOR REVIEW AND DISCUSSION

1. What is restitution? Does it work to deter criminal behavior? Why or why not? Explain.
2. How are restitution orders enforced?
3. Can probation or parole be revoked if restitution is not paid by the offender? Why or why not? Explain.
4. What are some interstate variations relating to the payment of restitution?
5. Can criminal restitution orders eventually be resolved through civil courts? Discuss.

37

High Anxiety Offenders in Correctional Settings

It's Time for Another Look

Shelley Johnson Listwan, Kimberly Gentry Sperber,
Lisa Murphy Spruance, and Patricia Van Voorhis

Adapted from Shelley Johnson Listwan, Kimberly Gentry Sperber, Lisa Murphy Spruance, and Patricia Van Voorhis, "High Anxiety Offenders in Correctional Settings: It's Time for Another Look." *Federal Probation* 68: 43–50, 2004.

Reprinted by permission from the Administrative Office of the U.S. Courts.

Over decades, various psychological classification systems have staked a clear position for the neurotic, high anxiety offender. We have accumulated evidence across four studies that find the neurotic group of offenders to be of particular interest to correctional practitioners and policy makers. They have made poor adjustments to prison, had the highest long-term recidivism rates, performed poorly in a cognitive skills intervention and assist in differentiating child molesters. The findings also illustrate that personality is an important factor across a number of different samples, lending support for the reliability of the Jesness Inventory.

Psychological, personality-based classification systems have been used since the 1960s to develop differential treatment and supervision plans for offenders (Van Voorhis, 2000). This approach assumed that, even apart from their risk of re-offending, offenders were not all alike and that no single treatment modality worked with all types of offenders across the full spectrum of correctional settings (Warren, 1971; Palmer, 1974). In support, the early proponents of differential treatment found that offenders who were placed in treatment modalities matched to personality characteristics were more likely to perform better than those who were inappropriately placed (Jesness, 1971; Palmer, 1974, 2002; Warren, 1983).

More contemporary writings place personality among a larger group of offender *responsivity* factors (Andrews, Bonta, and Hoge, 1990), including learning styles, motivation levels, intellectual functioning, and other traits, which are likely to become barriers to the success of some types of interventions. Notwithstanding the promising results of studies conducted through the 1970s and 1980s, reponsivity remains under-researched and seldom considered in correctional practice. Indeed, responsivity is a frequent topic of discussion in correctional policy meetings, non-empirical writings, and staff training, but it is seldom structured into current correctional practice or research.

This article summarizes the results of four recent studies that employed an offender-based personality typology (using the Jesness Inventory, 1996) to examine the importance of personality in prison adjustment, long-term offender recidivism, success in cognitive programming, and dynamics of child molestation. Across these samples of male offenders, we found a consistent pattern suggesting that high-anxiety offenders, those referred to as neurotic offenders on the personality classification systems, are distinct from other offenders in extremely important ways. The findings urge renewed consideration not only of offender personality but also of a distinct type of offender who receives limited attention in contemporary correctional treatment.

As noted in more detailed descriptions of the offender personality typologies (e.g., see Warren, 1971; Van Voorhis, 1994; Van Voorhis and Sperber, 1999), the neurotic personality type is one of four offender personality types common to the various personality classification systems (Megargee and Bohn, 1979; Quay, 1983; Jesness, 1988, 1996; Warren, 1983). The most common types and their descriptions are as follows:

I-level, as measured by the Jesness Inventory, identifies nine personality types. Among adults, these can be collapsed into the following four types (Van Voorhis, 1994) that are of primary interest to the present study: (a) antisocial, who are described as manipulative, hostile, and possessing antisocial values and peers; (b) neurotic, or highly anxious, defensive, and insecure; (c) dependent, described as dependent, followers, who do not evidence antisocial values/attitudes; and (d) situational, who are prosocial, conforming, and, at times, naive. The pattern across various I-level studies finds that types comprising the antisocial offenders (e.g., Aa, CFC, MP) and the neurotic offenders most often differentiate offenders in terms of their success in program (e.g., Heide, 1983; Jesness, 1971; Palmer, 1974, 2002; Warren, 1983), their offense patterns (e.g., Harris, 1979; Heide, 1992, 1999), and their prison adjustments (Van Voorhis, 1994).

In narrowing our focus to the neurotic offender, it is important to remember that anxiety can exist both as a state of mind and as a personality trait. The type of neuroticism discussed here does not relate to the general feeling of anxiety that most experience in response to situational pressures (e.g., anxiety over a licensing exam or a loved one's illness). Here we are concerned with anxiety as a trait, an enduring characteristic that more persistently influences individual perceptions and behavior. Studies conclude that individuals higher in trait anxiety are consistently more prone to perceive greater danger in their relationships and to respond with greater elevations of situational or state anxiety (Speilberger, 1985). Individuals with high trait anxiety, often called negative affectivity, tended to have a very negative view of themselves, to worry more often, and to dwell on frustrations and disappointments (Watson and Clark, 1984). Moreover, individuals high in neuroticism were shown to be more distressed on average in comparison to low neuroticism subjects and to have lower thresholds for responding to stressful events (Bolger and Schillings, 1991). Although some individuals may experience these feelings as a state of mind during times of stress, those high in negative affectivity manifest these feelings even in the absence of stress (Watson and Clark, 1984).

Although personality was neglected for many years in criminology, recent research finds it to be an important predictor of behavior. For example, research by Caspi, Moffitt, Silva, Stouthamer-Loeber, Kreuger, and Schmutte (1994) found that low constraint and negative emotionality were predictors of criminal behavior regardless of age, geographic location, race, and gender. Further, constraint and negative emotionality emerged as correlates among life-course persistent offenders (Kreuger, Schmutte, Caspi, Moffitt, Campbell, and Silva, 1994). Traits pertaining to negative emotionality and low constraint were also implicated in relationship difficulties (Moffitt, 1993), and health-risk behaviors (e.g., violent crime, alcohol dependence, sexual behavior, and dangerous driving habits. Finally, Agnew, Brezina, Wright, and Cullen (2002) found that "strain is more likely to lead to delinquency among those high in negative emotionality/low constraint" (p. 63). Importantly, the study also concluded that those high in negative emotionality and low in constraint did not engage in delinquency in the absence of strain.

Since their inception, correctional, psychological classification systems have staked a clear position for the neurotic, high anxiety, offender. With youth in California, these delinquents were diagnosed as either neurotic anxious or neurotic acting-out according to the Interpersonal Maturity Level (I-level) classification system (Warren et al., 1986; Palmer, 2002). In the Federal Bureau of Prisons, the Quay Adult Internal Management System (Quay, 1983) identified a neurotic anxious type for adults. The Quay System for juvenile offenders put forward a similar type (Quay and Parsons, 1972). Finally, the Megargee MMPI based Prison Typology (Megargee and Bohn, 1979) notes types Baker, George, and Jupiter. All are described as dealing with forms of trait anxiety.

Early writings offered some concerns about these individuals, as exemplified by the type descriptions of the neurotic offender. For example, sources asserted that neurotic offenders made poor adjustments to prison settings; needed to be placed away from predatory inmates; did not improve without intervention; and were likely to amplify rather than resolve acting-out behaviors when confronted by staff. Warren described this group of individuals as having a "good deal of internal 'wear and tear' involving anxiety, guilt, a 'bad me' self image, 'negative life script' distorted perceptions, and dysfunctional behavior." Delinquency has some private meaning and is not intended simply for material gain or as a response to peer pressure. It may involve acting out of a family problem, an identity crisis, or a long-standing internal conflict. These individuals may also show symptoms of emotional disturbance, chronic or intense depression, or psychosomatic complaints.

Both the Preston Topology Study (Jesness, 1971) and the Community Treatment Project (CTP) in California (Palmer, 1974, 2002; Warren, 1983) reported that outcomes were better for these youth under conditions of differential treatment that accommodated anxiety and targeted it for treatment. Differential treatment also involved "matching" offenders to officers and staff trained to counsel issues related to anxiety. When anxiety was accommodated, the neurotic delinquents showed more impressive treatment gains than most of the other groups (Palmer, 1974). But the development of correctional strategies for these offenders ceased in the 1970s.

Current thinking on offender therapy favors cognitive behavioral programs targeted to thinking skills, thinking errors, high risk situations, and coping strategies. This focus is well-supported by a large body of research, and confirmed by several meta analyses conducted in the 1990s. To facilitate consistent delivery, most current cognitive behavioral models are directed by manuals for facilitators. Some are scripted; most suggest activities such as role-playing exercises, thinking reports and group discussions. These are not intended to be confrontational, a well known difficulty for highly anxious offenders. One would think that an emphasis on how to think through difficult situations and to deal with emotions would be useful to such offenders; however the same models do not appear to have been developed with anxiety in mind.

In referring to offender anxiety as a "responsivity trait" (Andrews and Bonta, 1998; Andrews, Bonta, and Hoge, 1990), it is assumed to affect one's ability to succeed in correctional programs and environments. A number of authors suggest that we should consider these attributes when screening offenders into programs, so that they are not "harmed" by the intervention or expected to participate in an intervention that does not work. Unfortunately, once we have screened neurotic offenders out of programs (if we do) there appear to be no contemporary alternatives. Consequently, the current generation of offender programming has little to say, directly, about anxiety. Research examining these concerns is summarized below.

DESCRIPTION OF THE STUDIES

The four studies measured personality according to the Jesness Inventory (Jesness, 1996). In addition to 11 personality scales, the JI provides subtype scales, which correspond to earlier personality subtypes identified by the Interpersonal Maturity Classification System. Nine subtypes are put forward by the Jesness Inventory. For adults, these nine types may be collapsed further into four types (see Van Voorhis, 1994): (a) antisocial, (b) neurotic, (c) dependent, and (d) situational.

Study 1: The first study explored the comparative viability of several psychological classification systems for classifying adult male prison inmates. The relationship between the types identified by each classification system and prison adjustment emerged as an important issue. The study sampled two groups of federal inmates newly admitted to prison between September 1986 and July 1988; (a) 179 maximum custody inmates (response rate = 76%); and (b) 190 minimum custody inmates (response rate = 90%). At prison admission, the study participants completed detailed background interviews and several psychological inventories, including the Jesness Inventory. Inmates were tracked for 6 to 9 months. Follow-up data cited in this paper consisted of self-report measures of prison misconducts and stress. The self-report and staff measures were cumulative scales and had internal consistency (alpha values) greater than 0.70. Stress was measured by the Center for Epidemiological Studies Depression Scale (Radloff, 1977). The study utilized bivariate analyses. See Van Voorhis (1994) for a more detailed account of the measures and methodology of the study.

Study 2: The second study explored whether personality, as measured by the Jesness Inventory, was related to recidivism. A longitudinal design examined long-term recidivism rates for the study 1 cohort of federal prison inmates (n = 277) over a 10 to 12 year period.

Recidivism data, collected through NCIC in 1998, were available for approximately 85 percent of the time 1 sample. Even history analysis was employed to determine the relationship between the four collapsed Jesness Inventory types and outcome. Failure was defined as any new arrest and arrest for a specific charge including drugs, property offense, or violence. Control variables included race and a modified version of the Salient Factor Score (Hoffman and Beck, 1985). See Listwan (2001) for a more detailed account of the measures and methodology of the study.

Study 3: The third study, Phase II of the Georgia Cognitive Skills Experiment, examined the effectiveness of the Reasoning and Rehabilitation (R&R) (Ross and Fabiano, 1985) program on parolees across the State of Georgia. A focal issue of the study was whether some types of offenders responded differently to the cognitive skill intervention than others. Using an experimental design, male parolees were randomly assigned to either the R&R program group (n=574) or the control group (n=581) that received standard parolee services without the R&R program.

Program effectiveness was determined in part, by comparing experimental group and control group "failure" during a 30 month follow up period. Event history analysis was utilized and failure was defined as a return to prison. Control variables used in the study included risk, a history of violence, IQ, reading level, education, marital status, age, and race. See Van Voorhis, Spruance, Ritchie, Listwan, Seabrook, and Pealer (2001) for a more detailed account of the measures and methodology of the study.

Study 4: This study examined whether an existing offender typology—the Jesness Inventory—could differentiate among child molesters on such characteristics as denial, empathy, endorsement of cognitive distortions, and self-esteem. The study sample was comprised of 85 men convicted of a sexual offense against a minor; all were involved in correctional treatment at the time of the study. Each participant completed the Jesness Inventory as well as four other validated assessments designed to measure the dependent variables: Sex Offence Information Questionnaire Revised (Hogue, 1998), the Interpersonal Reactivity Index (Davis, 1983), the Abel and Becker Cognitions Scale (Abel, Gore, Holland, Camp, Becker, and Rathner, 1989), and the Rosenberg Self-Esteem Scale (Rosenberg, 1965). Additional data collected from each participant's program file measured offender demographics, offense characteristics, victim characteristics, and the offender's risk of reoffending as measured by the Static-99 (Hanson, 1997). The analysis used analysis of variance and analysis of covariance strategies. See Sperber (2003) for a more detailed discussion of the methodology and measures used in the study.

RESULTS

Study 1: Neurotic offenders had the highest proportion of self-reported aggression in both the maximum custody and minimum custody groups. Results were significant for the minimum custody sample ($p < 0.01$) but not the maximum custody group. More telling, perhaps, were findings for stress and depression experienced shortly into the prison term. Neurotic offenders scored the highest on the CESD scale. Results were statistically significant ($p < 0.05$) for both the minimum custody and maximum custody groups. On other measures, neurotic offenders performed similar to the antisocial type, or were not differentiated in any meaningful way from the other three personality types.

Study 2: The findings from the discrete-time, event history analysis of the effect of personality on recidivism indicated that personality contributed to the prediction of criminal behavior even when controlling for race and risk. More importantly, the highest probabilities for re-arrest were among the neurotics, followed by the antisocials, situationals, and dependents. The neurotics and antisocials had a significantly higher probability of experiencing re-arrest than the dependents.

The neurotics alone were significantly different from the other three types when predicting drug offenses. They were more likely to become involved in substance abuse than the other personality types, and they incurred the offenses in closer proximity to their release than the other offenders. Personality was not significant in the models predicting property or violent offenses.

Study 3: Phase II of the Georgia Cognitive Skills Experiment raised the question of whether offenders' personalities affected how they responded to a cognitive skills program, and the question was answered in the affirmative. Results from discrete-time, event history analysis indicated that neurotics responded adversely to the R&R program; neurotic offenders who participated in the program were returned to prison at significantly higher rates than neurotic offenders in the control group. Although only 35.3 percent of neurotic control group members recidivated, over half (54.8 percent) of neurotic experimental group members were reincarcerated by the end of the 30-month follow up period. The neurotic X experimental group interaction was significant (B = 0.80; p <0.05), as was the event history analysis model which included controls for risk level, history of violence, IQ, reading level, education, marital status, age, and race (model chi square = 103.25; p. <0.001). In contrast to the detrimental effects of the program on neurotics, parolees classified as antisocial, dependent, or situational improved slightly, though not significantly, by participating in the program (see Van Voorhis et al., 2002).

Study 4: While the results of this study supported the hypothesis that child molesters of varied personality types would differ on key psychological attributes, the extent to which the neurotic child molesters differed from the other personality types was of particular interest. For example, analysis of variance revealed that the personality subtypes differed significantly on three of the dependent measures—self-esteem, personal distress (an affective component of empathy), and fantasy (an intellectual component of empathy). The post hoc comparisons revealed that it was the neurotic child molester that was significantly different from the other three personality types. For example, neurotic child molesters had the highest score on the personal distress scale, meaning that they were the most likely to feel emotional discomfort in the presence of another's suffering. In addition, the antisocial offenders, situationals, and dependents scored similarly on the fantasy scale. Neurotics scored significantly higher, however, indicating that they were significantly more likely to identify with others on an intellectual level. The neurotic child molesters also evidenced significantly lower self-esteem scores than the other three groups.

CONCLUSIONS

In sum, we have accumulated evidence across four studies that find the neurotic group of offenders to be of particular interest to correctional practitioners and policy makers. They have made poor adjustments to prison, had the highest long-term recidivism rates, and appeared to have been harmed by the most prevalent correctional intervention in use at the present time. Moreover, the neurotic child molesters are different from other child molesters (as well as from stereotypes pertinent to child molesters) in ways that should factor into their treatment and therapy.

These findings are important for several reasons. First, they offer additional support to criminologists researching individual-centered theories of crime. The findings are in contrast to the earlier reviews of personality and crime (e.g., Schuessler and Cressey, 1950; Tennenbaum, 1977; and Waldo and Dinitz, 1967) and claims by researchers such as Vold and Bernard (1986), who argue that personality provides no theoretical relevance to understanding criminal behavior. While accumulating studies are finding a relationship between personality and criminal behavior, many of these studies are conducted with adolescents and young adults (Caspi et al., 1994; Caspi et al., 1997). The present studies note consistent results with respect to adult males.

Three of the studies (1 and 2 were of approximately the same sample) used different samples of offenders to explore the utility of the Jesness Inventory in predicting or differentiating offenders and their behaviors. The consistency of findings across different samples, added to the results of studies cited above, lends strong support to the external validity of findings regarding neurotic offenders.

Accumulating research carries implications for offender risk assessment, correctional management, and offender programming. Although research by Andrews, Bonta, and Hoge (1990) and Gendreau, Little, and Goggin (1996) find that personality is among the strongest predictors of criminal behavior, the "at risk" personality attributes typically referred to involves dimensions associated with antisocial ideation and psychopathy (Andrews and Bonta, 2003) rather than anxiety or neuroticism. Moreover, risk assessment instruments currently in use [e.g., Salient Factor Score (Hoffman and Beck, 1985), Level of Service Inventory-Revised (Andrews and Bonta, 1995), and Wisconsin Risk Assessment System (Baird, Heinz, and Bemus, 1979)] typically do not include measures of personality. Although there are good reasons for this, particularly against including anxiety, evidence is accumulating that anxiety may be a risk factor as well as a responsivity consideration.

More importantly, it may be a risk factor that is exacerbated by the prevailing correctional treatment modalities. To be cautious, this assertion is based upon only one study, whereas anxiety's importance as a risk factor appears across several studies. Even so, the finding pertaining to the cognitive skills intervention is of particular concern (Van Voorhis et al., 2001). Unfortunately, we cannot determine precisely why neurotic offenders become more prone to recidivism following participation in the cognitive skills program. It is possible that a group setting is not appropriate for offenders with neurotic personalities. The pressure of performing skills in front of peers and coaches who routinely evaluate and provide feedback on the use of the skills may further exacerbate their anxiety. Perhaps these facilitators or group members were too confrontational. Consideration might be given to curricular modifications, which could help such offenders to better deal with negative emotions and to develop skills for coping with anxiety-provoking situations. Perhaps these individuals would be better suited to anger management programming (e.g., see Goldstein and Glick, 1987) or to more clinical forms of intervention, but the alternatives have not been researched in the context that we are addressing.

Concerns might also be voiced for interventions that treat sex offenders as if they are all alike. It is not unusual, for example, for a sex offender program to target denial, empathy, and victim awareness. However, neurotic offenders often are not in denial and have capacity for empathy; they simply violate their own values. Again, programs that utilize a certain level of confrontation may be detrimental to, or at least less effective, with neurotic child molesters. Winn (1996), for example, notes that not all sex offenders respond well to confrontation. We may also need to revisit the issue of treating the self-esteem of these individuals. The correctional treatment literature abounds with warnings that self-esteem is not a risk factor and should not be the focus of offender therapy. However, to our knowledge, no studies attend to whether it might be a risk factor for some types of offenders. To further complicate matters, describing these child molesters as being introverted, insecure, and anxious yet possessing emotional empathy in no way suggests that they are "lower risk" offenders. Many of the neurotic child molesters in this study had previous convictions (63 percent). More specifically, many of them had a previous conviction for a sex offense (48.1 percent). Thus, it must not have been unusual for this group to violate their own values, which, for the most part, were prosocial.

Whatever the chosen alternatives, we are reminded poignantly of three assertions that emerged from the earliest research on neurotic offenders. First, they "do not get better on their own; they do need treatment" (Warren, 1983). Second, their antisocial behavior is amplified by anxiety-provoking situations, including some types of staff confrontations intended to correct behavior (Warren et al., 1966; Palmer, 2002). Third, when matched to appropriate rather than inappropriate interventions, they achieved more favorable results than other delinquents (Palmer, 1974); when they were not treated for their anxiety, their failure rate was atypically high. Appropriate treatment goals for these offenders involved reduction or resolution of internal conflicts, comfort with one's own needs and feelings, reductions in the inappropriate use of defense mechanisms, appropriate disengagement from the dysfunctional family problems, increased sense of self worth and improved capacity for enjoyment (Warren, 1983). Arguably, such treatment goals have not seen the light of day for a long time in this field.

QUESTIONS FOR REVIEW AND DISCUSSION

1. Who are high-anxiety offenders? What personality characteristics do they have? Discuss.
2. Discuss four studies where offender-based personality typologies were used to describe inmates. What were their general characteristics?
3. How does personality relate to classifying offenders for incarceration and subsequent institutional adjustment?
4. What are the general findings relating to recidivism among prisoners identified as high-anxiety offenders? Discuss.
5. What are some of the implications of these findings for offender risk assessment and treatment? How well can risk assessments identify offender needs and address them?
6. How can such assessments minimize recidivism of high-anxiety offenders? Discuss.

38

Managing Offenders with Special Health Needs

Highest and Best Use Strategies

Elizabeth Anderson
and Theresa Hilliard

Adapted from Elizabeth Anderson and Theresa Hilliard, "Managing Offenders with Special Needs: Highest and Best Use Strategies." *Corrections Today* 67: 58–61, 2005. Reprinted by permission from the American Correctional Association.

A major challenge for the corrections field is to develop effective strategies to address the unique requirements of offenders with special health needs. These requirements include appropriate housing, easily accessible health services, access to programming and effective release planning. To aim for the highest and best use of both physical plant and human resources, it is important to develop cost-effective, less restrictive strategies that mainstream offenders with special health needs, keeping them in the general population for as long as possible. These strategies promote independence and self-care in offenders. To the extent possible, nonmedical personnel and trained offenders can be used to assist special needs offenders. Since the vast majority of incarcerated offenders are released to the community, another benefit of these strategies is that they better prepare a special needs offender for making a successful transition to the community upon release. While most of these offenders return to the community, a small number may become sufficiently ill to be considered for compassionate early release.

When strategies that promote mainstreaming are not used, a likely outcome will be an approach that further institutionalizes offenders with special health needs and does not prepare them for release to the community. This approach medicalizes rather than normalizes the management of offenders with special health needs. At times, costly infirmary beds are used for some offenders who do not require the high level of care available there. Taking this approach can significantly increase the cost of incarceration for these offenders, as infirmary beds are among the most expensive beds within a prison to operate.

OFFENDERS WITH SPECIAL HEALTH NEEDS

There are many categories of patients with special health needs. They include the elderly, the terminally ill, patients with communicable and/or chronic diseases, offenders with physical disabilities, patients who are mentally disabled and those who are developmentally disabled. The size of some of these populations remains static. However, correctional institutions across the country are experiencing a rapid increase in both the number and proportion of elderly offenders.

Elderly Offenders

The combined impact of the graying of the overall population, sentencing policies, such as mandatory-minimum drug sentences and three-strikes laws, and continuing developments in medical science have led to significant increases in the number of older offenders in correctional institutions. There is no general agreement about the age at which offenders are considered to be elderly. In this article, elderly will be defined as offenders 50 years and older. This age has been recognized by researchers and health care professionals working in corrections and is supported by data on offenders incarcerated at the Washington State Department of Corrections. The elderly offender population is growing at a faster rate than the overall incarcerated population. In 1993, elderly offenders made up 6.7 percent of the Washington DOC population. In 2004, they had increased to 10.6 percent. During that same time period, the number of Washington's older offenders increased by 161 percent, while the overall offender population only increased 64 percent. With the aging of the baby boomers, the growth rate of the elderly offender population will continue to be high. This growth will drive a corresponding increase in the need for housing, health care services, programming and release planning services tailored to meet their needs.

Older offenders used a disproportionately large amount of the health care resources in the Washington DOC. In late 2004, they accounted for 16 percent of the on-site medical visits and 25 percent of the off-site medical trips. The elderly represented 48 percent of the admissions to community hospitals, which accounted for 51 percent of overall hospital costs. They represented between 40 percent and 50 percent of the DOC's patients with cardiac conditions, hypertension, diabetes and renal disorders. In fiscal year 2003, offenders 50 years and older accounted for 50 percent of the deaths.

While 42 percent of Washington's elderly offenders have multiple chronic conditions, it is important to note that the majority of older offenders (58 percent) do not. The Washington DOC has not done a detailed profile of these relatively healthier, older offenders, but it is a fair assumption that most of them are in the general population with no special provisions for housing, services or programming.

"Old" Young Offenders

Many offenders under age 50 are physiologically older than what would be expected given their chronological age. For many of these individuals, a history of drug abuse and multiple sexual partners, as well as not receiving health care on a regular basis prior to incarceration have contributed to their physiological aging. The housing, health services and programming needs of these individuals are very similar to those of elderly offenders. The population at Ahtanum View Corrections Center, Washington's minimum-security prison that is a secure assisted-living facility, reflects this similarity. While the majority of offenders at Ahtanum View are age 50 and over, typically about 40 percent of the institution's population is younger. The age range of offenders at Ahtanum View has included offenders from their 20s to their 90s.

Using data from the DOC's health services database, an offender having multiple chronic conditions was used as an indicator of health status. In October 2004, there were 1,710 offenders under the age of 50 who had more than one of the following chronic conditions: diabetes, HIV/AIDS, renal disease, cardiac conditions, chronic obstructive pulmonary disease, asthma and emphysema. These 1,710 offenders represented 11 percent of Washington's overall prison population; however, they accounted for a disproportionately high share of the use and cost of medical services. They were responsible for 19 percent of all community hospital admissions and 19 percent of community hospital costs.

The number of offenders 49 years and younger with multiple chronic conditions is more than double the 737 elderly offenders with these conditions. When planning for the future resources to support offenders with special health needs, DOCs with offender populations similar to Washington's should focus both on elderly offenders and on younger offenders who are in such poor health that they are high users of health services.

Physically Handicapped

The physically handicapped include individuals with impairments in mobility, vision, hearing and/or speech. The Washington DOC uses individual health status reports to alert staff to any special health care equipment, restrictions on activities and other considerations that offenders with special needs have. Data from these reports enable DOC staff to identify offenders with physical handicaps.

Mobility Impaired

A straightforward strategy to accommodate offenders who have difficulty walking is to preferentially assign them to facilities that are compliant with the Americans With Disabilities Act (ADA). For this to work, a correctional department has to have sufficient ADA beds at all custody levels. Concentrating offenders with impaired mobility in a few barrier-free facilities also supports developing programs to train other offenders to provide assistance such as pushing wheelchairs.

Four percent of the Washington DOC's offenders use canes, walkers or wheelchairs. The department's classification staff have been successful in concentrating these offenders in a few facilities. Obviously, placement in a disability-friendly environment is not the only factor in facility assignment. Monroe Corrections Center, the department's statewide medical referral center for the most seriously ill male patients, has the most mobility-impaired offenders. Excluding the male offenders at Monroe, 50 percent of those using canes and walkers and 76 percent of wheelchair users are concentrated at three fully ADA-compliant facilities.

Blind and Deaf Offenders

About 110 offenders in Washington's correctional facilities have significant visual or hearing impairments. Fewer than 20 of these individuals are totally blind or deaf. Accommodations need to be tailored to each individual's disability, environment and activities. In the late 1990s, the DOC established a new position, the deaf offender services manager, to work with deaf, and subsequently blind, offenders to set up accommodation plans. With appropriate accommodations, blind and deaf offenders can live in general population. However, at times, blind and deaf offenders have been assigned to live in infirmaries at institutions where staff are not knowledgeable about accommodating their special needs.

Some examples of accommodations blind offenders receive are mobility instruction, canes, and tape recorders for listening to books and recording correspondence. Blind offenders are also given computers capable of supporting their going to school and using the law library. Deaf offenders are given pagers to alert them to announcements on the prison's public address system. To support deaf offenders going to school and using the law library, they have access to computers, tutors and readers. Sign language interpreters are made available for activities such as health care appointments, classes and meetings with a deaf offender's classification counselor. In addition, smoke detectors designed for the deaf are installed in their cells.

SPECIAL MEDICAL HOUSING

Standard prison housing units get progressively more costly to build, staff and operate as the custody level of offenders they house increases. Similarly, there is a spectrum of special medical housing that is progressively more costly as the offenders they are designed for have increasing levels of medical and physical disability.

There are four levels of special medical housing: environmental support, assisted living, extended care and infirmary care. Highest and best use is achieved when offenders are assigned to the simplest and least restrictive setting that meets their needs and provides the appropriate support and services. The first two levels, environmental support and assisted living, are general population housing with straight-forward modifications such as ramps and grab bars. Residents typically go to the clinic for medical care. The two more complex levels, extended care and infirmary care, are designed and operated to care for patients who, if they were in the community, would be in a nursing home or in a hospice. Infirmary patients generally need a higher level of skilled care for short periods of time. For highest and best use, infirmary patients move to extended care as their condition improves. Extended care patients need less skilled care, but continue to need care over a long period of time.

Highest and best use is hard to achieve in the many prisons that only have general population housing units and infirmaries—the two ends of the spectrum. The full range of special medical beds needs to be available to patients at all custody levels. To estimate the number and type of special medical beds needed in the future, factors such as caseload forecasts by age cohort, changes in sentencing guidelines, and the demographics and health profile of offender populations should be considered.

Offenders with special health needs typically need assistance with one or more daily living activities. These activities include walking, dressing, using the toilet, bathing, eating, taking medications, and transferring to and from bed, a wheelchair, the bath and the toilet. Medication assistance includes reminding an inmate/patient when it is time to take medications, handing a container of medication to a patient and opening containers a patient cannot. This non-medical personal care is the same kind of assistance many people in the community give ailing and disabled relatives to support their living as independently as possible. In a prison setting, most of this assistance can be provided by non-medical personnel and trained, supervised offenders. National correctional standards allow an offender, working under staff supervision and with proper training, to assist impaired offenders on a one-on-one basis with most daily living activities. The standards do not permit offenders to assist patients with their medications.

Environmental Support

The environmental support housing level is a general population housing unit for offenders who can take care of themselves with very limited support. Physical plant modifications (e.g., grab bars, ramps, and handicapped-accessible toilets, sinks and bathing facilities) support independent living. It makes sense to place these units close to areas such as the dining hall and medical clinic and/or to make some services available in the unit (e.g., meals, pill lines and programming).

Assisted Living

Offenders living in these units can take care of themselves, but also have recurring need for support. With appropriate training and supervision, nonmedical personnel and offender volunteers can assist residents with daily living activities. Aides and licensed practical nurses can provide most of the additional help needed. Physical plant and location considerations are similar to environmental support units. Patients in these units typically go to the clinic for medical care.

Extended Care

Patients in these units need daily care over an extended period of time. Nursing aides and licensed practical nurses do much of the work since patients require a lower level of skilled care. Care is similar to what community nursing homes and hospices provide. Patients who are terminally ill or need ongoing care for chronic diseases, including Alzheimer's, or are in rehabilitation after a stroke or surgery, live in these units. Terminally ill patients can live in extended care units or in infirmaries, depending on the services they need.

Infirmary

Infirmaries provide skilled nursing care by registered nurses 24 hours a day, seven days a week. Since infirmaries are the costliest settings, the goal is to move patients to extended care as their condition improves. Infirmary patients include those who were recently discharged from hospitals and those who need observation to see if they should be sent to a hospital or emergency room. Patients also include those who are receiving intravenous or other advanced therapies and some who are terminally ill.

EARLY MEDICAL RELEASE

According to a 2003 correctional health care survey by the American Correctional Association, at least 17 states have compassionate early release programs for offenders with serious health problems who pose a low risk to public safety. This shifts the cost of care to payers such as Medicaid, Medicare, Veterans Affairs, private insurance or offenders' families. Some programs are limited to terminally ill offenders; others have broader eligibility.

To qualify for Washington's Extraordinary Medical Placement (EMP) program, offenders must be sufficiently ill to require costly care and pose a low risk to public safety. The community custody officers who supervise these offenders can return them to prison if their medical condition significantly improves or if they begin to pose a risk to public safety. In the first few years of the program (mid-1999 through 2003), 180 offenders were evaluated for EMP and 20 percent were placed in the community. Savings to the state averaged $16,400 for each EMP patient placed in the community.

Most offenders referred to Washington's EMP program did not qualify because they presented too high a risk to community safety. Others died or reached their release date before placement could be arranged. Finding appropriate community placement is difficult because many offenders do not have family able to care for them at home. In addition, nursing homes and other community facilities have limited vacancies and often will not accept offenders, due to concerns about their highly vulnerable residents.

A CHALLENGE FOR DOCS

Aging, chronically ill and disabled offenders are a varied population that will continue to challenge DOCs in the future. To manage these offenders effectively and cost efficiently, multiple strategies are needed. To begin, correctional administrators can evaluate the approaches used in the community to assist and care for people with similar problems and adapt them for use in correctional settings.

QUESTIONS FOR REVIEW AND DISCUSSION

1. Who are offenders with special health needs?
2. Why do special-needs offenders pose challenges to departments of corrections in the United States?
3. What sorts of special treatment must special-needs offenders have when reintegrating into their communities? Explain.
4. How much of a risk is posed by offenders with special needs? Are citizens at risk of being victimized by special-needs offenders? Why or why not? Explain.
5. How does assisting special-needs offenders reduce their recidivism and prevent crime?

39

Co-Occurring Substance Abuse and Mental Disorders in Offenders
Approaches, Findings and Recommendations

Stanley Sacks
and Frank Pearson

Adapted from Stanley Sacks and Frank Pearson, "Co-Occurring Substance Abuse and Mental Disorders in Offenders: Approaches, Findings and Recommendations." *Federal Probation* 67: 32–39, 2003.

Reprinted by permission from the Administrative Office of the U.S. Courts.

WHAT ARE CO-OCCURRING DISORDERS?

According to the Center for Substance Abuse Treatment (CSAT), Treatment Improvement Protocol (TIP), Substance Abuse Treatment for Persons With Co-Occurring Disorders,

> . . . Clients said to have co-occurring disorders have one or more mental disorders as well as one or more disorders relating to the use of alcohol and/or other drugs. A diagnosis of co-occurring disorders (COD) occurs when at least one disorder of each type can be established independently of the other and is not simply a cluster of symptoms resulting from the one disorder. (CSAT, 2003, Chapter 1)

Replacing older terms such as "dual diagnosis," "mentally ill chemical abusers," and "comorbidity," "co-occurring disorders" can encompass the full range of mental disorders, including depression, mood disorders, schizophrenia and personality disorders. This article summarizes the research on the prevalence of COD in offender populations, and the implications for treatment. Some principles and approaches guiding the treatment of offenders with COD are reviewed, the emerging evaluation research reports are reviewed, and recommendations for treatment and future research are provided.

PREVALENCE AND SERIOUSNESS OF THE PROBLEM

Prevalence denotes, within a specific population, the percentage of persons who have a particular disorder, while incidence denotes the percentage of a population with new cases (e.g., in a six-month period) (Merriam-Webster, 2003; Hendrie et al., 2001). In the 1980s and 1990s, substance abuse treatment programs reported that 50 to 75 percent of their clients had co-occurring mental disorders, while mental health clinics reported that between 20 and 50 percent of their clients had a co-occurring substance use disorder (see Sacks et al., 1997 for a summary of studies). The prevalence of mental illness and substance abuse among incarcerated offenders was examined by Powell, Holt, and Fondacaro (1997) in a review of 13 studies published between 1982 and 1995. The percentages of offenders who were reported to have diagnoses of common types of mental illness and substance use (not necessarily COD) compiled from the eight most recent of these studies (published from 1990 through 1997) are shown in Table 1.

Recent surveys by the Bureau of Justice found that "16 percent of State prison inmates, 7 percent of Federal inmates, and 16 percent of those in local jails reported either a mental condition or an overnight stay in a mental hospital" (Ditton, 1999). Direct evidence on the prevalence of COD among offenders has been reported, some of which indicates that the incidence of COD is increasing. *The Survey of Inmates of Local Jails—1983,* which compiled interview responses from 5,785 inmates in 407 institutions, categorized 15.4 percent as both mentally ill and substance abusing (Canales-Portalatin, 1995). A randomized, stratified sample of 1,829 delinquent youth ages 10–18 admitted to the Cook County (Chicago) Juvenile Temporary Detention Center found that nearly 50 percent of detainees were diagnosed with alcohol or drug dependence, and that almost 66 percent of boys and 73 percent of girls were diagnosed with one or

TABLE 1   Prevalence of some typical disorders as reported in studies of jails and prisons published 1990 to 1997

Disorder	N of Studies	Median %	Range
Alcohol dependence	8	73%	47% to 82%
Drug dependence	6	59%	32% to 64%
Antisocial	7	51%	41% to 64%
Depression	7	10%	5% to 17%
Dysthymia	7	7%	2% to 11%
Schizophrenia	6	4%	2% to 5%

Source: These statistics were computed from the data presented in Tables 1, 2, and 4 in Powell, Holt, and Fondacaro (1997). Some used 6-month criteria, others lifetime criteria; see the source for details.

more psychiatric disorders. These statistics provide the context for the incidence of COD, with 28 percent of the sample exhibiting both a conduct/behavior disorder and a substance abuse/dependence disorder (National Institute of Justice, 2000: 31; National Institutes of Mental Health, 2002).

A clinical assessment of offenders in the Colorado Department of Corrections shows trends of COD over the last decade. Kleinsasser and Michaud (2002), counting current diagnoses, not lifetime, report that mental disorders within this offender population increased from 3.9 to 14.0 percent between 1991 and 2001, and about three quarters of these had substance use disorders.

The challenges of treating clients with serious mental illness (SMI) and substance use disorders are apparent. A study of 121 clients with psychoses included 36 percent who were diagnosed with a co-occurring substance use disorder; this latter group spent twice as many days in hospital over the two years prior to treatment as did their non-substance abusing counterparts (Crome, 1999, p. 156; Menezes et al., 1996). Other studies (Drake et al., 1998) have documented poorer outcomes for clients who have SMI co-occurring with substance use disorders, in terms of higher rates of HIV infection, relapse, rehospitalization, depression, and risk of suicide. Involvement with the criminal justice system further complicates treatment for those with COD, and initiatives specific to the needs and functioning of COD offenders have been developed. The next section begins with a list of principles recommended by experts to guide the treatment of offenders with COD and is followed by a summary of some emerging programs.

APPROACHES TO TREATMENT FOR OFFENDERS WITH COD

In 1999, a meeting of major treatment policy makers introduced a model for COD levels of care, endorsed by the Substance Abuse and Mental Health Services Administration (SAMH-SA), which is defined by four "quadrants" (National Association of State Mental Health Program Directors and National Association of State Alcohol and Drug Abuse Directors, 1999). The quadrant model can be used both to design systems/programs and to determine whether or not a client's treatment is at the appropriate level of care. The disorders and needs of clients in each quadrant are: (1) Less severe mental disorder and less severe substance use disorder—treatment in outpatient setting of either mental health or chemical dependency programs, with consultation or collaboration between settings as needed; (2) More severe mental disorder and less severe substance disorder—treatment in intermediate level mental health programs using integrated case management; (3) Less severe mental disorder and more severe substance disorder—treatment in intermediate level substance use disorder treatment programs, with mental health program collaboration as needed; (4) More severe mental disorder and more severe substance disorder—treatment with intensive, comprehensive and integrated services for both substance use and mental disorders, available in a variety of settings (e.g., correctional institutions, state hospitals, or residential substance abuse treatment programs). Of course, COD is not just a health care problem; concerns of justice and legal rights are involved as well. Treatment should be delivered within the bounds of law and justice, not ignoring these principles (see, for example, Davis, 2003; Denckla and Berman, 2001, The Judge David L. Bazelon Center for Mental Health Law, 2003).

Diversion

In this context, diversion is a strategy of first identifying those COD offenders who are less of a threat to the community, then redirecting them away from the standard flow of criminal justice cases. For example, selected types of arrestees awaiting trial may be diverted to treatment prior to trial or to sentencing. Diversion saves criminal justice resources for more serious crimes and higher-risk offenders, and provides treatment to these individuals much sooner than is possible under normal criminal justice processing. Effective diversion emphasizes ". . . learning how to collaborate with law enforcement personnel. . . and ensuring that clients who are intensively monitored are also provided with adequate treatment to avoid jail recidivism" (Draine and Solomon, 1999: 56).

Screening and Assessment

A program is responsible to conduct screening that identifies those who might harm themselves or others, as well as those who show evidence of an incapacitating mental disorder. Preliminary evidence of COD is uncovered through a basic assessment, which also examines diagnoses, criminal history, and readiness for change, problems and strengths, to provide the counselor with sufficient data for treatment planning. Of course, standardized screening and assessment instruments should be used (CSAT, 2003); Peters and Hills (1997: 10–11) provide an extended listing of some recommended instruments for substance dependence and for mental health. Those researchers we have used and found valuable include, for substance dependence, the ASI (McLellan, Kushner, Metzger, Peters, et al., 1992); for mental health, the Beck Depression Inventory [BDI] (Beck, Steer, and Brown, 1996); the Brief Symptom Inventory [BSI] (Derogatis, 1993); and/or the Symptom Checklist 90 B Revised [SCL-90-R] (Derogatis, 1983).

For in-depth diagnoses, the Diagnostic Interview Schedule [DIS] (Robins, Cottler, Bucholz, and Compton, 1995) and the Structured Clinical Interview for DSM-IV B Patient Version [SCID] (First, Gibbon, Spitzer, and Williams, 1996), but both of these intensive diagnostic instruments require lengthy training even for staff with graduate degrees to learn exactly how to administer and how to score the interviews; also, an interview typically takes one to two hours to administer, and longer to score.

Osher, Steadman and Barr (2002) point out that, in addition to using appropriate instruments, it is important to gather information from other relevant sources (law enforcement, the court, family members) and to engage the offender in assessing his or her own needs. Any special circumstances (gender, age, language skills and comprehension, etc.) must be taken into account in the assessment.

Because symptoms typically change over time, often improving due to stressors or other factors, assessment should be repeated several times during the course of treatment (Peters and Hills, 1997: 25). A full description of the screening and assessment process and the available instruments (not specifically for offenders with COD, but which could be adapted) are found in the recent TIP for COD (CSAT, 2003).

Individualized Treatment Plan

"One size fits all" approaches to treatment of COD offenders simply will not work. Rather, "orientations and treatment activities should be flexibly designed for different diagnostic groups, individuals with different cognitive abilities, and different level of motivation for treatment" (Peters and Hills, 1997: 25). Again, the offender must be encouraged to participate in assessing his or her own needs and in developing his or her own treatment plan. It is especially valuable to consider the offender's input regarding past experiences with mental health or substance abuse treatment in terms of what worked and what didn't (Osher, Steadman, and Barr, 2002).

Pharmacological Treatment

Research has shown that treatment with particular medications is helpful for specific diagnoses of mental illness in particular individual circumstances (U.S. Department of Health and Human Services, 1999; see also National Institute on Drug Abuse, 1999). For example, pharmacological advances over the past decade have produced antipsychotic and other medications with greater effectiveness and fewer side effects (CSAT, 2003). It is generally helpful for mental health clinicians to obtain information about COD clients from the clients' substance abuse treatment counselors as well, in order to design effective treatment for both types of disorders. When desirable medication regimens are prescribed, careful monitoring should be used to ensure that medication compliance is maintained (Osher, Steadman, and Barr, 2002).

Integration of Treatment

> Integrated treatment refers broadly to any mechanism by which treatment interventions for COD are combined within the context of a primary treatment relationship or service setting. . . As such, integrated treatment reflects the longstanding concern within drug abuse programs for treating the whole person and recognizes the importance of ensuring that entry into any one system can provide access to all needed systems: in short, that clients face "no wrong door" in accessing treatment and services. (CSAT, 2003; Executive Summary)

Within offender populations the concept of integrated treatment should also include interventions that address criminal thinking, such as the cognitive-behavioral approaches designed for this purpose.

Experience within the mental health system has led to treatment models that integrate substance use services (CSAT, 1994; Drake and Mueser, 1996; Lehman and Dixon, 1995; Minkoff and Drake, 1991; Zimberg, 1993). In 1998, Drake and colleagues reviewed research emanating from studies conducted within mental health centers, concluding that comprehensive, integrated treatment, "especially when delivered for 18 months or longer, resulted in significant reductions of substance abuse and, in some cases, in substantial rates of remission, as well as reductions in hospital use and/or improvements in other outcomes" (Drake et al., 1998, p. 601). Similarly, studies within substance abuse treatment centers found that the integration of mental health services onsite improved both retention and outcome (Charney et al., 2001; Saxon and Calsyn, 1995; Weisner et al., 2001). The modified TC has demonstrated effectiveness among homeless clients with COD (De Leon, Sacks, Staines, and McKendrick, 2000). It is now recognized that treatment services for COD must be comprehensive (capable of responding to multiple issues), integrated (combining substance abuse and mental health treatment), and continuous (graduating through levels of care) (CSAT, 2003). These integrative models can be adapted for use within the criminal justice system.

Phases of Treatment

Many clinicians view clients as progressing through phases (Drake and Mueser, 1996; McHugo et al., 1995; Osher and Kofoed, 1989; Sacks et al., 1998). Generally, three to four phases are identified, including engagement, stabilization, treatment, and continuing care (aftercare). Psychoeducational approaches are common and clinically useful in the early stages of treatment to help individuals understand both their mental health disorder and substance abuse (Peters and Hills, 1997: 25). The middle phases should focus on mental health and substance abuse treatment, and on changes in criminal thinking and behavior and other problematic behavior patterns. Later phases emphasize community re-entry; the transition from treatment in prison to treatment in the community is especially important. Two crucial tasks are (1) to "identify required community and correctional programs responsible for post-release services" and (2) to "coordinate the transition plan to ensure implementation and avoid gaps in care" (Osher, Steadman, and Barr, 2002: 13-15).

Continuity of Care

Because both mental and substance use disorders tend to be chronic, and because recidivism likewise tends to recur, rehabilitation and recovery for offenders with COD is expected to take months, if not years. As clients move across different service systems, coordination (e.g., Morrissey et al., 1997) is needed to provide coherent care over time. This continuity is essential for the COD offender population, which is particularly susceptible to symptom recurrence, substance abuse relapse, and criminal recidivism.

Studies of criminal justice populations provide evidence of the benefits of continuity of care for those offenders not specifically identified as having COD. For example, at 3 years post-treatment, only 27 percent of those prison program completers who also completed an aftercare program were returned to custody, while three-fourths of the subjects in all other study groups were returned (Wexler et al., 1999b); similar findings were reported by Knight and colleagues (1999) and by Inciardi et al. (1997). Although these studies are subject to selection bias for entry into aftercare, the long-term outcomes suggest support for the use of aftercare as an essential element in sustaining positive treatment effects over time.

EXAMPLES OF PROGRAMMING

Over the past decade, interventions have been implemented to improve COD services delivered to offenders, and several programs for offenders with COD have been developed, most having some features in accord with the principles of effective treatment discussed above. This section provides examples of programming currently in place; however, research is needed to evaluate both the principles and the programs.

Diversion Approaches

Diversion programs can play a role before an offender is sent to jail to await trial (pre-booking diversion), while in jail awaiting trial, or while in jail awaiting sentencing.

PRE-BOOKING PROGRAMS

Pre-booking programs typically involved partnerships between the police and mental health professionals to deal with individuals who appear to have committed less serious offenses (e.g., misdemeanors) as a result of psychiatric problems (and who do not pose a risk of violence) by diverting them to mental health treatment instead of charging these offenders and having them await trial (Lamb, Shaner, Elliot et al., 1995). The other diversion programs summarized here are post-booking programs.

MENTAL HEALTH COURTS

In Mental Health Courts, the judge (as well as making the standard "judicial" decisions) typically takes a more active role than usual in the early stages of case processing. Although some mental health courts have a general caseload, most participants in the San Bernadino Mental Health Court have COD. This program admits defendants charged with nonviolent lower-level felonies, punishable by up to 6 years in prison, and defendants charged with misdemeanors for whom a jail term is otherwise likely. Clinical staff conduct interviews and screening, using a two- to three-week period to collect background information and to stabilize the client on medication. Upon admission, the offender is placed on probation, contingent upon compliance with an individualized treatment contract. Most participants are released into a board-and-care residential treatment facility. Case managers visit each client several times a week to ensure adherence to the treatment contract and delivery of appropriate treatment. Clients participate in a wide array of residential services, including group therapy, anger management, socialization skills, psychotherapy, medication therapy, chemical dependency treatment, budgeting skill training, and drug testing (Bureau of Justice Assistance, 2000b: Chapter 5).

JAIL DIVERSION PROGRAMS

In these programs the judge retains his or her standard role while another party plays a more active role in the screening and processing of potentially eligible psychiatric cases. For example, the District Attorney's Office may take on the screening work. The Kings County (Brooklyn, New York) *Treatment Alternatives for Dually Diagnosed Defendants* (TADD) identifies potential eligible offenders (by the nature of the charges, referrals from mental health or substance abuse treatment providers, etc.) for clinical assessment to determine whether the criteria of COD (diagnosis of both a DSM IV Axis I mental disorder and a substance abuse disorder) are met. The District Attorney's Office determines the plea offer for those who are eligible; if accepted in court, this leads to admission into TADD. Felons (62 percent of the participants) are placed in treatment for 16–24 months, while those with misdemeanor charges enter treatment for shorter terms. As reported this year, 47 percent of those entering TADD go directly into residential treatment, 22 percent are referred to outpatient facilities, 6 percent are placed in crisis beds pending residential treatment, and the remainder are referred to other forms of treatment. Successful TADD completion results in withdrawal of the guilty plea and the charges are dismissed; if the offender is unsuccessful, he or she is sentenced in accordance with the plea offer (District Attorney's Office Kings County NY, 2003).

JAIL OR PRISON APPROACHES

After reviewing seven dual diagnosis treatment programs in state and federal prisons for inmates with COD, Edens, Peters, and Hills (1997: 439) state in summary that

> Key program components include an extended assessment period, orientation/motivational activities, psychoeducational groups, and cognitive behavioral interventions, such as restructuring of "criminal thinking errors," self-help groups, medication monitoring, relapse prevention, and transition into institution or community-based aftercare facilities. Many programs use therapeutic community approaches that are modified to provide (a) greater individual counseling and support, (b) less confrontation, (c) smaller staff caseloads, and (d) cross training of staff. Research is underway in 3 of the 7 sites to examine the effectiveness of these new programs.

The Clackamas County Program (Oregon City, OR)

This program begins with pretreatment services for inmates with COD that explore psychoeducational and preliminary treatment issues, and that are provided by a substance abuse treatment counselor and a corrections counselor who is certified to provide substance abuse treatment services. On release, many of these inmates transfer to the *Corrections Substance Abuse Program,* a residential treatment program in a work release setting. On successful completion of the program, clients move to outpatient care in the community with continued monitoring by probation or parole.

The highest incidence of personality disorders among Clackamas County substance abuse treatment programs is found among offenders under electronic surveillance. A program for this difficult group relies on building skills to address such mental health issues as criminal thinking errors, anger management, and conflict resolution. *Bridges* is a specific subset within this program explicitly for clients who have COD, which provides both case management and treatment services. Since treatment for most of these clients is complicated by their severe and persistent mental illness and their history of failure in school and work, *Bridges* is intensive, step-wise, and structured, providing support and opportunity for clients to develop social and work skills (CSAT, 2003).

The Colorado Modified TC

Personal Reflections is a program for inmates with mental illness housed in a separate unit at the San Carlos Correctional Facility in Colorado. Therapeutic community (TC) principles and methods provide the foundation for recovery and the structure for the program of substance abuse and mental health treatment, and for a cognitive-behavioral curriculum focused on criminal thinking and activity. A positive peer culture facilitates behavior change, while psychoeducational classes increase the inmate's understanding of mental illness, addiction, the nature of COD, drugs of use and abuse, and the connection between thoughts and behavior. These classes also teach emotional and behavioral coping skills. Those who complete the prison program are eligible for a TC program in community corrections on release (see Sacks and Sacks, 2003 for a full description of the program).

Programming for Women Offenders

The WINGS Program at Riker's Island jail (New York City) provides voluntary substance abuse, mental health, and medical treatment services to women. The program includes group counseling, parenting skills classes, case management, and discharge planning (Barnhill, 2002). *TAMAR's Children* (Maryland) is designed for pregnant and post-partum women (with their infants) who are in state and local detention facilities. The program objective is to foster mother-infant attachments and to integrate the delivery of mental health services, substance abuse treatment, and trauma treatment (Barnhill, 2002).

RESEARCH ON OUTCOMES

This section reviews the emerging findings on outcomes of treatment for offenders with COD. Since relatively few studies have been published as yet, the outline of approaches from the preceding section is followed only roughly, and other outcome studies (e.g., Jail Case Management) have been included.

Jail Diversion Programs

In 1999, Steadman et al. found only three published reports on the effectiveness of jail diversion programs for those with COD. The first (Lamb, et al., 1995) assessed a pre-booking diversion program that teamed police officers and mental health professionals; the former provided transportation and skills in handling violence, while the latter contributed expertise in mental illness diagnoses and in dealing with psychiatric patients. The team made decisions for disposition of psychiatric crisis cases in the community, including those with a threat of violence or actual violence. In a six-month follow-up of the 224 cases under study, most of the troubled individuals were sent to hospitals for examination; only two were sent to jail. Similarly, a second study (Borum, Deane, Steadman, et al., 1998) examined pre-booking programs that showed promise in diverting those with mental disorders from jail while facilitating access to treatment. On average, only 6.7 percent of the "mental disturbance" calls resulted in arrest. The third study (Lamb, Weinberger, and Bross, 1999) reported on a post-booking program that provided mental health consultation to a municipal court. One-year follow-up data suggested that those who participated in the program had, on average, better outcomes than those who did not participate. Steadman et al. (1999) point out that, although these three research studies do provide useful information, the research methods employed were not rigorous enough to determine that the interventions were responsible for the observed outcomes.

A Multnomah County (Oregon) diversion program provides intervention treatment for offenders who are in psychiatric crisis, many of whom have significant alcohol and drug problems. A study (Gratton, 2001) comparing 73 offenders who were diverted to treatment to 133 who were sentenced to jail found that the jail group had lower re-arrest rates and better living situations at follow-up. The diversion group was using drugs more often than the jail group at the 3-month but not at the 12-month follow-up, possibly because of continued substance abuse treatment. The diversion group did report significantly higher mental health functioning after a year, suggesting the advantage of mental health services.

Prison Programs

Edens, Peters, and Hills (1997) describe the *Estelle Unit* in the Substance Abuse Felony Punishment Facility that contains mainly COD inmates in a modified TC operated by the Gateway Foundation for the Texas Department of Criminal Justice. Over a period of 9–12 months, at least 20 hours per week of treatment and education services are provided, including counseling for chemical dependency and relapse prevention. The authors cite Von Sternberg's (1997) unpublished report indicating high rates of retention in treatment, and lower rates of crime and drug use for graduates of the program, relative to a comparison group.

Van Stelle and Moberg (2000) conducted an outcome evaluation of the *Mental Illness-Chemical Abuse* (MICA) Program at Oshkosh Correctional Institution (Wisconsin), which included a comparison group of offenders who met *MICA* eligibility criteria, but who did not have enough time remaining on their sentences to participate in the experimental program. Logistic regression analyses revealed that *MICA* participants (both completers and dropouts) were more likely than those in the comparison group to be medication compliant, abstinent from substance use, and more stable at three months after release. These results suggest that medication compliance and resulting mental health stability may be associated with abstinence from substance use and perhaps to a decreased likelihood of recidivism. The authors note that only a small sample was available at the time of the evaluation, which qualifies the longer-term outcomes as preliminary.

In a study of the Colorado modified TC described above, Sacks and colleagues (2003) randomly assigned inmates with COD to either Modified TC or Mental Health treatment. Upon completion of prison treatment and release to the community, the Modified TC subjects could elect to enter an aftercare TC, while those in the Mental Health group were eligible to receive a variety of services in the community. The findings show an advantage for Modified TC treatment on measures of criminal behavior, particularly when prison and aftercare TC treatment are combined, as reincarceration at 12 months post-prison release for this group (5%) was significantly lower (p<.02) than for the Mental Health group (33%). These results support the principles of integrated treatment and continuity of care.

Jail Case Management

Godley et al. (2000) assessed a demonstration case management program for jailed individuals with COD. Program admissions were sentenced to probation, avoiding further time in jail, provided that they maintained compliance with the program. Case management services included screening, substance abuse treatment placement, progress monitoring for the court, graduated sanctions to increase treatment engagement, facilitate involvement of significant others, and referrals to various other support services. Of the 54 clients enrolled, six-month follow-up data were obtained for 41 participants, and showed statistically significant reductions in legal problems and improvements in symptoms.

FUTURE DIRECTIONS AND RECOMMENDATIONS

Treatment

1. Follow the five principles of treatment of clients discussed earlier (screening and assessment, individual treatment plans, integrated treatment, a phased approach, continuity of care), as well as the essential components of treatment for COD offenders (e.g., psychiatrically enhanced staffing, psychoeducational classes, criminal thinking and behavior interventions described in the COD TIP) (CSAT, 2003).

2. Extend the range of treatment available to offenders with COD. The modified TC is a promising approach (Sacks and Sacks, 2003; Sacks et al., 2003), while several other substance abuse methods translate effectively to the treatment of COD, e.g., motivational interviewing (Carey et al., 2001), cognitive behavioral approaches (Peters and Hills, 1997), contingency management (Petry, 2000; Petry et al., 2001) and relapse prevention strategies (Roberts et al., 1999).

3. Develop recommendations that will improve continuity of care; potential methods include the Modified TC, Assertive Community Treatment, and Intensive Case Management.

Research

1. Conduct a prevalence study of COD in adult offender populations that will examine the combined mental and substance abuse disorders, and delineate subgroups and age ranges, using sound procedures (clinical interview, record review, or standardized assessment instrument). This research will clarify the type and severity of COD in the offender population to inform policy and planning.

2. Survey services, staffing, resources, organizational characteristics, and integration of substance abuse and mental health treatment of existing COD prison programs. This information will inform program design by describing the environment and available resources.

3. Develop, refine, and test treatment approaches and strategies for offenders with COD (a) for in-prison treatment, (b) for successful transition to aftercare to promote continuity of care, and (c) for use of community resources to address the multiple needs of criminal justice clients with COD.

4. Conduct systems and economic analysis (a) to examine barriers both to treatment and to the integration of mental health and substance abuse services, and to elicit specific issues that generate public opposition, and (b) to study the costs of treatment and the benefits relative to costs.

CONCLUSION

Prevalence of COD in offender populations is high, and shows indications of being on the rise. Treatment principles that guide COD programming are now available, along with a variety of emerging program models and strategies, some of which show promising research results in terms of effectiveness. Additional program development, accompanied by rigorous evaluation research, is needed. The recently formed *Criminal Justice Drug Abuse Treatment Network* (National Institute on Drug Abuse, 2002) calls for an alliance among research, practice, and criminal justice to advance programs and research for substance abusing offenders. This initiative is particularly important to the COD offender population, which experiences unique difficulties and barriers to treatment, especially upon discharge from prison. A coordinated effort of practitioners, treatment providers, and criminal justice professionals is necessary to advance COD treatment for offenders while assuring that both public health and public safety concerns are met.

QUESTIONS FOR REVIEW AND DISCUSSION

1. What is meant by co-occurring substance abuse and mental disorders? Why are those conditions problematic for jails and prison administration? Explain.

2. What are the capabilities of most jails to deal with prisoners with co-occurring disorders?

3. How can diversion be of assistance to jail and prison officials in dealing with offenders with co-occurring disorders? What screening mechanisms are used to identify those with co-occurring disorders?

4. What are mental health courts? What are their goals?

5. What are jail diversion programs? What are their outcomes? Explain.

6. What treatment and research strategies are recommended for dealing with future populations of inmates with co-occurring disorders? Discuss.

40

"Debating the Effectiveness of Parole"

Anne Morrison Piehl

Adapted from Anne Morrison Piehl, "Debating the Effectiveness of Parole." *APPA Perspectives* 30: 54–61, 2006.

Reprinted by permission from the American Probation and Parole Association

"DOES PAROLE WORK?"

It sounds like a simple question. And most casual observers of criminal justice policy likely assume it is a question that the profession has a very good handle on. Recent commentary on this topic and the current symposium might prove baffling to an unsuspecting reader who happened upon this book.

And yet, this debate is routine for the field. The research reported by Amy L. Solomon, Vera Kachnowski, and Avi Bhati of the Urban Institute in "Does Parole Work? Analyzing the Impact of Postprison Supervision on Rearrest Outcomes" (2005) poses a question that has been posed frequently in the past. And while there is some disagreement about the answer, and whether it has changed over time, there can be no disagreement that it is a question that requires a clear answer. With three-quarters of a million people on parole supervision in the United States on any given day, society requires evidence on which to base key policy decisions such as: How many people should be on parole and for how long? Are some people more likely to have success on parole? How much parole supervision is enough? Which conditions of supervision are most efficacious for which parolees?

Does Parole Work? The Urban Institute Study

The Urban Institute report conducted their analysis of parole in the United States using data collected by the Bureau of Justice Statistics to study recidivism. This ambitious effort involved collecting and merging information from state and federal sources to create profiles of nearly 35,000 inmates released from state prisons in 1994. The data sample was drawn from prisoners in 15 states, and these include the larger states, so that the database is representative of two-thirds of all inmates in the nation. These profiles cover information on the inmates from their term in prison, their release, and for three years following release. The data underlying these profiles come from official criminal history records, so they include events that are essential to law enforcement in each jurisdiction, including date and type of arrests and convictions and, key to the Urban Institute report, date and type of release from prison.

The goal of the Urban Institute report was to provide the "big picture" about parole in America, using reliable information on a representative sample of inmates. Their research design necessarily would leave out much of the local detail that is essential to understanding how law enforcement is accomplished "on the street." At the same time, policy discussions frequently take place at the national level. Even in state or local discussions of policy, the first question is generally "what are other states doing?" So this report attempts to assess parole from the vantage point of "10,000 feet" elevation.

The Urban Institute researchers ambitiously tried to discern policy lessons and wisdom from the available data, but the quality of the extant data defies even their sophisticated analytical approach. I have used these data myself, and they do not allow the policy conclusions drawn in the Urban Institute report. Unfortunately, one cannot hope to answer the question of whether parole works either negatively or positively using their approach. There are statistical and substantive reasons for this conclusion. But before turning to these, and to the main question of whether parole works, we must begin by being clear about our definitions.

What Does "Parole" Mean?   The Urban Institute report begins by distinguishing between release type and supervision. There has been a sharp decrease in the proportion of inmates released due to the discretionary decisions of a parole board from 55 percent in 1980 to 22 percent in 2003 (Glaze and Pella, 2005). This trend resulted from policy choices in many states to put more determinacy into criminal sentences (Hughes et al., 2001), and also from the decisions of parole boards and inmates themselves to less aggressively seek discretionary release. Distinguishing between type of release and type and extent of supervision is essential to understanding how and whether parole works. However, much more work is necessary before we can claim to understand the salience of separating the decision about the timing of release from decisions about supervision intensity and length.

If the term "parole" was ever sufficient to describe the various state practices for monitoring ex-inmates in the community, it certainly is not sufficient now. Depending on the state, post-incarceration supervision can be provided by parole departments (some of which fall under departments of correction), probation departments, other entities, or some combination of these. In a shift from its historical role as providing an alternative to incarceration, probation now plays a substantial role in supervising adults following release from prison. An estimated 320,000 adults were supervised by probation following incarceration, which constituted 8 percent of the 4 million adults on probation at yearend 2002 (Glaze and Pella, 2005).

Across the United States, requirements for those under community supervision include a mix of elements, often crafted for individual offenders. Just as states vary in the way they organize post-incarceration supervision, they also vary in the extent to which they do it. Some states leave many released from prison unsupervised, while others require supervision of nearly all of those released. For some ex-inmates, terms under supervision may be decades long; for others, only a few months. In addition, what constitutes supervision at any given point is subject to interpretation. Intensive supervision in one state may mean monthly contact between a parolee and an agent in a regional parole office; in another, it may mean 24-hour electronic monitoring with officers in the field checking compliance of daily itineraries. In some systems, for some inmates, a continuum of supervision sanctions exists, allowing for progressive sanctioning for offenders in non-compliance with their terms of conditional release.

What Does "Work" Mean?   The Urban Institute report takes one definition of effectiveness of parole: reduction in recidivism. This is clearly a goal of parole supervision, but there are additional ways to operationalize the idea. Several recent reports on parole and prisoner reentry have developed and utilized the concept of parole "success" rates (Hughes et al., 2001; Travis and Lawrence, 2002). This statistic is defined as the number of parolees who completed their terms of supervision without having their parole revoked, being returned to jail or prison, or absconding, divided by the total number of parolees leaving parole in a given year. The success rate for the nation as a whole has hovered just above 40 percent for the past ten years (Glaze and Pella, 2005). Hughes et al. (2001) report that those released for the first time on the current sentence are much more successful than re-releases and that discretionary releases are substantially more successful than mandatory releases. The nationwide figures mask the tremendous amount of variation across states. Massachusetts was one of two states with the highest "success" rates (83 percent), and California had the lowest (21 percent).

The Bureau of Justice Statistics report notes that many factors affect measured "success" and cautions that these other factors may explain observed differences in this statistic. "When comparing State success rates for parole discharges, differences may be due to variations in parole populations, such as age at prison release, criminal history, and most serious offense. Success rates may also differ based on the intensity of supervision and the parole agency policies related to revocation of technical violators" (Hughes et al., 2001). Despite such qualifications, these "success" numbers have gained a fair bit of currency in the discussion of prisoner reentry. For example, Travis and Lawrence (2002) utilize the same measure to rank states, and Petersilia (2003) uses them to support an argument in favor of discretionary release.

Although these authors note that there are other factors one would like to examine in order to make sense of these numbers, the qualifications have not received the same attention as the raw numbers, though they are arguably more important. Reitz critiques these measures for being more a reflection of state policies than measures of the behavior of those supervised:

> *Simply put, it is a serious error to equate failure rates on postrelease supervision with the actual behavior of prison releases. The states are far too different in their revocation practices to allow us to consider the data compatible from state to state. In any jurisdiction, the number and rate of revocations depends to some degree on the good or bad conduct of parolees, to be sure, but it also depends at least as much on what might be called the "sensitivity" of the supervision system to violations. Sensitivity varies with formal definitions of what constitutes a violation, the intensity of surveillance employed by parole field officers, the institutional culture of field services from place to place, and the severity of sanctions typically used upon findings of violations. (Reitz, 2004)*

If these outcomes largely reflect policy differences, then they cannot be used to evaluate policies. In order to assess the effectiveness of parole, we must be able to identify which part of the observed difference is the result of behavior—of those supervised and of those doing the supervising. Only with clear information on individual and institutional behavior can we begin to know what works and to generalize that knowledge to other jurisdictions and other settings.

Success, as defined above, may well be a reasonable outcome measure for a supervising agency, when used with other statistics to evaluate performance. One could argue that parole agencies that improve their success rates are likely to have improved their operations. But comparing these measures across agencies is likely to lead to large errors. For example, it is likely that a thorough analysis of Massachusetts' stellar performance on this measure is largely driven by its limited reliance on post-incarceration supervision. In fact, that state is working to broaden its use of parole, as officials were worried that too many inmates were released with no community supervision, the result of determinate sentencing practices, reductions in the granting of discretionary release, and inmates deciding to finish out their terms rather than seek parole hearings (Piehl, 2002).

A more general approach to assessing the effectiveness of parole would begin by acknowledging that it proves difficult to understand post-release supervision as a separate program, distinct from the mechanisms that assign and provide it. Rather, any evaluation of supervision must begin with an understanding of the effects of the multiple system factors—laws, agencies, and practices—that govern who receives parole (or its equivalent), and the duration, intensity, and enforcement practices of the post-release supervision. The role of sentencing laws and practices has already been noted. In addition, the enforcement of the terms of conditional release may be affected by the actions of police and other law enforcement agencies working independently or cooperatively with correctional agencies. Crime sweeps enforcing nuisance laws may (intentionally or not) target recently released offenders and necessitate action by correctional agencies. Perhaps the most important question, from fiscal and justice perspectives, is whether jurisdictions respond too harshly to non-criminal violations of the terms of conditional release. Modest changes in the revocation rate translate into substantial changes in prison populations. Given these factors, considering post-release supervision as just one criminal sanction in a set of interrelated punishments may be the most appropriate way to judge whether it is "working."

Before concluding this section on parole effectiveness, it is worth remembering that the parole population has characteristics that are associated, not surprisingly, with poor success in the broader society (Petersilia, 2003). Recidivism rates are very high; nearly 50 percent of those released in 1994 were reconvicted for a new crime within three years of release (Langan and Levin, 2002). And, those released from prison and entering parole supervision are increasingly likely to have previously exited prison during the same criminal sentence (Blumstein and Beck, 2005). These facts represent the challenges that parole agents and agencies face every day.

Does Supervision Matter?

Last year I published a review of the evidence on the effectiveness of community supervision written with Stefan LoBuglio, chief of pre-release and reentry services for Montgomery County (Maryland) and a Ph.D. candidate at Harvard. In that work, we attempted to cull from the literature the evidence that would best inform judgments about effectiveness of parole. As you will see, the research literature is not sufficient to provide a detailed answer to this question, but does provide some insight, and suggestions for improving the research base. This section draws heavily on that earlier work (Piehl and LoBuglio, 2005).

An ideal test of whether post-release supervision of recent inmates reduces the probability of criminal re-offending would be based on the random assignment of a pool of soon-to-be released prisoners to either a treatment group that would provide post-release supervision, or to a control group that would have no supervision. With random assignment, a simple comparison of the rates of criminal activity across the two groups would provide definitive evidence on the effect of supervision. Unfortunately, there is an inherent problem with this research design: the outcome—recidivism—is intrinsically linked with supervision. In practice, increased supervision will likely lead to greater detection of rule violations and new criminal offenses. Furthermore, in non-experimental studies comparing the post-release criminal activity of offenders released under discretionary parole with those released under mandatory parole or released without supervision, selection bias proves problematic in drawing reliable inference. Parole boards will generally grant parole to those offenders who pose the least risk of re-offending and would be expected to have fewer arrests, on average, than those offenders who were turned down for parole, and those who received mandatory parole. This follows from parole board members doing their jobs as charged.

Another challenge to research in this area comes from difficulty in comparing offenders in prison to those under supervision. No matter how effective supervision services are, the risk to public safety will always be greater if an individual is supervised in the community rather than in prison. Studies of offender supervision typically compare offenders under different intensities and mixes of surveillance and treatment services. Necessarily, some behavior will be sanctioned by additional time behind bars. If there is any difference in the extent to which alternative programs rely on incarceration, then the outcomes are incomparable. Without a way to adjust for the differences in risk of further criminal activity or even violating conditions of supervision, it is impossible to credibly compare alternative supervision schemes over a substantial period of time.

Experimental Evidence on Intensive Supervision.   Over the past half century, periods of prison overcrowding have led some jurisdictions to implement intensive supervision programs both as a solution to divert offenders from prison, and to release inmates earlier from confined institutions into transitional programs. The few significant studies of intensive supervision conducted have focused on its effectiveness in reducing prison overcrowding without significantly increasing the public safety risk. In the 1950s, Richard McGee, noted penologist and then director of the California Department of Corrections, initiated a number of randomized research studies to determine the effectiveness of early parole as a function of offender risk and parole officer caseloads in the state. From a cost-benefit perspective, McGee concluded that intensive supervision was effective for offenders on the margin of choosing between criminal and law abiding behaviors, and not effective for either low risk offenders who may not have needed additional supervision to succeed or high-risk offenders who probably would have failed regardless of the nature of the supervision (Glaser, 1964).

The 1980s saw a resurgence of states' interests in Intensive Supervision Programs (ISP), touted as relatively low-cost intermediate alternatives to vastly overcrowded prisons. From 1986–91, the National Institute of Justice funded RAND to conduct a large randomized experiment of intensive supervision programs (ISP) in fourteen sites and nine states to assess their cost effectiveness. As reported by Petersilia and Turner (1993), who designed and oversaw the implementation of this evaluation, at the end of the one-year follow-up, 37 percent of the ISP treatment group had been rearrested as compared to 33 percent of the control group. Sixty-five percent of ISP offenders experienced a technical violation compared to 38 percent of the controls. Also, 27 percent of ISP offenders were recommitted to prison compared to 19 percent of the controls.

There are two ways to interpret these findings: either the program led to increased criminal behavior of those under heightened supervision (in the opposite direction of the anticipated effect), or the increased surveillance led to an increased probability of detection. If the latter is true, it is impossible to know whether there was in fact a deterrent effect that was overwhelmed by the surveillance effect. Also, the researchers speculated that the ISP may have sanctioned these infractions more harshly in an effort to shore up the credibility of the program (Petersilia and Turner, 1993). This too would obscure any true deterrent effect.

Although the evaluation could not provide any definitive evidence that increased supervision intensity provided public safety benefits, the highly elevated rate of technical violations for those in the treatment group suggests that the surveillance did in fact increase the rate of detection. Then the interesting question becomes whether technical violations are a proxy for criminal behavior. Experience in Washington State in the mid-1980s from a program that decreased the average number of conditions of release for probationers and de-emphasized the sanctions for technical violations does not support this hypothesis (Petersilia and Turner, 1993).

Despite the experience of hundreds of intensive supervision programs in this country and many studies, albeit few experimental, we still know very little about the effectiveness of these programs to reduce prison overcrowding or to reduce crime in detectable ways. The same issues that hinder our learning from many criminal justice practices are at work here. There is no consistency in the design and implementation of ISP programs; their surveillance and monitoring practices, caseloads, and their incorporation of rehabilitative requirements vary significantly both within and between programs. Some researchers have found that judges begin filling ISPs with lower-risk offenders who are not prison-bound—so called net widening—and believe that the investment of additional supervision resources for this population can backfire and lead to increased rates of violations and re-incarceration. However, if ISPs serve to enforce release conditions that were not previously being enforced under standard probation, and the detected infractions were directly or indirectly related to criminal activity, there could be a public safety benefit. Similarly, ISPs may serve to ensure the quicker detection and apprehension of violations by higher-risk offenders. Also, as McGee found, it is entirely possible that these programs may deter criminal offending from those offenders who are at the margins of choosing between licit and illicit behaviors. The bottom line is that the public safety benefit of intensive supervision programs relies on two mechanisms that have yet to be proven: the deterrence value of supervision, and the value of responding to technical violations to prevent crime.

The Connection Between the Release Process and the Extent and Effectiveness of Supervision.   Some analysts have used success measures to assess the efficacy of different approaches to prison release, comparing the outcomes of those released by a discretionary release process to the outcomes of those released at the completion of their sentences. In addition to the critiques offered above with regard to the way success is measured, there is a fundamental problem with this inference—it does not account for how

individuals are assigned to release status. That is, inmates who are released at the discretion of a parole board are likely to have a lower risk of recidivism than inmates whom a parole board chooses not to release. Further complicating matters is the variety of statutes that govern whether or not inmates with given criminal histories are eligible for discretionary release; differences in these laws across states will affect average success measures by release type. Research on this topic does not generally investigate whether discretionary release was available for those who were released at the expiration of their sentence.

Given that it is not straighforward to compare the effect of release type on the effectiveness of supervision in controlling the criminal behavior of those released from prison, what can be said about the connection between release policy and supervision? Mandatory release may or may not lead to a period of post incarceration supervision. Discretionary release generally leads to supervision for at least several months or the parole board would not take time to hear the case. When faced with an inmate who appears to pose a risk for public safety, a parole board must trade off the benefits and costs of discretionary release and the supervision opportunities that provides against the benefits and costs of keeping the inmate incarcerated until the maximum release date. For better or worse, under a policy of mandatory release, these tradeoffs are not considered on a case-by-case basis.

Inherently, discretionary release works against the notion that those least equipped to reintegrate should be subject to a period of post-release supervision from prison. Mandatory release polices provide a greater certainty that these individuals will receive supervision, but then raise a secondary resource allocation question. Certainly, if supervising all prisoners dilutes the intensity of supervision of high-risk offenders and needlessly interferes with the reintegration process of low-risk offenders, it could prove costly and counterproductive to making supervision "matter."

Critics of mandatory release call for a return to discretionary release in order to increase the incentives to encourage rehabilitative behavior among prisoners, and to balance disparities in sentences across offenders and jurisdictions. There are two other types of benefits of discretionary release that should also be considered. When making a release decision, a parole board can know about the inmate's plans: Does he have a job? Where will she live? Is there anyone who can vouch for these plans? Having established supports in place may be the most important determinant of successful reentry, and it is useful to require these before agreeing to release a person from confinement. Finally, the existence of discretionary release provides incentives for correctional institutions to provide rehabilitative opportunities and incentives for inmates to take advantage of these opportunities. It is a topic of lively debate whether the discretionary release process entails moral and practical benefits that are not just as easily achieved through other means (Petersilia, 1999; Reitz, 2004).

In the end, the issue of whether discretionary release is preferable to mandatory release has many dimensions in addition to its relationship to successful reentry following release from prison. From the perspective of reentry and public safety, release policy is important both to how parole outcomes are interpreted and to how other aspects of reentry and supervision are designed. Most states have some people released under the discretion of a parole board and others released at the end of their sentences. This fact suggests that the debate about "mandatory" versus "discretionary" should begin to consider the best way to support reentry in a system that contains multiple release types.

The Role of Changing Technology in Community Supervision.   New technologies have transformed the ability of supervising agencies to detect non-compliance among offenders, but now raise questions about whether we can learn too much and be forced to sanction without a clear benefit to public safety (Burrell, 2005). As technology becomes more effective and less expensive, it provides opportunities and challenges for supervising agencies. Faced with rising caseloads and few support resources in the community, the shift of supervising officers' roles from providing assistance to surveillance was probably inevitable, but certainly greatly accelerated by new technologies. Now, agencies could benefit from specific research on which technologies work best with certain types of offenders, and the development of best practices that would moderate the natural inclination to use technology excessively. This discussion brings us back to the need for a clear research agenda on what the goals of supervision are within the larger system of law enforcement.

Why Don't We Have Better Answers?

Why is it so hard to know the right answer to whether "parole works"? As some of the other commentators have noted, perhaps it is not very helpful to pose the question in this broad form. Rather, perhaps it is only really useful to assess effectiveness of any activity in a particular time and place. But this perspective is not sufficient. In other areas of social policy we seek to take advantage of tremendous cross-jurisdiction variation to build generalizable knowledge. The questions posed by the Urban Institute report are inherently difficult, but also immensely important to society.

A critical starting point is to accept that lively debate is necessary for making piecemeal progress toward an understanding of the empirical relationships at work. Too much money is being spent in this country, and too many people are living with their freedoms restricted, not to pursue (actively and systematically) a research agenda that is likely to assist making better policy choices. We now have plenty of descriptive information about those under supervision, but we need more and better information on other parts of the system. And we certainly need more and better studies of the actions of inmates, parole boards, field agents, judges, prosecutors, and others in response to the multiple goals and varied policies that govern criminal justice. Without more analysis of what each party is doing within the larger system, we will not be able to improve policies or practices, nor will we have reliable evidence on which to base recommendations.

One might think that the enormous variation in sentencing laws, discretionary release policies, and supervision practices across and within states would provide natural experiments from which to learn much about the effectiveness of supervision. However, as noted earlier, the inability to cleanly delineate differences in supervision practices from system differences makes inference from cross-jurisdictional comparisons suspect. It would certainly make cross-jurisdictional analyses better to have complete information on these system differences, something that is not easily attainable now. The fact that it is difficult to evaluate the effectiveness of supervision irrespective of system factors that determine who receives supervision, along with the duration, intensity, and enforcement of the terms of conditional release should lead us to consider alternative research strategies.

We also miss opportunities for developing research knowledge when political considerations dictate how resources are allocated. The Serious and Violent Offender Reentry Initiative authorized over $100 million to be spent on prisoner reentry programs, research, and evaluation. And it appears that this will be a missed opportunity for both practice and research. Grant funding was spread equally over 50 states, not strategically allocated to those jurisdictions with promising models and agency commitments. While some jurisdictions have put their money to good use, not all have done so. The result has been many marginal programs, most of which are likely to disappear with the funding. And with each program design so specific to its setting, and without a coordinated research effort to understand the drivers of program success, little generalizable knowledge will outlive the federal effort. It is a shame that such a large commitment may not result in reliable evaluation of the practice of prison release and community supervision.

What Research Agenda Would Shed More Light on These Questions?

We need a lively debate where people are open to refining their policy positions depending upon the outcomes of the research. That is, the debate should first emphasize the facts and ideas before turning to the solutions. And it may require substantial social investments to accomplish. The Moving to Opportunity experiments, designed to learn about the effects of neighborhoods on a variety of social outcomes (including some in criminal justice), cost the federal government as much as $70 million. Federal contracts for research ran about $1 million per year, and academic researchers raised another $7 million in research funding from 2000–2005 to extend the research capacities of the federal effort. Other substantial experimental efforts, like those that laid the groundwork for welfare reform, also required large amounts of funding. What this means is that one key element of a research agenda would be the development of a large-scale randomized experiment.

Another vital element of such an agenda should be the systematic collection of data from criminal justice agencies that are meaningful for cross-jurisdictional analysis. Of course, practices and laws vary by jurisdiction. As a result, under current data efforts, so does the meaning of the data elements. All large data sets for studying these questions have been based on administrative data defined by agencies in order to carry out their law enforcement functions. Therefore, it is possible to know whether an inmate was released due to a discretionary parole board decision or at the expiration of this sentence. But it is not possible to know which inmates were eligible for parole consideration, and whether it was the inmate or the parole board who decided against discretionary release. Nor do we know whether the corrections department facilitated the inmate's preparation for a parole hearing. Similarly, in trying to understand outcomes on supervision, we do not have systematic information on caseloads, standard expectations of parolees, or the behavior that did or did not trigger violations. Until we have a resource that defines policies and actions in a way that does not depend on the vagaries of each jurisdiction—that is, data collected for research, not for law enforcement—we will always be able to have debate over what, if anything, we have learned from non-experimental evidence.

As noted earlier, we cannot understand post-release supervision as a separate program distinct from the mechanisms that assign and provide it. Rather, any evaluation of supervision must begin with an understanding of the effects of the multiple system factors—laws, agencies, and practices—that govern who receives parole (or its equivalent), and the duration, intensity, and enforcement practices of the post-release supervision. Therefore, a third element of a research agenda is to conduct much more comprehensive evaluations that consider the system variables affecting supervision outcomes.

The fourth element of a research agenda is the one where we are currently doing the best—focusing on basic practices. For prisoners of certain attributes (offenses, age, employment/education history, return destination) what should be the supervision strategy?

How many times a month should these type of offenders report to supervising officers and what is the nature of this reporting relationship? For offenders who seem to pose a significant threat to public safety such as sexual predators, what type of technology proves most useful in providing round the clock surveillance, and what pharmacological and other treatment remedies are most effective? Does it make sense to front-load supervision services? Some of these studies have been conducted in Washington State and elsewhere. They are eminently doable, can have an immediate effect on practice, and take advantage of the existing variation in practice. To make the results generalizable to other locations, however, it is essential that research on a local effort contain sufficient information on the system factors that determine the characteristics of the target population and their incentives for compliance. Efforts to collect more information on cross-jurisdictional differences would benefit the effort to generalize studies of best practices.

The current symposium provides a challenge. Are we ready to put in place an ambitious research agenda that truly tests ideas about the best way to organize and apply community supervision? If so, it is reasonable to undertake an agenda that addresses the question from different levels, 10,000 feet and ground level, and evaluates innovative ideas and standard practices with equal intensity. This is the only way to increase the knowledge base.

QUESTIONS FOR REVIEW AND DISCUSSION

1. What was the Urban Institute study relating to parole and its effectiveness? Discuss.
2. Does parole work? Why or why not? Explain.
3. What are some key parole objectives? Are these objectives being achieved under the current system of parole in most states with parole systems? Why or why not? Explain.
4. How does regular supervision differ from intensive supervision? Does offender supervision seem to matter? Why or why not?
5. Should parole be automatic after an inmate has served a fixed portion of his or her time? Why or why not? Explain.
6. What can be done to deter parolees from reoffending?

41

Targeting for Reentry
Inclusion/Exclusion Criteria
Across Eight Model Programs

James M. Byrne
and Faye Taxman

Adapted from James M. Byrne and Faye Taxman, "Targeting for Reentry: Inclusion/
Exclusion Criteria Across Eight Model Programs." *Federal Probation* 68: 53–61, 2004.

Reprinted by permission from the Administrative Office of the U.S. Courts.

According to a recent Bureau of Justice Statistics (BJS) review of reentry trends in the United States, there were 1,440,655 prisoners under the jurisdiction of federal or state correctional authorities at year-end 2002 (Hughes and Wilson, 2002). During the year, there was a constant flow of offenders both into prison (close to 600,000 individuals) and out of prison (again, about 600,000). Offenders *entering* prison were either newly sentenced offenders (60 percent) or parole/other conditional release violators (40 percent). Offenders *leaving* state prison included drug offenders (33 percent), violent offenders (25 percent), property offenders (31 percent), and public order offenders (10 percent). About one in five of these reentry offenders were released unconditionally; the remaining offenders were placed under parole supervision. Overall, it is projected that 67 percent of these releasees will likely be rearrested and 40 percent will likely be returned to prison within three years of their release date, based on a recent BJS study (Langon and Levin, 2002). Clearly, a subgroup of the federal and state prison population appears to have integrated periods of incarceration into their lifestyle and life choices. The constant movement of these offenders into and out of prison has negative consequences not only for offenders but also for the community at large, including victims, family members, and community residents. What can and should the corrections systems do to "target" these offenders for specialized services and controls to improve reintegration into the community?

In the following article, we examine the offender targeting issue in detail, utilizing data gathered from our review of eight model Reentry Partnership Initiative Programs (see Taxman, Byrne, and Young, 2002 for an overview of research methodology). We begin by describing the changing patterns of federal and state prison admissions and releases. We then examine the target population criteria used in the eight model RPI programs and discuss the unique challenges presented by different offender groups, including repeat offenders, mentally ill offenders, sex offenders, and drug offenders. We conclude by identifying the relevant classification, treatment, and control issues that decision makers will have to address as they design and implement their own reentry processes for targeted offenders and/or communities.

1. REENTRY TRENDS: CHANGING PATTERNS OF PRISON ADMISSION AND RELEASE

The number of prisoners under state and federal jurisdictions has increased dramatically over the past eight decades. In 1925, there were 91,669 state and federal prisoners and the rate of incarceration was only 79 per 100,000 of the resident population. By the end of 2000, the number of incarcerated offenders rose to 1,321,137, which translates into a rate of incarceration of 478 per 100,000 residents. The change in the correctional landscape followed the shift in sentencing philosophy from rehabilitation to incapacitation, which grew out of frustration with offenders who refuse to change, the failure of rehabilitative programs to reduce recidivism, and the need to punish offenders for their misdeeds. Paradoxically, the incapacitation approach has resulted in more institutional-based punishment for offenders, but less community-based control of the returning home population.

Offenders are released from prison either conditionally or unconditionally. For the three out of four offenders released from prison conditionally in 1999, a supervised, mandatory release mechanism was used for 50.6 percent, some form of discretionary release via parole was used for 36.1 percent, and probation/other supervision was used for 13.3 percent. The remaining prison releasees—representing almost a quarter of the total release population (109,896—22.2 percent of all releasees) were sent back to the community "unconditionally," with no involvement of the state or federal government in overseeing their return to the community. That is, some type of supervised release (e.g., probation, parole, etc.) was not part of the reentry process. In the vast majority of these unconditional release cases (95 percent), the offender was released from prison due to an expiration of sentence.

Any discussion of the impact of our returning prison population on community safety must begin by recognizing the fundamental changes in release policy in this country over the past decade. Supervised mandatory release is now the most commonly used release mechanism by state prison systems, while the vast majority of federal offenders are released upon expiration of their sentence. Focusing for a moment on regional variations in release policy, we find that prison systems in the Midwest (35.4 percent of all releasees) and Western states (77.2 percent of all releasees) are more likely to rely on the supervised mandatory release mechanism than on either expiration of sentence or discretionary parole release. In the Northeast, the pattern is noticeably different: discretionary parole release is the most common release mechanism in these states (60 percent of all releases). This was also the pattern found in Southern states, although there is clearly a lower rate of discretionary parole releasees (33 percent of all releases) and more use of expiration of sentences (30 percent of all releasees) and/or supervised mandatory releasees (22 percent of all releasees) in this region.

Despite the growing trend toward the use of mandatory release mechanisms and away from discretionary parole release, we should emphasize that several states (21 in 1997) do not use this release mechanism at all. Six of them (Maine, Massachusetts, Ohio, Delaware, Florida, and Nevada) relied more often on expiration of sentence than on any other release option and in four of these states, supervised mandatory release was not available. Due to changes in parole practices, parole boards are reluctant to release offenders early. The growing trend is for more offenders to be released with either minimal time under community supervision, or without any community supervision condition at all. While some scholars observe that many offenders are better off without community supervision, due to the problem of technical violations and recycling of offenders from prison to community to prison (Austin, 2001), others observe that more supervision is required to manage the reintegration process and to reduce the potential harm that offenders released from prison and jail present to the community (Petersilia, 2000; Taxman et al., 2002). More research is needed in this area to determine the degree and level of supervised release (if any) that is useful to maximize community safety, but it certainly appears that changes in sentencing policies and release practices have likely had negative consequences for offenders and the communities to which they return.

Since many states have opted *not* to develop policies and procedures to allow supervised mandatory release, it is likely that more and more offenders will be "maxing-out" of prison in these jurisdictions. Do these offenders pose a greater threat to community safety than either the parole or mandatory release population? A recent study by the Bureau of Justice Statistics found that mandatory parolees are less likely to successfully complete parole than discretionary parolee discharges (Hughes, Wilson, and Beck, 2001). While we do not know the answer to the question about the relative effectiveness of different release mechanisms, it is important to continue to monitor this issue.

We do know that offenders are now serving a greater proportion of their sentences in prison and regardless of the *method* of release, they are returning to the community with the same problems (e.g., lack of skills to obtain employment, substance abuse problems, family problems, individual mental health and physical health problems, repeat offending behavior, etc.) that they had when they were first incarcerated (Maruna and Immarigeon, 2004). In addition, some offenders are returning to the community with *new* mental health, physical health, and personal (criminogenic) problems, due to such factors as negative institutional culture (Sparks, Bottoms, and Hay, 1996), increased incarceration period (Austin, 2001), the spread of communicable diseases in prison (RAND, 2003), and isolation from the community (Maruna and Immarigeon, 2004). While they were incarcerated, the communities they used to reside in may have improved (due to such factors as community mobilization and betterment activities, a better economy, community policing, etc.) or they may have deteriorated (due to economic downturns, increased gang activities, the spread of infectious disease, etc.). In either case, the community prisoner's return may be to quite a different community from the one they left. The longer offenders remain in prison, the more likely that there will be changes in family, peer associations, and neighborhood dynamics needing to be addressed during reintegration. All of these changes complicate reintegration, but they must be considered when designing and implementing offender reentry programs. As Gottfredson and Taylor (1986) demonstrated two decades ago, these person-environment interactions likely hold the key to understanding (and changing) the behavior of offenders released from prison.

2. OFFENDER TARGETING FOR REENTRY: AN OVERVIEW OF CURRENT PRACTICES

The Office of Justice Programs (OJP), in conjunction with a wide range of federal agencies involved in offender reentry directly or indirectly, has recently allocated 100 million dollars to help fund reentry initiatives in every state and U.S. territory, including Puerto Rico and the Virgin Islands. Beginning in 2002, 68 separate reentry programs have been designed, developed, and implemented, targeting a diverse group of juvenile and adult offenders. However, a recent BJS review of reentry trends revealed that in 2001, nearly half of all state prison releasees were from only five states.

It appears from our preliminary review of these programs that the OJP initiative will likely include only a *fraction* of these states' releasees, which makes the decision on whom to include and whom to exclude even more critical. Unfortunately, a detailed review of the initial development of the OJP reentry initiative has not been completed, although the Urban Institute has been selected to conduct the initial evaluation of this program. In the interim, we are left to sort through a large number of program descriptions (see OJP's web site for state-specific descriptions of reentry initiatives) and a small number of case studies and process evaluations.

Despite this evaluation research shortfall, it certainly appears that governors, legislators, and corrections administrators are jumping quickly onto the reentry bandwagon. The question we focus on in this article is straightforward: who (and where) should we target for reentry? To answer this question, we have examined the targeting criteria developed in eight model reentry partnership initiatives (RPI) programs identified by the Office of Justice Programs and recently included in a detailed multisite process evaluation conducted by the University of Maryland's Bureau of Governmental Research (for an overview, see Taxman et al., 2003b). It is our view that the targeting issues identified in the following review of the eight RPI programs will be applicable to 68 new reentry initiatives currently in development across the United States.

In general, the reentry programs we reviewed can be described as including three separate reentry phases: (1) the institutional phase, (2) the structured reentry phase, and (3) the community reintegration phase. However, considerable variation not only in the design, but also in the duration of each of these reentry phases appears to be related—in large part—to the specific targeting decisions made by program developers at each site. In the following section, we highlight the impact of offense, offender, and area-specific targeting decisions on each phase of reentry.

A. Targeting and the Institutional Phase of Reentry

Our review of RPI programs found considerable variation in what actually constitutes the "institutional" phase of offender reentry. In one jurisdiction (Burlington, Vermont), offenders were identified and selected to participate in the reentry program upon *entrance* to prison, during the initial prison classification process. In the remaining jurisdictions, identification of potential reentry participants occurred several months prior to the inmates expected *release* date (6 months to 1 year). Obviously, this basic decision has important ramifications for both the offender and the institution, particularly when participation in specific prison-based treatment programs is a feature of the reentry program. Regardless of when this phase of reentry began, it appears that inmates participating in the RPI programs we reviewed had access to programs and services not available to other inmates at these facilities. In this respect, treatment availability, access, and perhaps even quality represent important advantages linked to participation in the reentry programs we reviewed.

In the *institutional* phase of the reentry process, offenders who meet the RPI site's target population criteria are initially identified and contacted about possible participation in the reentry program. For offenders being released unconditionally, program participation is voluntary; however, conditional releasees may be required to participate as a condition of parole. Program developers at prospective RPI sites are faced with several difficult decisions regarding initial offender targeting. First, due to program size restrictions, RPI model programs at the sites we reviewed targeted specific release *locations* for reentry. Second, only a subgroup of all offenders to be released to these locations is usually targeted for potential reentry participation. Third, targeting may vary not only by location and offense type but also by the method of release (i.e., conditional vs. unconditional). And finally, program participation may be restricted to offenders who are at a certain level of institutional control (e.g., medium security), due to size limitations and/or institutional control concerns.

Regardless of exactly how the final group of RPI program participants is selected, the institutional phase is expected to include a range of offender programming options designed to prepare offenders for resuming their lives in the community. These program options would likely include education, vocational training, life skills, and of course, individual/group counseling. In three sites, the emphasis was on providing motivational readiness for treatment, in order to prepare the offender to make significant lifestyle changes as they return to the community. As we have noted in a separate report (see Taxman et al., 2003b), we maintain that reentry programs should be oriented toward preparing inmates for return to the community from the outset of their institutional stay. However, only one of the eight RPI models we visited (Burlington, VT) began the institutional phase during the first several months of an offender's incarceration. A much more common approach is to begin the institutional phase of the reentry program several months before the offender's targeted release date, but prior to the pre-release phase. In fact, several of the RPI programs we reviewed had the institutional phase folded into the structured reentry phase, making it difficult to determine where one phase ended and the next began.

B. Targeting and Structured Reentry

Structured reentry is the catchphrase for perhaps the most critical step in the offender's reentry process. During structured reentry, the offender must make the transition from institutional to community control. In the programs we reviewed, structured reentry began approximately 1 to 3 months prior to the offender's targeted release date and continued through the end of the offender's first month back in the community. It consisted of two distinct but interrelated stages (the in-prison and in-community stages), which were designed to offer a seamless system of transition from prison to community.

The structured reentry process requires coordination and collaboration between and among several distinct "partners" in the reentry process, including the offender, victim, community, treatment providers, police, and institutional and community corrections. As we have already observed regarding the *institutional* phase, "structured reentry" will likely be a different experience for offenders released conditionally than for those offenders (about 20 percent of all releases nationally) released unconditionally. However, the components of structured reentry likely will require the development of a plan for each returning offender targeted for participation, focusing on such basic issues as: (1) continuity of treatment, as offenders move from institutional to community treatment providers and address long-standing criminogenic factors (e.g., substance abuse, mental illness, repeat offending, etc.); (2) housing options; (3) employment opportunities; (4) family needs and services; and (5) victim/community concerns (e.g., safety, restitution, public health, reparation).

Some jurisdictions (i.e., Florida, Maryland, and Nevada) found it advantageous to move offenders closer to their release location during their last few months in prison to facilitate the community reintegration process. In theory, locating the offender closer to home should help him or her to renew family ties, obtain employment and secure appropriate housing and treatment. We suspect that these kinds of community linkages may actually be more important for offenders released unconditionally, without the specific forms of community treatment, supervision and control associated with the typical offender *conditional* release plan. For both conditional and unconditional releasees participating in a reentry program, it appears that some form of offender movement may be needed during the structured reentry phase, particularly if participation in a specific treatment program is a component of the reentry program and linkages need to be established to ensure provision/continuity of treatment.

C. Targeting and Community Reintegration

Phase III of the reentry programs we reviewed is referred to as the *community reintegration* phase. For many offenders leaving prison, the initial period of adjustment (i.e., the first one or two weeks after release) is actually *less* difficult than the subsequent period of community reintegration (see, e.g., Taxman, Young, and Byrne, 2003b). There are a variety of possible explanations for this phenomenon. First, keep in mind that essentially two groups of offenders are being released from prison: conditional and unconditional releasees. While both groups of offenders are offered similar support services (e.g., employment assistance, housing assistance, health care and treatment), conditional releasees are monitored by community supervision agents who have the power to revoke their parole if they refuse this "assistance." With the notable exception of sex offender registration, no such controls can be invoked for the unconditional releasee population, although the RPI initiative has pioneered the use of a number of informal social controls to induce offenders to fully participate in the reentry program. These informal social controls include the use of guardians and advocates in the community, who are available to assist the offender with reintegration, helping the offender make linkages with services, employers, and community groups (such as faith-based, self-help groups, etc.). The relationship that develops between guardians and returning offenders may have a positive influence on program participation and compliance.

It is certainly possible that after an initial period of compliance and participation, offenders from *both* groups will begin to return to earlier behavior patterns, such as gang participation or drug/alcohol abuse. For offenders under conditional release status, the use of behavioral contracts with clearly defined rewards and sanctions may reduce the number of offenders who backslide in this way. However, successful reentry programs must develop alternative mechanisms for fostering compliance among offenders released from prison unconditionally. For example, one site we visited proposed making "housing" assistance available to offenders actively participating in the reentry program. Stated simply, an offender may be released *unconditionally* from prison, but his or her participation in the reentry program is conditional on compliance with the program's rules and regulations (such as no drugs or alcohol, curfews, participation in treatment, etc.). If an offender wants to live in housing provided by the RPI, then he or she will continue to participate in treatment, remain employed, etc. In one RPI model we reviewed, housing is provided for up to 90 days. However, the program allows the offender to live in transitional housing for an additional 90 to 370 days for a minimal fee as the offender becomes stabilized in the community. For many offenders, housing may represent a more effective inducement than the threat of other sanctions (Taxman, Young, and Byrne, 2003b).

3. VARIATIONS IN TARGETING CRITERIA FOR REENTRY

Any discussion of offender reentry must begin by recognizing that urban areas, often with high concentrations of minorities, are "home" to the vast majority of returning inmates in the United States. Approximately 600,000 prison inmates returned to the community in 2002 alone (Hughes and Wilson, 2002); over half of these returning offenders were from five states (California, Florida, Illinois, New York, and Texas). To many observers, the answer to the question "whom should we target for reentry?" is straightforward: all releasees from our state and federal prison system, regardless of location, release status, conviction offense type, and/or criminal history. However, an examination of the target population criteria used to select offenders in the eight model RPI programs we reviewed presents a more pragmatic, stakes-oriented view of the targeting issue: do not place "high stakes" offenders (such as sex offenders) into a *new* reentry program.

This approach clearly fits the cardinal rule of correctional practice: inaugurate new initiatives by focusing on offenders who are likely to be compliant and less likely to create public outcry. The "low-risk/low-stakes" approach is promoted as a means to build community and stakeholder support for new concepts with the expectation that, if the innovation is successful, then corrections officials will expand the target population. In fact, many criminologists continue to argue that we are likely to see the largest reductions in offender recidivism when we target the highest-risk groups of offenders for program participation (Taxman, 2000). However, program developers may be less interested in recidivism reduction and more interested in the level of re-offending by program participants. When viewed in this light, the question becomes: how much recidivism is one willing (or able) to tolerate among offenders targeted for reentry?

All programs with offense restrictions specifically excluded sex offenders, utilizing information from both the offender's incarceration (or instant) offense and the offender's criminal history to identify ineligible offenders. In addition to restrictions on sex offenders, one jurisdiction places restriction on violent offenders, while another does not allow offenders who have ever committed a crime against children to participate. Another criterion used by staff at two sites was the psychological health of the offender. Offenders with a history of mental illness/psychological disorders are excluded from participation at these reentry sites. According to a recent review by Liebling (1999 as cited in Petersilia, 2000), approximately 1 out of 5 prison inmates report having a mental illness. Given the overlap among violent offenders, sex offenders, and mentally ill offenders, it appears that some RPI program developers used a multiple, offender/offense-based scheme to cast as wide a net as possible over the pool of multiple-problems offenders to exclude from the reentry programming.

We should emphasize that these ineligible offenders will still return to the community upon release, but they will do so without the specific support and control offered through the RPI effort at the eight sites we reviewed. Since a significant number of the unconditional release population who are "maxing out" of prison are sex or violent offenders, it appears that the very group of offenders raising the most community concern tends to receive the lowest level of correctional supervision and support. The paradox inherent in this decision is that it is precisely the group of offenders being excluded from reentry programs that would most likely benefit from participation in the programs, and that may present some of the greater public safety risks. Recent evaluation findings continue to demonstrate that larger gains in reducing recidivism are likely to occur with high-risk offenders who have a greater likelihood of committing new offenses (Andrews and Bonta, 1996; Taxman, 1998). As the RPI program grows and evolves, it is likely that many of the sites will expand the offender pool to include "high stakes" offenders. Three of the eight sites we visited understood this issue well enough to place no offense restrictions on reentry offenders for their specialized initiatives. In these jurisdictions, the key criterion was location. Reentry program developers reserve the reentry initiative to offenders returning to specific neighborhoods, regardless of their prior offense history, seriousness of current offense, or special needs (e.g., substance abusers, mentally ill).

4. OFFENDER-SPECIFIC REENTRY STRATEGIES: WHAT WORKS, WITH WHOM, AND WHY

As part of developing the RPI initiative, each jurisdiction had to consider the state of knowledge about the reintegration "challenges" posed by a wide range of institutionalized offenders. Decisions made about whom (and where) to "target" for specialized reentry programming will affect the structure and purpose of the RPI model being developed. As we have reported here earlier and in separate reviews (see Taxman et al., 2003b) high risk offenders, particularly sex offenders (however the pool is defined) have been excluded from participating in five of the eight model reentry programs we reviewed. Of course, sex offenders and other excluded offenders in these jurisdictions are still returning to the community, either on conditional or unconditional release status; they simply do not have access to the model programs, staff, services, and support that are being designed to maximize public safety. While such offense-based exclusion criteria may make sense to policy makers and program developers, they may actually make reintegration more difficult for "excluded" offenders.

What do we currently know about different types of offenders who will be returning to the community from our state and federal prison systems? The national statistics do not illustrate the tremendous variation in characteristics of offenders that occur by state and region. For program planners and developers, it is critical to examine state-specific (as well as region-specific) information about the characteristics of institutionalized offenders, and to design and implement reentry programs that are appropriate to the particular target population (offense type, offender type, demographic profile) and target area (e.g., urban, rural) included in the reentry initiative. In the following section we describe the unique reentry challenges presented by four groups of offenders: sex offenders, repeat offenders, substance abusing offenders, and mentally ill offenders. Although our focus is on *offenders,* we recognize that *communities* also will vary (e.g., tolerance, support, resources) in ways that will affect the offender reentry process.

A. Sex Offenders.   What is a sex offender? To many observers, the answer is obvious: anyone convicted of a sex-related crime. In 1997, for example, there were 1,046,705 offenders in our state prison system: 2.6 percent of these incarcerated offenders were convicted of rape, while another 6 percent were convicted of some other form of sexual assault. By comparison, only a fraction of the federal prison population (8 percent of 88,018 federal prisoners) would be classified as sex offenders. Many offenders currently in prison for other crimes have a criminal history that includes at least one sex offense conviction as an adult, and an unknown number of our state prison population have a juvenile record for sex offending. Taken together, approximately one in five offenders returning from state prison facilities to the community each year could be categorized as sex offenders. The sex offender category consists of a variety of behaviors that include, but are not limited to rapists, child molesters or pedophiles, exposures and other sexual deviancy. These groups of offenders pose a major classification, treatment, and control dilemma for public and community safety officials attempting to address the offender reentry issue. The different types of behavior imply different levels of treatment and control that are needed to address public safety issues (CSOM, 2001).

It needs to be pointed out that, as a group, sex offenders have comparatively lower recidivism rates than either drug or property offenders. However, *untreated* sex offenders have re-offense rates that are twice as high as sex offenders who receive some form of treatment (see, e.g., Alexander, 1999). Given these research findings, it is critical that RPI program developers think creatively about how to increase the treatment participation rates for sex offenders during all three of the reentry program's treatment phases. In those programs that exclude sex offenders, efforts will need to be made to explain the rationale for exclusion to residents of targeted communities. It is to be hoped that program developers in these jurisdictions will have more to fall back on than transfer mechanisms (via sexually dangerous offenders statutes) and sex offender registration.

B. Repeat Offenders.   Repeat offenders are those offenders who have a history of criminal behavior, including offenses that affect the quality of life of the communities. Nearly 60 percent of the federal prisoners and 83 percent of the state prisoners have at least one prior criminal conviction (Beck and Harrison, 2001). The classification issues for repeat offenders present enormous challenges to reentry planners. The repeat offender has violated the norms of the community, whether for a serious (e.g, murder, rape, robbery, assault, etc.) or minor (e.g., public disorder, etc.) offense. When viewed in the broader context of criminal "careers" (or crimes in the life course), an offender's current offense tends to be rather misleading, because it does not detail the offender's criminal history or the pattern of criminal behavior. For example, more offenders are in prison for public disorder offenses (up 114 percent in ten years), but their incarceration is more likely due to their criminal history than to the nature of the instant offense. Lynch and Sabol (2001) note that offenders in prison for violent offenses often have mental health and personal/behavioral issues that are not addressed in traditional prison treatment programs. For this reason, they are more likely to have behaviors that will carry over into the community. As a recent nationwide review of prison classification systems demonstrated (Hardyman et al., 2004), few prisons have a classification system that adequately assesses the offenders' criminogenic risk and need factors, therefore leaving reentry planners without a good understanding of the psychosocial functioning of the offender at the time of release from prison. Further, the complexity of criminal "careers" typologies generally (and offender crime trajectories in particular) underscores the need to identify subgroups of offenders at different states in their criminal careers.

A related category is the churners, or offenders that are in the prison-parole-prison cycle due to technical violations or new arrests while on supervision. As reported by Lynch and Sabol (2001), 36 percent of the prison releases in 1998 were prisoners who were released from a subsequent prison term on an original sentence. In other words, they had been in prison and released and then returned to prison for "mishaps" in the community. These repeat offenders present public safety challenges because they have already been unsuccessful in their reintegration; for these offenders, reentry applies equally to prison and community, which suggests the need to rethink our approach to this group of releasees.

C. Substance Abusers/Drug Offenders.   Most correctional administrators really recognize that most offenders are substance abusers, with national surveys noting that 80 percent of the state prisoners and 70 percent of the federal prisoners self-reported past drug and/or alcohol use (Ditton, 1999) and 16 percent reported committing the current crime to obtain funds for illicit drugs. A 1997 study of prisoners used the CAGE, a standard protocol in the field of alcohol assessment, finding that 24 percent of the offenders are alcohol dependent. The study did not use techniques to estimate the drug dependent population. However, as part of the Arrestee Drug Abuse Monitoring (ADAM), researchers found that nearly 80 percent of the offenders report past drug and/or alcohol use and 51 to 79 percent of the arrestees (with a median of 65 percent) have positive urinalysis at the time of the arrest for marijuana, cocaine/crack, heroine and opiates, methamphetamines, phencyclidine (PCP), and benzobiazepines. Using the DSM IV criteria to define drug dependency, 38 percent of the offenders were found to be dependent and in need of treatment. Actually, approximately half of the positive offenders (34 percent of all offenders) were considered heavy drug users based on the commonly accepted criteria of using drugs for at least 13 days per month (Taylor et al., 2001). Findings from ADAM indicate the offenders are not homogenous in their use patterns and in fact there is tremendous variation in their use of illicit substances. Marijuana, in most regions, continues to be the drug of choice. While offenders tend to test positive for one drug, behaviorally the dependent user tends to use an array of illicit substances depending on the availability.

The challenge for correctional officials is to identify the subgroup of returning offenders whose drug-alcohol dependency is directly associated with *other* forms of criminal behavior. This is the group that would most likely benefit from treatment and who pose a more immediate threat to public safety/security. Other drug users—entrepreneurs or recreational drug users—are less likely targets for substance abuse treatment programming, since their criminal behavior is not affected by their drug use (Chaiken and Johnson, 1988). A challenge exists to identify offenders who have substance-abusing behavior that increases their risk-taking in their criminal activities. Correctional administrators and treatment providers must develop a classification scheme that distinguishes between the substance abusers and the criminals. Such a scheme will allow RPI stakeholders to target offenders to appropriate treatment services, based on the need for cost-effective reentry strategies. As a number of researchers have suggested, different strategies must be developed based on an understanding of the specific state of an offender's addiction career and his/her criminal career.

D. Mentally Ill Offender/Dual Diagnoses.   Between 15 and 20 percent of the state prisoners have mental health issues that affect their normal functioning. A recent study of prisoners found that 14 percent had a mental health or emotional crisis in prison or were required to be admitted overnight. Nearly 10 percent of the offenders were using psychotropic medications within prison for their mental health issues, although six states had 20 percent of the offenders using medications (Hawaii, Maine, Montana, Nebraska, Oregon, and Vermont). A recent BJS study found that mental health services are commonly provided in maximum/high-security confinement facilities. Further, nearly 13 percent of the state inmates receive some type of mental health therapy, usually counseling (Beck and Maruschak, 2001). The prevalence of mental health disorders among the prison population carries over to the community, where medication and access to services are limited due to lack of health insurance. The needs of mentally ill offenders are just becoming more apparent as mental health issues are identified, especially related to the specific problem of providing treatment (both institutional and community-based) for the multiple problem offender (see, e.g. Lurigio et al., 2007). We know, for example, that mentally ill substance abusers fail in traditional substance abuse treatment programs at a significantly higher rate than other substance abusers. It is likely that similar failure patterns can be identified for the treatment of other offender problems (e.g., mentally ill sex offenders, mentally ill repeat offenders) that suggests that the multiple problem offenders require a different approach. Excluding mentally ill offenders and/or multiple problem offenders from the latest wave of reentry programs is obviously not the answer. Only a collaborative response from *both* mental health and corrections professionals (again, see Lurigio et al., 2007) can begin to address this target population's problems and needs.

5. CONCLUSIONS: OFFENDERS, COMMUNITIES AND THE NEED FOR CHANGE

Our review of the targeting criteria used in eight model reentry programs (in Massachusetts, Vermont, South Carolina, Florida, Washington, Nevada, Maryland, and Missouri) highlighted a number of critical issues that must be addressed by program developers. First, it appears that program developers—while agreeing that the reentry process includes three distinct, but interrelated phases (institutional) structured reentry, and reintegration)—are having difficulty clearly putting into operation each of these three program components. This problem is most noticeable in our review of the institutional phase of reentry; it is often unclear *when* this phase begins, *how* it should be distinct from the normal institutional programming and processes, and *where* the initial institutional phase of reentry should be located (e.g., should all reentry offenders reside in the same facility, on the same wing, etc., utilizing a therapeutic community model? Or should they simply have access to the same programs and resources, regardless of location?).

A second question that emerges from our review is: *Who* should be targeted for reentry? As we highlighted earlier, only a small proportion of all offenders currently in prison will be released to one of the specialized reentry programs described here. According to a recent BJS review of reentry patterns, *half* of the 600,000 adult prisoners released from state prison in 2001 came from the five states included in this report (California, Florida, Illinois, New York, and Texas). However, the target populations identified for these five states included *fewer than one thousand prisoners,* which represents less than 1/3 of 1 percent of all releasees from these five states. These selected inmates will be placed in programs funded by OJP's (100 million dollar) reentry initiative; about 9 million dollars was allocated to these five states for *adult* reentry programs, approximately $9,000 per offender released. Since only a fraction of the reentering prison population can be placed in this new wave of reentry programs, program developers need to consider carefully the criteria for selection they will utilize in their own jurisdictions.

Given limited resources, it certainly makes sense to begin by targeting specific *locations* for participation, perhaps based on an examination of previous release locations for each state's prison population. However, the danger inherent in restricting access to those offenders returning to a particular community or neighborhood is that (1) the program may actually *increase* the concentration of ex-offenders in a particular neighborhood, and (2) the identification of returning offenders in a specific area as reentry participants may result in the use of profiling strategies by local police (see Byrne and Hummer, 2004 for a discussion), which could have negative consequences for both offenders and communities.

Our review also revealed that program developers—often with a limited number of program placements—may exclude both high risk (to reoffend) and high stakes (to the programs' legitimacy) offenders from the initial target population. The problem inherent in this strategy is that it excludes from participation the very group of offenders most likely to need the services, support, and control provided by the reentry initiative. Since these offenders will be returning to the community anyway, program developers may want to consider the possibility that by expanding their target population, they may actually improve both community satisfaction and community safety (if the program actually delivers on its recidivism reduction goal). Of course, a larger target population requires additional funding for the reentry initiative, which may be difficult to obtain.

Finally, our discussion of the different offender types released from prison everyday—such as sex offenders, drug offenders, repeat offenders, and mentally ill offenders—emphasized the need to design *each* phase of the reentry process to address the reintegration issues raised by the specific target population selected for reentry. Since targeting decisions will vary from jurisdiction to jurisdiction, we anticipate that reentry program models will vary from site to site as well. However, we would recommend that program developers carefully consider whether their reentry program model can address the needs of the multiple-problem offender, since it is likely that—regardless of offense-specific, offender-specific, and location-specific targeting decisions—the majority of prisoners included in their program could be described as multiple-problem offenders.

QUESTIONS FOR REVIEW AND DISCUSSION

1. What are some general reentry trends among parolees? What are some of their characteristics? Describe.

2. What are some of the criteria used to make early-release decisions? Are these criteria effective in selecting the most eligible offenders for reentry? Why or why not? Explain.

3. What is meant by structured reentry? How important is community reintegration in a parolee's acceptance and adjustment?

4. Which types of offenders seem to be most inclined to repeat their criminal behaviors and recidivate upon release from prison?

5. Are there community mechanisms or interventions that might work in enhancing offender community readjustment? What are these mechanisms or interventions?

6. What is a therapeutic community model? What types of offenders are targeted?

7. Are there any reentry strategies that appear to be more promising than others? Why or why not? Discuss.

42

Environmental Corrections

A New Paradigm for Effective Probation and Parole Supervision

Francis T. Cullen, John E. Eck,
and Christopher T. Lowenkamp

Adapted from Francis T. Cullen, John E. Eck, and Christopher T. Lowenkamp, "Environmental Corrections: A New Paradigm for Effective Probation and Parole Supervision." *Federal Probation* 66: 28–37, 2002.

Reprinted by permission from the Administrative Office of the U.S. Courts.

Most Americans—such as the late Lou Gehrig in the last year of his life—manifest ambivalence about imprisoning one's "fellows." At times, opinion polls show that the public favors lengthy prison terms for offenders (Cullen, Fisher, and Applegate, 2000; Jacoby and Cullen, 1998). After all, the seven-fold increase in state and federal prison populations since 1970 has provoked only muted citizen opposition. And in several states the public have enthusiastically passed "three-strikes-and-you're out" laws Zimring, Hawkins, and Kamin, 2001).

Still, surveys also reveal that most Americans see prisons as potential schools of crime and doubt their deterrent effect. They are against merely warehousing offenders, and instead favor expanding rehabilitation programs. If offenders are not dangerous, Americans are willing to see if these wayward "fellows"—the ones who have "gotten bad breaks" as Lou Gehrig put it—can make it in the community (Applegate, Cullen, and Fisher, 1997; Cullen et al., 2000).

In fact, it is probably misleading to see prison and probation/parole as a strictly zero-sum phenomenon. For individual offenders, of course, the "in/out" decision—whether or not one goes to or is released from prison—is experienced as a zero-sum gaining or loss of freedom. But on a broad policy level, the growth of the incarcerated population to over

2 million offenders has not been accompanied by a commensurate reduction in the size of those under community supervision (Petersilia, 1997). As Petersilia (1997) shows, between 1980 and 1995 prison populations grew 237 percent; the comparable increase for parole was 218 percent and for probation was 177 percent. Numerically, the increase for probation—over 3 million—was about triple the 1.078 million increase for prisons. Furthermore, the number of convicted offenders under community supervision—which increased an average of 3.6 percent between 1990 and 2000—now stands at over 4.6 million. This statistic includes 725,500 offenders on parole and over 3.8 on probation (Bureau of Justice Statistics, 2001c).

The sheer number of offenders on probation and parole has created a crisis that, in many jurisdictions, is characterized by the twin problems of flat or shrinking resources and rising caseloads—estimated to be an offender-officer ratio of 30 to 1 for parole and 175 to 1 for probation (Camp and Camp, 1999; Petersilia, 1997, 2002; Reinventing Probation Council, 2000). This problem is daunting and, on one level or another, undoubtedly is implicated in any assessment of community supervision. For our purposes, however, we will suspend this broad contextual reality for much of our essay. Instead, we want to focus on the closely related, but analytically separate, issue of the *effectiveness of probation and parole supervision*. Simply put, if on any given day, 4.6 million convicted offenders are in our midst, one must question whether this is a wise policy to pursue. More precisely, the concern is whether we are supervising these offenders in the most efficacious way possible. Our main thesis is that the current practice of *community supervision could potentially be improved, perhaps dramatically, by adopting a new paradigm—a new way of thinking—about how best to supervise offenders on probation and parole;* we call this paradigm *environmental corrections.* But we do not wish to get too far ahead of ourselves, so let us pause for a moment before revisiting this matter in considerable detail.

THE NEED TO REINVENT COMMUNITY SUPERVISION

At present, American criminologists hold two incompatible views of probation and parole. First, most criminologists—representing a liberal or progressive position—see community supervision as the *lesser of two evils*: at least it is better than incarceration! There is no agenda as to how probation and parole might be accomplished more effectively. Rather, value inheres in community supervision only—or mainly—because it is *not prison*. In this scenario, prisons are depicted as costly and inhumane. They are seen as causing crime in two ways: by making those placed behind bars more criminogenic and by so disrupting communities—especially minority communities that lose high percentages of young males to incarceration—as to exacerbate crime's root causes (e.g., increase institutional disorganization) (see, more generally, Rose and Clear, 1998). Probation and parole are embraced because they are a lesser form of what Clear (1994) calls "penal harm"—a lesser form of the state's intervention into the lives of offenders. In this viewpoint, the more radical the state's *non-intervention,* the better (more generally, see Cullen and Gendreau, 2001; Travis and Cullen, 1994).

Second, a minority of criminologists—representing a conservative position—sees community supervision *as an evil.* John DiIulio is perhaps most noted for warning about the risks of failing to incarcerate offenders (Bennett, DiIulio, and Walters, 1996; DiIulio, 1994a, 1994b; Logan and DiIulio, 1992; see also, Piehl and DiIulio, 1995). For DiIulio, probation and premature parole are dangerous policies that allow not only petty offenders but also chronic and potentially violent offenders to continue their criminality. The social injustice of this policy, he claims, is that the victims of these offenders are disproportionately poor and minority inner-city residents; prisons, he says, "save black lives" (DiIulio, 1994a). He tells, for example, a "Philadelphia crime story," in which a cap on the local jail population by a federal judge led to offenders being given pre-trial release. The consequence, according to DiIulio (1994b, p. A21), was that "9,732 arrestees out on the street on pre-trial release because of her prison cap were arrested on second charges, including 79 murders, 90 rapes, 701 burglaries, 959 robberies, 1,113 assaults, 2,215 drug offenses and 2,745 thefts." The statistics nationally are even more startling. Writing with William Bennett and John Walters, DiIulio observes that convicted offenders in the community "do tremendous numbers of serious crimes, including a frightening fraction of all murders" (Bennett et al., 1996, p. 105). In 1991, for example, the 162,000 offenders who violated probation—who averaged 17 months under supervision in the community—were convicted of "6,400 murders, 7,400 rapes, 10,400 assaults, and 17,000 robberies" (Bennett et al., 1996, p. 105).

In a way, these two competing perspectives capture "realities" that are both correct. On the one hand, it is foolish to diminish the very real public-safety risk that offenders pose who are released into the community—to "deny their pathology" as Elliott Currie (1985) once put it. Research from life-course criminology now shows persuasively that there is a group of persistent offenders; some members of this group commit a few crimes annually and some a great number, but virtually all are lawless enough to be arrested and potentially incarcerated (see, e.g., Benson, 2002; see also, Piehl and DiIulio, 1995; Spelman, 2000). In this context, for 1992 the Bureau of Justice Statistics estimated that 17 percent of all those arrested for felonies were currently on probation (Petersilia, 1997, p. 183). In state prisons, almost 3 in 10 offenders were on probation when arrested; a similar proportion of death-row inmates report committing murder while they were on either probation or parole (Petersilia, 1997, p. 183). Only 43 percent of those under community supervision complete probation and parole successfully. Further, even discounting plea-bargaining and past criminal records, half of those on probation (52 percent) were placed on community supervision for committing a felony offense (Bureau of Justice Statistics, 2001c).

On the other hand, it is equally foolish to imagine that prisons are the sole solution to crime (Clear, 1994; Currie, 1998; Petersilia, 1992). In fact, it may be that the nation's thirty-year "imprisonment binge" (Irwin and Austin, 1994) is close to exhausting itself. Faced with spending $30 billion a year to administer correctional institutions, states are now "reversing a 20-year trend toward ever-tougher criminal laws—quietly rolling back some of their most stringent anticrime measures, including those imposing mandatory minimum sentences and forbidding early parole" (Butterfield, 2001; see also, Jasper, 2001). Furthermore, if prisons reduce crime, it seems likely that this is achieved mainly through incapacitation, not deterrence (Spelman, 2000; more generally, compare Lynch, 1999 with Nagin, 1998). There is beginning evidence, for example, that the longer offenders stay in prison, the higher their recidivism rate is when they are released (Gendreau, Goggin, Cullen, and Andrews, 2000). There also is research suggesting that compared to those imprisoned, re-offending is equal, if not lower, among those who are placed on probation (Cullen, Pratt, Miceli, and Moon, 2002; Petersilia and Turner, 1986; see also, Sampson and Laub, 1993). These findings are inconsistent with the view that prisons specifically deter offenders.

Where, then, do these various considerations leave us? First, in contrast to the desires of conservative commentators, the stubborn reality is that most offenders will not be incarcerated but will be placed under community supervision. And among those who are locked up, a high proportion will re-enter society in a reasonably short period of time—and perhaps more criminogenic than they were before being imprisoned (Petersilia, 1999; Lynch and Sabol, 2001; Travis, Solomon, and Waul, 2001). Second, in contrast to the implicitly rosy portrait that liberals often paint of the criminally wayward, many of these offenders placed in the community will be occasionally, if not high-rate, offenders. *In short, we are left with the inescapable necessity of supervising many potentially active, if not dangerous, offenders in the community.*

In this light, it is odd how little liberal commentators have had to say about the "technology" of offender supervision—that is, how to do it more effectively. They have remained silent for 30 years on methods of improving community-based supervision. In part, this silence represents a larger rejection of the social welfare role in corrections (Cullen and Gendreau, 2001), and the belief that the two sides of the probation/parole officer role—treatment and control—are in inherent conflict and render officers ineffective in their efforts to improve offenders (Rothman, 1980). Again, liberals have endorsed probation mainly as an alternative to prison, and what it should involve—its specific components—has been beside the point. We should note that in response to this failure to articulate a clear progressive vision of probation and parole, there is now a beginning movement to "reinvent" offender supervision under the name of "community justice" or the "broken windows" model (Clear, 1996; Clear and Corbett, 1999; Reinventing Probation Council, 2000). This revisionist thinking is noteworthy, however, precisely because it remains the exception to the rule (see also, Nevers, 1998; Leaf, Lurigio, and Martin, 1998).

In contrast, beginning in the 1980s, conservative commentators had much to say about how to "reform" community supervision: purge it of its social welfare functions and increase its policing and deterrence functions. We will revisit this matter soon, but we will give advance notice that this prescription has been detrimental to the practice of community supervision. It is a failed model (see, e.g., Cullen, Wright, and Applegate, 1996; Fulton, Latessa, Stuchman, and Travis, 1997; Gendreau, Cullen, and Bonta, 1994; Gendreau, Goggin, Cullen, and Andrews, 2000).

To reiterate, then, the purpose of the current paper *is to suggest a new paradigm or strategy for improving the community supervision of offenders.* Our effort, we believe, is both modest and promising. Our admission of modesty comes from the realization that we are, after all, proposing a conceptual framework, not a set of intervention techniques already proven to "work" in the real world. But despite their inherent limitations, new frameworks hold promise because they open up fresh possibilities of doing things; they are often a necessary, albeit not a sufficient, condition for change. In developing a different paradigm or way of thinking for probation and parole, we hope to provide advice where liberals have offered none and provide better advice than that furnished by conservatives.

The main premise of this enterprise is that effective correctional intervention must be based on *effective criminological research and theory* (see also, Andrews and Bonta, 1998). In this regard, we propose to borrow core insights from *environmental criminology*—a theory that links crime causation and crime reduction to the presence or absence of opportunities to offend—and to explore its implications for probation and parole supervision. In short, we wish to move *toward a paradigm of environmental corrections.*

Such an environmental approach will be novel but not fully new. Ideas often emerge simultaneously, though set forth in different contexts and with different emphases. The "community justice" or "broken windows" model mentioned just above foreshadows many of the insights we offer in this essay. Building on the ideas on community policing, problem-oriented policing, and a "broken windows" view of neighborhood disorder, a community justice model advocates probation/parole supervision that is proactive, neighborhood-based, linked to community groups and other justice agencies, restorative to victims, and concentrated in places where most crime occurs (for discussions of this model and related ideas, see Clear, 1996; Clear and Corbett, 1999; Karp and Clear, 2000; Kurki, 2000; Reinventing Probation Council, 2000). The clearest point of overlap between "community justice" corrections and environmental corrections is that both approaches believe that in supervising offenders, probation and parole officers should be *problem solvers,* sensitive to the *places* in which crime occurs, and enlist the assistance of both experts and *residents* in attempts to reduce crime events from transpiring.

The distinctiveness of environmental corrections is that its focus is, at once, more limited and more precise. Community justice is a broader paradigm that seeks to change the fundamental nature of corrections and, more generally, criminal justice—just as, for example, the rehabilitative ideal did during the Progressive Era and the "get tough" movement has more recently (Clear, 1994; Cullen and Gilbert, 1982; Rothman, 1980). Environmental corrections is compatible with the multifaceted shift inherent in the call for community justice, but it also can be part of a more incremental effort to reform existing community supervision. The key aspect of environmental corrections is not its revolutionary character but *its novel use of the insights of environmental criminology to illuminate how correctional supervision can lower recidivism by reducing offenders' opportunities to offend.* Advocates of community justice have offered similar insights (see, especially, Clear, 1996; Clear and Corbett, 1999), but they have stopped short of calling for a systematic environmental corrections that is explicitly tied to environmental criminology.

In the current essay, we follow the admonition of the Reinventing Probation Council, which advised that *"probation agencies must start thinking outside the box for public safety,* and design supervision strategies and programs for crime prevention and community betterment" (2000, p. 19; emphasis in original). We begin by discussing the central ingredients in crime and then make the commonsensical observation that, to reduce recidivism, community supervision must "do something about" each of these ingredients. Our special concern is with one of these ingredients—*opportunity*—and with how environmental criminology provides a theoretical framework for reconceptualizing the specific goals and means of offender supervision. This approach does require probation and parole agencies to "think outside the box," but not in ways that are counterintuitive or professionally demeaning. Instead, environmental criminology sees the insights of practitioners as integral to any effort to creatively redesign community supervision so that it makes the choice of returning to crime more difficult and less enticing.

CRIME IN THE MAKING—PROPENSITY AND OPPORTUNITY

For a criminal event to occur, two ingredients must converge in time and space: first, there must be a "motivated offender"—a person who has the propensity to commit the criminal act. Second, the person harboring a criminal propensity must have the *opportunity* to commit a crime (Cohen and Felson, 1979; Felson, 1995). This simple idea—that the recipe for making a criminal act is propensity and opportunity—holds potentially profound and complex implications for how to reduce crime. These implications have seldom been systematically or scientifically explored within corrections.

What Works with Propensity

Following the publication of Robert Martinson's (1974) classic review of research suggesting that treatment programs had "no appreciable effect" on recidivism, it became widely believed that "nothing works" in corrections (Cullen and Gilbert, 1982). Fortunately, this position is no longer tenable (Cullen, 2002; Cullen and Gendreau, 2000, 2001; MacKenzie, 2000). Research from available meta-analysis is now incontrovertible that correctional intervention programs—especially in the community—reduce recidivism (see, e.g., Andrews, Zinger, Hoge, Bonta, Gendreau, and Cullen 1990; Lipsey, 1992; Lipsey and Wilson, 1998; Losel, 1995; Redondo, Sanchez-Meca, and Garrido, 1999). These programs are especially effective in reducing reoffending when they are consistent with certain principles of effective intervention (Andrews, 1995; Gendreau, 1996; see also, Lurigio, 2000; Prendergast, Anglin, and Wellisch, 1995; Taxman, 2000). Such principles include: (1) using cognitive-behavioral interventions within the context of multi-modal programs; (2) targeting for change the known predictors of recidivism; (3) focusing on higher-risk offenders; (4) applying a sufficient dosage of treatment; and (5) providing appropriate aftercare.

The point here is that we are moving toward evidence-based corrections in which we have a good idea of the programmatic principles that induce offender change (Cullen and Gendreau, 2000; MacKenzie, 2000). The challenge is for probation and parole agencies to create programs based on the principles of effective intervention or to be "brokers" in which they place offenders into such programs as a core part of their correctional supervision requirements. The failure to attack offenders' propensity for crime through such programming no longer can be excused. Not doing so jeopardizes not only the offenders' chance for reform but also public safety. These assertions are strongly stated, but the knowledge base on "what works" in treatment is sufficiently developed that it is simply inexcusable (1) to use unproven intervention techniques or (2) to neglect treating offenders entirely (Gendreau et al., 1994).

The main thrust of this paper, however, is not with how probation and parole agencies should seek to reduce offenders' criminal propensities. As the literature cited above indicates, this issue is being addressed systematically and empirically. Instead, our chief interest is in the other ingredient to crime: access to the opportunity to offend.

What Does Not Work with Opportunity

From the beginning period in which community supervision was invented (Rothman, 1980), it was understood that "supervision" involved both trying to change offenders for the better *and* acting as an external source of control that, backed up by the threat of revocation, tried to keep offenders away from "trouble." When placed in the community, offenders often were given lists of "conditions" that spelled out the kind of situations they must avoid, including, for example, not frequenting bars, not having contact with criminal associates, and not carrying a weapon. There were also prescriptions of what offenders could do, such as staying employed and attending school. Embedded within these probation and parole "conditions" was the assumption that "going straight" was facilitated by offenders avoiding situations where *opportunities for crime* were present and frequenting situations where opportunities for crime were absent. Unfortunately, this core insight was never fully developed to its logical conclusion: the idea that a fundamental goal of community supervision was to *plan systematically with each offender on how precisely to reduce his or her opportunities for wayward conduct.*

As will be explored shortly in greater deal, opportunity reduction involves, among other factors, problem solving—that is, figuring out how to keep offenders away from situations in which trouble inheres. This approach requires, fundamentally, changing the *nature of supervision.* In contrast, efforts from the 1980s to the present to "intensively supervise" offenders—the deterrence-oriented "reform" advocated by conservatives—have sought mainly to change the *amount of supervision.* This strategy is akin to a police crackdown on crime in hopes of increasing the risk of detection or arrest as opposed to using police resources to solve the problems fostering neighborhood crime; even if the crackdown works for a specific period or for specific offenders, the effects tend to wear off over time because the underlying problems are not addressed. In any event, whether the literature involves narrative reviews, meta-analyses, or randomized experimental evaluations, the results are clear in showing that deterrence-oriented intensive supervision simply does not reduce recidivism (see, for example, Byrne and Pattavina, 1992; Cullen and Gendreau, 2000; Cullen et al., 2002; Cullen et al., 1996; Fulton et al., 1997; Gendreau et al., 1994; Gendreau, Goggin, Cullen, and Andrews, 2000; Gendreau, Goggin, and Fulton, 2000; MacKenzie, 2000; Petersilia, 1999; Petersilia and Turner, 1993). "There is no solid evidence," as Travis et al. (2001, p. 21) put it, "that solely increasing parole supervision will result in fewer crimes."

The weakness in the intensive supervision approach—the "pee 'em and see 'em" model as some officers call it—is that it is based on a crude understanding of crime. Efforts to specifically deter offenders through uncertain and distant threats of punishment are notoriously ineffective (Cullen et al., 2002). It may seem like good "common sense" that more intense monitoring would increase the deterrent capacity of community supervision. But its effects are diminished by two factors: it does not do much to change the underlying propensity to offend and it does not do much to change the structure of opportunities that induce "motivated offenders" to recidivate. In short, the two key ingredients to making crime—propensity and opportunity—are not transformed by increasing the amount of supervision. A new theory of supervision is needed—one that shows how to change the *nature* of supervision. It is to the conceptual building blocks of this approach that we now turn.

BUILDING ENVIRONMENTAL CORRECTIONS—LEARNING FROM ENVIRONMENTAL CRIMINOLOGY

Most criminological theories try to explain crime by variation in offender motivation and assume that criminal opportunities are ubiquitous. Environmental criminological theories, however, assume that the driving force behind crime is *opportunity,* because motivations to commit crimes, though variable, are common. In short, environmental criminologists believe that if you create an opportunity to commit crime, someone will eventually come to take advantage of it. To use an analogy from the baseball movie starring Kevin Costner, *Field of Dreams*: If you "build it"—in this case, a crime opportunity—offenders will "come."

A Core Theoretical Proposition

The insight from environmental criminology that opportunity is a salient criminogenic risk factor has important implications for the practice of corrections. If risk factors for crime are left untouched—or are targeted for change in ineffective ways—then offenders' chances of recidivating are increased. Conversely, effective correctional interventions have shown that they target and then change the risk factors underlying criminal behavior (Andrews and Bonta, 1998). Building on this insight, we offer the core proposition to our new paradigm of "environmental corrections": *The effectiveness of probation and parole supervision will be increased to the extent that officers systematically work with offenders, family and community members, and the police to reduce the extent to which offenders are tempted by and come into contact with opportunities for crime.* We suggest that the ineffectiveness of community supervision has, at least in part, been due to the failure to impact offenders' access to criminal opportunities.

Environmental Criminology

To develop a new approach to community correctional supervision, it is prudent to draw on that branch of the field that studies crime opportunities—a set of perspectives now grouped under the umbrella of *environmental criminology.* Scholarship in this area is both diverse and growing, and only its key components can be summarized here (for a more extensive review, see Bottoms, 1994). In this regard, four principles guide environmental criminology. First, offenders, like all people, are constrained in their movements by their daily routines and streetscapes, and these constrained movements bring offenders into contact with possible crime opportunities. Second, locations vary in the opportunities for crime they present to people with an inclination to commit crimes. Third, offenders, like all people, read their environments for clues as to what types of behavior are feasible. And fourth, offenders, like all people, make choices based on their perceptions of rewards, risk, effort, and ability to be "excused."

In short, environmental criminology investigates how offenders interact with their world and the consequences—including criminal acts—of these interactions. Three important variants of this approach can be found in the extant literature. We briefly review these approaches here.

Offender Movement and Offender Search Theory.   Offender search theory is based in the theories of transportation geography. People have "nodes" of activities—homes, schools, jobs, entertainment spots, shopping places, and so forth—and they travel between these nodes along routes. The routes and nodes network create the backbone of a "target" search area—not unlike a search area for a shopper except that the target is for crime and not for purchasing goods or services. Crime targets within sight of the routes and nodes are vulnerable to attack.

Offender search theory predicts that offenders look for targets around activity nodes and close to travel routes between nodes. This is called the "search area." When the search area overlaps with potential targets, there is a heightened chance of a crime. Targets far from search areas, however, have low probabilities of being victimized, and offenders moving through environments devoid of targets will get into little trouble.

Crime Hot Spots and Routine Activity Theory.   Offender search theory describes how people's routine movements structure the way they identify crime opportunities. Although it provides insight into those areas that will have many crimes and those that will have few crimes, this approach does not predict which targets will be selected within these areas. Notably, the selection of specific places—locations—for the commission of crimes depends on a host of site-specific conditions that, in combination, create an opportunity structure. The result is that a few places are repeatedly the sites of crime, whereas most places have few or no crimes. This concentration of crime at a few "hot spots" is similar to the concentration of criminal activity in a few repeat offenders.

What is it about *places* that make them either seemingly immune to criminal predation or the scene of repeated crimes? Routine activity theory explains this phenomenon. According to this approach, crimes occur when a "motivated offender" (a person with a propensity for crime) and an "attractive target" come together at the same time and place, and in the absence of people who are likely to prevent a crime. The inner triangle in Figure 1 depicts the three necessary elements for a crime to occur. Each of these three elements, however, has a potential "controller"—a person (or people) whose role it is to protect them (Felson, 1995). If a controller is present, then the opportunity for crime either is diminished or vanishes.

Thus, "handlers" control potential offenders. They are individuals with an emotional bond with the offender and who act in ways to keep the potential offender from offending. Parents, siblings, spouses, coaches, clergy, neighbors, and friends can be handlers. Offenders do not want handlers to know about any of their misdeeds. For this reason, offenders commit their crimes away from their handlers. Not surprisingly, very active offenders have few handlers in their lives, and these are not particularly effective. We note in passing that probation and parole officials can be considered "surrogate handlers."

"Guardians" control or protect targets (or potential victims, when the target is a person). Owners of things are the primary guardians of their property, though they may enlist others to act as guardians. Friends, neighbors, and colleagues protect each other from criminal predation, thus acting as guardians. Police officers can be considered surrogate guardians. Offenders shun targets with strong guardianship and seek targets with little or not guardianship.

All places are owned and controlled by someone or something. Owners, and their hired employees, are "managers." They are responsible for the smooth functioning of the

FIGURE 1
Routine Activity Theory's Crime Triangles

place. Managers include stores clerks, lifeguards, flight attendants, teachers in their class-rooms, bar tenders, librarians, and anyone employed to work at a location. Offenders avoid committing crimes against targets at locations with active managers.

When considered in its entirety, routine activity theory accounts for two important facts about crime. First, it explains why crime is extremely rare, given the ubiquity of crime targets. For a crime to occur not only do the three necessary elements have to come to-gether at the same time, but also there must be an absence of the three types of controllers. Such a combination of events occurs more frequently than we would like, but it is still rel-atively rare.

Second, it explains why crime is concentrated and, in fact, concentrated in three im-portant ways. Thus, crime is concentrated (1) in relatively few offenders—"repeat offend-ers"; (2) in relatively few victims—"repeat victims"; and (3) in a few places—repeat places or "hot spots" of crime. In each form of concentration, the reason is the routine absence of the three controllers when offenders meet targets (Eck, 2001).

Offender Choices and Situational Prevention.   Environmental criminology rests on the assumption that people—including offenders—make choices about what actions to take, given the circumstances they are in. This observation brings us to the third environ-mental criminological theory: situational crime prevention. This theory posits that offend-ers take into account four characteristics of situations; the possible rewards of offending; the risks of being detected by handlers, guardians, and managers; the effort it would take to attack the target and escape detection by possible controllers; and the excuses one could use to explain one's actions (Clarke and Homel, 1997). Environments may also be so structured that they stimulate situational motivations to offend (Wortley, 1997). In any event, because the offenders' decision calculus takes place moments before a crime, an intervention that occurs proximate to a crime situation will be more effective in preventing the given crimi-nal act than a more distal intervention. Furthermore, to the extent that active offenders have impaired cognitive abilities that make them more impulsive and take less account of past messages and future consequences, then situational prevention potentially has its greatest influence on the most troublesome people.

Practical Implications

Although useful in other ways, many criminological theories identify sources of crime—of-ten called "root causes" (e.g., inequality)—that provide few practical insights on how to pre-vent crime in the here and now. Environmental criminology is distinctive, however, in its identification of key elements of criminal acts that, at least potentially, are more amenable to manipulation. In particular, it focuses on factors proximate and integral to the criminal act—on factors that must converge in time and space or the crime will not occur. Accordingly, this perspective has more immediate practical implications on how to reduce criminal activity. Briefly put, crime is prevented by ensuring that offenders and targets do not converge at the same place and, if they do, that control or guardianship is present. Although we lack the space to review the research studies here, there is now voluminous evidence that policing and private interventions based on the principles of environmental criminology can achieve meaningful reductions in crime (see, e.g., Eck, 2002; Felson, 1995).

A NEW PARADIGM FOR CORRECTIONAL SUPERVISION

Probation and Parole Officers as Problem Solvers

Recidivism is due to offenders' retaining criminogenic motivation or propensity and their having access to opportunities for crime. Thus, to reduce reoffending, an important task for a probation or parole agency is to provide or place offenders into treatment programs, based on the principles of effective rehabilitation, that diminish their propensity for crime (Gendreau et al., 1994). The other task, however, is for probation and parole officers to reduce offenders' access to *crime opportunities*. In many agencies, this challenge will involve reconceptualizing the very nature of what offender *supervision* entails.

Even before the movement toward control-oriented supervision in the 1980s, it was common to distinguish two components of the officer's role: (1) as a counselor or human services provider, and (2) as a controller who "policed" offenders. As suggested previously, the flaw in the policing function of probation and parole officers was that it was based on the erroneous assumptions that effective supervision involved merely watching for and reacting to instances of offender misconduct. Much as in traditional law enforcement, they were acting as "crime busters." But as is well known, policing is in the midst of a paradigm shift that is transforming the role of police officers from that of "arrest makers" to "crime preventers" (Eck and Spelman, 1987). Whereas traditional enforcement involved vehicle patrols and reacting to reports of criminal incidents, problem-oriented policing values gaining knowledge or understanding about crime patterns (e.g., through mapping and other forms of analysis) and intervening proactively to prevent future criminal incidents from occurring. Opportunity blocking is the core technology of problem-oriented policing. Research suggests that problem-oriented policing is efficacious in lowering crime (Braga, Weisburd, Waring, Mazerolle, Spelman, and Gajewski, 1999; Sherman and Eck, 2002).

In this context, we are proposing that probation and parole officers reconceptualize their supervision function as involving not only watching and busting offenders but also problem solving. The key problem to solve, of course, is how to reduce offenders' access to criminal opportunities. This challenge is daunting but worth the effort: Given that opportunity is a major risk factor in reoffending, the failure to "pay attention" to opportunity reduction will increase the likelihood of recidivism and endanger public safety.

Reconceptualizing Supervision

At this juncture, we are going to offer ideas on what supervision oriented toward opportunity reduction might entail. These suggestions are informed, though not exclusively, by the concepts and insights of environmental criminological theories. We recognize that the recommendations we offer might appear on first blush—indeed, might be—"unrealistic," given the limited resources available. Regardless, although we trust that some specifics we offer might prove useful, our goal is to provoke a new wave of thinking about what it would mean if officers took seriously the task of keeping offenders away from crime opportunities.

Assessment.   Forward-looking agencies realize that, as in medicine, treatment interventions should be based on diagnosis. Instruments to assess offenders' risk and needs, such as the Level of Supervision Inventory, are now being used to classify high-risk offenders and to direct interventions (Bonta, 1996). In a similar way, officers would now complement risk-needs assessments with a diagnosis of the *role opportunity plays in the probationer's or parolee's offending*. Some insights might be gained by mapping in detail the locations (e.g., streets, bars) where past offending has taken place. It might also be useful to interview offenders and to use cognitive intervention techniques, such as "sequencing," in which offenders would describe, in very concrete ways, the steps or sequence of activities that lead them to search for and select crime opportunities and/or to wander into situations where "trouble happens." Further, officers might attempt to map out the routine activities of their supervisees to see whether crime opportunities inhere in their daily activities. Eventually, research studies could be undertaken to develop a "Crime Opportunity-Routine Activity Inventory" and/or other methods that would increase the ability of officers to assess how an offender under supervision creates or comes into contact with crime opportunities.

Working with Offenders. Informed by their opportunity assessment—and, more broadly, by environmental criminology—officers would focus on three tasks. First, with individual supervisees, they would try to *disrupt routine activities that increase crime opportunities*. As opposed to broad supervision conditions, such as "not associating with known felons," officers would seek to prohibit contact with specific people (e.g., past co-offenders), traveling on specific streets (e.g., outlined on a map given to offenders), and access to specific establishments (e.g., bars where trouble often ensues). Second, behavioral change involves not only extinguishing inappropriate conduct, but also replacing it with preferred alternatives. Officers thus might work with offenders to develop daily "activity calendars" scheduling prosocial activities (more generally, see Spiegler and Guevremont, 1998, pp. 326–327). This process might involve officers "brokering" prosocial activities—that is, developing rosters of "things to do" in the community or at home to lead offenders away from crime opportunities. Third, officers would see themselves not exclusively as "enforcing supervision conditions" but as *handlers of offenders*. Although the threat of revocation—a formal sanction—would necessarily loom in the background, the goal would be to exercise *informal social control* over offenders. This would entail using positive reinforcements for prosocial routine activities and building a "bond" with offenders. It might also involve taking whatever steps possible to increase the *effort* offenders would have to expend to access crime opportunities (e.g., challenging "excuses" for being in a forbidden location, responding as soon as possible when informed that an offender deviated from an agreed-upon calendar of activities).

Working with Family Members and the Community.   Ideally, officers would also attempt to enlist an offender's family, prosocial friends, and community members (e.g., minister, teacher) to assist in designing an opportunity reduction plan. Recall that these people are potential *handlers* of the offender. One strategy would be to have a "problem-solving conference" in which offenders and those in their intimate circle would jointly identify problematic routines and places and decide how these might be avoided. Because they are close on a daily basis to offenders, such intimates also might be able to supply positive reinforcements (e.g., praise, tickets to a ballgame, favorite meal) if offenders fulfill a "behavioral contract" to adhere to prosocial routines. As a last resort, they also might assist officers in knowing when offenders are backsliding into routines and places that place them at risk for crime.

Working with Community Place Managers.   Beyond those personally affiliated with offenders, officers might develop relationships with *place managers* in the community—from bartenders, to store owners, to parking lot attendants, to security guards, to police officers. These place managers could be used to contact probation and parole officers when offenders are entering locations where, in the past, trouble has emerged. The cooperation of place managers should be requested strategically, since many are unlikely to wish to be transformed into generalized informants. It might be possible, however, to secure their assistance to help monitor when a specific offender enters the place they are managing, especially if the goal is to head off trouble and make the managers' task of guardianship easier.

Although designed to reduce gang-related violence, Boston's "Operation Night Light" shows the potential impact of a probation-police model that is informed by environmental criminology and problem-solving principles (Corbett, Fitzgerald, and Jordan, 1998). In this intervention, judges imposed conditions of probation on specific offenders that included curfews and geographic restrictions on where youths could travel. Working in conjunction with police on a Youth Violence Strike Force, probation officers visit homes of targeted probationers in the evening hours and examine locations where juveniles "hang out" (e.g., playgrounds, street corners). There was suggestive evidence that the "Night Light" program reduced gang-related violence (see also, Morgan and Marrs, 1998).

In a similar vein, LEIN—the Law Enforcement Information Network—might be used to facilitate police assistance in opportunity reduction for supervisees. Each state has a system that allows police to check automobile registration information as well as an operator's license and criminal history when making a vehicle stop. Some jurisdictions have mandated that when a person is involved in a domestic crime, any "no contact" orders be entered into LEIN so that police can be aware of and enforce these orders. Other professions now advocate the entry of probation conditions into LEIN so that police know who is on community supervision, the nature of their conditions of probation/parole, and how to contact the supervising officer. Such a system would allow police to assist in the enforcement of curfews and restrictions on where offenders are allowed to travel or "hang out."

CONCLUSION—WHAT "WORKS" IN COMMUNITY SUPERVISION?

Corrections is entering an era of accountability in which credibility and funding will hinge increasingly on the ability of agencies to show that its practices "work" or are effective. To achieve reductions in offending, agencies would be wise to start with the realization that criminal acts are the product of offenders' propensity for crime and of their access to opportunities for crime. There is now a sizable literature on "what works"—the principles of effective treatment intervention—to reduce criminogenic propensities (Cullen, 2002; Cullen and Gendreau, 2000). Equally salient, research is clear on what does *not* work with opportunity reduction: broad-based attempts to monitor offenders (even intensely), threaten them with punishment, and then "bust" the "bad ones" (Cullen et al., 2002).

Taken together, these findings suggest two conclusions. First, agencies should either provide or serve as brokers for programs based on the principles of effective intervention. Second, a new paradigm—a new way of thinking—is needed to replace the failed paradigm that, in large part, has tried to use scare tactics to keep offenders away from crime opportunities. The purpose of this paper has been to sketch the components of this new approach to community supervision—a paradigm that we have called *environmental corrections*.

This name was carefully chosen, because it is rooted in the belief that sound correctional practices must be based on sound criminology—that is, based on viable theories and evidence on what causes crime. In this regard, environmental criminology has provided important insights into how opportunity is implicated in crime. It follows, we believe, that this knowledge can be used to establish an environmental corrections in which the key components of opportunity—offender thinking, routines, handlers, place management, and so on—are targeted for explicit intervention by probation and parole officers. A key aspect of this approach is that opportunity will be curtailed not only by threats of formal punishment for noncompliance, but more importantly by problem-solving officers who seek to expand informal control over offenders, to increase the effort offenders must exert to access crime opportunities, and to work with offenders to restructure and fill their lives with prosocial routines.

We recognize that translating theory into practice is fraught with a host of difficulties, not the least of which is that our ideas on reducing crime opportunities are likely to be labor intensive. In practical terms, this approach is likely to be cost effective primarily with high-risk offenders, who already often receive more intensive supervision. Furthermore, we have provided no hard data that our proposals will prove effective. Evaluation research will have to address a roster of issues before we can say that environmental corrections is a viable paradigm. Even with these qualifications, however, we are bold enough to suggest that environmental corrections holds considerable promise as a means to inspire new thinking and practice in the supervision of probationers and parolees.

QUESTIONS FOR REVIEW AND DISCUSSION

1. Is there a need to reinvent community supervision? Why or why not? Discuss.
2. What are "crime hotspots"?
3. What is routine activities theory? How does it influence offender crime choices?
4. What is meant by situational prevention?
5. What is the new paradigm for correctional supervision? Discuss.

43

"Evaluation Report of the Juvenile Mediation Program"

Robert R. Smith
and Victor S. Lombardo

Adapted from Robert R. Smith and Victor S. Lombardo, "Evaluation Report of the Juvenile Mediation Program." *Corrections Compendium* 27: 1–3, 19, 21, 2002.

Reprinted by permission from the American Correctional Association.

Mediation is a process in which a neutral individual aids parties in settling and negotiating a dispute. The Juvenile Mediation Program, which serves Brooke, Hancock, Marshall, Ohio, Tyler and Wetzel counties in West Virginia, works with school-age children and adolescents ages 6 to 18 and their families and/or guardians. The adolescents involved have been truant or have committed other status offenses or nonviolent crimes.

James R. Lee, chief probation officer in the First Judicial Circuit Court, established the program in 1997 and has been the program director since its inception. At that time, the program was called the Mediation/Arbitration Program and only served Brooke County. The following year, Hancock and Ohio counties were added; and in 1999, Marshall, Tyler and Wetzel counties were included. The program, now called the Juvenile Mediation Program, is funded by West Virginia Criminal Justice Services and the West Virginia Department of Health and Human Resources under the Juvenile Justice and Delinquency Prevention Act of 1974. Staff include a program director, program coordinator and two case managers.

PARTICIPANT ELIGIBILITY

Both status and nonviolent juvenile offenders from the six counties served are eligible to participate in the program. The program does not discriminate based on race, religion, gender, disability, marital status, sexual preference, economic status or national origin. No fees are charged for the mediation process or for any recommended services. All participants volunteer for services. If victims are involved, they are encouraged to attend meetings to be a part of the mediation process. Victims also are given an opportunity to participate in the overall program evaluation.

PROGRAM ELEMENTS

The Juvenile Mediation Program is not considered a formal legal process. It is best described as a process in which all involved parties join together to resolve differences without court involvement. The mediators' responsibilities include deciding the sincerity of the accused juvenile's remorse, determining a fair and just penalty for his or her wrongdoing and concluding if any services are necessary. The mediation hearing does not proceed without the juvenile's admission of guilt if a crime, not a status offense, is involved. A waiver of rights also must be signed to proceed. The waiver relinquishes the rights permitted at legal proceedings, such as having witnesses or lawyers present.

PROGRAM OBJECTIVES

Program objectives include working with eligible participants by scheduling mediation hearings and referring to appropriate services, their parents and others, such as legal guardians, victims, counselors and probation officers, to begin a dialogue about the status or nonviolent criminal offense and when necessary, initiating counseling or other services for offenders and/or their families. A written contract is negotiated for the families by the mediator who monitors participant progress through the contracted period at 30-, 60- and 90-day intervals. Contract service agencies may provide families with one or more services, including crisis intervention, behavior management, individual and/or group counseling, cognitive therapy, social skills, substance abuse treatment and psychological testing, depending on need.

Wraparound or support services, in addition to the aforementioned services, also are available through the mediation program based on an individual's severe truancy issues, maladaptiveness and familial dysfunctions. Those services include case management, individual treatment plans and intervention at schools, including development and monitoring of educational and behavioral goals, one-on-one supportive counseling, transportation and peer counseling. If participants demonstrate a need for extended help, i.e., clothing, food, holiday gifts, etc., they are referred to the Family Preservation Program, which is operated by the West Virginia Department of Health and Human Resources.

HOW THE PROGRAM WORKS

When a juvenile is charged with a status offense, such as underage drinking, or a crime, such as battery, a report is sent to the probation office in one of the six participating counties. A probation officer in that county reviews the case to determine if the juvenile is an appropriate candidate for the Juvenile Mediation Program. If he or she meets the eligibility criteria, the juvenile and family are asked to volunteer for the program. In situations in which the juvenile is involved in a crime, he or she also must admit guilt. Letters of apology, community service, tours of juvenile detention centers and monetary restitution are typical sanctions for nonviolent crimes. When all contractual requirements are satisfied, the mediator notifies the appropriate probation office. If the mediation fails, further action is taken by a social service agency, the court or both. The program is designed to last for a maximum period of 90 days and is terminated under one of three conditions:

- *Successful:* Juveniles must complete the required contractual agreement in 90 days. Participants who successfully complete the program will not be prosecuted, nor will their records be affected.

- *Unsuccessful:* Juveniles who fail to complete the required contractual agreement in 90 days will be referred to the probation department for further formal proceedings. Juveniles who re-offend during the 90-day period will be referred immediately for further prosecution.

- *Dismissal:* The mediator provides the recommendation for dismissal prior to disposition. It may be the result of a change of jurisdiction and usually is decided at the hearing.

All case information, except for public record information, remains confidential. Participants are asked to sign releases for such information when applicable.

VOLUNTEER MEDIATORS

The key element of the mediation program is built upon citizen volunteer mediators who are carefully screened and trained by program staff. A minimum of eight hours of volunteer mediator training is conducted on topics ranging from juvenile justice and criminal law to communication skills, listening techniques and victimization-related issues. Other volunteer mediator eligibility criteria include a minimum age of 21, a high school diploma or equivalent, and no criminal or Child Protective Services record. Current reading materials and videos related to violence, teen-age conflict and mediation, etc., are part of the mediator training. Since the program's inception, 75 volunteers have been trained and have participated in mediation processes.

MEDIATOR GUIDELINES

After a referral is made, screened and accepted, the volunteer mediator schedules a hearing. Program staff provide all parties involved with a letter explaining the procedures and times, dates and places of the hearings.

The volunteer mediator conducts the hearing and is responsible for attaining signatures on waivers and the 90-day contractual agreement. The mediator also is responsible for distributing copies of all paperwork to all parties, including program evaluation forms that are returned by mail to program staff. The mediator also explains to the parties that they have the right to request a hearing review if they are unsatisfied with any part of the program. The mediator is responsible for returning all hearing paperwork to program staff immediately after the hearing. If contract services are needed, the program coordinator makes all the arrangements. If monetary restitution is part of the 90-day contract, the maximum amount allowed is $500, and it is negotiated and monitored by the program director.

EVALUATION REPORT METHOD

Program participants included juveniles who committed status offenses, such as truancy, tobacco or alcohol consumption, incorrigibility, curfew violation or crimes, such as drug or drug paraphernalia possession, shoplifting, assault, battery and other offenses. From the program's inception July 1, 1997, through Dec. 31, 2000, 872 juveniles have participated.

A chi-square analysis was used to compare participant successful contract resolution frequencies for 670 participants across all counties served from July 1, 1997, through Sept. 30, 2000. A history of juvenile participation in the mediation program using fiscal year July 1 to June 30 reveals that in 1997, of the 55 participants, only one was unsuccessful; in 1998, of the 156 participants, five were unsuccessful; in 1999, of the 63 participants, 38 were unsuccessful; and for the first three months of fiscal year 2000, only one of the 58 participants was unsuccessful. In October, November and December of fiscal year 2000, 202 additional juveniles were served. However, because of a 90-day contract monitoring period, no data on contract resolutions were available as of the writing of this report. In addition, a frequency analysis was conducted using the 14-item, forced-choice Juvenile Mediation Program client evaluation form. There were 179 such forms returned for analysis.

A statistical analysis was made of the collected data. It was found that all counties represented a significant positive mediation effort for the program. These data further reflect that all counties do not significantly differ from one another in terms of overall mediation effectiveness. Indeed, the mediation program in the evaluated counties has demonstrated its effectiveness. The analysis revealed a significant positive program effect regarding participants' successful versus unsuccessful contract resolutions.

The 179 returned juvenile mediation client evaluation forms asked participants to evaluate the mediators' skills using a forced-choice, yes-no format. The questions were:

- Introduced and identified all individuals present;
- Explained the procedure satisfactorily;
- Exhibited knowledge of the case facts;
- Demonstrated an understanding of the law;
- Listened to the statements of all individuals;
- Encouraged involvement and participation;
- Showed awareness and concern of the conflict;
- Respected all opinions;
- Was cooperative;
- Created and maintained order; and
- Explained the findings of guilty and not guilty.

The following questions were not answered if the case was dismissed or there was a finding of no guilt:

- Discussed possible sanction requirements;
- Detailed actual sanction requirements; and
- Explained the consequences of failure to comply.

The overall analysis of the 14 items across participants (juvenile clients, juveniles' parents, victims and victims' parents) indicates that the mediation program is viewed by participants as significantly effective.

PROGRAM SUCCESS

In 1997, the Juvenile Mediation Program had projected a 70 percent successful contract-resolution mediation rate. Findings in this analysis, however, reveal a 93 percent successful mediation rate. Conclusions drawn from evaluation of the program are that the Juvenile Mediation Program significantly and positively resolves juvenile offenses without court involvement and participants' perceptions of the mediators' skills are positive. As such, the program represents a best practice that has state, regional and national implications such as high success rates and cost-effectiveness.

PROGRAM STRENGTHS

As a best practice model program, the Juvenile Mediation Program is steeped in a multisystematic (youths, parents, education, counselors, etc.), community-based, youth intervention paradigm. As part of this innovative program, it incorporates the following unique aspects:

Counseling services:
- Crisis intervention;
- Behavior management;
- Individual/family group counseling;
- Cognitive therapy;
- Skill development;
- Substance abuse treatment; and
- Psychological testing.

Wraparound services:
- Case management;
- Individualized intervention based on client needs;
- Interventions provided at school;
- Support for positive educational experience;
- Educational and behavioral goals developed and monitored;
- One-on-one supportive counseling;
- Transportation; and
- Peer counseling.

Another notable strength of the program is that two case managers successfully conducted the program in six counties. After being piloted for several years, the Juvenile Mediation Program now may be added to the professional literature concluding that such a program works and is, in fact, a best practice.

LIMITATIONS

While a comprehensive evaluation of the Juvenile Mediation Program did not identify any programmatic deficiencies, the only limitation is that it should be replicated statewide, regionally and nationally. It is highly recommended that any replication of this program be carefully modeled after the program using all the innovative components, such as counseling services, wraparound services, citizen volunteer mediators, etc.

IMPLICATIONS AND CONCLUSIONS

The highlight of the Juvenile Mediation program is that very few full-time personnel are needed to conduct such a program. Two case managers were employed to work with 670 youths from six countries. Again, when the program began in 1997, a 70 percent success rate was arbitrarily selected. As of Sept. 30, 2000, the actual rate of successful contract resolutions was 93 percent, or 625 of the 670 juvenile participants. As of July 1, 2001, all 625 juveniles have remained status and criminal offense-free. Of the 45 unsuccessful cases, to date, all have been involved in repeat status and/or criminal offenses since being terminated from the program. Of the program participant evaluations returned, all were favorable. The program's success is attributed to care and appropriate intervention.

QUESTIONS FOR REVIEW AND DISCUSSION

1. What is meant by juvenile mediation? What are some of its characteristics?
2. What is the Juvenile Mediation Program? What are its goals?
3. What were the program's strengths and weaknesses? Discuss.
4. How successful was the Juvenile Mediation Program? How was success measured?

44

Costs and Outcomes of a Work Ethic Camp

How Do They Compare to a Traditional Prison Facility?

Kurt D. Siedschlaw
and Beth A. Wiersma

Adapted from Kurt D. Siedschlaw and Beth A. Wiersma, "Costs and Outcomes of a Work Ethic Camp: How Do They Compare to a Traditional Prison Facility?" *Corrections Compendium* 30:1–5, 28–30, 2005.

Reprinted with permission by the American Correctional Association.

The Work Ethic Camp (WEC) is not a traditional prison nor is it a boot camp. The camp's philosophy is that behaviors and attitudes that reflect positive work ethics can be learned and transferred to all areas of an offender's life. The program is based on a cognitive approach that is designed to examine and challenge offender thinking patterns that support anti-social behavior to help them develop new ways of thinking. The WEC's treatment components include a cognitive-behavioral component, academic and vocational training, substance abuse treatment, physical training, group involvement, family dynamics and cognitive restructuring.

These treatment components are addressed through group methods. Offenders progress through a four-phase program that addresses changes in criminal thinking and behavior patterns. Cognitive-behavioral evaluation and the phase system are the foundation of the program. The WEC objectives are that offenders will:

1. Develop and enhance job-readiness skills to prepare them to obtain and maintain employment.
2. Develop life skills that will help them with money management, time management, family, daily living, relationships, leisure, education, and independent living.

3. Identify patterns of thinking and behavior that have resulted in past failures.

4. Develop a positive view of themselves and consider the harm they have caused their victims.

5. Become more responsible, improve their decision-making skills in the face of challenging situations, and enhance problem-solving abilities when faced with conflicts.

6. Be able to identify possible high-risk circumstances and strategies of how to avoid, cope with, or escape from trouble in the future (Wiersma and Siedschlaw, 2003; Nebraska Department of Correctional Services, 2002).

The WEC was designed with the expectation that offenders would complete the program within 120 days. However, the program can be extended to 180 days if treatment needs indicate that it is necessary. The program design calls for first-time, nonviolent felony offenders. One element of the screening process for offenders to be considered for the WEC is that they are physically and mentally able to complete the program. Many of the offenders are substance abusers. In fact, 103 offenders (39 percent) of the 272 in the WEC group were sent to the camp on drug-related charges. Thirty-nine percent of the remaining 169 offenders had prior drug and alcohol offenses on their records. The facility report for July 2004 indicated that 92 percent of the offenders at the camp were being treated for substance abuse (Nebraska Department of Correctional Services, 2004b). The report noted delays in offender programs as a result of offenders needing approximately 4 weeks to detoxify before they could apply themselves to the educational component of the program.

An evaluation of the WEC was conducted from February 2003 to May 2004. The original internal evaluation to be conducted did not include post-release outcomes; however, a request was made to include some indications of costs in relationship to outcomes. This article addresses that component of the evaluation: the costs and outcomes of the WEC compared to a population of offenders from a traditional prison facility.

State budgets are starved for cash, state prison systems are at capacity, and legislators and policy makers are looking for money-saving alternatives to prison (Madigan, 2003). Examination of the money invested in Nebraska's McCook Work Ethic Camp or any other correctional facility is a necessity in today's economic environment. The assessment of costs of a facility or program requires that consideration be given to exactly what is to be measured and how the cost of one program is compared with another. In today's environment, concepts such as rehabilitation, reintegration and restorative justice are not as critical as examination of the dollars expended and corresponding results achieved. The money expended relates directly to an effort to minimize cost. Money spent on government-sponsored programs may also be viewed as an effort to balance the use of the various programs with the expectations of the citizens of the state, the legislature, the executive branch of government, and the issue of public safety. Not all offenders are appropriate candidates for programs such as the WEC.

As of September 2004 the Federal Bureau of Prisons revised the cost of incarceration for inmates in the federal system, including community corrections centers, to $22,517 per year (Federal Bureau of Prisons, 2004). The annual cost for inmates in the Nebraska Department of Correctional Services (NDOCS) facilities, as of June 2004, averages $24,622 (Nebraska Department of Correctional Services, 2004a). Between 1982 and 2001, the federal government increased expenditures on corrections by 861 percent. The average annual increases are higher for corrections than any of the other components of the criminal justice system. State and local programs increased 9 percent per year, with the federal government correctional programs increasing an average of 13 percent per year (Bureau of Justice Statistics, 2004).

The problems of rising prison populations, operational costs, and recidivism rates are not new. As of February 2003, the Nebraska correctional population exceeded the design capacity by 33 percent (Nebraska Department of Correctional Services, 2004c). Nebraska opened a $6.67 million minimum-security WEC in April 2001 with an initial design capacity of 100 beds (Wiersma and Siedschlaw, 2003).

LITERATURE REVIEW

Greg Jones and Michael Connelly of the State Commission on Criminal Sentencing Policy laid out the common-sense elements for a review of the impact of a correctional program in 2001. Any review of the success of a correctional program must consider three dynamics: (1) how recidivism is counted; (2) the time frame for recidivism; and (3) the basis for making sense of the information on recidivism. That study showed that most correctional departments provide standard recidivism rates using 2- or 3-year follow-up periods; however, others provide rates up to 6 years (Jones and Connelly, 2004).

A study of 15 states and the representative recidivism rates uses the measurement of rearrest, reconviction, resentence to prison, and return to prison with or without a new sentence set within a time frame of 3 years as the criteria to examine the issue (Langan and Levin, 2002). The same study goes on to indicate that 51.8 percent of those released from prison were back in prison because they had received another prison sentence or because they had violated a technical condition of their release.

States are looking for alternatives to prison. And although they want something different from boot camps, states are focusing on highly accountable, highly structured short-duration treatment. Boot camp evaluations offer no evidence to indicate that future criminal behavior is reduced as a result of this type of intervention (Atkinson, 1995). One explanation why boot camps have not been effective in reducing recidivism is that they appear to lack the necessary focus on incorporating components of effective therapy (MacKenzie et al., 2001). The shift to short duration treatment programs, followed by close supervision, is being considered in Kansas, Wisconsin, Washington, Arkansas, Hawaii, Maryland, Mississippi, Missouri, Oklahoma, South Carolina and New Mexico (Madigan, 2003). The most successful correctional programs are believed to be those that address the cognitive functioning of offenders (Gendreau and Ross, 1979; Izzo and Ross, 1990).

Correctional programs are seeking new approaches addressing high recidivism rates and public disaffection for corrections and probation (Campbell and Wolf, 2001). Cognitive intervention programs (cognitive restructuring and cognitive skills) are not new to the corrections field. The movement began in Canada during the 1980s and has since emerged as the principal strategy used by Correctional Service Canada (Baro, 1999). Similar programs are used in many states, including Oregon, Michigan, Vermont, California and Colorado (Baro, 1999; French et al., 2000; Henning and Frueh, 1996; Husband and Platt, 1993; Powell, Bush, and Bilodeau, 2001; Withrow, 1994). Cognitive interventions are considered the preferred approach to rehabilitating offenders and are considered by many to be the most efficient and effective approach (Glick, 2003; Husband and Platt, 1993).

Andrews and Bonta (1998) identified criminogenic attitudes as primary predictors of criminal behavior. These include such things as anti-social history, anti-social attitudes and behaviors, anti-social associates, and values and beliefs that support criminal behavior. Cognitive interventions include cognitive restructuring, cognitive skills development, or both. Cognitive restructuring programs focus on changing the way offenders think; changing the values, beliefs, and attitudes that support their criminal lifestyle (Baro, 1999). Some programs also address deficits in education and substance abuse issues.

Henning and Frueh (1996) found a statistically significant difference among offenders who participated in Vermont's Cognitive Self-Change program. Program participants had a 20 percent reduction in recidivism compared with those who did not participate. Offenders who completed the Cognitive Skills Training program in Canada were readmitted for new convictions at a lower rate than the comparison group (Proportion, Fabian and Robinson, 1991). They also found that participants made positive changes in pro-social thinking and are better able to appreciate the perspectives of others.

In one of the largest controlled outcome studies conducted in Canada, Robinson (1995) noted a 20 percent reduction in official reconvictions for offenders who completed a cognitive skills training program. Robinson also noted that medium-need cases exhibited the greatest gains with a 52.2 percent reduction in official reconvictions. Drug offenders also showed lower recidivism.

A meta-analysis of correctional programs revealed that programs with a cognitive component were more than twice as effective as programs that did not (Izzo and Ross, 1990). Programs addressing thinking skills, problem-solving skills and social perceptions are more effective than those that do not (Ross and Fabiano, 1985).

More recent studies have also found cognitive-behavioral programs to be effective in reducing recidivism. Pearson et al. (2002) found that cognitive skills programs and cognitive-behavioral social skills development programs are associated with lower recidivism rates. In a second analysis of recent studies, Allen, MacKenzie, and Hickman (2001) found that in the majority of the studies on reasoning and rehabilitation, recidivism was reduced compared with those in control groups. However, they did find two studies with contradictory results.

METHODOLOGY

The principal factors considered in an effort to compare the results of the WEC program with the conventional prison program include cost of time served; offender similarities; a specific time frame for selection of the comparison group and an examination of the experiences demonstrated by offenders upon release into the community.

The study looked at all offenders received at the Nebraska Department of Correctional Services (NDOCS) and the WEC between February 1, 2003 and May 1, 2004. The population was controlled for the type of offense and prior record by selecting from department prison admissions only those offenders documenting a first-time felony sentence to a Nebraska adult facility. A review of the criteria for those offenders being considered for the WEC indicates that, by statute, offenders are to be nonviolent, first-time felony offenders between the ages of 17 and 35.

The offenses committed by the camp population included substance abuse charges, such as driving while intoxicated, and burglary, felony criminal mischief, theft, unlawful flight, criminal nonsupport, lesser assault, violation of protection order and accessory offenses. The NDOCS population was screened to consider those offenders with the same type of offenses as those offenders received at the WEC. Only those offenders received between February 2003 and May 2004 by NDOCS for the first time for nonviolent offenses were comparable to the WEC population.

The study included consideration of the 1,171 offenders who were admitted to the Nebraska Diagnostic and Evaluation Center during the study period. This number was reduced to 1,147 through screening of offense types from the data set provided by the NDOCS. This screening of offenders was conducted to eliminate offenders whose offenses or lesser offenses included a crime of violence. The NDOCS population had 661 offenders who had not been released and were still serving time as of July 31, 2004. Control for the basic offense types allowed a comparison of similar offenders sentenced to the adult prison system as those sentenced to the WEC.

Admissions to NDOCS revealed that of the 1,147 offenders received, 480 were released via direct discharge or parole. Direct discharges accounted for 237 of the releases. A total of 243 inmates were discharged under parole supervision. Twenty percent of the offenders released from NDOCS were female and 80 percent were male. The age range of these offenders was 18 to 46, with a mean age of 23 (Wiersma and Siedschlaw, 2004).

The first concern under consideration is the per diem cost of keeping individuals in the WEC as compared to the other adult correctional facilities. The significance of the money spent on camp participants is examined by comparing the average length of stay at the camp with the average length of stay of those offenders who were sent to NDOCS adult offender programs. The per diem cost and the relative length of stay is only one set of factors to be considered. The results of the stay at one institution or another must be compared to the performance of the offenders once they leave the institution.

The comparison of offenders from traditional prison programs and the WEC is made for several reasons. The camp was established as an alternative to prison, not as an alternative to community programs. The individuals selected for the camp fit a prescribed set of criteria and certain offenders are not eligible for the program. The original target population was first-time offenders who would have been sentenced to prison for a period of less than 3 years. While the analysis within the study suggested other criteria, the initial official criteria included that the offenders must:

1. Be nonviolent
2. Have no prior prison admission for felony convictions
3. Be between 17 and 35 years of age
4. Be guilty of an offense that has a maximum sentence of 10 years or less
5. Be determined to be mentally and medically fit
6. Not have been previously convicted of a crime under sections 28-319 and 28-320 of the Nebraska Revised Code. These code sections refer to first-degree sexual assault and a history of sexual assault or any other capital crime.
7. Have a recommendation for placement in the program from probation staff (Nebraska Department of Correctional Services, 1997).

The post-release performance of the various offenders within the study group was assessed through the use of state criminal history records. The state criminal history files and probation history files of each of the WEC participants and the state criminal history records of the 480 NDOCS offenders were researched following their release into the community. The criminal history records identified offenders who had been arrested and/or convicted subsequent to their release during the study period. This was the only avenue available at the time of this portion of the study to examine post-incarceration dynamics.

PROGRAM ADMISSIONS

Adult offenders received at the Nebraska Department of Correctional Services Diagnostic and Evaluation Center are immediately eligible for placement in any one of the adult facilities once they complete the 90-day intake and assessment period at the department's Lincoln Diagnostic Center. Offenders at the WEC are sentenced to the camp as a condition of intensive supervision probation (ISP).

LENGTH OF STAY

The length of time offenders spend at the WEC ranges from 120 to 180 days. The average length of stay at the camp was 115 days. Offenders were removed from the program early due to unsatisfactory performance, medical or mental health issues, or voluntary removal. The average length of stay for offenders received and then released from the NDOCS, during the time frame of this study, was 229.25 days or 7.38 months compared with 3.83 months for the WEC offenders received and released during the same time.

FACILITY COSTS

A new medium-/maximum-security facility in Tecumseh, Nebraska, opened in 2001, providing a design capacity for 960 offenders. The cost for construction of this facility was $72.6 million without the need to purchase land. The land was provided by the local governmental subunits. The construction cost per bed was $75,630.

Construction costs for the WEC, which required the purchase of land, was $6.67 million. The resulting construction, with a design capacity of 100, cost $66,625 per bed. To consider the cost of the facility equitably, it should be noted that there is no economy of scale in the current use of the camp facility. The camp could, without major cost, add another housing unit on the current campus and double its current capacity. The food service at the camp can accommodate twice the number of people it currently serves.

Many factors affect the cost of a facility. The facility at Tecumseh is a medium-/maximum-security complex. Hardware and physical facility costs are higher for a facility of a higher security level. The WEC is a community/minimum-security facility. Physical security costs are less and operational costs are less in a minimum-security program.

PROGRAM COSTS

The current design capacity at the WEC is calculated at 100. The design program at the camp sets a minimum 120-day stay. The average length of stay at the WEC was 115 days. Operating at its design capacity, the WEC has a cost of $43.69 per day. The average individual released in the community from the WEC costs Nebraska $5,024.35. The average length of stay within the remaining NDOCS facilities averages $76.53, resulting in an institutionalization cost per individual released of $17,525.37 or a total of $8,412,178 for the 480 offenders released from NDOCS.

WORK ETHIC CAMP OUTCOMES AND COSTS

Of the original 272 admitted to the WEC program, 222 completed the program and were released to ISP in the community. Fifty of the camp offenders did not complete the camp program due to the fact that they did not meet or did not maintain the standard established within the program. These offenders were returned to court for probation revocation.

Of the original WEC total population of 272, 73 offenders were arrested, 9 were convicted of a new crime, and 62 offenders were revoked, with 58 (21.3 percent) being sent to NDOCS or jail under probation revocation. All offenders in the WEC group who were arrested are included within the camp population of revocation figures. The arrest and incarceration of camp offenders resulted in 68 (25 percent) of the original 272 offenders being arrested and re-incarcerated. Thirty-five of the camp offenders had probation revocation pending at the completion of this study.

The total cost of providing WEC institutional services to 272 offenders with an average length of 115 days at $43.69 per day is $2,416,866. Of the 222 offenders who successfully completed the camp program, 155 were doing satisfactorily in the community at the study's completion.

The cost of providing the WEC program for all 272 offenders—$1,416,866 or $5,024 per offender—was considered as being wasted on those offenders who had been arrested, convicted or revoked, and are not in a satisfactory position in the community. If the entire cost of the program were placed on only those who have remained in the community (155), then the cost per successful camp participant would be $9,141.

TRADITIONAL PRISON OUTCOMES AND COSTS

The average offender from NDOCS was released in October 2003, providing an average of 10 months in the community at the time the study was completed. Ninety (18.7 percent) of the 480 offenders released from the correctional department were arrested within a 9-month period. These offenders were responsible for 152 arrests. These arrests included 64 felony arrests, 88 misdemeanor arrests, and 9 arrests for parole violations (Wiersma and Siedschlaw, 2004).

Of the 480 NDOCS offenders, 19 (3.9 percent) were convicted of a new offense and 9 (3.8 percent) of the 235 NDOCS offenders released on parole were returned to prison after parole revocation. If arrest is considered an unsatisfactory indicator for the group of 480 offenders released, with or without supervision, combined with the new convictions and parole revocations, the percentage of unsatisfactory NDOCS offenders is 24.5 percent.

If the cost of providing NDOCS services to all 480 offenders ($8.4 million) was factored as being wasted on those offenders who had been convicted of a crime or revoked from parole (28 persons) and the entire cost was placed on only those who did remain in the community (452), the institutional cost to obtain a successful offender in the community using the standard NDOCS programs is $18,611 per successful offender.

DISCUSSION AND CONCLUSIONS

Conducting a direct comparison of offenders completing a period of incarceration in NDOCS facilities to offenders released from the WEC is difficult. The cost of an offender's stay is relatively easy to calculate based on the cost per day of the facility and the length of stay. What proves elusive is establishing a direct correlation between the community release experience of NDOCS offenders and the camp offenders. Half the NDOCS offenders were directly discharged into the community without supervision. The remaining correctional department offenders were released under conventional parole supervision. Conventional parole may have only one personal contact per month with the offender.

The WEC camp offenders, by statute, are released under ISP. The level of supervision of offenders under ISP is markedly different. The average such client is seen personally about 6–8 times per month. No manner of direct comparison of the NDOCS offenders can be made to the WEC camp offenders because of the wide variation in supervision levels. Compounding the issue is the fact that half of the NDOCS offenders were direct discharges with no supervision or follow-up. The one number that is absolute is the number of offenders from either population who remain in the community without having demonstrated an arrest within the state criminal history files. The cost of obtaining a successful offender in the community ends up as the point of comparison for this study.

The cost of obtaining an offender in satisfactory status in the community, for this study, is based on the average cost per day, average length of stay, and the number of offenders from each program released during the period of the study who were successful or remained in the community at the completion of the study period. The prison population, in order to obtain an offender with a satisfactory status in the community, resulted in an incarceration cost of $18,611 for each offender. The community performance of this population demonstrated 9 new convictions for the group of offenders released into the community.

The initial results of the examination of the cost and relative success of individuals completing the WEC demonstrates a significant potential cost savings when compared to conventional prison sanctions. The shortfall of the study assessing the dynamics of the WEC is that the program is new and offenders released were only in the community for less than one year under community supervision. Some of the camp offenders had been released into the community for only a month or two. Most correctional departments provide standard recidivism rates using 2- to 3-year follow-up periods (Jones and Connelly, 2004). Due to circumstances beyond the control of the researchers, the time period of the current study did not allow for a long-term follow-up of the two offender groups.

The research will continue in regard to the WEC. It would be premature at this point to make any valid comparisons between the recidivism rates of those offenders completing the cognitive-behavioral programming at the WEC and offenders who were released from a traditional prison facility. But initial indications are that there is the potential for considerable cost savings without a significant increase of risk to the community when clientele are assessed and screened for appropriate characteristics, a program is operated effectively, and an effort is made to provide continuity between the program and transition back into the community. The results of this examination of the WEC offender compared with the NDOCS conventional program offender are entirely based on the lower costs of the WEC. In order to assess the true impact of the camp program, a longitudinal study must be completed that follows both sets of offenders under controlled dynamics for a minimum of 24 months after release. The effort to track these offenders and examine their employment and community experiences continues.

QUESTIONS FOR REVIEW AND DISCUSSION

1. What is the Work Ethic Camp? What are its aims or objectives?
2. Is the WEC better at reducing recidivism compared with traditional incarceration? Why or why not? Explain.
3. How can the cost factor be used as a measure of program effectiveness? Is it a valid measure? Discuss.
4. What relevance does the selection criteria for WEC have for the successfulness of the program?
5. How does WEC control or decrease criminal behavior? Explain.

45

Crimes Against Persons Age 65 or Older, 1993–2002

Patsy Klaus

Adapted from Patsy Klaus, *Crimes Against Persons Age 65 or Older, 1993–2002*. Washington, DC: U.S. Department of Justice, 2005.

According to the National Crime Victimization Survey (NCVS), persons age 65 or older generally experienced victimizations at much lower rates than younger groups of people from 1993 through 2002.

For the period 1993–2002 the elderly experienced nonfatal violent crime at a rate 1/20th that of young persons (4 per 1,000 age 65 or older versus 82 victimizations per 1,000 persons age 12–24). Violent crimes include rape, sexual assault, robbery, and aggravated and simple assaults.

Households headed by persons age 65 or older experienced property crimes at a rate about a fourth of that for households headed by persons under age 25 (93 per 1,000 households versus 406 per 1,000).

Purse snatching/pocket picking (personal larceny) was the only measured crime for which the elderly were victimized at about the same rates as most other age groups. Persons age 12–24 were the only group with higher rates of personal larceny than the elderly.

Although persons age 65 or older generally experienced lower victimization rates, when they were victimized they were most often the victims of property crimes, which include household burglary, motor vehicle theft and theft (table 1, figure 1). Property crimes accounted for 92% of victimizations affecting persons or households headed by someone 65 or older and 88% of victimizations against persons or households headed by persons age 50–64. In comparison, violent crimes comprised more than half the victimizations experienced by persons age 12–24.

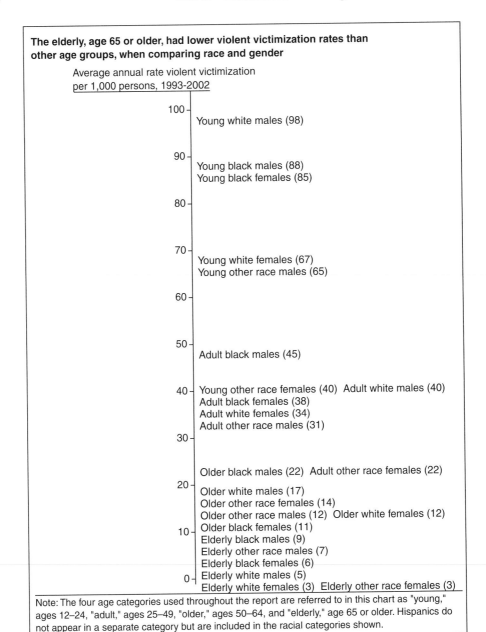

The elderly, age 65 or older, had lower violent victimization rates than other age groups, when comparing race and gender

Average annual rate violent victimization per 1,000 persons, 1993-2002

100 ─ Young white males (98)

90 ─ Young black males (88)
     Young black females (85)

80 ─

70 ─ Young white females (67)
     Young other race males (65)

60 ─

50 ─ Adult black males (45)

40 ─ Young other race females (40) Adult white males (40)
     Adult black females (38)
     Adult white females (34)
     Adult other race males (31)

30 ─

     Older black males (22) Adult other race females (22)

20 ─ Older white males (17)
     Older other race females (14)
     Older other race males (12) Older white females (12)
10 ─ Older black females (11)
     Elderly black males (9)
     Elderly other race males (7)
     Elderly black females (6)
 0 ─ Elderly white males (5)
     Elderly white females (3) Elderly other race females (3)

Note: The four age categories used throughout the report are referred to in this chart as "young," ages 12–24, "adult," ages 25–49, "older," ages 50–64, and "elderly," age 65 or older. Hispanics do not appear in a separate category but are included in the racial categories shown.

Compared to younger victims of personal crimes (rape/sexual assault, robbery, assault, and purse snatching/pocket picking), elderly victims were disproportionately victimized by thefts of their purses or wallets (figure 2). About 1 in 5 of personal crimes against the elderly were thefts compared to about 1 in 33 for persons age 12–49.

TABLE 1 Personal and Household Victimizations, by Type of Crime and Age, 1993–2002

Rates by Type of Crime 1993–2002	Total	Age of Victim			
		12–24	25–49	50–64	65 or older
All crimes					
Personal crimes total	39.9	84.5	38.4	15.5	5.4
Violent crime total	38.5	82.2	37.1	14.5	4.3
Rape/sexual assault	1.6	4.0	1.4	0.2	0.1
Robbery	4.3	8.4	4.2	1.9	1.0
Assault, total	32.7	69.8	31.6	12.4	3.2
Aggravated assault	8.1	17.5	7.8	2.9	0.9
Simple assault	24.6	52.3	23.8	9.5	2.4
Personal larceny	1.4	2.3	1.2	0.9	1.1
Property crimes total	231.5	406.3	282.2	188.5	93.1
Household burglary	41.1	82.1	46.4	33.6	22.8
Motor vehicle theft	12.5	22.4	15.4	10.2	4.5
Theft	177.9	301.8	220.4	144.7	65.8
Average annual					
Persons	221,841,700	49,465,940	102,193,620	38,048,660	32,133,480
Households	105,328,990	6,830,400	54,494,930	22,420,790	21,582,870

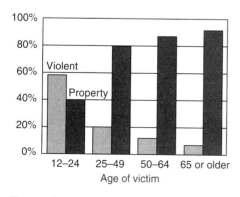

Percent of violent and property crimes, by age of victim, 1993–2002

FIGURE 1

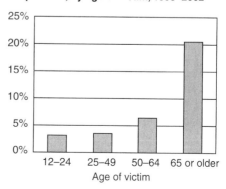

Purse snatching and pocket picking, as a percentage of all crimes against persons, by age of victim, 1993–2002

FIGURE 2

TRENDS IN VIOLENT AND PROPERTY CRIMES, 1993–2002

Nonfatal violence generally declined for most age groups between 1993 and 2002 (figure 3). The elderly had the lowest rates of any age group for nonfatal violence during this period. In recent years all rates have remained stable, after declining in earlier years. Rates for persons age 50–64 were stable during some of the years in which there were declines for younger age groups.

Murder, which is measured by the Federal Bureau of Investigation's Uniform Crime Reports, declined slightly for the elderly between 1993 and 1998 (figure 4). Since 1998 murder rates have remained stable for this age group. Persons age 65 or older had lower rates of murder than other age groups every year between 1993 and 2002.

Property crime victimizations declined for households headed by all age groups between 1993 and 2002 (figure 5). For persons age 65 or older, property crime rates in 2002 were less than half that of the rates in 1993 (63 per 1,000 households versus 133 per 1,000).

Rates of violent crime victimization per 1,000 persons, by age of victim, 1993–2002

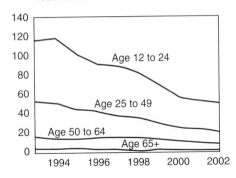

FIGURE 3

Murder rates per 10,000 persons, by age of victim, 1993–2002

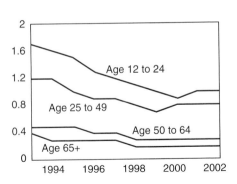

FIGURE 4

Property crime rates per 1,000 households, by age, 1993–2002

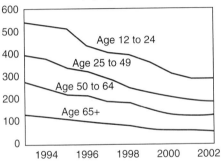

FIGURE 5

TABLE 2   Nonfatal Violent Victimizations, 1993–2002

	Age of Victim	
Total	12–64	65 or older
Percent facing weapons	25.7%	30.2%
Firearm	9.4	12.7
Knife	6.3	6.4
Other type	8.7	9.3
Don't know type	1.2	1.8
Percent resisting	71.0%	55.5%
Threatened/attacked with weapon	2.2	2.5
Threatened/attacked without weapon	27.9	15.3
Nonconfrontational resistance	29.5	24.9
Other or unknown type	11.3	12.9
Percent not resisting	29.0%	44.5%
Percent injured	25.9%	21.8%
Types of injury		
Serious	3.3	2.8
Minor	21.2	18.7
Rape without other injury	1.2	0.3*
Don't know type	0.1	0.0*

*Based on 10 or fewer cases.

VIOLENT VICTIMIZATION CHARACTERISTICS, 1993–2002

Compared to younger persons, the elderly are less likely to be victims of violence, but when victimized, persons age 65 or older—

- were equally likely to face offenders with weapons (30% versus 26%)
- were more likely to offer no resistance (45% versus 29%)
- were equally likely to receive serious injuries (3% for both groups) (table 2).

OFFENDERS IN VIOLENT CRIMES, 1993–2002

Persons age 65 or older, when compared with those age 12–64,—

- were somewhat more likely to face offenders who were strangers to them (53% versus 46%)
- were more likely to face offenders age 30 or older (48% versus 30%)
- were equally likely to face male offenders (about 79% versus 76%).

Characteristic of Violent Offender	Age of Victim	
	12–64	65 or older
Total	100%	100%
Relationship to victim		
Known to victim	31.7	23.6
Spouse/ex-spouse	5.1	2.4
Boyfriend/girlfriend	5.9	0.6*
Own child	0.9	2.6
Other relatives	4.0	4.1
Well-known person	15.8	13.9
Casual acquaintance	18.2	15.7
Stranger	46.3	52.5
Don't know relationship	3.7	8.2
Age 30 or older	30.2%	48.3%
Male	78.8%	75.6%

*Based on 10 or fewer cases

WHEN AND WHERE CRIMES OCCURRED
AND REPORTING OF CRIMES TO POLICE

Lower percentages of crimes against persons age 65 or older were committed at night compared to crimes against younger persons. About a fourth of violent crimes against the elderly were committed at night, compared to almost half of all violence against persons age 12–64. Similar differences existed for personal larceny (15% versus 34%) and property crime (21% versus 29%) (table 3).

About 46% of violent crimes and about 67% of property crimes against persons or households headed by persons age 65 or older occurred at or near their homes. The elderly were more likely than those age 12–64 to face these crimes while in or near their homes. Purse snatching/pocket picking rarely occurred near home for either persons age 65 or older or those under age 65 (5% versus 6%).

Compared to younger victims, persons age 65 or older were more likely to report violence (53% versus 44%) and purse snatching/pocket picking (42% versus 32%) to the police. Slightly over a third of all households, regardless of the age of the household head, reported property crimes.

TABLE 3   Characteristics of Crimes, 1993–2002

	Age of Victim	
	12–64	65 or older
Percent occurring at night		
Violence	45.8%	27.2%
Personal theft	34.4	14.8
Property crimes	29.2	20.9
Percent occurring at/near home		
Violence	27.0%	45.5%
Personal theft	5.4	5.8*
Property crimes	54.3	67.0
Percent reported to police		
Violence	43.9%	53.0%
Personal theft	32.1	42.3
Property crimes	34.7	35.5

Note: Some persons did not know when crimes occurred, especially property crimes.
*Based on 10 or fewer cases.
Of those persons age 65 and older who reported being a victim of violence, on the average during 1993–2002, approximately 22% were injured, and 1% reported sufficiently serious injuries to require their hospitalization (see Figure 6).

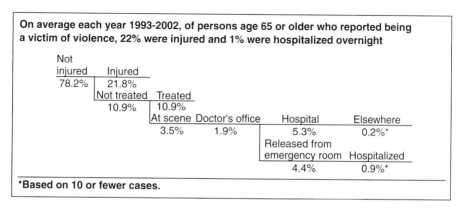

FIGURE 6

QUESTIONS FOR REVIEW AND DISCUSSION

1. Was there any increase in the victimization of persons age 65 or older during the 1993–2002 period? Why or why not? Explain.
2. What is the nature of crimes against the elderly?
3. What are some prominent trends in property and violent crimes against persons age 65 and older?
4. When and where are crimes against the elderly reported to the police?

46

Financial Crimes Against the Elderly

Kelly Dedel Johnson

Adapted from Kelly Dedel Johnson, *Financial Crimes Against the Elderly.* Washington, DC: U.S. Department of Justice, Office of Community Oriented Policing Services, 2003: 1–43, 37–48.

THE PROBLEM OF FINANCIAL CRIMES AGAINST THE ELDERLY

This guide addresses the problem of financial crimes against the elderly. It begins by describing the problem and reviewing risk factors. It then identifies a series of questions to help you analyze your local problem. Finally, it reviews responses to the problem and describes the conditions under which they are most effective.

Financial crimes against the elderly fall under two general categories: fraud committed by strangers, and financial exploitation by relatives and caregivers. These categories sometimes overlap in terms of target selection and the means used to commit the crime. However, the differences in the offender-victim relationships suggest different methods for analyzing and responding to the problem.

Fraud Committed by Strangers

Fraud generally involves deliberately deceiving the victim with the promise of goods, services, or other benefits that are nonexistent, unnecessary, never intended to be provided, or grossly misrepresented. There are hundreds of frauds, but offenders generally use a small subset of these against the elderly. The frauds typically occur within a few interactions.

- *Prizes and Sweepstakes:* These frauds generally involve informing the victim that he or she could win, or has already won, a "valuable" prize or a lot of money. The victim is required to send in money to cover taxes, shipping, or processing fees. The prize may never be delivered or, if so, is usually costume jewelry or cheap electronic equipment worth less than the money paid to retrieve it.

- *Investments:* Because many seniors live on fixed incomes, they often want to increase the value of their estate and ensure they have sufficient funds to meet basic needs. In investment scams, offenders persuade the elderly to invest in precious gems, real estate, annuities, or stocks and bonds by promising unrealistically high rates of return. The investments often consist of fake gemstones, uninhabitable property, or shares in a nonexistent or unprofitable company.

- *Charity Contributions:* Playing on some seniors' desire to help others, offenders solicit donations to nonexistent charities or religious organizations, often using sweepstakes or raffles to do so.

- *Home and Automobile Repairs:* Offenders may recommend an array of fraudulent "emergency" home repairs, often requiring an advance deposit. They may subsequently fail to do any work at all, start but not finish the work, or do substandard work that requires correction. Common frauds include roof repairs, driveway resurfacing, waterproofing, and pest control. The offenders are often transient, moving among neighborhoods, cities, and even states. Dishonest auto mechanics may falsely inform customers that certain repairs are needed, or they may bill for services or repairs that were not requested or were not completed.

- *Loans and Mortgages:* Seniors may experience cash flow shortages in the face of needed medical care or home repairs. Predatory lenders may provide loans with exorbitant interest rates, hidden fees, and repayment schedules far exceeding the elderlys' means, often at the risk of their home, which has been used as collateral.

- *Health, Funeral, and Life Insurance:* Many seniors are concerned about having the funds to pay for needed medical care or a proper burial, or to bequeath to loved ones upon death. Unscrupulous salespeople take advantage of these concerns by selling the elderly policies that duplicate existing coverage, do not provide the coverage promised, or are altogether bogus.

- *Health Remedies:* The elderly often have health problems that require treatment. Preying on this vulnerability, offenders market a number of ineffective remedies, promising "miracle cures." Unfortunately, given this false hope, many seniors delay needed treatment, and their health deteriorates further.

- *Travel:* Compared with younger adults, seniors often have more leisure time and are attracted to low-cost travel packages. However, many of these packages cost far more than market rates, provide substandard accommodations, or do not provide the promised services.

- *Confidence Games:* These frauds generally do not involve a product or service; instead, they include a broad array of deceitful scenarios to get cash from the elderly. The offender may pretend to be in a position of authority (e.g., a bank examiner), or otherwise trustworthy, concocting a story to get the victim to hand over cash, then disappearing. For example, the perpetrators of "lottery scams" claim to have won the lottery but to have no bank account in which to deposit the winnings. The offender promises the victim a premium in exchange for use of his or her account. After the victim makes a "good faith" payment to the offender, the victim never hears from the offender again.

In addition to variations in the type of product or service offered, frauds vary widely in the means used to commit them.

- *Telemarketing:* Offenders call people at home, using high-pressure tactics to solicit money for fraudulent investments, insurance policies, travel packages, charities, and sweepstakes. Fraudulent telemarketing operations are designed to limit the benefit to the customer while maximizing the profit for the telemarketer and for the highly efficient contact of a lot of potential customers.
- *Mail:* Fraudulent prize and sweepstakes operations often mail materials to a wide audience, relying on potential victims to "self-select" by returning a postcard or calling to indicate their interest. The mailings often look official, use extensive personalization (e.g., repeating the recipient's name in the text), include claims of authenticity, have contradictory content or "double-talk," and make a seemingly low-key request for the recipient to submit a small fee.
- *Face-to-face Contact:* Some frauds involving products and services (e.g., home and auto repairs) require face-to-face contact at either the victim's home or a business. Alternatively, a scammer gains entry to the victim's home by posing as a utility worker and distracts the victim while an accomplice burglarizes the home.

Successful frauds share common elements. The offenders gain trust and confidence through their charisma, by using a business name similar to that of a well-established organization, or by communicating a cover for the elder's well-being. They create the impression that the elder has been "chosen" or is "lucky" to receive the offer, and that such offers are rare. They encourage their victims to make an immediate decision or commitment to purchase products or services, which effectively limits the opportunity for consultation with others. Further, since the "special" offers are available to only a select group of customers, the offenders ask the victims to be discreet and not discuss the details, shrouding the transaction in secrecy and decreasing the chance of discovery by a family member, neighbor, or other concerned party. The frauds occur quickly, with little risk of exposure.

Financial Exploitation by Relatives and Caregivers

Unlike strangers, relatives and caregivers often have a position of trust and an ongoing relationship with the elderly. Financial exploitation occurs when the offender steals, withholds, or otherwise misuses their elderly victims' money, property, or valuables for personal advantage or profit, to the disadvantage of the elder. Their methods can include the following:

- simply taking the elder's money, property, or valuables;
- borrowing money (sometimes repeatedly) and not paying it back;
- denying services or medical care to conserve funds;

- giving away or selling the elder's possessions without permission;
- signing or cashing pension or Social Security checks without permission;
- misusing ATM or credit cards, or using them without permission;
- doling out the elder's money to family or friends; and
- forcing the elder to part with resources or to sign over property.

The tactics offenders use include deceit, coercion, intimidation, emotional abuse, or empty promises of lifelong care. Further, they usually try to isolate the victim from friends, family, and other concerned parties. By doing so, they prevent others from asking about the elder's well-being or relationship with the offender, prevent the elder from consulting with others on important financial decisions, and, perhaps most tragically, give the elder the impression that no one else cares about him or her.

In addition, relatives and caregivers sometimes exploit the following financial and legal arrangements:

- *Joint Bank Accounts:* Under the guise of helping the elder with his or her financial affairs, the offender has his or her name added to the elder's bank account, allowing the offender to deposit, withdraw, or transfer funds. The offender may threaten or coerce the elder into giving consent, or get consent despite the elder's limited capacity to make an informed decision.
- *Deed or Title Transfer:* The elder transfers ownership of property such as homes, real estate, or cars to the offender. This may occur as the result of force or intimidation, or as a "gift" or other transaction the elder does not fully comprehend.
- *Power of Attorney and Durable Power of Attorney:* These legal arrangements give a person the authority to manage the elder's affairs on the elder's behalf. When used properly, the legally appointed agent makes decisions that are in the elder's best interest. Misuse arises when the agent induces the elder to sign the document; makes decisions or transactions that benefit the agent, to the detriment of the elder; uses the power after it has been terminated; or uses the power for purposes other than what is intended.
- *Living Trusts and Wills:* To avoid potentially expensive probate fees and estate taxes, an individual can transfer property and other assets into a trust. The effectiveness of this legitimate estate-planning tool depends, of course, on the trustworthiness of the person appointed to manage the trust. In addition, through a variety of emotional appeals, a perpetrator may induce an elder to change his or her will, making the perpetrator the sole beneficiary upon the elder's death.

Distinguishing between an unwise, but legitimate, financial transaction and an exploitative transaction resulting from undue influence, duress, fraud, or lack of informed consent can be difficult. Suspicious transactions may be well-intentioned but guided by poor advice. Generally, financial exploitation involves a pattern of behaviors, rather than single incidents.

Related Problems

Financial crimes against the elderly share some characteristics with other crimes. Related problems requiring separate analysis and response include:

- identity theft,
- Internet fraud,
- check and credit card fraud, and
- prescription fraud.

Financial exploitation of the elderly may also occur in concert with other types of elder abuse, including:

- physical abuse,
- sexual abuse,
- emotional abuse, and
- neglect.

General Responses

The responses that follow are useful for addressing the problems of both fraud and financial exploitation. Strategies targeting the specific elements of each type of financial crime are discussed separately below.

1. *Creating multiagency task forces.* Elder fraud and financial exploitation cases are complex and require expertise in multiple areas, including:
   - law enforcement and investigation,
   - financial management,
   - insurance,
   - investments,
   - real estate,
   - probate law,
   - criminal law,
   - civil law,
   - mental capacity, and
   - social services for the elderly.

   It is unlikely that a single agency will have the necessary skills and resources for a multidisciplinary approach. Thus multiagency efforts are required, should include agencies and individuals with knowledge in the key areas, and should be tailored to the characteristics of the local problem.

2. *Working across jurisdictions.* Because both the victims and the offenders may live in and operate out of several jurisdictions, information-sharing among various law enforcement agencies is critical to building a solid case. A variety of federal, state, and local law enforcement agencies may need to be involved. Further, because financial exploitation often occurs in concert with other crimes, such as assault, neglect, and false imprisonment, multiple units within a given police agency may need to be involved.

3. *Improving reporting mechanisms.* It is widely agreed that underreporting dramatically skews available data on the prevalence of financial crimes against the elderly. The reasons for underreporting were discussed previously, but you

should pay attention to the specific barriers to reporting in your jurisdiction. Accurate descriptions of the local problem depend on better information about the type, frequency, and characteristics of various frauds.

4. *Training police to interview elderly victims of financial crimes.* Once the problem of underreporting has been tackled, intervention with offenders depends on the quality of information investigators can get from victims. There are two key areas in which focused training efforts are required: interviewing elderly victims, and investigating financial crimes.

   First, although certainly not the case for all seniors, many elderly victims have physical, sensory, memory, or other cognitive impairments that can interfere with an officer's attempt to gather information. It is therefore critical that officers are trained to identify such impairments and to respond with effective interviewing techniques. Improving officers' skills with elderly victims has been shown to improve the quality of investigations and to positively affect victims' subsequent attitudes, behaviors, and perceptions toward the police.

   Second, given the complexity of fraud and financial exploitation cases, investigators need to cover all of the relevant domains of inquiry. These should include victim characteristics (e.g., relationship to the offender, mental capacity, etc.), offense characteristics (e.g., telemarketing scam versus financial exploitation by a caregiver), and offender characteristics (e.g., relationship, frequency of contact), as well as detailed information about the elder's estate, financial arrangements, and relevant legal documents. Several investigation checklists are available to guide the development of a comprehensive inquiry.

5. *Decreasing victims' isolation.* Seniors who are isolated and have little contact with family, friends, caseworkers, and other concerned parties may be at increased risk of being victimized by fraudulent businesses. Decreasing this isolation through police welfare checks, neighborhood watches, and in-person outreach efforts can help to ensure that elders are aware of available resources they can turn to with questions and concern about potential scammers. Further, ongoing contact with family members can provide the means for ongoing monitoring of the elder's financial matters. The U.S. Postal Service has created a list of warning signs and various preventative measures for family and friends of seniors.

6. *Educating seniors and other concerned parties.* Although not effective as a stand-alone strategy, when used as part of a multifaceted response, outreach efforts should educate seniors about

   - types of scams operating in the area;
   - how to screen calls using caller-identification devices and answering machines;
   - suspicious behaviors and warning signs of fraudulent offers;
   - how to reduce unwanted solicitations by removing home addresses, phone numbers, and email addresses from marketing and junk mail lists;
   - how to investigate offers and potential purchases;
   - how to select qualified and reputable contractors;
   - how to end unwanted sales calls; and
   - how to report fraud.

7. *Identifying high-risk seniors.* Research has shown that offenders often repeatedly target past fraud victims using "mooch lists" and recovery room scams. Identifying seniors by risk level helps to target intervention efforts appropriately. High-risk seniors are those whom police, prosecutors, postal inspectors, or other agency personnel have identified as previous victims. Volunteers are dispatched to help the seniors prevent future victimization. They offer ongoing, in-person contact, providing not only emotional and moral support, but also tangible tools for combating fraud, such as reviewing daily activities, sorting through the mail, and evaluating telemarketing offers.

8. *Reversing the "boiler room."* These large-scale operations mail out postcards offering a free and guaranteed prize to the recipients. Those who respond to the telephone number listed receive detailed information on sweepstakes fraud and how to protect themselves. Working with senior volunteers, the U.S. Postal Service, consumer protection groups, and others, police may staff the hotlines and provide the information. Similarly, "reverse telethons" use operators with expertise in various types of fraud to answer callers' questions. Task forces established to combat the local elder fraud problem publicize, schedule, and recruit experts to offer advice to seniors, their families, and other concerned parties.

9. *Making it easier for people to hang up on telephone scams.* Studies have shown that many people have difficulty hanging up on telemarketers, even after they have decided they are not interested in the product or service being sold. An "Easy Hang Up" device has been used to help seniors end calls without fearing they are being rude or abrupt. Once the senior decides that a call is unwanted, he or she presses an activation button, and a short recorded message is played, such as "I'm sorry, this number does not accept this type of call. Please regard this as your notification and remove this number from your list. Thank You." The call is then disconnected.

10. *Launching undercover operations.* Although time-consuming and expensive, there have been several large-scale undercover operations to dismantle fraudulent telemarketing organizations. A key telemarketer vulnerability is the inability to be certain of whom they have called. In these operations, police officers and volunteers had their names added to "mooch lists" and posed as potential victims of telemarketing scams. Fraudulent organizations contacted them repeatedly, and the conversations were recorded and used as evidence. Such operations are usually conducted as collaborative efforts between federal, state, and local law enforcement, the AARP, and other senior advocacy organizations.

11. *Enacting proactive health care, legal and financial planning.* The best defense is a good offense. Programs to help people make health care and financial arrangements before they are necessary ensure that these decisions are made thoughtfully and with the person's voluntary and informed consent. Financial arrangements can vary from direct deposit of pension and Social Security checks and automatic payment of utility bills, to estate planning and the creation of powers of attorney. Professional help with such planning can be offered as part of community outreach activities implemented by a multidisciplinary team.

12. *Assessing statutes related to power of attorney.* Although power of attorney is a common tool that serves an important and legitimate purpose for many seniors, it is also vulnerable to abuse. Specific regulations governing powers of attorney

vary by state. Reviewing existing legislation and assessing current provisions for establishing, auditing, modifying, and canceling power of attorney are an important part of assessing the local problem. If existing statues are vulnerable to abuse, consider lobbying for the addition of protective safeguards.

13. *Screening caregivers.* Many states do not require in-home caregivers to undergo criminal background checks. By implementing such measures, people with a history of physical or financial abuse or neglect could be prevented from working as licensed caregivers. However, this strategy would affect only those caregivers hired through licensed agencies, and would not apply to informal caregiving arrangements.

14. *Training police and professionals involved in elders' affairs.* Police should be trained in the specific elements of fraud and financial exploitation. Further, reports from victims and other concerned parties are likely to be complex and may be confusing to both dispatchers and responding officers. Training for these individuals should focus on proper procedures for referring cases for investigation, and on ensuring that complainants understand how the case will be handled.

15. *Disseminating information as a stand-alone strategy.* Traditional approaches focused on raising public awareness have had limited success when used alone. Particularly when targeting elders with significant mental impairment, those who are isolated, and those who are in desperate financial situations, public information campaigns alone are insufficient for preventing financial abuse. Further, information campaigns that rely solely on the distribution of information (e.g., fliers, pamphlets) and do not feature any in-person interaction are among the least effective strategies for preventing crime.

16. *Enacting mandatory reporting laws.* Although they have shown some success in preventing and responding to child abuse, mandatory reporting laws have not been shown effective in preventing, identifying, or addressing financial abuse of the elderly. Training curricula generally include only the reporting requirements, and do not help officers to detect abuse or provide responsive services; in addition, sufficient resources are not allocated for quality investigations of all reports made.

17. *Bonding or registering telemarketers.* Although bonding and registration are often suggested to prevent fraud, there is no empirical research validating the effectiveness of such provisions. While legitimate businesses are likely to comply with such requirements, fraudulent organizations are not likely to be deterred by them. Further, it is unlikely that the average consumer would know to ask about bonding or registration, or that a fraudulent salesperson would tell the truth if asked about the company's compliance. In one jurisdiction, researchers discovered that fraudulent organizations found the registration requirement helpful, as being able to tell victims they were registered with the state brought a false air of legitimacy.

18. *Expanding existing statutes.* In the literature, there are many references to the need to expand the scope of existing statutes to promote the prosecution of financial crimes against the elderly, and to enhance applicable penalties. While enhanced sentences may offer some benefit in terms of specific deterrence, there is no empirical research indicating that such statutes result in increased prosecution rates. Further, such statutes have not been shown to have a general deterrent effect.

QUESTIONS FOR REVIEW AND DISCUSSION

1. What are some general types of crime against the elderly?
2. Why are the elderly prime targets for scams and fraud?
3. What is telemarketing? How can seniors combat telemarketers?
4. Can high-risk seniors be identified and assisted?
5. What roles can government play in minimizing fraud against the elderly?

47

What Is Telemarketing Fraud?

U.S. Department of Justice,
Criminal Division

Adapted from the U.S. Department of Justice, Criminal Division, *What Is Telemarketing Fraud?* Washington, DC: U.S. Department of Justice, Criminal Division, 1998.

Telemarketing fraud is a term that refers generally to any scheme to defraud in which the persons carrying out the scheme use the telephone as their primary means of communicating with prospective victims and trying to persuade them to send money to the scheme. When it solicits people to buy goods and services, to invest money, or to donate funds to charitable causes, a fraudulent telemarketing fraud operation typically uses numerous false and misleading statements, representations, and promises, for three purposes:

(1) *To make it appear that the good, service, or charitable cause their telemarketers offer to the public is worth the money that they are asking the consumer to send.* Fraudulent telemarketers, by definition, do not want to give consumers fair value for the money they have paid to the telemarketers. Because their object is to maximize their personal profits, even if the consumer suffers substantial financial harm, they will typically adopt one or both of two approaches: to fail to give the consumer anything of value in return for their money; or to provide items of modest value, far below what the consumer had expected the value to be on the basis of the telemarketers' representations. When the item is supposed to be a tangible "gift" or "prize" of substantial value, as in charity schemes or prize-promotion schemes, fraudulent telemarketers will instead provide what they term a "gimme gift." The "diamond watch" that the consumer thought would be worth many hundreds or thousands of dollars, for example, proves to be an inexpensively produced watch with a small diamond chip, for which the fraudulent telemarketer may have paid only $30 to $60.

(2) *To obtain immediate payment before the victim can inspect the item of value they expect to receive.* Regardless of what good or service a fraudulent telemarketer says he is

offering—investment items, magazine subscriptions, or office supplies, for example—a fraudulent telemarketer will always insist on advance payment by the consumer before the consumer receives that good or service. If consumers were to receive the promised goods or services before payment, and realized that the good or service was of little or no value, most of them would likely cancel the transaction and refuse payment.

Fraudulent telemarketers therefore routinely make false and misleading representations to the effect that the consumer must act immediately if he or she is to receive the promised good or service. These representations may suggest that the opportunity being offered is of limited quantity or duration, or that there are others also seeking that opportunity. In addition, fraudulent telemarketers usually persuade the victims to send their money by some means of expedited delivery that allows the telemarketers to receive the victims' payments as quickly as possible. For victims who have checks or money orders, the telemarketers use nationally advertised courier delivery services, which will deliver victims' checks by the next business day. For victims who have credit cards, the telemarketers obtain merchant accounts at financial institutions, so that the credit-card number can be processed immediately.

(3)   *To create an aura of legitimacy about their operations, by trying to resemble legitimate telemarketing operations, legitimate businesses, or legitimate government agencies.* Magazine-subscription schemes, for example, often tell consumers, "We're just like" a nationally publicized magazine-distribution organization, and in some cases have simply lied to consumers by stating that they are the nationally publicized organization. Telemarketers in "rip-and-tear" schemes or "recovery-room schemes" often falsely impersonate federal agents or other government officials to lend greater credibility to their demands for money.

Another factor that distinguishes fraudulent from legitimate telemarketing operations is "reloading." "Reloading" is a term that refers to the fraudulent telemarketer's practice of recontacting victims, after their initial transactions with the telemarketer, and soliciting them for additional payments. In prize-promotion schemes, for example, victims are often told that they are now eligible for even higher levels and values of prizes, for which they must pay additional (nonexistent) "fees" or "taxes." Because "reload" transactions typically demand increasingly substantial amounts of money from victims, they provide fraudulent telemarketers with their most substantial profits, while causing consumers increasingly large losses that they will never recoup voluntarily from the fraudulent telemarketers.

A third factor that distinguishes fraudulent from legitimate telemarketing operations is the fraudulent telemarketer's general reluctance to contact prospective victims who reside in the state where the telemarketing operation conducts its business. Fraudulent telemarketers recognize that if they contact victims located outside their state, any victims who later realize that they may have been defrauded are likely to be uncertain about which law enforcement agency they should contact with complaints, and less likely to travel directly to the telemarketing operation and confront the telemarketers about their losses.

Although many consumers apparently find it difficult to believe that there are people who will contact them on the telephone and lie and misrepresent facts in order to get their money, the reality is that at any given time, there are at least several hundred fraudulent telemarketing operations—some of them employing as many as several dozen people—in North America that routinely seek to defraud consumers in the United States and Canada.

Moreover, these schemes generally do not choose their victims at random. Fraudulent telemarketers routinely buy "leads"—that is, listings of names, addresses, and phone numbers of persons who have been defrauded in previous telemarketing schemes (and typically the amount of their last transaction with a fraudulent telemarketer)—from each other and from "lead brokers," companies that engage exclusively in buying and selling fraudulent telemarketers' leads. Although leads are relatively costly to the fraudulent telemarketer—as much as $10 or even $100 per lead in some cases—they also indicate to the fraudulent telemarketer which consumers are most likely to be persuaded to send substantial amounts of money that will far exceed the cost of the leads.

Firms giving references may provide the names of "touts" or "singers." "Touts" and "singers" are people who praise the telemarketer's services, but who actually are part of the scheme. Telemarketers also sometimes give as a reference an organization with a name similar to the "Better Business Bureau" ("BBB"), but which in reality has nothing to do with a legitimate local BBB.

QUESTIONS FOR REVIEW AND DISCUSSION

1. What is telemarketing fraud?
2. How can telemarketing fraud be recognized?
3. What are some of the "red flags" of fraud?

48

What Kinds of Telemarketing Schemes Are Out There?

U.S. Department of Justice,
Criminal Division

Adapted from the U.S. Department of Justice, Criminal Division, *What Kinds of Tele-marketing Schemes Are Out There?* Washington, DC: U.S. Department of Justice, Criminal Division, 1998.

In one sense, the nature and content of a telemarketing scheme to defraud is limited only by the ingenuity and skill of the scheme's organizers. Fraudulent telemarketers who observe that certain types of business, or certain business trends, are widely publicized in news media will incorporate references to such reports in their solicitations of victims. In practice, most fraudulent telemarketers operate one or more of the following types of schemes: charity schemes, credit-card, credit-repair, and loan schemes, cross-border schemes, Internet-related schemes, investment schemes, lottery schemes, office-supply schemes, "prize-promotion" schemes, "recovery-room" schemes, and "rip-and-tear" schemes.

CHARITY SCHEMES

Many people have a laudable desire to help those who are less fortunate by making donations to charitable causes. Fraudulent telemarketers have often exploited that desire, by devising schemes that purport to raise money for worthy causes. At various times, fraudulent telemarketers have falsely claimed, for example, that they were soliciting funds for victims of the Oklahoma City bombing or Mississippi Valley flooding or for antidrug programs. In one type of charity scheme, known as "badge fraud," fraudulent telemarketers purport to be soliciting funds to support police- or fire department-related causes.

Some of these schemes simply lie outright to would-be donors and give none of their proceeds to charity. Other schemes, to help maintain their aura of legitimacy, will donate a modest amount of their proceeds—typically no more than 10 percent—to a charitable cause so that they can show some evidence of their "legitimacy" to law-enforcement or regulatory authorities who may have received complaints about the schemes. In one scheme that resulted in successful federal criminal prosecutions, the schemes' organizers tried to enhance their appearance of legitimacy by sending the would-be donors "gimme gifts" and mounted plaques that thanked them for their contributions to a particular "foundation" (which was in fact an organization, run by former fraudulent telemarketers, that did nothing for people in need).

CREDIT-CARD, CREDIT-REPAIR, AND LOAN SCHEMES

Certain telemarketing schemes are devised to victimize people who have bad credit, or whose income levels may be too low to allow them to amass substantial credit. In many credit-card telemarketing schemes, telemarketers contact prospective victims and represent that they can obtain credit cards even if they have poor credit histories. The victim who pays the fee demanded by the telemarketer usually receives no card, or receives only a credit-card application or some cheaply printed brochures or flyers that discuss credit cards. In a variant of these schemes, the credit card that some consumers are given, after paying the fee to the telemarketer, requires the consumer to pay a company located outside the United States $200 or $300 and limits the consumer's charges on that card to an amount no greater than the amount of money the consumer has paid to the offshore company.

In advance-fee loan schemes, persons with bad credit are promised a loan in return for a fee paid in advance. Victims who pay the fees for the guaranteed loans have their names referred to a "turndown room"—that is, an operation, affiliated with the telemarketer, whose sole function is to notify the victims at a later date that their loan applications have been rejected.

Another way that fraudulent telemarketers try to take advantage of people with poor credit histories is by promising to "repair" their credit. Firms that promise that they can remove bankruptcies, judgments, liens, foreclosures and other items from a consumer's credit report, irrespective of the age or accuracy of the information, are misstating the facts. Judgments, paid tax liens, accounts referred for collection or charged off, and records of arrest, indictment, or conviction, may remain on a consumer's report for seven years, while bankruptcies may remain on the report for ten years. Credit reporting agencies are obligated by law to correct mistakes on consumers' reports. People with real errors on their reports can deal directly with the reporting agencies, or obtain assistance from the Federal Trade Commission with their problems. Credit repair agencies cannot generally succeed in eliminating accurate negative information from credit reports, despite the contrary claims of some firms.

CROSS-BORDER SCHEMES

Cross-border telemarketing schemes consist of telemarketing schemes—usually advance-fee loan schemes, investment schemes, lottery schemes, and prize-promotion schemes—where the scheme's operators conduct their telemarketing activities in one country and solicit victims in another country. Cross-border telemarketing schemes are appealing to some telemarketers because it further enhances the difficulties for consumers in reporting complaints and for law-enforcement agencies in investigating and prosecuting these schemes. To obtain certain kinds of evidence that they can use in legal proceedings, and to have criminal suspects extradited from foreign countries, law enforcement and regulatory authorities in the United States must use legal procedures that have been established by bilateral treaties with those countries. In some cases, those procedures provide opportunities for the criminal suspects to create substantial delays in legal proceedings by challenging the U.S. authorities' right to the evidence or the extradition of the suspect. A few fraudulent telemarketers have admitted to law enforcement authorities that they believe these delays can last long enough for victim-witnesses to die before they have an opportunity to testify in legal proceedings and receive some restitution of their losses.

INTERNET-RELATED SCHEMES

Many of the schemes to defraud that have been conducted exclusively by telemarketing are now being conducted partly or exclusively by the Internet. Consumers who have Internet access now regularly receive "spammed" E-mails—that is, unsolicited E-mails that purport to offer business or investment opportunities or opportunities to purchase computer-related or other goods or services. Much of the "spamming" invites consumers to telephone a particular telephone number, to visit a particular Webpage, or to mail funds to a particular address.

Many of these spammed E-mails, however, are sent by fraudulent schemes. In the past year, for example, federal and state authorities have actively pursued fraudulent schemes advertising on the Internet that included promotions for charities, investments such as pyramid schemes and Ponzi schemes, degrees from a fictitious educational institution, illegal raffles, and opportunities to sell coupon certificate booklets or to earn money at home by clipping coupons. According to the Internet Fraud Watch, a project of the National Consumers League, fraud reports to the Internet Fraud Watch increased substantially from an average of 32 per month in 1996 to nearly 100 per month in 1997. The Internet Fraud Watch also reported that for the period January–July, 1997, the top ten categories of Internet-related fraud complaints were:

1. Internet and online services that were misrepresented or never delivered;
2. General merchandise that was never delivered or not as advertised;
3. Auctions of items that were never delivered or whose value was inflated;
4. Pyramid- and multilevel marketing schemes in which profits are made from fees to join the scheme rather than sales of actual items;
5. Business opportunities that were substantially less profitable than advertised;
6. Work-at-home schemes that sold materials to consumers with false promises to pay for the work performed;
7. Prizes and sweepstakes schemes in which prizes were never awarded;
8. Credit-card offers in which consumers never received the promised cards;
9. Sales of self-help manuals that were misrepresented or never delivered; and
10. Magazine subscriptions that were never delivered or for which the scheme's affiliation with legitimate publishers was misrepresented.

INVESTMENT AND BUSINESS-OPPORTUNITY SCHEMES

Since the 1970s, many fraudulent telemarketers have offered a wide variety of spurious investment opportunities to would-be investors. The nature of the purported investments varies largely with what the telemarketers perceive, from widely publicized reports on business matters, to be the trends that less experienced or less sophisticated investors are most likely to consider attractive for high-profit investment. In the 1980s, for example, many telemarketing schemes offered "investments" in rare coins, precious metals, and so-called "strategic metals." In the 1990s, many telemarketing schemes turned to offering "investments" in items as diversified as "investment-grade" gemstones, ostrich farms, and telecommunications technology such as wireless cable systems for television broadcasting.

Where the investment item that the victim purchases is small enough to be held, such as gemstones or rare coins, fraudulent telemarketers often seal the items in a plastic container and ship the sealed container to the victim. The telemarketer also warns the victim not to open the container, as that would void the telemarketer's guarantee on those items. The true purpose of sealing the items in the container is to dissuade the victim from having the items independently appraised, as a genuine appraisal would inform the victim that the real market value of the items is far below what the telemarketer had represented.

LOTTERY SCHEMES

Fraudulent telemarketers have often used offers of "investing" in foreign lottery tickets or chances as a vehicle to defraud consumers. Although federal law forbids the importation, interstate transportation, and foreign transportation of lottery tickets or chances, many fraudulent telemarketers routinely contact people in the United States, through mailings, advertisements, and telephone calls, to solicit their involvement in foreign lotteries such as the "Australian Lottery" or "El Gordo." Victims often begin by paying as little as $5 or $10 for lottery chances. Many of those who do are later contacted by telemarketers who hold themselves out as "experts" in "investing" in lottery chances, and who solicit the victims for larger and larger amounts of money. Law enforcement authorities in the United States and Canada are aware of many instances in which victims have sent thousands, tens of thousands, and even hundreds of thousands of dollars to lottery telemarketers, after hearing repeated promises or guarantees of vast returns.

In reality, the telemarketers invest little or none of the victims' money in the lottery tickets or chances, and keep the money for themselves after paying salaries and other expenses of their fraudulent business. In some instances, where victims had been given certain lottery numbers by the telemarketers, and later learned independently that their numbers had won a real lottery, the victims were told that their winnings had been "invested" in other lottery tickets rather than being paid to them directly.

MAGAZINE-PROMOTION SCHEMES

A number of fraudulent telemarketing schemes in recent years have turned to offering magazine subscriptions, in part because of the apparent popularity of several nationally known magazine-promotion businesses that send mailings throughout the United States that advertise their multimillion-dollar prize contests. In a typical fraudulent magazine-promotion scheme, a telemarketer contacts a prospective victim and tells the victim that he or she has won a highly valuable prize or is to be given a highly valuable "gift," and falsely implies that the victim must purchase multiple magazine subscriptions to receive the award or gift. The victim is told the total price for the package of subscriptions, which can range from several hundred to several thousand dollars, but is not told which magazines he or she is to receive when the victim agrees to send money to the telemarketer. Instead, the telemarketer, after receiving the victim's money, sends the victim lists of magazines on which the victim can check off the magazines that he or she wants to order and which the victim then mails back to the telemarketer.

OFFICE-SUPPLY SCHEMES

One type of fraudulent telemarketing scheme that is directed specifically at the business community is the office-supply or "toner" scheme. In a typical toner scheme, an employee of the telemarketer first contacts a business under false pretenses to learn the make and model number of the copier used at that business. Within a day or two, a telemarketer then recontacts the business, this time falsely representing himself to be a representative of the copier company whose copier is being used at that business. The telemarketer falsely states that his company is about to increase the price of their toner, but that the company is prepared to offer the business a shipment of toner at the then-current price before the price increase goes into effect. If the business employee who answers the telemarketer's call agrees to have the toner shipped, the business thereafter receives an invoice for the toner without the toner, or receives a shipment of toner with the invoice.

This is known as "graymarket" toner—that is, toner that does not meet the quality specifications and requirements of legitimate copier companies. Businesses who use the graymarket toner often find that it clogs their copiers, requiring them to call their copier company for service. In many cases, businesses do not discover the true extent of the fraud until the copier company's service people repair the copiers and inform the businesses that the toner is not their company's toner and that there was no planned price increase.

PRIZE-PROMOTION SCHEMES

Over the years, law-enforcement and regulatory authorities have observed at least three varieties of telemarketing schemes that purport to offer prizes, awards, or gifts to consumers if the consumers buy certain goods or services or make supposedly charitable donations:

(1) The oldest of these schemes, which still is carried out in some areas of both the United States and Canada, involves a simply false statement to a prospective victim that he or she has won a particular highly valuable item, such as a car. Because the explicit promise of a valuable item that is never delivered provides clear evidence of fraudulent intent, participants in a number of these schemes were successfully prosecuted in the 1980s and 1990s.

(2) More recently, beginning in the late 1980s and early 1990s, some fraudulent telemarketers began conducting so-called "one-in-five" schemes. In a "one-in-five" scheme, the telemarketer contacts a prospective victim and represents that the victim has won one of five (sometimes four or six) valuable prizes. The telemarketer then lists the prizes for the

victim. All but one of the promised prizes would in fact have substantial value if awarded (such as a nationally known U.S.-manufactured car, a $3,000 cashier's check, and a $5,000 cashier's check); the remaining prize, however, was a "gimme gift" such as inexpensive "his and hers diamond watches," plastic dolphin statues, and gold rings.

Many telemarketers, in reading the award list to victims, deliberately included the "gimme gift" between two items of much higher real value, to make the victim believe that the "gimme gift's" value was somewhere between the value of the other two items. Although most "one-in-five" schemes invariably gave away only the "gimme gift," the telemarketers typically told victims who asked which prize they would be receiving that they could not give out that information because it would be "collusion" or "bribery." These explanations, while nonsensical, were developed to avoid having to tell prospective victims clearly false information about the prizes' value and the victims' chances of winning the far more valuable items.

(3) A variation on the "one-in-five" scheme is the so-called "mystery pitch" or "integrity pitch" (the latter term being more favored by fraudulent telemarketers). In a "mystery pitch," the telemarketer would tell a prospective victim that he or she had won something of substantial value, but refuse to tell the victim what the prize was because of professed concerns about "collusion" or "bribery." Some telemarketers apparently adopted the "mystery pitch" after seeing that other telemarketers were being successfully prosecuted in "one-in-five" schemes where the prizes were specifically listed for the victims.

In each of these variations of "prize-promotion" schemes, the telemarketers routinely "reload" victims by telling them that they have now qualified for higher levels of prizes, but that they must accordingly pay still more money to the telemarketers to cover the "fees" or "taxes" that the telemarketers claim are due on the prizes.

"RECOVERY-ROOM" SCHEMES

So-called "recovery-room" telemarketing schemes are schemes that often are extensions of other telemarketing schemes. As one or more telemarketing schemes gradually deprive victims of most of their funds, the victims become increasingly desperate to try to recover a portion of their losses, and increasingly concerned about the embarrassment that they would feel if they had to report the true extent of their losses to law enforcement. A telemarketer for a "recovery room" contacts the victim, and invariably claims some affiliation with a government organization or agency that is in a position to help telemarketing victims recover some of their past losses. Some telemarketers have falsely impersonated FBI, IRS, and Customs agents or attorneys in law firms, while others use more nebulous language to suggest a connection to a government agency (such as "I'm working with the court [or the district attorney]") in a particular city.

Because the telemarketers may have worked for the scheme that had previously defrauded the victims, they are well-equipped to disclose information about the amounts of the victims' past losses. This in turn gives the telemarketers additional credibility with the victims, who apparently believe that only a legitimate law-enforcement or other government agency could have access to such information. The telemarketers, posing as government officials, then tell victims that they must send a fee to them so that their money can be released by "the court" or otherwise delivered to the victims. This allows the telemarketer to deprive victims of even more money, while simultaneously encouraging the victims to believe that something is being done to protect their interests and causing the victims to postpone the filing of complaints with real law-enforcement or regulatory authorities.

"RIP-AND-TEAR" SCHEMES

As law-enforcement and regulatory authorities have become more vigorous in prosecuting fraudulent telemarketing, some fraudulent telemarketers have increasingly engaged in what are known as "rip-and-tear" schemes. What distinguishes a "rip-and-tear" scheme from other telemarketing schemes is simply the methods that the fraudulent telemarketers use to minimize the risks of detection and apprehension of the authorities. Instead of conducting their telemarketing from a single, fixed place of business, "rip-and-tear" telemarketers conduct their calls from various places, such as pay telephones, residences, and hotel rooms. Their contacts with prospective victims—who usually are repeat victims of past telemarketing schemes—involve explicit promises that the victims have won a valuable prize or are entitled to receive a portion of their past losses.

"Rip-and-tear" schemes often insist that the victims send the required "fees" to commercial mailbox facilities or by electronic wire transfer services, which create far less substantial paper trails than checks or credit cards and which allow the telemarketers to receive the victims' payments in cash. To create further difficulties for law enforcement, "rip-and-tear" telemarketers often hire persons to act as couriers to pick up the payments from the mailbox drop or wire transfer office; if law-enforcement agents pick up the payments and arrest the couriers, the organizers of the scheme are not tied directly to the delivery of the victims' funds. In some instances, law-enforcement authorities have reported that telemarketers appeared to be conducting countersurveillance—that is, watching to see whether they were under surveillance at pickup points, and engaging in evasive behavior.

QUESTIONS FOR REVIEW AND DISCUSSION

1. Is there a foolproof way of determining whether a telemarketer is a legitimate salesperson?
2. What steps should be taken if you suspect you're a victim of a fraudulent telemarketer?
3. How can you avoid becoming a victim of telemarketing? Discuss.

49

"Are Sex Offenders Dangerous?"

Lisa L. Sample
and Timothy M. Bray

Adapted form Lisa L. Sample and Timothy M. Bray, "Are Sex Offenders Dangerous?"
Criminology and Public Policy 3: 59–82, 2003.

Reprinted by permission of the American Society of Criminology.

Over the last decade, state legislatures spent an unprecedented amount of time and re-sources in addressing the behavior of sex offenders. Since 1990, sex offenders in at least 21 states have become "eligible" for civil commitment in mental health facilities after their re-lease from prison; in all 50 states, they have been made to register their addresses with law enforcement agencies, and they have had their residences and behaviors disclosed to the public. Some states introduced chemical castration and reintroduced execution as possible punishments for sex crimes. In Illinois, convicted sex offenders are now prohibited from public parks and school zones. Furthermore, currently all states mandate the drawing of DNA samples from convicted sex offenders, so they may be housed in databanks and used by law enforcement agencies to help identify criminal suspects and enact arrests (Stevens, 2001). Although these policies encompass a range of solutions from institutionalization to community-based alternatives, a common ideology pervades much of this legislation—a belief that without intervention or some sort of surveillance, sex offenders will never stop committing sex crimes.

Current sex offender policies are predicated on a notion of "once a sex offender, al-ways a sex offender." As one public official stated, "They will never stop. That [sex of-fending] is just what they do" (Sample, 2001). By implication, remarks such as these suggest that sex offenders are simply more dangerous than other criminal offenders because they exhibit a greater degree of compulsion for their crimes than that found for nonsexual offender groups. This perception of enhanced dangerousness provides a justification for current sex offender laws and the way in which they penalize sexual criminals far beyond the punishments other categories of offenders may receive. However, currently another perception of sex offenders is emerging and being used to justify the expansion of sex offender laws to nonsexual offenders, that which suggests that sex offenders begin offending by committing nonsexual crimes.

Research conducted on state DNA databases indicates that sex offenders partake in a variety of criminal activities before they commit an initial sex offense (Spaulding, 1999; Stevens, 2001; Willing, 2000). This evidence suggests that "gateway" or predicate offenses to sex offending may be discovered and the behavior addressed before offenders progress to sex crimes. In much the same fashion as marijuana has been identified as the "gateway" drug, currently burglary is being considered as the "gateway" offense to sex offending (Spaulding, 1999; Stevens, 2001; Willing, 2000). In accordance, at least 14 state legislatures have expanded DNA collection to persons convicted of burglary or possession of burglary tools in the hope that these offenders will be identified before their behavior manifests to sexual violence (Stevens, 2001). Furthermore, at least one state is currently considering expanding its sex offender registry to include persons convicted of burglary, robbery, or possession of burglary tools on the basis that these types of offenders have a high probability of committing future sex crimes.

The purpose of this paper is to highlight two common perceptions underlying sex offender laws, and the extension thereof, and to review them in light of current empirical evidence; the first being that sex offenders, more than any other group of offenders, are highly likely to repeat their crimes, and second, that some nonsexual crime types serve as predicate offenses to sexual offending. We acknowledge the sex offender laws, and their expansion, encompass a range of beliefs and assumptions about sex offenders beyond those we examine here. We also recognize the desires and intentions of public officials that lay behind these policies—primarily that of protecting the public from sexual harm and easing public fear. To this end, this commentary is not meant to dismiss the threat of sex offending, make light of the harm that victims endure, demean policy makers' judgments of the sex offender problem, or declare the current policies ineffective. Rather, based on our review, we will simply make the case that sex offenders may not be as dangerous as the laws would dictate or as we have been led to believe.

Our discussion begins with a review of the movement to enact the current sex offender laws and the public's support for these reforms. We then examine current evidence of sex offenders' levels of recidivism and nonsexual offenders' propensities to commit future sex crimes. Lastly, to further strengthen our argument, we include criminal history data from a single state to examine the probabilities of sexual and nonsexual offenders committing future sex crimes.

BACKGROUND

In the late 1980s and early 1990s, three specific incidents of sexual homicides against children were catalysts for much of the sex offender legislation we have today. In October 1989, Jacob Wetterling, 11, was abducted near his home in Minnesota by an armed masked stranger (National Criminal Justice Association, 1997). To date, he has still not been found. His case resembled that of a boy in a neighboring town who was abducted and sexually attacked earlier in the year. Both incidents are believed to have been committed by the same man, thus leading police to conclude they were searching for a repeat sex offender. Although the Wetterling abduction drew attention to the repetitiveness of sex offenders' behaviors, it was the homicides of Polly Klaas and Megan Kanka that brought this issue to the forefront of the policy agenda (Jenkins, 1998).

In 1993, the media widely disseminated the story of Polly Klaas, a 12-year-old girl who was abducted from her bedroom in California, sexually assaulted, and subsequently killed. Only one year later, the media reported that 7-year-old Megan Kanka was missing from her New Jersey home; she was later found sexually assaulted and murdered. Both Polly Klaas and Megan Kanka had been murdered by previously convicted sex offenders who had been released from prison. The parents of these murdered children actively lobbied state and federal legislators for remedies to address the repeat behavior of sex offenders. The results of their efforts have been witnessed nationwide.

In 1994, the Jacob Wetterling Crimes Against Children and Sexually Violent Offender Registration Act mandated that 10% of a state's funding under the Edward Bryne Memorial State and Local Law Enforcement Assistance grant program be used for establishing a state-wide system for registering and tracking convicted sex offenders (National Criminal Justice Association, 1997). The act also "strongly encouraged" states to collect DNA samples from registered sex offenders to be typed and stored in databases and used to clear crimes (p. 7). The Wetterling Act was soon amended by the passage of "Megan's Law" in 1996, which requires states to make sex offender registry information available to the public. Although states began complying with the Wetterling Act and its amendment by requiring blood samples and registry information from only those sex offenders convicted of violent sex acts against children, to date, all 50 states have expanded their registry, notification, and DNA laws to include persons convicted of a violent or nonviolent sex crime against any person regardless of their age.

The tragic deaths of these children who were murdered by previously convicted and released sex offenders not only initiated legal reform but also undoubtedly influenced our perceptions of sex offenders. These stories helped create an image of the sex offender as a compulsive recidivist who continues to present a danger to society despite any efforts at rehabilitation or reform. It is most likely this image that drives the public's support for the current sex offender laws.

Few scientific polls have been conducted to determine the public's opinions of sex offender laws, but those that have suggest that there is overwhelming support for sex offender registration, community notification, and DNA database laws. In 2001, the polling firm of MORI in Great Britain conducted a survey to determine if there was public support for "Sarah's Law," which is similar to our "Megan's Law" by giving the public access to a register of sex offenders (www.mori.com/diget/2001.) An overwhelming majority of those surveyed agreed that convicted pedophiles should be publicly named and people should know if a convicted pedophile lives in their neighborhood. Only 7% of those surveyed disagreed. In the United States, Phillips (1998) surveyed residents of the state of Washington to determine their support for community notification laws. Of the 400 residents surveyed, she found that more than eight out of ten respondents indicated that notification laws were very important, and the majority of respondents believed the laws would help reduce the chances of sex offenders committing another crime. More recently, Dundes (2001) surveyed a convenience sample of 416 persons in Maryland to determine their support for DNA databases. She found that 89% of those surveyed supported the inclusion of sex offenders and other violent felons in a DNA database to help facilitate more rapid apprehension of repeat offenders. Regardless of the scientific rigor of these surveys and polls, they suggest something that many of us already suspected. There is a belief among the public that sex offenders are highly likely to recommit sex crimes, and there is widespread support for current sex offender laws as a way to deter this repetitive behavior. However, there is also growing support for the extension of sex offender laws to nonsexual offenders on the basis that some offense types serve as "gateway" offenses to sex crimes.

Much of the information cited as evidence of the existence of a "gateway" offense to sex offending can be traced to three studies conducted on state DNA databases (Stevens, 2001; Willing, 2000). The Florida Department of Law Enforcement released the results of a study that found that 52% of the convicted rapists in that state's DNA database had previous convictions for burglary (Stevens, 2001; Willing, 2000). A similar study on Virginia's convict DNA database uncovered that in about half of the sex offense cases in which officers ran through and received a hit in the DNA database, the sample could be traced back to a convicted burglar (Stevens, 2001; Willing, 2000). These findings echoed the results from a British study conducted in 1998, which also found that more than three-quarters of rapists in the United Kingdom had burglary arrests in their pasts (Stevens, 2001; Willing, 2000). Findings such as these have led some state legislators to conclude that burglary is a predicate crime to sex offending, thereby necessitating the expansion of DNA collection, and possibly registration, to burglars or persons convicted of possessing burglary tools (Catabiana, 1999; Spaulding, 1999; Stevens, 2001; Willing, 2000). However, the logic of this conclusion is suspect. The studies frequently offered in support of burglary as a "gateway" crime are retrospective in nature, simply examining the pasts of current sex offenders and implying a pattern of escalation from burglary to sex crimes. Undoubtedly, sex offenders have many behaviors in their pasts from milk-drinking to school attendance, but it would be wrong to assert that school children or milk-drinkers go on to become sex offenders. As one colleague so eloquently put it, the researchers of these studies "have been looking through the wrong end of the telescope." In order to assert an increase in seriousness from burglary to sex crimes, prospective studies are needed to determine the degree to which burglars go on to commit sex offenses. Rather, the aforementioned studies can only speak to the degree to which sex offenders were once burglars, robbers, or thieves. Despite the illogical reasoning behind the extension of sex offender laws to nonsexual offenders, one study suggests that the public supports this expansion.

Dundes (2001) found that 77% of those surveyed supported expanding DNA databases to include all persons convicted of felonies, including both violent and nonviolent offenses, and 65% favored expanding DNA collection to all persons convicted of both felonies and misdemeanors. Although not specifically asked whether burglars go on to be sex offenders and should thereby be included in sex offender laws, it seems likely that these respondents would support such an action.

Although many believe that sex offenders exhibit high rates of recidivism and that burglars and robbers go on to become sexual criminals, empirical research offers little support for these notions. Several researchers have investigated, both retrospectively and prospectively, sex offending patterns among those offenders hospitalized, incarcerated, or under treatment for sex crimes (for reviews, see Furby et al., 1989; Becker and Hunter, 1992; and Hanson and Bussiere, 1998). Furby et al. (1989) reviewed 49 published sex offender recidivism studies and found that reported levels of reoffending among treated and untreated sex offenders ranged from 3.8% to 55.6%. The authors' results were consistent with Quinsey's (1984: 101) findings, and they agreed with his conclusion: "The differences in recidivism across these studies is truly remarkable; clearly by selectively contemplating the various studies, one can conclude anything one wants" (p. 27). More recently, Hanson and Bussiere (1998) conducted a meta-analysis of 61 studies examining reoffending patterns among sex offenders. They found that, on average, the sex offense recidivism rate was 13.4% during an average follow-up time of 4 to 5 years. They concluded, "The present findings contradict the popular view that sexual offenders inevitably re-offend. Only a minority of the total sample (13.4% of 23,393) were known to have committed a new sexual offense" (p. 357).

Although the aforementioned studies are enlightening, they did not compare sex offenders' rates of reoffending to those for other nonsexual offender groups. Given the way in which sex offender laws intimate that sex offenders are in greater need of supervision and management than other types of offenders not subject to these laws, this type of comparison is needed.

We found few studies that directly examine sex offenders' recidivism rates in comparison to that found for other groups. Most of these, however, suggest that sex offenders exhibit lower rates of reoffending than nonsexual offender groups (Langan and Levin, 2002; Hanson et al., 1995; Sapsford, 1998; Sipe et al., 1998. For example, Sipe et al. (1998) examined the adult arrest records of a group of adjudicated sexual and nonsexual juvenile offenders. They found that juvenile sex offenders were significantly more likely than nonsexual offenders to be arrested for sex crimes as adults. However, only a small percentage of both groups had an adult arrest for a sex crime (9.7% for sexual and 3.0% for nonsexual offenders). These authors also found that approximately 12% of juvenile nonsexual offenders were arrested as adults for other violent offenses and 32.6% for property crimes. These percentages were twice those found for juvenile sex offenders arrested as adults for other violent and property offenses (5.6% and 16.1%, respectively). In their investigation of recidivism rates among child molesters and nonsexual criminals, Hanson et al. (1995) found that 83.2% of nonsexual criminals were reconvicted over 15 to 30 years as opposed to approximately 62% of child molesters. More recently, Langan and Levin (2002) examined rearrest rates over three years for released prisoners in 15 states (N = 272,111). They found that those convicted of sexual assault (41.4%) and rape (46%) were among those with the lowest re-arrest rates when compared to other offender groups such as burglars (74%), robbers (70.2%), and thieves (74.6%). When examining rates of sexual re-offending, these authors found only 2.5% of released rapists were re-arrested for another rape within three years. Some sex offenders obviously recidivate. However, the empirical evidence to date does not seem to suggest that sex offenders have higher rates of recidivism than other groups of offenders and are thus in need of greater levels of surveillance and control.

In regard to the expansion of sex offender laws to non-sexual offenders, few researchers have directly examined the degree to which groups such as robbers or burglars go on to become sexual criminals. Blumstein et al. (1988) used transition matrices to examine specialization and escalation in offender patterns among 33,000 adults 17 years or older. They observed an increase in the seriousness of offending following arrests for aggravated assault. However, weaker levels of escalation were noted, especially for white offenders, following arrests for robbery, auto theft, and drugs. Also they noted, "white offenders exhibited high levels of de-escalation in seriousness following arrests for rape" (342). No increases in the seriousness of offending was observed following arrests for burglary or larceny. In contrast, using quasi-symmetry modeling, Britt (1996) noted significant patterns of escalation from drug, burglary, and larceny offenses to robbery and aggravated assault (217). These patterns were weak for both black and white offenders. He also found a weak pattern of escalation to rape, and a pattern of de-escalation to weapons and fraud violations. In sum, these studies offer mixed results regarding escalation in offending, suggesting that observed trajectories may be dependent on the race of offenders and the types of crimes for which offenders are initially arrested. More importantly, these findings provide little support for a belief in "gateway" offenses to sex crimes and even less support for the notion that burglary is the predicate offense to sexual offending.

In sum, sex offender legislation is unprecedented in its ability to penalize a specific type of offender *after* his/her judicially prescribed punishment has been served. Originally, no other category of offender was mandated to submit blood samples to DNA databanks, committed to mental health facilities after an imprisonment sentence was served, required to register an address with law enforcement officials, or had residence and criminal history disclosed to the public. Undoubtedly, several beliefs and intentions form the basis of these policies, but one belief appears inherent—that sex offenders, as a group, regardless of their race, gender, or offense, are compulsive offenders with higher rates of recidivism than other types of offenders display for their crimes (burglars for burglary, robbers for robbery, etc.). However, few studies suggest that sex offenders display a greater commitment to sex offending than other categories of offenders demonstrate for their crimes and thus deserve the enhanced levels of informal and formal surveillance that sex offender laws promote. Moreover, there is little empirical evidence to suggest that expanding sex offender laws to nonsexual offenders is justified on the grounds that some groups of offenders are likely to commit future sex crimes.

From the evidence presented here, we conclude that sex offender laws cannot be justified based on the assumption of unusually high rates of recidivism among sex offenders, nor can the expansion of these laws be justified on the notion of a likely predicate offense type. In an effort to provide further support for this conclusion, we offer the following case study of sexual and nonsexual offenders' recidivism in Illinois. We hope that this case study will further help to demonstrate that sex offenders are not more dangerous than other groups of offenders, when measured by repeat offending, and thus more deserving of the increased punitiveness of sex offender laws.

A CASE STUDY OF OFFENDERS' RECIDIVISM IN ILLINOIS

Data and Methods

For these analyses, we used criminal history information from 1990 to 1997 compiled by the Illinois State Police (ISP). The Illinois State Police serves as a central repository for information about arrests made in Illinois. All cities, counties, and municipalities, as well as universities, colleges, conservation, and railroad law enforcement agencies (1,082 reporting agencies in total), send their detailed arrest data to the ISP. These data then provide a reliable and comprehensive overview of all arrests made in the state over time.

Arrest rather than conviction data are preferred for this analysis for two reasons. Arrest data avoid downward bias resulting from plea bargains and charge reductions. Due to the mandatory registration of sex offenders upon conviction, it is likely that many offenders plead to nonsexual offenses in order to avoid future surveillance and stigma. In such cases, arrest charges more closely resemble the crime committed than the charge for which offenders plead guilty or are convicted.

Although there are advantages to using arrest data, there are also limitations. Arrest data allow for the inclusion of false positives, or people falsely accused of crimes. The Illinois State

Police does not receive clearance information, so to investigate the extent to which this may be a problem, we divided the number of arrestees listed in the UCR (1996) for sexual assault, robbery, nonsexual assault, burglary, and larceny into the number of those convicted for these crimes in state courts, as listed in the Bureau of Justice Statistics Sourcebook (1996), to estimate the extent to which arrests do not result in convictions nationwide. These findings indicate that the percent of sex offenders in the United States convicted for sexual assault (23.3%) is strikingly similar to the percent found for robbery (27.4%) and burglary (25.5%). The sexual assault percentage is somewhat higher than that found for nonsexual assault (13.3%). To the degree that the lack of criminal conviction represents a false accusation and Illinois resembles the nation as a whole, these data suggest that the fraction of persons falsely arrested for sex crimes would be roughly similar to that for other crime types.

Another limitation of official statistics is that they necessarily are limited to those persons who come to official attention. They also are susceptible to reporting bias and sometimes more accurately reflect police procedures than actual criminal occurrences. For investigations of sex-offending recidivism, some scholars suggest that the use of arrest data is particularly problematic because many sexual assaults are not reported to police (Bachman, 1998; Koss, 1996; Wood et al., 2000). However, the National Crime Victimization Survey (NCVS) (1995) indicates that sex crimes are reported to the police less frequently than some crimes but more frequently than others. There are also important group differences in the fraction of sex crimes reported.

The NCVS (1995) indicates that 32% of victims of rape and sexual assault ages 12 and older reported their incidents to police. This percentage was lower than reports of victimizations for robbery (60.6%), burglary (50.3%), and auto theft (74.4%), but it was the same or higher than the rate for simple assault (31.8%) and larceny (26.3%). When reports of rape/sexual assault are examined by race, the NCVS (1995) found that 52.1% of black victims reported their sexual assaults to police as compared to only 28.4% of whites. The percentage of reports for sexual victimization by blacks was greater than the percentage for nonsexual assault (45.5%) and comparable to their reporting of attempted robbery (54.2%). Age differences in reporting sex crimes to the police are pronounced. The NCVS found a greater proportion of victims ages 12 to 19 reported their sexual victimizations to police (42%) than their incidents of aggravated (40.2%) and simple nonsexual assault (24.4%). The reporting of sexual victimization for younger persons was higher than for persons 20–34 (26.7%) and 35–49 years of age (27.7%). Black victims and younger persons reported sexual attacks to the police in comparable proportions to their reports for nonsexual victimizations. These findings suggest that the under-reporting of sex crimes is highly uneven across different categories of victims, and therefore, the arrest data offer a somewhat more accurate picture of underlying victimization and offending patterns for some groups than others.

The under-reporting of criminal victimization to the police is a problem in all studies investigating recidivism. Not one of the eight index offenses listed in the UCR exhibited greater than 75% reporting to police (NCVS, 1995). However, arrest statistics are the only systematic data source available for the study of sex offenders who are not in custody or in treatment programs, they permit detailed comparison with other categories of offenders and crimes, and they afford a measure of recidivism through comparisons of rearrest probabilities across offense types.

The Illinois criminal history database includes the arrests of adults 17 years or older and comprises approximately 953,000 arrestees involved in 2,299,000 arrest events, which culminated in approximately 2,908,000 charges from 1990 to 1997. All charges occurring in conjunction with an arrest are included, which allowed us to characterize arrestees as specific "types" of offenders (i.e., sex offenders, burglars, robbers, etc.).

Our analyses examine sex offenders as a group, regardless of the age of their victims or the degree of sexual contact they had with their victims. We recognize that there has been evidence to suggest that sexual offenders with child victims recidivate at different rates than those with adult victims, and that those viewing or manufacturing child pornography may reoffend at different rates than do those who commit a violent sexual assault (Lieb et al., 1998; Marques et al., 1994; Quinsey et al., 1995, 1998). To date, however, all sex offenders in all 50 states are now required to provide blood samples and register with law enforcement agencies, despite their classification as pedophiles, rapists, or molesters, thus inferring that all sex offenders, regardless of their type, have a higher likelihood of reoffending than do their nonsexual offender counterparts. To assess this assumption, we then must look at sex offenders as a group, regardless of their type of offense or clinical classification.

To conduct these analyses, we first reduced the 10,688 Illinois statutes used to enact arrest charges into 24 general offense categories resembling those found in Part I and II of the UCR. These categories were created broadly and include attempts and all levels of aggravation, in order to examine the between-group differences in rearrests.

Once arrest charges were classified into general categories, we characterized arrestees as particular types of offenders. This could have been accomplished in several ways. Using 1990 as the base year, we considered classifying arrestees as a specific "type" based on their first arrest charge of the year. However, if an arrestee was charged with a burglary in January and a homicide in March, this categorization would label the arrestee as a burglar and under-represent serious violent felonies in the analysis. We also considered classifying arrestees by their most frequent charge in 1990, but again, if an arrestee's larceny charges outnumbered sex offense charges for the year, violent or sexual offenses would be lost. Ultimately, we characterized arrestees as a particular "type" based on their most serious charge for 1990, so that violent and sexual felonies were not under-represented in the analysis.

To determine the most serious charge, we created a hierarchy of offense types that resembles the offense seriousness scale recommended by Sellin and Wolfgang (1964). The hierarchy is based on the seriousness of the overall crime category, not necessarily the seriousness of the individual offense. Offense types were classified in terms of Class I offenses based on bodily injury, property loss, or property damage, with bodily injury being the most serious. Offense categories that did not include the elements needed for a Class I offense were then characterized as Class II offenses in order of seriousness based on the factors of intimidation; threat of property loss; primary, secondary, tertiary, and mutual victimization; and no victimization. For crimes such as stalking that did not exist in 1964, we used our own discretion when applying Sellin's and Wolfgang's (1964) characterization of offenses. Table 1 includes the 24 offense categories ranked form most to least serious, the number of charges in the dataset for each type, and their percent of total arrest charges.

Although most categories are self-explanatory, some need further elaboration. The sex offense category specifically includes all crimes for which Illinois offenders must register as a sex offender: manufacturing, distributing, or possessing child pornography; indecent solicitation of a child; sexual exploitation of a child; soliciting, patronizing, or pimping juvenile prostitutes; criminal sexual assault and abuse of both children and adults; and ritual abuse of a child. The weapons violation category includes only those crimes in which the firearm was not used, such as possession of an illegal firearm or improper sales. Crimes that

TABLE 1   Hierarchy of Offense Categories and Number and Percent of Charges 1990–1997

Offense Category	Number of Charges	Percent of Total	Offense Category	Number of Charges	Percent of Total
Homicide	34,340	1.20%	Weapons Violations	121,212	4.20%
Sex Offense	34,668	1.20%	**Stalking**	5,972	0.20%
Robbery	33,784	1.20%	**Public Order Offenses**	185,043	6.40%
Assault	660,291	22.70%	Drugs/Alcohol Viol.	445,060	15.30%
Kidnapping	7,191	0.20%	Driving Under Influence	1,475	0.10%
Abuse and Neglect	18,994	0.70%	Environmental Offenses	573	0.00%
Arson	3,386	0.10%	Business Offenses	62,333	2.10%
Burglary	124,568	4.30%	Sporting/Hunting Viol.	609	0.00%
Larceny	479,153	16.50%	Custody Violations	45,197	1.60%
Forgery	29,543	1.00%	Traffic/Vehicle Viol.	55,566	1.90%
Fraud	9,548	0.30%	Status Offenses	393	0.00%
Property Damage	339,734	11.70%	Other	209,742	7.20%
			Total	2,908,375	100.00%

include the discharge of a weapon fall within the assault, sexual assault, or homicide categories depending on the nature of the offense or harm committed. Custody violations include crimes that occur while directly under police or correctional custody, such as resisting arrest, contraband, and attempted escape. The status offense category includes statutes prohibiting the sale to or possession of alcohol by minors 18 to 21 years old. Finally, the "other" category includes crimes not elsewhere classified, such as election violations and bribery.

For several reasons, the following analysis is limited to the crime categories of homicide, sex offense, robbery, nonsexual assault, burglary, larceny, kidnapping, property damage, public order offenses, and stalking. First, Illinois Public Act 91-0528 expands the DNA database to include collection upon a conviction for several of these offenses, premised on the notion that offenders such as burglars, robbers, and kidnappers are more likely than others to commit future sex crimes. Stalking is included because it is also assumed to be a predicate offense to violent offending. The inclusion of the property damage, larceny, and public order categories permits comparisons of reoffending between violent and property crime types. Lastly, the homicide category is included because it represents the only offense judged to be more serious than sex crimes in most offense seriousness scales.

Rearrest serves as our measure for reoffending, which is one of the most common measures found in recidivism research (Prentky et al., 1995; Prentky et al., 1997; Rice et al., 1991; Quinsey, 1984; Quinsey et al., 1998). Using 1990 as our base year, we then performed analysis of variance on these data to evaluate differences between groups in future rearrest.

The use of rearrest as a measure for recidivism presents one last hurdle to overcome. The time arrestees spend in custody affects their opportunities to reoffend. To control for arrestees' "time off the street," we obtained Illinois Department of Corrections (IDOC) data from 1990 to 1997 (N = 161,296). These data include all the dates of inmates' entrance into

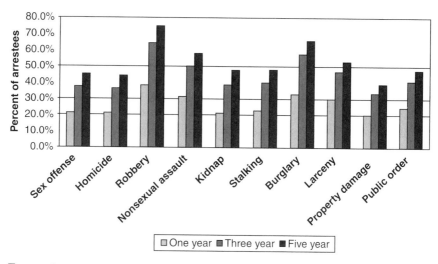

FIGURE 1

Percent of 1990 Arrestees Rearrested for any Offense within One, Three, and Five Years
(N = 146,918)

IDOC facilities and exit for reasons of completed time served, parole, escape, and work release; there was sufficient information in the IDOC file to match records to offenders in the criminal history file. We first calculated the percentage of arrestees incarcerated for each crime category in the analysis. We then removed from the analysis the arrestees who were not remanded to custody and calculated the average amount of time served by inmate groups by subtracting the date of admission from the date of exit. Although these data do not allow us to control for arrestees' time spent in local jails, the IDOC data offer a reasonable basis for estimating arrestees' opportunities to reoffend during the analysis period.

We recognize that rates of incarceration and length of time served vary across both sex offender types and individual offenders; however, our purpose in this study is not to highlight the recidivism rates of specific offenders or sex offender types. Rather, recidivism is examined only in relation to the assumption underlying sex offender laws: that sex offenders, as a group, reoffend at higher rates than do other offender types and are therefore in need of enhanced surveillance and control. These incarceration data are then simply offered to demonstrate that a sufficient number of sex offenders remained "on the street" and were available to offend during the analysis period and that differences in rates of reoffending across groups cannot solely be attributed to differences in imprisonment or time served.

Results

Figure 1 depicts patterns of rearrests among the listed offense categories for any offense. The differences in the percentages of reoffending among all offense categories for one, three, and five years proved to be statistically significant at the 0.05 alpha level, which is a predictable result given the size of the sample.

Similar to the findings at the national level, those arrestees whose most serious offense charge in 1990 was a robbery had the highest probability of rearrest (74.9%) within

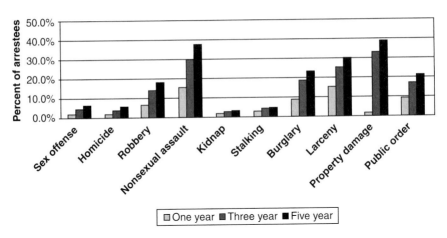

FIGURE 2
Percent of 1990 Arrestees Rearrested for the Same Offense within One, Three, and Five
Years (N = 146,918)

five years followed by arrestees charged with burglary (66%), nonsexual assault (58%), and
larceny (52.9%). Persons in the sex offense category had rearrest percentages of 21.3%,
37.4%, and 45.1% for any offense within one, three, and five years, respectively. These rates
are lower than those found for all other crime categories in the analysis except homicide
(44.2% within five years) and property damage (38.8%).

Sex offenders in Illinois do not appear to commit future offenses, in general, at a
higher rate than do other offenders. However, they may have higher levels of recidivism for
their crimes than other types of offenders exhibit for their particular offenses. Figure 2
shows the percentage of 1990 arrestees rearrested for the same offense within one, three,
and five years. Again, all group differences are statistically significant at 0.05.

Persons whose most serious charge in 1990 was property damage had the highest percentage of rearrests for their crimes in five years (38.8%) followed by those in the nonsexual assault category rearrested for assault (37.2% within five years) and persons in the
larceny category rearrested for larceny (30%). The sex offender category had a lower
offense-specific rearrest rate in five years (6.5%) than did arrestees in most other categories.
Robbers were rearrested for robbery (17.9%), burglars were rearrested for burglary (23.1%),
and those arrested for public-order offenses (21.4%) were rearrested for public-order crimes
in greater proportions than sex offenders were rearrested for sex crimes. Homicide (5.7%),
kidnapping (2.8%), and stalking (5%) were the only categories with lower offense-specific
rearrest rates within five years than sex offending, and those differences are very small.

Only a small percentage of sex offenders in 1990 in Illinois were rearrested for committing another sex crime within five years. However, it is then possible that sex offenders
were not the only group of offenders committing sex crimes, and some crime type may be
identified as the "gateway" offense to sex offending. Figure 3 depicts the percent of 1990
arrestees rearrested for a sex offense, as defined by those crimes for which offenders must
register as a sex offender in Illinois. Again, the differences in the percentages among offense categories for one, three, and five years are statistically significant.

Not surprisingly, arrestees whose most serious charge in 1990 was a sex offense have
the highest percentages of rearrest for a sex crime in one, three, and five years (2.2%, 4.8%,

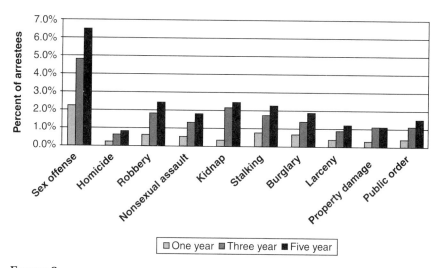

FIGURE 3
Percent of Arrestees Rearrested for a Sex Offense within One, Three, and Five Years (N = 146,918)

and 6.5%, respectively). Within five years, the robbery, kidnapping, and stalking categories all had between 2% and 3% of rearrests for sex crimes. Arrestees in the nonsexual assault, burglary, larceny, and public order categories had between 1% and 2% rearrests for sex crimes, and those in the homicide and property damage classifications had less than 1% rearrests for sex offenses. Note that no crime categories had higher than 6.5% of rearrests for sex crimes, which suggests that the overwhelming majority of offenders in all listed crime categories were not rearrested for a sex crime, including those persons classified as sex offenders.

The percentages of rearrest for listed offenses for sex crimes and for the same charges reported here are relatively low in comparison to other recidivism studies conducted on sex offenders, which consistently find that, on average, between 10% and 55% of sex offenders will be rearrested or reconvicted for new crimes (for reviews, see Furby et al., 1989 and Hanson and Bussiere, 1998). There are several possible explanations for this. First, many sex offender recidivism studies examine samples of sex offenders who have been incarcerated for their crimes. Under these circumstances, these types of sex offenders typically represent the worst-of-the-worst of the sex offending population. Their crimes were of such an egregious nature, or their offending histories were so long, that probation was not a viable option. One would expect higher rates of reoffending among samples of incarcerated sex offenders than we have found here for arrestees. Secondly, due to the potential mobility of the arrestees we examined here, they may have reoffended in another state. Our analysis would then underestimate recidivism because we have not captured these offenses in the Illinois criminal history database. Lastly, the low rates of reoffending found here may be a function of diminished opportunity. Arrestees may have been incarcerated and thus are no longer able to commit a new offense on the street. To investigate this possibility, we look to IDOC data.

Corrections data indicate that except for persons arrested for robbery (58.8%), the majority of all other types of arrestees spent no time in a state correctional facility from 1990 to 1997. Only 30.8% of persons arrested for a sex crime in 1990 were incarcerated in a state prison for some time during the period of the analysis, leaving almost 70% of offenders on the street with the opportunity to reoffend. In addition, approximately 85% of those arrested in 1990 for nonsexual assault, 87% of persons arrested for kidnapping, and 82% of persons arrested for larceny had no state prison sentence. Surprisingly, compared with sex offenders, a greater proportion of people arrested for burglary were incarcerated in state correctional facilities during the period. However, this may reflect the greater likelihood of persons arrested for sex offenses to "plead down" their charges.

Even if most sex offenders were not incarcerated over the seven-year period, those who were may have spent more time in prison than persons sentenced for other crimes. Illinois Department of Corrections data indicate that incarcerated sex offenders did spend more time, on average, in correctional facilities than other types of arrestees (27.7 months). However, this mean time served is less than three years and remains well within the window of the analysis. Those in the homicide and robbery categories, on average, spent two months fewer in custody than sex offenders (25.7 and 25.4, respectively), but recall that these are broad categorizations of offense types that include attempts and all levels of aggravation. With respect to homicide, the inclusion of attempts may be responsible for the appearance of shorter mean time served than found for the sex offense category. On average, persons in the other categories spent between one and two years in prison. The average time spent in custody for all those arrested and incarcerated for these offenses indicates that most had ample time to reoffend during the analysis period. Even so, it is possible that the difference in rearrest rates between sex offenders and others is due to the somewhat longer time spent in prison by the 31% of them who were incarcerated. It is unlikely, however, that all of the differences in rearrest percentages between sexual and nonsexual offenders can be attributed to time served.

SUMMARY AND CONCLUSION

To date, empirical research suggests that sex offenders are not as dangerous as sex offender policies would lead us to believe. Nationally, released sex offenders in 15 states had lower rates of recidivism than most other offender groups (Langan and Levin, 2002). When exploring recidivism patterns more closely in a single state, persons in the sex offense category had lower percentages of rearrests for any offense (45.1%) and for the same offense (6.5%) within five years than most other classifications of offenders. In fact, the overwhelming majority of sex offenders (93%) were not rearrested for another sex crime. This finding is surprising given the way in which DNA collection, registration, and notification provide law enforcement agents with ready-made lists of suspects for sex crimes or any other type of crime in which trace evidence is left on the scene. One would expect greater levels of rearrest among sex offenders than what has been observed here if for no other reason than they are the most highly visible group of offenders for law enforcement officers to question. Nevertheless, based on rates of reoffending, sex offenders do not appear to be more dangerous than other criminal categories and thereby deserving of the additional institutionalization and surveillance they receive after their judicial punishments have been served. In fact, to the extent that sex offender policies have been enacted based on sex offenders' levels of recidivism, research would indicate that robbers may be better candidates for DNA collection, registration, and community notification than sex offenders.

With regard to the existence of a "gateway" crime to sex offending, only small percentages of arrestees in Illinois were rearrested for sex crimes. Other than the sex offense category, no charge type had greater than 3% of arrestees rearrested for a sex offense. These results offer little support for the notion of predicate or "gateway" offenses to sex offending. Although the expansion of DNA collection and sex offender registration requirements to burglars and people possessing burglary tools would identify and monitor the approximately 2% of burglars who go on to commit a sex crime, it would also include the 98% of burglars who do not. To this end, the extension of sex offender policies to nonsexual offenders appears unjustified and would have little effect on preventing future sex crimes.

Although empirical research provides little support for sex offender laws on the basis of high rates of recidivism, as well as cast doubts on the existence of predicate offense types to sex crimes, most of the research cited or conducted here occurred over a short period of time, typically over three to five years. It is likely that higher levels of rearrest would be found over 10 or 20 years. Over a longer study period, a greater level of recidivism among sex offenders would likely emerge. Predicate or "gateway" offenses may be found. Future research should examine the behavior of sex offenders and other groups over longer periods. Moreover, the small percentages reported for rearrests for sex crimes may result from differences in the risk of conviction and incarceration between sex offending and other categories. However, national data and that from the IDOC suggest that differences in time spent off the street are not large enough to fully explain the reported differences in rearrest between persons arrested for sex offending and those arrested in other crime categories. To this end, another possibility needs to be explored. It is possible that the deterrent effect of current sex offender laws is responsible for the small percentages of rearrests that we observed.

Given DNA collection from sex offenders and the enhanced surveillance that registration and community notification creates, it is possible that these laws have suppressed incidents of sex offending. Sex offenders may recognize the greater likelihood of detection and apprehension and feel less free to commit their offenses. Likewise, current sex offender laws may also deter nonsexual offenders from committing an initial sex offense. After witnessing the social ostracism and isolation that sex offenders suffer as a result of registration and notification, burglars, robbers, and thieves may rethink the opportunity to commit an initial act of sexual violence. These possibilities need to be investigated before more classifications of offenders are included in sex offender policies and any further legislation is proposed.

Although current sex offender policies may deter sexual and nonsexual offenders, it is also possible that these effects may be hampered by the extension of these policies to more people and behaviors. Sex offender laws require law enforcement agencies to register sex offenders, track their residences, notify the public of their whereabouts, and apprehend registration violators in addition to the traditional crime-fighting and community service functions they are already expected to perform. Probation and parole officers have also accepted additional duties as a result of current sex offender laws. They are now required to hold public forums to disclose the whereabouts of released sex offenders. Notification laws have forced them to go to extraordinary lengths to find sex offenders housing and employment in a community that is opposed to their presence. They are mandated to perform more home visits to sex offender probationers and parolees, all while managing their nonsexual offender caseloads. The additional duties that sex offender laws require from law enforcement, probation, and parole officers undoubtedly taxes the time and attention of these already overworked criminal justice agents. The expansion of sex offender laws to nonsexual offenders would further increase the duties of these agents and possibly affect their ability to perform any of their duties effectively.

With every classification of offender that policy makers add to DNA collection or sex offender registries, they substantially increase the number of people law enforcement, probation, and parole agencies must monitor. For example, under a 1986 Illinois statute 3,609 sex offenders with child victims were potentially subject to DNA collection and registration, based on the 1990 arrest data. After the 1995 extension of this statute to include all sex offenders with child or adult victims, the number grew to 5,483, an increase of 52%. How effectively can criminal justice agents respond to this increase in workload? How effectively can they monitor a rapidly growing population of offenders? It seems reasonable to assume that the effectiveness and efficiency of sex offender laws may be diminished with their expansion to more people and behaviors. Agencies will be forced to spread their time and scant resources across an ever-increasing number of offenders and behaviors. As criminal justice agents attempt to manage this larger population of offenders, they would likely be less effective at monitoring the behavior and tracking the whereabouts of sex offenders, which is the group that policy makers originally hoped to control.

Criminal justice agents will not be the only group to be affected by the expansion of sex offender laws to nonsexual offenders. Current sex offender policies require a substantial financial commitment from the taxpayer. In 1999, the Illinois State Police received approximately $500,000 from the legislature to maintain the sex offender registry and place this information on the World Wide Web. Although this may sound like a large sum, it does not fully cover the costs of the computer mainframe, software, servers and printers, personnel salaries, training, and research needed to support registration and community notification laws. In addition, the Illinois Department of Corrections requested $115,000 to supplement the costs of the photography and computer equipment, development fees, and personnel salaries needed to take the photographs of sex offenders that are posted on the registration website. The maintenance of the sex-offender DNA databank also requires a sizeable financial commitment. In 1999, $950,000 of public funds were allocated to the ISP Forensic Division to maintain the DNA databank, take blood samples from both sexual and nonsexual offenders, and perform the scientific tests necessary to match evidence left at a crime scene to samples they possess. Despite the sum received to carry out these duties, the Forensic Division continues to run six months behind in matching crime scene evidence to database information. The addition of nonsexual offenders to registration and DNA databanks would undoubtedly increase the amount of funding needed from taxpayers and inevitably further slow the process of identifying DNA matches from crime scenes. A simple glance to the millions of federal funds available to reduce the backlog in DNA processing would suggest the existing infrastructure is nearing its saturation point. Although most would gladly open their wallets at the prospects of increased public safety and declines in sexual victimization, research suggests that the enhancements to public safety by expanding DNA collection and registration to burglars, robbers, or thieves would be minimal at best.

In this paper, we have examined two conceptions underlying sex offender laws, and their extension to nonsexual offenders: first, that sex offenders are more likely to recommit their crimes than are other criminal groups, and second, that some crime types, such as burglary, serve as "gateway" offenses to sexual offending. We did not find evidence in support of either of these assumptions. That is not to say that these policies are not justified on the grounds of other intentions or assumptions such as the particularly egregious nature of sex offending, especially against children, or the need to decrease the public's ever-growing fear of sexual victimization. Instead, this investigation simply serves to illustrate that criminal justice policies can be founded on misconception and that these misconceptions have financial consequences and can affect the likelihood of policies achieving their intended goals. We suggest that before further legislation is proposed and enacted to suppress criminal behavior, it would be wise to identify popular beliefs about the behavior, assess these conceptions against current empirical evidence, and then decide the most prudent course of action based on what we know about the prevalence, frequency, and etiology of the behavior, rather than basing our policies on what we simply believe to be true.

QUESTIONS FOR REVIEW AND DISCUSSION

1. Given what you have read in this particular study, do sex offenders pose more of a threat to society compared with other types of offenders? Why or why not? Discuss.

2. Are sex offenders more or less likely to repeat their crimes as compared with other types of offenders, such as burglars or robbers? Why or why not? Explain.

3. What are the purposes of sex offender laws? Are these purposes being fulfilled? Why or why not?

4. Can sex offending be prevented? Discuss.

50

"Assault Prevention"

City of Tempe, AZ

Adapted from the City of Tempe, AZ, *Assault Prevention*. Tempe, AZ: City of Tempe, 2005.

Sexual assault is a crime of violence, not sexual passion. It is meant to degrade, humiliate and control. The attacker can be a stranger or someone known and trusted. It can happen to anyone, at any time, at any place. The trauma of being assaulted is a shock from which many victims never fully recover.

No matter which form it takes, sexual assault is as much a problem today as it has been throughout history. While those most at risk are people between the ages of 10 and 29, it can happen to anyone at any age.

There is no portrait of a "typical" rapist. These men, like their victims, are all ages and come from all racial and social backgrounds. They can be college students, married men, doctors, teachers, or unemployed transients. Most are not crazy or deranged men looking for sex. In fact the majority of offenders are highly intelligent, married men with families and have ready access to consensual sex; but they rape to control, dominate and humiliate the victim.

The information below provides suggestions on how to avoid dangerous situations, ways to resist if threatened or attacked, and how to cope after an attack. The information is by no means complete. There are numerous community organizations that provide prevention programs and post-incident counseling to citizens and victims.

MYTHS AND FACTS ABOUT SEXUAL ASSAULT

MYTH: Sexual assault is a crime of passion and lust.

Sexual assault is a crime of violence. Assailants seek to dominate, humiliate and punish their victims.

MYTH: You cannot be assaulted against your will.

Assailants overpower their victim with the threat of violence or with actual violence. In cases of acquaintance rape or incest, an assailant often uses the victim's trust in assailant to isolate the victim.

MYTH: A person who has really been assaulted will be hysterical.

Survivors exhibit a spectrum of emotional responses to the assault: calm, hysteria, laughter, guilt, anger, apathy, shock. Each survivor copes with the trauma of the assault in a different way.

MYTH: Sexual assault is an impulsive act.

Seventy-five percent of all assaults are planned in advance. When three or more assailants are involved, 90% are planned. If two assailants are involved, 83%. With one assailant, 58% are planned.

MYTH: Assailants are usually crazed psychopaths who do not know their victims.

As many as 80% of all assaults involve either a known acquaintance, or someone the victim has had contact with, but does not know personally.

MYTH: Gang rape is rare.

In 43% of all reported cases, more than one assailant was involved.

MYTH: Many women claim they have been sexually assaulted because they want revenge upon the man they accuse.

Only 4–6% of sexual assault cases are based on false accusations. This percentage of unsubstantiated cases is the same as with many other reported crimes.

MYTH: Persons who dress or act in a sexy way are asking to be sexually assaulted.

Many convicted sexual assault assailants are unable to remember what their victims looked like or were wearing.

MYTH: All women secretly want to be raped.

While women and men may fantasize about being overpowered during sexual relations it is usually with a person of their choosing, whom they trust. They are in control of the fantasy. No one wants the physical and emotional pain caused by a sexual assault.

MYTH: Only young, pretty women are assaulted.

There is no such thing as a "typical victim." Both men and women are assaulted by both male and female assailants. Victims have ranged in age from newborns to 100 years old.

MYTH: It is impossible to sexually assault a man.

Men fall victim for the same reasons as women: they are overwhelmed by threats or acts of physical and emotional violence. Also, most sexual assaults that involve a male victim are gang assaults, by other males.

MYTH: If you do not struggle or use physical force to resist you have not been sexually assaulted.

If you are forced to have sex without your consent, you have been assaulted whether or not a struggle was involved.

STATISTICS

- Sexual assault continues to represent the most rapidly growing violent crime in America.
- Over 700,000 women are sexually assaulted each year.
- It is estimated that fewer than 50% of rapes are reported.
- Approximately 20% of sexual assaults against women are perpetrated by assailants unknown to the victim. The remainder are committed by friends, acquaintances, intimates, and family members. Acquaintance rape is particularly common among adolescent victims.
- Male victims represent five percent of reported sexual assaults.
- Among female rape victims 61% are under 18.
- At least 20% of adult women, 15% of college women and 12% of adolescent women have experienced some form of sexual abuse or assault during their lifetimes.
- Over 50% of the attacks occur in the home, and most of these are planned.
- In 85% of the cases, some type of direct force is used, whether it is choking, beating or plain physical force. A weapon is used one-third of the time.
- Rapists rarely attack once. They have one of the highest repeat rates of all criminals. More than 70% of those arrested for the crime are re-arrested within seven years.

PROFILES OF RAPISTS

The FBI has established four personality characteristics profiles for rapists. While most rapists will fit into one of the profiles, due to the fact that there are a variety of personalities, there is no one correct characteristic for a profile. Suspects may exhibit characteristics from one or more of the profiles.

Reassurance Rapist—81%

Motivation.   To resolve self-doubts by reassuring himself of his masculinity with no real intent to further harm his victim.

Style

- Surprise approach with force.
- Strikes between midnight and 5 am, usually at the victim's residence.
- Selects victims through voyeurism.
- Attacks victims who are alone or with small children.
- Negotiates with the victim.
- Does whatever the victim allows him to do.
- Attacks in his own residence or work area.

- Commits single assault.
- May keep a diary.

Social Interaction

- Few friends
- Self-concept as a loser
- Menial job with little public contact

Power Assertive Rapist—12%

Motivation.   To resolve self-doubts by reassuring himself of his masculinity with no real intent to further harm his victim.

Style

- Exploits opportunity after one or two dates
- Slaps, hits, curses, tears rather than removes clothes
- Waits 20–25 days between assaults
- Performs multiple assaults
- Disrobes victim
- Doesn't use mask or disguise

Social Interaction

- Flashy car
- Frequents singles bars
- "Hard hat" act
- "Macho" type

Anger Retaliatory Rapist—5%

Motivation.   To punish or degrade women by getting even; uses sex as a weapon for real or perceived injustices placed on him by women.

Style

- Acts spontaneously
- Commits assaults in his own area

Social Interaction

- Loner
- Minimal contact with others
- Works at "action jobs"

Anger Excitation Rapist—2%

Motivation.   Infliction of pain or erotic aggression

Style

- Uses premeditated con-style approach
- Immobilizes victim
- Assaults away from his area
- Uses weapon and/or tools of choice
- Usually records his assaults
- Learns quickly by experience
- Does not experience remorse

Social Interaction

- Family man
- "Good marriage"
- Compulsive
- Middle class

HOW TO REDUCE YOUR RISK OF BECOMING A SEXUAL ASSAULT VICTIM

While statistics say that most sexual assaults are premeditated, in some instances it is a "crime of opportunity," such as a date rape. The victim and suspect, for whatever reason, are at the same place at the same time. Whether the assault is one of opportunity or premeditation, there are simple precautions a person can follow to reduce, avoid, and even eliminate their chances of becoming a victim.

There are three locations where a person should be especially alert.

- While Driving
- At Home
- While Walking

While Driving

- Keep your car in good working order and the gas tank at least half full.
- Park in well-lighted areas and lock the doors, even if you'll only be gone a short time.
- Before returning to your car look around the parking lot for suspicious persons.
- When you return to your car have your key ready and check the front and rear seats and floor before getting in.
- Drive with all the doors locked.

- Never pick up hitchhikers.
- If you have a flat tire, drive on it until you reach a safe well-lighted, and well-traveled area.
- If your car breaks down, put the hood up, lock the doors, and put on the flashers. Use flares if you have them and tie a white cloth to the antenna. If someone stops to help, don't get out of the car, but roll down the window slightly and ask the person to call the police or a tow service for you.
- If you see another motorist in trouble, don't stop. Help by going to a telephone and calling the police for assistance.
- Exercise extra caution when using underground and enclosed parking garages. Try not to go alone.
- If you are being followed, don't drive home. Go to the nearest police or fire station and honk your horn. Or drive to an open gas station or other business where you can safely call the police. Don't leave your car unless you are certain you can get inside the building safely. Try to obtain the license plate number and description of the car following you.

At Home

- Make sure all windows and doors in your home can be locked securely, particularly sliding glass doors. Use the locks. Keep entrances well-lighted.
- Install a peephole in the door and use it.
- Check the identification of any sales or service person before letting him in.
- Don't let any stranger into your home when you're alone—no matter what the reason or how dire the emergency is supposed to be. Offer to make an emergency phone call while they wait outside.
- Never give the impression that you are at home alone if strangers telephone or come to the door.
- Get to know your neighbors—someone you can turn to if you're worried.
- If you live in an apartment, avoid being in the laundry room or garage by yourself, especially at night.
- If you come home alone and find a door or window open or signs of forced entry, don't go in. Go to the nearest phone and call the police.

While Walking

- Be alert to your surroundings and the people around you. Keep your head up and look alert.
- Stay in well-lighted areas.
- Walk confidently at a steady pace on the side of the street facing traffic.
- Walk close to the curb. Avoid doorways, bushes, and alleys.
- Wear clothes and shoes that give you freedom of movement. If you wear high heels at work, carry them with you and wear athletic shoes to work. You can change when you get there.

- Don't walk alone at night if possible. If you have to, be alert.
- Be careful when people stop you for directions. Always reply from a distance, and never get too close to the car. If you are in trouble, attract help any way you can. Yell something other people will understand, "Help," "Police," "Fire"!

IF YOU ARE ATTACKED

- Keep your head. Stay as calm as possible, think rationally and evaluate your resources and options.
- It may be more advisable to submit (this does not mean you consent) than resist and risk severe injury or death. Everyone has different strengths and abilities. You will have to make this decision based on the circumstances. But, don't resist if the attacker has a weapon.
- Keep assessing the situation as it is happening. If one strategy doesn't work, try another.
- Possible options in addition to nonresistance are negotiating, stalling for time, distracting the assailant and fleeing to a safe place, verbal assertiveness, screaming to attract attention and physical resistance.
- If you think fighting back/struggling may discourage the attack, remember **you have to hurt the rapist bad enough to create the time you need to escape.** Consider scratching with your fingernails, biting, poking in the eyes, kicking in the knee or groin, hitting on the nose, or jabbing the eyes or throat.
- Weapons such as guns, knives, and chemical sprays can easily be turned against you unless you are trained, and are not afraid, to use them. You must be prepared to possibly kill the attacker.
- If you are determined to carry some type of weapon, a chemical spray (such as pepper spray) is your best choice. It's non-lethal if used against you. Remember, you already have weapons with you, your keys, pens, pencils, etc. You also have your most important weapon, your brain.
- You may be able to turn the attacker off with bizarre behavior such as throwing up, urinating, or defecating.
- <u>**REMEMBER, THAT WHATEVER YOU DO, THE MOST IMPORTANT THING IS YOUR SURVIVAL.**</u>

Surviving a Sexual Assault

Fear, guilt and embarrassment may make it difficult to report the crime and tell those closest to you. After a severe emotional trauma, one needs the understanding and support of family and friends to help get through this difficult time. It is important to realize, however, that loved ones do not always know what to say or do to help. Well meaning advice or criticism about what happened is obviously painful. Keep in mind that their reactions can be the result of their own reluctance to accept the reality of everyone's vulnerability to crime. They can only do their best. It sometimes helps if you can let them know what you need.

A traumatic event like this leaves emotions raw and leaves people feeling vulnerable. It is normal to experience dramatic mood swings, to cry easily, to be irritable, or become upset over small things. You may have a startled response if you see someone who looks similar to your assailant or when you see something that reminds you of the crime. It is helpful to get counseling in order to deal with these feelings and to learn about the normal steps victims tend to go through after an assault.

Victims tend to go through several stages when coping with a sexual assault. General denial comes first, followed by a realization phase and then anger.

The Denial Stage

Initially, there may be denial with the victim shutting others out and avoiding the subject. This is often an attempt to believe that the assault did not happen. Disbelief can be protection from the overwhelming feelings associated with the trauma.

The Realization Stage

Denial is often followed by a realization phase where feelings begin to come out. Victims often lack trust in others. Fear of future assaults may cause you to isolate yourself. The most destructive feeling at this stage is a tendency to blame yourself for the assault. ***Don't blame yourself.***

The Anger Stage

Victims usually move next to a stage of anger. This is healthy when your feelings are directed toward your assailant. Sometimes your anger may be misdirected towards those around you. Let them know that you are not angry with them, but rather with what happened to you. The anger can cleanse because it indicates you are beginning to integrate the event into your life and move on without guilt.

Looking Ahead

Finally, you can begin to look ahead. You accept that it was terrible, but you realize it is over.

Suggestions

- Report the crime and cooperate with the police. Taking positive action against the assailant will help resolve your trauma. You will also be helping your community.

- It is your personal decision who else should be told about what happened. You have a right to privacy and only those you wish to tell need know about the incident.

- Express your feelings and needs to those who care. Be clear about what you want them to do or not do.

- It is very normal for feelings of fear to linger and these are often difficult to overcome. Do whatever you need to do to be safe. Talk to a counselor about ways to feel safe.

- Return to your normal routine as soon as possible. Everyday routine will help you regain a feeling of control in your life.

Reaction of Others

Your family and friends will also have mixed feelings and confusion over the crime. They may be uncomfortable around you because they may be afraid of making things worse. Common feelings are anger at the assailant, and frustration at not being able to direct that anger at the assailant. Marital relationships can become strained. The victim often feels uncomfortable resuming sexual relations following an assault. Most spouses or partners of the victim can accept these feelings intellectually, but still feel rejected or blamed in some way. Encourage your spouse or partner and other family members to seek help if they are having a hard time adjusting.

The Police Investigation

If an arrest was not made immediately, a detective will be assigned to investigate the case. You will probably be questioned several times in an effort to get as much information as possible about your assailant and the crime. Report any new information on the case to the detective assigned. You may be asked to help with an artist's drawing, take a polygraph or view a lineup. These are investigative tools. Without positive identification of the suspect, prosecution is not possible.

Going to Court

If the suspect is arrested, the suspect may be released from jail on bond or on their own promise to return for court. The judge will order him not to see you or talk to you. You should report any contact by the suspect or by anyone claiming to be the suspect's attorney to the police and county attorney immediately. Your interests will be represented by the County Attorney's Office shortly after an arrest is made and charges are filed.

You may be subpoenaed to testify at a preliminary hearing about what happened. During this hearing the judge listens to the facts to decide if there is "Probable Cause" for the case to go forward to Superior Court. This hearing is not to determine guilt or innocence, and there is no jury. The court process can take many months. This is normal so try not to be frustrated by the delays. Your Victim Assistance caseworker is available to give you the information and emotional support necessary to achieve a successful prosecution. Your input and participation will be important at various times to insure a just outcome.

VICTIMS' BILL OF RIGHTS

Crime victims have specific rights under Arizona Laws and the Rules of Criminal Procedure, which insure that the victim will be treated fairly.

- To be treated with fairness, respect, and dignity, and to be free from intimidation, harassment, or abuse, throughout the criminal process.
- To be informed, upon request, when the accused or convicted person is released from custody or has escaped.
- To be present at, and upon request, to be informed of all criminal proceedings where the defendant has the right to be present.

- To be heard at any proceeding involving a post-arrest release decision, a negotiated plea, and sentencing.
- To refuse an interview, deposition, or other discovery request by the defendant, the defendant's attorney, or other persons acting on behalf of the defendant.
- To confer with the prosecution, after the crime against the victim has been charged, before trial or before any disposition of the case and to be informed of the disposition.
- To read pre-sentence reports relating to the crime against the victim when they are available to the defendant.
- To receive prompt restitution from the person or persons convicted of the criminal conduct that caused the victim's loss or injury.
- To be heard at any proceeding when any post-conviction release from confinement is being considered.
- To a speedy trial or disposition, and prompt and final conclusion of the case after the conviction and sentence.
- To have all rules governing criminal procedure and the admissibility of evidence in all criminal proceedings protect victims' rights and to have these rules be subject to amendment or repeal by the legislature to ensure the protection of these rights.
- To be informed of victims' constitutional rights.

A victim's exercise of any right granted by this section shall not be grounds for dismissing a criminal proceeding or setting aside any conviction or sentence.

QUESTIONS FOR REVIEW AND DISCUSSION

1. What are four general myths about sexual assault?
2. What sorts of profiles of rapists has the FBI constructed? Describe them.
3. How can persons reduce their likelihood of becoming victims of sexual assault?
4. What is the Victims' Bill of Rights? What rights do victims have in sexual assault cases? Discuss.

51

Model Peer-Led Sexual Assault Prevention Programs
Lessons for Engaging and Empowering Youth

Michelle Harris
and Mark Bergeron-Naper, 1999.

Adapted from Michelle Harris and Mark Bergeron-Naper, *Model Peer-Led Sexual Assault Prevention Programs: Lessons for Engaging and Empowering Youth.* Boston: Massachusetts Department of Public Health.

Reprinted by permission of the Massachusetts Department of Public Health.

I. INTRODUCTION

In 1995, the Massachusetts Department of Public Health (MDPH) was notified that it would receive new Violence Against Women Act (VAWA) funding for sexual assault prevention initiatives through the Public Health and Health Services Block Grant from the Centers for Disease Control. To create a plan for these new funds, five public meetings were convened by the MDPH. The goal was to determine the need for community-based sexual assault prevention activities in the Commonwealth. Several priorities were identified based on the subsequent meetings. One of the priorities identified was to establish local sexual assault prevention and education demonstration projects, focusing on program development with both adolescent males 12–19 years of age and with cultural-linguistic minorities.

Five Sexual Assault Prevention Demonstration Projects were funded in 1997 to (1) provide community organization, primary prevention education and skill-building to target populations; and (2) change individual and community norms, attitudes, and behaviors about the serious legal, social, and public health problems of sexual assault. All programs used some form of a 'peers teaching peers' model and took into account the cultural beliefs and values of the community. Youth mentoring, leadership development and peer education were employed in each program.

The Massachusetts Department of Public Health began an evaluation project in 1998 to assess the process and effectiveness of the five demonstration projects. A focus group format was chosen as the method that would most fully elicit participants' perceptions of the impact and meaning of their program experiences. Focus groups were held at each site. Adolescent peer leaders identified four critical characteristics of adolescent sexual assault prevention programs that had a positive impact on them and their community. The four characteristics are:

- Promotion of a sense of belonging and connection to one's peers and community
- Incorporation of sexual assault prevention into every layer of the curriculum
- Provision of opportunities for participatory education and development of useful skills
- Modeling of the values of commitment and leadership

The focus group participants affirmed that their programs achieved these benchmark characteristics. Programs with the aforementioned characteristics successfully supported youth in understanding sexual assault prevention work as relevant and important to their lives and to their community. Programs were able to elicit and nurture participants' motivation and engagement around a potentially threatening set of issues, making it possible for these teens to incorporate program concepts into their lives.

II. DESCRIPTIONS OF THE DEMONSTRATION PROJECTS

Energia Positiva

Energia Positiva, part of the Holyoke Youth Alliance, educated 14 to 18 year old youth about sexual assault prevention and healthy relationships. This project, designed to offer Holyoke youth the opportunity to develop an understanding of their potential, worked with 15–20 youth. After receiving extensive training on sexual assault issues, the participants worked together to develop a theater presentation which they then performed throughout the community. Although the group primarily wrote and performed plays about sexual assault issues, they also worked on related projects including brochures, videos, and public service announcements geared to raise awareness of sexual assault and partner violence prevention. Serving primarily the Latino community of Holyoke, this project was intended to provide youth with the opportunity to learn about sexual assault prevention. This was accomplished through sharing and validating each others feelings and offering specific prevention information connected with group discussions of gender violence issues.

Mentor/Advocates for Respect and Safety Project

The Mentor/Advocates for Respect and Safety (MARS) project, a collaborative project between the Everywoman's Center and the Men's Resource Center of Western Massachusetts, focused on sexual assault prevention and youth empowerment. Mentor/Advocates were high school and college youth who underwent intensive training on sexual assault issues. Two after-school programs for middle school students, as well as various community outreach projects were established. The after-school programs were called *Life After School* and included single gender and co-ed discussion groups, interactive and creative activities, recreation and one-on-one mentoring. Community outreach activities included radio public service announcements, a youth mural project and pilot youth radio program, all focused on sexual assault prevention.

Latino Intergenerational Sexual Assault Prevention Project

The Latino Intergenerational Sexual Assault Prevention Project, or LISAPP, was intended to raise awareness about the problems and consequences of sexual assault in the Latino community of Chelsea. Sponsored by Centro Latino de Chelsea, this project was designed to educate and change the attitudes and behavior of both adults and youth in the community. The "training of trainers (TOT)" model was used in which participants acquired knowledge and skills which they integrated with their own life and cultural experiences. Participants then developed and made sexual assault prevention presentations to the broader community. Approximately 30 adults and youth participated in the project.

Teen Rape and Assault Prevention Project

TRAPP, the Teen Rape and Assault Prevention Project, began as a collaboration between Rape Crisis Services of Greater Lowell and Big Brother/Big Sister of Greater Lowell and, originally, was designed as a peer leadership program for males ages 15–18. It developed into a co-ed program of the Rape Crisis Services of Greater Lowell. TRAPP's primary goal was to initiate a community coalition of youth service providers and youth in a joint effort to change attitudes towards rape and sexual assault among teens. The project primarily served Cambodian and Latino youth in the schools and community through five high-school aged peer leaders who were trained on sexual assault issues. The youth learned public speaking, computer and media skills. Activities included skit creation and community presentations as well as sexual assault prevention web-site design.

Haitian Sexual Assault Prevention Project

The Haitian Sexual Assault Prevention Project, a program of the Haitian American Public Health Initiatives, worked with Haitian teens, ages 12 to 19, in the schools and the larger community. Originally working with only males, the program ultimately included both males and females. The project had two major goals. Participants promoted greater knowledge and understanding of the consequences of sexual assault in the local Haitian community. They also cultivated positive and non-violent individual and community norms to prevent sexual assault. Because locally-produced Haitian-language radio and cable shows are considered popular in this community, the participants created several public service announcements and an on-air radio and cable TV show that educated the community about rape and sexual assault. The project worked with high school-aged peer leaders who did both school and community-based presentations and assisted with a media campaign.

III. METHODOLOGY

In order to obtain support for this evaluation process, the facilitators first spoke with program staff about holding focus groups for program participants. Facilitators developed a series of questions that would address the youth's experiences during their involvement in sexual assault prevention activities. Program staff recruited youth who had participated to share their impressions and experiences in the program. Program staff explained to participants that the program could benefit from hearing the youth leaders' ideas but that their participation was voluntary and the conversations would be confidential. A focus group was held at each of the five program sites. A total of 38 youth, twenty-four females and fourteen males, participated.

The stated goals of the focus groups were: (1) to learn about participants' experiences and insights in youth programs; (2) to learn what motivated them to stay involved; and (3) to learn what they would want to change about the program. There were also three ground rules, which were confidentiality, respect, and one person talking at a time. Permission was requested to tape-record the conversations and participants were told that facilitators would be the only ones to hear the tapes, that their names would not be used, and finally that the tapes would be erased. Facilitators were able to ask and clarify questions and take notes as necessary. Each focus group lasted one hour, and one of the five groups used a Spanish translator. Following each focus group, facilitators debriefed and reviewed notes. They later listened to the tapes, coded and analyzed them for emergent themes.

IV. FOCUS GROUP FINDINGS

The four major themes that were emphasized in the focus groups are described below.

The Sense of Belonging and Connection to One's Peers & Community

"When we're here, we feel at home. We make decisions as a group and, over time, influence the message we're sending."

Most of the youth listed a variety of reasons for initially becoming involved in their local sexual assault prevention youth programs. The reasons included:

- wanting something to do after school
- wanting to stay off the streets
- making new friends
- interest in theater or media
- desire to improve quality of college applications
- giving back to the community

The youth, especially those involved for longer periods of time, spoke about the sense of belonging and the connection that they felt with one another and to their communities. When asked what they liked about the programs, youth spoke of working with each other, relationships with the adult facilitators and having a place to go where they felt understood and comfortable.

For some, to have a place to go was more of a physical need. They needed a place to go where they wouldn't be alone or feel unsafe. For others, it was much more of a psychological need. Some youth were relatively new to this country or were in search of a peer group. A few of the youth from Energia Positiva, for instance, were able to articulate that the program felt like "family," a place where they felt accepted and valued, where they could come, put down their bags, and not have to explain themselves. A few youth in each of the programs voiced that they had never experienced this feeling in other settings in their communities, especially at school. One youth said she liked the program because it felt safe to her and she didn't have to deal with discrimination. Several males said that if it were not for the program, they would probably be hanging out on the street, wasting time, and/or selling drugs.

When asked what gave them this sense of connection to one another and their community, the youth were unanimous that it was having a common purpose and developing genuine relationships that made the difference. To the youth, the sexual assault prevention message was a positive, meaningful one which they valued and shared as a group. Each group explained that they got some fulfillment and a sense of satisfaction from knowing that they were addressing real, but often hidden, community problems. Some youth had grown up with or known someone who had experienced sexual assault or partner violence, they understood how prevalent this problem is and the stigma that surrounds it. Being part of these programs meant standing up for themselves and their loved ones. It meant supporting and/or confronting their peers in school and thinking about the ways our society tolerates and supports sexual assault and partner violence.

Many of the youth talked about deciding to get involved as a way to give back to their community. For instance, a youth from TRAPP said, "I wanted to get more involved in the community because I like to help people." A youth from LISAPP described her motivation to share information and explain things that improve other people's lives. In this way, the youth saw themselves as useful members of the community and actively making it a better place to live.

The youth described the programs as increasing their confidence in themselves by being part of a team. A striking number of female adolescents described themselves as being shy and self-conscious at the beginning, and confident and comfortable now. One male youth also spoke to this point: "When we're here, we feel at home, we make decisions as a group and over time, influence the message we're sending." While in school they sometimes feel labeled or invisible, but in the sexual assault prevention programs they feel valued and responsible.

The Importance of Prevention

> "No one does much to change the roots of the problem. [The Kids] can talk about the things they're going through so they don't need to lash out about it. They can talk about it."

Prevention was a major theme that flowed through all five programs, but was especially emphasized by participants in the MARS Program. In each program, the youth articulated the goal of reducing and preventing sexual assault and partner violence. Each program interpreted this somewhat differently but all programs saw prevention as occurring through peer and, sometimes, adult education. The youth from Energia Positiva spoke about their use of theater as a means to convey the message of violence prevention. They described how watching as well as acting in the play evokes feelings aimed at influencing one's thinking and the choices one makes. Two of the older members said that this occurs because "you get into the role and take on the feelings of the character." Several youth said that by making the characters real and humorous, you can think about the issues more easily.

The youth from TRAPP shared this attitude about the use of drama. They described how they planned the use of skits about dating violence and sexual harassment as a way to spread their message. Youth from HAPHI and LISAPP seemed to rely more on public speaking to carry their message.

Unlike the other programs' efforts to reach a broad community through public speaking and theater, MARS focused primarily on educating groups of younger adolescents. With their more specific target audience in mind, peer leaders articulated that the MARS program brought alive the idea of prevention. They spoke of it frequently and listed it as their primary reason for becoming and staying involved.

When asked what they learned during the program, youth from MARS consistently spoke about the program being a "safe haven" for their younger peers, and the challenges of trying to influence younger adolescents' thinking about healthy norms in intimate relationships. The youth from MARS described this process as exciting and challenging. Many of the peer mentors described feeling frustrated by the negative influences of peer pressure on younger adolescents. One youth said, "we want to be on their level and support them, but sometimes we just want to tell them to do what worked for us." These youth spoke less about how the issues of sexual assault and partner violence impacted their own lives and relationships.

In contrast, the youth in the other four programs agreed that much of what they learned applied directly to their own lives. When asked what they had learned, several youth replied, "to think before I act," especially in situations where they are confronted by peer pressure or partner coercion. The females agreed that this was especially true in making decisions about who they should date and how to negotiate sexual decisions. For the males, 'thinking before acting' meant being more respectful of female friends, family members, and partners in their lives. One youth offered, for instance, that he had learned to show more respect and be more appreciative of his mother. A few other youth said that learning about the issues of sexual assault and partner violence made them more aware of and more able to recognize that their own teasing and name calling could be offensive or hurtful of others' feelings.

Another common response when asked what they learned was how to give and get respect and set standards in relationships. These concepts were voiced strongly by several female members of each group. The young women spoke about being "deserving of respect" and "not putting up with nobody who tries to abuse" them. When asked what they meant by abuse, they clearly articulated a continuum of abusive behaviors, including verbal manipulation, isolation, and degrading comments. They also described how the program taught them to identify and confront abusive behaviors and to ask for help from their peers or adults. While only some girls spoke with confidence about what they had learned, other girls nodded and listened intently.

Desire for Participatory Education and Useful Skills

"This is the most interesting and active thing I do all week."

The youth entered the programs with a range of knowledge and skill levels but over time they were generally able to enhance their skills and grow in their self-awareness. When asked what they learned about sexual assault and partner violence, they listed many topics and activities, including boundary-setting in relationships, effective communication, differentiating respect and power, sexual harassment, peer pressure, and gender roles. As a group, they identified trust-building games, role plays, and public speaking or theater experiences as being the most interesting and educational for them. According to the youth, this was because they were learning from their peers, through group interactions and through activities that made the issues real for them. Many of the youth described these activities as fun, a little scary, and hard at times.

When asked what they would think of learning about the issues without the activities, they said they would have been interested but not nearly as much. Some youth stated that the learning would not be as abundant and it would become much more intellectual and much less personal. For youth from MARS, several agreed with one youth's opinion that "this is the most interesting and active thing I do all week." Youth from each program indicated that learning had to involve real interactions among one another and had to involve input and thoughts about how the issues of sexual assault and partner violence apply to their own lives.

The participants' assessment of the value of individual activities varied. Many youth stated that the "trust games" were helpful at the beginning when they needed to feel safe and comfortable before being expected to work closely with their peers. One youth from Energia Positiva said, "the acting is hard, but it's fun cause the staff help us and because we get to make up a lot of the words until it [the play] makes sense to us." Youth from LISAPP and HAPHI were equally excited about their experience of learning through role plays. They spoke about how much fun it is to put yourself in a role and pretend to be someone different. They also described how useful it is to get feedback about how they look, act, and communicate their emotions on stage. One youth said, "I like the presentations when we did the dramas because it was fun and yet it felt so real." Youth from TRAPP also voiced their excitement at learning to present publicly. For instance, "we did an activity called 'The Spot Lights On You' where we had to go up and tell a story in front of the group, and then the group told us how we did and how we could improve."

Whether it was acting or public speaking, or in the case of the MARS program, mentoring their younger peers, the youth agreed that they were learning new skills. Many of the youth were glad to learn these skills because they could influence the lives of other young people and because they saw these skills as useful in other contexts, such as future careers. A few of the youth spoke about their desire to be actors, businesswomen, and to continue with community work. Some of the college age youth found that working with adolescents in the junior high schools in this program motivated them to plan on pursuing future careers as social workers and public health professionals.

The Value of Commitment and Leadership

"I like being recognized as the girl that helps us and passes on a good message."

When asked whether they would recommend this program to other young people their age, the youth gave an overwhelming "YES!" While not all of the youth completed the program, and some were more active than others, there was an overwhelming energy and sense of commitment that carried the groups forward. Most were quite pleased with the skills that they had learned and the work they had accomplished. Being in a play and/or speaking at a conference was something they enjoyed and helped motivate them to continue.

When asked why they stayed involved, several youth responded that they felt responsible to their communities, to their peers and to themselves. If they were late for play practice or unprepared for a community presentation, they felt they would hold back the team and let their peers down. But this sense of discipline and duty went beyond their peers. One youth said, "it's important that I finish what I started" and another youth chimed in saying, "yeah, I wanted to prove to my family and my community that I could complete something positive."

What was most striking about the youth's experience of working together and educating the community was how often they articulated pride in themselves as young community leaders. While some youth entered the programs with past leadership experience, for most youth, the program was their first opportunity to learn and apply new skills in a leadership role. As the participants spoke about this, they were clear to articulate how the experience of presenting and sharing information felt to them:

"It was like I was standing up there, all dressed up, watching them and they were probably thinking. 'Wow! Look at that guy, he knows something I don't know.' "

"You meet new people, learn stuff, show other people, teach them, they learn something, and you feel good that you made a change."

A common theme among the youth was their pride in being seen as knowledgeable and helpful. Some of the youth were surprised and flattered by the appreciation and recognition of others. As their confidence increased and their identities as leaders developed, they became even more active and committed to the work. The youth spoke about becoming more comfortable acting as advocates and confronting their peers in school around sexual assault issues. They talked about looking at their friends' relationships differently and being available if their friends are in danger. A youth from TRAPP talked about how he wore his TRAPP jacket to school which became a conversation starter with his peers and gave him the chance to talk about what he learned about sexual assault and rape prevention. A youth from Energia Positiva said that because of her experience acting in front of her peers, she now no longer feels embarrassed nor holds back in saying what she needs to say to people around her. Finally, a youth from HAPHI spoke about how important it is to stand up to other people's ignorance about sexual assault issues and to educate them. Even though she had been teased at school for being involved and talking about the issue, she felt like it was one of the most important things she had chosen to do. For the youth, overall, the sense of commitment to the issues, to their communities, and to one another is what really has strengthened the programs.

V. OBSERVATIONS & RECOMMENDATIONS

The final section of this report provides the youth's recommendations for improving the projects and for future development of these or similar projects.

Recommendations

Recommendations from the youth were varied. The youth from LISAPP and MARS wanted to spend more time doing trust-building games at the beginning and role-plays throughout the program. This suggestion came after explaining that these activities were their favorites but that they felt pressed for time or needed more direction from staff. For the youth from MARS, this suggestion was specific to practicing role-plays about how they interact with their younger peers and techniques they could try that might be more effective. Youth from Energia Positiva requested learning additional theater techniques and skills, including scenery, prop, and costume design and development. They also wanted to incorporate more dance and music into their shows. Youth from LISAPP suggested doing more speaking engagements in the community and tying these events to organized field trips. For instance, a youth suggested going to visit colleges and speaking with students there about college life while sharing violence prevention messages. Part of what came through with these comments was that they wanted more of what they already found positive. They also wanted increased opportunities to learn useful skills with the guidance of their peers and adults and to apply these skills in meaningful ways.

In discussing changes they would make if they were "in charge," youth said they would change and add to the physical space. Several youth talked about how they wished the program had its own space and could function more as a drop-in youth center. Youth from HAPHI, for instance, wanted a teen-focused space where they could easily stay off the streets and involve themselves in activities. For youth from Energia Positiva, having their own space would mean they would have more room to practice and they could expand their hours if staff were available. Finally, youth from MARS reported being happy using the school as their space but reported being unhappy with the restrictions placed on that space. Generally, the youth seemed to want to create a more teen-focused space.

Finally, the youth said they would recommend expanding their programs in overall size and resources. For them this would mean hiring more staff, attracting a greater number of youth and gaining increased community support. The youth asked for increased direction and assistance from staff members. They seemed to want more individual attention and increased mentoring from staff. While they were generally happy with these relationships, they wanted to be sure future staff would be both people they could relate to and people with a deep understanding of the issues of sexual assault and partner violence. A few youth from LISAPP talked about being touched by a staff member who had spoken with them about his own family member who was diagnosed with AIDS. The youth were struck by this staff person's honesty in explaining how his personal situation challenged his own homophobic assumptions about people living with AIDS.

Besides additional staff, the youth wanted to attract more young people their age who have genuine interest in the issues and want to actively participate. For them, this meant giving other young people a chance to do something positive for their community and having newer members in their peer group. For some of the programs, it would also mean offering more young people a stipend for participating. Youth from HAPHI and LISAPP, however, were concerned that some youth might come only to the program parties or just for the money and would not be reliable when the group needed them to help with the program. One teen suggested having clearer recruitment protocols and expectations, so that youth are accepted based on a variety of criteria and not just their interest in money. Another teen recommended rules about who can come to the parties or participate in the field trips based on their involvement. As discussed earlier, teamwork and commitment were crucial to these teens.

Some youth, from HAPHI and MARS in particular, pointed out the increased need for community support. For example, youth from MARS understood the importance of working with the schools but said they were not given access to schools to the extent they thought most efficacious. The youth discussed how the lack of community support limits their creativity and involvement. They were not sure, however, why the community was not more involved, or what they could do about it. Older members from HAPHI said they used to receive more support from the community and that the program was more fun in the past. To newer members, however, the program was still fun and the sexual assault prevention message was just as important.

Observations

The detail and breadth of the youth's recommendations were impressive and provide important guidance for future program planning. While the demonstration projects were primarily designed to educate youth on gender violence prevention, it may be inevitable that these programs will do much more than that.

As the youth stated, relationships were key for them. A high level of team/relationship building and mentoring skills was necessary for program staff. Expanded staff training and supervision could support advanced skill-building in staff self-awareness, communication techniques and content knowledge. Staff with adolescent social work, education, and youth development skills and experience could be effective in supporting the youth and their families as needed.

Findings indicate that youth gender violence prevention programs should be supported in building linkages within their communities. Working in coalitions can strengthen the sexual assault prevention message and improve the visibility of this issue. Particularly effective groups:

- meet on a regular basis
- are highly connected with the community
- are clear about their goals
- and include a diverse group of members (including youth who have participated in these types of programs)

Helping to plan, market, and publicize public events (e.g., health fairs, photography exhibits, the Clothesline Project, a "Take Back The Night" march, the "Yellow Dress" play) can galvanize support from the community while simultaneously educating its members. Finally, opportunities to promote training and share resources among these programs can enhance knowledge of and services to all youth. Such steps can also facilitate organizational linkages, service coordination and cross-referral.

As programs may grow in size, some might expand to include several overlapping areas or projects. This may mean having one group of youth involved in theater, another in dance, and another in media, or having phases of the program in which youth can decide how much they want to participate. To some extent, this existed at Energia Positiva, where youth worked for short lengths of time, and at LISAPP, where youth completed an initial training, then spoke in the community. While several of the youth requested increased opportunities for involvement and leadership, others wanted to know they could have time off when life got too busy or leave on good terms after completing one part of the program. This was especially a concern voiced by youth at LISAPP, where the training ended, but program activities continued. For this reason, use of multiple program components and program time periods or cycles seem to be effective strategies for involving more youth at a range of levels.

Finally, it is important for these types of programs to increase their knowledge and practice of incorporating useful evaluation tools into program activities. An assessment of peer leader attitudes and behaviors could be done at the beginning of the program, as early as the intake process or orientation sessions. Over time, these attitudes and behaviors could be assessed and change evaluated. In addition to filling out standard MDPH activity report forms to measure service outputs (e.g., number of presentations), some programs worked to create their own evaluations to measure service quality. However, further development, especially of impact measures, could yield even richer information. A combination of outcome and process measures could be used in order for program coordinators to know what they are doing, how they are doing it and how effective it is. Programs might expand upon current methods such as "before and after surveys," focus groups, youth/staff interviews and youth journals to measure changes in attitudes and behaviors. They could also consider increasing or incorporating regular 'rap sessions' or role-plays where youth can process their experiences and practice their skills. Ideally, the youth would help create and pilot these tools and use them in their outreach activities. The youth at Energia Positiva, LISAPP, and TRAPP, all spoke about beginning to integrate various evaluation tools into their peer outreach work.

Engaging young people in youth development-based programs may decrease risk for future perpetration and victimization.

QUESTIONS FOR REVIEW AND DISCUSSION

1. What are the purposes of sexual assault prevention projects?
2. What are the characteristics of adolescent sexual assault prevention programs?
3. Describe three different demonstration projects and their objectives.
4. What are the goals of focus groups? How do facilitators enhance the effectiveness of these types of groups? Discuss.
5. What are some reasons youth want to become involved in sexual assault prevention programs?
6. What are some strategies for preventing sexual assault?

Bibliography

ABDUL-JABBAR, K. (2000). *A Season on the Reservation: My Sojourn with the White Mountain Apache.* New York: Simon and Schuster, Inc.

ABEL, G. ET AL. (1989). "The Measurement of the Cognitive Distortions of Child Molesters." *Annals of Sex Research* 2: 135–153.

"ACHIEVING SUCCESS BEHIND BARBED WIRE." (1999). *WEAC News and Views* 35: 16.

ADAMSON, PATRICK B. (1991). "Some Comments on the Origin of the Police." *Police Studies* 14: 1–2.

ADMINISTRATIVE OFFICE OF THE U.S. COURTS. (1998). *Utah State Courts Report to the Community: The Changing Face of Utah Justice.* Washington, DC: Administrative Office of the U.S. Courts.

AGNEW, R. ET AL. (2002). "Strain, Personality Traits, and Delinquency: Extending General Strain Theory." *Criminology* 40: 43–71.

AKERS, RONALD L. (1994). *Criminological Theories: Introduction and Evaluation.* Los Angeles: Roxbury Publishing Company.

AKERS, R., AND C. SELLERS. (2004). *Criminological Theories: Introduction, Evaluation, and Application,* 4th ed. Los Angeles, CA: Roxbury Publishing Company.

ALBRECHT, S. L., AND M. GREEN. (1977). "The Attitudes of Blacks and Whites Toward City Services: Implications for Public Policy." In J. P. Crecine (ed.), *Financing the Metropolis: Public Policy in Urban Economies.* Beverly Hills, CA: Sage.

ALEXANDER, MARGARET. (1999). "Sexual Offenders Treatment Efficacy Revisited." *Journal of Research and Treatment* 11: 2.

ALLEN, L. C., D. L. MACKENZIE, AND L. J. HICKMAN. (2001). "The Effectiveness of Cognitive Behavioral Treatment for Adult Offenders: A Methodological, Quality-Based Review." *International Journal of Offender Therapy and Comparative Criminology* 45: 498–514.

AMERICAN PROBATION AND PAROLE ASSOCIATION. (2003). *Community Justice Position Statement.* Lexington, KY: American Probation and Parole Association.

ANDERSON, DAVID A. (1999). "The Aggregate Burden of Crime." *Journal of Law and Economics* 42: 611–642.

ANDERSON, STEPHEN V. (1995). *Evaluation of the Impact of Participation in Ohio Penal Industries on Recidivism.* Columbus, OH: Ohio Department of Rehabilitation and Correction.

ANDREWS, D. A. (1995). "The Psychology of Criminal Conduct and Effective Treatment." In James McGuire (ed.), *What Works: Reducing Reoffending.* West Sussex, UK: Wiley.

ANDREWS, D. A., AND J. L. BONTA. (1994). *The Psychology of Criminal Conduct.* Cincinnati: Anderson Publishing Company.

ANDREWS, D. A., AND J. L. BONTA. (1995). *The Level of Supervision Inventory—Revised LSI-R.* North Tonawanda, NY: Multi-Health Systems.

ANDREWS, D. A., AND J. L. BONTA. (1996). *The Psychology of Criminal Conduct.* Cincinnati: Anderson Publishing Company.

ANDREWS, D. A., AND J. L. BONTA. (1997). *Do We Need Theory for Offender Risk Assessment?* Ottawa, CAN: Correctional Service of Canada.

ANDREWS, D. A., AND J. L. BONTA. (1998). *The Psychology of Criminal Conduct,* 2nd ed. Cincinnati: Anderson Publishing Company.

ANDREWS, D. A., AND J. L. BONTA. (2003). *The Psychology of Criminal Conduct,* 3rd ed. Cincinnati: Anderson Publishing Company.

ANDREWS, D. A. ET AL. (1990). "Does Correctional Treatment Work? A Clinically Relevant and Psychologically Informed Meta-Analysis." *Criminology* 28: 369–404.

ANGLIN, M. D. (1988). "The Efficacy of Civil Commitment in Treating Narcotic Addiction." In C. G. Leukefeld and F. M. Tims (eds.), *Compulsory Treatment of Drug Abuse: Research and Clinical Practice.* Rockville, MD: National Institute on Drug Abuse.

APPLEGATE, BRANDON K., FRANCIS T. CULLEN, AND BONNIE S. FISHER. (1997). "Public Support for Correctional Treatment: The Continuing Appeal of the Rehabilitative Ideal." *Prison Journal* 77: 237–258.

ARROW, KENNETH ET AL. (1993). "Report of the NOAA Panel on Contingent Valuation." *Federal Register,* January 15, 58: 4601–4614.

ASHWORTH, A. (2002). "Responsibilities, Rights, and Restorative Justice." *Criminology* 42: 578–595.

ATKINS, H., B. K. APPLEGATE, AND G. F. HOBBS. (1998). "Mentally Ill and Substance Abusing Inmates: One Jail's Solution to Traditionally Fragmented Service Delivery." *American Jails* 12: 69–72.

ATKINSON, L. (1995). "Boot Camps and Justice: A Contradiction in Terms?" *Trends and Issues in Crime and Justice* (July).

ATTWELL, J., AND C. SAVILL-SMITH. (2004). "Mobile Learning and Social Inclusion: Focusing on Learners and Learning." In J. Attewell and C. Savill-Smith (eds.), *Learning with Mobile Devices.* London, UK: Learning and Skills Development Agency.

AUERHAHN, KATHLEEN. (1999). "Selective Incapacitation and the Problem of Prediction." *Criminology* (November).

AUGIMERI, L. K., K. GOLDBERG, AND C. KOEGL. (1999). *Canadian Children Under 12 Committing Offenses: Police Protocols.* Toronto, ON: Earscourt Child and Family Care Center.

AUSTIN, JAMES. (1997). *District of Columbia Department of Corrections Long-Term Options.* Washington, DC: National Council on Crime and Delinquency.

AUSTIN, JAMES. (1996). "The Effect of 'Three Strikes and You're Out' on Corrections." In David Shichor (ed.), *Three Strikes and You're Out.* Thousand Oaks, CA: Sage.

AUSTIN, JAMES. (2001). "Prisoner Reentry: Current Trends, Practices, and Issues." *Crime and Delinquency* 47: 314–334.

BACHMAN, RONET. (1998). "The Factors Related to Rape-Reporting Behavior and Arrest: New Evidence from the *National Crime Victimization Survey*." *Criminal Justice and Behavior* 25: 8–29.

BAILEY, WILLIAM G. (1986). *Police Science, 1964–1984: A Selected, Annotated Bibliography.* New York: Garland Publishing Company.

BAIRD, C., R. HEINZ, AND B. BEMUS. (1979). *The Wisconsin Case Classification/Staff Deployment Project.* Madison, WI: National Council on Crime and Delinquency.

BALDASSARE, M. (1986). "The Elderly and Fear of Crime." *Sociology and Social Research* 70: 218–221.

BARILLE, L. (1984). "Television and Attitudes About Crime: Do Heavy Views Distort Criminality and Support Retributive Justice?" In Ray Surette (ed.), *Justice and the Media: Issues and Research.* Springfield, IL: Charles C Thomas.

BARNES, ALLAN R. (2005). "Weed and Seed Initiative: An Evaluation Using a Pre/Post Community Survey Approach." Unpublished paper presented at the annual meeting of the Academy of Criminal Justice Sciences, Chicago.

BARNHILL, S. (2002). *Residential and Institutional Services: Visitation and Cohabitation Strategies.* Delmar, NY: National GAINS Center.

BARO, AGNES (1999). "Effects of a Cognitive Restructuring Program on Inmate Institutional Behavior." *Criminal Justice and Behavior* 26: 466-484.

BAROP, A. L. (1999). "Effects of a Cognitive Restructuring Program on Inmate Institutional Behavior." *Criminal Justice and Behavior* 26: 466–484.

BARR, H. (1999). *Prisons and Jails: Hospitals of Last Resort: The Need for Diversion and Discharge Planning for Incarcerated People with Mental Illness in New York.* Albany, NY: The Correctional Association of New York and the Urban Justice Center.

BARTOL, K. M., AND DAVID C. MARTIN. (1991). *Management.* New York: McGraw-Hill.

BASARAB, D. J., AND D. K. ROOT. (1992). *The Training Evaluation Process.* Boston: Kluwer Academic Publishers.

BATTISTICH, V. ET AL. (1997). "Caring School Communities." *Educational Psychologist* 32: 137–151.

BAUMER, ERIC ET AL. (1998). "The Influence of Crack Cocaine on Robbery, Burglary, and Homicide Rates: A Cross-City, Longitudinal Analysis." *Journal of Research in Crime and Delinquency* 35: 316–340.

BAUMER, T. L. (1978). "Research on Fear of Crime in the United States." *Victimology* 3: 254–264.

BAUMRIND, D. (1967). "Socialization and Instrumental Competence in Young Children." *Child Development* 38: 291–327.

BAYLEY, DAVID. (1996). "Measuring Overall Effectiveness." In Larry T. Hoover (ed.), *Quantifying Quality in Policing.* Washington, DC: Police Executive Research Forum.

BAYLEY, DAVID H., AND CLIFFORD D. SHEARING. (2001). *The New Structure of Policing: Description, Conceptualization, and Research Agenda.* Washington, DC: National Institute of Justice.

BAZEMORE, GORDON. (1992). "On Mission Statements and Reform in Juvenile Justice: The Case of the 'Balanced Approach.' " *Federal Probation* 56: 64–70.

BAZEMORE, GORDON. (1999). "The Fork in the Road to Juvenile Court Reform." *Annals of the American Academy of Political and Social Science* 564: 81–108.

BAZEMORE, GORDON. (2000). "Community Justice and a Vision of Collective Efficacy: The Case of Restorative Conferencing." In Julie Horney (ed.), *Policies, Processes, and Decisions of the Criminal Justice System.* Washington, DC: National Institute of Justice.

BAZEMORE, GORDON, AND CURT T. GRIFFITHS. (1997). "Conferences, Circles, Boards, and Mediations: The 'New Wave' of Community Justice Decisionmaking." *Federal Probation* 61: 25–37.

BAZEMORE, GORDON, AND DAVID R. KARP. (2004). "Community Service and Offender Reintegration." *Justice Policy Journal* 1: 1–37

BAZEMORE, GORDON, AND DENNIS MALONEY. (1994). "Rehabilitating Community Service: Toward Restorative Service Sanctions in a Balanced Justice System." *Federal Probation* 58: 24–35.

BAZEMORE, GORDON, AND JEANNE B. STINCHCOMB. (2000). "Restorative Conferencing and Theory-Based Evaluation." In Gale Burford and Joe Hudson (eds.), *Family Group Conferencing: New Directions in Community-Centered Child and Family Practice.* New York: Aldine de Gruyter.

BAZEMORE, GORDON, AND MARK S. UMBREIT. (2001). *A Comparison of Four Restorative Conferencing Models.* Washington, DC: Office of Juvenile Justice and Delinquency Prevention.

BECK, ALLEN, AND PAIGE HARRISON. (2001). *Prisoners in 2000.* Washington, DC: Bureau of Justice Statistics.

BECK, ALLEN, AND LAURA MARUSCHAK. (2001). *Mental Health Treatment in State Prisons.* Washington, DC: Bureau of Justice Statistics.

BECK, A. T., R. A. STEER, AND G. K. BROWN. (1996). *BDI-II Manual: Beck Depression Inventory.* San Antonio, TX: The Psychological Corporation.

BECKER, JUDITH V., AND JOHN A. HUNTER JR. (1992). "Evaluation of Treatment Outcomes for Adult Perpetrators of Child Sexual Abuse." *Criminal Justice and Behavior* 19: 74–92.

BEDAU, HUGO ADAM. (1992). *The Case Against the Death Penalty.* Washington, DC: American Civil Liberties Union, Capital Punishment Project.

BENEKOS, PETER J., AND ALIDA V. MERLO. (1995). "Three Strikes and You're Out!: The Political Sentencing Game." *Federal Probation* 59: 3–9.

BENNETT, WILLIAM J., JOHN J. DiIULIO JR., AND JOHN P. WALTERS. (1996). *Body Count: Moral Poverty and How to Win America's War Against Crime and Drugs.* New York: Simon and Schuster.

BENNIS, WARREN AND B. NANUS. (1997). *Leaders: Strategies for Taking Charge.* New York: HarperCollins.

BENSON, BRUCE L. (1996). *Privatization in Criminal Justice.* Oakland, CA: Independent Policy Report, Independent Institute.

BENSON, MICHAEL L. (2002). *Crime and the Life Course: An Introduction.* Los Angeles: Roxbury Publishing Company.

BESCI, ZSOLT. (1999). "Economics and Crime in the States." *Economic Review,* First Quarter.

BEST CONFERENCE. (1999). "Resolving Truancy Problems Through Mediation." Unpublished paper presented at the BEST Conference, Washington, DC.

BLACK, J., B. STEELE, AND R. BARNEY. (1995). *Doing Ethics in Journalism: A Handbook with Case Studies,* 2nd ed. Needham Heights, MA: Allyn & Bacon.

BLACKSTONE, ERWIN A., AND SIMON HAKIM. (1996). *Police Services: The Private Challenge.* Oakland, CA: Independent Policy Report, Independent Institute.

BLALOCK, HUBERT M. (1957). *Toward a Theory of Minority Group Relations.* New York: Wiley.

BLAU, PETER M. (1977). *Inequality and Heterogeneity: A Primitive Theory of Social Structure.* New York: Free Press.

BLOCK, CAROLYN REBECCA. (1998). "The Geo-Archive: An Information Foundation for Community Policing." In David Weisburd and Tom McEwen (eds.), *Crime Mapping and Crime Prevention.* Monsey, NY: Criminal Justice Press.

BLOUNT, WILLIAM R. (2003). "Does That Really Work? Evaluating Jail Programs, Procedures, Policies and Practices, Part I." *American Jails* 17: 80.

BLUMBERG, A. (1998). "ID Anti-Theft Efforts Stir Capitol Debate." *The Daily Recorder,* August 7, 1998: 7.

BLUMSTEIN, ALFRED. (1995). "Youth Violence, Guns and the Illicit Drug Industry." *Journal of Law and Criminology* 86: 10–36.

BLUMSTEIN, ALFRED, AND ALLEN J. BECK. (2005). "Reentry as a Transient State Between Liberty and Recommitment." In Jeremy Travis and Christy Visher (eds.), *Prisoner Reentry and Public Safety in America.* New York: Cambridge University Press.

BLUMSTEIN, ALFRED, AND JOEL WALLMAN (eds.). (2000). *The Crime Drop in America.* New York: Cambridge University Press.

BLUMSTEIN, ALFRED ET AL. (1988). "Specialization and Seriousness During Adult Criminal Careers." *Quantitative Criminology* 4: 303–345.

BOLGER, N., AND E. A. SCHILLINGS. (1991). "Personality and the Problems of Everyday Life: The Role of Neuroticism in Exposure and Reactivity to Daily Stressors." *Journal of Personality* 59: 355–386.

BONTA, JAMES. (1996). "Risk-Needs Assessment and Treatment." In Alan T. Harland (ed.), *Choosing Correctional Options That Work: Defining the Demand and Evaluating the Supply.* Thousand Oaks, CA: Sage.

BONTA, JAMES, SUZANNE WALLACE-CAPRETTA, AND JENNIFER ROONEY. (1998). *Restorative Justice: An Evaluation of the Restorative Resolutions Project.* Ottawa, Canada: Department of the Solicitor General Canada.

BONTA, J., S. WALLACE-CAPRETTA, AND J. ROONEY. (1999). *Electronic Monitoring in Canada.* Ottawa, Canada: Solicitor General's Office, Public Works and Government Services.

BORTNER, M. A., MARJORIE ZATZ, AND DARNELL F. HAWKINS. (2000). "Race and Transfer: Empirical Research and Social Context." In Jeffery Fagan and Franklin Zimring (eds.), *The Changing Borders of Juvenile Justice.* Chicago: University of Chicago Press.

BORUM, R., M. W. DEANE, AND H. STEADMAN ET AL. (1998). "Police Perspectives on Responding to Mentally Ill People in Crisis." *Behavioral Sciences and the Law* 16: 393–405.

BOSWELL, GWYNETH ET AL. (2002). "Working with Young Adults Sentenced to Life." *British Journal of Community Justice* 1: 77–89.

BOTTOMS, ANTHONY E. (1994). "Environmental Criminology." In Mike Maguire, Rod Morgan, and Robert Reiner (eds.), *The Oxford Handbook of Criminology.* Oxford, UK: Clarendon Press.

BOTTOMS, ANTHONY E. (1998). "Interpersonal Violence and Social Order in Prisons." In M. Tonry and J. Petersilia (eds.) *Prisons.* Chicago: University of Chicago Press.

BOWCOTT, OWEN. (1993). "Soldier Dies as IRA Bombers Ambush Patrol." *The Guardian,* February 10, 1993: 2.

BOWMAN, CATHY. (2005). "Involvement of Probation and Parole in Project Safe Neighborhoods." Unpublished paper presented at the annual meeting of the American Probation and Parole Association (July), New York.

BRAGA, ANTHONY A. ET AL. (1999). "Problem-Oriented Policing in Violent Crime Places: A Randomized Controlled Experiment." *Criminology* 37: 541–580.

BRAGA, ANTHONY A. ET AL. (2001). "Problem-Oriented Policing, Youth Violence and Deterrence: An Evaluation of Boston's Operation Ceasefire." *Journal of Research in Crime and Delinquency* 38: 195–225.

BRAITHWAITE, JOHN. (1989). *Crime, Shame, and Reintegration.* Cambridge, UK: Cambridge University Press.

BRAITHWAITE, JOHN. (2001). "Restorative Justice and a New Criminal Law of Substance Abuse." *Youth and Society* 33: 227–248.

BRAITHWAITE, JOHN. (2002). *Restorative Justice and Responsive Regulation.* New York: Oxford University Press.

BRATTON, WILLIAM, AND PETER KNOBLER. (1998). *Turnaround: How America's Top Cop Reversed the Crime Epidemic.* New York: Random House.

BRATTON, WILLIAM ET AL. (2004). "This Works: Crime Prevention and the Future of Broken Windows Policing." *Civic Bulletin* 35: 1–14.

BRESTAN, E. V., AND S. M. EYBERG. (1998). "Effective Psychosocial Treatments of Conduct-Disordered Children and Adolescents." *Journal of Clinical Child Psychology* 27: 180–189.

BRIDGES, GEORGE S., AND ROBERT D. CRUTCHFIELD. (1988). "Law, Social Standing, and Racial Disparities in Imprisonment." *Social Forces* 66: 601–616.

BRIDGES, GEORGE S. ET AL. (1993). *Racial Disproportionality in the Juvenile Justice System.* Olympia, WA: Washington Department of Social and Health Services.

BRILLON, Y. (1987). *Victimization and Fear Among the Elderly.* Toronto, Canada: Butterworths.

BRITT, CHESTER L. (1996). "The Measurement of Specialization and Escalation in the Criminal Career: An Alternative Modeling Strategy." *Journal of Quantitative Criminology* 12: 193–222.

BRITT, CHESTER L. (2000). "Social Context and Racial Disparities in Punishment Decisions." *Justice Quarterly* 17: 707–732.

BROOKS, T. R., AND M. PETIT. (1997). *Early Intervention: Crafting a Community Response to Child Abuse and Violence.* Washington, DC: Child Welfare League of America.

BROWNING, S. ET AL. (1994). "Race and Getting Hassled By the Police." *Police Studies* 17: 5–6.

BROWNLIE, E. B. ET AL. (2004). "Early Language Impairment and Young Adult Delinquent and Aggressive Behavior." *Journal of Abnormal Child Psychology* 32: 453–467.

BRYANT, J., R. A. CARVETH, AND D. BROWN. (1981). "Television Viewing and Anxiety: An Experimental Examination." *Journal of Communication* 31: 106–119.

BRYSON, JOHN M. (1995). *Strategic Planning for Public and Nonprofit Organizations: A Guide to Strengthening and Sustaining Organizational Achievement.* San Francisco: Jossey-Bass.

BUCK, GEORGE. (2002). *Preparing for Terrorism: An Emergency Services Guide.* Albany, NY: Delmar.

BURDON, W. M. ET AL. (2001). "Drug Courts and Contingency Management." *Journal of Drug Issues* 32: 73–90.

BUREAU OF JUSTICE ASSISTANCE. (1996). *National Survey of State Sentencing.* Washington, DC: Bureau of Justice Assistance.

BUREAU OF JUSTICE ASSISTANCE. (2000a). *A Second Look at Alleviating Jail Crowding: A Systems Perspective.* Washington, DC: U.S. Department of Justice.

BUREAU OF JUSTICE ASSISTANCE. (2000b). *Emerging Judicial Strategies for the Mentally Ill in the Criminal Caseload.* Washington, DC: Bureau of Justice Assistance.

BUREAU OF JUSTICE STATISTICS. (1996). *Sourcebook.* Washington, DC: U.S. Department of Justice.

BUREAU OF JUSTICE STATISTICS. (2001a). *Criminal Victimization in the United States, 1999.* Washington, DC: U.S. Department of Justice.

BUREAU OF JUSTICE STATISTICS. (2001b). *Criminal Victimization in the United States, 2000.* Washington, DC: U.S. Department of Justice.

BUREAU OF JUSTICE STATISTICS (2001c). *Probation and Parole Statistics: Summary Findings.* Washington, DC: U.S. Department of Justice.

BUREAU OF JUSTICE STATISTICS. (2004). *Justice Expenditure and Employment in the United States, 2001.* Washington, DC: U.S. Department of Justice.

BURNS, B. J., K. HOAGWOOD, AND P. MRAZEK. (1999). "Effective Treatment for Mental Disorders in Children and Adolescents." *Clinical Child and Family Psychology Review* 2: 199–254.

BURNS, B. J. ET AL. (1995). "Children's Mental Health Service Use Across Service Sectors." *Health Affairs* 14: 147–159.

BURNS, B. J. ET AL. (2000). "Comprehensive Community-Based Interventions for Youth with Severe Emotional Disorders: Multisystemic Therapy and the Wraparound Process." *Journal of Child and Youth Studies* 9: 283–314.

BURRELL, WILLIAM D. (2005). "Trends in Probation and Parole in the United States." *Back to the States.* Lexington, KY: Council of State Governments.

BURSIK, ROBERT J. (1988). "Social Disorganization and Theories of Crime and Delinquency: Problems and Prospects." *Criminology* 26: 519–551.

BURSIK, ROBERT J., AND HAROLD G. GRASMICK. (1993). *Neighborhoods and Crime: The Dimensions of Effective Community Control.* Lexington, MA: Lexington Books.

BUTTERFIELD, FOX. (1995). "Many Cities in the U.S. Show Sharp Drop in Homicide Rate." *New York Times,* August 13, 1995: 1, 10.

BUTTERFIELD, FOX. (1996). "Major Crimes Fell in '95, Early Data By FBI Indicate." *New York Times,* May 6, 1996: A1, A14.

BUTTERFIELD, FOX. (1998). "Reasons for Dramatic Drop in Crime Puzzles the Experts." *New York Times,* March 29, 1998: A14.

BUTTERFIELD, FOX. (2001). "States Easing Stringent Laws on Prison Time." *New York Times,* September 2, 2001: 1, 16.

BYRNE, JAMES, AND APRIL PATTAVINA. (1992). "The Effectiveness Issue: Assessing What Works in the Adult Community Corrections System." In James Byrne, Arthur Lurigio, and Joan Petersilia (eds.), *Smart Sentencing: The Emergence of Intermediate Sanctions.* Newbury Park, CA: Sage.

BYRNE, JAMES M., AND DON HUMMER. (2004). "Examining the Role of the Police in Reentry Partnership Initiatives." *Federal Promotion* 68: 62–68.

BYRNE, J. M., F. S. TAXMAN, AND D. YOUNG. (2003). *Emerging Roles and Responsibility in the Reentry Partnership Initiative: New Ways of Doing Business.* Washington, DC: National Institute of Justice.

CAIN, TRAVIS ANN. (2002). *JUMP.* Washington, DC: Office of Juvenile Justice and Delinquency Prevention.

CALIFORNIA DEPARTMENT OF CORRECTIONS. (2000). *California Prisoners and Parolees: 2000.* Sacramento, CA: Offender Information Services Branch, Department of Corrections.

CALIFORNIA DEPARTMENT OF CORRECTIONS. (2001a). *CDC Facts: Third Quarter 2001.* Sacramento, CA: Offender Information Services Branch, California Department of Corrections.

CALIFORNIA DEPARTMENT OF CORRECTIONS. (2001b). *CDC Facts: Fourth Quarter 2001.* Sacramento, CA: Offender Information Services Branch, California Department of Corrections.

CALIFORNIA DEPARTMENT OF CORRECTIONS. (2001c). *Office of Substance Abuse Programs: Weekly In-Prison Population Report.* Sacramento, CA: Office of Substance Abuse Programs, California Department of Corrections.

CALIFORNIA HIGH-TECH TASK FORCE COMMITTEE. (1997). *Combatting High-Tech Crime in California: The Task Force Approach.* Sacramento, CA: California High-Tech Task Force Committee, June, 1997: 3.

CAMERON, DANE A. (1997). "Three Strikes Law: The Legislature as Judge." Paper presented at the Western Political Science Association Conference, Tucson, AZ, March 13–15.

CAMP, CAMILLE GRAHAM, AND GEORGE M. CAMP. (1999). *The Corrections Yearbook 1999.* Middletown, CT: Criminal Justice Institute.

CAMPBELL, M., AND J. E. CUEVA. (1995). "Psychopharmacology in Child and Adolescent Psychiatry: A Review of the Past Seven Years." *Journal of the American Academy of Child and Adolescent Psychiatry* 34: 1262–1272.

CAMPBELL, R., AND R. V. WOLF. (2001). *Problem Solving Probation.* Washington, DC: Center for Court Innovation, Bureau of Justice Assistance.

CANALES-PORTALATIN, D. (1995). "Comorbidity of Mental Illness and Substance Use in Jail Populations." *Journal of Offender Rehabilitation* 22: 59–76.

CARAMANIS, C. (1999). "Literacy Education Presents a Challenge in the Correctional Setting." *M.A.J.P.S. News.*

CAREY, K. B. ET AL. (2001). "Enhancing Readiness-to-Change Substance Abuse in Persons with Schizophrenia: A Four-Session Motivation-Based Intervention." *Behavior Modification* 25: 331–384.

CARLSON, J. (1985). *Prime Law Enforcement.* New York: Praeger Publishers.

CARNEVALE, DAN. (2002). "White House Official Asks Colleagues to Help Create National Computer-Security Strategy." *The Chronicle of Higher Education,* April 19, 2002: 12.

CASCIO, B. (2000). "Communication and Teamwork." *Corrections Insight* 17: 12–13.

CASPI, A. ET AL. (1994). "Are Some People Crime-Prone? Replications of the Personality-Crime Relationship Across Countries, Genders, Races, and Methods." *Criminology* 32: 163–195.

CASPI, A. ET AL. (1997). "Personality Differences Predict Health-Risk Behaviors in Young Adulthood: Evidence from a Longitudinal Study." *Journal of Personality and Social Psychology* 44: 112–126.

CATTABIANI, MARIO F. (1999). "Dent Bill to Expand DNA Database." *Allentown Morning Call,* March 26, 1999: B1.

CENTER FOR MEDIA AND PUBLIC AFFAIRS. (1997). *In 1990s TV News Turns to Violence and Show Biz.* Washington, DC: Center for Media and Public Affairs.

CENTER FOR SEX OFFENDER MANAGEMENT. (2001). *Case Studies on CSOM's National Resource Sites,* 2nd ed. Silver Springs, MD: Center for Effective Public Policy.

CENTER FOR SUBSTANCE ABUSE TREATMENT. (1994). *Assessment and Treatment of Patients with Co-Existing Mental Illness and Alcohol and Other Drug Abuse: Treatment Improvement Protocol Series, Number 9.* Rockville, MD: Center for Substance Abuse Treatment.

CENTER FOR SUBSTANCE ABUSE TREATMENT. (2003). *Substance Abuse Treatment for Persons with Co-Occurring Disorders: Treatment Improvement Protocol (TIP) Series.* Rockville, MD: Substance Abuse and Mental Health Services.

CHAIKEN, MARCIA, AND BRUCE JOHNSON. (1988). *Characteristics of Different Drug-Involved Offenders.* Washington, DC: U.S. Department of Justice.

CHARNEY, D. A., A. M. PARAHERAKIS, AND K. J. GILL. (2001). "Integrated Treatment of Comorbid Depression and Substance Use Disorders." *Journal of Clinical Psychiatry* 62: 672–677.

CHILD WELFARE LEAGUE OF AMERICA. (1997). *Sacramento County Community Intervention Program.* Washington, DC: Child Welfare League of America.

CHILDREN'S RESEARCH CENTER. (1993). *A New Approach to Child Protection: The CRC Model.* Madison, WI: National Council on Crime and Delinquency.

CHILDRESS, R., V. TALUCCI, AND J. WOOD. (1999). "Fighting the Enemy Within: Helping Officers Deal with Stress." *Corrections Today* 60: 63.

CHIRICOS, T., S. ESCHOLZ, AND M. GERTZ. (1997). "Crime, News, and Fear of Crime: Toward an Identification of Audience Effects." *Social Problems* 44: 342–357.

CHIRICOS, T., K. PADGETT, AND M. GERTZ. (2000). "Fear, TV News, and the Reality of Crime." *Criminology* 38: 755–785.

CHRISTENSEN, J., J. SCHMIDT, AND J. HENDERSON. (1982). "The Selling of the Police: Media, Ideology, and Crime Control." *Contemporary Crisis* 6: 227–239.

CHRISTIE, N. (1977). "Conflicts as Property." *British Journal of Criminology* 17: 1–15.

CIVIKLY-POWELL, JEAN. (1999). "On Humor and Being Yourself: Humor Should Enable You and Your Students to Relax." *Thriving in Academe* (August): 6–10.

CLARKE, RICHARD A. (2002). "White House Official Asks Colleges to Help Create National Computer-Security Strategy." *The Chronicle of Higher Education,* April 19, 2002: 12.

CLARKE, RONALD V., AND ROSS HOMEL. (1997). "A Revised Classification of Situational Crime Prevention Techniques." In Stephen P. Lab (ed.), *Crime Prevention at the Crossroads.* Cincinnati: Anderson Publishing Company.

CLARKE, RONALD V., AND MIKE HOUGH. (1984). *Crime and Police Effectiveness.* London, UK: Her Majesty's Stationery Office, Home Office Research Study No. 79.

CLEAR, TODD R. (1984). "Correctional Policy: Neo-Retributionism, and the Determinate Sentence." In George F. Cole (ed.), *Criminal Justice: Law and Politics,* 4th ed. Monterey, CA: Brooks/Cole Publishing.

CLEAR, TODD R. (1994). *Harm in American Penology: Offenders, Victims, and Their Communities.* Albany: State University of New York Press.

CLEAR, TODD R. (1996). "Toward a Corrections of 'Place': The Challenge of 'Community' in Corrections." *National Institute of Corrections Journal* (August): 52–56.

CLEAR, TODD R., AND RONALD P. CORBETT. (1999). "Community Corrections of Place." *APPA Perspectives* 23: 24–32.

CLEAR, TODD R., AND DAVID R. KARP. (1999). *The Community Justice Ideal.* New York: Westview.

CLEAR, TODD R., AND DAVID R. KARP. (2000). "Toward the Ideal of Community Justice." *National Institute of Justice Journal* (March): 21–27.

CLEMENT, KEITH E. (1998). "The Impact of Three Strikes Laws on State Prison Populations." Paper presented at the annual meeting of the Western Political Science Association, Los Angeles, CA, March 19–21.

CNN. (2003). "Bombs Kill at Least 20 in Downtown Casablanca." *CNN.com,* May 19, 2003.

COCOZZA, J. J. (1992). *Responding to the Mental Health Needs of Youth in the Juvenile Justice System.* Seattle, WA: The National Coalition for the Mentally Ill in the Criminal Justice System.

COHEN, LAWRENCE E., AND MARCUS FELSON. (1979). "Social Change and Crime Rate Trends: A Routine Activities Approach." *American Sociological Review* 44: 588–608.

COHEN, MARK A. (1988). "Pain, Suffering, and Jury Awards: A Study of the Cost of Crime to Victims." *Law and Society Review* 22: 537–555.

COHEN, MARK A. (1998). "The Monetary Value of Saving a High Risk Youth." *Journal of Quantitative Criminology* 14: 5–33.

COHEN, MARK A., TED R. MILLER, AND SHELLI B. ROSSMAN. (1994). "The Costs and Consequences of Violent Behavior in the United States." In Albert J. Reiss, Jr. and Jeffrey A. Roth (eds.), *Understanding and Preventing Violence: Consequences and Control of Violence,* Vol. 4. Washington, DC: National Research Council, National Academy Press.

COHEN, MARK, ROLAND T. RUST, AND SARA STEEN. (2002). *Measuring Public Perceptions of Appropriate Prison Sentences: Executive Summary.* Washington, DC: U.S. Department of Justice, National Institute of Justice.

COHEN, R. (1995). *Probation and Parole Violators in State Prison, 1991.* Washington, DC: Bureau of Justice Statistics.

COHN, A.W. (2003). "Chicken Little Says the Sky May Be Falling!" *Journal of Offender Monitoring* 16: 2–4.

COLE, DAVID. (1999). "Discretion and Discrimination Reconsidered: A New Response to the New Criminal Justice Scholarship." *Georgetown Law Journal* (May) 87: 1059–1093.

COLEMAN, JAMES E. JR. (1998). "The ABA's Proposed Moratorium on the Death Penalty." *Law and Contemporary Problems* 61: 1–231.

CONDUCT PROBLEMS PREVENTION RESEARCH GROUP. (1999a). "Initial Impact of the Fast Track Prevention Trial for Conduct Problems: I." *Journal of Consulting and Clinical Psychology* 65: 631–647.

CONDUCT PROBLEMS PREVENTION RESEARCH GROUP. (1999b). "Initial Impact of the Fast Track Prevention Trial for Conduct Problems: II." *Journal of Consulting and Clinical Psychology* 67: 648–657.

CONKLIN, JOHN. (2003). *Why Crime Rates Fell.* New York: Allyn and Bacon.

CONLY, C. (1999). *Coordinating Community Services for Mentally Ill Offenders: Maryland's Community Criminal Justice Treatment Program.* Washington, DC: U.S. Department of Justice.

CONNELLY, L. (1999). *Implementing Effective Offender Supervision Practices and Programming: Electronic Monitoring.* Lexington, KY: American Probation and Parole Association.

COOK, P. J., AND D. A. GRAHAM. (1977). "The Demand of Insurance and Protection: The Place of Irreplaceable Commodities." *Quarterly Journal of Economics* 91: 143–156.

COOK, PHILIP J., AND JOHN H. LAUB. (2002). "After the Epidemic: Recent Trends in Youth Violence in the United States." In Michael Tonry (ed.), *Crime and Justice: A Review of Research,* Vol. 29. Chicago: University of Chicago Press.

COOK, PHILIP J., AND JENS LUDWIG. (2000). *Gun Violence: The Real Costs.* New York: Oxford University Press.

COOPERSMITH, S. (1969). *Implications of Studies on Self-Esteem for Educational Research and Practice.* Washington, DC: U.S. Government Printing Office.

CORBETT, RONALD P., BERNARD J. FITZGERALD, AND JAMES JORDAN. (1998). "Operation Night Light: An Emerging Model for Police-Probation Partnership." In Joan Petersilia (ed.), *Community Corrections: Probation, Parole, and Intermediate Sanctions.* New York: Oxford University Press.

CORK, DANIEL. (1999). "Examining Space-Time Interaction in City-Level Homicide Data: Crack Markets and the Diffusion of Guns Among Youth." *Journal of Quantitative Criminology* 15: 379–406.

CRAWFORD, ADAM, AND TIM NEWBURN. (2003). *Youth Offending and Restorative Justice.* Portland, OR: Willan.

CROME, I. B. (1999). "Substance Abuse and Psychiatric Comorbidity: Towards Improved Service Provision." *Drug Education, Prevention, and Policy* 6: 151–174.

CRONIN, AUDREY KURTH. (2003). *Terrorists and Suicide Attacks.* Washington, DC: CRS Report for Congress, Congressional Research Service.

CROWE, A. H. ET AL. (2002). *Offender Supervision with Electronic Technology.* Lexington, KY: American Probation and Parole Association.

CRUTCHFIELD, ROBERT D., GEORGE S. BRIDGES, AND SUSAN R. PITCHFORD. (1994). "Analytical and Aggregation Biases in Analyses of Imprisonment: Reconciling Discrepancies in Studies of Racial Disparity." *Journal of Research in Crime and Delinquency* 31: 166–182.

CULLEN, E. (1997). "Can a Prison Be a Therapeutic Community?: The Grendon Template." In E. Cullen, L. Jones, and R. Woodward (eds.), *Therapeutic Communities for Offenders.* New York: Wiley.

CULLEN, FRANCIS T. (2002). "Rehabilitation and Treatment Programs." In James Q. Wilson and Joan Petersilia (eds.), *Crime: Public Policies for Crime Control.* Oakland, CA: ICS Press.

CULLEN, FRANCIS T., BONNIE S. FISHER, AND BRANDON K. APPLEGATE. (2000). "Public Opinion About Punishment and Corrections." In M. Tonry (ed.), *Crime and Justice: A Review of Research,* Vol. 27. Chicago: University of Chicago Press.

CULLEN, FRANCIS T., AND PAUL GENDREAU. (1989). "The Effectiveness of Correctional Rehabilitation: Reconsidering the Nothing Works Debate." In L. Goodstein and D. MacKenzie (eds.), *American Prisons: Issues in Research and Policy.* New York: Plenum.

CULLEN, FRANCIS T., AND PAUL GENDREAU. (2000). "Assessing Correctional Rehabilitation: Policy, Practice, and Prospects." In Julie Horney (ed.), *Policies, Processes, and Decisions in the Criminal Justice System.* Washington, DC: U.S. Department of Justice.

CULLEN, FRANCIS T., AND PAUL GENDREAU. (2001). "From Nothing Works to What Works: Changing Professional Ideology in the 21st Century." *Prison Journal* 81: 313–338.

CULLEN, FRANCIS T., AND KAREN E. GILBERT. (1982). *Reaffirming Rehabilitation.* Cincinnati: Anderson Publishing Company.

CULLEN, FRANCIS T. ET AL. (1996). "Control in the Community: The Limits of Reform?" In Alan T. Harland (ed.), *Choosing Correctional Interventions That Work: Defining the Demand and Evaluating the Supply.* Thousand Oaks, CA: Sage.

CULLEN, FRANCIS T. ET AL. (2002). "Rehabilitation." In Alex R. Piquero and Stephen G. Tibbetts (eds.), *Rational Choice and Criminal Behavior: Recent Research and Future Challenges.* New York: Routledge.

CURRIE, ELLIOTT. (1985). *Confronting Crime: An American Dilemma.* New York: Pantheon Books.

CURRIE, ELLIOTT. (1998). *Crime and Punishment in America: Why the Solutions to America's Most Stubborn Social Crisis Have Not Worked: And What Will.* New York: Metropolitan Books.

DAHLGREN, DANIEL C. (2005). "Emotional Sociology and Juvenile Delinquency: The Value of Interpreting Emotional Subculture of Gangs." Unpublished paper presented at the annual meeting of the Academy of Criminal Justice Sciences, Chicago.

DAILY MAIL. (1993). "Bombs Set Shops Ablaze." May 10, 1993: 5.

DAS, DILIP K. (1986). "Police and Community in America: Influences from Across the Atlantic." *Police Studies* 9: 138–147.

DAVIS, M. H. (1983). "Measuring Individual Differences in Empathy: Evidence for a Multidimensional Approach." *Journal of Personality and Social Psychology* 44: 113–126.

DAVIS, W. N. (2003). "Special Problems for Specialty Courts." *American Bar Association Journal* 89: 32–37.

DELEON, G. (1993). "What Psychologists Can Learn from Addiction Treatment Research." *Journal of Addictive Behaviors* 7: 103–109.

DELEON, G. (2000). *The Therapeutic Community: Theory, Model, and Method.* New York: Springer Publishing Company.

DELEON, G. ET AL. (2000). "Modified Therapeutic Community for Homeless MICA's: Treatment Outcomes." *Journal of Substance Abuse* 26: 461–480.

DENCKLA, D., AND G. BERMAN. (2001). *Rethinking the Revolving Door: A Look at Mental Illness in the Courts.* Washington, DC: Center for Court Innovation.

DEROGATIS, L. R. (1983). *SCL-90-R: Administration, Scoring and Procedures Manual II for the Revised Reversion and Other Instruments of the Psychopathology Rating Scale Series.* Towson, MD: Clinical Psychometric Research.

DEROGATIS, L. R. (1993). *BSI Brief: Symptom Inventory Administration, Scoring and Procedures Manual.* Minneapolis, MN: National Computer Systems, Inc.

DIIULIO, JOHN J. JR. (1994a). "The Question of Black Crime." *The Public Interest* 117: 3–32.

DiIULIO, JOHN J. JR. (1994b). "A Philadelphia Crime Story." *Wall Street Journal,* October 26, 1994: A21.

DISHION, T. J., J. McCORD, AND F. POULIN. (1999). "When Interventions Harm: Peer Groups and Problem Behavior." *American Psychologist* 54: 755–764.

DISTRICT ATTORNEY'S OFFICE KINGS COUNTY, NY. (2003). *Treatment Alternatives for Dually Diagnosed Defendants (TADD).* http://www.brooklynda.org/DTAP/TADD.htm (May 27, 2003).

DITTON, P. M. (1999). *Mental Health Treatment of Inmates and Probationers.* Washington, DC: Bureau of Justice Statistics.

DITTON, PAULA M., AND DORIS JAMES WILSON. (1999). *Truth in Sentencing in State Prisons: Bureau of Justice Statistics Special Report.* Washington, DC: U.S. Department of Justice.

DOMINICK, J. R. (1973). "Crime and Law Enforcement in the Mass Media." In C. Winick (ed.), *Deviance and Mass Media.* New York: McGraw-Hill.

DOOB, A., AND G. MacDONALD. (1979). "Television Viewing and Fear of Victimization: Is the Relationship Causal?" *Journal of Personality and Social Psychology* 25: 432–444.

DOOLEY, MICHAEL. (1996). "Restorative Justice in Vermont: A Work in Progress." In (IS, Inc. (ed) *Community Justice: Striving for Safe, Secure and Just Communities.* Washington, DC: National Institute of Corrections.

D'OVIDIO, ROBERT, AND JAMES DOYLE. (2003). "A Study on Cyberstalking: Understanding Investigative Hurdles." *FBI Law Enforcement Bulletin* (March): 10–17.

DRAINE, J., AND P. SOLOMON. (1999). "Describing and Evaluating Persons with Serious Mental Illness." *Psychiatric Services* 50: 56–61.

DRAKE, R. E., AND K. T. MUESER. (1996). *Dual Diagnosis of Major Mental Illness and Substance Abuse Disorder II: Recent Research and Clinical Implications: New Directions for Mental Health Services.* San Francisco: Jossey-Bass, Inc.

DRAKE, R. E. ET AL. (1998). "Review of Integrated Mental Health and Substance Abuse Treatment for Patients with Dual Disorders." *Schizophrenia Bulletin* 24: 589–608.

DUNDES, LAUREN. (2001). "Is the American Public Ready to Embrace DNA as a Crime Fighting Tool? A Survey Assessing Support for DNA Databases." *Bulletin of Science, Technology, and Society* 21: 369–375.

EASTERN STATE PENITENTIARY. (2004). *Eastern State Penitentiary.* http://www.easternstate.com/ history/sixpage.html (May 20, 2004).

ECK, JOHN E., AND WILLIAM SPELMAN. (1987). *Problem-Oriented Policing in Newport News.* Washington, DC: Police Executive Research Forum.

ECK, JOHN E. (2001). "Policing and Crime Event Concentration." In Robert Meier, Leslie Kennedy, and Vincent Sacco (eds.), *The Process and Structure of Crime: Criminal Events and Crime Analysis.* New Brunswick, NJ: Transaction.

ECK, JOHN E. (2002). "Preventing Crime at Places." In Lawrence W. Sherman, David P. Farrington, and Brandon K. Walsh (eds.), *Evidence-Based Crime Prevention.* New York: Routledge.

ECK, JOHN E., AND EDWARD MAGUIRE. (2000). "Have Changes in Policing Reduced Violent Crime? An Assessment of the Evidence." In Alfred Blumstein and Joel Wallman (eds.), *The Crime Drop in America.* New York: Cambridge University Press.

EDENS, J. F., R. H. PETERS, AND H. A. HILLS. (1997). "Treating Prison Inmates with Co-Occurring Disorders: An Integrative Review of Existing Programs." *Behavioral Sciences and the Law* 15: 439–457.

ELIAS, R. (1992). *The Politics of Victimization.* New York: Oxford University Press.

ELIAS, R. (1993). *Victims Still: The Political Manipulation of Crime Victims.* Newbury Park, CA: Sage.

ELLIOTT, B. (1984). "Individualized Treatment Within a Peer Group Treatment Program." Paper presented at the October meeting of the Midwestern Criminal Justice Association, Chicago.

ELLIOTT, DELBERT S. ET AL. (1996). "The Effects of Neighborhood Disadvantage on Adolescent Development." *Journal of Research on Crime and Delinquency* 33: 389–426.

ELLIOTT, W.N., AND G.D. WALTERS (1997). "Psychoeducational Drug Abusing Clients: The Lifestyle Model." *Journal of Drug Education* 27: 307–319.

ENGEN, RODNEY L., AND SARA STEEN. (2000). "The Power to Punish: Discretion and the Sentencing Reform in the War on Drugs." *The American Journal of Sociology* (May) 105: 1357–1395.

EREZ, EDNA, AND P. R. IBARRA. (2004). "Electronic Monitoring of Domestic Violence Cases: A Study of Two Bilateral Programs." *Federal Probation* 68: 15–20.

ERICSON, R., P. BARANEK, AND J. CHAN. (1987). *Visualizing Deviance.* Toronto, Canada: University of Toronto Press.

ERON, L. D. ET AL. (in press). *A Cognitive-Ecological Approach to Preventing Aggression in Urban Inner-City Settings.* Chicago: Metropolitan Area Child Study Research Group, University of Illinois.

ERVIN, L., AND A. SCHNEIDER. (1990). "Explaining the Effects of Restitution on Offenders: Results from a National Experiment in Juvenile Courts." In B. Galaway and J. Hudson (eds.), *Criminal Justice, Restitution, and Reconciliation.* New York: Willow Tree Press.

ERWIN, B. (1990). "Old and New Tools for the Modern Probation Officer." *Crime and Delinquency* 36: 61–75.

ESTEP, R., AND P. MacDONALD. (1984). "How Prime-Time Crime Evolved on TV, 1976–1983." In R. Surrette (ed.), *Justice and the Media.* Springfield, IL: Charles C Thomas.

FABELO, TONY. (2000). *Goal Met: Violent Offenders in Texas Are Serving a Higher Percentage of Their Prison Sentences.* Austin, TX: Criminal Justice Policy Council.

FAGAN, JEFFREY, AND GARTH DAVIES. (2001). "Street Stops and Broken Windows: Terry, Race, and Disorder in New York City." *Fordham Urban Law Journal* 28: 457–504.

FAGAN, JEFFREY, FRANKLIN ZIMRING, AND JUNE KIM. (1998). "Declining Homicide in New York City: A Tale of Two Trends." *Journal of Criminal Law and Criminology* 88: 1277–1323.

FARABEE, DAVID, M. L. PRENDERGAST, AND M. D. ANGLIN. (1998). "The Effectiveness of Coerced Treatment for Drug-Abusing Offenders." *Federal Probation* 62: 3–10.

FARABEE, DAVID ET AL. (1999). "Barriers to Implementing Effective Correctional Drug Treatment Programs." *Prison Journal* 79: 150–163.

FARRINGTON, DAVID P. (2003). "Developmental and Life-Course Criminology: Key Theoretical and Empirical Issues." *Criminology* 41: 221–255.

FAULKNER, SAMUEL S., AND CYNTHIA A. FAULKNER. (2004). "Poverty as a Predictor of Child Maltreatment: A Brief Analysis." *Journal of Poverty* 8: 103–106.

FAUTEK, P. K. (2001). *Going Straight.* Lincoln, NE: Winters Club Press.

FEDERAL BUREAU OF INVESTIGATION. (2003). *Uniform Crime Reports.* Washington, DC: U.S. Government Printing Office.

FEDERAL BUREAU OF PRISONS (2004). *Federal Incarceration Cost Estimates, 2000–2003.* Washington, DC: Federal Bureau of Prisons.

FELD, BARRY C. (1999). "Rehabilitation, Retribution, and Restorative Justice: Alternative Conceptions of Juvenile Justice." In Gordon Bazemore and Lode Walgrave (eds.), *Restorative Juvenile Justice: Repairing the Harm of Youth Crime.* Monsey, NY: Criminal Justice Press.

FELDMAN, PAUL. (1994). "LA Homicides Drop 28% in 1st Half Along with Other Crimes." *Los Angeles Times,* August 6, 1994: B1–B2.

FELKER, D. W. (1974). *Building Positive Self-Concept.* Minneapolis, MN: Burgess Publishing Company.

FELSON, MARCUS. (1995). "Those Who Discourage Crime." In John E. Eck and David Weisburd (eds.), *Crime and Place: Crime Prevention Studies,* Vol. 4. Monsey, NY: Criminal Justice Press.

FELSON, MARCUS. (1998). *Crime and Everyday Life,* 2nd ed. Thousand Oaks, CA: Pine Forge Press.

FIELD, G. (1984). "The Cornerstone Program: A Client Outcome Study." *Federal Probation* 48: 50–55.

FIELD, G. (1989). "A Study of the Effects of Intensive Treatment on Reducing the Criminal Recidivism of Addicted Offenders." *Federal Probation* 53: 51–56.

FIELD, G. (1998). "From the Institution to the Community." *Corrections Today* 60: 94–97, 113.

FIELDS, SCOTT A., AND JOHN R. McNAMARA. (2003). "The Prevention of Child and Adolescent Violence: A Review." *Aggression and Violent Behavior* 8: 61–91.

FINN, M. A., AND S. MUIRHEAD-STEVES. (2002). "The Effectiveness of Electronic Monitoring with Violent Male Parolees." *Justice Quarterly* 19: 293–312.

FINN, PETER. (1998a). *The Delaware Department of Correction Life Skills Program.* Washington, DC: U.S. National Institute of Justice.

FINN, PETER. (1998b). "The Orange County, Florida Jail Education and Vocational Programs." *American Jails* 12: 9–28.

FIRST, M. B. ET AL. (1996). *User's Guide for the Structured Clinical Interview for DSM-IV Axis I Disorders: Research Version SCID-I, Version 2.0.* New York: Biometrics Research Department, New York State Psychiatric Institute.

FIRST, MICHAEL B., MIRIAM GIBBON, R.L. SPITZER, AND J.B. WILLIAMS (1996). *DSM-IV Casebook.* Washington, DC: American Psychiatric Press.

FISHMAN, M. (1981). "Police News: Constructing an Image of Crime." *Urban Life* 9: 371–394.

FLORIDA DEPARTMENT OF JUVENILE JUSTICE. (1999). *National Comparison from State Recidivism.* Tallahassee: Florida Department of Juvenile Justice.

FORD, D., AND A. K. SCHMIDT. (1985). "Electronically Monitored Home Confinement." *NIJ Reports* 2: 6.

FOSDICK, RAYMOND B. (1920). *American Police Systems.* New York: Macmillan.

FRANKEL, MARVIN E. (1972). *Criminal Sentences: Law Without Order.* New York: Basic Books.

FRAZIER, CHARLES E., AND SOON R. LEE. (1992). "Reducing Juvenile Detention Rates or Expanding the Official Control Nets: An Evaluation of a Legislative Reform Effort." *Crime and Delinquency* 38: 204–218.

FRENCH, A., J. KIMBLE, C. SLUSSER, AND E. WALTON. (2000). "Cognitive Self-Change Programs: Opportunity Through Teamwork." *Corrections Today* 62: 94–97.

FRIEDMAN, LAWRENCE M. (1993). *Crime and Punishment in American History.* New York: Basic Books.

FRISBIE, W. PARKER, AND LISA NEIDERT. (1977). "Inequality and the Relative Size of Minority Populations: A Comparative Analysis." *American Journal of Sociology* 82: 1007–1030.

FULTON, BETSY ET AL. (1997). "The State of ISP: Research and Policy Implications." *Federal Probation* 61: 65–75.

FURBY, LITA, MARK R. WEINROTT, AND LYN BLACKSHAW. (1989). "Sexual Offender Recidivism: A Review." *Psychological Bulletin* 105: 3–30.

GABLE, R. K. (1986). "Application of Personal Telemonitoring to Current Problems in Corrections." *Journal of Criminal Justice* 14: 167–176.

GARAFALO, J. (1977). *Public Opinion About Crime: The Attitudes of Victims and Nonvictims in Selected Cities.* Washington, DC: U.S. Government Printing Office.

GARAFALO, J. (1981a). "Crime and the Mass Media: A Selective Review of Research." *Journal of Research in Crime and Delinquency* 18: 319–350.

GARAFALO, J. (1981b). "The Fear of Crime: Causes and Consequences." *Journal of Criminal Law and Criminology* 82: 839–857.

GARVEY, STEPHEN P. (1998). "Freeing Prisoners' Labor." *Stanford Law Review* 50: 339–398.

GATHRIGHT, G. (1999). "Conflict Management in Prisons: An Educator's Perspective." *Journal of Correctional Education* 50: 142–147.

GEHRING, T. (2000). "A Compendium of Material on the Pedagogy-Androgogy Issue." *Journal of Correctional Education* 51: 151–163.

GENDREAU, PAUL. (1996). "The Principles of Effective Intervention with Offenders." In Alan T. Harland (ed.), *Choosing Correctional Options That Work: Defining the Demand and Evaluating the Supply.* Newbury Park, CA: Sage.

GENDREAU, PAUL, FRANCIS T. CULLEN, AND JAMES BONTA. (1994). "Intensive Rehabilitation Supervision: The Next Generation in Community Corrections." *Federal Probation* 58: 72–78.

GENDREAU, PAUL, C. GOGGIN, F. T. CULLEN, AND D. A. ANDREWS. (2000). "The Effects of Community Sanctions and Incarceration in Recidivism." *Forum on Corrections Research* 12: 10–13.

GENDREAU, PAUL, CLAIRE GOGGIN, AND BETSY FULTON. (2000). "Intensive Supervision in Probation and Parole." In Clive R. Hollin (ed.), *Handbook of Offender Assessment and Treatment.* London, UK: John Wiley.

GENDREAU, PAUL, T. LITTLE, AND C. GOGGIN. (1996). "A Meta-Analysis of the Predictors of Adult Offender Recidivism: What Works?" *Criminology* 34: 575–607.

GENDREAU, PAUL, AND B. ROSS. (1979). "Effective Correctional Treatment: Bibliotherapy for Cynics." *Crime and Delinquency* 25: 463–489.

GERBNER, G. ET AL. (1980). "The Mainstreaming of America: Violence Profile No. 11." *Journal of Communications* 30: 10–29.

GIFFORD, SIDRA LEA. (2002). *Justice Expenditure and Employment in the United States, 1999.* Washington, DC: U.S. Department of Justice.

GILLERMAN, MARGARET. (1996). "Bush: E. St. Louis Good Guys Winning." *St. Louis Dispatch,* June 18, 1996.

GLASER, D. (1964). *The Effectiveness of a Prison and Parole System.* Indianapolis, IN: Bobbs-Merrill Company.

GLASER, D., AND R. WATTS. (1992). "Electronic Monitoring of Offenders on Probation." *Judicature* 76: 112–117.

GLAZE, LAUREN E., AND SERI PELLA. (2005). *Probation and Parole in the United States, 2004.* Washington, DC: Bureau of Justice Statistics.

GLICK, B. (2003). "Cognitive Programs: Coming of Age in Corrections." *Corrections Today* 65: 78–82.

GODLEY, S. H. ET AL. (2000). "Case Management for Dually Diagnosed Individuals Involved in the Criminal Justice System." *Journal of Substance Abuse Treatment* 18: 137–148.

GOLDMAN, S. K. (1999). "The Conceptual Framework for Wraparound: Definition, Values, Essential Elements, and Requirements for Practice." In B. J. Burns and S. K. Goldman (eds.), *Promising Practices in Wraparound for Children with Serious Emotional Disturbances and Their Families.* Washington, DC: Center for Effective Collaboration and Practice, American Institutes for Research.

GOLDRING, J. (1997). *Quick Response Therapy.* Northvale, NJ: Aronson.

GOLDSTEIN, A. P., AND B. GLICK. (1987). *Aggression Replacement Training: A Comprehensive Intervention for Aggressive Youth.* Champaign, IL: Research Press.

GOODMAN, MARC. (2001). "Making Computer Crime Count." *FBI Law Enforcement Bulletin* (August): 13.

GORDON, M., AND D. GLASER. (1991). "The Use and Effects of Financial Penalties in Municipal Courts." *Criminology* 29: 651–676.

GOTTFREDSON, D. C., AND W. H. BARON. (1992). *Deinstitutionalization of Juvenile Offenders: Summary.* Washington, DC: National Institute of Justice.

GOTTFREDSON, DENISE C., RICHARD J. MCNEIL, AND GARY D. GOTTFREDSON. (1991). "Social Area Influences on Delinquency: A Multilevel Analysis." *Journal of Research in Crime and Delinquency* 28: 197–226.

GOTTFREDSON, S., AND R. TAYLOR. (1986). "Person-Environment Interactions in the Prediction of Recidivism." In J. Byrne and R. Sampson (eds.), *The Social Ecology of Crime.* New York: Springer-Verlag.

GRABER, D. (1980). *Crime News and the Public.* New York: Praeger Publishers.

GRATTON, J. (2001). "Jail Diversion for Persons with Co-Occurring Disorders." *Criminal Justice Abstracts* 34: 26–59.

GRAVES G. ET AL. (1985). *Developing a Street Patrol: A Guide for Neighborhood Crime Prevention Groups.* Boston, MA: Neighborhood Crime Prevention Council, Justice Research Institute.

GREENBERG, M. T., AND C. A. KUSCHE. (1993). *Promoting Social and Emotional Development in Deaf Children: The PATHS Project.* Seattle, WA: University of Washington Press.

GREENLEY, J. R. (1992). "Neglected Organizational and Management Issues in Mental Health Systems Development." *Community Mental Health Journal* 28: 371–384.

GREENWOOD, P. W., AND S. TURNER. (1993). "Evaluation of the Paint Creek Youth Center: A Residential Program for Serious Delinquents." *Criminology* 31: 263–279.

GRISET, PAMELA L. (1991). *Determinate Sentencing: The Promise and the Reality of Retributive Justice.* Albany, NY: State University of New York Press.

GROSSMAN, D. C. ET AL. (1997). "Effectiveness of a Violence Prevention Curriculum Among Children in Elementary School." *Journal of the American Medical Association* 277: 1605–1611.

GUILIANI, R. W. (2002). *Leadership.* New York: Talk Miramax Books, Hyperion.

GUILIANI, R. W., AND HOWARD SAFIR. (1998). *COMPSTAT: Leadership in Action.* New York: New York Police Department.

GUNN, P. (1999). "Learner and Instructor Needs in a Correctional Setting." *Journal of Correctional Education* 50: 74–82.

GUNTER, B. (1987). *Television and Fear of Crime.* London, UK: John Libbey.

HAAB, TIMOTHY C., AND KENNETH E. McCONNELL. (1997). "Referendum Models and Negative Willingness to Pay: Alternative Solutions." *Journal of Environmental Economics and Management* 32: 251–270.

HAGAN, JOHN. (1992). "The Poverty of a Classless Criminology: Presidential Address, American Society of Criminology." *Criminology* 30: 1–19.

HAGAN, JOHN. (1994). "The New Sociology of Crime and Inequality in America." *Studies on Crime Prevention* 3: 7–23.

HAGEMAN, MARY JEANETTE. (1985). *Police-Community Relations.* Beverly Hills, CA: Sage.

HAGHIGHI, B., AND J. SORENSEN. (1996). "America's Fear of Crime." In T. J. Flanagan and D. R. Longmire (eds.), *Americans View Crime and Justice: A National Public Opinion Survey.* Thousand Oaks, CA: Sage.

HALE, C. D. (1981). *Police Patrol: Operations and Management.* New York: Wiley.

HALL, E. A., D. M. BALDWIN, AND M. L. PRENDERGAST. (2001). "Women on Parole: Barriers to Success After Substance Abuse Treatment." *Human Organization* 60: 225–233.

HALL, S. ET AL. (1978). *Policing the Crisis: Mugging, the State, and Law and Order.* London, UK: Macmillan.

HAMMER, MICHAEL, AND JAMES CHAMPY. (1993). *Reengineering the Corporation: A Manifesto for Business Revolution.* New York: Harper Business.

HANSON, R. K. (1997). *The Development of a Brief Actuarial Risk Scale for Sexual Offense Recidivism.* Ottawa, CAN: Department of the Solicitor General of Canada.

HANSON, R. KARL, AND MONIQUE T. BUSSIERE. (1998). "Predicting Relapse: A Meta-Analysis of Sexual Offender Recidivism Studies." *Journal of Consulting and Clinical Psychology* 60: 348–362.

HANSON, R. KARL, HEATHER SCOTT, AND RICHARD A. STEFFY. (1995). "A Comparison of Child Molesters and Nonsexual Criminals: Risk Predictors and Long-Term Recidivism." *Journal of Research in Crime and Delinquency* 32: 325–337.

HARCOURT, BERNARD E. (2001). *Illusion of Order: The False Promise of Broken Windows Policing.* Cambridge, MA: Harvard University Press.

HARDYMAN, P., J. AUSTIN, AND J. PEYTON. (2004). *Prison Intake Systems: Assessing Needs and Classifying Prisoners.* Washington, DC: National Institute of Corrections.

HARLAND, A. T. (1981). *Restitution to Victims of Personal and Household Crimes.* Washington, DC: Bureau of Justice Statistics.

HARMON, JOHN. (1999). "Terrorism: It's Getting Less Disciplined, More Dangerous." *Cox News Service*, March 31, 1999.

HARRIS, G. (1995). *Overcoming Resistance: Success in Counseling Men.* Lanham, MD: American Correctional Association.

HARRIS, P. W. (1979). "The Interpersonal Maturity of Delinquents and Non-Delinquents." *Dissertation Abstracts International.* University Microfilms, State University of New York.

HARRIS, PATRICIA M. (ed.). (1999). *Research to Results: Effective Community Corrections.* Lanham, MD: American Correctional Association.

HARRISON, L. D., AND S. S. MARTIN. (2000). *Residential Substance Abuse Treatment for State Prisoners Formula Grant: Compendium of Program Implementation and Accomplishments.* Newark, DE: Center for Drug and Alcohol Studies, University of Delaware.

HART, H. L. A. (1968). *Punishment and Responsibility: Essays in the Philosophy of Law.* Oxford, UK: Clarendon Press.

HART, W. (1987). *The Art of Living: Vipassana by S.N. Goenka.* San Francisco: Harper and Row.

HARVARD LAW REVIEW. (1966). "Anthropotelemetry: Dr. Schwitzgebel's Machine." 80: 403–421.

HAWKINS, DARNELL F. (1993). "Crime and Ethnicity." In Brian Forst (ed.), *The Socio-Economics of Crime and Justice.* Armonk, NY: M.E. Sharpe.

HAWKINS, DARNELL F. (1999). "What Can We Learn from Data Disaggregation? The Case of Homicide and African Americans." In M. Dwayne Smith and Margaret Zahn (eds.), *Homicide: A Sourcebook of Social Research.* Thousand Oaks, CA: Sage.

HAWKINS, J. D. ET AL. (1999). "Preventing Adolescent Health-Risk Behaviors by Strengthening Protection During Childhood." *Archives of Pediatrics and Adolescent Medicine* 153: 226–234.

HAWKINS, R., AND S. PINGREE. (1980). "Some Progress in the Cultivation Effect." *Communication Research* 39: 193–226.

HAYES, HENNESSEY, AND KATHLEEN DALY. (2003). "Youth Justice Conferencing and Re-Offending." *Justice Quarterly* 20: 725–764.

HEATH, L., AND K. GILBERT. (1996). "Mass Media and Fear of Crime." *American Behavioral Scientist* 39: 379–386.

HEGELIN, ROBERT. (1994). "A Flurry of Recidivist Legislation Means 'Three Strikes and You're Out.'" *Journal of Legislation* 20: 68–82.

HEIDE, K. (1992). *Why Kids Kill Parents: Child Abuse and Adolescent Homicide.* Columbus, OH: Ohio State University Press.

HEIDE, K. (1999). *Young Killers: The Change of Juvenile Homicide.* Thousand Oaks, CA: Sage.

HEIDE, K. M. (1983). "An Empirical Assessment of the Value of Using Personality Data in Restitution Outcome Prediction." In W. S. Laufer and J. M. Day (eds.), *Personality Theory, Moral Development, and Criminal Behavior.* Lexington, MA: D.C. Heath and Company.

HENDRIE, H. C. ET AL. (2001). "Incidence of Dementia and Alzheimer's Disease in Two Communities." *Journal of the American Medical Association* 285: 739–747.

HENNEPIN COUNTY ATTORNEY'S OFFICE. (1995). *Delinquents Under 10 in Hennepin County.* Minneapolis, MN: Hennepin County Attorney's Office.

HENNING, K. R., AND B. C. FRUEH. (1996). "Cognitive-Behavioral Treatments of Incarcerated Offenders: An Evaluation of the Vermont Department of Corrections Cognitive Self-Change Program." *Criminal Justice and Behavior* 23: 523–541.

HENRY, V. E. (2002). *The COMPSTAT Paradigm: Management Accountability in Policing: Business and the Public Sector.* New York: Looseleaf Law Publications.

HERBERT, BOB. (1995). "Good News for the City." *New York Times,* August 11, 1995: A15.

HERRENKOHL, T. I. ET AL. (2001). "School and Community Risk Factors and Interventions." In R. Loeber and D. P. Farrington (eds.), *Child Delinquents: Development, Intervention, and Service Needs.* Thousand Oaks, CA: Sage.

HICKMAN, J. L. (1998). "Our Ever-Changing Local Jail Population." *American Jails* 12: 53–56.

HILL, K. G. ET AL. (1999). "Childhood Risk Factors for Adolescent Gang Membership: Results from the Seattle Social Development Project." *Journal of Research in Crime and Delinquency* 36: 300–322.

HILLIS, BRADLEY J. (1995). "Approaches to Internet Access: A Primer for Managers of Courts and Law Firms." *ILP Newsletter* (January): 1–3.

HILLSMAN, S. (1990). "Fines and Day Fines." In M. Tonry and N. Morris (eds.), *Crime and Justice: A Review of Research,* Vol. 12. Chicago: University of Chicago Press.

HILLSMAN, S., AND J. A. GREENE. (1992). "The Use of Fines as an Intermediate Sanction." In J. M. Byrne, A. J. Lurigio, and J. Petersilia (eds.), *Smart Sentencing: The Emergence of Intermediate Sanctions.* Newbury Park, CA: Sage.

HINDELANG, M. J. (1974). "Public Opinion Regarding Crime, Criminal Justice, and Related Topics." *Journal of Research in Crime and Delinquency* 11: 101–116.

HOCKSTADER, LEE. (2001). "Two Suicide Bombers Kill at Least 10 in Jerusalem: Attacks, Nearby Car Blast Wound 170 in Heart of City." *Washington Post,* December 2, 2001: A1.

HOFER, H. (2000). "Notes on Crime and Punishment in Sweden and Scandinavia." Paper presented at the 115th International Training Course. Tokyo, JAPAN: United Nations Asia and Far East Institute for the Prevention of Crime and the Treatment of Offenders.

HOFFMAN, JOHN P. (2001). "A Contextual Analysis of Differential Association, Social Control, and Strain Theories of Delinquency." *Social Forces* 81: 753–785.

HOFFMAN, P. B., AND J. L. BECK. (1985). "Recidivism Among Released Federal Prisoners: Salient Factor Score and Five-Year Follow-Up." *Criminal Justice and Behavior* 12: 501–507.

HOGUE, T. E. (1998). "The Sex Offense Information Questionnaire: The Development of a Self-Report Measure of Offense-Related Denial in Sexual Offenders." Unpublished doctoral dissertation, Cardiff, University of Wales.

HOLDEN, G. A., AND R. A. KAPLER. (1995). "Deinstitutionalizing Status Offenders: A Record of Progress." *Juvenile Justice* 2: 3–10.

HOWELL, J. C. (1995). *Guide for Implementing the Comprehensive Strategy for Serious, Violent, and Chronic Juvenile Offenders.* Washington, DC: U.S. Department of Justice.

HOWITT, P. S., AND E. A. MOORE. (1991). "The Efficacy of Intensive Early Intervention: An Evaluation of the Oakland County Probate Court Early Offender Program." *Juvenile and Family Court Journal* 42: 25–36.

HSER, Y., M. D. ANGLIN, AND K. I. POWERS. (1993). "A 24-Year Follow-Up of California Narcotics Addicts." *Archives of General Psychiatry* 50: 577–584.

HSER, Y. ET AL. (2001). "A 33-Year Follow-Up of Narcotics Addicts." *Archives of General Psychiatry* 58: 503–508.

HUANG, WILSON W. S., AND MICHAEL S. VAUGHN. (1996). "Support and Confidence: Favorable Attitudes Toward the Police Correlates of Attitudes Toward the Police." In T. J. Flanagan and D. R. Longmire (eds.), *Americans View Crime and Justice: A National Public Opinion Survey.* Thousand Oaks, CA: Sage.

HUGHES, K. W. (1990). "*Florida Star v. B.J.F.:* Can the State Regulate the Press in the Interest of Protecting the Privacy of Rape Victims?" *Mercer Law Review* 41: 236–257.

HUGHES, T., AND D. WILSON. (2002). *Reentry Trends in the United States.* Washington, DC: U.S. Department of Justice.

HUGHES, T., AND D. J. WILSON. (2003). *Reentry Trends in the United States: Inmates Returning to the Community after Serving Time in Prison.* Washington, DC: Bureau of Justice Statistics.

HUGHES, THOMAS, DAVID WILSON, AND ALLEN BECK. (2001). *Trends in State Parole, 1990–2000.* Washington, DC: U.S. Department of Justice, Bureau of Justice Statistics.

HUSBAND, S. D., AND J. J. PLATT. (1993). "The Cognitive Skills Component in Substance Abuse Treatment in Correctional Settings: A Brief Review." *Journal of Drug Issues* 23: 31–42.

IFCC. (2004). *IFCC 2002 Internet Fraud Report.* Washington, DC: IFCC.

INCIARDI, J. A. (1996). "The Therapeutic Community: An Effective Model for Corrections-Based Drug Abuse Treatment." In K. Early (ed.), *Drug Treatment Behind Bars: Prison Based Strategies for Change.* Westport, CT: Praeger Publishers.

INCIARDI, J. A. (2003). "The Irrational Politics of American Drug Policy: Implications for Criminal Law and the Management of Drug-Involved Offenders." *Ohio State Journal of Criminal Law* 1: 273–288.

INCIARDI, J. A. ET AL. (1997). "An Effective Model of Prison-Based Treatment for Drug-Involved." *Journal of Drug Issues* 27: 261–278.

IRWIN, K. (2004). "The Violence of Adolescent Life: Experiencing and Managing Everyday Threats." *Youth and Society* 35: 452–479.

IRWIN, JOHN, AND JAMES AUSTIN. (1994). *It's About Time: America's Imprisonment Binge.* Belmont, CA: Wadsworth.

ISRAEL, MARK, AND JOHN DAWES. (2002). "'Something from Nothing': Shifting Credibility in Community Correctional Programs in Australia." *Criminal Justice: The International Journal of Policy and Practice* 2: 5–25.

IZZO, R. L., AND R. R. ROSS. (1990). "Meta-Analysis of Rehabilitation Programs for Juvenile Delinquents: A Brief Report." *Criminal Justice and Behavior* 17: 134–142.

JACKSON, J. L., J. W. DEKEIJSER, AND J. A. MICHON. (1995). "A Critical Look at Research on Alternatives to Custody." *Federal Probation* 59: 43–51.

JACOB, H. (1971). "Black and White Perceptions of Justice in the City." *Law and Society Review* 6: 69–89.

JACOBY, JOSEPH E., AND FRANCIS T. CULLEN. (1998). "The Structure of Punishment Norms: Applying the Rossi-Berk Model." *Journal of Criminal Law and Criminology* 89: 245–312.

JASPER, DEBRA. (2001). "Prison Expenses Straining Budget: Some Lawmakers Consider Alternatives to Incarceration." *Cincinnati Inquirer,* May 28, 2001: A1, A9.

JENKINS, PHILIP. (1998). *Moral Panic, Changing Concepts of the Child Molester in Modern America.* London, UK: Yale University Press.

JESNESS, C. F. (1971). "The Preston Typology Study: An Experiment with Differential Treatment in an Institution." *Journal of Research in Crime and Delinquency* 8: 38–52.

JESNESS, C. F. (1988). "The Jesness Inventory Classification System." *Criminal Justice and Behavior* 15: 78–91.

JESNESS, C. F. (1996). *The Jesness Inventory Material.* North Tonawanda, NY: Multi-Health Systems.

JOANES, ANA. (2000). "Does the New York City Police Department Deserve Credit for the Decline in New York City's Homicide Rates? A Cross-City Comparison of Policing Strategies and Homicide Rates." *Columbia Journal of Law and Social Problems* 33: 265–311.

JOHN DOBLE RESEARCH ASSOCIATES AND JUDITH GREEN. (2000). *Attitudes Toward Crime and Punishment in Vermont: Public Opinion About an Experiment with Restorative Justice.* Englewood Cliffs, NJ: John Doble Research Associates.

JOHN HOWARD SOCIETY. (2000). *Electronic Monitoring.* Edmonton, Alberta, Canada: John Howard Society.

JONES, A. (2005). "A Tagging Tale: The Work of the Monitoring Officer: Electronically Monitoring Offenders in England and Wales." *Surveillance and Society* 2: 581–588.

JONES, G., AND M. CONNELLY. (2004). *Prison vs. Alternative Sanctions: Trying to Compare Recidivism Rates.* Baltimore: Maryland State Commission on Criminal Sentencing Policy.

JONES, M. B., AND D. R. OFFORD. (1989). "Reduction of Antisocial Behavior in Poor Children by Nonschool Skill-Development." *Journal of Child Psychology and Psychiatry and Allied Disciplines* 30: 737–750.

JUSTICE RESEARCH AND STATISTICS ASSOCIATION. (1999). *Juvenile Justice Evaluation Needs in the States: Findings of the Formula Grants Program Evaluation Needs Assessment.* Washington, DC: Justice Research and Statistics Association.

JUSTICE RESEARCH AND STATISTICS ASSOCIATION. (2005). *The Weed and Seed Strategy.* Washington, DC: Justice Research and Statistics Association.

KAPLAN, MORTON H. (1999). "When You Speak, Do They Listen?" *New York Times*, April 16, 1999:2.

KARMEN, ANDREW. (2000). *New York Murder Mystery: The True Story Behind the Crime Crash of the 1990s.* New York: New York University Press.

KARP, DAVID R. (2001). "Harm and Repair: Observing Restorative Justice in Vermont." *Justice Quarterly* 18: 727–757.

KARP, DAVID R. (2004). "Birds of a Feather: A Response to McCold." *Contemporary Justice Review* 7: 59–68.

KARP, DAVID R., AND TODD CLEAR. (2000). "Community Justice: A Conceptual Framework." In Charles M. Friel (ed.), *Boundaries Changes in Criminal Justice Organizations.* Washington, DC: National Institute of Justice.

KARP, DAVID R., AND TODD R. CLEAR. (2002a). "The Community Justice Frontier: An Introduction." In David R. Karp and Todd R. Clear (eds.), *What Is Community Justice? Case Studies of Restorative Justice and Community Supervision.* Thousand Oaks, CA: Sage.

KARP, DAVID R., AND TODD R. CLEAR. (eds.). (2002b). *What Is Community Justice? Case Studies of Restorative Justice and Community Supervision.* Thousand Oaks, CA: Sage.

KARP, DAVID R., JODI LANE, AND SUSAN TURNER. (2002). "Ventura County and the Theory of Community Justice." In David R. Karp and Todd R. Clear (eds.), *What Is Community Justice? Case Studies of Restorative Justice and Community Supervision.* Thousand Oaks, CA: Sage.

KARP, DAVID R., AND LYNNE WALTHER. (2001). "Community Reparative Boards in Vermont." In Gordon Bazemore and Mara Schiff (eds.), *Restorative Community Justice: Repairing Harm and Transforming Communities.* Cincinnati: Anderson Publishing Company.

KARP, DAVID R., GORDON BAZEMORE, AND J. D. CHESIRE. (2004). "The Role and Attitudes of Restorative Board Members: A Case Study of Volunteers in Community Service." *Crime and Delinquency.* 50: 487–515.

KARP, DAVID R., MARY SPRAYREGEN, AND KEVIN DRAKULICH. (2002). *Vermont Reparative Probation Year 2000 Outcome Evaluation: Final Report.* Waterbury, VT: Vermont Department of Corrections.

KAZDIN, A. E. (1985). *Treatment of Antisocial Behavior in Children and Adolescents.* Homewood, IL: Dorsey Press.

KELLAM, S. G., AND G. W. REBOK. (1992). "Building Developmental and Etiological Theory Through Epidemiologically Based Preventive Intervention Trials." In J. McCord and R. E. Tremblay (eds.), *Preventing Antisocial Behavior: Interventions from Birth Through Adolescence.* New York: Guilford Press.

KELLAM, S. G. ET AL. (1994). "The Course and Malleability of Aggressive Behavior from Early First Grade into Middle School: Results of a Developmental Epidemiologically-Based Preventive Trial." *Journal of Child Psychology and Psychiatry* 35: 259–281.

KELLING, G. L. (1995). "How to Run a Police Department." *City Journal* 5: 4.

KELLING, GEORGE L. (1974). *The Kansas City Preventive Patrol Experiment: A Summary Report.* Washington, DC: The Police Foundation.

KELLING, GEORGE L., TONY PATE, DUANE DIECKMAN, AND CHARLES E. BROWN. (1974). *The Kansas City Preventive Patrol Experiment: A Summary Report.* Washington, DC: Police Foundation.

KELLING, GEORGE L., AND WILLIAM BRATTON. (1998). "Declining Crime Rates: Insiders' Views of the New York City Story." *Journal of Criminal Law and Criminology* 88: 1217–1232.

KELLING, GEORGE L., AND C. COLES. (1996). *Fixing Broken Windows: Restoring Order and Reducing Crime in Our Communities.* New York: Free Press.

KELLING, GEORGE L., AND WILLIAM H. SOUSA JR. (2001). *Do Police Matter? An Analysis of the Impact of New York City's Police Reforms.* New York: Manhattan Institute Civic Report.

KEMPF-LEONARD, KIMBERLY, PAUL E. TRACY, AND JAMES C. HOWELL. (2001). "Serious, Violent, and Chronic Juvenile Offenders: The Relationship of Delinquency Career Types to Adult Criminality." *Justice Quarterly* 18: 449–478.

KENNEDY, DAVID. (1998). "Pulling Levers: Getting Deterrence Right." *National Institute of Justice Journal* (July): 2–8.

KENNEDY, DAVID ET AL. (2001). *Reducing Gun Violence: The Boston Gun Project's Operation Ceasefire.* Washington, DC: National Institute of Justice.

KERLE, K. (1998a). *American Jails: Looking to the Future.* Boston: Butterworth-Heinemann.

KERLE, K. (1998b). "Jail Programs." *American Jails* 12: 5.

KESSLER, DAVID A. (1985). "One- or Two-Officer Cars? A Perspective from Kansas City." *Journal of Criminal Justice* 13: 49–64.

KILPATRICK, D., C. EDMUNDS, AND A. SEYMOUR. (1992). "Rape in America: A Report to the Nation." In *The National Women's Study.* Charleston, SC: Medical University of South Carolina National Crime Victims Research Treatment Center; Arlington, VA: National Center for Victims of Crime.

KIRKPATRICK, D. L. (1998). *Evaluating Training Programs: The Four Levels.* San Francisco: Barrett-Koehler Publishers.

KLASSKIDS. (2001). *Megan's Law in All 50 States and Victims' Rights in the 50 States.* http://wwwklaaskids.org/pg-legmeg.htm (February 21, 2001).

KLEIN, R. (1991). "Preliminary Results: Lithium Effects in Conduct Disorders." Unpublished paper presented at the 144th annual meeting of the American Psychiatric Association. New Orleans, LA.

KLEINSASSER, L. D., AND J. T. MICHAUD. (2002). "Identifying and Tracking Seriously Mentally Ill Offenders in the Colorado Department of Corrections." Presentation to the Mental Health in Corrections Consortium, Washington, D.C.

KNIGHT, K., D. D. SIMPSON, AND M. L. HILLER. (1999). "Three-Year Reincarceration Outcomes for In-Prison Therapeutic Community Treatment in Texas." *Prison Journal* 79: 337–351.

KNITZER, J. (1982). *Unclaimed Children: The Failure of Public Responsibility to Children and Adolescents in Need of Mental Health Services.* Washington, DC: The Children's Defense Fund.

KONTOS, LUIS, DAVID BROTHERTON, AND LUIS BARRIOS (eds.). (2003). *Gangs and Society: Alternative Perspectives.* New York: Columbia University Press.

KOOISTRA, P. G., J. S. MAHONEY, AND S. D. WESTERVELT. (1998). "The World According to Cops." In M. Fishman and G. Cavender (eds.), *Entertaining Crime: Television Reality Programs.* New York: Aldine de Gruyter.

KOSS, M. (1996). "The Measurement of Rape Victimization in Crime Surveys." *Criminal Justice and Behavior* 23: 55–69.

KRAUSS, CLIFFORD. (1996). "Now, How Low Can Crime Go?" *New York Times,* January 28, 1996: D5.

KRUEGER, R. F. ET AL. (1994). "Personality Traits Are Linked to Crime Among Men and Women: Evidence from a Birth Cohort." *Journal of Abnormal Psychology* 103: 328–338.

KUPPERSTEIN, L. (1971). "Treatment and Rehabilitation of Delinquent Youth: Some Sociocultural Considerations." *Acta Criminologica* 4: 11–111.

KURKI, LEENA. (2000). "Restorative and Community Justice: A Conceptual Framework." In Michael Tonry (ed.), *Crime and Justice: A Review of Research,* Vol. 27. Chicago: University of Chicago Press.

KUSOW, A. M., L. C. WILSON, AND D. E. MARTIN. (1998). "Determinants of Citizen Satisfaction with the Police: The Effects of Residential Location." *Policing* 20: 655–664.

KUSTER, B. (1998). "Methods to Increase Educational Effectiveness in an Adult Correctional Setting." *Journal of Correctional Education* 49: 67–72.

LAB, STEVEN P. (2004). *Crime Prevention: Approaches, Practices and Evaluations,* 5th ed. Cincinnati: Anderson Publishing Company.

LACAYO, RICHARD. (1996). "Law and Order." *Time,* January 15, 1996: 48–54.

LAFREE, GARY. (1988). *Losing Legitimacy: Street Crime and the Decline of Social Institutions in America.* Boulder, CO: Westview.

LAGRANGE, R., AND I. F. FERRARO. (1989). "Assessing Age and Gender Differences in Perceived Risk and Fear of Crime." *Criminology* 27: 697–717.

LAMB, H. R., ET AL. (1995). "Outcome for Psychiatric Emergency Patients Seen by an Outreach Police-Mental Health Team." *Psychiatric Services* 46: 1267–1271.

LAMB, H. R., L. E. WEINBERGER, AND B. H. GROSS. (1999). "Community Treatment of Severely Mentally Ill Offenders Under the Jurisdiction of the Criminal Justice System: A Review." *Psychiatric Services* 50: 907–913.

LAMB, S. (1996). *The Trouble with Blame: Victims, Perpetrators, and Responsibility.* Cambridge, MA: Harvard University Press.

LANCOT, N., AND M. LEBLANC. (1996). "The Participation of Boys in a Marginal Gang: A Phenomenon of Selection and Opportunities." *Canadian Journal of Criminology* 38: 375–400.

LAND, KENNETH C., PATRICIA L. MCCALL, AND LAWRENCE E. COHEN. (1990). "Structural Covariates of Homicide Rates: Are There Any Invariances Across Time and Social Space?" *American Journal of Sociology* 95: 922–963.

LANDSVERK, J., AND A. GARLAND. (1999). "Foster Care and Pathways to Mental Health Services." In P. Curtis and G. Dale (eds.), *The Foster Care Crisis: Translating Research into Practice and Policy.* Lincoln, NE: University of Nebraska Press.

LANAGAN, PATRICK A. (1998). "America's Soaring Prison Population." *Science* 151.

LANGAN, P., AND D. LEVIN. (2002). *Recidivism of Prisoners Released in 1994.* Washington, DC: U.S. Department of Justice.

LARDNER, JAMES (1997). "Can You Believe the New York Miracle?" *New York Review,* August 14, 1997: 54–58.

LATIMER, JEFF, CRAIG DOWDEN, AND DANIELLE MUISE. (2001). *The Effectiveness of Restorative Justice Practices: A Meta-Analysis.* Ottawa, CAN: Department of Justice Canada.

LAW ENFORCEMENT NEWS. (1997). "UCR Forecasts 5th Consecutive Crime Dip." February 14, 1997: 5.

LEAF, ROBIN, ARTHUR LURIGIO, AND NANCY MARTIN. (1998). "Chicago's Project Safeway: Strengthening Probation's Links with the Community." In Joan Petersilia (ed.), *Community Corrections: Probation, Parole, and Intermediate Sanctions.* New York: Oxford University Press.

LEASE, MATTHEW L., AND TOD W. BURKE. (2000). "Identity Theft: A Fast-Growing Crime." *FBI Law Enforcement Bulletin* (August): 8–12.

LEE, M. (1901). *A History of Police in England.* London, UK: Methuen and Company.

LEHMAN, A. F., AND L. B. DIXON. (1995). *Double Jeopardy: Chronic Mental Illness and Substance Use Disorders.* Chur, Switzerland: Harwood Academic Publishers.

LEUKEFELD, C. G., AND F. M. TIMS. (1988). *Compulsory Treatments of Drug Abuse: Research and Clinical Practice.* Washington, DC: U.S. Government Printing Office.

LEVITT, STEVEN D. (1997). "Using Electoral Cycles in Police Hiring to Estimate the Effect of Police on Crime." *American Economic Review* 87: 270–290.

LEVITT, STEVEN D. (2002). "Deterrence." In James Q. Wilson and Joan Petersilia (eds.), *Crime: Public Policies for Crime Control.* Oakland, CA: ICS Press.

LEVRANT, SHARON ET AL. (1999). "Reconsidering Restorative Justice: The Corruption of Benevolence." *Crime and Delinquency* 45: 3–27.

LICHTER, L., AND S. LICHTER. (1983). *Prime Time Crime.* Washington, DC: Media Institute.

LIEB, ROXANNE, VERNON QUINSEY, AND LUCY BERLINER. (1998). "Sexual Predators and Social Policy." *Crime and Justice: A Review of Research* 23: 43–114.

LILLY, J. R. ET AL. (1993). "Electronic Monitoring of the Drunk Driver: A Seven-Year Study of the Home Confinement Alternative." *Crime and Delinquency* 39: 462–484.

LINDSMITH CENTER. (2000). http://lindesmith.org/library/focal18.html (May 8, 2000).

LIPSEY, MARK W. (1992). "Juvenile Delinquency Treatment: A Meta-Analytic Inquiry into the Variability of Effects." In Rolf Loeber and David P. Farrington (eds.), *Serious and Violent Juvenile Offenders: Risk Factors and Successful Interventions.* Thousand Oaks, CA: Sage.

LIPSEY, MARK W., AND DAVID B. WILSON. (1998). "Effective Intervention for Serious Juvenile Offenders." In Rolf Loeber and David P. Farrington (eds.), *Serious and Violent Juvenile Offenders: Risk Factors and Successful Intervention.* Thousand Oaks, CA: Sage.

LISKA, A., AND W. BACCAGLINI. (1990). "Feeling Safe by Comparison: Crime in the Newspapers." *Social Problems* 37: 360–374.

LISTWAN, S. J. (2001). "Personality and Criminal Behavior: Reconsidering the Individual." UMI Digital Dissertation Abstracts.

LOCHMAN, J. E. ET AL. (1993). "Effectiveness of a Social Relations Intervention Program for Aggressive and Nonaggressive Rejected Children." *Journal of Consulting and Clinical Psychology* 61: 1053–1058.

LOCK, J., AND G. D. STRAUSS. (1994). "Psychiatric Hospitalization of Adolescents for Conduct Disorder." *Hospital and Community Psychiatry* 45: 925–928.

LOEBER, R., AND D. P. FARRINGTON (eds.). (1998). *Serious and Violent Juvenile Offenders: Risk Factors and Successful Interventions.* Thousand Oaks, CA: Sage.

LOEBER, R., AND FARRINGTON, D. P. (eds.). (2001). *Child Delinquents: Development, Intervention, and Service Needs.* Thousand Oaks, CA: Sage.

LOGAN, C., AND J. DIIULIO JR. (1992). "Ten Deadly Myths About Crime and Punishment in the United States." In G. F. Cole and M. G. Gertz (eds.), *The Criminal Justice System*, 7th ed. Belmont, CA: Wadsworth.

LOGAN, CHARLES H., AND JOHN DIIULIO (1992). *Myths About Crime and Punishment.* Madison,WI: The Wisconsin Policy Research Institute for Criminal Justice.

LOSEL, FREDERICH. (1995). "The Efficacy of Correctional Treatment: A Review and Synthesis of Meta-Evaluations." In James McGuire (ed.), *What Works: Reducing Reoffending.* West Sussex, UK: John Wiley.

LOVEDAY, BARRY. (2004). "Police Reform and Local Government: New Opportunities for Improving Community Safety Arrangements in England and Wales." *Crime Prevention and Community Safety: An International Journal* 6: 7–19.

LOWE, L. (1995). *A Profile of the Young Adult Offender in California Prisons.* Sacramento, CA: Office of Substance Abuse Programs, California Department of Corrections.

LUDWIG, JENS, AND PHILIP J. COOK. (2001). "The Benefits of Reducing Gun Violence: Evidence from Contingent-Valuation Survey Data." *Journal of Risk and Uncertainty* 22: 207–226.

LURIGIO, ARTHUR J. (2000). "Drug Treatment Availability and Effectiveness: Studies of the General and Criminal Justice Populations." *Criminal Justice and Behavior* 27: 495–528.

LURIGIO, ARTHUR J. ET AL. (2004). "The Effects of Serious Mental Illness on Offender Reentry." *Federal Probation* 68: 45–52.

LURIGIO, ARTHUR J. ET AL. (2007). "The Effects of Specialized Supervision on Women Probationers: An Evaluation of the POWER Program." In R. Muraskin (ed.), *It's a Crime: Women and Justice, 4/e.* Upper Saddle River, NJ: Prentice Hall/Pearson.

LYNCH, JAMES, AND WILLIAM SABOL. (2001). *Prisoner Reentry in Perspective.* Washington, DC: Crime Policy Report, U.S. Department of Justice.

LYNCH, MICHAEL J. (1999). "A Further Look at Long Cycles and Criminal Justice Legislation." *Justice Quarterly* 16: 431–450.

LYONS, JAMES A. (1997). *Characteristics of Inmates Discharged 1995.* Albany, NY: New York Department of Correctional Services.

MACKENZIE, DORIS LAYTON. (2000). "Evidence-Based Corrections: Identifying What Works." *Crime and Delinquency* 46: 463.

MACKENZIE, D. L., AND S. DE LI. (2002). "The Impact of Formal and Informal Social Controls on the Criminal Activities of Probationers." *Journal of Research in Crime and Delinquency* 39: 243–276.

MACKENZIE, DORIS LAYTON, ET AL. (2001). *A National Study Comparing the Environments of Boot Camps with Traditional Facilities for Juvenile Offenders.* Washington, DC: U.S. Department of Justice.

MADIGAN, E. (2003). *States Eye Drug Treatment Instead of Prison.* http://www.stateline.org/stateline/?pa=story&sa-showstoryInfo&id=300449.

MAGUIRE, B. (1988). "Image vs. Reality: An Analysis of Prime-Time Television Crime and Police Programs." *Crime and Justice* 11: 165–188.

MAGUIRE, KATHLEEN ET AL. (1998). *Sourcebook of Criminal Justice Statistics.* Albany, NY: Hindelang.

MAGUIRE, MIKE, ROD MORGAN, AND ROBERT REINER (eds.). (2002). *The Oxford Handbook of Criminology.* Oxford, UK: Oxford University Press.

MALTZ, M. D., A. GORDON, AND W. FRIEDMAN. (1991). *Mapping Crime in Its Community Setting: Event-Geography Analysis.* New York: Springer-Verlag.

MAINPRIZE, S. (1996). "Elective Affinities in the Engineering of Social Control: The Evolution of Electronic Monitoring." *Electronic Journal of Sociology.* Online: http://collection.nic.bnc.ca/100/2001/3000/ejofsociology/2003/v07/n03/mainprize.html.

MALONEY, DENNIS, GORDON BAZEMORE, AND JOE HUDSON. (2001). "The End of Probation and the Beginning of Community Justice." *APPA Perspectives* 25: 22–30.

MANGAN, TERANCE J., AND MICHAEL G. SHANAHAN. (1990). "Public Law Enforcement/Private Security: A New Partnership?" *FBI Law Enforcement Bulletin* 62: 18–22.

MANHATTAN INSTITUTE (2000). *Transforming Probation Through Leadership: The "Broken Windows" Model.* New York: Manhattan Institute.

MANNING, PETER K. (1984). "Community Policing." *American Journal of Police* 3: 205–227.

MANNING, PETER. (2003). *Policing Contingencies.* Chicago: University of Chicago Press.

MAPLE, JACK, AND CHRIS MITCHELL. (1999). *The Crime Fighter: Putting the Bad Guys Out of Business.* New York: Doubleday.

MARANS, S., AND M. BERKMAN. (1997). *Child Development-Community Policing: Partnership in a Climate of Violence.* Washington, DC: U.S. Department of Justice.

MARCHANT, P. (2005). "What Works? A Critical Note on the Evaluation of Crime Reduction Initiatives." *Crime Prevention and Community Safety: An International Journal* 7: 1460–1480.

MARLATT, G. A., AND J. L. KRISTELLER. (1998). "Mindfulness and Meditation." In W. R. Miller (ed.), *Integrating Spirituality in Treatment: Resources for Practitioners.* Washington, DC: American Psychological Association.

MARQUES, JANICE K. ET AL. (1994). "Effects of Cognitive-Behavioral Treatment on Sex Offender Recidivism: Preliminary Results of a Longitudinal Study." *Criminal Justice and Behavior* 21: 28–54.

MARSH, H. (1991). "A Comparative Analysis of Crime Coverage in Newspapers in the United States and Other Countries from 1960 to 1989: A Review of the Literature." *Journal of Criminal Justice* 19: 67–80.

MARTIN, S. S. ET AL. (1999). "Three-Year Outcomes of Therapeutic Community Treatment for Drug-Involved Offenders in Delaware: From Prison to Work Release to Aftercare." *Prison Journal* 79: 294–320.

MARTINEZ, STEVEN M. (2004). *Testimony of FBI Assistant Director Steven M. Martinez Before the House Government Reform Committee's Subcommittee on Technology, Information Policy, Intergovernmental Relations, and the Census.* Washington, DC: U.S. Government Printing Office.

MARTINSON, R. (1974). "What Works? Questions and Answers About Prison Reforms." *The Public Interest* 35: 22–54.

MARUNA, S., AND R. IMMARIGEON (eds.). (2004). *After Crime and Punishment: Pathways to Offender Reintegration.* Portland, OR: Willan Publishing.

MARUNA, S., R. IMMARIGEON, AND T. LEBEL. (2004). "Ex-Offender Reintegration: Theory and Practice." In S. Maruna and R. Immarigeon (eds.), *After Crime and Punishment: Pathways to Offender Reintegration.* Portland, OR: Willan Publishing.

MARVELL, THOMAS B., AND CARLISLE E. MOODY JR. (1997). "The Impact of Prison Growth on Homicide." *Homicide Studies* 1: 205–233.

MAWBY, R. I., AND S. WALKLAKE. (1994). *Critical Victimology: International Perspectives.* London: Sage.

MAXWELL, GABRIELLE, AND ALLISON MORRIS. (1993). *Family, Victims and Culture: Youth Justice in New Zealand.* Wellington, NZ: Victoria University of Wellington, Social Policy Agency and Institute of Criminology.

MAXWELL, GABRIELLE, AND ALLISON MORRIS. (1997). "Family Group Conferences and Restorative Justice." *Journal on Community Corrections* 8: 37–40.

MAXWELL, GABRIELLE, ALLISON MORRIS, AND TRACY ANDERSON. (1999). *Community Panel Adult Pre-Trial Diversion: Supplementary Evaluation.* Wellington, NZ: Institute of Criminology, Victoria University of Wellington.

MAYER, G. R., AND T. W. BUTTERWORTH. (1979). "A Prevention Approach to School Violence and Vandalism: An Experimental Study." *Personnel and Guidance Journal* 57: 436–441.

McCLELLAN, A. T. ET AL. (1993). "The Effects of Psychosocial Services in Substance Abuse Treatment." *Journal of the American Medical Association* 269: 1953–1959.

McCOLD, PAUL. (2004). "Paradigm Muddle: The Threat of Restorative Justice Posed by the Merger with Community Justice." *Contemporary Justice Review* 7: 13–36.

McCOLD, PAUL, AND BENJAMIN WACHTEL. (1998). *Restorative Policing Experiment: The Bethlehem Pennsylvania Police Family Group Conferencing Project.* Pipersville, PA: Community Service Foundation.

McDEVITT, JACK. (2005). "Evaluating Project Safe Neighborhoods in the District of Massachusetts." Unpublished paper presented at the annual meeting in March of the Academy of Criminal Justice Sciences, Chicago.

McDONALD, P. P. (2002). *Managing Police Operations: Implementing the New York Crime Control Model: COMPSTAT.* Belmont, CA: Wadsworth.

McELREA, FREDERICK W. (1996). "New Zealand Youth Court: A Model for Use with Adults." In Burt Galaway and Joe Hudson (eds.), *Restorative Justice: International Perspectives.* Monsey, NY: Willow Tree Press.

McGARRELL, EDMUND. (2005). "Comprehensive Examination of the Project Safe Neighborhoods Initiative." Unpublished paper presented at the annual meeting in March of the Academy of Criminal Justice Sciences, Chicago.

McGEE, ZINA T., AND SPENCER R. BAKER. (2002). "Impact of Violence on Problem Behavior Among Adolescents." *Journal of Contemporary Criminal Justice* 18: 74–93.

McGLOTHLIN, W. H., M. D. ANGLIN, AND B. L. WILSON. (1977). *An Evaluation of the California Civil Addicts Program.* Rockville, MD: National Institute on Drug Abuse.

McHUGO, G. J. ET AL. (1995). "A Scale for Assessing the Stage of Substance Abuse Treatment in Persons with Severe Mental Illness." *Journal of Nervous and Mental Disease* 183: 762–767.

McIVOR, GILL. (1993). "Community Service by Offenders: Agency Experiences and Attitudes." *Research on Social Work Practice* 3: 66–83.

McLAUGHLIN, EUGENE, AND JOHN MUNCIE (eds.). (2001). *Controlling Crime,* 2nd ed. Thousand Oaks, CA: Sage.

McLELLAN, A. T. ET AL. (1992). "The Fifth Edition of the Addiction Severity Index." *Journal of Substance Abuse Treatment* 9: 199–213.

MEEHAN, A., AND M. PONDER. (2003a). "How Roadway Composition Matters in Analyzing Police Data on Racial Profiling." *Police Quarterly* 5: 306–333.

MEEHAN, A., AND M. PONDER. (2003b). "Race and Place: The Ecology of Racial Profiling African-American Drivers." *Justice Quarterly* 19: 399–430.

MEGARGEE, E., AND M. BOHN. (1979). *Classifying Criminal Offenders: A New System Based on the MMPI.* Beverly Hills, CA: Sage.

MELTON, A. (1995). "Indigenous Justice Systems and Tribal Society." *Judicature* 70: 126–133.

MENEZES, P. R. ET AL. (1996). "Drug and Alcohol Problems Among Individuals with Severe Mental Illness in South London." *British Journal of Psychiatry* 168: 612–619.

MERCER, RON, MURRAY BROOKS, AND PAULA TULLY BRYANT. (2000). "Global Positioning Satellite System: Tracking Offenders in Real Time." *Corrections Today* 62: 76–80.

MERRIAM-WEBSTER. (2003). *Medical Dictionary.* http://www.merriam-webster.com/cgi-bin/mwmednlm (June 6, 2003).

MESSIGNER, SHELDON L., AND P. E. JOHNSON. (1977). *California's Determinate Sentencing Statute: History and Issues.* Washington, DC: National Institute of Law Enforcement and Criminal Justice.

MESSNER, STEVEN F., AND RICHARD ROSENFELD. (1998). "Social Structure and Homicide: Theory and Research." In M. Duane Smith and Margaret A. Zahn (eds.), *Homicide: A Sourcebook of Social Research.* Thousand Oaks, CA: Sage.

MILLER, LINDA S., AND KAREN M. HESS. (1994). *Community Policing: Theory and Practice.* Minneapolis/St. Paul: West Publishing Company.

MILLER, ROD. (1997). "Inmate Labor in the 21st Century: You Ain't Seen Nothin' Yet." *American Jails* 11: 45–52.

MILLER, TED R., MARK A. COHEN, AND BRIAN WIERSEMA. (1996). *Victim Costs and Consequences: A New Look.* Washington, DC: National Institute of Justice.

MINKOFF, K., AND R. DRAKE. (1991). *Dual Diagnosis of Major Mental Illness and Substance Disorder.* San Francisco: Jossey-Bass.

MITCHELL, ROBERT C., AND RICHARD T. CARSON. (1989). *Using Surveys to Value Public Goods.* Washington, DC: Resources for the Future.

MOFFITT, T. E. (1993). "Life-Course-Persistent and Adolescent-Limited Antisocial Behavior: A Developmental Taxonomy." *Psychological Review* 100: 674–707.

MONTROSS, K. J., AND J. F. MONTROSS. (1997). "Characteristics of Adult Incarcerated Students: Effects on Instruction." *Journal of Correctional Education* 48: 179–186.

MOORE, ELIZABETH. (1996). "Doling Out Services: The Push for Privatization Is Strong, But Will Unions, Taxpayers, Stand for It?" *Newsday,* April 15, 1996: C1.

MOORE, G. E., AND D. P. MEARS. (2001). *Strong Science for Strong Practice: Linking Research to Drug Treatment in the Criminal Justice System.* Washington, DC: Urban Institute.

MORGAN, M. (1983). "Symbolic Victimization and Real-World Fear." *Human Communication Research* 9: 146–157.

MORGAN, TERRY, AND STEPHEN D. MARRS. (1998). "Redmond Washington's SMART Partnership for Police and Community Corrections." In Joan Petersilia (ed.), *Community Corrections: Probation, Parole, and Intermediate Sanctions.* New York: Oxford University Press.

MORRIS, ALLISON. (2002). "Critiquing the Critics: A Brief Response to Critics of Restorative Justice." *British Journal of Criminology* 42: 596–615.

MORRIS, ALLISON, GABRIELLE MAXWELL, AND JEREMY ROBERTSON. (1993). "Giving Victims a Voice: A New Zealand Experiment." *Howard Journal of Criminal Justice* 32: 304–321.

MORRIS, NORVAL. (1974). *The Future of Imprisonment.* Chicago: University of Chicago Press.

MORRIS, NORVAL, AND MICHAEL TONRY. (1990). *Between Prison and Probation: Intermediate Punishments in a Rational Sentencing System.* New York: Oxford University Press.

MORRIS, NORVAL, AND DAVID J. ROTHMAN. (1995). *The Practice of Punishment in Western Society.* New York: Oxford University Press.

MORRIS, S. M., H. J. STEADMAN, AND B. M. VEYSEY. (1997). "Mental Health Services in United States Jails." *Criminal Justice and Behavior* 24: 3–19.

MORRISSEY, J. ET AL. (1997). "Service System Performance and Integration: A Baseline Profile of the ACCESS Demonstration Sites: Access to Community Care and Effective Services and Supports." *Psychiatric Services* 48: 374–380.

MOYNAHAN, J. M. (1999). "Jail Officer Stress: There Is a Choice." *American Jails* 13: 71–78.

MTA COOPERATIVE GROUP. (1999a). "A 14-Month Randomized Clinical Trial of Treatment Strategies for Attention Deficit-Hyperactivity Disorder." *Archives of General Psychiatry* 56: 1073–1086.

MTA COOPERATIVE GROUP. (1999b). "Moderators and Mediators of Treatment Response for Children with Attention Deficit-Hyperactivity Disorder." *Archives of General Psychiatry* 56: 1088–1096.

MUMOLA, CHRISTOPHER. (1999). *Substance Abuse and Treatment, State and Federal Prisoners, 1997.* Washington, DC: Bureau of Justice Statistics.

MURPHY, D. (2002). "The NRF Vipassana Recidivism Study: Final Report." Unpublished manuscript.

MURPHY, GERALD R., AND MARTHA R. PLOTKIN. (2003). *Protecting Your Community from Terrorism: Strategies for Local Law Enforcement.* Washington, DC: Police Executive Research Forum.

MURPHY, H. A., J. M. HUTCHINSON, AND J. S. BAILEY. (1983). "Behavioral School Psychology Goes Outdoors: The Effect of Organized Games on Playground Aggression." *Journal of Applied Behavioral Analysis* 16: 29–35.

MUSE, F. M. (1998). "A Look at the Benefits of Individualized Instruction in a Juvenile Training School Setting: How Continuous Progress Accelerates Student Performance." *Journal of Correctional Education* 49: 73–80.

MYERS, MARTHA, AND SUSETTE M. TALARICO. (1987). *The Social Contexts of Sentencing.* New York: Springer-Verlag.

NAGIN, DANIEL S. (1998). "Criminal Deterrence Research at the Outset of the 21st Century." In Michael Tonry (ed.), *Crime and Justice: A Review of Research,* Vol. 23. Chicago: University of Chicago Press.

NAGIN, DANIEL S. (2001a). *Costs and Benefits of Crime Prevention, Crime and Justice 28.* Chicago: University of Chicago Press.

NAGIN, DANIEL S. (2001b). "Measuring Economic Benefits of Developmental Prevention Programs." In S. Welsh, D. Farrington, and L. Sherman (eds.), *Costs and Benefits of Preventing Crime.* Boulder, CO: Westview Press.

NATIONAL ADVISORY COMMISSION ON CRIMINAL JUSTICE STANDARDS AND GOALS. (1973). *Task Force Report on Juvenile Justice and Delinquency Prevention.* Washington, DC: Law Enforcement Assistance Administration.

NATIONAL ADVISORY COMMISSION ON CRIMINAL JUSTICE STANDARDS AND GOALS (1973). *Report of the National Advisory Commission on Criminal Justice Standards and Goals.* Washington, DC: U.S. Government Printing Office.

NATIONAL ASSOCIATION OF STATE MENTAL HEALTH PROGRAM DIRECTORS AND NATIONAL ASSOCIATION OF STATE ALCOHOL AND DRUG ABUSE DIRECTORS. (1999). *National Dialogue on Co-Occurring Mental Health and Substance Abuse Disorders.* Washington, DC: National Association of State Alcohol and Drug Abuse Directors.

NATIONAL CENTER FOR POLICY ANALYSIS. (1999). *Crime and Punishment in America: 1999.* Washington, DC: National Center for Policy Analysis.

NATIONAL CENTER FOR VICTIMS OF CRIME. (1987). *Victims' Rights and the Media.* Arlington, VA: National Center for Victims of Crime.

NATIONAL CENTER FOR VICTIMS OF CRIME (1994). *Recommended Guidelines for Talk Shows and Crime Victim Guests.* Arlington, VA: National Center for Victims of Crime.

NATIONAL COMMISSION ON CORRECTIONAL HEALTH CARE. (2002). *The Health Status of Soon-to-Be Released Inmates,* Vol. I. Washington, DC: Office of Justice Programs.

NATIONAL CRIME VICTIMIZATION SURVEY. (1995). *Criminal Victimization in the United States.* Washington, DC: U.S. Department of Justice, Bureau of Justice Statistics.

NATIONAL CRIMINAL JUSTICE ASSOCIATION. (1997). *Sex Offender Community Notification.* Washington, DC: National Criminal Justice Association.

NATIONAL GAINS CENTER. (1994). *Applying the Research to Improve Mental Health Services in Jails: A Workshop Summary.* Delmar, NY: National GAINS Center.

NATIONAL INSTITUTE ON DRUG ABUSE. (1999). *Principles of Drug Addiction Treatment.* http://165.112.78.61/PODATI.html (June 20, 2002).

NATIONAL INSTITUTE ON DRUG ABUSE. (2002). *National Criminal Justice Drug Abuse Treatment Services Research System.* Bethesda, MD: National Institutes of Mental Health.

NATIONAL INSTITUTE OF JUSTICE. (1997). *Three Strikes and You're Out Policies.* Washington, DC: National Institute of Justice.

NATIONAL INSTITUTE OF JUSTICE. (2000). *At a Glance: Recent Research Findings.* Rockville, MD: National Institute of Justice.

NATIONAL INSTITUTES OF MENTAL HEALTH. (2002). *RELEASE: Psychiatric Disorders Common Among Detained Youth.* http://www.nimh.nih.gov/events/prjuveniles.cfm (March 19, 2003).

NATIONAL PROBATION SERVICE. (2005). *Total Electronic Monitoring Caseloads and Latest Monthly New Starts as of 28 February 2005.* Online: http://www.probation.homeoffice.gov.uk/output/Page137asp#Statistics.

NATIONAL RESEARCH COUNCIL. (2004). *Fairness and Effectiveness in Policing.* Washington, DC: National Academy Press.

NAYLOR, K. (1983). "Positive Classroom Conditions Through the Workshop Way." Unpublished master's thesis. Provo, UT: Brigham Young University.

NEBRASKA DEPARTMENT OF CORRECTIONAL SERVICES. (1997). *Incarceration Work Camp Program Statement: Final Report.* Lincoln, NE: Nebraska Department of Correctional Services.

NEBRASKA DEPARTMENT OF CORRECTIONAL SERVICES. (2002). *Information Handbook and Offender In-House Rules.* Lincoln, NE: Nebraska Department of Correctional Services.

NEBRASKA DEPARTMENT OF CORRECTIONAL SERVICES. (2004a). *Annual Cost Report: Fiscal Year 2004.* Lincoln, NE: Nebraska Department of Correctional Services.

NEBRASKA DEPARTMENT OF CORRECTIONAL SERVICES. (2004b). *Demographics Report, Work Ethic Camp, July 2004.* Lincoln, NE: Nebraska Department of Correctional Services.

NEBRASKA DEPARTMENT OF CORRECTIONAL SERVICES. (2004c). *Director of Facilities Report.* Lincoln, NE: Nebraska Department of Correctional Services.

NELSON, C. M., R. B. RUTHERFORD, AND B. I. WOLFORD. (1996). *Comprehensive and Collaborative Systems That Work for Troubled Youth: A National Agenda.* Richmond, VA: Eastern Kentucky University.

NEVERS, DAN. (1998). "Neighborhood Probation: Adapting a 'Beat Cop' Concept in Community Supervision." In Joan Petersilia (ed.), *Community Corrections: Probation, Parole, and Intermediate Sanctions.* New York: Oxford University Press.

NEWBURN, TIM ET AL. (2002). *The Introduction of Referral Orders and the Youth Justice System.* London, UK: Home Office.

NEW YORK POLICE DEPARTMENT. (1994). *The Compstat Process.* New York: New York Police Department, Unpublished document, BM 754.

NIEMEYER, MIKE, AND DAVID SHICHOR. (1996). "A Preliminary Study of a Large Victim/Offender Reconciliation Program." *Federal Probation* 56: 30–34.

NOLAN, JAMES T., AND LAURIE SOLOMON. (1977). "An Alternative Approach in Police Patrol: The Wilmington Split-Force Experiment." *The Police Chief,* November: 58–64.

NOLEN, L. (1999). "Byline: A Day in the Life: A Unique Training Opportunity for a Correctional Educator: Blast Off to Space Camp." *Journal of Correctional Education* 50: 110–111.

NUGENT, WILLIAM ET AL. (2001). "Participation in Victim-Offender Mediation and Reoffense: Successful Replication?" *Research on Social Work Practice* 11: 5–23.

O'BRIEN, SANDRA ET AL. (2002). *Who Are We Serving and How We Are Doing: Third Evaluation Report on BARJ Programs in Vermont.* Waterbury, CT: Department of Social and Rehabilitation Services.

OFFICE OF JUVENILE JUSTICE AND DELINQUENCY PREVENTION. (1995). *Delinquency Prevention Works.* Washington, DC: Office of Juvenile Justice and Delinquency Prevention.

OFFICE OF JUVENILE JUSTICE AND DELINQUENCY PREVENTION. (1997). *Reaching Out to Youth Out of the Mainstream.* Washington, DC: Office of Juvenile Justice and Delinquency Prevention.

OFFICE OF JUVENILE JUSTICE AND DELINQUENCY PREVENTION. (1999). *Justice Department Program Focuses on Reducing Truancy: Chronic Absenteeism Predictor of Future Delinquency.* Washington, DC: Office of Juvenile Justice and Delinquency Prevention.

OFFICE FOR VICTIMS OF CRIME. (1996). *Special Report on Victims of Gang Violence.* Washington, DC: U.S. Department of Justice.

OFFICE FOR VICTIMS OF CRIME. (1998). *New Directions from the Field: Victims' Rights and Services for the 21st Century.* Washington, DC: U.S. Department of Justice.

OLDENETTEL, D., AND M. WORDES. (1999). *Community Assessment Centers.* Washington, DC: U.S. Department of Justice.

OLISS, PHILIP. (1995). "Mandatory Minimum Sentencing: Discretion, The Safety Valve, and the Sentencing Guidelines." *University of Cincinnati Law Review* 63: 1851.

OLIVER, M. B., AND B. G. ARMSTRONG. (1995). "Predictors of Viewing and Enjoyment of Reality-Based and Fictional Crime Shows." *Journalism and Mass Communication Quarterly* 72: 559–570.

OLIVERO, J. MICHAEL. (2005). "Youth at Risk and Measures of Psychopathy." Unpublished paper presented at the annual meeting in March of the Academy of Criminal Justice Sciences, Chicago.

OLSON, D. E., AND G. F. RAMKER. (2001). "Crime Does Not Pay, But Criminals May: Factors Influencing the Imposition and Collection of Probation Fees." *Justice System Journal* 22: 29–46.

OLWEUS, D. (1991). "Bully-Victim Problems Among School Children: Basic Facts and Effects of an Intervention Program." In K. Rubin and D. Pepler (eds.), *The Development and Treatment of Childhood Aggression*. Hillsdale, NJ: Erlbaum.

OSGOOD, D. WAYNE, AND A. L. ANDERSON. (2004). "Unstructured Socializing and Rates of Delinquency." *Criminology* 42: 519–549.

OSGOOD, D. WAYNE, AND JEFF M. CHAMBERS. (2000). "Social Disorganization Outside the Metropolis: An Analysis of Rural Youth Violence." *Criminology* 38: 81–115.

OSHER, F. C., AND L. L. KOFOED. (1989). "Treatment of Patients with Psychiatric and Psychoactive Substance Abuse Disorders." *Hospital and Community Psychiatry* 40: 1025–1030.

OSHER, F. C., H. J. STEADMAN, AND H. BARR. (2002). *A Best Practice Approach to Community Reentry from Jails for Inmates with Co-Occurring Disorders: The APIC Model*. Delmar, NY: The National GAINS Center.

OTTO, R. K. ET AL. (1992). "Prevalence of Mental Disorders Among Youth in the Juvenile Justice System." In J. J. Cocozza (ed.), *Responding to the Mental Health Needs of Youth in the Juvenile Justice System*. Seattle, WA: The National Coalition for the Mentally Ill in the Criminal Justice System.

OUSEY, GRAHAM C., AND MATTHEW R. LEE. (2002). "Examining the Conditional Nature of the Illicit Drug Market-Homicide Relationship: A Partial Test of the Theory of Contingent Causation." *Criminology* 40: 73–102.

OUTLAW, M. C., AND R. B. RUBACK. (1999). "Predictors and Outcomes of Victim Restitution Orders." *Justice Quarterly* 16: 847–869.

PACKER, HERBERT L. (1968). *The Limits of the Criminal Sanction*. Stanford, CA: Stanford University Press.

PALMER, T. (1974). "The Youth Authority's Community Treatment Project." *Federal Probation* 38: 3–13.

PALMER, T. (2002). *Individualized Intervention with Young Multiple Offenders*. New York: Routledge.

PAN, H. ET AL. (1993). "Some Considerations on Therapeutic Communities in Corrections." In J. A. Inciardi (ed.), *Drug Treatment and Criminal Justice*. Newbury Park, CA: Sage.

PAPY, J., AND R. NIMER. (1991). "Electronic Monitoring in Florida." *Federal Probation* 55: 31–33.

PARADE MAGAZINE. (1997). "Do You Believe What Newspeople Tell You?" Arlington, VA: Newseum and The Roper Group.

PARENT, D., AND B. SNYDER. (1999). *Police-Corrections Partnerships*. Washington, DC: U.S. Department of Justice.

PARENT, DALE ET AL. (1996). *Key Legislative Issues in Criminal Justice: The Impact of Sentencing Guidelines*. Washington, DC: National Institute of Justice.

PARKER, K. (1993). "Fear of Crime and the Likelihood of Victimization: A Bi-Ethnic Comparison." *Journal of Social Psychology* 133: 723-732.

PARKER, K., AND M. C. RAY. (1990). "Fear of Crime: An Assessment of Related Factors." *Sociological Spectrum* 10: 29–40.

PARKER, K., A. ONYEKWULUJE, AND K. MURTY. (1995). "African-Americans Attitudes Toward the Local Police: A Multivariate Analysis." *Journal of Black Studies* 25: 396–409.

PARKS, G. A., AND MARLATT, G. A. (1999). "Relapse Prevention Therapy for Substance-Abusing Offenders: A Cognitive-Behavioral Approach." In Edward Latessa (ed.), *What Works: Strategic Solutions: The International Community Corrections Association Examines Substance Abuse*. Lanham, MD: American Correctional Association.

PARRY, C. D. ET AL. (2004). "Trends in Adolescent Alcohol and Other Drug Use." *Journal of Adolescence* 27: 429–440.

PATCHIN, JUSTIN, AND SAMEER HINDUJA. (2005). "Bullies Move Beyond the Schoolyard: A Preliminary Look at Cyberbullying." Unpublished paper presented at the annual meeting in March of the Academy of Criminal Justice Sciences, Chicago.

PATTERSON, G. R., AND M. E. GUILLION. (1968). *Living with Children: New Methods for Parents and Teachers.* Champaign, IL: Research Press.

PAYNE, D. M., AND ROBERT C. TROJANOWICZ. (1985). *Performance Profiles of Foot Versus Motor Officers.* East Lansing, MI: National Neighborhood Foot Patrol Center, Michigan State University, Community Policing Series No. 6.

PEAK, KENNETH J. (1993). *Policing America: Methods, Issues, and Challenges.* Englewood Cliffs, NJ: Prentice Hall.

PEARSON, F. S., D. S. LIPTON, C. M. CLELAND, AND D. S. YEE. (2002). "The Effects of Behavior/Cognitive-Behavioral Programs on Recidivism." *Crime and Delinquency* 48: 476–496.

PELISSIER, B. ET AL. (2000). *TRIAD Drug Treatment Evaluation Project.* Washington, DC: Federal Bureau of Prisons.

PERRY, JOHN G., AND JOHN F. GORCZYK. (1997). "Restructuring Corrections: Using Market Research in Vermont." *Corrections Management Quarterly* 1: 26–35.

PETERS, R. H., AND H. A. HILLS. (1997). *Intervention Strategies for Offenders with Co-Occurring Disorders: What Works?* Delmar, NY: National GAINS Center.

PETERSILIA, JOAN. (1992). "California's Prison Policy: Causes, Costs, and Consequences." *Prison Journal* 72: 8–36.

PETERSILIA, JOAN. (1997). "Probation in the United States." In Michael Tonry (ed.), *Crime and Justice: A Review of Research,* Vol. 22. Chicago: University of Chicago Press.

PETERSILIA, JOAN. (1998). "A Decade of Experimenting with Intermediate Sanctions: What Have We Learned?" *Federal Probation* 62: 3–9.

PETERSILIA, JOAN. (1999). "Parole and Prisoner Reentry in the United States." In Michael Tonry and Joan Petersilia (eds.), *Crime and Justice: A Review of Research,* Vol. 26. Chicago: University of Chicago Press.

PETERSILIA, JOAN. (2000). "When Prisoners Return to the Community: Political, Economic and Social Consequences." *Sentencing and Corrections* 9: 1–7.

PETERSILIA, JOAN. (2002). "Community Corrections." In James Q. Wilson and Joan Petersilia (eds.), *Crime: Public Policies for Crime Control.* Oakland, CA: ICS Press.

PETERSILIA, JOAN. (2003). *When Prisoners Come Home: Parole and Prisoner Reentry.* New York: Oxford University Press.

PETERSILIA, JOAN, AND SUSAN TURNER. (1986). *Prison Versus Probation in California: Implications for Crime and Offender Recidivism.* Santa Monica, CA: RAND.

PETERSILIA, JOAN, AND SUSAN TURNER. (1992). "An Evaluation of Intensive Probation in California." *Journal of Criminal Law and Criminology* 82: 610–658.

PETERSILIA, JOAN, AND SUSAN TURNER. (1993). "Intensive Probation and Parole." In Michael Tonry (ed.), *Crime and Justice: A Review of Research,* Vol. 17. Chicago: University of Chicago Press.

PETERSON, RUTH D., AND JOHN HAGAN. (1984). "Changing Conceptions of Race: Towards an Account of Anomalous Findings of Sentencing Research." *American Sociological Review* 49: 56–70.

PETRY, N. M. (2000). "A Comprehensive Guide to the Application of Contingency Management Procedures in Clinical Settings." *Drug and Alcohol Dependence* 158: 21–22.

PETRY, N. ET AL. (2001). "Contingency Management Interventions: From Research to Practice." *American Journal of Psychiatry* 158: 1–9.

PHILADELPHIA POLICE DEPARTMENT. (2003). *The COMPSTAT Process.* Philadelphia: Philadelphia Police Department.

PHILLIPS, DRETHA M. (1998). *Community Notification as Viewed by Washington's Citizens.* Pullman, WA: Washington State Institute for Public Policy.

PIEHL, ANNE MORRISON. (2002). *From Cell to Stress: A Plan to Supervise Inmates After Release.* Boston: Massachusetts Institute for a New Commonwealth.

PIEHL, ANNE MORRISON, AND JOHN J. DiIULIO JR. (1995). " 'Does Prison Pay?' Revisited: Returning to the Crime Scene." *The Bookings Review* (Winter): 21–25.

PIEHL, ANNE MORRISON, AND STEFAN F. LOBUGLIO. (2005). "Does Supervision Matter?" In Jeremy Travis and Christy Visher (eds.), *Prisoner Reentry and Public Safety in America.* New York: Cambridge University Press.

PIEHL, ANNE MORRISON ET AL. (2003). "Testing for Structural Breaks in the Evaluation of Programs." *Review of Economics and Statistics* 85: 550–558.

POLLOCK, JOHN, AND JAMES MAY. (2002). "Authentication Technology: Identity Theft and Account Takeover." *FBI Law Enforcement Bulletin* (June): 1–4.

POWELL, T., J. BUSH, AND B. BILODEAU. (2001). "Vermont's Cognitive Self-Change Program: A 15-Year Review." *Corrections Today* 63: 116–120.

POWELL, T. A., J. C. HOLT, AND K. M. FONDARCARO. (1997). "The Prevalence of Mental Illness Among Inmates in a Rural State." *Law and Human Behavior* 21: 427–438.

PRANIS, KAY. (1998). "Promising Practices in Community Justice: Restorative Justice." In American Probation and Parole Association (ed.), *Community Justice: Concepts and Strategies.* Lexington, KY: American Probation and Parole Association.

PRENDERGAST, M. L., M. D. ANGLIN, AND J. WELLISCH. (1995). "Treatment for Drug-Abusing Offenders Under Community Supervision." *Federal Probation* 59: 66–75.

PRENDERGAST, M. L., AND W. M. BURDON. (2001). "Integrated Systems of Care for Substance Abusing Offenders." In C. Leukefield, F. Tims, and D. Farabee (eds.), *Treatment of Drug Offenders: Policies and Issues.* New York: Springer.

PRENDERGAST, M. L., J. WELLISCH, AND M. WONG. (1996). "Residential Treatment for Women Parolees Following Prison Drug Treatment: Treatment Experiences, Needs and Services." *Prison Journal* 76: 253–274.

PRENDERGAST, M. L. ET AL. (1999). *A Process Evaluation of the Forever Free Substance Abuse Treatment Program.* Los Angeles: Drug Abuse Research Center.

PRENTKY, ROBERT A., RAYMOND A. KNIGHT, AUSTIN F. S. LEE, AND DAVID D. CERCE. (1995). "Predictive Validity of Lifestyle Impulsivity for Rapists." *Criminal Justice and Behavior* 22: 106–128.

PRENTKY, ROBERT A., RAYMOND A. KNIGHT, AND AUSTIN F. S. LEE. (1997). "Risk Factors Associated with Recidivism Among Extrafamilial Child Molesters." *Journal of Consulting and Clinical Psychology* 65: 141–149.

PRESIDENT'S TASK FORCE ON VICTIMS OF CRIME. (1982). *Final Report.* Washington, DC: President's Task Force on Victims of Crime.

PRESSER, LOIS, AND PATRICIA VAN VOORHIS. (2002). "Values and Evaluations: Assessing Processes and Outcomes of Restorative Justice Programs." *Crime and Delinquency* 48: 162–188.

PROJECT SAFE NEIGHBORHOODS. (2005). "Project Safe Neighborhoods." Unpublished paper presented at the annual meeting in March of the Academy of Criminal Justice Sciences, Chicago.

PROPORTION, F. J., E. A. FABIAN, AND D. ROBINSON. (1991). *Focusing on Successful Reintegration: Cognitive Skills Training for Offenders.* Ottawa, CAN: Correctional Service of Canada, Research and Statistics Branch.

PURKEY, W. W. (1970). *Self-Concept and School Achievement.* Englewood Cliffs, NJ: Prentice Hall.

QUAY, H. C. (1983). *Technical Manual for the Behavioral Classification System for Adult Offenders.* Washington, DC: U.S. Department of Justice.

QUAY, H. C., AND L. PARSONS. (1972). *The Differential Behavioral Classification of the Juvenile Offender.* Washington, DC: U.S. Department of Justice.

QUILLEN, CHRIS. (2002). "Mass Casualty Bombings Chronology." *Studies in Conflict and Terrorism* 25: 293–302.

QUINSEY, VERNON L. (1984). "Sexual Aggression: Studies of Offenders Against Women." In David N. Weisstub (ed.), *Law and Mental Health: International Perspectives,* Vol. 1. New York: Pergamon.

QUINSEY, VERNON L., ARUNIMA KHANNA, AND P. BRUCE MALCOLM. (1998). "A Retrospective Evaluation of the Regional Center Sex Offender Treatment Program." *Journal of Interpersonal Violence* 13: 621–644.

QUINSEY, VERNON L., MARNIE E. RICE, AND GRANT T. HARRIS. (1995). "Actuarial Prediction of Sexual Recidivism." *Journal of Interpersonal Violence* 10: 85–105.

RAND CORPORATION. (2003). "Prisoner Reentry: What Are the Public Health Challenges?" *RAND Research Brief.* Santa Monica, CA: RAND, RB-6013-PSJ.

RADLOFF, LENORE S. (1977). "The CES-D Scale: A Self-Report Depression Scale for Research in the General Population." *Applied Psychological Measurement* 1: 385–401.

RAPHAEL, STEVEN, AND JENS LUDWIG. (2003). "Prison Sentence Enhancements: The Case of Project Exile." In Jens Ludwig and Philip J. Cook (eds.), *Evaluating Gun Policy: Effects of Crime and Violence.* Washington, DC: Brookings Institution Press.

RAUDENBUSH, S.W., AND A.S. BRYK (2002). *Hierarchical Linear Models 2/e.* Thousand Oaks, CA: Sage.

REDONDO, SANTIAGO, JULIO SANCHEZ-MECA, AND VINCENTE GARRIDO. (1999). "The Influence of Treatment Programs on the Recidivism of Juveniles and Adult Offenders." *Psychology, Crime, and Law* 5: 251–278.

REENTRY POLICY COUNCIL. (2004). *Charting the Safe and Successful Return of Prisoners to the Community.* Lexington, KY: Council of State Governments.

REGAN, CLAIRE. (2004). "UDA Blamed for Hoax Alerts." *Belfast Telegraph,* January 16, 2004.

REIMAN, J. (1998). *The Rich Get Richer and the Poor Get Prison: Ideology, Class, and Criminal Justice.* Boston: Allyn and Bacon.

REINER, R. (1985). *The Politics of the Police.* New York: St. Martin's Press.

REINVENTING PROBATION COUNCIL. (2000). *Transforming Probation Through Leadership: The "Broken Windows" Model.* New York: Center for Civic Innovation at the Manhattan Institute.

REITH, M. (1999). "Viewing Crime Drama and Authoritarian Aggression: An Investigation of the Relationship Between Crime Viewing, Fear and Aggression." *Journal of Broadcasting and Electronic Media* 43: 211–221.

REITZ, KEVIN. (2004). "Questioning the Conventional Wisdom of Parole Release Authority." In Michael Tonry (ed.), *The Future of Imprisonment in the 21st Century.* New York: Oxford University Press.

RENZEMA, M., AND E. MAYO-WILSON. (2005). "Can Electronic Monitoring Reduce Crime for Moderate to High-Risk Offenders?" *Journal of Experimental Criminology* 1: 1–23.

RICE, J., AND B. ANDERSON. (1990). "Gerbner's 'Cultivation Hypothesis' Revisited: A Cultivation Analysis of Data from the Media Crime Prevention Campaign in the United States, 1980." Unpublished paper presented at the American Sociological Association, Washington, D.C (August).

RICE, MARNIE E., VERNON L. QUINSEY, AND GRANT T. HARRIS. (1991). "Sexual Recidivism Among Child Molesters Released from a Maximum Security Psychiatric Institution." *Journal of Consulting and Clinical Psychology* 59: 381–386.

RICHARDSON, JAMES F. (1970). *The New York Police: Colonial Times to 1901.* New York: Oxford University Press.

RIFKIN, A. ET AL. (1997). "Lithium Treatment of Conduct Disorders in Adolescents." *American Journal of Psychiatry* 154: 554–555.

RIVERS, J., AND T. TROTTI. (1989). *South Carolina Delinquent Males: A Follow-Up into Adult Corrections.* Columbia, SC: South Carolina Department of Youth Services.

ROBERT, PHILIPPE. (2003). "The Evaluation of Prevention Policies." *European Journal of Crime, Criminal Law, and Criminal Justice* 11: 114–130.

ROBERTS, J., AND A. DOOB (1986). "Public Estimates of Recidivism Rates: Consequences of a Criminal Stereotype." *Canadian Journal of Criminology* 28: 229–241.

ROBERTS, L. J., A. SHANER, AND T. A. ECKMAN. (1999). *Overcoming Addictions: Skills Training for People with Schizophrenia.* New York: W.W. Norton and Company.

ROBINS, L., L. COTTLER, K. BUCHOLZ, AND W. COMPTON. (1995). *Diagnostic Interview Schedule for DSM-IV (DIS-IV).* Rockville, MD: National Institute on Mental Health.

ROBINSON, D. (1995). *The Impact of Cognitive Skills Training on Post-Release Recidivism Among Canadian Federal Prisoners.* Ottawa, CAN: Correctional Service of Canada, Research Division.

ROCHE, DECLAN. (2003). *Accountability in Restorative Justice.* New York: Oxford University Press.

ROSE, DINA R., AND TODD R. CLEAR. (1998). "Incarceration, Social Capital, and Crime: Implications for Social Disorganization Theory." *Criminology* 36: 441–479.

ROSE, S. J., A. ZWEBEN, AND V. STOFFEL. (1999). "Interfaces Between Substance Abuse Treatment and Other Health and Social Systems." In B. S. McCrady and E. B. Epstein (eds.), *Addictions: A Comprehensive Guidebook.* New York: Oxford Publishing Company.

ROSEBROUGH, T. R. (1999). "Teaching to the Brain in the College Classroom." *The Teaching Professor* 13: 2–3.

ROSENBERG, M. (1965). *Society and the Adolescent Self-Image.* Princeton, NJ: Princeton University Press.

ROSENFELD, RICHARD. (2002). "The Crime Decline in Context." *Contexts* 1: 25–34.

ROSENFELD, RICHARD. (2004). "The Case of the Unsolved Crime Decline." *Scientific American* 290: 68–77.

ROSHIER, B. (1973). "The Selection of Crime News by the Press." In S. Cohen and J. Young (eds.), *The Manufacture of News.* Beverly Hills, CA: Sage.

ROSICA, B. A., AND C. M. WALL. (1997). "VisionQuest: A New Direction in Education Leadership for Teaching Troubled Youth." *Journal of Correctional Education* 48: 187–191.

ROSS, DAVID H. (1995). "The Clutter in California Criminal Law." *California Journal* (October): 46–59.

ROSS, R. R., AND E. A. FABIANO. (1985). *Time to Think: A Cognitive Model of Delinquency Prevention and Offender Rehabilitation.* Johnson City, TN: Institute of Social Sciences and Arts.

ROTHMAN, DAVID J. (1980). *Conscience and Convenience: The Asylum and Its Alternatives in Progressive America.* Boston: Little, Brown.

ROUNTREE, PAMELA W., KENNETH C. LAND, AND TERANCE MIETHE. (1994). "Macro-Micro Integration in the Study of Victimization: A Hierarchical Logistic Model Analysis Across Seattle Neighborhoods." *Criminology* 32: 387–414.

ROY, S. (1993). "Two Types of Juvenile Restitution Programs in Two Midwestern Counties: A Comparative Study." *Federal Probation* 57: 774–802.

ROY, S. (1997). "Five Years of Electronic Monitoring of Adults and Juveniles in Lake County, Indiana: A Comparative Study on Factors Related to Failure." *Journal of Crime and Justice* 20: 141–160.

RUBACK, R. B., J. N. SHAFFER, AND M. A. LOGUE. (2004). "The Imposition and Effects of Restitution in Pennsylvania: Effects of Size of County and Specialized Collection Units." *Crime and Delinquency* 50: 168–188.

RUFFIN, RUSSELL. (1999). "Lakewood Police Utilize Private Security." *Law Enforcement Television News.* Denver, CO: Cherokee Productions.

SACCO, V. (1995). "Media Constructions of Crime." *Annals of the American Academy of Political and Social Science* 539: 141–154.

SACCO, V., AND B. FAIR. (1988). "Images of Legal Control: Crime News and the Process of Organizational Legitimation." *Canadian Journal of Communication* 32: 114–123.

SACKS, S., G. DELEON, A. L. BERNHARDT, AND J. Y. SACKS. (1998). *Modified Therapeutic Community for Homeless Mentally Ill Chemical Abusers: Treatment Manual.* New York: National Development and Research Institutes, Inc.

SACKS, S., AND J. Y. SACKS. (2003). "Modified TC for MICA Inmates in Correctional Settings: A Program Description." *Corrections Today* 65: 41–45.

SACKS, S., J. Y. SACKS, G. DELEON, A. L. BERNHARDT, AND G. L. STAINES. (1997). *Modified Therapeutic Community for Mentally Ill Chemical Abusers.* (In *Federal Probation* 67, No. 2, p. 38.)

SACKS, S. ET AL. (2003). *Modified Therapeutic Community for Homeless Mentally Ill Chemical Abusers.* New York: National Development and Research Institutes.

SAMPLE, LISA L. (2001). "The Social Construction of a Sexual Offender." Ph.D. dissertation. Unpublished.

SAMPSON, ROBERT J., AND W. BYRON GROVES. (1989). "Community Structure and Crime: Testing Social Disorganization Theory." *American Journal of Sociology* 94: 774–802.

SAMPSON, ROBERT J., AND JOHN H. LAUB. (1993). *Crime in the Making: Pathways and Turning Points Through Life.* Cambridge, MA: Harvard University Press.

SAMPSON, ROBERT J., AND JOHN H. LAUB. (1993). "Structural Variations in Juvenile Court Processing: Inequality, the Underclass, and Social Control." *Law and Society Review* 27: 285–311.

SAMPSON, ROBERT J., S. RAUDENBUSH, AND F. EARLS. (1997). "Neighborhoods and Violent Crime." *Science* 227: 918–924.

SANBORN, JOSEPH B. (1994). "Remnants of *Parens Patriae* in the Adjudicatory Hearing: Is a Fair Trial Possible in Juvenile Court?" *Crime and Delinquency* 40: 599–615.

SAN MATEO COUNTY. (2005). *Electronic Monitoring Program.* San Mateo, CA: Sheriff's Office, Custody Division, San Mateo County.

SANOW, ED. (2003). "COMPSTAT, the Real Cops on the Dots." *Law and Order,* August: 4.

SAPSFORD, ROGER J. (1998). "Further Research Applications of the 'Parole Prediction Index.' " *International Journal of Criminology and Penology* 6: 247–254.

SARKAR, DIBYA. (2002). "Homeland Security Focuses Coordination." http://www.cw.com/fdw/articles/2002/0401/news-home-04-01-02.asp.

SAXON, A. J., AND D. A. CALSYN. (1995). "Effects of Psychiatric Care for Dual Diagnosis Patients Treated in a Drug Dependence Clinic." *Journal of Consulting and Clinical Psychology* 63: 1022–1031.

SCHMERMANN, SERGE (1997). "Bombings in Jerusalem: The Overview." *New York Times,* September 7, 1997:A1.

SCHIFF, MARA, GORDON BAZEMORE, AND CARSTEN ERBE. (2001). *Tracking Restorative Justice Decision-Making in the Response to Youth Crime: The Prevalence of Youth Conferencing in the United States.* Ft. Lauderdale, FL: The Community Justice Institute, Florida Atlantic University.

SCHMIDT, A. K. (1988). *The Use of Electronic Monitoring by Criminal Justice Agencies.* Washington, DC: National Institute of Justice.

SCHOENWALD, S. ET AL. (2000). "Multisystemic Therapy Versus Hospitalization for Crisis Stabilization of Youth: Placement Outcomes 4 Months Post-Referral." *Mental Health Services Research* 2: 3–12.

SCHUESSLER, K. F., AND D. R. CRESSEY. (1950). "Personality Characteristics of Criminals." *American Journal of Sociology* 55: 476–484.

SCHUMACHER, M., AND G. KURZ. (1999). *The 8% Solution: Preventing Serious, Repeat Juvenile Crime.* Thousand Oaks, CA: Sage.

SCHWITZGEBEL, R. K. (1965). *Streetcorner Research: An Experimental Approach to the Juvenile Delinquent.* Cambridge, MA: Harvard University Press.

SCHWITZGEBEL, R. L. (1969). "A Belt from Big Brother." *Psychology Today* 2: 45–47.

SCHWITZGEBEL, R. L., AND R. M. BIRD. (1970). "Sociotechnical Design Factors in Remote Instrumentation with Humans in Natural Environments." *Behavior Research Methods and Instrumentation* 2: 99–105.

SCHWITZGEBEL, R. K. ET AL. (1964). "A Program of Research in Behavioral Electronics." *Behavioral Science* 9: 233–238.

SECRET, PHILIP E., AND JAMES B. JOHNSON. (1997). "The Effect of Race on Juvenile Justice Decision Making in Nebraska: Detention, Adjudication, and Disposition, 1988–1993." *Justice Quarterly* 14: 445–478.

SEIFFERT, J. M. (1984). "Alexandria's Citizen Awareness Program." *FBI Law Enforcement Bulletin* 53: 16–20.

SELLIN, THORSTEN, AND MARVIN E. WOLFGANG. (1964). *The Measurement of Delinquency.* New York: Wiley.

SEPER, JERRY. (2000). "Justice Sets Up Web Site to Combat Internet Crimes." *Washington Times,* May 9, 2000: A6.

SEYMOUR, A., AND L. LOWRANCE. (1988). *Crime Victims and the News Media.* Ft. Worth, TX: National Center for Victims of Crime.

SHERMAN, LAWRENCE W., AND JOHN E. ECK. (2002). "Policing for Crime Prevention." In Lawrence W. Sherman, David P. Farrington, and Brandon C. Welsh (eds.), *Evidence-Based Crime Prevention.* New York: Routledge.

SHIELDS, PATRICIA M., CHARLES W. CHAPMAN, AND DAVID R. WINGARD. (1983). "Using Volunteers in Adult Probation." *Federal Probation* 47: 57–64.

SHOVER, NEAL, AND WERNER J. EINSTADTER. (1988). *Analyzing American Corrections.* Belmont, CA: Wadsworth Publishing Company.

SHRAWDER, J. (1999). "Secrets of Success—Tough Questions." *Teaching for Success: The Journal of Critical Success Factors: Teaching* 11: 1.

SHUFORD, J. A., AND H. T. SPENCER. (1999). "Experiential Conflict Resolution for Prison Staff." *Corrections Today* 61: 96–104, 156.

SIMPSON, D. DWAYNE. (2001). "Modeling Treatment Process and Outcomes." *Addiction* 96: 207–211.

SIMPSON, D. DWAYNE, AND H. J. FRIEND. (1998). "Legal Status and Long-Term Outcomes for Addicts in the DARP Follow-Up Project." In C. G. Leukefeld and F. M. Tims (eds.), *Compulsory Treatment of Drug Abuse: Research and Clinical Practice.* Washington, DC: U.S. Government Printing Office.

SIMPSON, D. DWAYNE, AND K. KNIGHT. (2001). "The TCU Model of Treatment Process and Outcomes in Correctional Settings." *Offender Substance Abuse Report* 1: 51–53, 58.

SIPE, RON, ERIC L. JENSEN, AND RONALD S. EVERETT. (1998). "Adolescent Sexual Offenders Grow Up: Recidivism in Young Adulthood." *Criminal Justice and Behavior* 25: 109–124.

SKINNER, B. F. (1969). *Contingencies of Reinforcement: A Theoretical Analysis.* New York: Appleton-Century-Crofts.

SKOGAN, W., AND M. MAXFIELD. (1981). *Coping with Crime.* Beverly Hills, CA: Sage.

"SMALLER CLASSES INCREASE POOR STUDENTS' TEST SCORES." (1999). *Adult Basic Education News in Wisconsin.*

SMITH, B., R.C. DAVIS, AND S.W. HILLENBRAND (1989). *Improving Enforcement of Court-Ordered Restitution.* Washington, DC: State Justice Institute.

SMITH, P., C. GOGGIN, AND P. GENDREAU. (2002). *The Effects of Prison Sentences and Intermediate Sanctions on Recidivism: General Effects and Individual Differences.* Ottawa, Canada: Public Works and Government Services, Solicitor General's Office.

SMITH, R. L., AND R. W. TAYLOR. (1985). "A Return to Neighborhood Policing: The Tampa, Florida Experience." *Police Chief* 52: 39–44.

SMITH, WANTLAND J. (1991). "Private Sector Development: A Winning Strategy for New Police Stations, Sheriff's Stations, and Jails." *The Police Chief* (August): 29–33.

SOLNIT, A. J. (2000). *The Cost and Effectiveness of Jail Diversion: A Report to the Joint Standing Committee of the General Assembly.* Hartford, CT: Connecticut's Department of Mental Health and Addiction Services.

SOLOMON, AMY L., VERA KACHNOWSKI, AND AVI BHATI. (2005). *Does Parole Work? Analyzing the Impact of Postprison Supervision on Rearrest Outcomes.* Washington, DC: Urban Institute.

SOURCEBOOK OF CRIMINAL JUSTICE STATISTICS ONLINE. (2005). "Persons Under Jail Supervision." Online: http://www.albany.edu/sourcebook/wk1/1614.wk1.

SPARKS, R., A. BOTTOMS, AND W. HAY. (1996). *Prisoners and the Problem of Order.* Oxford: Clarendon Press.

SPAULDING, TOM. (1999). "State Wants DNA Samples from Convicted Burglars." *Sarasota Herald Tribune*, November 16, 1999: 1B.

SPELMAN, WILLIAM. (2000). "What Recent Studies Do (and Don't) Tell Us About Imprisonment and Crime." In Michael Tonry (ed.), *Crime and Justice: A Review of Research,* Vol. 27. Chicago: University of Chicago Press.

SPIEGLER, MICHAEL D., AND DAVID C. GUEVREMONT. (1998). *Contemporary Behavior Therapy,* 3rd ed. Pacific Grove, CA: Brooks/Cole.

SPIELBERGER, C. D. (1985). "Anxiety, Cognition, and Affect: A State-Trait Perspective." In A. H. T. J. Maser (ed.), *Anxiety and the Anxiety Disorders.* Hillsdale, NJ: Lawrence Erlbaum Associates Publishers.

STANCHFIELD, P. (2001). "Clarifying the Therapist's Role in the Treatment of the Resistant Sex Offender." In B. K. Welo (ed.), *Tough Customers: Counseling Unwilling Clients.* Lanham, MD: American Correctional Association.

STEADMAN, HENRY J. ET AL. (1999). "Comparing Outcomes for Diverted and Nondiverted Jail Detainees with Mental Illness." *Law and Human Behavior* 23: 615–627.

STEADMAN, H.J. ET AL. (1999). *Law and Psychiatry: Mental Health Courts.* Marion County, IN: Mental Health Diversion Program.

STEELE, P. A., J. AUSTIN, AND B. KRISBERG. (1989). *Unlocking Juvenile Corrections: Evaluating the Massachusetts Department of Youth Services: Final Report.* Washington, DC: National Institute of Justice.

STEINBERG, ANNIE, JANE BROOKS, AND TARIQ REMTULLA. (2003). "Youth Hate Crimes: Identification, Prevention, and Intervention." *American Journal of Psychiatry* 160: 979–989.

STEURER, S. (2000). *Best Practices: The Correctional Education Program.* Baltimore: Maryland State Department of Education.

STEVENS, AARON P. (2001). "Arresting Crime: Expanding the Scope of DNA Databases in America." *Texas Law Review* 79: 921–961.

STINCHCOMB, JEANNE B. (2001). "Using Logic Modeling to Focus Evaluation Efforts: Translating Operational Theories into Practice Measures." *Journal of Offender Rehabilitation* 33: 58.

STINCHCOMB, JEANNE B. (2005). *Corrections: Yesterday, Today, Tomorrow.* Lanham, MD: American Correctional Association.

ST. LOUIS POST-DISPATCH. (June 30, 1992). "Guidelines on Privacy Issues," B1.

STOUTHAMER-LOEBER, M., R. LOEBER, AND C. THOMAS. (1992). "Caretakers Seeking Help for Boys with Disruptive and Delinquent Child Behavior." *Comprehensive Mental Health Care* 2: 159–178.

STRANG, H. (2002). *Victim Participation in Restorative Justice.* London: Oxford University Press.

STRANG, HEATHER ET AL. (1999). *Experiments in Restorative Policing: A Progress Report on the Canberra Reintegrative Shaming Experiments (RISE).* Canberra, AUS: Australian National University.

STUART LITTLE. (1999). Culver City, CA: Columbia Pictures, Columbia TriStar Home Video.

STUMPF, HARRY P., AND JOHN H. CULVER. (1992). *The Politics of State Courts.* New York: Longman.

STUMPF, HARRY P., AND JOHN H. CULVER. (1998). *American Judicial Politics,* 2nd ed. Upper Saddle River, NJ: Prentice Hall.

STUTLER, THOMAS R. (2000). "Steadling Secrets Solved: Examining the Economic Espionage Act of 1996." *FBI Law Enforcement Bulletin* (November): 11–16.

SUGG, D., L. MOORE, AND P. HOWARD. (2001). "Electronic Monitoring and Offending Behavior: Reconviction Results for the Second Year of Trials of Curfew Orders." *Findings.* London, UK: Research, Development, and Statistics Directorate, #141, Home Office.

SURETTE, R. (1990). *The Media and Criminal Justice Policy: Recent Research and Social Effects.* Springfield, IL: Charles C Thomas.

SURETTE, R. (1998). *Media, Crime, and Criminal Justice: Images and Realities,* 2nd ed. Belmont, CA: Wadsworth Publishing Company.

SZOSTAK, E. W., AND J. MARROW. (2001). "From Conflict to Mutual Respect: Programs for Offenders with Mental Illness and/or Substance Use Disorders in Albany, New York." *American Jails,* September/October 15: 42–47.

TAKAYAMA, J., A. BERGMAN, AND F. CONNELL. (1994). "Children in Foster Care in the State of Washington: Health Care Utilization and Expenditures." *Journal of the American Medical Association* 271: 1850–1855.

TAXMAN, F. S. (1998). *Reducing Recidivism Through a Seamless System of Care: Components of Effective Treatment, Supervision, and Transition Services in the Community.* Greenbelt, MD: University of Maryland.

TAXMAN, F. S. (2000). "Unraveling 'What Works' for Offenders in Substance Abuse Treatment Services." *National Drug Court Institute Review* 2: 93–133.

TAXMAN, F. S., J. BYRNE, AND D. YOUNG. (2002). *Targeting for Reentry: Matching Needs and Services to Maximize Public Safety.* Washington, DC: National Institute of Justice.

TAXMAN, F. S., D. YOUNG, AND J. M. BYRNE. (2003a). *From Prison Safety to Public Safety: Best Practices in Offender Reentry.* Washington, DC: National Institute of Justice.

TAXMAN, F. S., D. YOUNG, AND J. M. BYRNE. (2003b). *Offender's Views of Reentry: Implications for Processes, Programs, and Services.* Washington, DC: National Institute of Justice.

TAXMAN, FAYE, DOUGLAS YOUNG, JAMES BYRNE, ALEXANDER HOLSINGER, AND DONALD ANSPACH. (2002). *From Prison to Public Safety: Innovations in Offender Reentry.* Washington, DC: National Institute of Justice.

TAYLOR, BRUCE G. ET AL. (2001). "The Validity of Adult Arrestee Self-Reports of Crack Cocaine Use." *American Journal of Drug and Alcohol Abuse* 27: 399–419.

TAYLOR, BRUCE G. ET AL. (2001). *ADAM Preliminary 2000 Findings on Drug Use and Drug Markets.* Washington, DC: U.S. Department of Justice.

TENNENBAUM, D. J. (1977). "Personality and Criminality: A Summary and Implications of the Literature." *Journal of Criminal Justice* 5: 225–235.

THE JUDGE DAVID L. BAZELON CENTER FOR MENTAL HEALTH LAW. (2003). *Suspending Disbelief: Moving Beyond Punishment to Promote Effective Interventions for Children with Mental or Emotional Disorders.* Washington, DC: Bazelon Center for Mental Health Law.

THE TIMES. (1993). "Hijacked Drivers Chose to Risk Death." April 27, 1993.

THOMAS, C. W., AND J. M. HYMAN. (1977). "Perceptions of Crime, Fear of Victimization, and Public Perceptions of Police Performance." *Journal of Political Science and Administration* 5: 305–317.

THOMASON, T., AND A. BABBILI. (1988). *American Media and Crime Victims: Covering Private Individuals in the Public Spotlight.* Ft. Worth, TX: Texas Christian University.

TOOMBS, THOMAS G. (1995). "Monitoring and Controlling Criminal Offenders Using the Satellite Global Positioning System Coupled to Surgically Implanted Transponders." *Criminal Justice Policy Review* 7: 341–346.

TOWNSHIP OF EVESHAM, NJ POLICE DEPARTMENT. (2001). *Megan's Law: A Message from the Attorney General.* http://www.twp.evesham.nj.us/eve_pd_ml.hun (February 21, 2001).

TRAVIS, JEREMY. (2000). *But They All Come Back: Rethinking Prisoner Reentry.* Washington, DC: U.S. Department of Justice, Office of Justice Programs.

TRAVIS, JEREMY, AND FRANCIS T. CULLEN (1994). "Radical Non-Intervention: The Myth of Doing No Harm." *Federal Probation* 48: 29–32.

TRAVIS, JEREMY, AND S. LAWRENCE. (2002). *Beyond the Prison Gates: The State of Parole in America.* Washington, DC: The Urban Institute.

TRAVIS, JEREMY, AMY SOLOMON, AND MICHELLE WAUL. (2001). *From Prison to Home: The Dimensions and Consequences of Prisoner Reentry.* Washington, DC: The Urban Institute.

TREMBLAY, R. E. ET AL. (1990). "The Montreal Prevention Experiment: School Adjustment and Self-Reported Delinquency after Three Years of Follow-Up." Unpublished paper presented at the annual meeting in November of the American Society of Criminology. Baltimore, MD.

TROJANOWICZ, ROBERT C., AND DENNIS W. BANAS. (1985a). *Job Satisfaction: A Comparison of Foot Patrol Versus Motor Patrol Officers.* East Lansing, MI: National Neighborhood Foot Patrol Center, Michigan State University, Community Policing Series No. 2.

TROJANOWICZ, ROBERT C., AND DENNIS W. BANAS. (1985b). *Perceptions of Safety: A Comparison of Foot Patrol Versus Motor Patrol Officers.* East Lansing, MI: National Neighborhood Foot Patrol Center, Michigan State University.

TROJANOWICZ, ROBERT C., AND MARK H. MOORE. (1988). *The Meaning of Community in Community Policing.* East Lansing, MI: National Neighborhood Foot Patrol Center.

TRULSON, CHAD R., JAMES W. MARQUART, AND JANET MULLINGS. (2005). "Towards an Understanding of Juvenile Persistence in the Transition to Young Adulthood." Unpublished paper presented at the annual meeting in March of the Academy of Criminal Justice Sciences, Chicago.

TSOUDIS, OLGA. (2000). "Relations of Affect Control Theory to the Sentencing of Criminals." *Journal of Social Psychology* (August) 140: 473–485.

TURNER, MICHAEL G. ET AL. (1995). "Three Strikes and You're Out Legislation: A National Assessment." *Federal Probation* 59: 16–35.

UMBREIT, MARK S. (1993). *How to Increase Referrals to Victim-Offender Mediation Programs.* Waterloo, CAN: Fund for Dispute Resolution.

UMBREIT, MARK S. (1994). *Victim Meets Offender: The Impact of Restorative Justice and Mediation.* Monsey, NY: Willow Tree Press.

UMBREIT, MARK S. (1995). "Holding Juvenile Offenders Accountable: A Restorative Justice Perspective." *Juvenile and Family Court Journal* 46: 31–42.

UMBREIT, MARK S. (2000). *The Restorative Justice and Mediation Collection: Executive Summary.* Washington, DC: Office for Victims of Crime.

UMBREIT, MARK S. (2003). *Facing Violence: The Path of Restorative Justice and Dialogue.* Monsey, NY: Criminal Justice Press.

UMBREIT, MARK S., AND ROBERT COATES. (1993). "Cross-Site Analysis of Victim-Offender Mediation in Four States." *Crime and Delinquency* 39: 565–585.

UMBREIT, MARK S., ROBERT COATES, AND BETTY VOS. (2001). "The Impact of Victim-Offender Mediation: Two Decades of Research." *Federal Probation* 60: 24–29.

UMBREIT, MARK S., AND SUSAN STACEY. (1996). "Family Group Conferencing Comes to the U.S.: A Comparison with Victim-Offender Mediation." *Juvenile and Family Court Journal* 47: 29–38.

UMBREIT, MARK S., AND HOWARD ZEHR. (1996). "Restorative Family Group Conferences: Differing Models and Guidelines for Practice." *Federal Probation* 65: 29–33.

UNIFORM CRIME REPORT. (1996). Washington, DC: Federal Bureau of Investigation.

U.S. BUREAU OF THE CENSUS (2000). *2000 Census.* Washington, DC: U.S. Government Printing Office.

U.S. DEPARTMENT OF HEALTH AND HUMAN SERVICES. (1999). *Strategies for Integrating Substance Abuse Treatment and the Juvenile Justice System: A Practice Guide.* Washington, DC: U.S. Department of Health and Human Services.

U.S. DEPARTMENT OF JUSTICE. (1998). *Project RIO.* Washington, DC: U.S. Department of Justice.

U.S. DEPARTMENT OF JUSTICE. (2006). *Persons Under Correctional Supervision 2005.* Washington, DC: U.S. Department of Justice.

U.S. DEPARTMENT OF STATE. (2003). *Patterns of Global Terrorism.* Washington, DC: U.S. Department of State.

U.S. FEDERAL TRADE COMMISSION. (2003). *FTC Releases Top 10 Consumer Complaint Categories in 2003.* Washington, DC: U.S. Federal Trade Commission.

U.S. GENERAL ACCOUNTING OFFICE. (2004). *High-Performing Organizations: Metrics, Means, and Mechanisms for Achieving High Performance in the 21st Century Management Environment.* Washington, DC: U.S. General Accounting Office.

UNITES STATES SENTENCING COMMISSION. (1984). *United States Sentencing Commission Guidelines.* Washington, DC: United States Sentencing Commission.

VANDERZELL, JOHN H. (1966). "The Jury as a Community Cross-Section." *The Western Political Quarterly* 19: 136–149.

VAN SOEST, DOROTHY ET AL. (2003). "Different Paths to Death Row: A Comparison of Men Who Committed Heinous and Less Heinous Crimes." *Violence and Victims* 18: 15–33.

VAN STELLE, KIT R., AND D. PAUL MOBERG. (2000). *Outcome Evaluation of the Wisconsin Residential Substance Abuse Treatment Program: The Mental Illness-Chemical Abuse (MICA) Program at Oshkosh Correctional Institution, 1998–2000.* Madison, WI: Department of Preventive Medicine Center for Health Policy and Program Evaluation, University of Wisconsin Medical School.

VAN STELLE, KIT R., AND D. PAUL MOBERG (2000). "Reducing Offender Drug Use." *NIJ Journal* (July): 21–23.

VAN VOORHIS, P. (1994). *Psychological Classification of the Adult Male Prison Inmate.* New York: State of New York Press.

VAN VOORHIS, P. (2000). "An Overview of Offender Classification Systems." In P. Van Voorhis, M. Braswell, and D. Lester (eds.), *Correctional Counseling and Rehabilitation.* Cincinnati: Anderson Publishing Company.

VAN VOORHIS, P., AND K. G. SPERBER. (1999). "When Programs Don't Work with Everyone: Planning for Differences Among Correctional Clients." *Corrections Today* 61: 38–42.

VAN VOORHIS, P. ET AL. (2001). *The Georgia Cognitive Skills Experiment Outcome Evaluation, Phase One.* Atlanta, GA: Technical Report Submitted to the Georgia Board of Pardons and Parole.

VERMONT DEPARTMENT OF CORRECTIONS. (2003). *A Job and a Place to Live.* Waterbury, CT: Vermont Department of Corrections.

VEYSEY, B. M., H. J. STEADMAN, S. SALASIN, AND S. M. WELLS. (1995). *Double Jeopardy: Persons with Mental Illnesses in the Criminal Justice System.* Washington, DC: U.S. Department of Health and Human Services.

VISCUSI, W.K. (1998). "Value of Risks to Life and Health." *Journal of Economic Literature* 31:1912–1946.

VITIELLO, MICHAEL. (1997). "Three Strikes: Can We Return to Rationality?" *Journal of Criminal Law and Criminology* 87: 395–481.

VOLD, G. B., AND T. J. BERNARD. (1986). *Theoretical Criminology,* 3rd ed. New York: Oxford University Press.

VON HIRSCH, A. (1998). "Penal Theories." In M. Tonry (ed.), *The Handbook of Crime and Punishment.* New York: Oxford University Press.

VON STERNBERG, L. (1997). "Retention Rates of Participants in a Therapeutic Program in the Texas Department of Criminal Justice." Unpublished paper. Huntsville, TX: Texas Department of Criminal Justice.

WADDINGTON, P. A., AND Q. BRADDOCK. (1991). "Guardians or Bullies? Perceptions of the Police Amongst Adolescent Black, White, and Asian Boys." *Policing in Society* 2: 31–45.

WALDO, G. P., AND S. DINITZ. (1967). "Personality Attributes of the Criminal: An Analysis of Research Studies, 1950–1965." *Journal of Research in Crime and Delinquency* 4: 185–202.

WALKER, S., C. SPOHN, AND M. DELONE. (1996). *The Color of Justice.* Belmont, CA: Wadsworth.

WALKER, SAMUEL. (1992). *The Police in America: An Introduction,* 2nd ed. New York: McGraw-Hill.

WALKER, SAMUEL. (1998a). *Popular Justice: A History of American Criminal Justice,* 2nd ed. New York: Oxford University Press.

WALKER, SAMUEL. (1998b). *Sense and Nonsense About Crime and Drugs,* 4th ed. Belmont, CA: Wadsworth Publishing Company.

WALSH, A. (1998). "Jail: The First Link in Our Chain of Collaboration." *American Jails,* March/April: 51–59.

WALSH, A. (2000). "Should Jails Be Messing with Mental Health or Substance Abuse? A Tale of Joining Forces." *American Jails,* March/April: 60–66.

WALSH, J., AND D. HOLT. (1999). "Jail Diversion for People with Psychiatric Disabilities: The Sheriff's Perspective." *Psychiatric Rehabilitation Journal* 23: 153–160.

WALTERS, G.D. (1990). *The Criminal Lifestyle: Patterns of Serious Criminal Conduct.* Newberry Park, CA: Sage.

WALTERS, G.D. (1998). *Changing Lives of Crime and Drugs: Intervening with Substance Abusing Offenders.* New York: Wiley.

WALTERS, G.D. (2001). "Overcoming Resistance to Abandoning Criminal Lifestyle." In B.K. Welo (ed.), *Tough Customers: Counseling Unwilling Clients.* Lanham, MD: American Correctional Association.

WARR, M. (1984). "Fear of Victimization: Why Are Women and Elderly More Afraid?" *Social Science Quarterly* 65: 681–702.

WARREN, M. (1971). "Classification of Offenders as an Aid to Efficient Management and Effective Treatment." *Journal of Criminal Law, Criminology, and Police Science* 62: 239–268.

WARREN, M. (1983). "Applications of Interpersonal Maturity Theory to Offender Populations." In W. S. Laufer and J. M. Day (eds.), *Personality Theory, Moral Development, and Criminal Behavior.* Lexington, MA: Lexington Books.

WARREN M. ET AL. (1966). *Interpersonal Maturity Level Classification: Diagnosis and Treatment of Low, Middle, and High Maturity Delinquents.* Sacramento, CA: California Youth Authority.

WATSON, D., AND L. CLARK. (1984). "Negative Affectivity: The Disposition to Experience Aversive Emotional States." *Psychological Bulletin* 96: 465–490.

WAX, EMILY. (2002). "Suicide Bombers Kill 12 at Resort in Kenya: Hotel Hosted Israelis, Missiles Fired Nearby at Plane." *Washington Post,* November 29, 2002: A1.

WEAVER, J., AND J. WAKSHLAG. (1986). "Perceived Vulnerability to Crime, Criminal Experience, and Television Viewing." *Journal of Broadcasting and Electronic Media* 30: 141–158.

WEBSTER-STRATTON, C., AND M. A. HAMMOND. (1997). "Treating Children with Early-Onset Conduct Problems: A Comparison of Child and Parent Training Interventions." *Journal of Consulting and Clinical Psychology* 65: 93–109.

WEEDON, JOEY R. (2004). "The Foundation of Re-Entry." *Corrections Today* 66: 6.

WEISHEIT, R. A., L. E. WELLS, AND D. N. FALCONE. (1995). *Crime and Policing in Rural and Small-Town America: An Overview of the Issues.* Washington, DC: Bureau of Justice Statistics.

WEISNER, C. ET AL. (2001). "Factors Affecting the Initiation of Substance Abuse Treatment in Managed Care." *Addiction* 96: 705–716.

WEISSBERG, R. P., H. A. BARTON, AND T. P. SHRIVER. (1997). "The Social-Competence Promotion Program for Young Adolescents." In G. W. Albee and T. P. Gullotta (eds.), *Primary Prevention Works: Issues in Children's and Families' Lives,* Vol. 6. Thousand Oaks, CA: Sage.

WEST, MARTY L. (1993). "Get a Piece of the Privatization Pie: Private Security Agencies." *The American Society for Industrial Security, Security Management* 37: 54.

WEXLER, H. K. (1996). *The Amity Prison TC Evaluation: Inmate Profiles and Reincarceration Outcomes.* Sacramento, CA: California Department of Corrections.

WEXLER, H. K., J. BLACKMORE, AND D. S. LIPTON. (1991). "Project REFORM: Developing a Drug Abuse Treatment Strategy for Corrections." *Journal of Drug Issues* 21: 469–490.

WEXLER, H. K., AND C. LOVE. (1994). "Therapeutic Communities in Prison." In F. Tims, G. DeLeon, and N. Jainchill (eds.), *Therapeutic Community: Advances in Research and Application.* Rockville, MD: National Institute on Drug Abuse.

WEXLER, H. K. ET AL. (1992). "Outcome Evaluation of a Prison Therapeutic Community for Substance Abuse Treatment." In G. Leukefeld and F. M. Tims (eds.), *Drug Abuse Treatment in Prisons and Jails.* Rockville, MD: National Institute on Drug Abuse.

WEXLER, H. K. ET AL. (1999a). "The Amity Prison TC Evaluation: Reincarceration Outcomes." *Criminal Justice and Behavior* 26: 147–167.

WEXLER, H. K. ET AL. (1999b). "Three-Year Reincarceration Outcomes for Amity In-Prison Therapeutic Community and Aftercare in California." *Prison Journal* 79: 312–336.

WHITE, J. R. (1998). "Team Building in the Mountain State: Teaching Cognitive Behavioral Group Skills and Building Alliances Between Inmate Services and Correctional Officers." *American Jails* 12: 19–22.

WICHARAYA, TAMASAK. (1995). *Simple Theory, Hard Reality: The Impact of Sentencing Reforms on Courts, Prisons, and Crime.* Albany, NY: State University of New York Press.

WIERSMA, B., AND K. SIEDSCHLAW. (2003). "Nebraska's Work Ethic Camp: The First Year." *Corrections Compendium* 28: 1–4, 29–31.

WIERSMA, B., AND K. SIEDSCHLAW. (2004). *The Work Ethic Camp, McCook Nebraska: An Evaluation and Assessment.* Private report, pp. 29, 95.

WIESNER, M., AND M. WINDLE. (2004). "Assessing Covariates of Adolescent Delinquency Trajectories: A Latent Growth Mixture." *Journal of Youth and Adolescence* 33: 431–442.

Will, J. A., and J. H. McGrath. (1995). "Crime, Neighborhood Perceptions, and the Underclass: The Relationship Between Fear of Crime and Class Position." *Journal of Criminal Justice* 23: 163–176.

Williams, T., M. Azbrack, and L. Joy. (1982). "The Portrayal of Aggression on North American Television." *Journal of Applied Social Psychology* 12: 360–380.

Willing, Richard. (2000). "Many Rapists Were Thieves First: Results May Lead to Taking of DNA for Lesser Crimes." *USA Today*, July 10, 2000: 3A.

Wilson, J. J., and J. C. Howell. (1993). *A Comprehensive Strategy for Serious, Violent, and Chronic Juvenile Offenders.* Washington, DC: U.S. Department of Justice.

Wilson, James Q., and George Kelling. (1982). "Broken Windows." *Atlantic Monthly,* March: 29–38.

Wilson, James Q., and Joan Petersilia. (2004). *Crime: Public Policies for Crime Control.* Oakland, CA: Institute for Contemporary Studies Press.

Wilson, William J. (1987). *The Truly Disadvantaged: The Inner City, the Underclass, and Public Policy.* Chicago: University of Chicago Press.

Wilson, William J. (1996). *When Work Disappears: The World of the New Urban Poor.* Chicago: University of Chicago Press.

Wilson, O. W., and Roy C. McLaren. (1977). *Police Administration,* 4th ed. New York: McGraw-Hill.

Withrow, P. K. (1994). "Cognitive Restructuring: An Approach to Dealing with Violent Inmates." *Corrections Today* 56: 112–116.

Wolff, N. (1998). "Interactions Between Mental Health and Law Enforcement Systems: Problems and Prospects for Cooperation." *Journal of Health, Politics, Policy, and Law* 23: 133–174.

Wood, Raymond M., Linda S. Grossman, and Christopher G. Fichtner. (2000). "Psychological Assessment, Treatment, and Outcome with Sex Offenders." *Behavioral Sciences and the Law* 18: 23–41.

Wortley, Richard. (1997). "A Classification Technique for Controlling Situational Precipitators of Crime." *Security Journal* 14: 63–82.

Wright, B. A. (2004). *Educating for Diversity.* New York: The John Day Company, 26–28.

Wright, Lawrence. (2004). "The Terror Web." *The New Yorker*, August 2, 2004, 26–28.

Yin, P. (1980). "Fear of Crime Among the Elderly: Some Issues and Suggestions." *Social Problems* 27: 492–504.

Yochelson, S., and S. E. Samenow. (2000). *The Criminal Personality: A Profile for Change.* New York: Aronson.

Zamble, E., and V. L. Quinsey. (1997). *The Criminal Recidivism Process.* London, UK: Cambridge University Press.

Zarkin, Gary A., Sheryl C. Cates, and Mohan V. Bala. (2000). "Estimating the Willingness to Pay for Drug Abuse Treatment: A Pilot Study." *Journal of Substance Abuse Treatment* 18: 149–159.

Zaro, D. (2000). "The Self-Actualized Correctional Educator." *Journal of Correctional Education* 51: 191–192.

Zillman, D., and J. Wakshlag. (1985). "Fear of Victimization and the Appeal of Crime Drama." In D. Zillman and J. Bryant (eds.), *Selective Exposure to Communication* 13: 141–156.

Zimberg, S. (1993). "Introduction and General Concepts of Dual Diagnosis." In J. Solomon, S. Zimberg, and E. Shollar (eds.), *Dual Diagnosis: Evaluation, Treatment, Theory and Program Development.* New York: Plenum Medical Book Company.

Zimring, Franklin E. (1998). *American Youth Violence.* New York: Oxford University Press.

Zimring, Franklin E., Gordon Hawkins, and Sam Kamin. (2001). *Punishment and Democracy: Three Strikes and You're Out in California.* New York: Oxford University Press.